DATE DUE

NOV 0 7 1991	
4 1997	

AMERICAN SEATING FURNITURE 1630–1730

AMERICAN SEATING FURNITURE 1630–1730

AN INTERPRETIVE CATALOGUE

BENNO M. FORMAN

A WINTERTHUR BOOK

W. W. NORTON & COMPANY

NEW YORK   LONDON

THIS PROJECT HAS BEEN SUPPORTED BY FUNDS FROM THE NATIONAL ENDOWMENT FOR THE ARTS, THE NATIONAL ENDOWMENT FOR THE HUMANITIES, THE FORD FOUNDATION, AND THE FRIENDS OF WINTERTHUR

Published simultaneously in Canada by
Penguin Books Canada Ltd.,
2801 John Street, Markham, Ontario L3R 1B4.
Printed in the United States of America

Printed and bound by
Balding + Mansell International Limited, Wisbech, England

First Edition

ISBN 0-393-02516-0

W. W. Norton & Company, Inc.,
500 Fifth Avenue, New York, N.Y. 10110
W. W. Norton & Company Ltd.,
37 Great Russell Street, London WC1B 3NU

1 2 3 4 5 6 7 8 9 0

FOR
Elizabeth Varley Forman
and
Lisa Marian Forman
Geoffrey Varley Forman
Sybil Isadora Forman

CONTENTS

THE CATALOGUE

EDITORIAL
STATEMENT

This book contains three essay sections and six catalogue sections, each of which has an essay and from seven to twenty-seven extensive catalogue entries. The ninety-two pieces of early American seating furniture in the Winterthur Museum collection that are the focus of Benno Forman's discussion in the catalogue section of the book are given entry numbers. All other illustrations, including close-up details of the ninety-two chairs, are designated as figures, and these 194 pictures are numbered continuously throughout the book. In addition, the book is replete with references to other chairs that are illustrated in various readily available books.

The catalogue entries and captions begin by identifying the object, place of origin, earliest and latest possible dates of manufacture, and, where known, woods and dimensions. The inclusion of a Linnaean name for the woods indicates that the wood has been microanalyzed. Dimensions are provided, both in inches and in centimeters. Objects in public collections are identified accordingly; however, individual or private owners are not identified by name. For the ninety-two

chairs, stools, and couches in the catalogue entries, Forman has designated each chair by the possible label(s) that might have been used at the time the chair was made. These labels are based on terms found in craftsmen's account books, correspondence, wills, and inventories of that particular colony.

The following abbreviations are used in captions and catalogue entries:

OH	overall height	SH	seat height	H	height
OW	overall width	SW	seat width	W	width
OD	overall depth	SD	seat depth	D	depth

In all catalogue entries the number following the provenance line is the Winterthur Museum accession number.

The footnotes and text use short-title references to books, articles, and manuscripts; the full citation for each is given in the bibliography. A concordance, preceding the index, lists by accession number all the Winterthur chairs, stools, and couches that are illustrated in this book.

BENNO M. FORMAN (1930–1982)

FOREWORD

BENNO M. FORMAN
AN APPRECIATION

I was very touched to be asked to write a foreword to this eagerly awaited book which makes a classic contribution to the great tradition of American furniture studies. Benno Forman became a cherished friend during the dozen or so years when he established himself as one of the most celebrated members of the international community of furniture historians; yet, it is strangely difficult, perhaps especially so for an Englishman, accurately to describe his achievement because it embraced infinitely more than published research and was all the more remarkable since behind it there did not lie many years of training and experience. I propose therefore to recall the lively personal qualities which created Benno's famous reputation, inspired affection on both sides of the Atlantic, and sometimes caused waves. Future generations of readers will be curious to know what kind of man the author was and something of the enthusiasm, faith, and advocacy he brought to furniture.

I had corresponded with Benno Forman long before our memorable first meeting at the Furniture History Society conference held in Norwich during September 1969. He came renowned as a man of versatile interests, a true expert devoted to his work, and one who had discovered early that to share information generously was the best way to open up a subject and was repaid tenfold. His rich personality and immense knowledge soon turned him into a conference character. He attended four of these autumn gatherings between 1969 and 1981, often bearing gifts, and his presence, besides ensuring that no piece of oak furniture, however coarse and shoddy, ever passed without comment, also guaranteed a jolly time. Benno's quality as a teacher was readily apparent when he spoke spontaneously about furniture at the houses we visited.

However, he will be fondly remembered by intimate friends for his scathing comments on, say, the dullness of investment collections, the misdeeds of timber analysts, or howlers in the latest popular guide to antiques. Benno's boisterous humor enlivened many late night sessions over a bottle of duty-free malt whisky and a pipe. In the best academic tradition he enjoyed being irreverent, as he put it "one of the rowdy boys"; no scholar can be earnest the whole time. Were Queen Anne's last words really "With my death a great age of chair legs ends"?

As a mature student at Winterthur (1966–68) Benno became convinced that the attention given to seventeenth-century American furniture had never been equal to its artistic and historical importance. It had, to be sure, been the object of some frequently rather antiquarian research, but in the climate of the late 1960s when he arrived on the academic scene curators and collectors were mostly prejudiced in favor of elegant eighteenth-century masterpieces. With crusading zeal and a ruthless passion for work, Benno set about cutting a fresh swath through his chosen subject. The "Forman factor" emerged under the inspired tutelage of Charles Montgomery who encouraged him to apply modern research techniques to early colonial furniture. Benno's sharp stylistic and technical analysis, illuminated by exhaustive documentary searches, was consistently professional, but his most original contribution was, to my mind, an acute awareness of the relevance of regional traditions in English oak furniture. His eager pursuit of this approach not only established new bearings in the subject but inspired English colleagues, myself included, who had previously closed their minds to the challenge to start investigating local design types and decorative preferences. His lectures and articles also moved several exceptionally able young American students including Robert F. Trent and Robert Blair St. George to follow his example. They, like all worthy disciples, rapidly became competitive while he was driven to ever greater exertions; thus a healthy spirit of rivalry developed which always heralds major advances in any academic discipline where formerly hardly anyone really cared. As the recipient of many inquisitive letters I gladly remember how Benno stimulated fieldwork that led on to exciting discoveries in the English countryside. He was no isolationist, and others who shared this experience will wish to join me in quoting Shakespeare's apt tribute: "It was you who hath marked forth the way that led us hither."

Cataloguing is one of the most demanding tasks because it is always so easy to postpone tackling another entry on the grounds that a more urgent lecture must be prepared or a book review handed in on time. Benno wrote to me in January 1980 of "the sheer fun and exhilaration and the exhaustion from drudgery" that went into the compiling of his book. On an earlier occasion he complained that he could no longer work regularly after midnight and urged me not to delay finishing my own Chippendale volumes. For a time I found it hard to understand why the Winterthur catalogue was taking so long, and even suspected Benno of becoming a little desultory until he mentioned in passing that most of the entries covered several pages and each section was to be prefaced by a major historical essay. Clearly he planned a massive interpretive work very different in scale from earlier titles in the series. Perhaps his scheme was overambitious, possibly in pursuit of excellence he aimed too high.

Benno, like I suppose most of us who have embarked on similar enterprises, kidded himself that his project was nearer completion than was actually the case. The pressures on him must have been intense, and, as we now know, he did not live to oversee publication. However, Benno had capital friends who, while expressing a very human mixture of sadness and fury that not all the text was as far forward as they had been led to believe, rallied round and unselfishly channeled their best energies into finishing the work. The result of this collaborative effort is truly impressive, and its influence will be enormous. The language of the catalogue is studied and vigorous; the breadth, detail, and precision of the entries marks a significant advance on nearly all previous works of this kind, and the prefatory essays, particularly the section on woods, are going to be of inestimable value. No archival research was too irksome, while the "archaeological" interpretation of each object—an approach learned from Charles Montgomery and then even further refined—stamps the book with indelible quality.

Only close friends can be fully aware of the anguished doubts that lie behind certain statements. Benno knew so much that he was sometimes desperately unsure about the origin of unprovenanced items. Ultimately he would probably have been the first to admit that his survey amounts to an interim report on the Winterthur collection. Yet nobody can ever accuse him of skimping research. Having bitterly complained that English colleagues had neglected basic fieldwork, he spent weeks searching country churches for woodwork that might prove a point, while many trips to the UK were combined with journeys to Germany, Holland, Scandinavia, and even the Channel Islands in the quest for evidence. The result of all this activity and commitment is one of the best books on furniture ever written. Finally, it is fitting that, by passing on his knowledge and inspiring affection, Benno happily ensured that there were loyal friends qualified and willing to undertake the completion of this catalogue; its publication is a triumph.

CHRISTOPHER G. GILBERT
Temple Newsam House
Leeds, England

PREFACE

When Benno M. Forman accepted a fellowship in the Winterthur Program in Early American Culture in 1966, a single great division shaped the field of early American furniture study. On one hand, he felt pressed by an obligation to become a "connoisseur" capable of judging an object's artistic merit in relation to universal standards of quality. After all, the virtue of developing one's visual memory and powers of instant recall had been an honored mandate of curatorial training ever since the early eighteenth century. Gentle *arrivistes* such as Jonathan Richardson had insisted outright that the purpose of being a connoisseur was to develop "a delicacy of eye to judge of harmony, and proportion, of beauty of colours, and accuracy of hand. . . . To be a good connoisseur," he explained, "a man must be as free from all kinds of prejudice as possible; he must moreover have a clear, and exact way of thinking, and reasoning; he must know how to take in, and manage just ideas; and throughout he must have not only a solid, but an unbiased judgment." From this idea flowed a more subtle corollary. In being able to assess the quality of an object, the connoisseur should be able to evaluate people as well. A good connoisseur, Richardson insisted, "must be conversant with the better sort of people" in order to progress.

On the other hand, the new term, *context*, a word itself borrowed by American social historians of the day from anthropologists and linguists, demanded that the understanding of an object's function and meaning be based not on universal standards imposed on the object by the connoisseur, but on standards of excellence and use recognized by the culture of its creator. The obligation of the connoisseur was to pronounce transcendental judgment; the duty of the con-

textual historian of furniture was to reconstruct the systems of fashion, transmission, and replication that framed an object as it moved through a specific social structure. Whither lieth the truth?

Finding himself an inmate of a house divided, Forman did the only thing possible. Following the lead of his mentor, Charles F. Montgomery, he set about to build a career dedicated to proving that connoisseurship and context are not opposed, but part of the same process of intellectual exploration. This realization freed him to find significance in details that might otherwise escape notice. The probing examination of seat-framing techniques on eighteenth-century Philadelphia chairs, for example, enabled him to identify securely some construction methods as Germanic in origin and others as definitely English. Or, at another level of inquiry, he relentlessly pursued the stylistic sources for the cane chair from Boston to London, to northern Europe, and finally to the Iberian peninsula. As he discovered patterns in both the style and the structure of early American furniture, he checked their validity through the microanalysis of wood samples, in the terse phrasing of probate records, and in the frustrating tangles of family genealogy. Indeed, he always maintained that any great student of furniture history must also be an authority on documentary research, botany, chemistry, and the history of technology. In short, Benno became a scholar who left few stones unturned. His was a total vision, a view of historical method that linked the dry details of scientific research with grander arguments about cultural development and social change. Benno's quest began where others had left off; in particular, he sought to extend the respective work on English and Iberian colonial furniture of Robert W. Symonds and Robert C. Smith. The end of his ambitious research, as we see in this volume, was nothing less than to construct a cultural history of American seating furniture and the woodworking trades from 1630 to 1730.

With this interpretive catalogue of the early seating furniture in the Winterthur collection, Forman brings to American decorative arts an expansion of a basic concept he learned from George Kubler's *Shape of Time*: the realization that centers of artistic energy are often best illuminated by activity on their periphery. In fact, Forman found much of the significance of American furniture history to reside in its ability to shed light on production in London, Amsterdam, and the Rhineland. It was this basic discovery that led him throughout his productive career to explore early American urban furniture above all else, objects produced in centers like Boston, Salem, New York City, Philadelphia, Baltimore. His fascination with urban furniture was in part due to his lively emotional response to its formal complexity; he was drawn to the visual drama of "high-style" objects. As he once explained it, they were the objects that sang to him. He also found these objects intellectually intriguing. He was challenged by the complexities of urban shop production that he knew stood behind their undulating facades, shimmering veneered surfaces that distract the eye from the money-saving shortcuts they conceal. As he searched for answers to endless lists of new questions, his research led him back principally to England. Working both in London and in rural districts, Forman established firm antecedents for early American work. Perhaps more significantly, he was able to see colonial furniture styles as an extension of documented patterns of geographic and social diffusion within English society. In so doing, he was fully astride a recognized trend within social history that saw early American culture less as an exceptional break from "Old World" structures than as a continuation of them.

Benno was able to inspire greatness in others as this book—his book—undoubtedly will. He was good at urging others to excel. As his English colleagues like Christopher Gilbert, Peter Thornton, Margaret Swain, and Anthony Wells-Cole will readily attest, his infectious enthusiasm inspired them to begin working with renewed energy on overlooked corners of Britain. In the process, they produced a series of fine publications; the regional furniture exhibitions and catalogues published by Gilbert and Wells-Cole at Temple Newsam, Swain's tightly argued articles on needlework, and Wells-Cole's ongoing research on mannerist print sources for late sixteenth- and seventeenth-century English woodwork. Forman also drove his acquaintances in continental museums—T. H. Lunsingh Scheurleer, Elisabet Hidemark, and others—to begin working with new intensity on their own local sources. As did their European counterparts, his American colleagues found in Benno an unequalled critic, a willing coconspirator who always found time to answer letters in remarkable detail. Forman considered many people his professional allies: university professors, antiques dealers, interested craftspeople, and other museum professionals. So it is that John T. Kirk, Albert Sack, Joe Kindig, John D. Alexander, Jr., and Frank Horton, to name just a few, will all welcome the appearance of this volume.

Forman was also an inspiring and exacting teacher and from 1968 until his death in 1982 was the pedagogical backbone of the Winterthur Program in Early American Culture. A course with Forman was a genuine apprenticeship in the logic of formal analysis, basic and elegant writing, exacting connoisseurship skills, documentary research methods, and whatever broader cultural concepts were worrying him at the time. While many students of old furniture never got past the details, Benno loved to ponder big questions. He was always ready to argue about the definition of *style*, how ideas moved through society, who was responsible for their transmission, and how difficult it is to make style correlate with issues of social class. Indeed, many of today's leading museum professionals were his pupils or colleagues: Wendy A. Cooper, Brock Jobe, Dean F. Failey, Patricia E. Kane, Cathryn J. McElroy, and Philip D. Zimmerman among others. The list is simply too long to mention everyone.

Perhaps most of all, Forman contributed to the working lives and intellectual growth of his colleagues at Winterthur Museum. As he did with students and professional friends, he believed in the basic creative potential of his fellow employees. He also believed that creative people benefit from constant dialogue. His own enthusiasm helped sustain, among others, Nancy Goyne Evans through much of her definitive study of American windsor furniture, and Susan B. Swan in her work on early American textile history. For everyone whom Forman inspired to excel, this book—the first comprehensive survey of early seating furniture at Winterthur Museum, really the first major cultural history of furniture to be published in America—will be a welcome sight. During its fifteen-year preparation, many people wondered why it was taking so long. "Why isn't it finished?" colleagues often asked him. And Benno would smile or frown and simply say, "Because I don't know all the answers yet." But that was his modest way of deflecting a more basic truth. The real reason why Forman's catalogue quickly became the most often-quoted unfinished book in America was that he willingly sacrificed his own time to help others learn.

Although this catalogue is meticulously researched, amply illustrated, and long, its preparation was never more than one part of Forman's wonderfully complex identity as a person. Indeed, his personality almost defies qualification. Besides his all-consuming interest in American furniture, he also made time to develop skill in photography, and some of the clear images his lens captured grace the pages of this volume. He was a wonderful piano player, an accomplished musician who always looked at perfect ease when perched on the bench in front of his baby grand—the only piano we know of with William and Mary–style legs. He was also a connoisseur of cooking and fine wine. Finally, he was an enthusiast of small foreign cars, each of which seemed smaller, faster, and brighter in color than the one before.

This volume, then, is an imperfect artifact of a man who always feared that he never completely understood the artifacts that other people left behind. Because of Forman's premature death, the community of scholars of American material culture has lost one of its leading lights, one of its most generous thinkers. The sheer amount of information that Forman held in his head was staggering. It is all lost. His plans to continue working on the early case furniture and tables in the Winterthur collection are also lost. His brilliant gift as a teacher, a leader who did much to shape the high standards of museum scholarship in America today, is lost to future generations of graduate fellows in the Winterthur Program in Early American Culture. It is also a loss to the many devotees of antiques collecting who never had the pleasure of hearing him deliver a public lecture. And in a very real sense, his death was a personal loss to his wife, Elizabeth V. Forman, and to his children, Lisa, Geoffrey, and Sybil. Benno always looked forward to the day when he could present them with his book, his gift to them for the many sacrifices they made on his behalf. Although he and they were sadly deprived of that moment, this volume is dedicated to his family—his greatest supporters, his closest friends.

Upon his death, some sections of Forman's manuscript were more developed than others. In part this was the outcome of his changing interests. Between 1978 and 1982, for example, he spent much of the time perfecting his understanding of the leather chair industry in Boston, New York, and Philadelphia, with the result that the introduction to "Carved Topp'd, Plain Topp'd, and Crook'd-Back Leather Chairs" and the catalogue entries that follow it were in excellent shape. Other sections, especially those in which other scholars had made recent new discoveries, needed completion and minor revisions. As this manuscript was completed, we undertook to write sections that Forman had intended to include, complete sections that he had outlined or only partially drafted, or revise existing sections if new information had since surfaced that might affect the general nature of the argument or the accuracy of the entry. Specifically, Robert St. George rewrote some passages in the chapter on woodworking artisans and, with the helpful advice of Michael Palmer, John D. Alexander, Jr., and Harry Alden, made minor corrections to the chapter on woods. He also rewrote substantial segments of the introduction to turned chairs, revised some of those entries, and wrote others that were previously undrafted. In addition, he wrote catalogue entries for leather chairs, couches, and stools and edited the entire manuscript several times. Robert Trent substantially revised Forman's introductory essay to upholstered chairs, including new attributions for some objects, and rewrote a few object entries. He drafted the essay on easy chairs, a portion of the book that Forman never began. He also revised and extended Forman's previously published piece on the development of the joined chest of drawers in America for republication in *Winterthur Portfolio* (vol. 20, no. 1 [Spring 1985]: 1–48). This was an essay that Forman had planned to include in his projected companion volume on early American case furniture, a book that he was working on simultaneously with this one.

In his general editorial capacity, Robert St. George was aided greatly by the publications staff of Winterthur Museum. As director of the Publications Office, Ian M. G. Quimby enthusiastically supported the swift completion of this project from the outset and encouraged efforts to secure funding to make its final publication possible. The brunt of the editorial task fell on Catherine E. Hutchins, associate editor. She was the ideal person to edit the Forman catalogue, having worked closely with him on his last two major publications. She knows his idiosyncratic stylistic preferences, his feeling for the rhythm of a strong sentence, his attention to the precise details of good prose. While we were called upon to oversee and make any necessary amendations to what Forman had already written, Kate deserves all the credit for turning it into a readable book.

From the very beginning of this project in February 1982, we have labored to enhance what we, having been his students, understood as Forman's own thinking on a given topic and have throughout scrupulously avoided imposing our conclusions on his data. As a result, we feel confident and pleased that this volume represents the publication and faithful completion of Forman's own scholarship, although in places an inevitable editorial presence may be detected.

How, then, should this book be read? The answer is simple: It should be read in the spirit that Forman lived and worked, in a spirit of demanding generosity. Although there is much new information in this volume that will be useful to students of early American furniture in a direct way, this book is also a monument to Forman's own rigorous method of study. Building his discipline and approach on the foundations laid by his noteworthy predecessors in the study of seventeenth-century American furniture—individuals like Irving W. Lyon, Wallace Nutting, Clair Franklin Luther, and Helen Park—Benno moved to connect objects and documents, products and processes. The remarkable depth of the present volume demonstrates how demanding the "Forman method" can be. He worked for fifteen years and, with the exception of brilliant essays on the heart and crown chairs of late eighteenth-century Connecticut, Delaware valley slatback chairs, and Pennsylvania German furniture, never took his study past the 1740s. Yet students confronting the impressive detail in this book should not be dismayed or left wondering what remains for them to study. The areas left to study are the rest of the eighteenth century, the complex vista of the nineteenth and twentieth centuries, the impact of industrialization on established shop production, the exact relationships between urban and rural styles, and the tentative linkages between the study of historic artifacts and labor history.

Each of these topics is a virtual frontier. Each presents a new challenge to universalize the methods of inquiry that Forman worked so hard to develop. After reading through his book, some may claim that Forman's field, the study of American furniture history, is still young. But we can all agree that it has grown stronger for his efforts.

ROBERT BLAIR ST. GEORGE
and ROBERT F. TRENT

ACKNOWLEDGMENTS

Benno Forman had many friends who shared ideas and research with him, including: Pauline Agius, Richard E. Ahlborn, Celia Alberici, John E. Alden, Edward P. Alexander, John D. Alexander, Jr., Kenneth L. Ames, Elizabeth Rhoades Aykroyd, James Ayres, Margit Baad, W. Baer, Cynthia Blake Baldwin, Jairus B. Barnes, Linda R. Baumgarten, Geoffrey Beard, Louise Conway Belden, W. F. Bennet, Robert Bishop, John Bivins, Jr., Mary C. Black, Roderic H. Blackburn, Col. and Mrs. Miodrag Blagojevich, John Bly, Philip H. Bradley, Carl Bridenbaugh, David S. Brooke, Michael K. Brown, Kathryn C. Buhler, Patricia R. Bullen, Georgia Brady Bumgardner, Joseph T. Butler, Patricia M. Butler, Patrick H. Butler III, Richard M. Candee, George Carlisle, Barbara G. Carson, Cary Carson, Skip Chalfont, Victor Chinnery, Lillian B. Cogan, Wendy A. Cooper, Suzanne Corlette Crilley, Abbott Lowell Cummings, Larry Curry, Phillip H. Curtis, James J. F. Deetz, Bernward Deneke, Gail L. Dennis, Charles G. Dorman, Antoinette F. Downing, William L. Dulaney, Philip H. Dunbar, Samuel R. Durand, Penelope S. Eames, William Voss Elder III, Frederick G. Emmison, Nancy Goyne Evans, Frank P. Ewing, Dean F. Failey, Jonathan L. Fairbanks, Dean A. Fales, Martha Gandy Fales, Anne Farnam, Donald L. Fennimore, Eugene S. Ferguson, George J. Fistrovich, Oscar P. Fitzgerald, E. McClung Fleming, Edward T. Fogg, Wendell D. Garrett, Beatrice B. Garvan, Donna-Belle Garvin, James L. Garvin, Lawrence D. Geller, Christopher G. Gilbert, Benjamin Ginsburg, Cora Ginsburg, Constance Godfrey, Dudley Godfrey, Anne C. Golovin, William L. Goodman, Carol Gordon, Alan Gowans, Thomas A. Gray, Barry A. Greenlaw, Wallace B. Gusler, Robert Haines, Joseph W. Hammond, Roland B Hammond, David A. Hanks, John Hardy, Thompson R. Harlow, John Harrison, Tony Harrison, Ingmar Hasselgreen, Helena Hayward, John Hayward, Morrison H. Heckscher, Mrs. William Heidgerd, Elisabet Hidemark, Elizabeth Hill, Sinclair H. Hitchings, Graham Hood, Frank L. Horton, Charles F. Hummel, Conover Hunt, Bryden Bordley Hyde, Gervase Jackson-Stops, Simon Jervis, Brock W. Jobe, Fred J. Johnston, Phillip M. Johnston, Edward T. Joy, Neil Duff Kamil, Patricia E. Kane, Wendy Kaplan, Myrna Kaye, John S. Kebabian, James O. Keene, Joseph P. Kindig, Jr., Joseph P. Kindig III, John T. Kirk, Ruth Matzkin Knapp, Nancy D. Kolb, Terry H. Kovel, Dwight P. Lanmon, Anne T. Larin, David Learmont, Barbara Brown Lee, Bernard Levy, S. Dean Levy, Bertram K. Little, Nina Fletcher Little, Robert Logan, Margaretta M. Lovell, T. H. Lunsingh Scheurleer, Charles T. Lyle, William H. MacDonald, Cathryn J. McElroy, Milly McGehee, Susan Mackiewicz, Mervin Martin, John W. Melody, Charles F. Montgomery, Florence M. Montgomery, Caroline Morris, John D. Morse, Milo M. Naeve, Christina H. Nelson, Irene R. Norton, Richard C. Nylander, Scott Odell, Gabriel Olive, Joseph K. Ott, Michael R. Palmer, Peter J. Parker, Andrew Passeri, Roger Peers, Donald C. Peirce, Eleanor Perley, Ruth Piwonka, Dorothy Potter, Lois Olcott Price, David Pye, Ian M. G. Quimby, Nicholas Quinn, Richard H. Randall, Jr., Bradford L. Rauschenberg, Mary Lyn Ray, George J. Reilly, Paula N. Reiss, Nancy L. Restuccia, Nancy E. Richards, William Rieder, S. Dillon Ripley, 2d, Lynn Springer

Roberts, Ellen M. Rosenthal, Rodris Roth, Darrett B. Rutman, Albert Sack, Harold Sack, Robert Sack, Frances Gruber Safford, Robert Blair St. George, Gordon Saltar, Carol C. Sanderson, Richard H. Saunders, Herbert F. Schiffer, Margaret B. Schiffer, Karol A. Schmiegel, Arlene Palmer Schwind, Margo Scott, L. Corwin Sharp, Nancy Rivard Shaw, Raymond V. Shepherd, Jr., Sarah B. Sherrill, Bruce T. Sherwood, Jane Rittenhouse Smiley, Deborah A. Smith, James Morton Smith, Malcolm S. Smith, Nancy A. Smith, John J. Snyder, Jr., Frank H. Sommer III, Joseph Peter Spang III, William Stahl, Joan Stevens, David Stockwell, Stanley Stone, Colin M. Streeter, Susan Burrows Swan, Scott T. Swank, John A. H. Sweeney, Kevin M. Sweeney, Paul Swenson, Beatrice K. Taylor, Peter K. Thornton, Robert F. Trent, Charles van Ravenswaay, R. J. van Wandelen, Gilbert T. Vincent, Fred Vogel III, John Walton, Barbara McLean Ward, Gerald W. R. Ward, David B. Warren, William L. Warren, Deborah Dependahl Waters, Lura Woodside Watkins, Carolyn J. Weekley, Martin Eli Weil, Anthony Wells-Cole, Winsor White, and Philip D. Zimmerman.

Thanks also go to those museums and historical agencies in the United States, England, Scotland, Wales, Sweden, West Germany, Spain, Portugal, and Italy whose staff members handled numerous research and study requests and photographic orders.

Special thanks go to the many members of the support staff at Winterthur: Alberta M. Brandt, Kathryn K. McKinney, George J. Fistrovich, and Wayne B. Gibson, handled the numerous requests for in-house photography; Eleanor McDonald (Neville) Thompson, Beatrice K. Taylor, Bert R. Denker, and E. Richard McKinstry supplied assistance in the library; registrarial staff members Karol A. Schmiegel, Lauren L. Chapin, and Marian P. Blakeman, working with art handlers James Patterson and Maynard Cash and supervisor Everett Boyce, facilitated object study; the staff of the word processing center, especially Cheryl Calvetti and Deidre McPherson along with Ann Marie Keefer, Jane M. Mellinger, and Linda A. Carson typed numerous drafts of the manuscript; long-time office secretaries Patricia R. Bullen and Sandra S. Mitchell typed the early drafts; Carol K. Baker, Marjorie W. Cross, Suzanne C. Hamilton, Neidra E. Karrer, Joyce H. Longworth, Clare G. (Chinx) Noyes, Barbara C. Shellenberger, Mary-Hammond Sullivan, Anne Y. Wolf, Marilyn G. Wolf, and Jane P. Wright, and many other Winterthur guides did special work on objects and offered additional insights. Thanks also go to the Winterthur Publications Office staff: Ian M. G. Quimby, Catherine E. Hutchins, Gerald W. R. Ward, Patricia R. Lisk, Alma F. Sorber, and Florence Pratt; to the staff at W. W. Norton: James L. Mairs, Jeremy N. Townsend, and Amy Silin; and to book designer Margaret Wagner.

INTRODUCTION

BENNO M. FORMAN

To explain all nature is too difficult a task for any one man or even for any one age. 'Tis much better to do a little with certainty and leave the rest for others that come after you than to explain all things by conjecture without making sure of anything.

ISAAC NEWTON

Friends and acquaintances who have watched this catalogue develop might wonder why it took so long to do. The answer is quite simple: It was pointless for me to write a catalogue of this museum's collection of early seating furniture until I had studied it sufficiently well and compared it with pertinent examples in other collections. Only after that process was complete could I say something insightful about seating furniture. I am sure that every historian, no matter what his or her specialty, feels a similar need, but in the present case it seemed particularly appropriate because when I first became interested in seventeenth-century furniture and Charles F. Montgomery agreed to advise my master's thesis on the topic in 1966, three monumental works towered over the field—Irving W. Lyon's classic *Colonial Furniture of New England* (the first and still the greatest work of American furniture scholarship) and Wallace Nutting's *Furniture Treasury* and *Furniture of the Pilgrim Century*. The first and third are now reprinted, the second has never been out of print. Any book that would cover similar ground should say more than they did or it does not deserve to be published.

Early furniture has recently begun to appeal to furniture collectors again, but the scarcity of such furniture in its own time has meant that only a few great examples have come onto the market since the 1920s, which in turn means that collecting seventeenth-century American furniture could never become a popular sport. Monograph literature on the subject prior to 1970 reflects this lack of enthusiasm. Prior to the revived interest represented by the model articles and catalogues of an intrepid band of devotees within the past decade, only sporadic flurries of publication occurred, notably in 1938/39 when Dr.

Lyon's son, Irving P., published six articles on Thomas Dennis, and in 1952 when Helen O'Boyle Park published a reexamination of the younger Lyon's work. This meant in 1968, when I went to work as Mr. Montgomery's research assistant, that considerable research lay ahead, for not only would the project have to be done virtually from scratch, but the writings of others and the objects published by them would have to be subjected to critical examination.

It quickly became clear that no other body of seating furniture is less documented than the examples made in Europe and America during the seventeenth century. On the one hand a body of written documents survives to show that the first settlers of New England, New York, and southward possessed a copious supply of furniture, and on the other hand a body of surviving furniture exists that looks as if it ought to have been made in the time and locations that the documents cover. Putting the two together is a task that is easier to conceive mentally than to accomplish in fact.

The earliest American seating furniture has fascinated collectors for over a century and has been displayed in the historical museums of our country even longer. That a lore should have developed about it is only natural, and the fascination these objects generate has, to a great extent, complicated the task of sorting them out. Like the documents and objects themselves, each bit of lore must be explored, weighed, and assessed for the germ of truth that may lurk within it.

Early in the process of surveying the Winterthur collection for this catalogue, two things became clear. First, that the collection itself, containing about 100 examples of seating furniture made between 1630 and 1730, which makes it the most extensive in the country, nonetheless lacked certain forms and regional examples; second, that the story began well before the earliest example in the collection was made and extended beyond the advent of the so-called Queen Anne style. Thus a catalogue confined to the furniture at Winterthur alone would provide neither a comprehensive view of the regional styles that were made in America prior to 1730 nor a coherent picture of the way in which those styles got here. From the start it did not seem that a mere catalogue of the objects themselves would be true to the modern standards of scholarship that not only suggest that we find out as much as the object itself can tell us but demand that we place the object in its proper temporal context to understand its relevance to social history and the broader sweep of our early culture.

The furniture historian's task would be simple if the colonies strung out along the eastern seaboard of the present United States had been settled by a homogeneous cultural group from a single place. But that was not the case. Englishmen who had lived in Holland settled in Plymouth Colony, English dissenters of many persuasions and members of the Church of England, including Welshmen, Scotsmen, and Irishmen, settled throughout the rest of New England, Swedes set down in the Delaware valley, Dutchmen founded New York, Germans found their way into the Hudson valley—all before 1650. Moreover, these settlers came from a variety of urban, village, and rural traditions. Many Londoners settled in Boston, while both East Anglians and West Countrymen moved out into its agrarian hinterlands. In the fourth quarter of the century, while early seventeenth-century styles were still being made in the provinces of Europe, a number of Londoners, West Countrymen, Welshmen, and Germans (from the northern and western German principalities), came to Pennsylvania and settled where the Swedes had preceded them. During this same period, Lancastrians settled in the upper Connecticut River valley; craftsmen from the Island of Jersey—English in fact, but somewhat French in cultural traditions—came to Boston, Salem, Connecticut, and Long Island; French Huguenots came to Boston, Rhode Island, and New York; and Scotsmen came to New Jersey. The intermingling of local European cultural traditions, attitudes, and tastes is embodied in the furniture of each area.

Our understanding of American seating furniture in the styles popular before 1730 is further complicated by the reflection of the attributes of other movements which an art historian might describe as "late Renaissance classicism with northern European mannerist overtones followed closely by early baroque ideas." Because these styles were international in their time, the question of whether certain aspects of them were brought to America by Englishmen working in the northern European manner or northern Europeans working in their native styles continually confounds us. To tell the story of American furniture between 1630 and 1730 with any pretence to accuracy or, for that matter, to simple honesty, has required that we begin by exploring the continental European impulses that inspired it. Moreover, early in our research it became apparent that these impulses cannot be viewed as an initial activity that merely started the cultural ball rolling, but were

continually felt each time a new craftsman emigrated, taking with him a new local tradition or a reflection of the latest fashions in his homeland. These impulses account for the richness and variety of American furniture and their intermingling accounts for its uniqueness, but they also complicate the process of analysis so that, at times, the task of sorting out the threads have come to dead ends that can only be described by the word *failure*. In the light of this tangled skein, I hope that this book will be read in the spirit that I have written it: it was never intended to be the final word on the subject but rather a guide to future research and an immediate stimulus to younger scholars who should not be discouraged by the appearance of an attempt at definitiveness that its slow production might seem to indicate. In actuality, the study of American furniture is in its infancy.

As is true of many recent scholars in American decorative arts, the teaching of Charles Montgomery has shaped much of my thinking over the years. Early in my career he impressed one particular idea in my mind: It is not enough for a student to ferret out the facts and present them, one must comment upon them as well. To make such an assessment was not a privilege but an obligation; the person who has looked over any particular body of materials in all likelihood knows more about it than anyone else and, therefore, must try to abstract its general tenor. It is this process of making informed generalization on the basis of available facts that to some extent defines the trend of current scholarship in the decorative arts. The construction of theories, based upon general experience, has found its way into this book often, not with the intention of explaining problems away, but in the hope that we will narrow the range of probabilities in our generation and enable future students of this body of furniture to develop techniques by which to get at fresh ideas

In addition to this theorizing, I fear that I have fallen into a trap that the history of art sets for those who would write about it. I have felt it incumbent upon me to articulate those particular qualities that seem to set many of the examples of furniture that I have seen over the years apart from their fellows. This is a dangerous business for it involves a subjectivity that is currently out of vogue, but I have found that, with familiarity, the forms and workmanship of this first century of American furniture reveal a haunting beauty and fascination that must be verbalized. Undoubtedly this was the intent of some of the anonymous craftsmen whose chairs are pictured in this book, for many of them paid great attention to design and exercised considerable care in execution. By way of apology, I can say that I have found myself so sympathetic to the attitude of Giorgio Vasari, who wrote *Lives of the Artists* (1568) for the edification of collectors, that I have been seduced by it. Vasari states:

When I first undertook to write these lives, it was not my purpose to make a mere list of the artists or a catalogue of their works. This I could have done by means of a chart or table, without using my own critical judgment. But historians do not content themselves with a simple narrative of events. They must investigate the means by which successful results have been attained, and the points about which errors have been made. Being persuaded that history is the mirror of human life, they set forth the underlying currents, the character of events, for from these details men learn the true government of life. This, then, is the purpose of history. There is, besides, the pleasure of reading about the past as though it were the living present.

When I undertook to write the history of the noblest masters of our arts, I determined to be a true historian so far as I was able, wishing above all to honor the arts and those who labor in them. I have tried not only to tell what has been done, but to distinguish the better from the good, and the best from the better. I have also sought to discriminate among the different methods, processes, and even the various fantasies, inventions, and modes of treatment of the artists. [1]

I have no doubt that my criteria for the judgment of beauty, like those of Vasari, are not eternal, for no commentator can hope to do better than to express a personal view of the aesthetic values of the time, and my intention has been no more than that. Here will be found, perhaps, an indication of the taste of our age in regard to this subject for the future to muse upon.

Many people who will use this book will be disappointed to find that it does not deal with every piece of early furniture illustrated in the books of Wallace Nutting, Luke Vincent Lockwood, and Esther Singleton, now unfortunately no longer reliable guides to early furniture of American origin. The reasons that this was not done are cogent. First, many of these objects cannot be found today and cannot be dealt with adequately on the basis of their photographs alone. Second, had this been attempted, this book would have become so unwieldy and difficult to use that the main contours of the period under discussion would have become lost in a morass of details. Instead, I have opted to show the broad outline of representative and influential objects to which many others can be related. This book is primarily a catalogue of the earliest seating furniture in Winterthur Museum and as such the collection determined the direction of the research that was undertaken to elucidate it. But, with the generous assistance and forbearance of many private collectors and numerous museums in America and Europe, additional pertinent and illuminating objects have been included.

The form of this catalogue was inspired by that used by Charles Montgomery in his catalogue of Winterthur's federal-style furniture, but since seventeenth-century styles mark the beginning of furniture making in this country, it seemed appropriate to discuss the backgrounds of our origins as fully as possible. The Winterthur collection is composed largely of New England, New York, and Pennsylvania furniture. Since the collection itself concentrates on these areas, so does this catalogue. The collection has no recognizable examples of southern furniture of this early period; as a result, the South is largely neglected in the text. The stereotypical view of the South as an area largely dependent upon imported European goods for house furnishings is not explored by this catalogue, although it is obvious that this idea can apply only to the uppermost stratum of society. The absence of information about the towns in the seventeenth-century South precludes a conceptual study of the sort that we are able to do for areas farther north, a problem that is further complicated by the low survival rate of southern furniture which means there are scant clues upon which to base a theoretical framework to flesh out with facts unearthed by research. It is difficult, for example,

to generalize about seventeenth-century turned chairs in the South when only a handful of unrelated examples have survived. Thus, this book, like most studies of American colonial furniture, reflects a northern bias.

Winterthur's original collection was not formed with an eye toward representing every geographical area and every possible mutation of style. Anyone who ever visits the museum quickly realizes that Henry Francis du Pont was attracted to furniture of outstanding aesthetic qualities, exemplary workmanship, fine woods, and unusual details. This peculiar twentieth-century standard, by which he measured all of the objects that he added to his collection, caused him to choose a great deal of early furniture that subsequent research suggests was made in Boston, a town whose continually developing metropolitan atmosphere caused its furniture to manifest those qualities of design, workmanship, and materials that appealed to a highly refined taste both at the time it was made and at the time it was collected, for no collector that I have ever known has aspired to collect ordinary objects. As a consequence, these pieces of furniture have imposed a bias upon the documentary research undertaken for this book and that bias seems to suggest that Boston, from the very first years of settlement until the middle of the eighteenth century, was one center that established styles. The importance of an urban area in the development of material culture has been stated with consummate elegance by Sir Uvedale Price (1747–1829) who wrote toward the end of the eighteenth century that "[a]ll the fine arts have been brought to their greatest perfection where large bodies of men have been settled together: for wealth, emulation, and comparison are necessary to their growth." [2] Of course, the technique of analyzing unidentified objects on the basis of their relationship to urban examples—what might be called the "great city theory of history"—is an old model and is useful, but only up to a point. Its major fault is that it tends to ignore the evidence that many localities had established their own traditions early, had no contact with Boston economically, and cared little what the fashions were in that metropolis. The model further neglects the fact that many localities were as much in direct contact with European styles as was Boston and that influences from abroad were not necessarily filtered through the shops of Boston on their way to the other towns of America.

Despite its shortcomings, the idea that the furniture of a large urban area influenced the taste in its hinterland has been adhered to in this book in the belief that, while not perfect, it is more workable than no model at all in a time period whose furniture is poorly represented by documented examples. In many instances, its validity can now be demonstrated. In the instances where it has not worked, we are seldom any wiser.

The introductions to the various sections of the catalogue deal with the main strands of pertinent European traditions insofar as they can be unraveled, and insofar as they reflect the traditions that appear in the furniture at Winterthur. This catalogue is not intended as a study of all European traditions, and I hope will not be read as such. We have been able to ask many more questions than European monographs have been able to answer. European scholarship for over a century has given primary consideration to what may be called "art furniture," and research has been conducted in rather traditional art historical terms. As such, it differs greatly from American studies. By European standards much of the seventeenth-century American furniture has precious little to recommend it. An ornate piece of furniture for a member of a royal court was not only beyond the imagination of American craftsmen of the seventeenth and early eighteenth centuries but beyond the aspirations of their clientele as well. According to our present view, such stuff was not appropriate to the vast majority of the members of colonial society divided between a conservative agrarian group and a conservative middling urban group which lacked a hereditary aristocracy at the top but had a large laboring class at the bottom. Surprisingly enough, a few early inventories, such as those of Theophilus Eaton, a London merchant turned governor of Connecticut, and John Cotton, ministerial conscience of New England, give us a tantalizing glimpse of unexpectedly opulent furniture and furnishings, totally at odds with our preconception of what ought to have been appropriate to life in the Puritans' colonial society.

A second thrust of more recent vintage in the study of European furniture has been ethnographically oriented and has concentrated on peasant furniture. The American equivalent is generally referred to as "folk art" and does not correspond to the kinds of early furniture in the Winterthur collection. Those few American examples which fall into this category are undatable and usually have been treated as late manifestations of recognizable styles rather than as vernacular objects. If I had to characterize the social classes for which the early furniture at Winterthur was made, I would have to say two things. First, any use of the word *class* when discussing seventeenth-century American society must be qualified. The colonists were part of a society which recognized as legitimate certain aspects of deferential aristocracy while at the same time they accepted increasingly more rigid separations between the various social groups. Thus the concept of "social class" was only beginning to emerge during the seventeenth and early eighteenth centuries. Second, most of the furniture at Winterthur was originally owned by members of these emergent middle and upper classes, the colonial counterparts of the European middling orders and prosperous rural yeomen. Regrettably little has been written about the furniture of these classes in Europe. And the major weakness in American museum research and collecting in the twentieth century has been the insular concentration on American-made furniture to the exclusion of contemporary imported European-made items which served as models of taste and as prototypes to American-trained craftsmen. It may already be too late to attempt such a study. If it were done, it would likely invalidate a number of the conclusions that have been reached as to the originality, uniqueness, and meaning of American furniture.

The documents that relate to American furniture of the early period and the conditions under which the furniture itself has survived have prompted scholars to ask questions somewhat different from those our European colleagues ask. Indeed, the documents as much as the nature of the objects themselves have conditioned the direction of American furniture studies. One of the prime objectives of the last quarter century in American furniture history has been to define the regional character of furniture. Work during the past decade has attempted to substitute the word *local* for *regional*, with the result that much of the best effort of the present generation of scholars has been devoted to determining more precisely where surviving pieces of furniture actually originated. Unlike silver, it is not stamped with a maker's mark; unlike houses, it does not tend to stay put. Progress, the expansion of cities, the peripatetic restlessness of Americans, economic pressures, accidental destruction, disdain for objects no longer in fashion, absolute misrepresentation by dealers at their worst, and even the mania for collecting antiques that has preserved objects, have all served to uproot furniture from the locality in which it was made, blurring the trail which historians must follow in order to identify specific pieces of furniture and to understand them as documents of the culture that produced them. In many instances, this book can scarcely go beyond a vague estimation as to the provenance of a piece of furniture, so time-consuming is the task of tracking down related, better documented examples. I feel no need to apologize for this, and see it rather as a contribution in drudgery by my colleagues and myself upon which another generation can build. We only hope that no need will arise to do again in the immediate future what we have already done, but the need to carry it further and deeper remains.

This book is also devoted to a detailed analysis of the seating furniture in the Winterthur collection itself—doubtless to the point of tedium for the casual reader—for often the only clues to the origins or date of a piece of furniture are contained in what can be deduced from the details of its materials and construction. The necessity for studying a piece of furniture as the document of itself—second-best evidence—is to a great extent conditioned by the nature of the survival of artifacts. Why should a piece of furniture that was out of fashion or broken beyond repair or inconvenient in bulk or useless in form have been kept from destruction in the days before avid antiques collecting? We assume that survival has been subject to chance, influenced by all the whims of discarding and retaining that countless previous owners impress upon an object. It is therefore pointless to pretend that in this random pattern of survival the furniture, made as it is of such frangible organic materials as wood, vegetable fiber, and cloth, could escape the past unscathed and unaltered. How many houses of the colonial period have escaped new wings, altered roof lines, front porches, dormer windows, plastered ceilings, and the like? Few have, but all have a story to tell, and the accumulated knowledge that can be scavenged here and there makes each fragment the stuff of history. Furniture is the same, and it is the belief of the staff at Winterthur that it ought to be treated the same way. A fragment that reveals something about the life of the past is to be considered a document and ought to be treasured for study, and moreover, displayed, even though its full aesthetic impact may not be conveyed because of changes or loss of parts.

The reasons for changes to a piece of furniture fall roughly into three categories: changes made to continue its useful life, changes that have been made to restore it to its original appearance, and changes that have altered its original form to make it more desirable or collectable. It is clear that these changes proceed from different human motives. The first is honest, the second is altruistic, and the third pernicious. Nevertheless, all three exist, and all three must be considered, and that is, in itself, a tedious process.

To some extent, the introductions to each section of the catalogue can be read as a more or less narrative discussion of the furniture of the period. But to read them this way will not give the whole picture, because these introductions are designed to cover the basic background of the form and period with the objects in the catalogue in mind, to discuss some of the significant related forms and important objects that are not represented in the Winterthur collection, and to raise ideas and problems more appropriate to the form as a class or group than to any individual object. A number of artifacts in the Winterthur collection, as in any collection, do not fit into the mainstream that these introductions attempt to deal with, and they are considered individually in the catalogue entries. The collection contains objects about which sufficient identifying data to pinpoint the places of origin have not survived. This prevents us from fitting such pieces into a broader picture, in which case they are not considered in the introduction to a section and their catalogue entries are often short. In other instances, the present state of knowledge left little to say about some specific pieces of furniture after the broad outline had been presented in the introduction. In a few instances, the entries are long and introduce additional detailed material. This has been consciously done so that the data that make up the book are placed where they are most pertinently illustrated by surviving furniture.

Throughout the course of writing this book, I have struggled to reduce complexity to clarity; no hope of reducing it to simplicity was ever entertained. Subheadings divide the introductions into more digestible bites. Introductions end with summations which sift the main ideas from the welter of factual materials. In some cases I could only hope to write a summary that attempted to state concisely the bare bones of the factual materials in the section; in others the conclusions introduce new materials that view the factual materials from points of view that are different from the themes developed in the introductions. In a few cases, where sufficient examples have survived or where sufficient material is available, the conclusions deal with the most difficult of all problems to synthesize—how the objects were used, what they meant to their owners, and why they look as they do. Needless to say, the nature of the documents that survive precludes the attempt to do this with every form represented in the catalogue.

It was obvious from an early date that it would be impossible to include as many illustrations as was desirable to illuminate graphically all those points that are best illustrated by photographs. As a compromise, I have not shown a number of significant objects which have been previously published and are readily accessible. Hardly any collector who will read this book does not already possess a well-thumbed copy of Wallace Nutting's *Furniture Treasury*. The same may

be said of Luke Vincent Lockwood's *Colonial Furniture in America*. Likewise, it is now unnecessary to own a run of *Antiques* for access to the pertinent articles cited here since Robert F. Trent's well-edited reprint of most of them, somewhat nostalgically entitled *Pilgrim Century Furniture* by the publishers, is available.

The visual evidence is supplemented by the written records. But language, like the objects, has changed, been added to, subtracted from, and otherwise modified in the centuries of use that separate us from the seventeenth century. Words and objects have both survived from that century, but it is not now as clear to us as it was then to those who used them, what words were applied to what objects. The *Oxford English Dictionary* (*OED*), normally a sufficient key to unlock the problems of language, is essentially a literary dictionary. Its quotations usually show when a word first began to be used, but its definitions do not invariably reveal the subtle details of character that differentiated the now obsolete forms of furniture used by our ancestors, or the processes by which these pieces were made. Consequently, I offer a definition of these terms at their first mention in the book and include notes on their household or craft uses that are deduced from or proven by English and American documents dating from the seventeenth and eighteenth centuries.

The order in which this catalogue is arranged will doubtless seem strange to many readers who may have to search about a bit to find what they are looking for. I have read many catalogues in the past decade in the attempt to find a format that would make the information in this one available in the most efficient manner possible and at the same time satisfy the multiple aims of what my former colleague John D. Morse called "a catalogue, plus." The problem of how to retrieve information is one that always plagues researchers. This book will doubtless be used as a reference work, since a person would have to be hearty indeed to pick it up and read it from beginning to end. But consistent with the aim of writing a narrative history, it is more or less arranged on a chronological framework. My ideal is that no concept that has not been previously introduced should be used to demonstrate a point, all the while recognizing that what is common knowledge to one reader may be opaque to another. Since this book deals extensively with the techniques used to produce furniture—the most objective data we have to go on—it seemed that the book should be arranged to accommodate the study of those techniques in a reasonably coherent manner. This led to a dilemma: should the study begin with the joiner or the turner, the two craftsmen whose work dominated the period being considered? Because it was impossible to say that one was more important than the other, I decided to consider both as simultaneously as possible. The products of both of these trades embody the same general aesthetic impulses and decorative vocabulary. Further, the work of both crafts is often found in a single piece of furniture, and to separate them artificially for the purpose of exposition is needlessly arbitrary. With an awareness of trade structure and individual artisans in mind, I quickly realized that the point of view concerning furniture that has been almost universally adopted in catalogues is that of the collector or the historian as aesthetician. As a corrective, which has perhaps become overcorrected, I have tried to approach connoisseurship from the point of view of the man who was making the furniture and who was earning a living by selling it.

While each chapter thrusts onward in time from earlier to later, and is arranged chronologically according to stylistic changes, each furniture form is completely discussed before we move on to any others. For example, upholstered chairs were first being made in this country around 1655, when wainscot chairs were still much in vogue; however, upholstered chairs are not introduced in the catalogue until after *all* the wainscot chairs have been discussed.

A further problem of arrangement arises because all the chairs made prior to 1730 in America did not evolve from a single earlier one. For example, slat-back chairs were made in two distinct styles. One derived from the ornamental and proportional schemes common in the early seventeenth century, the other derived from cane chairs in what, for lack of a better term, we call the "William and Mary style." In the interest of narrative coherence, therefore, the story of the turned and joined chairs of seventeenth-century date is interrupted by the introduction of the story of the cane chair, since the later turned and joined chairs can be better understood if we compare them with the cane-chair aesthetic that inspired them.

The catalogue entries are arranged both chronologically and geographically beginning with New England followed by those from New York and the Middle-Atlantic colonies. In those instances when a form appeared in the Middle-Atlantic colonies before it did in New England, the earlier piece takes precedence. Generally the geographical arrangement follows the chronological one, for the forms of furniture that are made in America are generally first made in the urban areas of New England, predominantly in Boston, where the furniture industry was well developed within the first two decades of settlement.

Much of the catalogue, and a significant portion of each introduction as well, is devoted to the exercise known as connoisseurship. The implied techniques of connoisseurship that underlie this book are spelled out in the first chapter, "Connoisseurship and Furniture History." It is perhaps a moot point as to whether that subject should be brought to the reader's attention at the beginning of the book or at the end. Each location has its difficulties. On the one hand, the reader has a right to know the limitations of the study and the attitudes and biases of the author. On the other hand, most of the statements of principle in the chapter are derived from the materials in the rest of the book, so that it is possible that the critical reader will find himself disturbed by unsupported statements that go contrary to ingrained ideas. The chapter, therefore, should be read as an inquiry into the bases of common knowledge and not as an invitation to Armageddon.

Much of this book is devoted to the investigation of the details and techniques that are the basis for critical judgments about a body of furniture that has only within the last fifteen years been looked at with a critical eye. In many cases, the details elude interpretation; in others, the process of con-

noisseurship has not provided sufficient information. In many cases I have forced myself to make judgments which I hope posterity will confirm, but if it does not, I can only hope that I have not needlessly misled future students, whom I urge to get at the facts I was unable to discover. Each generation must rewrite history in its own image. In that way knowledge increases as historians mellow.

Those of us who work at Winterthur Museum are convinced that the objects that have survived from the past are documents of American life that are not duplicated in written records. But, like the latter, they are not always self-expressive, so our ability to perceive their meaning depends upon an understanding that is the result of study and interpretation. For example, the story of the destruction of the virgin forests of eastern America by the wood-consuming economy of colonists who gave little or no thought of conservation or replenishment is implicit in these objects. It has an inescapable parallel in our age, and the warning is clear.

Every historian hopes to find Truth. My aim has been more modest. I have hoped merely to find some truths and to uncover what insights I could into the life of the people who used this furniture, its meaning to them and, perhaps most important of all in the absence of verbal documents on the point, to synthesize or make a composite of the way in which the craftsmen may have seen it and may have thought about it. One thing has become clear in the process: This furniture shows that much of the groundwork for the industrial revolution of the nineteenth century is found in techniques practiced by furniture craftsmen in the seventeenth century.

This book has been written during the tenures of two directors of Winterthur, Charles van Ravenswaay and James Morton Smith. Both have been exceedingly patient about the time it has consumed, and both have subscribed to the notion inherent in it: that to transcribe what everyone else has said over the years about this body of furniture and the age in which it was made was not enough. The time has come to look at this material anew, and to look at it from the inside out. In many cases we are convinced that we have succeeded, in others we have certainly fallen into the trap of being too credulous. I once remarked to furniture historian Colin Streeter how unusual it was that Luke Vincent Lockwood, Wallace Nutting, Percy McQuoid, and R. W. Symonds, fine connoisseurs all, could have been gulled into publishing, as antique, furniture that could not have been more than fifteen or twenty years old. "Ah," he responded, "but they were taken in by the forgeries that were made for *their* generation." Undoubtedly, future generations will find that we have been taken in by the forgeries that were made in our honor. The principle that emerges from this is that it is hard to think beyond the limits of one's own time. The self-evident fact or scrap of information that misinforms is as much a pitfall today as it was for Thomas Johnston of London in 1595.

Manie are the woonders & mermailes in this world, and almost incredible, were it not that experience teacheth the contrarie: for who could bee preswaded to beleeue that the Owstridge could eate or deuoure cold & hard Iron, or that hote burning Iron could not hurt her stomacke, were it not that it hath and is daylie seene and knowne.[3]

Indeed, in the preparation for this catalogue, I have read enough books and manuscripts from the sixteenth through the nineteenth centuries that I often find myself falling into the verbal expressions and habits associated with those writings. One convention common to them all was a foreword or a preface usually entitled "The Author's Apology to the Readers." Such a disclaimer seems an idea too good to resist, although the false humility generally couched therein often barely conceals a hearty conceit. One such apology written by a man who obviously intended never to publish another book, is too appropriate not to quote in full. It is the preface to the anonymously published (and partially plagiarized, hence the anonymity) *General Description of All Trades*.

Now there remains only for me to request the *candid* Reader, that, upon his meeting with here and there some little things, that may not exactly tally with his Knowledge or Judgment, he will not immediately condemn the Whole, or major Part, which he knows nothing of: But consider how many different Persons must have been consulted, to gain so much Intelligence as is herein communicated; and add to this the Oddness and Variety of Men's Tempers, on being asked three or four civil Questions, the answering which was no Trouble, nor could be any Detriment; yet some were shy, others jealous; some testy, others sour, nay, some quite angry, thinking one was come as a Spy to steal the Secrets of their Trade; And, besides all this, several of the same Trade or Business were met with who gave very different Accounts.[4]

I can happily say that during the course of work on this, I met with odd tempers only twice. All the rest whom I have solicited have shared a goodness of spirit that has added what richness of detail this book possesses.

NOTES

[1] Vasari, *Lives of the Artists*, p. 41.
[2] Lauder, *Sir U. Price on the Picturesque*, p. 328.
[3] Thomas Johnston, *Cornucopiae, or Divers Secrets*, as quoted in Ferguson, *Bibliographical Notes*, 1: pt. 4, p. 14.

[4] *General Description of All Trades*, preface.

AMERICAN
SEATING
FURNITURE
1630–1730

CHAPTER 1

CONNOISSEURSHIP AND FURNITURE HISTORY

In every physical science we have carefully to distinguish between the facts which form its subject-matter and the theories by which we attempt to explain these facts, and group them in our scientific systems. The first alone can be regarded as absolute knowledge, and such knowledge is immutable, except in so far as subsequent observation may correct previous error. The last are, at best, only guesses at truth, and, even in their highest development, are subject to limitations, and liable to change.
JOSIAH PARSONS COOKE,   New Chemistry

The word *connoisseurship* has taken on such precious connotations in the recent past that many people who rifle through the pages of this book and see it here will be repelled and read no further. The word can easily evoke an effete and elitist image of highly cultivated persons lightly passing value judgments and altogether giving themselves up to the hedonistic enjoyment of vague verbalization about the aesthetic qualities of art objects. A definition in the *Oxford English Dictionary* (*OED*) does little to dispel this image. *Connoisseurship*, it says, is a "critical acquaintance with works of art or matters of taste."[1] What questions this blithe definition leaves us with! To what end can we be critical about matters of taste— essentially private conclusions—when taste is the one thing that sane people do not dispute? And what does *acquaintance* mean? If the lexicographers had instead used the word *knowledge*, which we understand to be the sum of study and experience, then it would be clear that the connoisseur *earns* the right to be critical, and connoisseurship becomes an active experience. But *acquaintance* is a word of casual detachment, a word that places a certain distance between the connoisseur and the subject of the criticism. In this relationship, *acquaintance* is not a matter of doing anything about anything, it is merely a take it or leave it mental state, possibly a state of mild interest or momentary diversion, but not of concern.

And what can the word *critical* mean in the *OED* definition? Whether it means seeking what is wrong with something or seeking what is right with it, the word implies a judgmental decision, and, conjoined with the words *acquaintance* and *taste*, places the act of connoisseurship in a realm of subjectivity which ignores that connoisseurship in the visual arts is invariably directed to something that is concrete. To those who would form significant collections, this definition is unacceptable because of its frivolous overtones; it is unacceptable to historians because it calls for no backbone of a discipline founded on the analysis of data; and it is unacceptable to the present generation of young scholars who bring a sense of purpose along with dedication and trained minds to the study of the furniture maker's art.

It may seem pointless to take to task a definition in a book that is primarily concerned with literary rather than real problems, but the exercise is necessary if only to show that this definition, like many in the physical sciences, is not eternal. Words change with the needs of the people who use them. This century-old definition fails to convey the remotest suggestion of the richness of the Latin root, *cognoscere*, from which the word *connoisseurship* is derived. Every first-year Latin student quickly learns that *cognoscere* is translated "to know," but time and experience teach that it must also on occasion be translated "to observe, to perceive, to recollect, to inform one's self," and, as if these were not tasks enough for one who truly wants to know, "to learn," and finally, "to understand." This string of meanings is a roadmap to connoisseurship, and connoisseurship in all these senses is what this book is about.

Whereas connoisseurship is knowledge gained from experiencing objects with our senses, furniture history is knowledge of what it was possible for an object to have been in its time. The connoisseur derives knowledge from the object itself; the furniture historian derives knowledge from documents that are essentially independent of the object. If a would-be connoisseur does not know the history of a form of furniture or the history of the technology used to make it or the history of the materials of which it is made and something about the people who could have made it and owned it, then the connoisseurship can only mirror this lack of knowledge. The historian who does not have a feeling for the way the object was executed or a sense of the way its design affected the process, and who is insensitive to details of structure and to the distinguishing traits that different societies have impressed on the artifacts they made, cannot know at what moment in time or where in space to begin the search that may reveal the meanings of the objects. The disciplines of the connoisseur and the historian are not the same, but in the best of all possible worlds their techniques and attitudes are combined in the historian of objects.

Far from the flights of fancy that have at times in the past characterized the connoisseurship of furniture, modern connoisseurship yields understanding through the careful analysis of both objects and written documents. In this process the documents are mute, while the mind is active. Jacob Bronowski characterized human thought as being of two different types, scientific and intuitive.[2] The scientific thinker builds each step of a complex idea upon the previous one, proceeding from the known to the unknown in an orderly manner. Intuitive thought, in contrast, stimulates the mind to make quick associations in a nonverbal way, to proceed by analogy from resemblances, something on the order of what happens to us when we come into contact with a work of art. Both of these types of thinking have historically been used to convey messages, the one by precise denotative expression, the other by evoking connotations or images in the mind. Both types of thinking have motivated furniture making and furniture buying in past cultures, and furniture historians must use both types of thinking to get at the ideas which have inspired the furniture that forms the subject matter of their studies. They must be prepared to deal not only with logic but with inspired illogic as well, for these are attributes of the ways human beings think, and both have been used to translate thoughts into objects.

If a piece of furniture is the result of a professional process, we can learn a great deal about it through research. We know, for example, that in the past furniture was made according to the crafts practiced by different tradesmen and that these crafts were taught and learned in a rational way, governed by certain rules devised to promote the good of the group. Objects of art made according to those rules—in short, the objects that can be fitted into the long tradition of historical craftsmanship—can be subjected to analysis. We know that objects were made according to the technological abilities of the societies in which the craftsmen who made them were working, although we also know that in every historical period technologies have existed yet, for one reason or another, have not been used. Further, we know that the possible ways of making an object were defined by the available materials. If this were all, the museums in which furniture is housed would be museums of industrial archaeology, presided over by historians of technology and culture. The objects themselves would be little more than "anthropological curiosities," as art historian Rudolf Wittkower once characterized them. But we know also that the furniture of the past represents something *more* than technological history because it is ornamented and because it has formal qualities.

Sometimes the form of a piece of furniture is itself ornamental. More often, the ornament is an added embellishment. Psychologists may someday prove that craftsmen add ornamentation to objects because they have an uncontrollable urge to ornament, but it is certain that ornamentation has been sought by buyers throughout history—a fact that need be supported by no documents other than craftsmen's bills that demonstrate that embellishment costs money. It follows, then, that ornamentation and fashionable shapes conveyed a message to the buyer, and it seems fair to assume that the buyer intended to convey this message to anyone who would see the piece of furniture. The message may have been so innocent as "I delight in ornamented furniture," or so naive as "I am rich because I can afford ornamented furniture," or "I am pious because I eschew ornamentation," or so self-righteous as "I am rich and am of the elect but I am pious because the ornamentation I have chosen is a group of religious symbols," or one of a number of other ideas we can no longer conceive because the cultures of which historical furniture was once a living part have been forgotten—a part of what English historian Peter Laslett called "the world we have lost." Yet, the failure to understand is ours; the message is still there if we wish to learn to read it.

The craftsman who decorates furniture uses the vocabularies of the sculptor, the architect, and occasionally the painter, and furniture with these types of ornament has found its way into numerous museums that do not deal with technological history. In these museums, the ornamental character of this furniture is enjoyed by visitors and pondered by scholars. A few of these objects possess significant form, but each example on which ornamentation was attempted was clearly made as beautiful—let us not hesitate to use the word—as its maker could make it. That beauty is a part of such objects suggests that such pieces were intended to have a significance somewhat deeper than the mere fact of their utilitarian existence.

The embodiment of form in a piece of furniture and the addition of ornament to it cannot be an accident. Both permit the designer and maker to stimulate an emotional response in the way that a persuasive actor, an easel painter, a sculptor, a poet, or a musician can. (Indeed, only in the relatively recent past have the words *artisan* and *artist* taken on exclusive meanings.) No one could argue that any piece of furniture might have the rich ambiguity of a great poem, or might evoke the same diversity of conflicting human experience that a great painting portrays, or convey the same poignancy as a classic drama, or directly stimulate emotions as a piece of music does. The beauties of these arts are different from those of furniture. This difference, in a hierarchy of values defined by our ideas of what constitutes serious art, does not mean that the artful aspects of furniture lose their power to stimulate us even though the vocabulary in which those artful aspects are realized is not of our generation. The artistry mankind embodies in its artifacts has a way of transcending time, a way of being eternally present. We are remiss if we believe that a chair had no function in the culture that produced it beyond being something to sit on or that a court cupboard had no role beyond being a convenient place from which to serve food. Long-forgotten roles and functions are never obvious in furniture that has been out of use or out of fashion for many generations; they must be recovered by scholarship. The frustration of all historical scholarship is that the reconstructed picture will always be imperfect; the breath of life, with all its ambiguity, is missing.

Since humanistic researchers know that their recovery of the past is destined to yield an imperfect picture, they must scrutinize the theoretical concepts and generalizations to ascertain that these arise from the data and not from wishful thinking. A furniture historian cannot afford to be less rigorous with the materials than any other modern scientist. If we suppress subjectivity for a moment, put aside considerations of the accidents of survival and the ravages of time, and pursue connoisseurship with the detachment of the scientific disciplines, we can analyze only three aspects of a piece of furniture objectively: the materials of which it is made, the workmanship with which it is executed, and the design that it embodies.

The study of American seventeenth-century furniture is relatively routine when we deal with the materials of which it is made. Microanalysis, the microscopic examination of the anatomical structure of a minute sample of wood, quite often enables us to state with reasonable accuracy what species of tree a piece of furniture is made from. If that species is indigenous to the western hemisphere and not the eastern, we can state with accuracy in which hemisphere the wood grew, and if documentary evidence can be introduced to demonstrate that the wood in question was not shipped from one hemisphere to another, we can state with some assurance that objects made of that wood were made where the wood grew. In this respect, American furniture historians during the past quarter century have had a tremendous advantage over our predecessors, regardless of their reputations or scholarship, for we can now speak with confidence on this one point. Using microanalysis, we can identify a body of furniture of American origin on the basis of which relationships can be perceived, research can be undertaken, and generalizations can be made.

The other two aspects of connoisseurship—workmanship and design—are much less objective, but their intricacies and complexities can be partially unraveled by close observation and analysis, research, logic, and a steadfast determination to allow the imagination to be stimulated only by collected data.

Nothing guarantees that we, like our predecessors, shall not also often go wrong, for furniture history is a humanistic discipline and not a science.

That workmanship and design are not literally objective qualities capable of quantification or impersonal analysis does not license us to approach furniture history in a purely emotional way simply because a piece of furniture can affect us emotionally. We shall commit a grave error if we deprive ourselves of the systematic examination of all the materials relating to furniture without classifying them in as orderly a way as possible, without grouping together those aspects of the furniture of a culture that fall together naturally, and without seeking to abstract from them the general principles that the furniture of many cultures may have in common. Above all, we err if we do not use the most valuable tool of the scientific method available to use—model making, the construction of hypotheses based upon the existence of available data with the objective of giving direction to the search for *missing* data in the ultimate hope of arriving at understanding.

If the content of a book such as this is to go beyond mere description, we need to synthesize a great deal of data. We need, for example, to use contemporary documents to tell us about the craftsmen who made furniture. Sometimes the results of our research exceed our greatest expectations, and we can actually trace the seemingly random wanderings of a fashion by identifying patterns of immigration and movements of craftsmen. Sometimes we have good information about these craftsmen and can construct a picture of how they practiced their trades in their communities. When we learn to see the furniture that they made as a document, our knowledge advances by quantum leaps.

A piece of furniture can sometimes illuminate virtually every detail of how its maker executed it, what tools he used, even where he got his nails or screws. We can sometimes tell if the maker was clever or slovenly. Sometimes we can tell whether he war right-handed or left-handed or had a sense of humor. On occasion we can perceive whether he respected his materials, did his work as if he loved it or was a day laborer working merely for pay. Gathering this kind of information becomes more than a mundane chore; it becomes an exhilarating experience through which we can, for a moment, touch the personality of a human being from the past in a way that is seldom available to us through any other medium, for in an object we have both thought and deed.

Research can eventually illuminate all of this for us. But with the results of the research in, we are still dealing only with those things that are susceptible to rational thought, to systematic recovery, no matter how disorderly or random the materials, no matter how accidental their survival. All this tells us little about the intuitive aspects of the man who designed any given object or the thoughts of the men who made it. To divine the complexity of sensations that influenced even the dullest craftsman represented in this catalogue defies our powers. Of course these problems are not new to the study of the arts; they are new only to the study of eastern North American furniture made prior to 1730. And those who have studied the phenomenon of the artistic impulse have left us hints that may be applied to the work at hand. Over the years a vocabulary has developed that we can now use to discuss the problems inherent in understanding furniture. Unlike the denotative language of mathematics, the vocabulary of the decorative arts has little precision and therefore requires some explanation, for words still slip and slide with imperfection, as T. S. Eliot pointed out a generation ago. Vocabulary is, of course, necessary, and words are useful when we define them narrowly.

One of the difficult words in the vocabulary of furniture history is *design*. Design is inherent in every made object. Design is the fruit of a person's thought about the way an object should look and function. It is, in addition, the outline of a solution to a problem. A design may represent a system that a society has embraced to define its own aims or a self-conscious device used by a craftsman to attain an end, but in another sense design also appears to be a quality that a person not bred to the society that used it or someone who is not a craftsman can perceive. In 1748, one author noted, "Design is not of interest only to the architect, for under this name in general is comprehended form [and] ornament. . . . It ought to enter into the plan of all education; for men of the first order, in order to acquire taste, of which design is the soul; for all well-born men for their personal use, and for artisans in order that they may advance and distinguish themselves in their professions."[3] For many generations, the aesthetic enjoyment of design was left to "men of the first order." Indeed, until very recently, design has meant little more to furniture historians than an opportunity to verbalize their subjective reactions to the appearance of an object. *Design* has been a term that is usually preceded by the adjectives *good* or *bad*, which of course tell us much about the attitudes of the connoisseur and the times, little about the object in question, and still less about the historical subjectivity of those seventeenth-century individuals we are interested in knowing more concretely. Many furniture historians now realize that the phrases good design and bad design relate to notions that properly fall under the study of the history of taste and do not in fact relate to the qualities of objects at all. Connoisseurs must be strong-minded, indeed, to avoid confusing the design that underlies an object with the workmanship that has been used to realize it.

When a casual student of furniture gets hold of an eighteenth-century design book, the great temptation is to look at the pretty pictures and skip over the quaint prose that precedes them. Such books have survived when most of the objects of their time have perished, and the sheer beauty of the laid paper, the vitality of the engraved line, the impasto of copperplate printing, all exert a subtle call to the senses. The flowing ideas of the designs themselves become part of an artistic expression that make us tend to see a printed design as a thing of beauty and lead us to believe that the design was conceived of as an end in itself with no allusion to function. But a designed thing must *do* something (although a design that satisfies function need not be aesthetically pleasing). A chair may offer rest for the weary and functionally satisfy the requirement of design in that respect, but if we were to put it on a pedestal in a museum and shine a spotlight on it, the interrelationship of its parts might not please our taste. The

reverse is also true: many an aesthetically stimulating chair design offers no pleasure to the sitter. Furniture historian John Gloag once delightfully imagined a customer's commission to Thomas Chippendale: "Good chairs, Mr. Chippendale, that comfort your body without creasing your coat. 'Slife, would you have me rise from table with a garland pressed betwixt my shoulders?"[4]

Modern thinkers, however, do not always support the mutual exclusiveness of design and form. David Pye has done more than any other contemporary student of aesthetics to help us recover a nonsubjective basis for verbalizing the relationship between an object and its design. Pye suggests that the only judgment one can make of an object is whether or not its workmanship realizes the design from which it was taken. If it does, then it must, by definition, be a successful object.[5] Pye's brilliant and innovative approach also shows that a design and the workmanship used to realize it are inextricably linked, a notion that has commonly been neglected by students of furniture. Once we learn to think of a design as something more than a beautiful picture, then the idea of *designs for making* unlocks the possibility of identifying the unknown work of America's colonial craftsmen on the basis of their known work; it takes the technique of attribution out of the realm of the subjective and gives it an objective basis.

If a design for making is actually a set of instructions to a craftsman on how to realize a design, the instructions, often repeated, will result in parts that are more or less uniform each time they are made, hence as nearly identical to each other as the human eye and hand can make them using imperfect materials such as wood and imprecise tools. Euclid said it best when he postulated that "things equal to the same thing are equal to each other." Designs for making may be as complex as a set of plans or specifications, or as simple as a single stick upon which a craftsman has cut notches to give him the dimensions for every element of a turned chair. Usually these designs survive from the colonial period in the form of wooden patterns or templates. Indeed, templates are occasionally noted in estate and shop inventories of craftsmen. From such templates, woodworkers could make many pieces of furniture, virtually identical in shape and dimensions, and that they did so is confirmed by objects in the museum collections of our country. Pye has aptly named the results of this process *the workmanship of certainty*. The point of a professional craftsman's employing the workmanship of certainty in his trade is that it is easier, more efficient, and more profitable to make objects exactly alike than it is to make them slightly different from each other.

The ideas of designs for making and the workmanship of certainty contain one further concept that is crucial to the process of furniture connoisseurship: they imply that the man who conceives the design for an object need not be the man who makes it. A classic illustration of the implications of a design is in even so fanciful a book of patterns as Thomas Chippendale's *Gentleman and Cabinet-Maker's Director*.[6] We now understand that Chippendale put together this book of engraved illustrations to advertise the capabilities of his shop, but when an order for furniture to be made from his designs went to his workshop from the showroom, you may be sure

Fig. 1. Chairs. From Chippendale, *Gentleman and Cabinet-Maker's Director*
(1762), pl. 13. (Winterthur Library.)

that the man who was to make the furniture (and that man was *not* Chippendale) had a set of patterns to guide him in cutting out the parts.

This method is reflected by the very title of the book, and the plan is carried through in the illustrations. The gentleman (who may have more money than taste) is told what fashionable furniture is; the cabinetmaker is told how to make it. Take, for example, figure 1. At first glance it is an awkward picture made by an artist who could not decide whether he wanted to draw the chairs in two dimensions or three. On closer inspection, it becomes apparent that a suggestion of three-dimensional perspective has been worked into the engraving primarily to suggest to a gentleman what a finished Chippendale chair might look like. Those parts of the chair which carry the stylistic burden—the front legs and the back from the seat up—are drawn in two dimensions and these give the craftsman who will make the chair a set of plans that he can enlarge with a pantograph or a sector to create the two-dimensional patterns from which the chair, indeed countless sets of chairs, can be made.

For the social and economic historian, the idea that patterns were used to create a multiplicity of examples of the same object shows that shop practices in the so-called preindustrial age were not so quaint as we have been led to believe. It relieves the art historian of the necessity of invoking the muse of invention more than once for each form that a craftsman made and explains how the craftsman was able to sustain his creativity through the process of replication. For the connoisseur, it means that the patterns of various pieces of furniture can be recreated, can be taken from the objects that have survived, and

can be used to remove attribution from the realm of a gentlemanly, educated guess and place it instead upon an objective footing.

More than a century passed between the time that the first furniture was made in America and Chippendale's *Director* was published, which means that the shops of the colonies' earliest furniture makers undoubtedly differed from those of the following century. But the greatest difference between the later products of Chippendale's shop in London and those earlier ones of an American craftsman, such as Peter Blin in Wethersfield, Connecticut, or Henry Messenger in Boston, is that Blin and Messenger physically made the furniture that they designed. Blin's designs, and those of his contemporaries may have existed on paper or in templates, perhaps brought from Europe when they emigrated, but more likely, they existed only in their heads and hands, the product of training ingrained by custom—what we call *workmanship of habit*. These designs came to life each time an object was made from them.

As connoisseurs we must make evaluations. Can we use Pye's standards to make judgments about furniture? Can we say that pieces of furniture are "good" or "bad" if we do not know what the designs were like that the furniture was meant to realize? Pye's stringent criteria—originally suggested for students of modern design—point the way out of the judgmental void. Although few colonial designs have survived, in many instances a number of objects made from the same design have. If we examine these objects and find that they are virtually alike, it seems reasonable to assume that the maker corrected any minor design errors after making the first and before making the second example, and therefore the subsequent pieces closely followed the design that he intended them to realize. This analysis works if the designer was also the maker, a situation that we assume closely approximates the realities of most American rural or village furniture shops throughout the colonial period. It also is a valid analysis for an urban shop—even when the designer was not the maker—because the necessities of competitive production meant that a master's journeymen and apprentices used patterns that resulted in exact replication. The furniture produced from these patterns must accurately represent the design from which they were taken, always assuming that the master of the shop or someone under his direction was the designer and pattern maker.

Such criteria as these, however, do not take into account that the vast majority of the colonial furniture in the museums and private collections of our country cannot be identified as to the towns of origin, let alone the shops. Most of these pieces of furniture have no surviving relatives, and this places an extra burden upon the connoisseur, the essence of whose method is comparison. The unique item offers only a mass of data, some of which will, of course, be familiar but much of which will only be generally analogous to the accumulated information that constitutes knowledge. The unique item offers the connoisseur no source for direct comparison and no basis on which to form a judgment. The historian side of the connoisseur warns that no man-made object from the age in which craftsmen learned their trades by serving an apprenticeship can be unique. The apprenticeship method of passing on knowledge from one generation to the next, if it has no other significance, means that every object has its precedent and is itself precedent to another related object.

In the absence of absolute standards for judging furniture, as casual observers we have felt the need to introduce more subjective ones that reflect the temper of our times. We have even developed a vocabulary to express these ideas. We equate age with rarity, rarity with value, and value with price. The American tradition of admiring success—whether it be in terms of the best or the biggest or the most elaborate or the rarest or the most expensive—has been with us since the arrival of the first English settlers. As the prices of these antiquities soar out of view and money loses its value, we cannot imagine that the objects of our affections can be less than perfect. We find it difficult to imagine that a handmade item from an age so different from our own can have shoddy joints, rough backs, slapdash painting, or inferior materials. Such notions do not agree either with our mental image of an age in our history in which an honest day's work was given for a full day's pay or with the prices these objects now command.

We have an equally difficult time reconciling the apparently useless workmanship lavished on colonial furniture with our conception of the conservative lives that our ancestors led. Nonetheless, we admire elaborate objects for their complexity, allowing that complexity may have been an end in itself; we see furniture with a lot of workmanship lavished on it as "rich" and admire its "quality"; the simple examples we label "chaste," equate them with what we conceive to be the "Puritan plain style," and attempt to project into them the virtue of Puritan simplicity; those examples with painted carving we marvel at as a continuation of the medieval practice of polychroming; those with the traditional ornamentation that was common in the Middle Ages (especially when the embellishments are roughly executed) we label "vernacular" or "folk" or even "naive," enjoy their charm, but shake our heads and comment on the lack of sophistication in the craftsmen who executed them.

When we look dispassionately at the value judgments, we are forced to admit that we do not have history, nor have we said anything that modern scholars would consider very important or even accurate about the furniture. The intuition of the present-day commentator is not that of the craftsman who made the object or that of the people who used it and brings us no closer to historical truth after all. What has happened is that the artistic aspects of these objects have seduced us, perhaps just as their makers intended them to, and we have felt constrained to comment on the experience. Our emotional reaction to the form or to the skill with which the piece of furniture was designed and wrought tends to overwhelm any other considerations. A piece of furniture that excites the imagination transports the furniture historian from the mundane world of court records, which recite joyless tidings of men in conflict, to a realm of beauty, the concept of which is as subjective as the public records are objective. Our verbal rhapsodies reflect our inner needs. We want the objects we consider beautiful to have been made by virtuous men, and we are disturbed when we find, for example, that Thomas Dennis, the best-known American furniture maker of the seventeenth century, was a liar who claimed that he had felled six trees on Ipswich Common (which he had permission to do) when in fact he had felled eighteen; in addition to stealing from the community, he stole some nails that were left in an unattended small boat; he overcharged for his work; he did not live up to his monetary obligations to his apprentice; and he did not pay his bills.[7] In this case, and many others, the virtue is in the objects and not the man.

When we look at Pye's criterion for the successful execution of a design in the light of historical research, we find a hidden subtlety that would elude us if we accepted the notion that a design is but a solution to a mechanical problem. The very fact that execution adds an evocative element to the design indicates something more than a literal solution to a problem has occurred: behind the created object lies the motive of the customer in ordering it. It is clear that the owner of a new object wishes to express something by possessing it, and if we can read the object fully, we learn that it says just as much about the customer as it does about the designer who conceived it and the craftsman who executed it.

Historians and collectors often differ in regard to what is important about a piece of old furniture. Many public institutions and private collectors have traditionally been concerned with aesthetic appeal and have put their collections together accordingly. Their furniture contains some explicit information—the materials of which they are made and the techniques used to make them—but most of the pieces cannot be associated with a craftsman; consequently, such institutions and collectors have generally ignored the craftsman's role. In a few, relatively rare instances, a piece of furniture can be associated with a maker's shop, and this has enhanced its price in the modern-day marketplace. In contrast, furniture historians prefer to collect furniture that has something of a document about it. They incline to be as interested in the person and the society behind the furniture as the furniture itself, not only because social history is fashionable in scholarly circles today, but because surviving artifacts are the enactment of men's efforts, thoughts, and feelings. The furniture contains information about an aspect of colonial life that we do not readily find in written sources. If a piece of furniture happens to be considered beautiful, the beauty is no impediment to a furniture historian, but the absence of beauty is no impediment either.

To do the job properly, the furniture historian attempts to establish some of the basic facts about objects from within documents. That these documents tend to provide information about people and not objects makes the furniture historian a social historian, thereby converting necessity to virtue. Generally, the people historians can learn the most about are not the people who were using or making the specific objects that historians are studying. Written documents, therefore, are not enough, and the historian must learn to look to an additional source: the object as the document of itself.

The two sources of information—documents and objects— are not only dissimilar in kind and therefore require the historian to develop different techniques for getting at the information each contains, but they are also dissimilar in the type of information that they convey. The furniture historian deals more frequently in analysis and argument than in proof. As a consequence, the writings of modern students of furniture abound in a tedious preoccupation with the processes of identifying specific examples and locating them in place and time—information that is not self-evident in the furniture itself. Occasionally students can show, by history of ownership or by kinship to related and better documented examples, that a piece of furniture came from a certain place. Or they may place it in time by using objective criteria, such as a carved date. The methods by which an object is made are also good evidence. If those techniques are consistent with those commonly used in a specific place and time, the piece of furniture may in fact be what it appears to be. But more of the students can only guess the date and place and do so on the basis of the style.

Style is one of the words we abuse when we deal in quick and easy communication. The *OED* gives twenty-eight substantive definitions for *style*, no one of which quite conveys the sense in which historians and other writers use the word in dealing with the cultural and aesthetic ramifications of an object. *Style*, in the most abstract sense and in the most stilted language, is "a kind, sort, or type, as determined by manner of composition or construction, or by outward appearance."[8] It is thus a manner of executing a work or performing an operation and by extension represents those aspects of appearance embodied in an object that give it distinction and make it recognizable. It may be as small as the manner of expression that is characteristic of a single craftsman or as large as a body of expressions that typify a civilization, overwhelming enough to characterize an age or a culture.

A design or system of design can combine ideas and forms in such a compelling way that it captures the imagination of all who see it or the products made from it. When such a system of design is sufficiently elaborated so that it becomes recognizably different from what came before or after, we refer to it as "a style," examples of which can be perceived in the work of Crispin van der Passe, Jean Berain, Daniel Marot, Charles Percier, and Pierre-François-Lénourd Fontaine, and the Bauhaus School.

An increased proficiency in our understanding of style has made us complacent. One direction in which the study of style has gone has been to treat style as an independent discipline. We have thought of historical styles as being absolute, immutable, universally spread throughout the cultures that used them and possessed of attributes that are observable, hence quantifiable. We have theorized that styles were conceived of, designed, made, introduced, accepted, and left to cast their grand shadows over a generation until a subsequent generation rejected the aesthetic of its elders. In our unending search for absolute certainty—a residuum of nineteenth-century aspirations but an end that modern scientific measurement denies the possibility of attaining—we have attempted to work such ideas as these into quasi-scientific theories that explain the attributes of undocumented furniture. One such theory is the concept of periodization, the idea that a given object can be equated with a given period of time because it is made in a certain style.

The theory of periodization is based upon the observation that styles have historically succeeded each other. According to this theory, once a new style becomes dominant, the earlier style becomes insignificant. In practical terms, the theory is often embodied in such statements as "the William and Mary style was popular from 1700 until 1725 at which time it was succeeded by the Queen Anne style." Terminology aside— since it does not really seem to matter what we verbally tag a style so long as the people with whom we wish to communicate understand what we are talking about—these dogmatic statements contain a host of assumptions and prompt a great number of questions. What objects made in 1700 indicate that styles had changed? Does 1700 represent the date at which the William and Mary style was introduced or the date at which the style became common, or prevalent, or quantifiable? Were no objects in this style made after 1725 or was the style merely no longer dominant after that date? Do these dates apply to America, or to America and England, or to America, England, Holland, and France? Do they apply to the city and the country alike? Do they apply to all social and economic levels in the city? And above all, where is the information that supports these assertions?

Even if we substitute the word *popular* for *dominant*, as some writers have done, the same questions arise. How many objects and how many documents are necessary to indicate popularity? The idea of periodization, with its strong implication of a sequence of styles following each other with clockwork regularity, gives a spurious sense of legitimacy to itself and a sense of relief to those who use it, because the theory validates the physical law that states no two objects can occupy the same place at the same time.

More than a century has passed since the appearance of the

theory of dating on the basis of style. Bit by bit this rough-and-ready tool of early furniture historians has been transformed into the axiom, "style equals date of manufacture." Brooking no contradiction in the popular literature, the axiom remained unquestioned so long as the criterion for judging the style of a piece of furniture was the *quality* of its design and execution. But then in many circles any furniture whose design and workmanship were not of what was deemed to be splendid quality did not matter much and hence did not affect the equation. Modern furniture historians tend to be less cavalier. The present generation of young scholars are so bold as to see furniture as one expression of the way in which an entire society lived, and they want to understand it all. An axiom, they feel, is only so good as the data that supports it; consequently they have begun to refine the style-equals-date equation by asking not only when a style appears in culture but also where a style comes from and how the particular manifestation of a style in a particular society comes about, for the "how" governs the "when."

It is obvious that one true, correct, and simple answer to any of these questions does not exist. Students of history long ago recognized the ethnic attributes of some groups of furniture, such as the *kas* of the Dutch in New York, and extended this consciousness of an ethnic style to describe furniture that is not necessarily ethnic, such as that particular favorite among the writers of the early twentieth century, "Dutch chairs" (meaning those with crook'd legs). But phrases and associations do not answer questions about style, they merely characterize them. The question of how styles come about is deeper and more complex than that.

Too often, casual students of American furniture have accepted a style as a "given," assuming that the basic research into these questions had been done generations ago. When we look back, however, we find that earlier scholars held wildly erroneous ideas, or simply glossed over the problem, or confronted it only theoretically. One of the most common theories, that styles "develop," has been advanced by numerous American and a few British writers in the past half century. Development appears to be a perfectly plausible concept when we look at the vast number of objects from the past that express a similar stylistic idea but are not demonstrably copies of each other. The existence of these similar objects is forceful evidence that style is an idea and that the variations of the idea are a sign of development. *Development*, however, is a word that has an overtone of orderly growth in one specific linear direction, and this overtone may be misleading because we cannot assume that developmental relationships exist among a heterogeneous collection of unidentified objects that have in common only the style in which they are made. The problem with the idea of development that a collection of undated objects does not address is when the "development" took place. It is easy to show that a style develops *after* it becomes known to a wide circle, but this begs the question. The real question is: Does a style become a style by the slow accretion of ideas, or is a style invented all at once?

Evidence can be found to support both points of view, and it is difficult to chose one to the exclusion of the other. If we define styles broadly and base our conclusions upon an arrangement of objects that have attributes of an earlier style mixed in with those of a new one, a gentle development with the accretion of new ideas added to older forms indeed seems to be the way styles came about. The problem is that the data upon which the conclusion is based is faulty. A meaningful conclusion can only be reached by surveying as orderly an arrangement of identified objects as we can muster. If we have estimated the dates of the objects in any sequence on the basis of the answer we have been taught the sequence ought to reveal, we should not be the least surprised when our expectations come true!

If, on the other hand, we define the attributes of a style rather narrowly, excluding those objects that contain elements of an earlier style, and base our conclusions on historical research into documents, we could come to the opposite conclusion. We could argue that in almost every case, major styles were first presented to the world as inventions, that is, as something new, although the men who invented these styles doubtless struggled through a period of development—perhaps *synthesis* is a better word—in arriving there.

The questions of the origins of styles are particularly acute in cultures that did not invent the styles in which their craftsmen worked. Colonial New England, for example, derived its notions of what was stylish from English ideas on the subject. But English craftsmen who dealt in fashionable furniture after 1650 modeled their versions of each current style on what was being made on the Continent. By the time the ideas reached New England, they were not secondhand, but thirdhand. This argues strongly for the idea that current styles were well formed by the time they reached the urban centers in America. In a sense, it supports the hypothesis that styles were for all practical purposes introduced inventions that were adopted by American craftsmen, although these may have been old inventions by the time they arrived.

In later furniture history, numerous well-documented instances of the invention of a style can be found. The way in which they came about suggests that the principles involved were not new at the time—they are merely better documented. The French empire style is a classic example. It was made to order by Percier and Fontaine specifically for the purpose of dissociating the furniture of Napoleon's France from that of the Bourbon monarchy (Louis XVI style) and to replace it with the one with attributes that evoked the military successes of the emperor (directoire style). If each major international style comes about through the imaginative efforts of designers who are giants, any development of any style must occur after its invention and introduction and not through a gradual amalgamation of partly formed notions.

A style may be carried beyond the national boundaries by the emigration of a craftsman or designer, as well as by the shipment of designs, templates, or a piece of furniture. If a style is transmitted by any of these methods, any development of it in that new place must come after its introduction and cannot express or contain suggestions of a growth toward the style. If this idea is correct, we are confronted with a seeming *contretemps*. A diligent furniture historian can point out that preechoes (a favored poetic but logic-defying term used by students of art) of what we have been pleased to call the empire style are found in the work of Giambattista Piranesi in Italy and of Charles Heathcote Tatham in England some years before Percier and Fontaine formally synthesized that style. But this serves to confuse the later phase of the neoclassical movement with a rather narrower instrument, originated for political and propagandistic purposes, that constituted Percier and Fontaine's achievement.

While we can say that the empire style was invented in a moment, it is essential to distinguish between the moment of its creation and the time it took to translate the drawings of it into objects. It is apparent that the French palaces and public buildings of Napoleon's time were not furnished in an instant and that the style doubtless became elaborated as the actual work was done. In a very like sense, the Chippendale style was not fixed. It has what we now know are Chippendale's personal earmarks, which make it recognizable and distinguish it from the rococo style as practiced in France and England, but it was not a static conception, which is readily apparent when we look at the actual products that emerged from Chippendale's shop instead of the design book that made his name famous. Christopher G. Gilbert's meticulous survey of that shop's documented work reveals why Chippendale operated one of the two or three leading furnishing establishments in London: the shop was a leader precisely because it did not stand still. Chippendale was a fertile and innovative creator who had exemplary imagination and talent, but in a real sense his customers forced him to exercise whatever natural innovative talent he may have possessed.[9] Considering that most of his patrons among the nobility and the affluent gentry knew each other, it is obvious that he had to offer each of them a product that varied from what he had sold to the others.

Another idea that the alternation of historical styles has evoked is embodied in the word *cyclical*, the concept being that styles have followed each other in cycles. We can easily support this notion by showing that furniture styles have generally followed each other in a more or less predictable way: periods of classicism have been followed by periods that can only be described as romantic; a generation of highly ornamented objects has been followed by a generation of furniture whose aesthetic depends upon severity; surfaces that are carved or molded in high relief have been succeeded by shining veneers.

Insofar as *cyclical* suggests recurrent patterns in which styles grow and then subside in popularity the notion has some merit. It is at best, however, an after-the-fact analysis. The idea of a cycle connotes a measured regularity, but regularity does not appropriately suggest the way in which styles actually follow each other in a specific place at a specific time. The styles enjoyed by the tastemakers of colonial America do not gently waft in and gracefully retreat, as the interpretation of data furnished by household inventories might lead us to believe; groups of inventories tell us only what people had when they died and not when they got it. It now seems more realistic to believe that styles replace each other abruptly. They explode onto the scene! As they become known throughout the circle of those to whom it is important to be stylish and percolate down the social and economic scale and outward from fashionable centers, they set off a continuing series of secondary explosions. First the big bang, then smaller bangs, and then still smaller bangs until nothing is left but a few restrained pops. By that time, the tastemakers, or perhaps a new set of tastemakers, are setting off a new big bang. For those who initiate this sequence, no development has occurred, only change, dynamic and drastic. If styles occur in waves, they are more like tidal waves than breakers!

If a style consists of an amalgamation of form and content, then it is possible that the attributes of either form or content can be grafted onto an object to give it the flavor of the style. Can a piece of furniture that has a style grafted onto it be said to be *in* a style or has the style merely been suggested by use of one or more of its attributes? Does putting a California cabernet sauvignon in a bottle shaped like one from Bordeaux make the wine a claret? Does adding rococo ornament to a design for a Georgian looking-glass frame, as Matthias Lock did in 1744, make it a Chippendale looking-glass frame?[10] Each of us will answer these questions differently, depending upon what point we are trying to get the data to demonstrate, but if we were to think in the purest of terms, the answer would have to be that adding new ornament to an old form does not make a new style. To be most accurate, we would have to say that the style defines its attributes but, ironically, the attributes may connote the style without defining it. A pain in the jaw is the symptom of a toothache, it does not cause it.

The person who would think of a style in abstract terms must exert considerable mental effort to hold its image in mind without embodying the idea in an object. Because this is such a difficult task, for the past century furniture history has been taught as if the characteristic attributes of an object define its style and as if these attributes can be abstracted and verbalized. While this may be pedagogically sound procedure, the result is flawed because the intellectual dismemberment of a style for didactic purposes artificially disintegrates the three units— form, ornament, and content—that cause a style to be a style in the first place. In the interest of historical accuracy, styles and their attributes must be seen for what they really are: abstractions drawn from the observation of a number of undated and probably undatable objects that we summarily group according to their casual resemblances and label with catch phrases that ease our problems of communication and definition. Certainly nothing is wrong with this, if it is the best we can do, for the process of organization must begin somewhere. At the same time, we must be aware that this is all we have done and remain ever cautious when we use these labels.

In the same way that a series of objects can be arranged to show how a style comes into being, a series of objects in a specific style can be arranged to show that a style is undergoing change during the entire time that it is being made. While the first of these can lead us badly astray, the latter arrangement can yield real results that further our understanding. The very idea of being in style guarantees that any succession of objects made to gratify the need to be stylish must be part of a continuous process of change to satisfy the definition of being in style. Change supports the notion that fixed styles do not universally dominate periods of time. The history of art reveals that many styles can be popular in a given place at the same time, and the possible permutations of those styles are as diverse as the human beings who make the objects. The pervasive notion that styles are confined to rather closely dated periods in a given place is incapable of being proved. Indeed, research into the history of furniture fails to confirm the idea of periodization; while we may sometimes find evidence of when a style is introduced and begins to enjoy its first popularity, we usually have no idea when its successor obliterates it. Research also shows that styles do not disappear at the same rate throughout the various levels within a culture.

While the idea that fully formed "pure" styles are introduced into derivative cultures must remain an intellectual possibility, the actual fact is we cannot show that this happened very often in colonial America. For one thing, the real life practice of a craft by a man who must earn his livelihood by what he makes does not conform to the perfect intellectual model we construct to explain the objects he ought to produce. In actual practice, the conception of what a style should be like in America was inevitably influenced by individuals in Europe who continued to make their own versions of the style and whose various ideas were continually being introduced into America in the same way that the original ideas of the style had been: migration of craftsmen, shipment of patterns or drawings or furniture.

The process of transmitting stylistic ideas requires time and calls the popular style-equals-date axiom into further question. If transmission occurs over a period of time and consists of numerous individual interpretations of an idea, then style-equals-date can only be a clue that invites furniture historians to investigate the documentable manifestations of a stylistic idea in a specific place at a specific time and to relate it to similar local manifestations in other locales. In short, we ought to explore specific embodiments of various styles much more thoroughly before we attempt to make broad generalizations. So far, the history of furniture, with a few grand exeptions, has been written the other way around. Our overall view of the history of our furniture ought to be thought of as little more than a conceptual or theoretical framework, subject to constant correction, rather than as the answer to all of our questions.

Like all aspects of human endeavor, styles cannot be divorced from specific cultural contexts. The idea that a piece of furniture is a reflection of the culture that made it is not new. It was very much a part of the philosophy of the earliest collectors of artifacts from the American past, those who saw individual pieces of ancient, hopelessly out-of-fashion furniture as having a mystical quality that linked the present to previous generations, as relics of the people who had founded a society that later generations enjoyed. The Reverend William Bentley of Salem, Massachusetts, noted in his diary when he received the turkey-work couch from the Appleton family, "All were willing honourably to dispose of to a friend of the family what they feared to destroy & dared not disgrace."[11]

The historian of furniture cannot ignore the context in which furniture was enjoyed when it was new and the changing attitudes toward it over the centuries. Context is as much a part of the object as the materials of which it is made. The turkey-work couch is now in the Essex Institute. We do not see the couch in the same way that its original owners (incidentally *not* the Appletons) did at the end of the

seventeenth century, nor as Bentley did at the beginning of the nineteenth. In order to do the job properly, therefore, furniture historians must be more than connoisseurs of objects; they must try to recover from history the ways in which the objects were perceived in the past. From such study comes meaning, and meaning is a part of the content of an object.

No student of furniture will ever admit to having sufficient data from which to work, and the lack of data often leads to oversimplified statements about the context in which the furniture of the past was made and used. Oversimplifications lead us to believe that we have achieved an understanding we have not. We are constantly tempted to see long-dead cultures as monolithic, as if the culture of a civilization that is simple in comparison to ours was absolutely simple, as if all of the activities of that culture were centered on a single set of values, and as if hints of these values are to be found in every artifact the culture produced. While this may be true of so-called primitive cultures, none of the communities that produced the furniture in this book could be described as such. For every Jacobite in New England there was a commonwealth's-man; for every practicing Congregationalist at Ipswich, there was a closet Anglican in Boston and a Baptist in Rhode Island. We expect a great deal if we demand that a piece of furniture reflect all of these opinions. Indeed, it is likely that furniture will not. The way any given piece of furniture looks could be traced to any of a number of different sources within a community. Economic, ethnic, religious, and political differences among customers can lead to distinctive tastes in furniture. And the appearance of furniture is further influenced by the background and skills of the craftsman.

These variables suggest that in a complex society new stylistic attributes appear on the furniture at different times on different levels for different tastes. Although it seems a cliché, the idealized image of the village craftsman working away at his craft under the spreading chestnut tree has a germ of truth in it. For the independent rural woodworker, time was measured in part by the rhythms of the agricultural year. Documentary evidence repeatedly reveals that he was a professional in every way when he was working at his trade, but he and his sons and apprentices—if he had them—also spent a predictable amount of time plowing and sowing in the spring, mowing hay in the summer, and harvesting in the fall. The reward of a life wedded to the soil and the seasons is that a person learns the nature of continuity; the penalty is that the horizon circumscribes his world.

Potential customers in agricultural communities are normally conservative. In such seventeenth-century communities the majority of the furniture makers had little impetus to change either their ways of working or their styles, and, not surprisingly, few newly immigrated craftsmen who held new or fashionable ideas sought to settle in these communities. Yet the furniture collections do show that on more than one occasion the devil whispered in the ear of a prospering villager and inspired him to commission a work in the latest style, a piece that stated his perception of his rightful place among his neighbors and his consciousness of rank, order, and precedence.[12] A customer can certainly demand the latest style, but when the local craftsman makes that piece of furniture will it be in the latest fashion? Obviously the ideas of both maker and customer are conditioned not by the attributes of a style but by what they perceive that style to be, and the result is always tempered by the abilities of the craftsman. Village craftsmen often advertised in the provincial newspapers that they made furniture in "the newest and latest taste, as well as it is made in Boston or London," but when we look at the furniture we can identify from their shops, we find that rarely would we confuse it with Boston or London productions.

Much village-made furniture is instantly recognizable. It often *suggests* a style without being in the style. Individual examples generally have proportions different from what we expect a piece of stylish furniture to have—taller, skinnier, squatter. Their ornament is often sparse or, conversely, excessive. The motifs of the ornament suggest the style but are not those we would expect a cosmopolitan craftsman to have used. Connoisseurs who appreciate both the prototype and the variant are fortunate; the whole wide range of human endeavor is theirs to enjoy. Other connoisseurs are less fortunate; they interpret the village-made variation as aberrant and therefore "distorted"; they see only exaggeration and interpret it as "naive"; they are unable to understand the object as a product of a craftsman who was attempting to work in a style for which he was not trained.

If we espouse the point of view that the customers of these craftsmen intentionally seek the bizarre and the grotesque, then we must be prepared to explain away the pressure to conform, which all social groups exert on their members. Is it not, after all, social pressure that makes a customer want an object in a new style in the first place? If that person is in a place where precise information as to what constitutes the new style is as difficult for him to come by as it is for the craftsman who is to make it for him, can he not be excused for accepting something that, according to his perceptions, fills the bill?

By and large, a craftsman learns not only the way in which to make an object in his master's shop but the style in which to make it, and he is understandably reluctant to cast aside all that he has learned by experience in order to work at something that is new to him and perhaps unproved. The result is that much new style furniture made in colonial America carries with it strong overtones of the previous style and sometimes, in village furniture, of the one before that. Because we have known for some time that this is often the case, furniture historians have found it convenient to introduce into our thinking the concept of time lag, or style lag, with its unavoidable note of condescension, to explain why this furniture looks the way it does. Increased attention to the documents that illuminate the provincial furniture of Europe, however, has revealed that Europeans on the same social and economic levels as the yeomen of seventeenth-century America have just about the same kinds and quantities of household furniture as their American counterparts, and that their furniture stands in about the same stylistic relationship to the furniture of the places from which they derive their notions of what is fashionable as the American examples do.

If the village craftsmen were the only craftsmen at work in colonial America, the national inferiority complex that has long gone hand in hand with the concept of time lag might be understandable, if not completely justifiable. But, the busy seaports of colonial America supported an aggressive furniture industry. These ports acted as a magnet to emigrating European craftsmen and to foreign trade, much of it speculative. New styles or variations of them arrived in America from London and Bristol in the same way (if not quite so often) as they arrived in Bristol from London and in London from Holland and France, with every new shipment of furniture and every newly arrived craftsman. The craftsmen in these American seaport towns were different from the romanticized picture we have painted of their village counterparts. We can document that the realities of urban competition among the craftsmen guaranteed that any newly arrived ideas quickly appeared in the work of every furniture maker who was in the business of selling fashion. Even if we lacked documentary evidence on this point, the concept of time/style lag in cosmopolitan centers poses an almost insurmountable logical problem. How could we ever have seriously imagined that a two-month sea voyage, by an emigrating craftsman who, say, had worked in the latest London manner, could cause him to regress twenty-five years in his art, a possibility that must inevitably require him to work in a style that was passé when he received his training?

Indeed, newspaper advertisements throughout the colonial period tell us the very opposite is true. What craftsman would fail to capitalize on his capacity to work "in the latest and best London manner" if that boast would help him break into the already competitive marketplace in his adopted land? In short, unless specific causes can be adduced to explain a delay in the transmission of ideas—a war in progress, religious or political scruples against being fashionable, lack of money with which to buy new fashions, export items consisting of old stock shipped to the colonials to be got rid of—we have no reason to assume that a customer in a seaport town who wanted a piece of furniture in the newest fashion was hampered by anything but the time it took a ship to bring the model or a maker from Europe. The only lag that enters into the equation is the time it takes for style to percolate down to the social and economic level that will permit exportation.

All cultures that derive notions of fashion from another culture, perhaps all complex cultures, are characterized to some extent by the persistence of old and comfortable styles; this persistence is what we often confuse with lag. In addition, the occasional object that bears a late date and does not conform to our preconceptions of what a style should have been like in America at that time, taints our view of the entire oeuvre. Such pieces of furniture attract our attention unduly while objects that can be identified as having been made when the style was young are elusive.

Prudent connoisseurship demands that we distinguish between the work of urban and village craftsmen, and the gradations in the products of each. In colonial American society during the first century of English settlement, two strains of the furniture-making arts ran parallel to each other through time, and neither was confined to the town or the countryside. One strain represents the work of craftsmen who came early and perpetuated their techniques and attitudes as they trained their apprentices. When styles changed, such craftsmen grafted the attributes of the new style onto forms that they could execute with old techniques, for life and art had to go on. The second strain represents the new styles brought in by the continual influx of new craftsmen who had been specifically trained to make them. It is thus clear that only a part of the furniture made by craftsmen in America represents an old tradition perpetuating initial impulses; the rest is the product of newly introduced ideas.

In a society open to new immigrants, stylistic change is a persistent force. The culture is not subject to once-in-a-generation or once-in-a-style introductions of ideas from outside. If we look at furniture made in geographically or intellectually isolated areas of America prior to the nineteenth-century introduction of factory methods and an efficient transportation that made the current taste available to everyone, we perceive an exciting paradox of human behavior in which stylistic emphases run counter to each other. On the one hand, in communities that experienced little infusion of new ideas about anything, furniture often becomes simplified, consistent with the expectations of its customers. The images of the prototypes from which their furniture was originally taken have become indistinct, blurred with passing time. In short, the makers forget. On the other hand, in equally isolated places, forms and ornament become more complex, more elaborate, taking on a life of their own, according to the sensibilities of individual makers, so that the effects they produce seem excessive and exaggerated when their furniture is compared with the prototypes. In both situations, which could conceivably occur simultaneously on different social or economic levels within a single community, forms and ornament can evolve into entities that have no recognizable prototypes, European or American.

Both of these situations can be described by the concept of evolution, although to call the process of becoming simpler rather than more complex "evolutionary" runs contrary to the popular late nineteenth-century conception that evolving forms move to a higher and therefore better state. *Evolution*, however, is patently the wrong word to apply to a provincially made object that has merely acquired attributes reflecting fashionable changes in the larger or parent culture. The piece of furniture in the derivative culture has not evolved, nor has the craftsman who made it. In American-made furniture, evolution might be observable if we were able to gather together a body of work made in one maker's shop over a period of time. In such a group the attributes that account for change in appearance ought to come about by a logical elaboration of the possibilities inherent in the original style; they ought to represent the mind of the craftsman subjecting the original idea to his individual sensibility, rather than changes in the community's ideas of style. In such instances, the work of some American craftsmen does appear to evolve. A classic example is the Philadelphia Chippendale-style high chest of drawers. It is something that did not exist in the parent culture, and by all rights can be said to have evolved in our country. Of course, others may argue that it is merely a form that became outmoded in the parent culture a generation earlier and in America this form is really an idea that persisted past its time with up-dated ornament.

In the seventeenth and eighteenth centuries, craftsmen continually offered variations on the themes of their times; some were accepted by the public and were sold in great quantities, others were not. From the former, the commercially successful examples, which are of necessity the ones that survive in quantity, we furniture historians have our conception of style of the times; from the latter pieces, which we have never been able to cope with successfully, we tend to see only the details that evoke the idea of the familiar style and to ignore the variations from the norm that show innovation. Of course, even the touches that we interpret as novel may not have been original in the derivative colonial culture. We can never be sure that further research might not reveal that an immigrant craftsman came into contact with an episode of furniture making in England that has escaped our attention.

Fashion is the attentive handmaiden of style. Like style, it is an idea in the mind, an abstraction. It is a tyrant. Those who submit to its tyranny find it to be often illogical, sometimes painful. When it is embodied in an object, it is always expensive, for no new fashion is ever cheaper than the one it replaces. Fashion is often arbitrary and exists for no reason other than to excite admiration, and that, too, is part of its meaning. Its technique is contrariness in the pursuit of novelty. When new styles appear, they first appear among those classes who can afford to cast off the old for the new, and in the process those people gain something more valuable than the money they will spend.

Any method of connoisseurship must consider the effects of fashion on stylistic ideas. In practical terms, furniture historians using independent written documents can often show that a new style has appeared in a certain place, which enables us to equate the visible manifestation of that style with a moment in time. But, while this is demonstrably true for the furniture made for the most fashion-conscious classes in colonial America, the attempt to apply this idea to the broader spectrum of American society is less successful because many pieces of surviving furniture are not stylistically pure.

In the past we have suggested that stylistically impure furniture, containing as it does attributes of more than one style, should be dated according to its latest feature, and we have referred to such furniture as transitional. In the process we have made *transitional* the most abused word in the vocabulary of connoisseurship. In the same way that a style can be made at any time following its introduction, so can the attributes of a new style be grafted onto a piece of furniture whose form is rooted in an earlier style. While many pieces of furniture may indeed have been made in the space of time between the passing out of one style and the coming in of a new, this hypothesis is rarely, if ever, capable of being proved by an object that has been removed from its context because proof demands independent documentary evidence, evidence we often cannot adduce.

In theory, if we understand the attributes of styles in the colonial era, we ought to be able to recognize an object whose appearance suggests that it was made in a period of transition. Reality, unfortunately, rarely conforms to this theory for the simple reason that objects are visible in space, while transition is a concept that deals with time. When we look at specific pieces of furniture whose date of manufacture we cannot place on the basis of style, some of them seem ahead of their times, others behind. Can both be transitional? This alluring, popular word conceals a trap for the unwary. As long ago as 1915, Edward Gregory, with persuasive charm, noted:

Students of old furniture who carry their investigations beyond the point at which it is fairly easy to distinguish one period from another, may be tempted to agree with a worried amateur collector who, in despair of ever arriving at a true designation, declared that he believed all specimens in existence were nothing more than transitional. This declaration is a very much wiser and more profound one than it looks at first sight, for in a sense all art is transitional. It typifies the age in which it is produced, but also partakes of what has gone before, and illustrates a movement in thought which is bound to develop in the future.[13]

Gregory faced the problem that everyone who attempts to write about the broad sweep of furniture history encounters, the problem of what to call these styles so that readers can understand the objects being discussed. Undoubtedly, Gregory would be amused to find us still debating questions of designation some sixty years later. Yet is "what to call it" really what we want to learn about the furniture of the past? Ours must be a frivolous discipline, indeed, if our greatest concern is what cubbyhole of language an object ought to be fitted into. It is doubtful that we can ever come up with terms that will be simple enough to use in conversation and complex enough to encompass within their definitions the great diversity of attributes and their variations that constitute our ideas of a style, not to mention the accidents of history, the visions of patrons, and the individual quirks of craftsmen, each of whom perceives the world about him from a slightly different point of view.

The problem of designation runs deep. Things have the habit of becoming what we call them, and a name tends to become the definition of the object without explaining it. In furniture nomenclature we speak of "Queen Anne chairs," yet the style owes little to Queen Anne, who died many years before the style gained currency; nonetheless, the ambiguous label endures.

Does Gregory also err in logic? How can an object forecast the future? If it intimates an idea that is in the future, then the future is not *in* the future. At any given moment, a limitless number of possible futures exist depending on choices and influences. An object does not represent a figurative point on a straight line from the past to the future, as teachers often find it convenient to pretend, but is rather a point prior to many alternative futures, and only hindsight reveals which one of many possible pasts it came from. Styles are defined by historians and not by the craftsmen who make things in those styles.

Here is the heart of the problem of transition. How it is possible for a craftsman to make a piece of furniture with attributes of a new style unless those attributes are already present in his culture? How can a craftsman make a transition to a new style if the new style does not already exist? If it does not exist, then how can he know what he is supposed to be making a transition to? It ought to follow, therefore, that no piece of furniture made in a derivative culture is absolutely

transitional in time, although it may represent the personal transition of a craftsman or designer from one style to another. Once the personality of an individual craftsman is introduced into the equation, then the relentless passage of time in the life of the style is suddenly halted and what is done becomes less an imperative and more a personal option. The object that a craftsman produces can properly be said to be transitional in style, but we cannot infer from this fact when it was made.

An even more pointed question arises about the arts of a derivative culture. How can we distinguish derivative objects from objects reflecting the process of development in the craftsman's culture? In other words, how can we be sure that what we might perceive as evidence of the development of a style in a derivative culture is not in fact an object copied from an object that is itself transitional in style? This possibility is always present when the culture is simultaneously derivative and dynamic. When we are able to trace styles and their attributes back through documents or documented examples of furniture to the originating culture, we see that form and content of a style do not invariably travel as a unified entity.

Where is the still point in this turning world? When is the moment in which a style is defined in its own time? There can be only one answer to this: it is defined at the moment that it is invented, or if a culture does not invent it, then it is defined at the moment it is introduced into that culture. This is its high moment. This is the moment of novelty that animates all the subsequent desires to possess the style. And yet, it is obvious that this is only one aspect of the life of the style, for the style does not stand still. Gregory was on the very brink of enunciating a principle that would have made him immortal in the eyes of future connoisseurs and furniture historians, the simple thought that change itself is a constant.

History has taught us that new styles radiate outward to new places over a period of time. The designers who first gave life to the styles perpetuated in England and America during the period that concerns us lived in continental Europe. In a sense, every craftsman who lived outside this select circle of inventors was derivative, and his ideas were provincial.

The words *derivative*, *provincial*, *colonial*, and *dependent* as I have used them here are not pejorative, for the invention of something truly new is a great rarity in human experience. Most ideas are derived from new combinations of what has gone before or from a shift of emphasis. The decorative ideas that held sway the first half of the seventeenth century were essentially a revival of classicism with a few twists of fantasy added. The presence of a great deal that is old in something that is new is usual, for this is the way that mankind perpetuates its hard-won achievements. Continuity is found in the furniture crafts because the apprenticeship system guarantees that it will be there. Every craftsman has a strong tie to the past because he learned his craft from his master who was trained in the past. When a master passes his craft on to his apprentices, much of the heritage goes with it. In *The History of the Royal Society* (1667), Thomas Sprat comments in rather depressing terms on the dark side of this fact. "Those men," wrote Sprat,

who are not peculiarly conversant about any one sort of Arts, may often find out their Rarities and Curiosities sooner than those who have their minds confin'd wholly to them. If we weight the Reasons why this is probable, it will not be found so much a Paradox, as perhaps it seems at the first Reading. The Tradesmen themselves, having had their hands directed from their Youth in the same Methods of Working, cannot when they pleas to easily alter their custom, and turn themselves into new Rodes of Practice. . . . Especially having long handled their Instruments in the same fashion, and regarded their Materials, with the same thoughts, they are not apt to be surpriz'd much with them, nor to have any extraordinary Fancies, or Raptures about them.

These are the usual defects of the Artificers themselves: Whereas the men of freer lives, have all the contrary advantages. They do not approach those Trades, as their dull, and unavoidable, and perpetual employments, but as their Diversions. . . . There is also some privilege to be allow'd to the generosity of their spirits, which have not bin subdu'd, and clogg'd by any constant toyl, as the others. Invention is an Heroic thing, and plac'd above the reach of a low, and vulgar Genius. It requires an active, a bold, a nimble, a restless mind: a thousand difficulties must be contemn'd, with which a mean heart would be broken: many attempts must be made to no purpose: much Treasure must sometimes be scatter'd without any return: much violence, and vigor of thoughts must attend it: some irregularities, and excesses must be granted it, that would hardly be pardon'd by the severe Rules of Prudence. All which may persuade us, that a large, and an unbounded mind is likely to be the Author of greater Productions, than the calm, obscure, and fetter'd indeavors of the Mechanics themselves.[14]

Sprat may be accurate, but we must remember that his statements are conditioned by his vision, which was confined to the gentle class from which the members of the Royal Society, hence his intended readers, came. Had Sprat studied in the London furniture shops of his time, he would have seen ingenious innovations occurring every day, and he would also have seen, had he but known it, the foundations of modern industrial production. Moreover, if Sprat had ever served an apprenticeship with a vital master, rather than analyzing the situation as an uninvolved observer, which historians are prone to do, he would have realized that many masters had an inventive resiliency, a way of coping with the unanticipated, an instinct for survival that they did indeed pass on to their apprentices.

Were craftsmen as dull as Sprat portrays them, the propensity to stasis that the apprenticeship system encourages would have frozen furniture history eons ago. We would all still be sitting on klismos chairs or on oak stools without backs. This is visibly not so, which means that change has been as important a force in furniture history as tradition. American furniture in the seventeenth century did not remain the same as the European prototypes because the men who made it did not remain the same as they would have had they remained in Europe. And American furniture could not avoid changing from its prototypes because the conditions under which it was made differed from those of Europe. During the initial period of migration from England to New England, entire parishes often moved, under the leadership of ministers, and settled as single units. Such movements resulted in the establishment of a way of life founded on a bodily transfer of ideas to a new community. Among these ideas were preferences for the furniture the families were accustomed to in England. But

chance could place parishes from very different places in close proximity in New England. In many regions a single joiner served two or more communities. Thus it is not surprising that many a Yorkshireman who settled in the Bay Colony's town of Rowley found himself sitting in a wainscot chair made by an Ipswich joiner from Devonshire.

New England furniture is not innovative in the second quarter of the seventeenth century, nor is the English furniture that inspired it. Political and social unrest had had its impact on the arts. Another aspect of life that mitigated against innovation in this period was the newness of the colonial settlement. The craftsmen were transplanting familiar ideas onto a new terrain. Typically, ideas that are removed from the mainstream of an integrated cultural life, where give and take keeps them vital, have one of two things happen to them: either they develop according to the influences of the new context— which are undeniably different from those in the homeland— and go on to new glories of elaboration and complexity, or, within a generation or so, they descend to a meaningless ritual and uninspired repetition that may not even be relevant to the new environment. The relatively unstartling nature of the furniture produced by furniture craftsmen during the first half century of colonial settlement is further compounded by the fact that striking innovations have seldom been made for the middling social orders, who are, indeed, the sort of people that became the first settlers of America.

As the second generation came to maturity around the beginning of the third quarter of the seventeenth century, old patterns of exclusiveness began breaking down. New colonists from a variety of places in England were settling in the older colonial communities; old masters were taking apprentices from new families who had a slightly different cultural background; new master craftsmen were taking apprentices from older families; new customers were bespeaking products that suited their own tastes rather than the taste of the craftsman who was to make them; and new stylistic ideas were making their way into America.

Change can be readily perceived when previously distinct cultural groups with individualistic practices come into contact with each other. As the presence of a Dutch-born king on the English throne changed tastes in England, the institutionalization of the Anglican church brought a new taste to Massachusetts for some people and an old taste for others. Like adversaries in an ancient Greek drama, cultural groups with fundamentally different beliefs may have mistrusted or tended to remain aloof from each other, but because they depended upon each other for survival, they could not avoid the kinds of contact that finally resulted in the transmission of some characteristics to each other. Nowhere in early eighteenth-century America was more vital furniture produced than in Pennsylvania where Swedes, Englishmen, Welshmen, and Germans mingled. Yet the juxtaposition need not be so dramatic as that to occur; members of the Dutch Reformed Church and Huguenots in New York, sharing contiguous bits of land with Englishmen, also did it.

The effect of cultural differences among furniture makers becomes obvious on their products once we learn to look for it, but the impact of the demand for a new style on an individual craftsman is more subtle and perhaps more important. To the historian of William and Mary furniture, for example, the question of how designers and craftsmen actually confronted the problem of making a piece of furniture in this new style looms large. William and Mary–style case furniture was not made by ringing a few stylistic changes on the joined furniture of the seventeenth century; it represents the complete rejection of an old aesthetic, in which ornament was applied to a surface, for one in which the surface itself is rich, and, more important, it represents the replacement of an entire craft. The joiner, who used pinned mortises and tenons and oak panels, was supplanted by the cabinetmaker, who used dovetails to hold together pine-board cases and covered the surfaces with hardwood veneers. A master joiner confronted with this situation had only two choices: He could either quit making furniture or teach himself to work in the new style. The public records of New England confirm that the first alternative was chosen by some, the collections of our museums show that the second was chosen by others.

This extreme example illustrates the craftsman's dilemma in a specific moment that is visibly evident without reference to any document other than the furniture itself, but actually the situation it represents occurs repeatedly throughout the history of furniture each time a new style is introduced. What London joiner making low-back oak chairs with rudimentary turnings and turkey-work upholstery in 1645 could have imagined that in twenty-five years his sons and, if he lived long enough, he himself would be making beech or walnut chairs with floral-carved crest rails, twist-turned legs, and woven cane uphol-stery? What must it have been like to be John Gaines of Ipswich, who learned as an apprentice to make spindle-back chairs with turned legs and arms, who made them as a master for a decade or more, and who suddenly found that his customers wanted banister-back chairs with carved feet, arms, and crest rails that, if they could not be procured from him, could be gotten elsewhere? If such craftsmen are to survive in their trades, they must learn to be designers and sometimes teach themselves a new craft.

Can we infer from a piece of undocumented furniture whether it was made by a craftsman who had been taught to make furniture in a new style or by one who taught himself? Often we can. At its best, a piece of furniture in a new style made by a man who was trained to work in that style will have an almost academic air. It will perhaps convey the feeling that form and content, or if you prefer, the techniques of execution and design, without placing value judgments on them, are inseparable from each other. It will evoke the image of its European ancestry. Each of its parts will be proportioned to the others and will follow a modular scheme that can be mathematically expressed today. Each part will reveal the qualities of workmanship expected from an academic shop, which means that each different craft will be performed professionally by a master of the craft needed to produce it. It may even contain physical evidence of new tools employed or new techniques of construction developed expressly to satisfy the design objectives of the new style.

In contrast, a piece of furniture made by a craftsman who has taught himself to work in a new style can easily betray an older aesthetic in shape or proportions or can be identified because it may be made with techniques that are older than the style suggests. This is certainly true of most of the village cabinetmaking of eighteenth-century new England, most examples of which have pinned mortise-and-tenon joints that carry down through successive decades a lingering echo of the age of joinery. The vocabulary of the new style may be grafted onto an older form, or the new shapes may have about them an exaggeration or attenuation, "misunderstood" we call them, without understanding ourselves how they came to be. The new details will generally be taken from readily available prototypes, and these prototypes will rarely be of European origin. The object will have the earmarks of the new style without being exactly *in* the new style. And if we do not painstakingly try to find out when and where they were made, we might very well be inclined to date them earlier than they really are and dub them "transitional."

Do craftsmen under the one influence produce "good" furniture and the others produce "bad"? Perhaps these are not the proper questions to ask. Many connoisseurs are exhilarated by Gaines's chairs because they know that John Gaines, trained as a turner, taught himself how to carve crest rails, arms, and feet. They admire the freshness, vitality, and imagination of these in spite of—or perhaps *because* of—their departures from the style of their Boston counterparts. Others esteem only Philadelphia Chippendale with tamely symmetrical rococo-esque ornament, ludicrously lavished on case furniture forms that had been out of use two styles earlier in London, or chairs that are as close as possible to the pictures in Chippendale's *Director*, ignoring that their stumpy rear legs are a carryover from the previous style that should have been out of fashion in Philadelphia and was never in fashion in England, at best qualifying such chairs for the label "transitional."

Transitional these chairs are, but transitional only for the craftsman who is making them, for every craftsman whose career spans a working lifetime of a quarter century must experience stylistic obsolescence and the necessity of making a personal transition in the style of the furniture he produces. If this is so, then the straight-line "development" of furniture styles, as taught by books that are too simple, is doubly pernicious, for a style does not undergo one development, but hundreds simultaneously. These developments run parallel to each other, and they do not begin and stop at the same time. In fact, there are as many developments of a style as there are shops producing objects in that style, and each of these developments represents a stylistic idea subjected to the individual talent of a designer or designer/craftsman. The particular problem for the individual craftsman is how to capture the earmarks of a style in his own work, and by the standards of those who look for striking expressions of the individual spirit, the craftsman who slavishly copies a prototype gets no points.

Considering all of the possible factors that can affect the way that an object may appear to its historian, the task that Johann Joachim Winckelmann set for himself in writing his *History of Ancient Art*, and by simplification for all art historians since, is difficult. Winckelmann's object was "to show the origin, progress, change and downfall of art, together with the different styles of nations, periods, and artists, and to prove the whole, as far as it is possible, from the ancient monuments now in existence."[15] The modern scholar would publicly quibble only with the word *downfall*, since it implies a lack of detachment from the subject that is not fashionable today: we are now content to study change, to suggest the reasons for it, and its meaning. But no one would quibble with the rest of Winckelmann's objectives, and those are the objectives of this book.

NOTES

[1] *OED*, s.v. "connoisseurship," 1.

[2] See Bronowski, *Ascent of Man*, pp. 13–56, 411–38.

[3] Diderot and d'Alembert, *Encyclopédie*, s.v. "dessein en architecture" (author's translation).

[4] Gloag and Walker, *Home Life in History*, p. 243.

[5] Pye, *Nature and Art of Workmanship*, pp. 13–24. See also, Pye, *Nature of Design*, pp. 21–39.

[6] Chippendale, *Gentleman and Cabinet-Maker's Director*.

[7] *Essex Quarterly Courts*, 4:349, 5:316, 6:72, 4:455, 423.

[8] *OED*, s.v. "style," 22.

[9] Gilbert, *Life and Work of Thomas Chippendale*.

[10] See, for example, Heckscher, "Lock and Copland," pl. 2.

[11] Bentley, *Diary*, 4:595. See also Trent, "History for the Essex Institute Turkey Work Couch," pp. 29–37.

[12] See Eames, "Furniture in England, France and the Netherlands," p. xvii.

[13] Gregory, *Furniture Collector*, p. 1.

[14] Sprat, *History of the Royal Society*, pp. 391–92.

[15] Lodge, *History of Ancient Art*, pp. 149–50.

CHAPTER 2

THE WOODS USED IN AMERICAN FURNITURE

~

Except in places where the timber had been destroyed, and its growth prevented by frequent fires, the groves were thick and lofty. The Indians so often burned the country, to take deer and other wild game, that in many of the plain, dry parts of it, there was but little small timber. Where lands were thus burned there grew bent grass, or as some called it, thatch, two, three and four feet high, according to the strength of the land. This, with other combustible matter, which the fields and groves produced, when dry, in the spring and fall, burned with violence and killed all the small trees. The large ones escaped, and generally grew to a notable height and magnitude. In this manner the natives so thinned the groves, that they were able to plant their corn and obtain a crop.

BENJAMIN TRUMBULL,   Complete History of Connecticut

The society and culture Europeans established in New England three and a half centuries ago differed so much in every particular from today's that it is difficult to visualize. We are dependent upon electronics for communication; brick, iron, asbestos, gypsum, and lime for shelter; steel and aluminum for transportation; petrochemicals for fertilizer; and fossil fuels for warmth. Our ancestors communicated ideas by the spoken and written word, traversed distances on foot or horseback or in carts or ships, collected manure for fertilizer, and used wood for virtually everything else.

A tourist in search of New England's past will find little more than a few quaint and picturesque towns that time has passed by. Most of the vista is filled with commuter traffic and fellow tourists speeding past endless suburban sprawl and thriving electronics plants, abandoned farms and textile mills —themselves curious relics of progress—silt-filled rivers meandering to ports that only pleasure craft visit, and thousands of acres of scrub pine. In only one place, the restored Iron Works at Saugus, Massachusetts, can the modern visitor find a small suggestion of the grandeur of the forest of mixed hardwoods and conifers that once covered this land and that now can be conjured up only in the mind's eye by reading the descriptions of contemporary observers.[1] In the museum at

Saugus is the remnant of a giant oak log more than four feet in diameter that once supported an anvil and absorbed the shock of the 500-pound water-driven trip-hammer that thumped down upon it once every two seconds, twelve hours a day for more than twenty years.

It is fitting that the single memento of this forest should be a piece of oak since the oak was the tree most familiar to immigrant Englishmen. Their homes had been framed with it, the case furniture they had known was made of it, the ships that had brought them to the new world were built of it, and laws and customs governing its ownership and use were part of every Englishman's life. The landscape of New England, despite the praise heaped upon it by eager London propagandists, in many ways resembled that which the settlers had long known in their native shires. Its overall climate and terrain permitted and even encouraged the establishment of a pattern of living based on the one that settlers had been familiar with in Europe.[2] But unlike Europe, America possessed wood in abundance, virtually free for the taking. Indeed, wood was so plentiful that Francis Higginson, the minister to the settlers at Cape Ann, Massachusetts, wrote to friends in England in the late summer of 1629 with a note of awe: "Here we have plenty of fire to warm us, and that a great deal cheaper than they sell billets and fagots in London; nay, all Europe is not able to afford to make so great fires as New England. A poor servant here, that is to possess but fifty acres of land, may afford to give more wood for timber and fire as good as the world yields, than many noblemen in England can afford to do. Here is good living for those that love good fires."[3] Limitless as the forest appeared, the first of many laws regulating the cutting of oak trees on the lands held in common by all the settlers were soon passed—at Ipswich in 1634 and at Salem two years later.[4]

William Wood, author of *New England's Prospect* (London, 1634), lived in Massachusetts between 1629 and 1633 and has the distinction of being the first naturalist to commit to print a short catalogue of the useful types of woods he had observed here. Almost all of them found their way into furniture during the first century of settlement. Wrote Wood:

The land affords . . . good store of Woods, & that not onely such as may be needfull for fewell, but likewise for the building of Ships, and houses, & Mils, and all manner of water-worke about which Wood is needefull. The Timber of the Countrey growes straight, and tall, some trees being twenty, some thirty foot high, before they spread forth their branches; generally the Trees be not very thicke, though there be many that will serve for Mill posts, some beeing three foote and a halfe o're. And whereas it is generally conceived, that the woods grow so thicke, that there is no more cleare ground than is hewed out by labour of man; it is nothing so; in many places, divers Acres being cleare, so that one may ride a hunting in most places of the land, if he will venture himselfe for being lost: there is no underwood saving in swamps, and low grounds that are wet, in which the English get Osiers, and Hasles, and such small wood as is for their use.

Though many of these trees may seeme to have epithites contrary to the nature of them as they grow in England, yet are they agreeable with the Trees of that Countrie. The chiefe and common Timber for ordinary use in Oake, and Walnut: Of Oakes there be three kindes, the red Oake, white, and blacke; as these are different in kinde, so are they chosen for such uses as they are most fit for, one kind being more fit for clappboard, others for sawne board, some fitter for shipping, others for houses. These Trees affoard much Mast for Hogges, especially every third yeare, bearing a bigger Acorne than our English Oake. The Wallnut tree is something different from the English Wallnut, being a great deale more tough, and more serviceable, and altogether as heavie: and whereas our Gunnes that are stocked with English Wallnut, are soone broaken and cracked in frost, beeing a brittle Wood; we are driven to stocke them new with the Country Wallnut, which will indure all blowes, and weather; lasting time out of minde. These trees beare a very good Nut, something smaller, but nothing inferiour in sweetnesse and goodnesse to the English Nut, having no bitter pill. There is likewise a tree in some part of the Countrey, that beares a Nut as bigge as a small peare. The Cedar tree is a tree of no great growth, not bearing above a foot and a halfe square at the most, neither is it very high. I suppose they be much inferiour to the Cedars of Lebanon so much commended in holy writ. This wood is more desired for ornament than substance, being of colour red and white like Eugh, smelling as sweete as Iuniper; it is commonly used for seeling of houses, and making of Chests, boxes, and staves. The Firre and Pine bee trees that grow in many places, shooting up exceeding high, especially the Pine: they doe afford good masts, good board, Rozin and Turpentine. Out of these Pines is gotten the candlewood that is so much spoken of, which may serve for a shift amongst poore folkes;

but I cannot commend it for singular good, because it is something sluttish, dropping a pitchie kinde of substance where it stands. Here no doubt might be good done with saw mils; for I have seene of these stately highgrowne trees, ten miles together close by the River side, from whence by shipping they might be conveyed to any desired Port. Likewise it is not improbable that Pitch and Tarre may be forced from these trees, which beare no other kinde of fruite.

For that countrey Ash, it is much different from the Ash of England, being brittle and good for little, so that Wallnut is used for it. The Horne-bound tree is a tough kind of Wood, that requires so much paines in riving as is almost incredible, being the best for to make bolles and dishes, not being subject to cracke or leake.[5]

Among these woods, oak was the key ingredient in the way of life the seventeenth-century New England settlers quickly established. It supplied the principal beams and girts with which they and their descendants framed houses for three centuries. It was the favorite wood for cooking in their picturesque, inefficient fireplaces whose large size guaranteed that wood would become scarce within a century.[6] The relative density of oak caused it to burn slowly; it was an excellent source of fuel. Its ashes were leached to make potash, part of which was used locally to make soap, the rest shipped to England for the glassmaking industry. Early settlers discovered that the sawdust of the red oak tree made a yellow dye whose brilliance and permanence were superior to anything they had known in England. Colliers used oak in large quantities to make a superior quality charcoal that the blacksmiths of the colony soon preferred. And friendly Indians taught the early colonists that boiled acorns, if not appetizing, were at least filling when the seasonal larder ran low.

EARLY METHODS OF CONVERTING TIMBER TO LUMBER

The oak tree also furnished the first settlers with clapboards for the sides of their houses and shingles for the roofs when the driving rains of New England proved too harsh for the wattle-and-daub walls and thatched roofs that many of the new settlers had been accustomed to in England. Shingles and clapboards could be quickly split out of a freshly cut oak log with only a few tools, and split, or riven, wood survived the sustained exposure to rain and ice much better than sawn stuff.[7]

Most of the oak used in the earliest case furniture that went into these houses was also riven out of logs and then sawn into shorter lengths, referred to as "bolts." Oak, cedar, and many other woods with straight long fibers and an absence of knots lend themselves to this technique. The greatest advantage to riving wood instead of sawing it, from the craftsman's point of view, is that riving can be done quickly by one man—no small advantage for a labor-poor society that is in a hurry to convert a natural product into a useful state. Riving tools are few and simple, and the "axes, . . . frow [froe], . . . beetle ring & 4 wedges" listed in the 1646/47 inventory of Michael Carthrick of Ipswich, who called himself a "carpenter" in his will, indicate the two processes by which it was done.[8] For logs already sawn into bolts, a maul and a froe are all that are needed. The maul, a piece of roughly shaped wood somewhat like a short thick softball bat, is used to strike a froe that has been placed against the end grain of the wood being split. The iron blade of the froe is wedge-shape in section, about a foot long, not particularly sharp, and looks something like a knife whose handle has been put onto the blade at a right angle. The handle projects upward to be grasped with one hand. The blade is struck with the maul and driven into the wood. Then the handle is worked to and fro to split the wood.[9] The "200 of clapboards" listed in Carthrick's inventory were riven by the second process, which required a different set of tools and a different technique. To make clapboards, a knot-free log of the desired length is laid on the ground. An indentation parallel to the length of the tree and at right angles to the annular rings is made with an axe on the upper side of the log near one end. Wooden wedges, whose heads are kept from spreading by iron "beetle rings" fastened about their necks, are driven into the gash with a large wooden maul, or beetle, whose head also had beetle rings around its extremities to keep it from spreading, and the log is split.[10]

For virtually all seventeenth-century case furniture (fig. 2) and wainscot chairs, wide, thin, tapering sections of riven oak, taken from trees of rather large diameter, were squared into panels and their edges were feathered to fit inside the joined frames.[11] These frames consist of rails, stiles, and muntins, also riven but then squared on three sides with a drawknife or plane. Wood worked up in this manner is easily recognizable because one of the two broad sides of each piece is usually an almost perfect radial plane, while the side opposite it is often only moderately worked and retains some of the natural taper of the original rift (fig. 3). More thinly riven wood was used for drawer fronts and sides, and the most thinly riven of all for drawer bottoms. Riving can almost be done in less time and with less effort than it takes to tell about it, so easily can oak be worked with hewing hatchet and plane along the fibers that run the length of the tree.[12]

Oak has additional advantages besides the capacity to be worked quickly. A major one is that it does not tend to warp, or cast, upon drying. Because it does not warp, oak can be riven and worked with a great deal of its natural moisture still in it.

When oak is riven on a radial plane—that is, along any plane that radiates outward from the center of the trunk to the bark—the plane of the rift splits downward through sections of the ray structure of the tree, here and there revealing flecks of the rays that speckle the surface of the wood. These flecks have often been found charming, even beautiful, by a number of furniture historians, but it is unrealistic to think of them as anything but an incidental consequence of using either riven or quartersawn wood. Since a large proportion of the furniture made from riven wood in the seventeenth century was painted when it was new, one can scarcely argue that the flecks were a consciously sought decorative device.

Boards and planks that are uniformly rectilinear in section are more often the product of sawing rather than riving. Sawing involves considerably more labor. Unlike shaving a riven board along the direction of its long fibers, sawing along

Fig. 2. Detail of back of chest of drawers showing typical panel-framed construction. Ipswich, Mass., 1678. (Winterthur 57.541.)

Fig. 3. Detail of back side of cupboard showing woods cut along radial plane (left) and transverse plane (right). (Winterthur 57.542.)

the long fibers of the wood violates natural tensions within the wood because it cuts tangentially through the fibers instead of separating them. Consequently, sawn boards must be carefully stacked and dried to minimize the effects of the unequal loss of moisture (warping). This implies that some time must elapse between the sawing of the boards and their use.

Sawing, nonetheless, had its place in the fabric of colonial life and was used at any early date. The time-honored method of producing boards by sawing is for two sawyers to work together with a long, thick saw at something called a "sawpit." The name suggests a hole in the ground, and in at least one instance such a method was employed in seventeenth-century New England. Making preparations to build its first meeting-house in January 1637/38, the town of Dedham voted "To allowe for digging of Pitts 12: foote in length 4½. foote broad [and] 5: foote deepe [2s]. 6d" and "To alowe for saweing Pyne board 5s & for spliting 6s p Centm   And for ye breaking Carfe of 2. foote deepe 3d p foote Running measure." After deliberation, the townsmen found that "John Morse vundrtaketh to pforme the same, & hath liberty to take what helpe he pleaseth"; those carpenters he chose were "to haue for makeing of pitholls 12d ye payer."[13] Yet by the time most New England villagers began processing their own building timbers, the most common sawing technique they seem to have used was the one most popular in England at the time of emigration, consisting of a scaffold or trestle arrangement of wood (put together in any of a number of ways) upon which a squared log could be laid. One man, known as "the topman," stood atop the log and guided the saw along a straight line. The other man, known as "the pitman," stood under the log and provided the muscle power to pull the saw down, for the saw cut only on the downward stroke. The topman then pulled it back up, and the procedure was repeated. Professional pit sawyers were always engaged in pairs and, as seems to be the story for the laboring man throughout history, the pitman, who did the hard work, received a 40 percent share while the topman, who possessed the skill to follow a straight line, received 60 percent. A sawpit of this type can be set up anywhere. Although pit-sawn oak is the norm in seventeenth-century furniture from London, where the sawyers company held sway, virtually no pit-sawn wood has been found in American furniture.[14]

Pit sawing was at best a slow and rather laborious method of obtaining boards and plank for building a new country and could in no way keep up with the demand. Ironically, the means to a greater supply of boards and plank had already been established before the first great influx of colonists to Massachusetts Bay in the 1630s. In Maine and New Hampshire, where great stands of timber stood close to vigorous streams, water-powered sawmills were already producing boards and plank for export.[15] Mills of this type (fig. 4) spread rapidly throughout the colonies, and virtually every township had one before the end of the century. The wood most commonly sawn in these mills was pine, and the low appraised value placed upon numerous chests and boxes in fairly early inventories suggests that pine quickly found its way into American furniture. In contrast to New England, mill-sawn boards of fir and spruce used in some seventeenth-century English furniture were imported from the Continent and rarely found their way inland from the urban seaports at which they landed.

In many ways, the presence of Englishmen operating sawmills in seventeenth-century New England was revolutionary. In contrast to continental Europe, England had no long tradition of mechanical sawing. With respect to the large stands of timber near rapidly flowing streams, America was like those places in Europe where mill sawing was done, and both differed from England. The New England timberlands were either owned in common by the residents of the various townships or by absentee proprietors who were unable to protect their interests. In England, every square foot of land and the timber on it was owned by someone who lived not very far away. But the single element that made mill sawing a natural option from the very beginning of settlement in New England was the scarcity and, therefore, the expense of skilled laborers of any sort. If boards were to be supplied in any quantity and at reasonable cost, mechanical means would have to provide the

Fig. 4. Water-powered sawmill. From Edward Williams, *Virginia's Discovery of Silke Wormes . . .*, facing p. 75. (Beinecke Rare Book and Manuscript Library, Yale University.)

labor. Further, no restrictions or laws mitigated against this, in contrast to England where the sawyer's trade—like all handicrafts that provided employment in that overpopulated country —was protected by custom and statute.

Insofar as production was concerned, the sawmill, with its blade tirelessly moving up and down as the water passed over its mill wheel, outdistanced the amount of work that a pair of pit sawyers could produce by a ratio of more than 7 to 1.[16] Pit sawing, therefore, persisted in America only in those places where water power was insufficient to permit mill sawing, where compass sawing—such as the rounded shapes needed in shipbuilding—was required, or where woods other than those normally capable of being sawn by the mills were needed.

WOOD IDENTIFICATION

Many collectors of American furniture confess that they know little about woods and the technology used to make furniture from them and indeed seem disinclined to learn. The advances that scholars have made over the past quarter century reveal that connoisseurship is inseparable from a knowledge of the history of technology and of the relatively small number of woods used to make American furniture. The ability to recognize the woods used in America prior to 1730 can be achieved with a little practice. This knowledge provides a surer way to recognize American furniture than do all the books on furniture styles that have ever been written. Indeed, the failure to learn and study these facts can easily result in expensive errors for collectors and reputation-shattering ones for historians.

Not the least of the problems facing the student of furniture who would deal with woods is what to call them. A wood is usually known by a common name that either characterizes some visible aspect of the tree as it stands in the forest or tells where a type of tree likes to grow or denotes some aspect of the wood after it is wrought into lumber, usually its color. Evocative names like "Swamp Maple," "Tulip Poplar," "Foxtail Pine," "Quaking Aspen," and "Stinking Cedar" are often too imprecise or confusing to be of much use. Popular names are occasionally applied to a number of different trees; for example, any maple found growing in a swamp might be a swamp maple, although that would be hard to know when we see it in a piece of furniture. Others merely describe varieties of a species, or characteristics that are common to numerous different species, and are unnecessarily misleading, attaching the name of one family to a tree which belongs to an entirely different one. Tulip Popular or Tulip Tree, also known as Yellow Poplar, is a classic case in point, for it is not a poplar (genus *Populus*), but is a member of the genus *Liriodendron* and thus part of the magnolia family.

Of course, we can call something by any name we care to, but we must always be prepared for the consequence, which in this case is the inability to communicate with precision. Far from being affected or self-consciously erudite or pompously pedantic, we need to refer to the woods from which furniture is made by some unambiguous terminology, and in the case of woods, we are fortunate in having a terminology that is recognized throughout the world, the International Rules of Botanical Nomenclature, based upon the Linnaean system.

The process of utilizing this vocabulary involves some effort. To identify a wood precisely, ideally one should have a limb of the tree with the bark and leaves on it and flowers and, if possible, the mature fruit—a situation that seldom occurs in nature. Since the closest a furniture collector could come to this situation would be to possess an Adirondack chair or a piece of rococo garden furniture, the ideal is rarely approximated. All that we have to deal with is the wood after it has been made into furniture, and that is almost impossible to identify with precision by eye. Experience has taught all who have tried it, and made an expensive mistake, to be wary. Indeed, continued contact with antique-furniture woods is the one realm of human existence where familiarity breeds caution instead of confidence!

The mark of an informed student of furniture is the willingness to confess that one does not know for certain what a wood is and to call the wood anatomist for help. If advanced collectors and dealers admit the difficulty of invariably being able to distinguish between walnut and mahogany, who will be so bold as to bet a fortune that the unaided eyes can tell the difference between eighteenth-century West Indian mahogany and nineteenth-century African mahogany, or between an unvariegated cut of European walnut and the American species? Indeed, examples of the same species will reflect the conditions under which they grew. Walnut from Salem, Massachusetts, can look very different from a piece that grew near Norfolk, Virginia; a piece of wood from a tree that grew at the dry top of a hill will be less porous and hence look different from a piece from another tree of the identical species that grew along a stream at the bottom of the same hill. In many cases, on the same tree the heartwood is a different color from the sapwood. The absence or presence of minerals in the soil also can impart different colors to the wood of trees of the same species. Most confusing of all is the interposition of a murky

veil that consists of shellac or varnish or both, or paint, or paint that has been removed, or wax, or grime, or some combination of them all, or that invention of the devil, linseed oil which polymerizes on the surface of a piece of furniture like a sticky plastic and, when mixed with turpentine and vinegar, makes it smell like a green salad. Added to the difficulties impeding the gross identification of woods are two final ones. A great variety of related species of the same genus that grew in different parts of colonial America and that were made into furniture do look the same. Second, there are closely related European species of some woods that are visually indistinguishable from their American counterparts.

The surest way out of the conflicting tangle of possibilities is for the collector or curator to call upon a person who does microanalysis—the microscopic examination of the anatomical structure of a minute sample of wood—to determine what tree the wood came from. [17] Microanalysis is practiced by the professional botanist who is a microanatomist. This scientific work is based upon the fact that the anatomy of many species of trees differs slightly from its fellows, and those differences can be observed and tabulated. But in the same way that science today no longer expects 100 percent accuracy in its results, microanalysis can perhaps be forgiven its shortcomings as well, for it, too, does not provide absolute certainty at all times. Microanalysis does, however, offer a systematic approach to the problem of identifying furniture woods—in striking contrast to the benign neglect or rough guesses that were common prior to the time Russell H. Kettell first used it in *Pine Furniture of New England* (1929) and Charles F. Montgomery, aided by Gordon K. Saltar, raised it to the level of a refined art when he regionalized American federal-style furniture with it (1966).

Considering that microanalysis enables us to speak with confidence about the one objective piece of information we can have about a piece of furniture—the wood it is made from— we are amazed that hostility toward the use of the technique lingers in some circles. I have known more than one charismatic dealer in antique furniture who professed to have no faith in microanalysis, convinced a few good clients of its irrelevance, and as a consequence retired rich.

Microanalysis is work for a specialist, not the sort of thing that the average collector dabbles in for himself. It has proved to be a reliable technique within its self-acknowledged limitations. For this book the furniture at Winterthur and in many other related collections has been tested and retested as the data upon which our knowledge is based have increased. Our object has been to be able to speak with confidence about the woods that were used in American furniture prior to 1730.

Regardless of whether one cares to become a microanatomist or merely wishes to look at furniture with an informed eye, it is important to think for a moment about wood before it is ever made into a piece of furniture. [18] The tree as it grows in the forest is a complex structure, composed of cells like any other living organism. These cells are arranged in a distinctive manner for each family of trees, and their characteristics can be systematically observed and tabulated. Despite the incredible diversity of woods that nature has produced, trees can only be arranged into two categories according to their general

KEY

A   Pith
B   Cambium
C   Bark
D   Annual growth rings
    D_1 Spring growth
        highly porous
    D_2 Summer growth
        less porous
E   Transverse plane
F   Radial plane
G   Tangential plane

1   Top of giant ray
1a Side of giant ray
1b End of giant ray
2   Top of fine ray
2a End of fine ray
3   End of pore or vessel
3a Side of pore

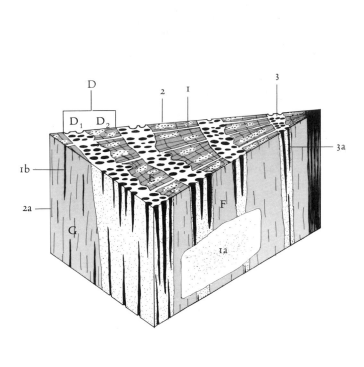

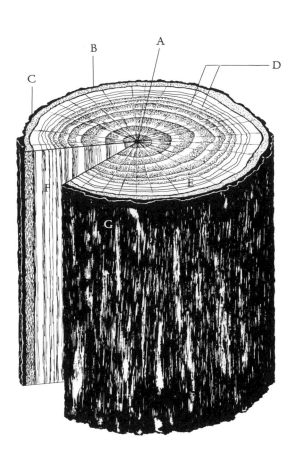

Fig. 5. Two cross-sectional views of red oak (*Quercus rubra*). (Drawing: Robert Blair St. George and Wade Lawrence.)

structure: softwoods (conifers and their relatives) and hardwoods. As far as precise description goes, hard and soft are not the best imaginable terms to use because many of the so-called hardwoods are softer than a number of the softwoods, and vice versa. Botanists long ago discovered that all of the trees in each of these two great classes have a distinctive, objective characteristic that sets all the trees of one type apart from all the trees of the other. They avoid confusion by referring to the hardwoods as "porous" woods, because of the easily visible ringlike pore structure, and the softwoods as "nonporous," because they lack such visible vessel structures. The exterior of most furniture, including the examples in this book, is made of one or more of the porous woods; some of the interiors have parts made of nonporous woods such as conifers. A typical ring-porous hardwood, the red oak, is illustrated in figure 5 and is of singular importance to furniture study in that it is a species native only to the North American continent.

When a ring-porous tree first sprouts from its seed, it consists almost entirely of pith (A)—a heterogeneous aggregation of cells (fibers) insusceptible to microidentification—and bark. Soon after the sprout begins to grow, a sheath of highly specialized cells between the pith and the bark known as the cambium, or cambium layer, (B) take over the job of making a tree. The cells in the cambium manufacture by cell division two other kinds of cells. Toward the inside of the tree they make wood; toward the outside they make bark (C). Like pith, bark is insusceptible to microidentification. Each year, a new layer of wood is formed around the previous year's growth as the tree grows both upward and outward. This layer of wood represents the tree's annual growth (D) and is most easily perceived on a transverse section of a stump, log, or limb where it is referred to in common parlance as an annular ring. In moist years the annual growth is greater than in dry years, and for that reason the rings are not uniform in thickness. The annular ring in a tree consists of two types of growth, the rapid spring growth or early wood (D_1), which produces in the red oak example highly porous, spongy-looking wood, and the slower summer growth or late wood (D_2), which is usually noticeably less porous and hence produces wood that is rather more solid.

When we look closely at a piece of wood from this tree, with a 10-power magnifying glass, we notice many things that are not readily visible to the naked eye. The illustration to the left in figure 5 shows a wedge cut out of the log at the right. This wedge, very close in section to what a seventeenth-century furniture maker obtained when he rived an oak log, shows the planes from which the microanatomist gathers his facts. The most obvious planes—at the top and bottom of the sample— do not come about through the process of riving, but represent two parallel, transverse cuts across the diameter of the log. This view of the wood is commonly referred to as end grain or, in the language of the botanist, the transverse plane (E). The planes represented by the tapering sides of the sample are called radial planes (F), and the plane that is perpendicular to both the radial and transverse planes is called the tangential plane (G). A piece of wood can be cut in any direction for the purposes of furniture making, but any given piece of wood contains an infinite number of these planes and every sample taken from a piece of furniture will have a perfect example of each of them within it somewhere.

Trees are all constituted along the same general lines. Having stated in no uncertain terms that it is foolhardy to try to distinguish unfamiliar examples of American furniture from European examples without wood analysis, in fact we can safely identify one group of wood—red oak—and it appears only in American furniture. To understand how we can say this underlines the importance of understanding the general features of all ring-porous wood and, for the student of seventeenth-century furniture, those of the oaks in particular.

Fig. 6. A comparative view of the tangential planes of white oak (left) and red oak (right). The pores of the white oak (*Quercus alba*) are filled with the resinous tyloses; those of the red oak (*Quercus rubra*) are clear.

OAKS

The most characteristic attribute of any oak is that it has easily visible giant medullary rays (see fig. 5). The rays are visible on the transverse plane as an aggregate of prominent cells that radiate outward from the center of the tree. They grow perpendicular to the annular rings and through them. Yet oddly enough, in porous woods, such as oak, maple, and beech, they create the planes of structural weakness that make riving so efficient.[19] Rays also appear in the other planes of the sample (remember that the tree is three-dimensional), but they look different in each. On the radial plane, they are shiny and may appear dark *or* light in color, depending on how the light happens to strike them. If we have a perfect cut—which we rarely do—they are more or less rectilinear in appearance (1a) where the cut slices through them. But because rays do not grow in exactly straight lines, the entire side of one is almost never exposed, their full depth from top to bottom is seldom seen. On the tangential plane, the full height of the cross section of rays is visible. The elongated ends (1b) appear dark and wide in the middle and taper to points. After looking at these through his microscope Gordon Saltar described them as looking like "canoes filled with caviar." In mature red oaks, the ends of these giant rays are rarely as much as one inch long on the tangential plane; in mature white oaks, they may attain a length of several inches. In addition to giant rays, the oaks have finer rays that are visible on both the transverse (2) and tangential planes (2a), but they are difficult to see without magnification.

The growth ring (D) on the transverse plane reveals the story of a tree's life cycle. The portion of each year's growth nearest to the center of the red oak tree appears for the most part as many large pores (3). These pores are actually the ends of the long vessels that conduct water and nutrients from the roots to the leaves when the tree is growing. They form a ring because they are the first cells (D_1) that the cambium produces each spring, and they are formed next to the last growth of the previous year, which is very different in appearance. They thus add, all around the trunk of the tree, a distinctive, readily visible layer of early wood (D_1) that marks the beginning of the creation of a new growth ring. Some of these vessels will also be visible on the radial and tangential planes (3a) where they have

been sliced through by the tool that cut the sample. The tubular vessels look the same on both planes.

The amount of moisture available to a tree growing in the temperate zone decreases as spring turns into summer and, in the case of ring-porous trees such as the red oak, the character of the wood that the tree manufactures changes as well. The vessels produced during summer growth (D_2) are somewhat smaller, fewer in number, and barely visible on the radial and tangential planes without magnification. Because these vessels are smaller and the rate of growth is less rapid, the wood produced in the summer growth portion of the annular ring is denser than the spring growth. Many trees produce a minute but definite line at the point where the summer growth comes to an end, but the red oak is not one of them. Some wood samples, especially those from trees that grow in the tropics where seasonal variation in the climate is small, do not show any dynamic difference between summer and spring growth, and many trees that grow in temperate climates are genetically constituted in such a way that the difference between spring and summer wood is scarcely visible on the transverse plane. In contrast to the oaks, which along with ash, chestnut, elm, locust (*Robinia pseudoacacia*), hickory, and mulberry are ring-porous woods, most of the other trees that grow in the temperate zone and are used in furniture (for example, tulipwood, basswood [genus *Tilia*], beech, birch, and the maples) have pores that are usually fairly uniform in size and are evenly diffused throughout the annular growth. These latter are diffuse porous woods; further discussion of their anatomy is irrelevant here.

A student of furniture needs only one more bit of anatomical information to obtain a rough and ready means of distinguishing between the American red oak that is found in a great deal of American seventeenth-century furniture and white oak, the type that is invariably found in English furniture. White oak possesses an easily visible feature—tylosis —that is less often present in red oak.[20] Tyloses are cellular structures that form in the vessels of the white oak tree as those vessels cease to conduct fluids. Tylosis eventually dries out and, as Saltar expresses it, "looks like dried Coca-Cola." Figure 6 is an enlargement of the tangential plane of a sample of white oak (*left*) and one of red oak (*right*) as each looks with the aid of a 10-power magnifying glass. The walls of the vessels of the red oak are ribbed, but no tylosis is visible. The vessels of the white oak, on the other hand, are so clogged with tylosis that the walls cannot be seen clearly.

The differences between the red oak and the white oak illustrate how careful observation and a little knowledge enable a student of furniture to distinguish one important furniture wood from another and provide the layman an insight into the principles upon which the wood anatomist works. In most cases, especially those that involve the separation of American species of wood from closely related European species, the task is far more complex and depends upon factors that have not even been considered here. Such factors as the width of rays, measurable only in microns, the presence or absence of calcium oxylate crystals in the parenchema, the manner in which the pits meet each other—in fact dozens of variables in parts of the tree's anatomy—make microanalysis a full-time and highly specialized trade in which attributes must be observed and tabulated with painstaking accuracy.

Once a furniture historian has determined what wood or woods a piece of furniture is made of, the real task begins. Having found red oak in a piece of furniture, for example, three questions must then be asked: Was red oak the only oak used in American furniture? Was red oak indigenous only to America in the seventeenth century? And if so, was red oak ever a successful article of commerce in the export trade from America? Questions like these must be asked of every wood once it is identified, and they lead us into another field of study where research must be undertaken. In this case, it might be called "The History of American Woods since the Settlement of America by Europeans," a study that is in its infancy.

Historically, two kinds of oak (genus *Quercus*) were used in American furniture: white oaks (subgenus *Lepidobalanus*) and red oaks (subgenus *Erythrobalanus*). Each is roughly distinguishable to the eye by the characteristic color of its heartwood, which is reflected in its common name. Within each subgenus are a number of varieties, but, for practical purposes, *Quercus alba* may be considered the historically most important white oak and *Quercus rubra* the most important red oak in furniture making.

Although white oak was used in both European and American furniture, red oak never appears in English furniture of the seventeenth century. The latter was not native to England, and none grew there until 1691 when Bishop Compton of Fulham planted some in his garden for ornamental purposes.[21] The open vessels in a red oak board allow water to pass freely through it, in contrast to boards of the white oak family, whose tyloses effectively seal the vessels. The open vessels of red oak readily absorb moisture, an invitation to fungi and bacteria. Red oak could not survive the long voyage to England in the hold of a seventeenth-century ship without decay, and, after a few disastrous attempts, no shipments of red oak were made to England. The earliest description of the problem is that of 1696, when a trial cargo was shipped to Deptford for use by the Royal Navy. The inspector of the shipment wrote, "the wood in general is of very tender and 'frow' substance mingled with red veins and subject to many worm holes with signs of decay."[22] Since white oak was invariably used in English furniture with which American examples might be confused visually, and since red oak was not an article of commerce, it is highly probable that any piece of early furniture made of red oak is of American origin.

While this detailed discussion may seem rather more than a casual reader cares to know, it has been introduced here to underscore the importance of properly identifying the wood of which a piece of furniture is made. In this case, proper identification and a small knowledge of the history of a specific wood obviate the need for microanalysis. But this is one of the few exceptions. No serious step toward understanding a piece of furniture can be taken without such observations as this, for close observation and the detailed recording of data are the heart of connoisseurship and not optional acts to be indulged in as whimsey dictates.

Unfortunately, American white oak cannot yet be separated by microanalysis from most of the European species of white oak. The furniture craftsmen of seventeenth-century New England generally preferred to work with red oak, but specific individual shops in both Massachusetts Bay and Connecticut, out of habit, personal preference, or availability, worked with the white variety.[23]

Although we cannot invariably separate American and English furniture of white oak even with wood analysis, knowledge of the way in which American as opposed to English craftsmen worked the oak that they used in seventeenth-century furniture can aid the connoisseur in a general way. Like all rules of thumb, exceptions will be found, but, generally, white oak used in seventeenth-century American furniture was of excellent quality and was riven; English craftsmen rarely rived oak after the middle of the sixteenth century both because the clear grades needed for riving were rare, and hence expensive, and because riving was wasteful. When American craftsmen sawed white oak to use inside a piece of furniture, such as drawer sides, or for boxes, they generally sawed it into rather thick pieces, usually more than ½" (more than 1.3 cm) thick. English craftsmen, even in rural areas, usually sawed their oak much thinner, commonly less than ½" (less than 1.3 cm). Because oak was scarce in seventeenth-century England and poorer grades or cuts that came dangerously close to knots were used, the longitudinal cell pattern of English oak in furniture is often quite irregular. In America, where oak was plentiful, knotty oak was almost never used. Indeed, as a general rule, the skimpiness of the size of scantling used throughout European furniture contrasts quite clearly with the profligate use of scantling on American examples throughout the colonial period. When European white oak was quartersawn, the wood revealed an easily recognizable ray figure—something like the stripes of a zebra (fig. 7)—that is a result of cutting near but not quite on the radial plane.[24] Riving, if properly done, follows the rays, and on every piece of riven oak at least one side is a true radial plane, thus the "zebra stripe" is rarely seen in American furniture. The color of European white oak generally differs from that of American white oak as well. Especially after it has oxidized somewhat through exposure to air, European white oak generally changes to a silvery gray color that, once seen, will never be forgotten; American white oak tends to remain a yellowish white. Finally, seventeenth-century oak furniture

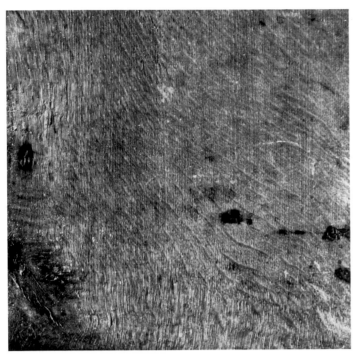

Fig. 7. Detail of quartersawn European white oak which has a distinctive striped ray structure. (Photo: Benno M. Forman.)

Fig. 8. Detail showing the underside of one of the mill-sawn red-oak joists and the white-pine floorboards from the hall of the Seth Story house, Essex, Mass., 1684, now installed at Winterthur Museum. (Photo: Winterthur.)

that has remained in England throughout the eighteenth century appears to have been waxed and polished to a smooth, shiny, and quite hard surface. If it remained there through the nineteenth century, it was often treated to an overall coat of brown stain, inside and out, which is recognizable and may even still smell of linseed oil. Nineteenth-century English fakes have also often been treated to this finish. American oak furniture rarely received either of these finishes during the seventeenth century. Instead, it was either forgotten or painted. If the former, it has a rather dry, bleached look. If the latter, traces of paint pigment invariably remain in the exposed vessels of the wood, even if the paint has been removed.

It is no accident that many of the immigrant furniture makers of seventeenth-century America soon learned to prefer the trees of the red oak family to their more familiar cousins of the white variety. Red oak's greater porosity meant that it was less dense and therefore much easier to rive and plane. Equally important, the foliage and branches of forest-grown red oak sprout toward the top of the tree, leaving a long, strong, branch-free, hence knot-free, expanse of trunk. Since this trunk could be riven perfectly by a technique well known to the rural woodworkers who first settled New England, it is little wonder that red oak became popular among the makers of furniture.

Although references to mill-sawn oak appear in the records as early as 1658, only rarely have we observed mill-sawn oak in the early furniture of New England.[25] The reason for this may be tied to two facts: Sawn oak boards dry out at the rate of only one inch per year; and as the boards dry, the wood hardens, toughens, and warps. Considering the level that sawing technology had attained in the early seventeenth century, pit sawing would have put furniture made primarily of seasoned oak beyond the means of most early colonists. Mill sawing might have diminished the cost had not the toughness of oak and the relatively feeble torque of water-powered sawmills combined to make this method almost as slow and expensive as pit sawing. Furthermore, in order to make the most of its inherent strength, oak was quarter sawn, a process that involved considerable additional handling of the log (and increased its cost at the mill), rather than flat sawn like most woods intended for plank and boards. Only one instance of mill-sawn oak in a piece of American furniture has been observed and that is a Sudbury, Massachusetts, communion table that has mill-sawn stretchers and rails.[26] The table is now at the Wadsworth Atheneum, Hartford.

Mill-sawn oak was used in house-building. The Seth Story house, from which the Seventeenth Century Room at Winterthur Museum was taken, was built in 1684. The room has mill-sawn joists of red oak (fig. 8), undoubtedly run by the owner and builder of the house, Seth Story, at the sawmill he had inherited from his father, William, four years earlier. The mill and house were located at The Falls (now Essex Falls) of the Chebaggo River in the south parish of seventeenth-century Ipswich Township, then known as Chebacco Parish. Because oak is a relatively dense wood the saw kerfs in mill-sawn oak are spaced at $\frac{1}{4}''$ to $\frac{3}{8}''$ (0.6 to 1.0 cm) intervals. In contrast, the cuts on the softer pine boards above the joists in the illustration are $\frac{1}{2}''$ to $\frac{3}{4}''$ (1.3 to 1.9 cm) apart.

Oak was the most popular wood used in furniture in northern Europe for centuries prior to the settlement of America. It was abundant in the New World and the relatively large amount of expensive and elaborately worked furniture that has survived from our seventeenth century convincingly argues that oak was considered stylish. Oddly enough, in contrast to related furniture from northern Europe, oak was seldom used in New England for *turned* chairs, although turned oak certainly appears on the wainscot chairs and joint stools dating from the same period.

CONIFERS

White pine (*Pinus strobus*) was being milled into boards and planks in eastern Massachusetts before the Puritans ever saw Boston Bay. But mill-sawn pine is not found as a primary wood in the fine, joined furniture of that area prior to the style of the 1670s. Here is an example of a technological achievement that existed but was not used, despite its sensible character, by the craftsmen working between 1630 and 1660, the only explanations for which can be the grip of habit and the expectations of their customers.

Conifers seem to have been the woods of the carpenter in the seventeenth century, and pine is the primary ingredient of the American six-board chest. It was also used for the lids and bottoms of oak-sided boxes and desks and probably was used for leather-covered cradles and trunks, although no surviving American examples of the latter dating from the seventeenth century have been identified.

New England in the seventeenth century was rich in conifers of many sorts, and a regional preference of craftsman's use—obviously tied to the natural distribution of the trees themselves—is apparent in the appearance of different pines in the furniture of different areas. The Bay Colony craftsmen who relied upon the forests in northeastern Massachusetts and southern New Hampshire and Maine mostly worked with white pine. Those in Plymouth Colony added riven white cedar (*Thuja occidentalis*), also known as arbor vitae, to the repertoire. In the Connecticut River valley, a member of the yellow pine group (resinous, or pitch, pines) is often found, although the exact species has not yet been identified (perhaps *Pinus rigida Miller*). This pine also occasionally appears in the furniture of New York. Another member of the yellow pine group, appears in early Pennsylvania furniture. Other related yellow pines were used in Virginia.

The presence of a mill-sawn conifer in a piece of seventeenth-century furniture is not prima facie evidence of its American origin. Mill-sawn spruce (genus *Picea*), for example, was a mainstay of northern European furniture in this period and along with various firs (genus *Abies*) was shipped to England in great quantities. These woods are easily recognized because boards made from these trees reflect the nature of the trees themselves. Both spruce and fir have a great many branches, and boards made from them have numerous knots. Removing these branches prior to mill sawing was the sort of laborious task that American loggers in the colonial period did not have to do: white pine with its long clear trunk was abundant, so spruce and fir were ignored. The European and American species of spruce and fir cannot be differentiated by micro-analysis, but when these woods are encountered in a piece of furniture, I assume the piece of furniture is of European origin unless the conifer is found in conjunction with an identifiable American hardwood that was not shipped to Europe during the colonial period. Usually spruce and fir are indiscriminately referred to as "deal" in English books on furniture. A deal was originally a unit of measurement and was understood to refer to a board or plank 9″ or more wide, no more than 3″ thick and at least 6′ long (22.9 × 7.6 × 183.9 cm). The word has subsequently come to be applied to the wood itself and, as casually used today, causes considerable confusion.

Mill-sawn pine as a secondary wood, appears to have been used more commonly in the oak furniture of Connecticut earlier than in eastern Massachusetts; it first appears in the datable furniture of Boston and Essex County in the 1670s. As a primary wood, pine began to be substituted there for oak panels in furniture of the following decade. Because most of the wood used for six-board chests is planed on both surfaces, it is virtually impossible to determine if it was mill sawn or pit sawn, although the bottoms of a few chests reveal that they were mill sawn. Such chests were popular and inexpensive case furniture made by both joiners and carpenters; so, too, were coffins. By the time mill-sawn lumber came into wide use for finer and more complex furniture—roughly 1700 to 1720—cabinetmakers were replacing joiners as the dominant furniture producers of their day. Mill-sawn lumber is easily recognized by the regular marks that an up-and-down saw blade leaves as it passes through the log. These marks are always absolutely parallel to each other and are spaced from ½″ to ¾″ (1.3 to 1.9 cm) apart, depending on the power of the mill in which the wood was sawn. They are generally, but not invariably, perpendicular to the edge of the board, depending on whether the blade in the mill that sawed the log was perpendicular to the bed on which the log rested or was angled to the work so that the blade entered the log bit by bit on the downward stroke and disengaged easily on the upward one.

In the eighteenth century, British makers of picture frames appear to have discovered the joys of working with American white pine, but little record of the shipment of white pine boards to Europe in the seventeenth century has survived. Shipping records do reveal that mill-sawn white pine boards were sent from New England to the southern mainland colonies and the West Indies in the latter years of the seventeenth century. Surviving furniture confirms that the practice continued throughout the eighteenth century, for New England white pine is a common secondary wood in the furniture of Charleston, South Carolina. Mill-sawn white pine, from either New England or the Hudson River valley, also appears in the early eighteenth-century case furniture of New York City, a happenstance that has, in the absence of better evidence, often caused this furniture to be attributed to a New England rather than a New York origin.

Like oak, white pine was not generally a turned-chair maker's wood. White pine turns well but lacks sufficient strength for chair construction; it is too soft for chair joints. However, the somewhat harder yellow pine of the middle colonies and southward is occasionally found in a turned state, usually as table legs, newel posts, and the like. (The wainscot chair illustrated in catalogue entry 19 has its original seat of white pine, and its original rear panel was also white pine.)

SYCAMORE

In 1678 the presence of another mill-sawn wood can be documented in the furniture of Essex County, Massachusetts. American sycamore (*Platanus occidentalis*) appears as the bottom of two drawers in the Staniford-Heard family chest of drawers and plentifully throughout the Woodbury family cupboard, dated 1680, both of which are in the Winterthur collection. The distinctive marks of the waterpowered vertical-motion sawmill is visible on the bottom of the middle shelf and on the undersides of the drawers. Sycamore, not to be confused with the Eurasian maple (*Acer pseudoplatanus*) that is called "sycamore" in Great Britain, was a justifiably popular wood among the first sawmill operators of Essex County. Sometimes called buttonwood, sycamore was a hardwood that sawed easily. It was moderately light in weight, had a compact grain structure, and, as English naturalist John Josselyn noted during his visit to New England in 1670, it "was a stately tree growing here and there in the valleys," which means it was convenient to the streams on which sawmills were located.[27] Sycamore retained its shape well after being moistened and bent, so it was occasionally used to make the slats of chairs, although ash was more commonly used.

TULIPWOOD

Another wood popular with mill sawyers, perhaps before the seventeenth century was over, was tulipwood or tulip tree (*Liriodendron tulipifera*), commonly called tulip poplar or yellow poplar today although the tree is of the magnolia family and is not related to the genus *Populus*. The tree is a native American species but did not grow naturally in the cold climate of eastern Massachusetts and does not appear to have been cultivated there until the nineteenth century, although it may have grown in the southern part of the state, near Rhode Island.[28] It is commonly found in furniture of coastal Connecticut, New York, and Pennsylvania. Virtually all the early furniture in which tulipwood was used is of board construction, and usually if tulipwood was the primary wood, the piece is painted, a time-honored practice in Europe. The "white workers" of the Lowlands deliberately chose soft and smooth woods for case furniture that was to have painted decoration.[29] In America tulipwood was occasionally used for turned work but, because it is weak, was rarely used in turned chairs. Like the conifers, it is essentially a carpenter's wood.

THE MAPLES

Among the woods most commonly found in American seventeenth-century furniture and the wood preferred above all others by turners were maples of two general types, roughly classified as hard maples and soft maples. The reason that seventeenth-century English writers classified these woods this way is clear to us today: a fingernail will scarcely penetrate the surface of a hard maple while it easily makes an impression on the surface of a soft maple. The species of hard maple that is most commonly found in furniture is Eurasian sycamore, *Acer pseudoplatanus*, a tree that was rare in England prior to the late sixteenth century and not indigenous to the western hemisphere, although it is common now.[30] When it does turn up in a piece of American furniture prior to 1750, it most often does so in the form of boards rather than turned members since its hardness does not encourage working with man-powered tools.

According to Saltar, American hard or sugar maple, *Acer saccharum*, cannot easily be separated from the European hard maple by microanalysis. While this wood is not common in the earliest furniture of New England, it sometimes appears as boards in simple eighteenth-century furniture that from this style looks to have been made at a somewhat earlier date. Generally, we should not expect to find *Acer saccharum* in turned work. Its relative rarity in the earliest American furniture may be accounted for by its cold-loving nature. It grew in areas where timber was not cut in the initial years of settlement. In the event that microanalysis reveals that a stylistically early piece of furniture contains one of the hard maples, additional evidence ought to be sought to demonstrate its American origin.

Soft maples, on the other hand, are commonly found in American chairs from the middle of the seventeenth century onward, but the fly in the ointment is that the soft maple of England, the English field maple (*Acer campestris*) was a common turner's wood prior to the settlement of America. Joseph Moxon referred to it by the name "soft maple" in 1681 and described it as a favorite wood among turners.[31]

While the soft maples of England and America cannot be easily distinguished from one another by eye, Saltar was occasionally able to separate them by microanalysis, although his test was not infallible. Despite praise from Moxon, English field maple does not appear to have been a very commercial wood and was used primarily for small turnings and possibly for treen ware, as veneer, and as inlay or stringing, but rarely for furniture making. Even though several responsible authorities have voiced doubt that timber-sized examples were available to craftsmen in seventeenth-century England, because the tree survives today as little more than a large bush in hedgerows, the possibility that it was used for furniture cannot be totally dismissed. A number of mature soft maples can be found to-day throughout England, and the Wood Museum at Kew contains a cross section of the trunk of a botanically identified example more than two feet in diameter.[32] A careful though unsystematic search for furniture made of soft maple in the museums and country houses of England has generally gone unrewarded, which suggests that it is not a wood that found its way into commerce and hence might not be expected in London-made furniture. This in turn suggests that any furniture made of it in England during the period 1630–1730 would likely be of a provincial nature that could easily be confounded with its American counterparts.

The soft maples of America exist in a number of species, among which are the red maple (*Acer rubrum*), the striped maple (*Acer pennsylvanicum*), and the silver maple (*Acer saccharinum*). It is not clear which of these is referred to by John Evelyn as the "Virginia Maple," but whichever it is, he reports it was far superior to beech and was "not yet cultivated in England."[33] There is some difficulty in differentiating between the silver maple and the striped maple by microanalysis, but because silver maple is another tree that prefers a cold climate and thus was likely to grow at high elevations, the likelihood of its being logged in the seventeenth century and hence finding its way into furniture diminishes.

Maple first appears on New England case furniture in the form of applied half spindles and as the giant balusters of court cupboards. It was also used to make table legs and sometimes the framing members of the earliest chamber or dressing tables. It is common in the so-called Cromwellian style, leather and turkey-work upholstered chairs made in urban America from about 1655 until almost the end of the seventeenth century and in upholstered chairs made throughout the eighteenth century.

BEECH

Beech, by far the most popular wood used by northern European turners, has not yet been found in seventeenth-century-style American spindle-back or slat-back chairs. Two Cromwellian-style leather chairs with twist-turned legs in Massachusetts collections are made of beech (not micro-analyzed) and have been reported as being of American origin. If these chairs were made in America, then they probably dated from the third quarter of the seventeenth century, were made in Boston, and are the earliest New England chairs containing this wood. The straight-turned, Boston examples in this style are usually made of maple with seat and back rails of oak or maple or a mixture of both.

An axiom among many dealers in American furniture and old-time collectors is that any chair made of beech is of European origin. As is true with most assumptions that are unsupported by objective facts, this axiom has been as much a hindrance to understanding as a help. In fact, beech was used by urban chairmakers in America producing chairs in the late seventeenth and early eighteenth-century style, and, as the catalogue that follows suggests, some extraordinary and unexpected pieces of furniture were made in the colonies during that period. While European beech (*Fagus sylvatica*) and American beech (*Fagus grandifolia*) look identical to the eye, they can be separated from one another by microanalysis, although the test is laborious.[34]

Where maple was available, beech was rarely used. This cannot be attributed to an inherent inferiority of American beech to American maples, because the physical qualities of the woods are so strikingly similar as to be almost interchangeable.[35] The scarcity of beech in American chairs, as opposed to its ubiquitous presence in northern European chairs, is the result of several factors. Although beech trees are plentiful in New England, mature examples tend to have rotten cores and have been attacked by fungi or insects. It is not uncommon to fell a perfectly healthy looking specimen of beech and find only a shell with relatively little usable timber in it. Maple, on the other hand, has all the best qualities of beech—closeness of grain, a strong ray structure—and turns and polishes well. It does not appear to be markedly superior to beech in work-ability, but because of its smaller rays, it takes a strain better. Considering that maple was less susceptible to rot and insect damage and was plentiful, it is easy to see why American chairmakers preferred maple to beech.

Beech was rarely used on case furniture as an exterior wood. It does, however, appear as the front panels on a so-called Hadley chest in the Winterthur collection and is exceptional there.

WALNUT

The rare appearance of walnut in the earliest surviving New England furniture or references to it in the earliest inventories of Massachusetts speak more loudly than any other documents of material culture as to the social level in England from which the first settlers of New England came. Sixteenth- and seventeenth-century English inventories indicate that considerable walnut furniture was present in the homes of the aristocracy. Indeed, in 1635 Gervase Markham exhorted English gentlemen to "make choyse of the finest Walnut-tree you can find, . . . for joyned Tables, Cubbords, or Bedsteads."[36]

Despite the widely held belief that walnut furniture did not become popular in America until after 1700, "a walnutte chair" stood in the parlor of the Reverend John Norton of Boston on April 24, 1663 (the earliest reference to that wood so far discovered in a New England inventory), and predictably enough, Norton was a man whose profession placed him socially and economically among New England's aristocrats.[37] If this piece of furniture was of American origin and not a family heirloom from another age and a different life, it was made of black walnut (*Juglans nigra*). The black walnut—so called because of the dark color of its heartwood—is a native American tree, indigenous to this hemisphere and separable from the European species, *Juglans regia*, by microanalysis. Another species of walnut, familiarly known as butternut (*Juglans cinerea*), is also indigenous to America. Butternut has not been found in any of the furniture for which microanalyses have been performed for this book. Its grain is similar in appearance to black walnut, but it is usually lighter in color than its cousin. Walnut that has been bleached by exposure to the light—a common occurrence with English furniture—could easily be mistaken for butternut.

The best quality European walnut from the furniture maker's point of view exhibits dark striations and hence a striking figure that the American variety never possesses. These desirable cuts of European walnut, sometimes taken from the roots of the tree, are referred to as "Grenoble" or "French" walnut or even "Circassian" in contemporary literature, but they are merely different names for the single, northern European species *Juglans regia*, or English walnut. Equally striking cuts of this wood—often from diseased malformations on the trees known in England as "burrs" and in America as "burls"—were commonly used as veneers in European furniture. "Fiddles" and "crotches," either from the root area or from the point at which two major stems of the tree diverge, were cut into veneers and were used in both England and

America. European walnut of ordinary quality also found its way into furniture of lesser quality. This wood can easily be confused with the general run of American black walnut since the cane chairs and dressing tables of the 1690–1730 era that are made of walnut in England are stylistically similar to contemporary American examples made of the American species. Generally walnut was used rather skimpily, that is, thinly cut, in Europe. Contrary to popular notions and to some of the comments by early observers, American walnut is considered a delicacy by some insects and is, like the English variety, often found in a worm-eaten condition. This is particularly true of furniture that has spent most of its life in coastal New England or on Long Island.

The tests used to separate American walnut from the European species by microanalysis are not widely known, but they are positive and convincing. American walnut exhibits a thickening of the cell walls, crystals of calcium oxylate are deposited in its cells.[38] The absence of these characteristics in a walnut sample usually results in its being pronounced European.

Black walnut was used as an ornamental wood on a court cupboard (Winterthur 66.1261) dated 1680 and probably made in the vicinity of Salem, Massachusetts. The presence of black walnut in a chest owned by the Society for the Preservation of New England Antiquities (SPNEA) further suggests that black walnut was used for decorative purposes a generation earlier. Yet walnut furniture cannot be said to have ever become common in New England during the eighteenth century. The wood was used as a veneer in William and Mary furniture, but surviving solid walnut furniture and documentary references to it in Massachusetts are scarce. It seems likely that this is so because the walnut was a relatively rare tree in Massachusetts, the wood apparently coming onto the market literally as a windfall on those occasions when an old tree died or was accidentally destroyed. Even in the nineteenth century black walnut grew in Massachusetts only "in small numbers, or solitary," and it is doubtful that large stands of the tree were consumed in the early years of the eighteenth century. When walnut first became a stylish wood in New England, Boston's woodworkers imported it from Virginia.[39] In Pennsylvania furniture, black walnut is as common as oak is rare. Since the English taste that influenced the earliest settlers of Pennsylvania in the 1680s was not materially different from that affecting New Englanders, it is logical to conclude that walnut furniture is rare in New England because the tree itself was rare.

A notion persists among collectors of American furniture that "Virginia walnut" was shipped to Europe in large quantities after 1709 and found its way into much furniture. The origin of this popular conception has been difficult to trace, but it seems to be based upon an inference drawn from the following oft-reprinted remarks of John Claudius Loudon that date from 1838: "It is a remarkable fact in the history of this [walnut] tree, that, in the winter of 1709, the greater part of the walnut trees of Europe, and more especially of Switzerland, France, and Germany, were killed; or so far injured, as to render it advisable to fell the trees. The Dutch, at that time, foreseeing the scarcity of walnut timber that was likely to ensue, bought up all the trees that they could procure, in every

direction, and sold them again, according to the demand, for many years afterwards, at a greatly advanced price."[40] The documents do reveal a trickle of American walnut into Europe, particularly England, toward the end of the seventeenth century, but they also show that it was mostly used for interior woodwork. Furthermore, eighteenth-century English furniture made of American black walnut is virtually unknown in England today.

Especially with black walnut furniture, the question continually arises as to whether or not a piece of furniture made solely of an American wood can definitely be attributed to an American origin. The question is particularly important insofar as black walnut is concerned, for if we can answer this question in the affirmative, then the range of fine early American-made chairs is extended by several significant examples. To confirm or deny the proposition depends on our ability to demonstrate whether black walnut was an article of commerce and shipped in quantity from the colonies to Europe, particularly to England.

All evidence from New England indicates the major timber export was white pine for ship masts.[41] Farther south, in colonial Pennsylvania, where every other tree must have been a walnut, the colonial records are mute. The absence of references in Pennsylvania records is somewhat at odds with the statement made in 1630 by William Strachey, former secretary of the Virginia colony: "black walnutt . . . is returned [to England] . . . yearly by all shipping from [Virginia], and yields good profit, for yt is well bought up to make waynscott, tables, cubbordes, chairs and stooles of a delicate grayne and cullour like ebonie, and not subject to worms."[42] Walnut furniture from the seventeenth century is not likely to confuse a collector or curator today. Indeed, it may have been this walnut that John Evelyn knew and admired when he glowingly praised its virtues in *Sylva* (1664) and recommended its cultivation to his countrymen: "[The] black [walnut] bears the worst *Nut*, but the timber [is] much to be preferred, and we might propagate more of them if we were careful to procure them out of Virginia, of all the most beautiful and best worth planting," although he hastens to concede, "those of *Grenoble* come in the next Place, and are much prized by our Cabinetmakers." Evelyn continues, "[I]n truth, were this Timber in greater Pleanty amongst us, we should have far better *Vtensils* of all Sorts for our Houses, as *Chairs, Stools, Bedsteads, Tables, Wainscot, Cabinets*, &c. instead of the more vulgar Beech, subject to the Worm, weak and unsightly; but which, to counterfeit and deceive the unwary, they wash over with a *Decoction* made of the *green Husks* of *Walnuts*, &c. I say, had we Store of this Material, especially of the *Virginian*, we should find an incredible Improvement in the more stable *Furniture* of our Houses."[43]

In 1692 William Brathwayte used black walnut extensively in the wainscotting, dadoes, and cornices of his great mansion, Dyrham Park, Gloucestershire. Yet the wood was not universally admired. William Fitzhugh, a planter in Stafford County, Virginia, found little market for it in the West Country of England when he sent a consignment of walnut plank in June 1695 to George Mason, his Bristol merchant. According to Fitzhugh's letters, Mason was not able to sell it for three years. Fitzhugh ruefully wrote, "I shall never trouble Bristol Market more with any Walnut plank . . . your Bristol price did not answer my expectation." Turning to London, Fitzhugh sent "ten 3 inch plank" to John Cooper in London on July 26, 1698, with the "hope it will come to a good market," but he died in 1701 before it was sold.[44]

Undoubtedly other planters in America were shipping black walnut to England throughout the seventeenth century, but the evidence for it is scanty. That indefatigable furniture researcher R. W. Symonds has suggested that American walnut was not used in English furniture to any great extent until the reign of George I (1714–1727). By way of documentation, he shows that the list of importations into London from Michaelmas (September 29) 1697 to Michaelmas 1698 itemized only "161 walnut boards at 3s. 6d. per plank" plus 54 walnut planks valued at £16.5 from Virginia and Maryland.[45] To some extent Symonds's assertions are borne out by the furniture made of walnut that survives in the museums and country houses of England today: in the pre–1720 styles, English case furniture is veneered with the easily recognized European walnut.

On the other hand, furniture of black walnut was much admired in America, and in at least two instances, furniture in this wood was ordered from London by Americans. On February 20, 1712/13, James Logan of Philadelphia wrote to his factor, John Askew in London for "2 finest Virginia Walnut Chairs at 9s or 9s 6[d] ye same wth those I had of [Robert] Gam[m]age at ye Crown in Panels [St. Paul's] Ch[urch] Yard[,] wth Paws at ye feet designed to suit ye others." About five months later, he augmented the order: "I would have ye two black walnut chairs I wrote for made up half a Dozen besides an Armed one, to suit those I have."[46] Another American, Samuel Sewall of Boston, admired black walnut and in the late winter of 1719/20 made a memorandum of the furniture he had ordered from England on the occasion of his daughter Judith's marriage. Included among the many items were "A True Looking Glass of black Walnut Frame of the newest Fashion (if the Fashion be good), as good as can be bought for five or six pounds. . . . A duzen of good black Walnut Chairs, fine Cane, with a Couch. A Duzen of Cane Chairs of different figure, and a great Chair, for a chamber; all black Walnut."[47]

While two Americans definitely had a taste for English furniture made of black walnut—assuming that they got what they ordered—other considerations mitigate against American walnut's being a popular article of commerce. Transporting any wood to England from America advanced its price by 100 percent to the importer. By the time it was resold to a craftsman, it had increased in price even more. This means that only a furniture maker who had customers willing to purchase items made of expensive woods could afford it, and this in turn means that the wood could only be used in expensive furniture. When we combine this fact with the knowledge that the figure of American walnut was considered inferior to that of European walnut—which it admittedly is—the likelihood of finding much American walnut in English furniture is slim.

If the English prejudice against American walnut did not continue unchecked until the mid nineteenth century, it re-surfaced then when walnut furniture again became popular. The author of Blackie and Son's *Cabinet Maker's Assistant* complains in 1853 that the shortage of walnut in Europe has caused the cabinetmakers of London to have recourse "to the black Virginia walnut, or *Juglans nigra*, a considerable quantity of which is now imported into Britain from America. . . . In quality it is decidedly inferior to that of European growth, as is indicated by the price, which is only 4d. per superficial foot" as opposed to that from Italy, which is sold in London for 9d. to 1s. per foot. "What we have seen," the author continues, "is of a dull uniform brown, having little of the figure which is necessary in ornamental furniture. It is, however, servicable when wrought in the solid, for the inferior parts of articles of which the principal parts are veneered with finer wood."[48]

Two black walnut cane chairs of extraordinary quality, described in the catalogue below, are believed to be of Philadelphia origin, and make the question of the possible use of American walnut by English furniture makers of more than academic interest. The design and workmanship of these chairs are far above the average of what a collector who has learned all one can know about early eighteenth-century chairs from New England examples might expect in an American chair. If these chairs were not made in this country—always a possibility—they have probably been here since they were two months old, which, while not the same thing as being natives, at least makes them naturalized citizens and important documents of taste if not of craftsmanship.

ASH

Ash is a common turned-chair maker's wood that grew plentifully in the forests of New England. One American variety, commonly known as black ash (*Fraxinus nigra*), can be positively identified and separated from *Fraxinus excelsior*, the major European species. Other American species are not so easily separated. Despite William Wood's statement in *New England's Prospect* that American ash was "good for little," we commonly find that colonial chairmakers used it for turned chairs, although documents suggest that in the seventeenth century it was most frequently used to make oars. Ash boards, stiles, and rails are almost unknown in New England seventeenth-century joined furniture (see catalogue entry 40, below). Ash burls, and maple as well, were used as veneers on American furniture in the William and Mary style. Ash used in this way is easily distinguished from maple because of its prominent, summer-growth pores, usually cut through at an angle and quite a prominent part of the figure in the veneer. Ash veneer also appears in English furniture of this period.

One use of ash that has generally gone unnoticed was for bottoming chairs. André Michaux, French botanist who commented on American trees in the early nineteenth century, noted that the wood of the black ash, which he called *Fraxinus sambucifolia*, "may be separated into thin, narrow strips [and] . . . is selected in the country for chair-bottoms and riddles [coarse seives]."[49] Documentary sources do not reveal how early such splint seats were installed on the chairs of New England, but it is possible that they were put on turned chairs in the middle colonies, where they are called "checked seats," from the late seventeenth century onward.

BIRCH

Birch (genus *Betula*) rarely appears in American furniture before the latter years of the eighteenth century, although it was occasionally used earlier instead of maple for turned elements. An outstanding example of this is visible on the legs of the high chest of drawers believed to have been made in 1720 (Winterthur 66.1306). Birch could easily have been used in the villages of New England throughout the eighteenth century, where the choice of woods was greater than in the cities, and where some craftsmen apparently used any wood that came to hand.

Birch is another cold-loving tree and is rarely found in early furniture made south of northern New England. It is a common wood in the furniture of French Canada, much of which can be separated from its New England counterparts only on the basis of stylistic details or techniques of construction that can be traced to French rather than English traditions. Birch is also a common wood in northern European furniture, and only one American species, *Betula lenta* commonly called "sweet" or "black" birch, occasionally can be separated from the European species. If a piece of furniture made of birch has stylistic characteristics that do not permit it to be precisely equated with a well-known school of American craftsmanship or does not possess additional woods that can be positively identified as being American, the best course is to compare it with known northern European examples, particularly those of Norway, Sweden, and northern Germany.

POPLAR

The appearance of poplar (genus *Populus*) in a piece of furniture a decade ago invariably resulted in its being pronounced European. However, the investigation of early turned chairs for this book reveals that poplar was a fairly common wood among the seventeenth-century turners of eastern Massachusetts, particularly in the area around Boston (see catalogue entries 1 and 14). The wood has the rather nondescript appearance of birch but is softer than birch or maple. It was also used for the turned legs of William and Mary furniture made in Boston.

OTHER WOODS

A few additional woods found their way into furniture made in New England prior to 1730, but their occurrence is extremely rare. Among them is chestnut, occasionally found as boards in eastern Massachusetts furniture. Elm has been observed so rarely that no regional pattern in its use can be suggested. Hickory, a highly favored wood among windsor-chair makers in the eighteenth century, appears only in the Cromwellian-style spindle-back chairs associated with the New Jersey/New York area. These chairs are similar to those illustrated in catalogue entries 11 and 12, below, neither of which contain hickory. These two do, however, contain cherry and are among the rare instances of the use of that wood prior to 1725. In Pennsylvania, cherry was also used in wainscot chairs of the so-called Chester County type. When used in this way, the cherry was generally stained to resemble walnut.

Admittedly the foregoing list of common woods used in American furniture prior to 1730 is based on the few surviving documents and those pieces of furniture whose survival is at best an unrepresentative selection of what once existed. It is foolhardy to attempt to make generalizations on the basis of such evidence, for many woodworkers must have made quantities of furniture out of the woods that casually came to hand. They did not hold themselves accountable to furniture historians of the future who might try to impose some order or some rationale on their choices. At best, therefore, the materials outlined above and considered below are an estimate, and no warranty exists to guarantee that any single piece of furniture outside the sampling discussed here will conform to our notions of what the general rules should be.

To the reader with imagination, the catalogue of woods above will seem quite short, for the seventeenth-century forests of eastern North America abounded in types of trees that have not even been mentioned here. Conspicuous by their absence are a number of woods that are common in northern European furniture of which related species grew in colonial America. It is only logical that a craftsman who confronted the bountiful American forest could have chosen a much broader palette with which to work than has been itemized here. Where is the elm, so dear to the hearts of the provincial cabinet- and chairmakers of England? Where are the mulberry, the bog oak, and the fruitwood that English writers have told us much of their furniture of this period contains? Where are the holly and the boxwood that these same writers tell us were used for stringing and inlay? Where are the spruce and fir, so popular in the furniture of northern Europe?

No simple answers will encompass all the questions that arise when we consider the choices that American furniture makers made when they came to select the woods they would work with. Some of the questions can easily be dispensed with because they deal with myths and not facts. When microanalyzed fruitwood almost invariably turns out to be beech—one need only look at the twisted shapes of growing pear and apple trees to see why they could never become commercial furniture woods. Bog oak turns out to be good, sound, honest white oak that has been stained black or has become blackened by oxidation or smoke or otherwise colored by the accidents of time. Although an occasional mulberry may have found its way into an English craftsman's shop, a specimen of its use that has been confirmed by microanalysis has not found its way into the literature.[50]

The leading factor that influenced an immigrant woodworker to select the woods that he would use in his trade does not seem to be so much what was available in the forest as the set of habits and the technology that he brought with him from

Europe. The qualities of some woods, such as oak, ash, and the conifers, suited the purposes for which they had been chosen long before America was heard of, and they were not to be abandoned hastily. Some of these woods, particularly oak, also suited the techniques with which they were fabricated into scantling and then into furniture. They had been fired in the crucible of experience and had been found worthy. Indeed, due to its desirable rivability, American red oak was a wood better suited to the existing English riving tradition than English oak itself.

Maple, which had not been generally available in England, quickly found a place in the hearts of American furniture craftsmen, particularly those who did turning. This wood was readily available, and while not markedly superior to beech in workability, it supplied more usable lumber from a tree of a given size than a beech of the same size was liable to, and for this reason it became commercially available and widely used.

Situations like the one that caused maple to become popular make us pause for a moment to reexamine our mental reconstruction of what it must have been like for a European-born furniture maker to confront the American forest of mixed hardwoods and pine. If a craftsman settled in a village, where the forest was just down the road, he could select any wood he wanted. Nothing prevented him from going into the forest and felling a tree. Thomas Dennis, for example, a joiner of Ipswich, had common rights and permission in 1671 to fell six trees for his trade. The court records of Essex County, Massachusetts, tell us that Dennis and his servant/apprentice, Josias Lyndon, did just that and "wrought [them] into bolts ... in Ipswich woods on the south side of the river."[51]

In a more urban area the craftsman relied upon others for his wood; the choice was not in his hands but in those of the people who provided wood to the town. James Symonds, a joiner of Salem, about fifteen miles south of Ipswich, was a commoner, just like Thomas Dennis, but between 1679 and 1682 Symonds's chief source of boards and bolts was the stock of merchant Jonathan Corwin, who had in turn received them in exchange for goods from sawyers and rivers elsewhere in Essex County. Symonds was not Corwin's only customer for wood: joiners John Launder and John Neal and chairmaker John Macmillion also bought their wood from him.[52] The woods that merchants like Corwin had in stock carries us further afield. Elm, for example, might well have been unknown in Salem furniture, not because it was unavailable, although some evidence suggests that certain species of elm are rare in Massachusetts, but because the elm trees that were there may have been too large to handle with available technology.[53] Birch is another wood that is rare in early Massachusetts furniture because the examples worth converting into lumber may have grown where they could not be efficiently harvested.

The picture that emerges from this complex of circumstances is that the American craftsman's ability to select any wood he pleased from the virgin forest—the idyllic dream—was restricted because of commercial considerations over which he had little control. Despite the tales of many early writers on European furniture, it is likely that European craftsmen operated in the same way.

As life in the colonies grew more assured and New England's ships took the produce of their fishing grounds southward, return cargoes brought a few exotic woods, already items in international commerce from the American tropics, back to the urban seaports. Some of these woods found their way into furniture prior to 1700. An unexpected one is lignum vitae, a dark, heavy, oily wood primarily used for making the pulleys in blocks for ships' tackling. Two others, also used ornamentally, were cocobolo, a variety of rosewood (genus *Dalbergia*) and *Cedrela* (spp.), a member of the mahogany family, often mentioned by Wallace Nutting as "Spanish cedar." The use of such woods was rare and exceptional.

The distribution of the various species of woods was influenced by the soils in each locale, the nature of the climate and any microclimates, and the biological characteristics of the trees themselves that enable them to thrive under certain conditions but do less well under other conditions. Even the habits of the real first settlers of New England, the Indians, affected the distribution of trees that Europeans would find.

The American holly (*Ilex opaca*) provides as good an example as any of the influence of climate. This wood is generally encountered as a shrub east of the Hudson River, and attains its greatest size as a tree in Louisiana.[54] It was therefore unavailable for cabinetmaking in Massachusetts. Climate also affects the range of spruce (genus *Picea*), one of the most common woods in northern European furniture. In Europe it was often used in gilded carvings, as drawer linings, as the core upon which veneer was laid, and in the frames and backs of looking glasses. A glance at the map of the world will show that the Baltic region, from which most European spruce was obtained, lies in the same latitudes as Canada in this hemisphere, and since spruce is a cold-loving tree, it does not grow much south of Canada, northern New York State, Vermont, hinterland New Hampshire, and Maine.[55] Its genetic character causes it to grow branches all along its trunk, which means that it seldom yields a clear board without knots. A better alternative existed in the abundant white pine (*Pinus strobus*), and so the spruce was generally rejected by the lumbermen of colonial America. The white pine, which also thrives in a cold climate, is genetically different from the spruce in that its branches tend to appear at the top of the tree. Because it has fine working characteristics and is abundantly available throughout New England, it became the leading commercial wood of colonial America.

The white pine was not ubiquitous at the time the first settlers came to New England. The microclimate of the relatively sheltered Connecticut River valley permitted an intrusion of the yellow pine group—generally known as southern yellow pine—that mingled with the white pine. The Indians periodically burned the woods along parts of the valley to provide better grazing grounds for the animals they hunted. The fires destroyed the seedlings of the white pine but did not affect the seedlings of the taeda pine, which survive heat better, and so, to the amazement of furniture historians, "southern" yellow pine appears in the furniture of the Connecticut River valley.[56] An equally important custom of the Indians influenced the woods that would appear in the furniture in Boston. The Shawmut peninsula on which Boston was established was devoid of wood when the settlers first arrived. This peninsula, jutting out into Massachusetts Bay and joined to the mainland by a narrow neck, had been used by the Indians, perhaps for centuries, as a place to graze animals. Because the land had been cleared, the peninsula was an ideal place to farm and build a town, except that it had no wood for building. Wood, therefore, had to be brought there from outlying areas. In 1660, Samuel Maverick recorded that Malden, Braintree, and Hingham were towns that furnished Boston with timber for its "many Artificers." Much timber was also imported from New Hampshire and, slightly later, Maine.[57]

Furniture historians are accustomed to seeking out the types of wood that appear in a piece of furniture to enable them to suggest its place of origin with some accuracy. The theory runs that if a native wood grew in a certain place, but not in another, a piece of furniture containing that wood could with reason be attributed to that area. The theory is eminently workable so long as we take into account that some woods became articles of commerce at a surprisingly early date. The white pine is a classic case in point. Good evidence has survived to show us that white pine was shipped from the New England colonies to New York, South Carolina, and the West Indies. Furniture that contains this wood must be interpreted in the light of man's meddlesome interference with nature and not as prima facie evidence that an object was created in the place to which the wood is native. If history worked in simple ways, we would very likely believe that all mahogany furniture of the eighteenth century was made in either Cuba or South America.

CONCLUSIONS

Decorative-arts historians believe that understanding an object begins with the analysis of the materials of which it is made. Furniture in the preindustrial age was, obviously, made of wood. What is far from obvious, however, is that the social, economic, technological, and cultural ramifications of the use of wood are complexly interrelated and, upon close examination, reveal in microcosm how the early generations of settlers in New England first began to diverge from the ways of the cousins and brothers they left behind in England.

We could begin a study of the material life of the first settlers at almost any point and it would show how the North American continent began to mold Europeans into Americans. The climate, for example, was different from that to which Englishmen were accustomed—colder in our North, hotter in our South—and this variable was superimposed onto existing cultural patterns to affect the selection of materials for the houses the settlers built. Clapboards were therefore needed on braced-frame houses to protect the nogging or wattle and daub that was generally only whitewashed or plastered over in England, and shingles from the plentiful forests replaced thatch (although isolated references to thatchers and thatched roofs occur here and there in the records for an uncommonly long time). The climate also affected the height of rooms inside: low ceilings were built where it was necessary to conserve heat, high ones where it was desirable to dissipate it.

These factors led to other choices. Settlers rived clapboards and shingles, using a technique once common in England, but in the 1630s more closely tied to Scandinavian and German building traditions.[58] The height of rooms required modifications to the proportions of interior woodwork and the furniture that went into them. Extremes of temperature and climate further necessitated two sets of clothing—one for hot weather, one for cold—and that in turn required having a place to store the out-of-season clothes. The inevitable result of these and a dozen other differences is that accustomed ways were adjusted to meet the needs of new circumstances, and that new furniture forms were concocted to accommodate new needs or practices.

Another variable that affected the way of life of Englishmen in America is that there was no such thing as the typical immigrant, no median or mean that averages out human personality and experience, and thus there was no typical furniture and no typical way of making it. Indeed, in this period—to some extent even today—there was no typical Englishman; the society was stratified socially (although social mobility has long distinguished England from its continental neighbors). Moreover, England in the seventeenth century was highly regionalized, and the settlement of America thrust together people of very different backgrounds in new environments, a situation which guaranteed that Americans would soon be different from Englishmen, an idea confirmed by modern sociological studies: the ability to hold onto old ways of doing things cannot persist with the same force and meaning when the conditions that support those ways change.

Further, the act of moving from an economy of scarcity to an economy of plenty, as these seventeenth-century Europeans did, was bound to affect not only the way people used the material world around them but their attitude toward it. That nature endowed the eastern part of North America with vast forests that could support wood-consuming European colonies in the seventeenth century is a truism, but its corollary is inescapable, for the new settlers were not only wood consumers but also farmers and graziers. The very different needs of the agrarian culture that the immigrants established in the midst of the forest (as opposed to the one that the Indians had enjoyed on the same lands) and the urban areas that the agrarian areas supported, affected the immigrants as well as the forest. Attitudinally, if the cloak of the vast forest did not actually breed lawlessness, it at least bred contempt for conventional attitudes toward some aspects of the culture the settlers had left behind. A good example is the way in which they continued the sometime English tradition of poaching upon the land owned by absentee proprietors. The forest of America seemed to stretch onward to infinity, and what royal favorite at court in England could do anything about a tree or two borrowed from the lands he had never seen and could not police?

Hand in hand with this attitude toward institutions whose sanctity had never been questioned in over-populated, law-conscious England went a willingness to try out new things that had rarely been done or were, for that matter, needed at home. One of the most obvious of the new things to be tried out on a large scale in America was the sawmill, a device that was rare in England for three reasons. The first two are inextricably intertwined: a scarcity of water power near large stands of publicly owned timber. Added to these was the desire to protect the livelihood of men engaged in the sawyer's trade.[59] By way of contrast, in America, abundant streams flowed through forests owned in common by the villagers or, it seemed, owned by nobody, and the labor to exploit these forests to meet the demand for lumber was scarce. The sawmill—a device that was common on the European continent—was an easy solution, and its affect on English colonists was inevitable: Men who had never seen pine boards at home learned how to build mills to saw logs and to use boards in houses and furniture. They learned to accept the presence of mill-sawn pine boards as a matter of course.

Less obvious is the effect of abundance of oak—the preferred furniture wood of the seventeenth-century joiner—on the way that American craftsmen fabricated that hardwood for use. Riving, the technique that creates usable materials quickly but is wasteful of wood, was once common in England when much of the country was covered with forests and wood was plentiful. By the middle of the sixteenth century, demand had begun to outstrip supply, so wood of the high quality that lent itself to riving became scarce, and riving became equally rare, probably surviving only in rural areas.[60] We now have some slight evidence that the abundance of excellent quality oak in New England enabled joiners who had been dependent upon sawyers for their boards in London to begin to rive wood for themselves when they took up their trade in America. Indeed a joiner could produce for himself a greater quantity of usable panels and rails in a given amount of time than two pit sawyers could. The use of riving has deeper implications for students of oak furniture. Any wood that is riven must have had a special quality in addition to the quality of clearness—moisture.

The replacement of the joiner's tradition by the cabinetmaker's has been so complete that it is often difficult for students of furniture to think back to a time when it was not desirable to work with wood that is virtually dry. The theme haunts the wood selection and description section of Blackie and Son's *Cabinet Maker's Assistant*, a book that effectively documents the problems of the cabinetmaker as far back as the time that the craft was introduced into the Anglo-American tradition.[61] As pointed out in the previous chapter, two of the attributes that distinguish the craft of the early cabinetmaker from that of the joiner are the use of boards for case furniture, as opposed to the joiner's frames and panels, and the use of veneer for surface decoration, as opposed to carving and/or painting. Both of these cabinetmaker's techniques require well-seasoned woods. For example, if the ground upon which the veneer is to be glued has much moisture in it, the glue breaks loose as the wood shrinks and the veneer pops up and cracks. If the veneer is not well dried, it shrinks, and its joints pull apart. Much cabinetmaker's work done in both England and America

during the period in which joiners were teaching themselves how to be cabinetmakers reveals these problems. The lesson of how necessary it is to work with well-seasoned wood was learned so long ago that the tradition of working with wet wood had to be recalled to our collective consciousness.

While it has long been obvious that oak stiles, rails, and crests that were destined to have carved decoration must have been carved before the oak dried out to its final hardness, no one was prepared for the fact that the joiner's principal method of mortise-and-tenon construction with riven wood was also based on working the wood while it was still green, or wet. The evidence has always been there and doubtless has been observed by countless furniture restorers and conservators over the years. But until the inquiring mind of furniture specialist John D. Alexander, Jr., caused him to look critically at the joiner's craft more freshly than anyone else in our generation has been equipped to do, we did not fully realize that most of the joiner's case furniture made in seventeenth-century America was made from wood that retained most of its original moisture content.[62] If worked while wet, oak works easily, precisely, and *quickly* from an economic standpoint. Alexander's discovery that much of the riven oak that went into the furniture of seventeenth-century New England had a high moisture content makes more vivid than ever the statement that Wallace Nutting made more than half a century ago. Nutting, a sensitive connoisseur of New England's earliest furniture who proves to have been wiser than we often suggest, wrote, "Our ancestors did not always do work in the slowest and the hardest way, although such an impression has their strenuous life made, that some authors seem to presume that the fathers preferred a hard way to an easy one."[63]

The question of a supply of wood is far from one of mere academic historicism. The situation for a craftsman living in Ipswich, where the forests are a few blocks away, is different from that of a craftsman who lives on Cornhill in Boston. The village craftsman could procure his wood from a standing tree; the craftsman in Salem or Boston had to procure his from a lumber merchant. This meant that the village craftsman could practice a totally different type of woodworking, one in which unseasoned wood was worked by ancient techniques, while his urban cousin, who could never be sure of the moisture content of the wood that came his way, was forced to use different techniques. So strongly is the myth of the rugged independent craftsman of colonial times implanted in our minds that we cannot conceive of an urban craftsman who is interdependent, not independent, and whose ways of doing things are controlled by factors that are independent of him. The ways in which his work must differ from that of the village craftsman is a theme that will develop in this book as specific instances occur.

[1] See Jorgensen, *Guide to New England's Landscape*, esp. pp. 179–207, for a corrective view of the idea of a "primeval forest" that covered New England. For a modern study of its meaning and historical uses, see Carroll, *Timber Economy*. Carroll also evokes the impression that the forest made on the first settlers in "Forest Society of New England," pp. 13–36.
[2] See Tyack, "Immigration from East Anglia to New England," p. 413.
[3] Young, *Chronicles of the First Planters*, p. 254.
[4] Waters, *Ipswich in the Massachusetts Bay Colony*, 1:68.
[5] Wood, *New England's Prospect*, pp. 16–18. This book appears to be the source of numerous similar reports by subsequent authors who wrote about New England but never visited it. The "tough" walnut tree that Wood describes seems to resemble the hickory (genus *Carya*), a tree that did not grow in England and was thought by early observers to be a type of walnut.
[6] William Douglass, a Scottish physician who lived in Boston from 1718 until his death in 1752, wrote ca. 1749, "Even the firewood near Boston is much exhausted. We are under the necessity of fetching it from the province of Main, and the territory of Sagadahock" (*Summary Historical and Political*, 2:69).
[7] The word "riving" rarely occurs in the public records of New England, generally because it is a concept that does not fit into the nature of those documents. "Rift-wood" is occasionally mentioned. "Clapboard" is a corruption of the phrase "cleft-board"—a board that is split or riven. The few seventeenth-century clapboards that have survived, such as those on the Fairbanks House, Dedham, Mass., reveal the wedge-shaped profile of riven wood.
[8] *Essex Probate*, 1:64. For a good description of these tools, essentially unchanged from their seventeenth-century form, see Salaman, *Dictionary of Tools*.
[9] *Essex Probate*, 1:64. The word "to-ward" survives in our language, but its opposite, "from-ward," from which both fro and frow appear to be contracted, does not.
[10] By December 1621, the settlers in the Plymouth Colony were exporting clapboards to England; see Bradford, *Of Plymouth Plantation*, p. 92; Bishop, *History of American Manufactures*, 1:95.
[11] The panels used in seventeenth-century chests and wainscot chairs average about 10¼″ (26 cm) and 15″ (38.1 cm) in width, respectively. Each panel is worked from a radial section of a large tree with the sapwood and pithwork excluded.
[12] Moxon's late seventeenth-century pictorial description of a joiner's shop emphasizes these tools (see fig. 16).
[13] *Town and Selectmen*, p. 39, details the meeting of January 18, 1637/38; I am indebted to Robert Blair St. George for this reference.
[14] A possible exception may be a chest of drawers with doors owned by the Pennsylvania Historical Museum Commission and displayed at Pennsbury Manor. This chest of drawers, which appears to all intents and purposes to be a typical London example, has hackberry (*Celtis occidentalis*) drawer sides. Hackberry is an indigenous American tree and if the drawer sides are original, as they appear to be, then the chest of drawers ought to be of American origin. The framing members of the piece of furniture are made of pit-sawn oak.
[15] See Forman, "Mill Sawing in Seventeenth Century Massachusetts," pp. 110–30, 149.
[16] Forman, "Mill Sawing in Seventeenth Century Massachusetts," pp. 118–19.
[17] The book which deals most comprehensively with the anatomy of American woods is Panshin and de Zeeuw, *Textbook of Wood Technology*; see also the exquisitely illustrated discussion in Core, Côté, and Day, *Wood Structure and Identification*. An outstanding study of European woods is Greguss, *Holzanatomie*. For a useful work in identifying standing trees, consult Little, *Audubon . . . Field Guide*, and Symonds, *Tree Identification Book*.
[18] Although most microanalytic work is now regularly done by wood anatomists, many identifications do not demand the eye of the specialist. For an excellent introduction to wood identification using a simple 10-power hand lens, see Hoadley, *Understanding Wood*, ch. 3.
[19] The effects of rays on the relative strength of both hardwoods and softwoods are presented in Hoadley, *Understanding Wood*, ch. 1.
[20] While the distinction between oaks of the white and red groups is often made on the basis of the respective presence or absence of *tylosis*, in actuality *tylosis* is occasionally present in the vessels of the woods of the red oak group. Yet, as wood researcher Michael Palmer has explained to me, the occurrence of *tyloses* in the red oaks "is not a consistent feature as with the woods of the white oak [group]. In red oak specimens . . . I have noticed localized occurrences of *tyloses* in almost every specimen. In other words, the presence or absence of *tyloses* is not a strongly supportive clue in making an identification with regard to the oaks. One should look for other, more reliable features . . . such as the size and number of late wood pores. The red oaks possess fewer, larger, and more thick-walled late wood pores than do the white oaks" (Palmer to Forman, December 2, 1980).
[21] Loudon, *Arboretum et Fruticetum Britannicum*, 3:1880.
[22] Calendar of State Papers, Colonial Series, American and West Indies, 1696–97, p. 10, as quoted in Albion, *Forests and Sea Power*, p. 24.
[23] For example, many pieces of white oak are illustrated and described in Kane, *Furniture of the New Haven Colony*.
[24] Quartersawn wood is that in which the saw cuts along the long grain are made as closely as possible to a 90° angle to the annular rings, however in commercial sawing this is practically never attained, and the various angles between 45° and 90° are generally accepted as constituting quarter sawing.
[25] Forman, "Mill Sawing in Seventeenth Century Massachusetts," p. 122.
[26] See Trent, "Joiners and Joinery of Middlesex County, Massachusetts" (conference report), p. 140 and fig. 8.
[27] John Josselyn as quoted in Robinson, *Flora of Essex County*, pp. 95–96.
[28] Robinson, *Flora of Essex County*, pp. 31, 169.
[29] Lunsingh Scheurleer, "Dutch and Their Homes," pp. 13–14.
[30] As late as 1640, John Parkinson in *Theatrum Botanicum*, wrote of the sycamore, that "it is nowhere found, wild or natural, in our land, that I can learn; but only planted in orchards or walkes for the shadows sake" (as quoted in Johns, *Forest Trees of Britain*, p. 49).
[31] Joseph Moxon, *Mechanick Exercises* (1703), reprinted (1970) as *Moxon's Mechanick Exercises*, pp. 198, 73.
[32] Maxwell, *Trees*, p. 62; also A. F. Mitchell, Forest Research Station, Forestry Commission, Wrecclesham, Franham, Surrey, to Forman, July 16, 1973.
[33] Evelyn, *Silva*, p. 65.
[34] This information is based upon a dozen years of experience and acquaintance with Gordon Saltar, a wood anatomist for Winterthur Museum. Saltar's tests for American beech have been confirmed by Her Majesty's Forest Products Laboratory at Prince's Risborough, England, but they have never been published by Saltar. I am satisfied that his test is accurate, although I regret that I have never been informed by Saltar as to what factors his estimates are based upon. [Editor's note: Research is currently being undertaken to verify Saltar's techniques.]
[35] The table of basic stresses for clear material in the U.S. Department of Agriculture, *Wood Handbook*, p. 105, gives the same figures for beech and maple (black and red) in the following four categories: extreme fiber in bending, compression perpendicular to the grain, compression parallel to the grain, maximum horizontal shear and modulus of elasticity.
[36] Markham, *English Husbandman*, p. 57; I am indebted to Ian M. G. Quimby for this reference.
[37] Suffolk Probate, 4:149.
[38] Miller, "Reticulate Thickenings in some Species of *Juglans*," pp. 898–901; I am indebted to Michael A. Palmer for this reference.
[39] Emerson, *Report on the Trees and Shrubs Growing Naturally in the Forests of Massachusetts*, p. 186. Robinson, *Flora of Essex County*, p. 96, notes that the black walnut is "occasionally cultivated from the western states." He continues, "we have received specimens of the nuts of this tree from Mr. J. C. Peabody of Newburyport, gathered in a place near that city where he thinks the trees are indigenous, but this seems under careful consideration to be hardly probable." Evidence that walnut was imported into Boston in the eighteenth century is contained in Jobe, "Boston Cabinet Woods," p. 252.
[40] Loudon, *Arboretum et Fruticetum Britannicum*, 2:1426.
[41] Albion, *Forests and Sea Power*, p. 31.
[42] Lowenthal, "History in Houses (Dyrham Park)," p. 868; I am indebted to Bradford L. Rauschenberg for calling this reference to my attention.
[43] Evelyn, *Silva*, pp. 58, 59.
[44] Davis, *William Fitzhugh and His Chesapeake World*, pp. 339, 361, 367; I am indebted to Arlene Palmer Schwind for calling this book to my attention.
[45] R. W. Symonds, "Turkey Work, Beech and Jappanned Chairs," p. 392. The Symonds papers at Winterthur do not contain any additional pertinent references to this matter.
[46] James Logan to John Askew, March 20, 1712/13, and August 1, 1713, correspondence book, Logan Papers, HSP; I am indebted to Bradford L. Rauschenberg for this reference. I am indebted to Colin M. Streeter for pointing out that Robert Gammage's premises were "at the crown" in St. Paul's churchyard. See also Heal, *London Tradesmen's Cards*, p. 61.
[47] Samuel Sewall [to Samuel Stroke], Memoranda [February 20, 1719/20], Sewall, *Letter-book*, 2:106. The items arrived in August 1720 (Sewall, *Diary*, 2:259–60).
[48] *Cabinet Maker's Assistant* (London: Blackie & Son, 1853), reprinted as Blackie and Son, *Victorian Cabinet Maker's Assistant* (1970), p. 23. This is the most sophisticated and informative and very likely most important *vade mecum* to historical cabinetmaking in print.
[49] Michaux, *North American Sylva*, 3:113. Ash splint is made by pounding the log and crushing the porous early wood, causing the annular ring to delaminate.
[50] That fruitwood is usually beech has been determined by examination of a number of pieces of furniture in England. Blackie and Son voice their disdain for what is commonly called bog oak in the *Cabinet Maker's Assistant*, ch. 2, pp. 18, 19. Mulberry is a close relative of ebony and is among a small group of sometimes dark-colored woods that grow in the northern temperate zones. Pieces of veneer that do not exhibit a very dark heartwood surrounded by a very light sapwood are almost certainly not mulberry. Burls of mulberry would be hard to identify by microanalysis. All evidence indicates that its use was very occasional in seventeenth-century England. Mulberry might easily be mistaken for olivewood and walnut veneers, by far the more common woods used by urban cabinetmakers. An amusingly disdainful discussion of mulberry is to be found in Hinckley's invaluable, *Directory of Historic Cabinet Woods*, pp. 93–95.
[51] *Essex Quarterly Courts*, 4:349.
[52] May 31, 1680, January 11, 1682/83, et passim, Corwin ledger.
[53] Emerson, *Report on the Trees and Shrubs Growing Naturally in the Forests of Massachusetts*, p. 299.
[54] Sargent, *Manual of the Trees*, pp. 669–70.
[55] For distribution of the white spruce (*Picea glauca*), the most common North American species, see Fowells, *Silvics of Forest Trees*, p. 318.
[56] Judd, *History of Hadley*, pp. 97–99. Judd points out that the burnings were continued by the English settlers; he also notes the presence of yellow pine and the absence of white pine (pp. 295, 430–31).
[57] Waters, "Maverick's Account of New England," pp. 236–39. See also Forman, "Mill Sawing in Seventeenth Century Massachusetts," pp. 117–23.
[58] See Cummings, *Framed Houses of Massachusetts Bay*, pp. 128–130.
[59] Company of Joyners, leaf 95 verso, quotes a complaint dated March 25, 1633, which says that in that year only 58 freeman sawyers were at work in London and asserts that "all the said ffree Sawyers are not able to perform the Eighth part of the labor and business for sawing within this City, Liberties and adjacent places." The complaint continues that between 1613 and 1633 the sawyers hired only foreigners to work for them and increased the prices of their work so that they were taking "sometimes Three pence and sometimes ffour pence for sawing a Curfe [kerf?] of Wainscott which was then done for Three half pence." An additional complaint, dated January 26, 1687/88, leaf 96 recto, informs us that the sawyers company were employing all of the sawyers in London so that the joiners and carpenters of the city could not

get any sawing done, and were forced to buy their wood from the freeman sawyers at high prices.

[60] *Moxon's Mechanick Exercises*, p. 84, refers to the stile and rail of a joiner's frame as "quarters," suggesting a persistence in terminology in London from an earlier time when these parts were riven and truly were quarters, although there is no suggestion in his chapter on joinery that riving was still a technique employed by joiners in his time.

[61] Blackie and Son, *Victorian Cabinet Maker's Assistant*, ch. 2, pp. 6, 7, 10, 11, 18, 49 et passim.

[62] In his excellent *Make a Chair From a Tree*, Alexander develops the role of wet-wood construction in slat-back, shaved-chair construction. Since the publication of that seminal work, he has continued to probe the implications of his findings, and has presented persuasive evidence to the author that *most*, if not all, joined furniture made in seventeenth-century America was built using principles similar to those that guided the production of round-tenon and round-mortise chairs as will be discussed in the chapter on joined furniture, below. Progress in the direction that Alexander's work suggests is slow, however, for the simple reason that verification depends on our being able to examine *disassembled* seventeenth-century examples—a need with which few working curators can comply. As a result, more data is needed before conclusive results can be published. That seventeenth-century carpenters used green wood in house construction certainly supports Alexander's theory; Cummings, *Framed Houses of Massachusetts Bay*, p. 11, quotes Sir William Petre's surveyor in 1566 to the effect that Chignall Hall, Essex, was "builded moostly with greene tymber, as yt semeth, for the houses yeld and shrink in every parte." I am deeply indebted to John D. Alexander, Jr., for pointing out to me that parts of framed-and-paneled furniture can be fabricated from unseasoned wood.

[63] Nutting, *Pilgrim Century* (2d ed.), p. 22.

CHAPTER 3

SEVENTEENTH-CENTURY WOODWORKING CRAFTSMEN AND THEIR CRAFTS

Every living thing leaves traces of what it was; man alone leaves traces of what he created.

JACOB BRONOWSKI,   Ascent of Man

Anyone familiar with American history could logically assume that our earliest furniture ought to have been made shortly after the earliest dates of settlement recorded in our annals. The surviving documents of the colonies shed little light on this subject, and only a handful of furniture made during the first generation of settlement can be identified with certainty. Our search for early furniture is complicated by the additional problem of how to recognize it. In contrast to the earliest American written records, whose dates are generally a part of the documents themselves and therefore self-evident, modern historical method requires that an artifact be substantiated by evidence beyond the mere fact of its existence. The search for such corroborative evidence does not have a long tradition.

In the 1840s, when a small group of Americans first became interested in the artifacts of their past, no particular collecting emphasis was placed on furniture made in the colonies nor was any particular value attached to possessing it. An artifact conferred status on its owner by the assertion that one's ancestors had brought it over, preferably on the *Mayflower*. When the historians who wrote the nineteenth-century town histories of New England dealt with furniture, they often confected pedigrees to suit their ideas of what should have been

rather than what actually was. On occasion, traditions of importation have gotten attached to objects that we now know, from microscopic wood analyses, are of American origin. These pieces of furniture form a core. Regrettably, wood analysis is not routinely used in most American museums, is almost unknown in most historical societies, and is anathema to many dealers. The result is that systematic investigation of the physical properties of furniture is not always a simple task.

In the absence of relevant factual material, writers have often devised theories about what the earliest furniture of New England may have looked like. Those theories based on wish fulfillment have usually proved wrong. Soundly constructed hypotheses, on the other hand, have successfully led us to many objects that in fact can be demonstrated to date from this first century of colonial settlement.

The first theory that early students of American furniture developed was inferred from the difficult living conditions encountered by the early settlers of America. Because these conditions were perceived as primitive, early students of seventeenth-century artifacts assumed that the furniture used by the settlers was crude. Anthropologists and sociologists in the twentieth century have demonstrated that this assumption is only partly true. It is obvious, for example, that harsh living conditions do not rob a craftsman of his skills or his conception of what an object for a specific purpose must look like. A trained joiner from a civilized English town does not, upon arrival in the New World, make a primitive bench out of half a log (a material hard to come by in any case) to serve as a joint stool any more than his fellow settlers abandon verbal communication and revert to sign language.

It is, however, equally clear that some needs will be satisfied by nonskilled means in a community where skilled labor is in short supply. A broadside published in London in 1622 forecasts that nonprofessional furniture would be made in the new settlements and that this furniture would coexist with familiar, highly articulated, contemporary items brought from home or made here by trained craftsmen. This broadside, windily entitled "The Inconveniences that Have Happened to Some Persons which Have Transported Themselues from *England* to *Virginia*, without Prouisions Necessary to Sustaine Themselues . . . ," advises emigrants to take, in addition to the apparel, victuals, arms, household implements, and tools of husbandry:

	[£ s. d.]
Two broad Axes at 3.s.8.d. a piece	— 07 04
Fiue felling Axes at 18.d. a piece	— 07 06
Two steele hand sawes at 16.d. a piece	— 02 08
Two two-hand-sawes at 5.s. a piece	— 10 —
One whip-saw, set and filed with box, file, and wrest	— 10 —
Two hammers 12.d. a piece	— 02 00
Three shouels 18.d. a piece	— 04 06
Two spades at 18.d. a piece	— 03 —
Two augers 6.d. a piece	— 01 00
Sixe chissels 6.d. a piece	— 03 00
Two percers stocked 4.d. a piece	— 00 08
Three gimlets 2.d. a piece	— 00 06
Two hatchets 21.d. a piece	— 03 06
Two froues to cleaue pale 18.d.	— 03 00
Two hand-bills 20.d. a piece	— 03 04
One grindstone 4.s.	— 04 00
Nailes of all sorts to the value of	02 00 —
Two Pickaxes	— 03 — [1]

The presence of tools like these in the earliest household inventories of New England demonstrate that settlers generally heeded the advice in the broadside. Much of the furniture that could have been made with such tools must have been rough in execution, for smoothing planes are conspicuously absent from the list. This knowledge, however, does not greatly aid us in identifying pieces of this furniture in time, were we to encounter them today, for it is clear that the physical circumstances confronted by the first settlers in America recurred as they or their descendants pushed the frontier inland: furniture was produced that filled a need, and little attention was paid to the niceties of style and ornament that leisure and conspicuous consumption permit.

In a sense, simple utilitarian furniture is timeless, but its form and structure must follow accustomed models. In most cases the forms of such furniture express the use to which each is put. Moreover, furniture that is made because it is needed has little pretension to style and is distinguishable from century to century only when it contains evidences of technological change that we can date from our knowledge of technological

history. The difference between a board chest made in Plymouth in 1630 or Toledo in 1780 or Dodge City in 1880 might only boil down to whether wrought, cut, or wire nails can be found in it. The historian can make few intelligent comments about nonprofessional furniture because its makers are not governed by the predictable forces that years of research have revealed their more systematic compatriots responded to.

The picture that nonprofessional furniture presents, however, is only part of a larger picture and is the part we cannot deal with. The periods in which the settlers in Virginia huddled in tents and those at Philadelphia dwelt in riverbank caves and those in New England lived in wigwams were relatively short, as we look back on them now, although it would have been another thing to have lived in such conditions. The records reveal that in the next phase of settlement skilled craftsmen arrived, bringing with them the cultural heritage of Europe. These craftsmen did not produce rude dwellings and furniture. It is obvious now, as it should have been all along, that they could not do this because they simply did not know how. Theirs were the sophisticated skills of centuries of orderly development, and those skills were wed to the concepts of design that are manifest in the surviving objects.

Independent documentation of the objects produced by these civilized techniques, as with the early do-it-yourself examples, is often not available, a contretemps that would seem to leave us with an insoluble problem insofar as verifying their date of manufacture is concerned. But an alternative exists, and that is the study of the object itself as a document of itself. This technique combines the study of the history of design with the history of technology and places objects in time. The history of design tells us where objects should fall in relationship to the trends of European art as we understand them, and that is the matter to which the catalogue below addresses itself. Technological history, in this case, means the recovery of the methods and tools that furniture craftsmen used and the customs associated with their crafts at the time that America was settled.

The earliest surviving documents of English and Dutch America contain the names of our first professional woodworkers. Some of the trades that they followed are familiar to us today because they still survive. No one needs to be told what a carpenter, an upholsterer, a cabinetmaker, a carver, or a chairmaker does. Each one still does it today. Other craft designations such as "joiner" and "turner" have disappeared from the American language. We cannot even conceive what the products of these crafts looked like without the effort of historical recovery. It is something like reading a play by Shakespeare in which the words appear to be the same as those we use today, but the full comprehension of the experience eludes us because the words themselves no longer mean what they did 400 years ago.

The random nature of surviving documents always hampers historical reconstruction, and this is certainly true of the references to the American craftsmen whose activities are analyzed here. Even in the highly ordered society that dominated western civilization in the seventeenth century, human beings did not live their lives like a clockwork mechanism, and no single self-employed individual would have completely conformed to the general picture that emerges in this chapter. Documents show that many woodworking craftsmen in the young colonies performed a variety of tasks in order to survive economically. What a craftsman did in real life may bear little relationship to the word or two that he used in a legal document as a shorthand description of his trade. Enough records do remain, however, to permit us to sketch the outlines of the furniture-making crafts in seventeenth-century Anglo-America as practiced by the great majority of craftsmen, particularly those who lived in towns. The possible exceptions to the general rule, which doubtless apply to many of the individuals mentioned in this book, will have to be ignored for the moment. The evidence that survives in written documents and in the furniture itself confirms the general idea that most furniture makers stuck to their crafts and performed them in a regular and orderly manner in the ways tried and proved by constant practice over the centuries and handed down from father to son and from master to apprentice in their most efficient and perfected state.

THE CARPENTER

Carpenters were undoubtedly the first woodworkers to practice their trade in the new settlements, building houses where none had existed before. They also made furniture. Carpenter-made furniture, when it has survived at all from the seventeenth century, is difficult for the modern scholar to identify. Because furniture making was not the primary result of the carpenter's efforts, we have traditionally assumed that carpenter-made furniture was simple in form and construction —plain boxes, board chests, benches, cupboards, tables, and the like. We have also assumed that carpenters decorated their case furniture with a few moldings run with a plane or with simple and traditional intaglio designs carved into the surface, both of which offer the art historian little to contemplate. But little evidence has survived to indicate that these assumptions are correct. Indeed, modern studies reveal that it is possible, indeed probable, that many seventeenth-century woodworking craftsmen labeled as carpenters in the early records of colonial America emigrated from rural villages in England where craft activities were not governed by guilds. As a consequence, these craftsmen had learned and practiced the full range of their art, which included joinery, just as their ancestors had done for centuries before the two trades branched off from each other. Thus, the greatest impediment to our understanding the furniture that they produced lies in the fact that the documents that enumerate the forms that they made do not tell us either the techniques that they used to make them or the ornamentation that they put upon them. There are a few exceptional surviving pieces of furniture that have some documentary reason for being attributed to men who are called carpenters in the records, such as the communion table believed to have been made late in the seventeenth century by Stephen Jaques of Newbury[port], who was undoubtedly a joiner by training. Their furniture barely hints at the ingenuity of this class of craftsmen, who framed houses with joints more complex and

clever than any used in furniture.[2] Nonetheless, if we are to believe an indenture dated August 2, 1653, a full generation after the initial settlement of Plymouth Colony, a young carpenter who had just finished his apprenticeship was expected to set up as a journeyman (one who works by the day) with the following tools furnished by his master: "one broad axe, two playnes, two Augers and a sett of Chissels; & an hand saw."[3]

While the distinction between a carpenter and a joiner was doubtless clear to the men who practiced each of those crafts in the seventeenth century, the line between them was not invariably clear to their contemporaries. We cannot always tell, for example, from a household inventory containing tools but not mentioning whether the testator was a carpenter or a joiner, what his trade in fact was. The kitchen of George Phillips, who died in Boston in 1644, contained his tools: "5 sawes, 3 axes, 3 yron wedge wth carpenters and Joyners tooles . . . £1:10:00." Phillips was, perhaps like many of the first generation immigrant craftsmen, prepared for virtually any woodworking emergency: he also possessed "a turning lath[e]."[4] In 1653, Thomas Wifford of Northumberland, England, charged his friend, Paul Sympson, then en route to Maryland, to have the tasks of carpenter, joiner, and upholsterer performed for him. He ordered Sympson, "when Nayles and Carpenter can be had[,] to build . . . a fifteen foot house Square with a welch Chimney, the house to be floord & lofted with Deale boards and lined with Riven boards on the inside with a handsome Joined Bedstead, one small Joyned Table and Six Joined Stooles and three wainscott Chaires, and to furnish the . . . room with bedding curtains & ballance [valance] Chamber Linnen and all other things fitting & Convenient."[5] This commission would certainly have required a versatile carpenter, one who also plied the needle. It is, of course, likely that Wifford anticipated the carpenter would not necessarily do all these tasks himself but would instead contract to have them done. It is doubtful that a carpenter sewed up curtains any more often than he did the work of the trained plasterer, assuming that the "welch Chimney"—doubtless a pejorative term as it is used here— was a catted chimney made of a timber frame, filled with wattles, and finished with a coat of fine clay daub.

From the language used in contemporary craftsmen-client contracts, it is often difficult to tell if indeed the contracting carpenter actually intended to do the work agreed upon. A contract filed among the papers of the Quarterly Court held at Ipswich, Massachusetts, on March 26, 1661, however, lists work that could have been executed by a carpenter. It was

made, Sept. 27, 1659, with William Averell, carpenter, by Richard Jacob, both of Ipswich: Said Averell was to erect a building 18 feet square and 13 feet stud, to provide clapboards and shingles for the said building and to lay them; to lay three floors with joist and board; to make 4 windows too stole windows of 5 Lights apeece and to Claristory windows of 4 Lights apeece also a garret window to Casements betwene studs pertitions and dors to Close the Roms Compleat as allso to Remoue A Little Rome and Close it to his house and mak it tite betwene allso to make a table and frame of 12 to 14 foot Long and a joyned forme of 4 foot Long and a binch Behind the table.[6]

The amount paid was £12, and Averell agreed to have the work completed by the last of August. He not only agreed to make a board bench, as might be expected of a carpenter, but also to make a joined form, of the type only a joiner should have made in urban England. What this document most plainly shows is that in a rural village, such as Ipswich in 1659, a craftsman identified with one trade would not hesitate to turn his hand to another.

Obviously the techniques a carpenter uses to frame a house are close to those used by a joiner to frame a table or a piece of case furniture. But when we come to examine the best surviving case furniture of New England, we find that sawn boards are rarely used to any extent, particularly in the urban examples. Historically, distinctions between joiners and carpenters in England have not been documented earlier than 1386 when the *OED* shows the word *joiner* to be in use. The classic distinction between the two crafts is pointed out by the anonymous author of *A General Description of All Trades* (1748): "Carpentry and Joinery, that Part especially belonging to House-work (and even Undertaking, or furnishing of funerals) are often performed by the same Persons, though the work of [the Joiner] is much lighter and reckoned more curious than that of Carpenters; for a good *Joiner* can often do both well, but every *Carpenter* cannot work at joinery."[7] Although it is possible to read this quotation too literally, we now understand that the trades of the carpenter and the joiner may have been drawing together once more by the 1740s after several centuries of separation and that joiners were well on their way to being supplanted by cabinetmakers as the primary makers of furniture.

Fig. 9. Detail of framing techniques used on a cabinet door, probably from Windsor, Conn., 1650–80. (Winterthur 59.2324.) Note the grooves cut to hold the inset panel and the design of the tenons in the top rail. (Photo: Benno M. Forman.)

THE JOINER

The product of the joiner's craft is called "joinery" or "joined work," but the techniques used to produce it are much older than the name that distinguishes it from carpentry. Joseph Moxon, whose *Mechanick Exercises or the Doctrine of Handy-Works Applied to the Arts of Smithing, Joinery, Carpentry, Turning, and Bricklaying* presents the most coherent picture of England's woodworking trades, poetically stated, "joinery is an Art Manual, whereby several Pieces of Wood are so fitted and join'd together by Straight-line, Squares, Miters or any Bevel, that they shall seem one intire piece."[8] The technique basically consists of making a frame of wood, square or rectangular in section, that is held together by mortise-and-tenon joints (fig. 9) and fastened with wooden pins. Such a frame can be fitted to other frames to form the lower structure of tables, or the bases of cabinets, or stools and chairs. These frames can be grooved on their inner perimeters, and feather-edged boards can be fitted into them (see fig. 2) to form panels that can be used to wainscot walls and to make case furniture, the heads and testers of beds, and joined chairs with paneled backs. Typical furniture produced by the joiner, as opposed to the carpenter, is listed in a decision reached by the London Court of Aldermen to settle a suit between these two trades in 1632. Joiners were entitled to the exclusive manufacture of:

All sorts of Beadsteads whatsoever (onlie except Boarded Bedsteads and nayled together).

All sorts of Chayres and stooles which are made with mortesses or tennants.

All tables of wainscotte wallnutt or other stuffe glewed with fframes mortesses or tennants.

All sorts of formes framed made of boards with the sides pinned or glewed.

All sorts of chests being framed duftalled pynned or glued.

All sorts of Cabinets or Boxes duftalled pynned or glued.[9]

The framing technique of the joiner is a scaled-down and simplified version of the framing technique of the house carpenter, but the seventeenth-century joiner used smaller tools and had more of them. The possession of more and smaller tools obviously permitted the joiner to produce work of more intricate detail and finer scale than the average carpenter could aspire to. Joined work is usually, but not invariably, embellished with planed moldings and carving. The planed, decorative grooves on seventeenth-century American case furniture—sometimes executed with a plane, sometimes with a scraping tool called a "scratch stock"—may be the last vestige of what was once a widespread decorative technique that we call "linenfold" carving but that, according to one remarkable document, was called "drapery" work in sixteenth-century England. Such work was executed by joiners using planes, with a touch of carving at the ends of the folds to give the illusion of textile hangings.[10] Inasmuch as considerable labor was expended in creating it, a piece of joined furniture usually commanded a fairly high price; thus in an inventory, a joined object can often be recognized by the valuation placed upon it.

Detailed statements about the sort of work joiners did in seventeenth-century America are rare. Surviving bills are only marginally informative, and since seventeenth-century joiners' account books are nonexistent, modern researchers are dependent on estate inventories and an occasional contract between customers and joiners. An unusually detailed contract between a ship owner and a Boston joiner named John White reveals a great deal about joinery in its prime.

Articles of Agreement Indented concluded the [blank] Day of Decemb anno Dom One Thousand Six hundred Eighty and ffive Between John White of Boston in New England joynor on the one part and Arthur Tanner of Boston afforesd marriner on the other part are as ffolloweth Imp[rimi]s The s[ai]d William [John?] White for the considerations herein exprest doth Covenant promise bind and oblige himself his heires estate and adm[inistrator]s to doe and performe all Such Joynors worke in and upon the Ship Which william Greenough is now building for the sd Tanner on the Stocks in Sd Greenoughs Building yard as is herein mentioned & expressed.

Vizt:

To Plane and rabbitt the upright of the Sterne
To Plane and rabbitt all necessaryes for the Territts
To Plane the great cabbin Deck
To make a Bulkhead & doors to that cabbin
With two Close cabbins & settlebed with turn'd ballasters and a Table in three parts with a Cupboard & all Lockers convenient with Shutters for the light and to ceile it after the best manner
To Imbow [i.e., run a molding upon] all railes that shall be placed on sd Ship with a ffife raile
To Ceile [ceiling; a synonym for joining] the roundhouse & make in it two Cabbins and a Table wth Lockers, and too lights wth Shutters to them
To plane the Bulkeheads & make a table on the Quarter Deck: and Chaire & binacle with Hen Coops convenient
To Plane the planks in the Steeridge & round the beames & to make foure hanging Cabbins and a binnacle wth one Close Locker wth a Lock to the Same
To make foure close Cabbins between decks & a Saile room wth a grateing bulkhead for the gun roome & to round the beames
To Plaine the Bulk head of the Steeridge & the Innboard plank along the side to make all such Gangways the master sees meet. To plane all Gunwales & round house & bulk head of the forecastle & to make in the forecastle two Cabbins and Two Lockers & to plane the planks of the Beake hedd All which abovementioned worke with what more Joynors work fitt for sd Ship & not herein mentioned is to be done and finished to the masters content and in good and workemanlike order in every respect by the ffifteenth day of may next ensuing the day of the date hereof if required.[11]

Carving was the most common decorative technique used by the first joiners in rural New England, and many joiners

Fig. 10. Detail showing the scribe marks on a carved panel of a chest attributed to John Thurston, Dedham or Medfield, Mass., 1639–45. (Winterthur 57.539.)

were capable of ornamenting their work this way. In more metropolitan centers, especially where ships were fitted out, carving was traditionally a separate and distinct branch of the joiners' trade. According to the strict definition of carving promulgated by the London Court of Aldermen in 1632, "carved workes" were "either raised or cutt through or sunck in with the Grounde taken out being wrought and cutt with carving Tooles without the use of Plaines."[12]

The abstract floral carving found on the most ambitious New England furniture of the early seventeenth century was laid out with a rule, a square, and a pair of compasses (also called dividers); the scribe marks that served as the original plan are often still visible (fig. 10). A remarkable misericord of indefinite date, from Saint Nicholas Church, Lynn Regis, Norfolk, England (fig. 11), shows a master carver—doubtless the very master who executed the misericord itself—scribing a design with a pair of compasses, although the joint of the compasses has been broken off.[13] Lying on the panel are the square and rule. Additional work that has already passed through the master's hand is being executed by two journeymen behind him, while an apprentice is bringing the pot of beer or ale to which all artisans were customarily entitled as a matter of right during the course of a day's work.

Although compass, square, rule, and scribe were the traditional tools used to lay out most of the carving on American joined furniture, this was not the only method. Many Connecticut River valley chests known as "Hadley chests" appear to have been laid out with the aid of a template, which very roughly positioned the pattern on the stiles, rails,

Fig. 11. Detail of misericord from St. Nicholas Church, Lynn Regis, Norfolk, England, sixteenth century. (By permission of the Board of Trustees, Victoria and Albert Museum, London, England.)

Fig. 12. A turner at his lathe. From Croker, Williams, & Clark, *Complete Dictionary of Arts and Sciences*, 3: pl. 133, fig. 2. (Winterthur Library.)

drawer fronts, and panels. The field of each panel was then carved with a narrow gouge *ad libitum*, as the fancy of the joiner more or less directed, and with considerable variety from maker to maker and time to time. Freehand laying out of patterns, however, seems to have been uncommon, if indeed examples of it can be found at all, although on occasion, the design was not carefully planned for symmetry.

Joiners who were capable of doing carving are rarely identified as "carvers" in the records of New England's villages; however, often a joiner's inventory will list carvers tools. In other cases, lawsuits occasionally reveal that a joiner did carving. Such is the case with a deposition sworn in a case at a Quarterly Court held in Ipswich, Massachusetts, in March 1682, in which Thomas Dennis deposed that Grace Stout "had bought a carved box with a drawer in it of him in 1679"; this item is the sole documentary evidence that joiner Dennis was also a carver. The information that Phineas Pratt—the earliest joiner known to have been working in Plymouth Colony and hence in New England—was also a carver comes down to us in a somewhat more bizarre way. Pratt, who had joined Weston's colony at Weymouth (between Boston and Plymouth) in 1622, wrote a history, entitled "A Declaration of the Affairs of the English People that First Inhabited New England," in 1662. Although Pratt's narrative was concerned with things other than the joiner's trade, he does record the following curious conversation with an Indian, who also carved, that occurred in 1623. According to Pratt, the Indian said, in broken English, "'me heare you can make the Lickness of men & of women, dogs & dears, in wood & stone. Can you make [words missing]. . . .' I said, 'I can see a kniue in yor hand, wth an Ill favored ffase upon the haft.' Then he gave it into my hand to see his workmanship." A specialist whose sole occupation was that of a "carver" does not appear in the public documents of New England until Edward Budd of Boston is so identified in a Suffolk County deed of January 4, 1668.[14]

THE TURNER

The trade of the turner has been greatly neglected in studies of early furniture until recent years, which is difficult to understand because the turner was just as important as the joiner among the furniture makers of the seventeenth century, and numerous extraordinary examples of turning have found their way into the great collections of our nation. Moreover, the lathe—the tool that distinguishes the turner's work from that of other workmen—is the tool that is used to make tools, and as such it was an important factor in establishing other trades during the period.

Turned furniture was made by rotating long pieces of wood, which had been roughly shaped to a more or less cylindrical form, between the two metal points in a lathe, and by cutting away the unwanted portion of the cylinder with a type of chisel known as a "gouge" (fig. 12). The turned cylinders were then assembled into furniture by fitting the rounded ends of cross pieces into auger holes drilled into upright members. The products, generally known as turned work or "turnery," consisted primarily of chairs, footstools, spinning wheels, balusters for staircases, pulleys for ships, hubs for wheels, and wooden plates called "trenchers." The technique of turning is ancient; examples of turned work have survived in the tombs of Egypt; others are pictured in frescoes unearthed at Pompeii and Herculaneum. Turners are not recorded by that name in all the communities of New England from the beginnings of their histories, but no village, indeed, no farm could have long functioned without someone nearby who practiced that art. Very often he was known as a wheelwright, and he made turned chairs as well as wheels.

In the incorporated cities and towns of England, the crafts of the joiner and the turner had been kept nominally separate by the rules of the companies or guilds, each of which jealously guarded the privilege of practicing his own "art and misterie."[15] The surviving records of the Aldermen's Court of the City of London, however, show that theory did not always work out in practice. The following decision, concerning a case adjudicated in 1632 gives us a rare insight into the differences between these crafts as well as specific information about the art of the turner.

We have called before us as well the M[aster] & W[arden] of Compy of Turners as also the M & W of Compy of Joyners. It appeareth that the Compy of Turners be grieved that the Compy of Joyners assume unto themselves the art of turning to the wrong of the Turners. It appeareth to us that the arts of turning & joyning are two several & distinct trades and we conceive it very inconvenient that either of these trades should encroach upon the other and we find that the Turners have constantly for the most part turned bed posts & feet of joyned stooles for the Joyners and of late some Joyners who never used to turn their own bedposts and stool feet have set on work in their houses some poor decayed Turners & of them have learned the feate & arte of turning which they could not do before. And it appeareth unto us by custom that the turning of Bedposts Feet of tables joyned stools do properly belong to the trade of a Turner and not to the art of a Joyner and whatsoever is done with the foot as have treddle or wheele for turning of any wood we are of opinion and do find that it properly belongs to the Turner's and we find that the Turners ought not to use the gage or gages, grouffe [groove] plaine or plough plaine and mortising chisells or any of them for that the same do belong to the Joyners trade.[16]

In rural England and in both rural and urban New England furniture-makers' guilds did not exist, so it was not unusual to find a turner and a joiner at work in the same shop (fig. 13). In some villages, the same furniture craftsman was frequently accomplished in both crafts.[17]

Fig. 13. Carved panel showing a rural English woodworking shop, 1590–1610. Oak with some gilding; some of the original red and green paint is still visible in the men's breeches and the woman's skirt; H 14½″ (36.8 cm), W 28½″ (72.4 cm). (Private collection.)

THE CABINETMAKER

In the last quarter of the seventeenth century, the cabinetmaker began to replace the joiner first in England and then in America as the most important maker of case furniture. Once established, cabinetmaking was almost invariably distinguished in documents from joinery, and the men who practiced cabinetmaking in New England were rarely referred to by any other trade designation despite the efforts of decorative arts writers in the 1930s and 40s to designate all joiners as "cabinetmakers"). While American cabinetmakers were all accomplished joiners, not all joiners were cabinetmakers.

No literary description of the cabinetmaker's trade in England predates the one that appears in R[obert?] Campbell's *The London Tradesman* (1747).

The Cabinet-Maker is [the Upholsterer's] right-hand Man; he furnishes him with Mahogany and Wallnut-tree Posts for his Beds, Settees of the Same Materials, Chairs of all Sorts and Prices, carved, plain, and inlaid, Chests of Drawers, Book-Cases, Cabinets, Desks, Scrutores, Buroes, Dining, Dressing, and Card Tables, Tea-Boards, and an innumerable Variety of Articles of this Sort. The Cabinet-Maker is by much the most curious Workman in the Wood Way, except the Carver; and requires a nice mechanic Genius, and a tolerable Degree of Strength, though not so much as the Carpenter; he must have a much lighter Hand and a quicker Eye than the Joiner, as he is employed in Work much more minute and elegant. A Youth who designs to make a Figure in this Branch must learn to Draw; for upon this depends the Invention of new Fashions, and on that the Success of his Business. He who first hits upon any new Whim is sure to make by the Invention before it becomes common in the Trade; but he that must always wait for a new Fashion till it comes from Paris, or is hit upon by his Neighbour, is

never likely to grow rich or eminent in his Way. A Master Cabinet-Maker is a very profitable Trade; especially, if he works for and Serves the Quality himself; but if he must serve them through the Chanel of the Upholder, his Profits are not very considerable. A Journeyman who knows his Business may have a Guinea a week; and if he works Piece-Work, and applies with tolerable Diligence, may earn thirty shillings and some weeks two Guineas.[18]

By the time Campbell's description was published, cabinetmaking had been established in the American colonies for more than fifty years.

The first man called a cabinetmaker to come to America from England was John Clark who is listed in Boston's *Book of Strangers* upon his arrival on October 31, 1681. Yet we have been unable to identify him as a practitioner of his trade in Boston after that date. Nine years later John Goodson of Philadelphia wrote to a friend in England and noted that "one Cabinet-maker" was working in that town on August 24, 1690, but Goodson fails to identify the cabinetmaker by name.[19]

Oddly enough, the word *cabinetmaker* appears only once in the Minutes of the Court of the Worshipful Company of Joyners of London between 1669 and 1695, and that was in 1692 when James Hawford was "admitted into the freedom of this Compa[ny] by patrimony, being a Cabinetmaker or Joyner by Trade."[20] Despite the rarity of documentary mention of the cabinetmaker's trade, cabinets were executed in England for the Prince of Wales in 1619. The order of "The Procession to the King's [James I] Funeral, 1625," lists "Cabbynett-makers" among the "Artificers of the Roabes," although the exact nature of the cabinets that they made is not entirely certain. The craft was apparently so rarely practiced among the joiners of England prior to the 1680s that it is not even mentioned by Joseph Moxon or by Randle Holme, who assiduously followed Moxon's book in matters pertaining to the woodworking crafts.

The abilities of cabinetmakers were disparaged well into the eighteenth century by such important commentators upon English life as Batty Langley, whose hostility apparently stemmed from cabinetmakers' inattention to the study of the orders of architecture and the schemes of proportion derived from them. In May 1740, Langley dipped his pen in venom and wrote, "Cabinet Makers, were originally no more than Spurious Indocible Chips, expelled by Joiners, for the

Superfluity of their Sap. . . . Tis a very great Difficulty to find one in Fifty of them that can make a Book-Case &c. indispensably true, after any one of the Five Orders; without being obliged to a Joiner for to set out the Work and make his Templets to work by." During the century that had passed between the early notices of cabinetmaking in London and Langley's time, the origins of that trade in England had been obscured. This probably indicates that in Langley's lifetime many furniture-making joiners must have abandoned their traditional trade for the more profitable one of cabinetmaking. Certainly the construction techniques we have come to associate with the cabinetmaker had been in use in London since at least the third quarter of the sixteenth century by Protestant craftsmen from continental Europe who had sought refuge from the religious wars that racked the Lowlands.[21]

The products of the cabinetmaker are easily distinguished from those of the joiner. Where the primary technique of the joiner is the pinned frame and panel, the cabinetmaker uses board construction; where the primary joint of the joiner is the mortise and tenon, the cabinetmaker uses the dovetail (visible in German furniture [fig. 14] long before it can be documented in surviving English furniture); where the primary surface ornamentations of the joiner are carving, planed grooves, applied spindles and moldings, and polychrome painting, the cabinetmaker uses veneers; and where the joiner usually uses hardwood, such as oak or walnut to frame his cases, the cabinetmaker commonly uses a conifer under his veneer.

Examples of the cabinetmaker's craft appear in northern Europe in the sixteenth century—earlier in Italy. The craft appears to have emerged from the virtually indistinguishable trades of the coffermaker and the trunkmaker, craftsmen who covered cases of boards with leather in the same way that the cabinetmaker used veneer (fig. 15). The American strain of cabinetmaking, primarily using hardwoods rather than veneered softwoods, appears only after English-trained cabinetmakers had introduced the William and Mary style and the construction techniques associated with it into New England.[22] Specific techniques and the variations from them that give American furniture its individuality and, in some cases, help us to identify its place of origin are discussed in the catalogue below.

THE TOOLS OF THE JOINER

Many collectors of American furniture profess no interest in tools and the ways in which they were used, a curiously self-defeating attitude, since a knowledge of hand tools, the marks that they make, and the ways in which they could be used are better insurance against making a collecting error than are all the books on art ever published. Virtually every piece of colonial American furniture still bears the marks of the tools that were used to make it, and these marks are often the only objective clues that tell us not only how the object was made, but *when*. To the colonial craftsman the adage "Time is money" had a grimly serious meaning. Every craftsman's income was governed by how much work he could produce in a day. With the pressure always behind him to turn out as

Fig. 14. Albrecht Dürer, *Birth of the Virgin.* 1503–4. Woodcut; H 11⅝″ (29.5 cm), W 8 5/16″ (21.0 cm). From Talbot, *Dürer in America*, pl. 39. Note the lateral dovetail construction of the board chest.

much work as possible, a craftsman did not lavish workmanship on the parts of his furniture that were not visible, which means that he did not remove tool marks from places that were not meant to be seen, such as the bottoms and backs of drawers, the backs of case furniture, and inside joints.

The history of tools is not of mere academic interest to the tool buff, and it is of the utmost significance to the collector and curator because the marks that these ancient hand tools made are the best objective sources that exist for the study of old furniture. Furthermore the absence of such marks is reason to question the date and origin of a purported piece of early furniture. Tool marks on furniture can be equated with the verbal documentation supplied by colonial inventories to give us information about craft practices that cannot be gained in any other way. Together the marks of tools and manuscript documents of colonial America generally confirm the assertions made by Joseph Moxon in *Mechanick Exercises*, thereby making that book a useful guide rather than a quaint literary curiosity surviving from a time that has disappeared from our conscious thought.

Moxon was a printer and globemaker by training. His descriptions of simple joiner's, turner's, and carpenter's tools and their employment were based upon personal experience and have the ring of authority because he actually used such tools in his daily labors. More esoteric tools which he did not use, such as the device attached to a lathe used for turning "swash work," were beyond his descriptive powers (as a reader of the book soon learns) because he was simply not familiar with them. W. L. Goodman, distinguished British historian of tools, maintains that when Moxon interviewed other artisans to plumb their knowledge, these sly tradesmen would often leave out a crucial step, so that Moxon's directions are at times incomplete.[23] Some of the rest of Moxon's data, particularly the form of a number of the tools shown in his engravings, were plagiarized from André Félibièn, *Des Principes de l'architecture, de la sculpture* (Paris, 1676) and offer little solace to the student of the distinctive character of Anglo-American tools.

Two illustrations from Moxon's book (figs. 16 and 17) depict many of the same tools possessed by Thomas Scottow, the earliest Boston joiner whose inventory itemizes tools.

Fig. 15. Coffretier-Malletier-Bahutier. From Diderot, *Recueil de planches, ... les arts méchaniques*, 1: 247. (Winterthur Library.)

Scottow had come to New England from Norwich, Norfolk, in 1634 as a mature workman. His inventory, submitted for probate on January 18, 1661/62, listed "25 plaines, one long saw, three hand saws, a paire of compasses, 3 Augers, 2 hold fasts, 3 benches, 25 chissells, files & other tooles, 2 Axes & a frow, 6 chissels & other working tooles & lumber [i.e., miscellaneous items] and boardes." In the "cellar" of his home was "a lathe and six turning tooles" valued at 12*s*. In the "yard" was "a parcell of wood," "a parcell of bolts," and "pannels &c."[24] The most illuminating feature of Scottow's inventory is that it illustrates the working habits of a provincial English joiner who had settled in an urban area in New England and worked as a joiner but also did his own turning, unfettered by urban English custom or guild restraints. And one of the work benches in his shop was doubtless used by his son, John, who survived him.

In 1675, George Cole, a young joiner from the village of Lynn, Essex County, Massachusetts, was killed in King Philip's War. Cole, who had been trained by John Davis, a joiner and son of Jenkin Davis, a joiner who had emigrated from Bristol, England, in 1634, may be considered a "third generation" craftsman. His inventory, proved on November 30, 1675, contains most of the joiner's tools mentioned by Moxon, with a few unusual turns of phrase that typify many American inventories. It included:

3 saues, 8s.
2 goynters & foreplaine, 6s.
3 smothing plains & a draing knife, 3s. 6d.
2 plan[e]s & 2 revolving plains, 10s.
4 round plains, 5s.
3 rabet plains, 4s.
3 holou plains, 3s. 6d.
9 Cresing plains, 10s. 6d.
6 torning tools, 9s.
3 plaine irons & 3 bits, 1s. 6d.

1 brase stok, 2 squares & gorges
1 brod ax & 1 fro, 2s.
holfast, 1s. 6d.
hamer, 1s. 6d.
6 gouges, 2s.
9 Chisels, 5s.
2 ogers & 1 draing knife, 3s.
1 bench hooks, 2 yoyet irons, 1s.
a gluepot, 1s. 6d. . . . .
for what work he has done in his shop, 1[£]. 10s.[25]

The feature of these inventories that identify both Cole and Scottow as joiners rather than carpenters is the large number of planes of all sorts that they both possessed—25 by Scottow, 30 by Cole—including 9 creasing (molding) planes.[26] Also present in Cole's shop were gauges to scribe tenons and mortise holes, turning tools, a froe for riving wood, and numerous other tools mentioned by Moxon.

THE TOOLS OF THE CABINETMAKER

The earliest American cabinetmaker's inventory is that of Charles Plumley of Philadelphia, taken on December 15, 1708. Plumley had come to Philadelphia at the age of 10 and must have trained under a cabinetmaker who was already there. He could not have been at work for himself much before 1695, but he was definitely working there in 1698. During his short but documented career, Plumley accumulated an extraordinary number of tools and a great deal of fine furniture that he probably made himself. His inventory is one of the key documents of American furniture history and is transcribed in Appendix 1. It contained "2 Mahogany Planks 36½ feet at 16d. p[er foot] £2:8:8," the earliest mention of that wood in an American craftsman's inventory, and "4 Center bitts," the

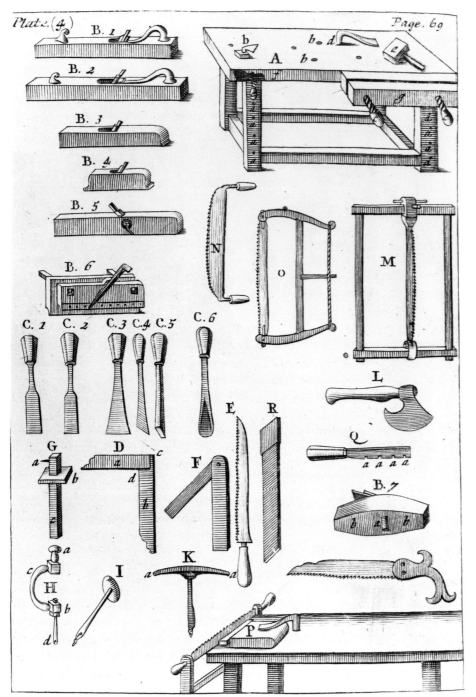

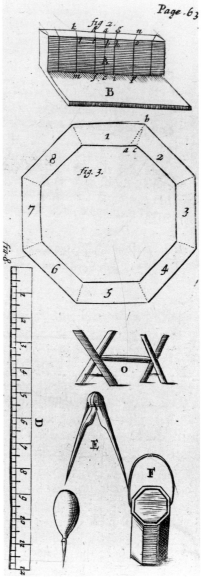

Fig. 16. Joiners tools. From Moxon, *Mechanick Exercises* (1703), pl. 4, facing p. 69. (Winterthur Library.) Moxon used the following labels:

A. *Work-bench*
  a. Holes for pins
  b. *Hook*
  b. *Holes* for *Hold-fast*
  c. *Bench-Screw* [here a double screw]
  d. *Hold-fast*
  e. *Mallet*
  f. *Table*
  g. *Bench-Screw* [or vise]

B. [*Planes*]
  1. *Fore Plane* [with convex arch blade]
  2. *Joynter* [with flat blade]
  3. *Strike-Block*
  4. *Smoothing-Plane*
  5. *Rabbet-Plane*
  6. *Plow*
  7. *Block-Plane*
    a. *Mouth*
    b. *Tongue*
    b-a-b. *Sole*

C. [*Chisels*]
  1. *Former Chissel*
  2. *Paring-Chissel*
  3. *Former Chissel*
  4. *Skew-Former*
  5. *Mortess-Chissel*
  6. *Gouge*

D. *Square*
  a. *Handle*
  b. *Tongue*
  c. *Outer Square*
  d. *Inner Square*

E. *Compass Saw*
F. *Bevil*
G. *Gage*
  a. *Tooth*
  b. *Oval*
  c. *Staff*

H. *Piercer*
  a. *Head*
  b. *Pad*
  c. *Stock*
  d. *Bitt*
I. *Gimlet*
K. *Augre*
  a-a. *Handle*
  b. *Bit*
L. *Hatchet*
M. *Pit-Saw*
N. *Whip-Saw*
O. *Bow-Saw*
P. *Whetting Block* or *Rub Stone*
Q. *Saw Wrest*
R. *Mitre Square*
[S]. *Tennant Saw*
    [located above the lower table]

Fig. 17. Joiners tools. Detail from Moxon, *Mechanick Exercises* (1703), pl. 5, facing p. 63. (Winterthur Library.) Moxon used the following labels:

fig. 2. *Mitre-Box*
  A. *Upright*
  B. *Bottom-piece*
  The italic letters represent *Kerfs* struck with the *Bevil* at various angles and sawn

fig. 3. *looking-glass frame* [plan]
  a-b. Square end of piece 2
  b-c. Bevel you work the piece to
  a-b-c. Tenon on the under side

D. *Rule*
E. *Compasses*
F. *Glew Pot*
[G.] *Pricker* or *Awl* [next to Glew Pot]
O. *Trussel*

earliest reference to this type of bit so far found in England or America. A "parcell of olive wood and other Veinarys [veneers] £1:16:0; 6 ffeneaireing screws [clamps] . . . 6[s.]; 76 lb. of Glew . . . 8[s.] 8[d.]," and enough tools and hardware to accomplish the most complex commission entitle Plumley to be called a "cabinetmaker," although he is not identified as such in any document. The only problem is that no veneered or mahogany Philadelphia furniture from this period has thus far been identified.[27]

In contrast, a considerable amount of veneered New England furniture in the William and Mary style has survived, which makes the study of the earliest Boston cabinetmaker's inventory—that of William Howell—of more than passing interest. Howell was first recorded in Boston in the summer of 1714. Where he came from or how long he had been there is not known. He died of fever in December 1717 at the age of 40. The inventory of Howell's shop, taken at the height of the popularity of the William and Mary style in Boston, makes a striking contrast to the inventories of joiners Scottow and Cole.

1 Long Jointer 5[s.] To 1 Short Jointer 4[s.] To 1 Old Jointer 2[s.]
1 Strick [strike] block & Smoothing Plain 3[s.]
1 pair of Hollow & round Plains 2[s.]
2 Quarter Rounds 4[s.] To 2 Phillisters 1[s.] 6[d.]
one Rabiting Plain & one austickle 4[s.]
one Small Round & one tooth Plain 1[s.]
4 old Plains 1[s.] To 2 Old Smoothing Plains 1[s.]
1 pair bitt Stock & 3 bitts & one Drill 2[s.] 6[d.]
1 Phillister & bed Plain 1[s.] To 8 old Chisels 3[s.]
2 old Rasps & 4 old Files 1[s.] To 3 half round files 1[s.] 6[d.]
1 pr. of Large Iron Compasses 1[s.] To 1 Hand Saw 3[s.]
1 fine Saw 3[s.] To 1 Small Saw 6d
1 inch Auger & 2 Large Gimblets 9[s.] 6[d.]
1 Finereing Hammer & Pinchers 2[s.]
2 Handsaw sets 1[s.]
a pr. of Hinges & 3 Duft tails 2[s.]
2 Glew Potts 4[s.] To a piece of Nus skin 1[s.]
2 pound of Bees wax 3[s.]
80 lb. of Lead £1.
Walnut Fenere £8:18:00. . . .
a leaf of a tea table 7[s.] 6[d.]
15 lb. of glew 15[s.] To one clock and head case £18:1:3.
Walnut tree at Mr. Edes 10[s.] 6[d.]
1 pr. shells and box 2[s.]
12 Pillars for a Chest of Draws 9[s.]
1 Saw and Frame £3
2 feet for a bedstead with Pillars 4[s.]
shingles Clapboards & Laths £4.[28]

Many of the items listed here are worthy of closer analysis. For example, Howell's "Phillister" planes (line 4) are of the type used for making the rabbets in which the squares of glass, or lights, of a sash window are set. The "pair of Hollow & round Plains" (line 3), valued at the rather slight sum of 2s., were perhaps a small pair of matched planes, one of which cut a hollow, or concave, profile, while the other cut a round, or convex, profile, such as is often found on early drop-leaf or gateleg tables, and might indeed have been used on the "leaf of a tea table" (line 21). An item that is only rarely found in joiners' inventories is prominent here: the "piece of Nus skin" (line 17), valued at 1s., was the skin of the nurse fish or dogfish,

a relative of the shark, and was the colonial woodworker's equivalent of sandpaper.

From the list of tools and raw materials in Howell's inventory, it is a simple task to reconstruct the entire process of making and veneering a piece of William and Mary–style case furniture, as performed by a Boston cabinetmaker in the early decades of the eighteenth century. "Walnut Fenere" (line 20), highly valued at £8.18, could easily have been cut by Howell and his apprentice from a "Walnut tree," like the one "at Mr. [Edmond?] Edes" (line 23) with the "Saw and Frame" (line 26). The "fine Saw" (line 12) would have been used for cutting this wood further or possibly for cutting the dovetails that held the drawers together. The drawer fronts and other parts of the carcass were roughed up with the "tooth plain" (line 6) in order to provide small furrows in which the "glew" (line 22) from the "glew Potts" (line 17) would stay when the "Walnut Fenere" (line 20) was pressed onto it with the particular type of flat-faced tool known as a "Finereing [veneering] Hammer" (line 14). "Lead" weights (line 19), of which Howell possessed 80 pounds, were placed on the work until it dried. The irregularities of the veneered surface and excess glue were removed with the "Nus skin" (line 17), and the whole was perhaps polished, in the English manner, with "Bees wax" (line 18).

The style of furniture Howell was making is also clear from his inventory: "12 Pillars for a Chest of Draws" (line 25) in 1717 can only refer to turned legs for high chests, and "2 feet for a bedstead with Pillars" (line 27) is the only documentary allusion yet found that gives any hint as to what an American bedstead in the William and Mary style may have looked like. Finally, the shingles, clapboards, and lath in the last line show that this cabinetmaker was not above doing a little carpentry.

What is not found in Howell's inventory is as significant as what is there. Where, for example, is the burl maple veneer, which is by far the most popular surface found on Boston's surviving William and Mary furniture? Perhaps it was a commodity that was purchased as needed from specialists who made a profession of supplying it. And where are the lathe and turning tools with which the turned legs, or pillars, for a chest of drawers were made? The absence of these tools suggests that surviving Boston furniture of this period may confirm that turned legs were made in only three or four distinct patterns and were purchased by most of Boston's cabinetmakers from two or three craftsmen who specialized in turning and supplied legs to one and all.

THE TOOLS OF THE TURNER

The art of the turner was practiced in New England as early as that of any woodworking craftsman, and it was very different from that of the joiner. Turned work has always had limited stylistic possibilities. Because of the nature of their craft, turned-chair makers established a distinctive strain that recognizably persists throughout the history of American furniture.

The tools and implements of a fully furnished master turner's shop are second in complexity to the sawmill in colonial America and are somewhat more varied than those of the joiner. While Moxon could illustrate joiner's tools in two plates, he required four to illustrate those of the turner. Basically, the tools are all devoted to cutting away wood as it turns on either a great lathe (fig. 18) or a pole lathe (fig. 19). "Rose work," "swash work," "screws," "twist work," and two-axis turning can all be executed by skillful turners but require separate tools and devices that make explanation of the more esoteric aspects of the crafts complex.[29]

The earliest New England inventory listing turner's tools is that of Joseph Harbye, who died at sea on the way to Boston in 1638. Harbye's estate contained 5 "wimbles [braces], a goudge, felling axe, 1 new leather sute" (such as most artisans wore in England), as well as "Chissels & turning tooles" worth 2s.[30] While the evidence for Harbye's being a turner is circumstantial, the inventory of Thomas Baynley [Bagnley], who died in Concord, Middlesex County, Massachusetts, in May 1643 clearly shows that he was a carpenter and turner. His tools, owned in partnership with Francis Barker, consisted, in part, of 6 "plaine yrons," 4 augers, 2 holdfasts, 3 axes, 3 mortising chisels, 2 gouges and 2 "hooke tools," 3 turning chisels, 1 handsaw, 1 clapboard ax, 3 wedges, 2 rubbing stones, 1 bench hook, 1 spokeshave and 3 planes, 2 small bits and 3 small gouges, 1 "jointer" and 2 "plaine yrons," and 1 "skrew" and "pin to turne."[31] The screw and pin are illustrated in figure 19 at letters *d* and *f*. George Barrell, a cooper of Boston, who possessed a great number of tools of all sorts, died in the same year. His inventory contained "a turne," an English dialectical synonym for *lathe*, and 15 turning chisels which he appears to have used in his trade, perhaps for making bungs and spigots.[32]

The inventory of Thomas Wickes of Salem, recorded in June 1656, is the earliest that unquestionably reveals some of the products of the turner's craft in Massachusetts. Wickes, who had come to Charlestown in 1636, settled in Salem in 1639 and is the first turner to appear in the records of that town. His estate included the following: "flagges" valued at £2.10; "working timber," £1.10; "made ware as greene Chayres, wheeles & Reemes," £5; "plank & boards," £1; and "tooles," £6.[33] Despite its brevity, the inventory reveals much. "Flagges" were used for the seats of turned chairs, and "flag chairs" or "flag bottomed chairs" are much more frequently listed in the inventories of Essex and Suffolk counties than "rush bottomed" ones, which are mentioned more frequently in Middlesex County inventories. It is possible that the same aquatic plant is being referred to in both places since the difference between the twisted leaves of the "flag" (probably *Acorus calamus*), and those of the most common bulrush (genus *Scripus*) might not be readily discernible to the untrained eye. Both of the plants grew in coastal Massachusetts in the seventeenth century. The use of the word *flag* as opposed to *rush* can probably be traced to English regional speech dialects. Since no seventeenth-century turned chairs with the original flag or rush seats have been examined by the author during the course of preparing this book, it is virtually impossible to verify these conjectures. In the Wickes inventory and indeed in all the inventories quoted in this book, the use of words such as *flag* record the speech patterns and perceptions of the individual

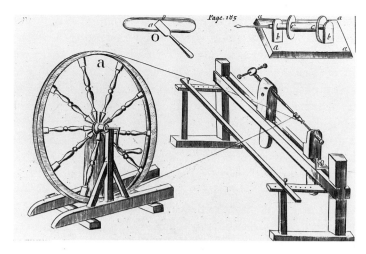

Fig. 18. Turners tools. From Moxon, *Mechanick Exercises* (1703), pl. 14, facing p. 185. (Winterthur Library.) Moxon used the following labels:

a. *Great Wheel*
O. *Chissel* lying aslant the work
 a-b. cutting angle

Drill-Bench [in right corner]
 a-a. Thick board
 b,b. *Stiles* [a pair]
 c-c. *Rowler*

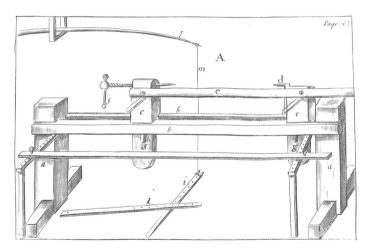

Fig. 19. Turners tools. From Moxon, *Mechanick Exercises* (1703), pl. 12, facing p. 163. (Winterthur Library.) Moxon used the following labels:

A. *Lathe* [pole lathe]
 a. *Legs* or *Stiles*
 b. *Cheeks* [sides]
 c. *Puppets*
 d. *Pike*
 e. *Rest*
 f. *Handle* of the *Screw*

g. *Tennants* of the *Puppets*
h. *Wedge*
i. *Treddle*
k. *Cross-Treddle*
l. *Pole*
m. *String*

who took the inventories and not what the actual object itself may have been in fact. The Wickes (probably pronounced "Weeks") inventory was taken by Hilliard Veren, a merchant of Salem who came from Salisbury, England, and Thomas Cromwell, called both a physician and a tailor, whose place of origin is not recorded. The word *flag* was very likely not Veren's, but Cromwell's, who may have had some familiarity with turnerly things inasmuch as his brother Philip was a wheelwright.[34]

The mention of wheels in the Wickes inventory seems perfectly straightforward, except that it is not immediately clear whether they were spinning wheels or cart wheels, both indifferently called "wheels" in seventeenth-century inventories and both made by turners in that period. The otherwise incomprehensible word *reems*, with which it is joined, may be a variant spelling of *rims*, which, unfortunately, still does not clarify the issue. "Made ware" in the shop indicates that Wickes not only executed bespoke work but apparently had some stock made up in advance. The reference to "green" might be construed as a mistranscription for "treen," or wooden dishes, which were turner's products, were it not that "green chairs" are mentioned a number of times in the English inventories of the same era. Additionally, the presence of such chairs in household inventories suggests that the impulse to believe that such chairs were made of unseasoned, or "green," wood is likewise unfounded. In all probability, green chairs were simply chairs painted green. Although no chairs with original green paint have survived from the seventeenth century, unpainted chairs in that period appear to have been referred to as "white."[35]

Edward Browne, a turner who was in Ipswich in 1637, was making both chairs and treen ware at the time of his death in 1659. He had in his shop "work done toward chaires," "3 wheeles, finished lennen," "Wheeles, woolen & linnen not finisht," "6 trayes, dishes, trenchers, & payles." He also had 11 chairs in his household—a large number for this early date.[36]

Treen ware is abundantly present in the shop of Nathaniel Adams, Sr., a turner in Boston whose inventory was taken on November 1, 1675. The large variety and quantity of items in Adams's shop form a striking contrast to the rather meager equipment and store of merchandise that his village and rural contemporaries possessed and plays havoc with the conventional notion of how colonial craftsmen practiced their trades. The comparison of Wickes's inventory with Adams's shows not only the contrast between rural and urban craftsmen's shops but also the differences between village and urban craftsmen's ways of life. The village turner, like the village joiner, farmed during the appropriate part of the year and rarely had a large stock of furniture made up for sale, which suggests that he made furniture mostly to order. The urban turner, who had no farm to occupy his time, usually had a stock of goods for sale in his shop, which suggests that he worked at his trade year round. From this stock he not only could satisfy local demand, including the goods he sold to customers from the countryside who came to the urban area to sell their produce and purchase manufactured items, but also had stock that he could send out in the coastal trade on short notice when the occasion arose. In Adams's Boston shop were:

	[£ s. d.]
7 doz of Large wooden Platters at 8s. pr. doz: is	2:16:00
6 doz. of hollow turnd ware at 6s. pr. doz: is	1:16:00
8 grosse of taps [for kegs] at 5s. pr. grosse is	2:00:00
5 grosse & five doz. of trenchers at 8s. pr grosse is	2:03:04
4 grosse of woodden Spoones at 4s. pr. grosse	0:16:00
1 doz. of woodden Sives at	0:09:00
15 new Chaires at 2s. pr. ps.	1:10:00
48 chaires unbottomed at 18s. pr. ps.	3:12:00
4 grosse of Sive Rimmes at 3s. doz: is	7:04:00
timber at the wharfe	5:00:00
a p[ar]cell of Sive rimmes	10:00
a pcell of wheele rimmes	1:00:00
a pcell of flagges for Chaire Bottoms	10:00
a pcell of turner's tooles	3:00:00
1 great wollen whele	5:00

5 doz: & 3 wicker fanns at 5s. pr. pc. is	15:00:00
3 wicker basketts	4:00
2 wicker Cradles	10:00
a pcell of Shovells & three half bushells	5:00
8 pare of Bellows at 3s. pr. ps. is 16[s.]	
7 Haire Sives & two Lawne [fine cloth] Sives at 15d. pr. ps.	11:03
. . . a pcell of refuse [useless] Sive bottoms	8:00
1 dozen of Lawne Sive bottoms	10:00
Severall peeces of old Lumber, Stuffe and Blockes [for ship's rigging] only hewd for torneing	1:10:00
20 hundred of Lanthorne's hoarnes at 7s. pr. hundred is	7:10:00[37]

Unlike his village equivalents, Adams appears to have dealt in imported goods. At 5s. apiece, the "wicker fanns" must be large ones of the type used for winnowing grain. It is possible that they were made in Boston, perhaps of osiers (willow) or other supple woods, but no evidence has yet emerged from the public records of this period to indicate that anyone there was following that trade. Items of this type are logical candidates for importation from England where wages were much lower and such labor-intensive goods, including transportation costs, were competitively priced. The same is true of the sieves, which he had likely either purchased from a local merchant or imported from England directly. Evidence of the former is preserved among the letters of Samuel Sewall of Boston. On July 15, 1686, William Needham requested him to order "6 duz. of Lawne Sive bottoms not of the largaest size: all to be bordered with redd leather, for the white leather rotts, the Lawne being drest with Allome." On October 24, 1691, Sewall made a memorandum "To send for Tho. Hunt, Turner," from whom Sewall planned to order more than 20 dozen sieves of varying coarseness and 16 dozen strainers. In all likelihood turners like Hunt and Adams added turned handles to sieves, a practice confirmed by analogy through the many European warming pans that have survived from the colonial period with handles of American woods. The lawn sieves were fine and appear to have been generally used for sifting (bolting) flour. Adams's references to wicker cradles and to 15 new chairs at 2s. each raise another issue. Wicker chairs and cradles are relatively common in American and English inventories of the seventeenth century. The latter were used for obvious purposes, the former as invalid chairs or for a woman recovering from childbirth.[38] One further point of fascination with the Adams inventory is the mention of "timber at the Wharfe," which confirms that the wood used by Boston's craftsmen was imported into the town.

The American inventory that itemizes the greatest number of turning tools is that of Joseph Carpenter of Rehoboth in the Plymouth Colony, recorded on May 20, 1675. Carpenter, born and perhaps trained in England, was the son of William Carpenter, a carpenter by trade, who was in New England in 1635. Carpenter was primarily a wheelwright who may have combined a bit of joinery with his turning. Since his inventory indicates that he was the only turner in his village, he doubtless made chairs for his neighbors. The shop contained:

	[£ s. d.]
spokes and timber for Worke	5
2 broad axes	15
a croscutt and a hand saw	10

2 adds	10
a frow and a holdfast	5: 6
2 beatle rings and 4 wedges	10
2 hatchetts	5
a viz	2
a spoke shave & Gripers	5
a _____arre and screw & bo_____ and turning tools	16
plow plaines and a Ioynter	1: 5: 0
a great Ioynter	5
a [l]ave screw and turning tooles	1: 4: 0
a square & spokeshave	6
2 bursses 1 Great gouge	18
5 augers 3 wrybitts	1:01:00
2 paire of plyers	3
3 plaine Irons	2: 6
wimble bitts and a sett	4: 6
2 smale saues and a scribe	4
a hamer and a mrkeing tool	2
a maderell	1: 6
red occur and Glew	1
smale nailes for wheeles	1
a burning Iron	1
2 paire of compasses & prickers	2: 6
working benches	5
6 spinning wheeles	1: 10:00[39]

The inventory of his father's or grandfather's estate taken April 21, 1659, contained several similar, or possibly the same, tools: a crosscut saw, an adz, beatle rings, a jointer, turning tools, a spokeshave, bursses, and a gouge.[40]

Stylistic changes came and went in colonial New England prior to the introduction of the windsor chair without any basic changes to either the techniques of the turned-chair maker or the appearance of his products. The employment of water and, later, steam power to drive the lathes in America's chairmaking shops in the nineteenth century made these inexpensive chairs even more inexpensive or relatively fancier for the same money, but otherwise the craft of the turned-chair maker remained fairly static. Variations from straight turning are rare. What, for want of a contemporary name, we can call "two-axis turning" was introduced into urban New England sometime between 1650 and 1660. Turning of this type appears on leather upholstered chairs in the Cromwellian style, and the technique for accomplishing it is discussed in the section devoted to leather chairs. The only additional major innovation introduced into American turned-chair making, other than the use of cane (*Calamus rotang*) as a bottoming material, is a new type of seat framing, which can also be traced to the introduction of the cane chair. Instead of using turned or turned-and-shaved seat lists set into auger holes in the legs (fig. 20a), a seat frame consisting of flat, horizontal lists, mortised and tenoned on the front corners and intersected by a round tenon turned on the upper end of the front legs, is occasionally found in village chairs (fig. 20b). While turned chairs more or less reflect the vocabulary of changing styles, the increasing popularity of slat-back chairs in eighteenth-century New England is perhaps the only major change that occurs in the trade. Contemporary records reveal what these chairs were called in their time. When John Corning, a turned-chair maker living in Beverly, Massachusetts, died in 1734, for example, his shop contained "11 two backed New Chairs" valued at 23s. 6d. and "9 two backed new Chairs without

Fig. 20. Detail showing different ways of framing seats. (Winterthur 57.1367 [left], 59.2499 [right].)

bottoms" at 18d. each. Corning's shop also contained "36 bundles of flags for Chairs" valued at 10s.[41]

One of the curious aspects of early inventories is that no devices such as the ones illustrated in figures 21 and 22 are clearly identified by name; yet a chair cannot be as easily made without them as it can be with them. These tools have gone by a number of names in their time. Joseph Moxon calls the one he illustrated a "sweep" and says that it is used for marking circles on a globe. Since Moxon was a globemaker and not a chairmaker, he may be forgiven for not telling how a chairmaker used it. Randle Holme also calls it a "sweep." Roubo illustrates a highly sophisticated and accurate version of this adjustable tool and calls it a "*compas à verge.*"[42] Basically the tool, whose name may be literally translated as "edge compass," was a device to help the chairmaker mark the places on the uprights where the crosspieces intersect them. The purpose is to insure that the crosspieces are parallel to each other and to the floor. Numerous authors in the past have suggested that a simple stick with nails driven through it, such as those illustrated in figure 23, was used for this purpose. While this idea has the merit of being a logical solution to the problem, actual attempts to recreate the process of using such a marking stick have usually resulted in a mess: it is difficult to hold steady a thin, vibrating stick with not very sharp wrought nails protruding from it and apply pressure to all the points simultaneously in such a way that they make a single, neat circle around the perimeter of a chair leg turning in a lathe. The examples in figure 23 were collected by the late William MacDonald from either the Bayard or the Clayton chair shop operating in Allentown, New Jersey, in the nineteenth century.[43] Such a stick could be used to mark a point on a leg or stile that was to be drilled for a crosspiece. The stick was

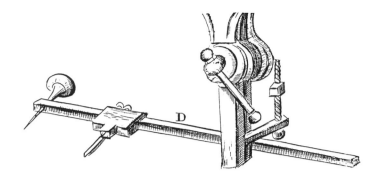

Fig. 21. Turners sweep. Detail from Moxon, *Mechanick Exercises* (1703), pl. 16, facing p. 212. (Winterthur Library.)

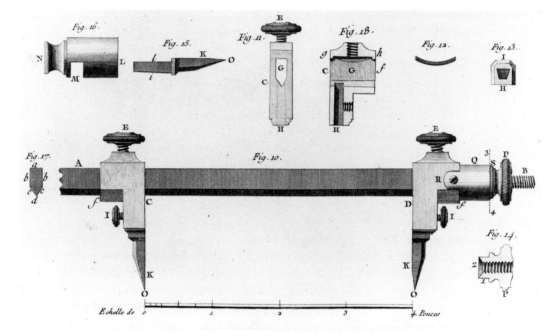

Fig. 22. Compas à verge. Detail from Hulot, *L'art du tourneur mécanicien* (1775), pl. 12. (Winterthur Library.)

Fig. 23. Chairmakers marking sticks. Bayard or Clayton chair shop, Allentown, N.J., nineteenth century. (Monmouth County Historical Association, Freehold, N.J.)

merely placed in contact with the leg, and the protruding head of the nail was tapped with a hammer. That such sticks were used in this manner is given credence by the many nineteenth-century chairs that lack scribed lines on the uprights at the juncture with the crosspieces. Furthermore the stick on the right in the illustration is curved—just about at the proper angle to have been used in this fashion on curved pieces of wood such as appear as the bent rear stiles of countless "mule-eared," slat-back "kitchen" chairs, often referred to today as "oyster shucking chairs." How much earlier than the first part of the nineteenth century the tapping, as opposed to scribing, technique was used cannot now be estimated, but it is possible that many early chairs without scribed lines may well be the antiques they seem to be rather than forgeries.

In the colonial period, however, turners commonly used some technique to scribe uniform radii around the posts of their chairs, to indicate both where crosspieces go and where ornamental elements occur. If a turned-chair maker positions his auger holes consistently with these lines, an error that might spoil a chair is less readily made, but exactly how this was done in the seventeenth century is documentarily elusive. Doubtless many ways of doing this were hit upon. One solution to the problem was documented by Allen H. Eaton in the 1930s: "Jim Gosnell, believed to have descended from an English group of chairmakers . . . worked about twenty-five years ago in the neighborhood of Tryon [in North Carolina]. He used what he called a 'measuring stick' upon which he laid out his chair pattern. He could neither read nor write nor did he use figures, but by marks or notches on the stick, he was able to register the lengths for the posts, rungs, the size of the seat, and all other dimensions needed for the complete design, and he made chairs accurately from these marks on a single stick."[44] Indeed notches on the edge of a stick laid on the rest of a turner's bench permit a turner to place his "grooving hook" or similar sharp gouge precisely and steadily against a turning chair leg and thus to inscribe quickly the precise and carefully controlled lines.

The technological aspect of the art of the turned-chair maker is a totally absorbing topic once it is opened and could occupy the remaining pages of this book were we to deal with it in the detail it deserves. We have not, for example, discussed the ramifications of the ways that chairmakers used uncured (green or wet) wood for their uprights, into which they pounded dried rungs that "swelled into" the round mortises, as a means of holding a chair together. Nor have we gone into the great number of ways by which we can trace in chairs the national or even, in a few cases, regional origins of the immigrant chairmakers in this country. These ideas and many others are appropriately discussed when specific examples of the techniques can be observed on a surviving chair in the chronological survey that follows.

THE CHAIRMAKER

From the mid 1680s on, the word *chairmaker* begins to crop up in New England documents. References such as the one to Benjamin Gray who is listed as a "turner alias chairmaker" in 1699 and numerous others where a craftsman is sometimes called a "turner" and sometimes called a "chairmaker" could easily lead to the presumption that at some point in the history of the crafts the title "turner" was dropped in favor of "chairmaker."[45] While it is certainly true that chairs were always the primary product of those turners who did not specialize in a particular product, such as pulleys for ship tackling, it is a curiosity that "chairmaker" does not occur in the records of colonial America until about the time that cane chairs began to come into fashion. Indeed cane chairs combine the arts of the joiner and the turner, and "chairmaker" was generally first used in urban areas to refer to men who practiced this combined art. From this point of view, the New England craftsmen who made chairs upholstered in leather in the Cromwellian style were as much "chairmakers" as those who upholstered their chairs in cane; however, all the American inventory evidence that has been found concerning the former indicates that they called themselves "joiners" and were known to their compatriots by that craft designation.

Specific instances that confirm the existence of an urban craftsman who combined joinery and turning are the various documents that refer to Thomas Stapleford. He is called a "chairmaker" in a Boston document dated 1684. Eleven years later, after he had moved to Philadelphia, Stapleford is referred to as a "Chair fframe maker" in another Boston document. In 1717, he billed James Logan of Philadelphia for the following: "a large oval Table" £3.15, "a large Pine Table" 25s., and "a Pallet Bedstead" 25s. Clearly these items represent more than simple turner's work and suggest that parts of Stapleford's earlier chair frames were made with joiner's techniques, just as these later products were. At the time of his death in 1739, Stapleford willed to his daughter additional "chairmaker's" work, which undoubtedly combined the turner's art with that of the joiner, in the form of "half a dozen Cane chairs . . . to be finished at the Charge of my Estate by my Executors."[46]

Although it was not published until 1748, the statement by the anonymous author of *A General Description of All Trades* sums up the craft of the chairmaker as it stood in London, as well as in the urban centers of America from about 1700 on.

Though this Sort of Household Goods is generally sold at the Shops of the *Cabinetmakers* for all the better Kinds, and at the Turners for the more common, yet there are particular *Makers* for each.

The Cane-chair-makers not only make [cane chairs] . . . but the better Sort of matted, Leather bottomed, and Wooden Chairs, of all which there is great Variety of Goodness, Workmanship and Price; and some of the Makers, who are also Shop Keepers, are very considerable Dealers, employing from 300 to upwards of 500£. in the Trade. The Work is pretty smart, the Hours from six to nine; and a Journeyman's Wages 12s. a week.

The white Wooden, Wicker and ordinary matted Sort, commonly called Kitchen-chairs, and sold by Turners are made by different Hands, but are all inferior Employs.

Those covered with Stuffs, Silks &c. are made and sold by the Upholsterers.[47]

Although it does not appear in the lists of tools in books dealing with colonial woodworking, an important "new" tool, the center bit, which is particularly useful to the cane-chair maker, finds its way into use in America around the beginning of the eighteenth century. The earliest documentary reference to this tool in America occurs in the 1708 inventory of Charles Plumley (see Appendix 1). His "4 Center bitts and 1 dott bitt" were valued at 5s.[48] The center bit differs from the pod auger in that it has a point which enables the chairmaker to drill holes with great precision and little effort. Such holes do not need to be started with a gimlet. Experiments with pod augers by Winterthur's former furniture conservator, Mervin Martin, and by furniture specialist John D. Alexander, Jr., of Baltimore reveal that the pod auger is particularly suited to drilling holes in wood that retains a great deal of its natural moisture. The pod auger does not drill dry wood as nicely. The center bit in its many guises is a bit that does very well on cured wood, such as would more likely be found in an urban craftsman's shop, where moisture content was difficult to control. The center bit does not "walk" or move out of place as round pointed bits do, and its chisel-shape foot is particularly advantageous in helping to cut a precise hole through the long grain of the wood at angles difficult to master with a pod auger (see catalogue entries 53 and 54). So far, center bits have been found prior to 1750 only in the inventories of America's urban craftsmen, and the earliest instances of its use have been observed on urban cane chairs. This sort of bit is particularly useful for drilling holes in the front corners of the seat frame of the cane chair where the craftsman wants as deep a hole as possible through a relatively thin mortise-and-tenon joint, in order to maximize adhesion when the short, round tenon on the upper end of the front leg is glued into place. In an extremely early illustration, a center bit is called a "borer with auger" (fig. 24).[49]

Fig. 24. Tools used for boring logs. *P*: a borer with auger, *Q*: a wider borer. Detail from a plate in Agricola, *De re metallica* (1556), p. 177. (Winterthur Library.) I am indebted to Joseph W. Hammond for calling this to my attention.

CRAFT ORGANIZATION IN NEW ENGLAND

The foregoing brief and very general outline of the crafts and tools of the various types of furniture makers who worked in America during the seventeenth century is a place to begin the study of the furniture that has survived from the earliest years of New England's history, but it does not tell the whole story. What furniture looks like was as much affected by the ways in which the lives of the craftsmen who made it were organized as it was by the tools, materials, and styles with which the craftsmen worked. To understand the significance of the interrelationship of the crafts as they were practiced, their role in society, and how these roles changed in America and differed from practices in England requires the connoisseur to look deeper into social history.

The working craftsmen who produced furniture in America all came from what is commonly referred to as "the artisan class" in Europe, but they came from both rural and urban backgrounds and, as a consequence, established two distinct strains of furniture making in this country. The life of the rural craftsman in England at the time that America was settled was governed by a number of laws, some of which had been periodically enacted and reenacted since 1349. The most influential of these laws was the Statute of Artificers, promulgated in 1562/63. This statute required, among other things, that every person who intended to practice a trade should spend seven years learning it and imposed upon the

justices of the peace of the realm the duty of meeting in each locality once a year to establish wages for each kind of industry.[50] Superficially these laws appear to bypass the prerogatives of the guilds in the various cities, but in reality they merely extended rules that already existed to the rural areas and established a civil mechanism for administering them.

Guilds, or "companies," as they were called in the seventeenth century, were a phenomenon of town life in the Middle Ages. Charters, which amounted to an exclusive license to practice a trade (we would call them "monopolies" today) were purchased by guilds. In London, charters came from the crown; in smaller towns, they were granted by the local governing body. The charters gave the companies certain privileges and responsibilities. While craft guilds existed in every incorporated town in medieval England, all crafts were not represented by guilds in all towns. London, York, and Chester, for example, appear to be the only cities that had guilds composed exclusively of joiners in seventeenth-century England. Guilds existed for three reasons: First, to limit the number of men working in given trades within the town and thus control nonmember competition; second, to keep the price for the work done by members as high as possible; and third, to maintain control over the quality of work produced for sale in the town. In most cases they also provided for members who became indigent or for the widows of deceased members.[51]

While guilds were unquestionably declining in power during the first half of the seventeenth century because of the population explosion of the sixteenth century, the very fact that they had existed for several centuries conditioned the habits that had governed craft life in the towns, not so much by force of law as by strength of custom. The greatest effect that this custom exerted was to confine the practice of each craft to members of the guild of that craft. As far as furniture craftsmen were concerned, this meant that joinery was exclusively practiced by joiners and that turnery was confined to turners. A complaint to the Court of Aldermen of the City of London on November 3, 1622, resulted in the following statement, recorded in the Minutes of the London Company of Turners.

At this courte complaint being made againste William Gryme for putting his apprentice to worke at the trade of Turning wthin a Joyners, to make turners worke for the Joynr to the [deprivation?] of the company of Turners, wch was more fitting to be done at home, at the Turners howse, because the Joyners by such means will come acquainted with the Turners trade in tyme may come to do the like work themselves for their own uses, to the great damage of a great number of this mistery.

The court ordered "Mr. Gryme . . . to take his apprentice back home to work."[52]

In contrast to the practice in London and other towns which had guilds, the separation of woodworking trades was virtually unknown in the rural villages where it was not uncommon for the talents of the carpenter, joiner, carver, turner, and wheelwright to be combined in one man, especially in those villages which could not possibly give full employment to specialists in any one of these trades.

The question of how the crafts would be administered in Massachusetts Bay arose very soon after settlement. From the craftsman's point of view, no problem existed during the first years. In each settlement there was plenty of work to do and not enough skilled craftsmen to do it. From the customer's point of view, it was a different matter. As early as 1633 John Winthrop confided to his journal that a "scarcity of workmen has caused them to raise their wages to an excessive rate, so as a carpenter would have three shillings a day," when twelve pence would have been more in accord with the rate in England.[53] The leaders of the colony never questioned the universally held idea that labor and prices should be controlled. The only question was how to do it. Should workmen be controlled by legislation, in the manner of the Statute of Artificers which governed craft life in rural England, or should guilds be chartered as was done in the incorporated towns?

Both were tried. On October 1, 1633, the General Court of the Massachusetts Bay Company ordered that "master carpenters, sawyers, masons, clapboard rivers, bricklayers, : . . joiners, . . . etc., should not receive more than two shillings a day without meals, and not more than fourteen pence a day . . . [with] board."[54] A similar law is spelled out in considerably greater detail in the minutes of the General Court of the Colony of Connecticut for June 7, 1641. In those records, very much in the manner of English laws of the same period, it was noted:

Forasmuch as the Court haueing lately declared their apprhensions to the Country conserneing the excesse in wages amongst all sorts of Artificers and workemen, hopeing thereby men would haue bine a law vnto themselues, but finding little reformation therein, The said Court hath therefore Ordered, that sufficient able Carpenters, Plow writs, Wheelewrits, Masons, Joyners, Smithes and Coopers, shall not take aboue 20d. for a dayes worke from the xth of March to the xith of October, nor aboue 18d. a day for the other prte of the yeare, and to worke xi howers in the day the summer tyme, besids that wch is spent in eateing or sleeping, and ix howers in the wynter: also, mowers, for the type of mowing shall not take aboue xx d. for a dayes worke.

It is Ordered, also, that all other Artificers, or handicrots men and cheife laborers shall not take aboue xviij d. a day for the first halfe yeare as aforesaid, and not aboue 14d. pr day for the other prte of the yeare; and wtsoeuer worke is lett or taken by the great or prsell by any workemen, laborers or artificers wtsoeuer, shall be valued by the prportion aforesaid.

Also, Sawyers shall not take aboue 4s. 2d. for slitt worke or three inch planke, nor aboue 3s. 6d. for boards, by the hundred. Also, boards shall not be sold for aboue 5s. vi d. the hundred.[55]

Seven years later, the second method of control—the guild system—was tried in Boston. On October 18, 1648, the cordwainers and the coopers each felt themselves numerous enough to petition the General Court for permission to "become a company." The petitions were granted "for a period of three years and no longer." The charters of the two companies were not renewed at the expiration of their terms; when the hatmakers applied for a similar privilege in 1672, they were told to reapply when they "shall make as good hats

and sell them as cheape as are affoorded from other parts."[56] They never reapplied.

The hesitancy to charter companies is understandable: after all, the Massachusetts Bay Company was a chartered organization itself, and the right of the General Court, or assembly, to charter others was, at best, legally tenuous. After this early flirtation with the guild system, it became evident that practice in New England, both urban and rural, would follow rural English practice: control of craftsmen of the same trade as well as disputes among craftsmen of different trades were handled by the civil government consisting of town magistrates and appointed civil judges.

It is no accident that Boston was the town where the guild system was tried. The Puritan founders of New England envisaged an essentially agrarian community, similar to the villages from which men like John Winthrop had come. They did not contemplate that Boston would become a large town, with men living in it from many places, not the least of which was London.

An important demographic study listing 2,885 heads of households who came to New England between 1630 and 1650 and whose places of origin can be determined shows that the greatest numbers of emigrants came from the eastern and southern counties of England, predominately East Anglia and the city of London. Suffolk provided 298 of these adult males, Essex 266, Kent 197, Devonshire 175, Norfolk 169, Somerset 153, or about 45 percent of the emigrants. London's 203 emigrants constituted 7 percent.[57] If woodworking craftsmen emigrated in the same ratio as other citizens, these counties provided almost half of the woodworking craftsmen in New England before 1650.

The statistical abstraction agrees with the genealogical research into the places of origin of New England's joiners and turners, for the vast majority of them came from country towns. If the craftsmen who came to America brought the craft habits and the ways of thinking of their native areas to the places in the New World where they settled, it should come as no surprise that the vast majority of New England furniture bears a resemblance to the kind of furniture that was being made in provincial England. This fact also accounts for the recognizably regional character of much American furniture. No wonder the work of Thomas Mulliner from Ipswich, Essex, who settled in Branford in New Haven Colony, looks so different from the work of William Searle from Ottery St. Mary, Devonshire, who settled in Ipswich, Massachusetts; or that the work of both these men and their descendants looks so different from the work of John Symonds from Great Yarmouth, Norfolk, who settled in Salem, Massachusetts, for the local craftsmen in each of these localities in England, isolated from each other, produced furniture that reflected the style preferences, habits of use, and tastes of the different localities in England from which they came.

As might be expected, a significant portion of that small percentage from London who had no taste for grubbing with a hoe gravitated toward urban rather than rural areas to settle down, and in fact, four of the earliest furniture craftsmen who came from London settled in Boston: John Davis, a joiner, embarked on the *Elizabeth*, from London, on April 15, 1635;

Thomas Edsall (alias Hedsall), a turner, departed London on the "17th Aprill, 1635 In the *Elizabeth and Anne* to New England"; Ralph Mason, a joiner, from St. Olave's Parish, Southwark, embarked July 4, 1635, for Boston; and Henry Messenger, yet another joiner from London, was in Boston by 1641, when his son John was born.[58] It seems clear that this contingent of London craftsmen, all of whom continued to practice their trades, must have accounted for an important part of the furniture made in Boston during their time and that this furniture must have had stylistic and technical overtones of the furniture being made in London when they left. It is likely, for example, that these craftsmen introduced the dovetail as a furniture joint into America. On the basis of this fact, we have been able to identify a London strain of American furniture that originated in Boston.[59]

But we have not been able to identify *all* the schools of furniture making in Boston. Craftsmen from rural England also settled there. Thomas Scottow, the joiner who came from Norwich, Norfolk, and died in Boston in 1661, was one of them. We could perhaps have spotted him as a joiner from an unincorporated English village purely on the basis of his inventory (among the joinery tools were "a lathe and six turning tooles") but it is unlikely that we shall ever identify his work unless we someday can isolate the Norwich school of joinery in England.[60] We can say, however, that Scottow must have found a niche in the taste and temper of Boston or he would not have succeeded as a joiner. While he may have contributed his mite to the style and techniques of Boston craftsmanship, it is more likely that he either found it expedient to absorb the earmarks of the London style or catered to a non London taste among Boston's settlers.

Mason, Messenger, Edsall, and Scottow all had sons who continued to practice the family trade in a second and, in some cases, a third generation. Whatever styles and techniques these men worked in were without doubt perpetuated by these sons, because the apprenticeship system guarantees that this will be so. Indeed, the concept and practice of apprenticeship was the single most important aspect of both the Statute of Artificers and the guild system to affect American craft life and its products.

The custom of passing on the techniques of a trade by having an apprentice serve with a master was well established in England by the fourteenth century. Acceptance of the principle of apprenticeship in New England can be noted as early as June 14, 1642, when the General Court felt compelled to legislate on the matter of "the great neglect in many parents and masters in training up their children in learning, labor and other imployments which may bee profitable to the commonwealth."[61] The Court set up the machinery by which the selectmen of each town, with the aid of the local courts and magistrates, should oversee the proper education of the young; apprenticeship was the method by which this was to be accomplished.

Concern for the proper training of the young was reiterated in a law of 1648 that, in addition, elaborated on the need of parents and masters to attend the matters of literacy and religious education as well. The sense of this law was embodied, virtually without change, in the revision of 1658,

published as *The Code of 1660.* The aims of the system must have been neglected throughout the colony, however, for in 1668 the court published an enforcing act.[62] The language of this act as stated in an order from the Salem court to the constable of Topsfield is filled with sincere passion on this point.

It is required of the selectmen that they see that all . . . youth under family Government be taught to read perfectly the english tongue, have knowledge in the capital laws, and be taught some orthodox catechism, and that they be brought up in some honest imployment, profitable to themselves and the commonwealth . . . the prevalency of the former neglect notwithstanding, . . . you are required to take a list of the names of those young persons . . . who doe not serve their parents or masters as children, apprentices, hired servants or journeymen ought to do, and usually did in our native country.[63]

A typical craftsman's apprenticeship indenture of this period was recorded among the deeds of Plymouth Colony.[64] It varies only from the usual agreement of this time in that it does not specify that the apprentice be taught a catechism.

1653   BRADFORD GOVR
The 2cond of August 1653

Memorandum That Thomas Savory senior of Plymouth and Ann his wife Doe by these prsents covenant with Thomas Lettice of Plymouth aforesaid Carpenter; That theire sonn Thomas Savory Juni aged five yeares or thereabouts on the 15th Day of March last past before the Date heerof shall Remayne and continue with the said Thomas Lettice untill hee bee of the age of one and twenty yeares; During which time the said Thomas Savory the younger is to bee with the said Thomas Lettice after the mannor of an apprentice; And the said Thomas Lettice is to find unto his said apprentice During the said time meat Drinke apparrell washing and lodgin and all other necssearies fitt for one in his Degree and calling and to teach an Instruct his said apprentice in the arte or trade of an house carpenter in as able mannor as himselfe can prforme it, likewise During the aforsaid tearme of tim the aforsaid Thomas Savory is to Doe and prforme unto his said master all faithfull service and not to neglect his said masters business nor absent himselfe from the same by night or Day without Lycence from his said Master; hee shall not marry or contracte himselfe in marriage to any During the said tearme hee shall not Imbezell purloyne or steale any of his goods or Reveale any of such seacrets that ought to bee kept but shall behave himselfe in every Respecte as an obeidient and faithful servant ought to Doe as well in word as in Deed furthermore the said Thomas Lettice covenanteth by these prsents that the said Thomas Savory shalbee by him or his appointment and att his charge Taught to Read and write the English Tongue; And incase the said Thomas Lettice shall Decease before his said apprentice attaine the age of one and twenty yeares That notwithstanding the said Thomas Savory the younger shalbee and Remayne with Ann the wife of the said Thomas Lettice the Remayneder of his time unexpired During her widdowhood but incase shee marry againe then the said Thomas Savory the younger shalbee free And incase the said Thomas Savory the younger Doth continue with the wife of the aforesaid Thomas Lettice untill his time bee expired then shee is to Doe and prforme all such conditions as the said Thomas Lettice on his prte should have Donn: and prformed excepting onely the Teaching of the Trad of a carpenter abovementioned or causing the same to bee taught which shee is heerby wholly freed from; and Lastly when the tearme of time abovementioned is by the said Thomas Savory the younger fully attained; that then the said Thomas Lettice or Ann his wife (in case shee bee the longer liver) shall provide for and Deliver unto theire said apprentice two suites of apparell viz one for best and another for working Daies and alsoe hee the said Thomas Lettice or Ann; his wife shall Deliver unto theire said apprentice certaine Carpenters tooles videlicett one broad axe two playnes two Augers and a sett of Chissels; & an hand saw; In Witnesse of the prmises that they shalbee faithfully prformed the prties abovesaid have heerunto sett to their hands

in the prsence of   THOMAS LETTICE [mark]
NATHANIELL MORTON   THOMAS SAVOREY[65]

In addition to being the vehicle by which craft techniques were passed on from one generation to the next, the settlers of Massachusetts Bay used the apprentice system to attain four social ends. First, in order to prevent a child from becoming a burden on the community the courts used it to apprentice to fit masters the children of either destitute or deceased parents. Second, the courts would apprentice, to a person of good character, a child who had an "unfit" (immoral) parent or parents. Third, apprenticeship was used to assure supervised religious instruction and to encourage literacy. Finally, the system was an approved method of acquiring cheap and reasonably reliable labor, as it had been in England.

By 1660, however, trouble had developed in Boston. Although it is not clear whether demand for manufactured goods had outreached supply or a general looseness in administration of the law was to blame, the quality of workmanship had declined, and the problem became the concern of the July 20 town meeting:

Whereas itt is found by sad experience that many youthes in this Towne, being put forth Apprentices to severall manufactures and sciences, but for 3 or 4 years time, contrary to the Customs of all well governed places, whence they are uncapable of being Artists in their trades, besides their unmeetenesse att the expiration of their Apprentice-ship to take charge of others for government and manuall instruction in their occupations which, if nott timely amended, threatens the welfare of this Towne.

Itt is therefore ordered that no person shall henceforth open a shop in this Towne nor occupy any manufacture or science, till hee hath compleated 21 years of age, nor except hee hath served 7 years Apprentice-ship, by testimony under the hands of sufficient witnesses. And that all Indentures made betweene any master and servant shall bee brought in and enrolled in the Towne's Records within one month after the contract made, on penalty of ten shillings to bee paid by the master att the time of the Apprentices being made free.[66]

Two practices outlined in the statement emphasize how New England's methods varied from urban England's habits. First, the requirement that an apprentice must be 21 years of age before he could open a shop had been a specification in rural England since the promulgation of the Statute of Artificers in 1562/63, but in the incorporated towns and cities of England the minimum age for a master workman was 24, and required two years of service as a journeyman.[67] Second, the town of Boston indicated the desirability and necessity of exercising

control over the trades that required apprenticeship, and said that the town would regulate this aspect of its life *through the civil courts*. This, too, was similar to rural English practice, where such control was supervised by the civil government—justices of the peace and town magistrates—and unlike London, in which guild courts policed their own members virtually without interference.

Despite the efforts of all concerned, Boston's laws still could not be enforced. Perhaps the city was growing too fast. Perhaps growth continued to breed demand for cheap goods with quality not a consideration. Or perhaps, most of all, the model of the Statute of Apprentices was not viable in an urban context. Whatever the cause, a petition of May 23, 1677, shows the state at which matters had arrived: the artisans of Boston, arguing "that whereas a very considerable part of the Town of Boston doth Consist of Handy craftsmen, whose outward subsistence doth depend upon gods Blessing in the dilligent use of their callings, & many of us . . . finding ourselves under great disadvantages by the frequent Intruding of Strangers from all parts," asked the selectmen to protect their interests by enforcing court orders already on the books. "Especially those Orders," they urged, "Referring to the Admission of Inhabitants, and also that Order referring to the good of Trades, Providing that Trades-men shall fullfill a Sufficient Apprenticeship & be proficients in Their Calling before they set up their Trades."[68]

History does not record that any action was taken on the petition. This inaction had profound consequences on the appearance and quality of American furniture for two centuries. The document clearly reveals that two distinct classes of furniture were then being made in Boston. On one level, the furniture was well made, perhaps stylistically conservative, but certainly built in the traditional way. On the other level, shoddy merchandise was being made, perhaps for the less well-to-do or the less discriminating tastes, or perhaps merely for a class of people who needed furniture and could not afford the work of the prestigious joiners who signed the petition.

The Boston craftsmen, in claiming that "the way of our subsistence being so much differing from other towns," suggested what the documents of these towns reveal: a different pattern of craft life had emerged in the countryside surrounding Boston. For one thing, the usual practice of a craftsman in rural areas was to divide his time between working at his craft and farming, as the tools of husbandry and tracts of farmland in craftsmen's inventories reveal. It was also common for him to sell the labor of his sons and apprentices to other farmers at harvest time. The shops of rural craftsmen were often in their own houses, whereas Boston craftsmen often rented shop space in other, more centrally located buildings particularly after 1660.[69] Rural craftsmen only occasionally employed a journeyman, but journeymen were common in Boston. Moreover, small towns could seldom support more than one furniture craftsman at a time: it was usual for a new craftsman to appear in a village only after the death of his predecessor. Such was the case, for example, with Thomas Dennis, a joiner from England who did not move from Portsmouth, New Hampshire, to Ipswich, Massachusetts, until after the death of

William Searle in 1667, although Dennis had purchased land in Ipswich several years earlier.

In urban areas, different circumstances caused craftsmen to develop different institutions. The numerous lawsuits that fill the records of the Suffolk County Court of Common Pleas reveal that Boston's craftsmen commonly worked for each other, and not always harmoniously. While a piece of joined furniture in rural New England was very likely made by a single craftsman and his apprentice from beginning to end, there is evidence that some joiners in Boston relied on turners to supply turned pieces from the very moment that the turners set up shop. This de facto separation of the crafts had nothing to do with the artificial separation that a guild system might have encouraged, although it might originally have occurred among the group of joiners who came from London and had always relied upon specialist turners and perhaps specialist carvers like Edward Budd who by the 1660s was living in Boston.[70]

In Salem—the second largest town in New England at the end of the seventeenth century, but much smaller than Boston —a system of cooperation rather than competition developed. The main part of the furniture trade was concentrated in a small area on Essex Street, just off the southerly side of the Common (now Washington Square) where joiners James Symonds, Nathaniel Silsbee, and John Lander (Launder), lived, as did Benjamin Gray, a turner/chairmaker, in the last quarter of the seventeenth century. At first glance, this concentration of workmen with closely related trades might seem to be a lingering vestige of medieval urban craft life, where certain streets in towns sheltered all of the practitioners of the same trade. But Symonds, Lander, Silsbee, and Gray were all second and third generation Americans whose fathers had come from rural, not urban England, and had no memory of this practice. Of course, it could always be a coincidence, but a more likely theory is that these craftsmen were developing a new (for them) institution, similar to an ancient one, on the basis of mutual interest.

An important factor in this situation may be traced to the apprenticeship system. The seventeenth-century joiner's trade in Salem was dominated from its very beginning by the lengthened shadow of one man, John Symonds. Symonds, who came from Great Yarmouth, Norfolk, was in Salem before 1636, when the written records of the town begin. Symonds had two sons, James and Samuel. Samuel was trained by his father and moved to Rowley Village (now Boxford), where he, in turn, may have trained Nathaniel Capen, the only son of the parson of neighboring Topsfield. Samuel Symonds also employed a journeyman named Joshua Bisson, who later moved to Beverly, where he lived and worked well into the eighteenth century. John Symonds, prior to his death, had begun to train John Pease who finished his training with James Symonds. Pease moved to Enfield, Connecticut, where we can be certain he made furniture in the Symonds manner. James Symonds also trained at least two of his own sons, John II and Thomas, and possibly Edward Norris III, who later married Symonds's daughter, Mary. He also trained Nathaniel Silsbee. Silsbee in turn may have trained John Marsh, who by 1690 was living in Rappahannock, Virginia,

and who was the eldest son of Silsbee's sister, Mary. The only joiners in Salem who escaped the influence of Symonds were John Lander, who may have been trained in Boston, and Joseph Neal, who may have been trained by his elder brother, John, always called a carpenter in the records.[71]

This inbreeding by a group of craftsmen is of great significance. It illustrates the tightness of a community of workmen, related not only through training but also by ties of blood (much like the parallel situation among American silversmiths), and in turn accounts for the generic resemblance of antique furniture that consistently turns up today in specific locales. Further, it offers a reasonable basis for regional attribution of otherwise undocumented furniture, in the absence of better information.

A coin, of course, has two sides, and the second side of this one is that not all craftsmen remained in the community where they trained. Their departure, not always a matter of choice but one of economics, was inherent in the apprenticeship system. Assuming that the system works perfectly, seven years after a master has taken an apprentice there will be two masters of the same craft in a community where formerly only one had worked. At that time, each master takes a new apprentice, for he cannot practice his craft without one. In seven more years, two new masters have appeared, bringing the total to four masters working in a town that fourteen years earlier had supported only one. Unless the town has grown— and many did not—enough work cannot be found for all. The pressure on the less settled master to migrate becomes strong, and through this migration specific stylistic ideas and technical methods were diffused throughout colonial America. The implications of this dissemination mean that connoisseurship will not be easy. How are we to say that similar pieces of furniture were actually made in the same place even in so limited a span of time as the sixty-five years of the seventeenth century in which American rural furniture underwent very little recognizable change? Sixty-five years represents only two generations in the life of a family, but it is nine seven-year generations of craft life. What certainty our understanding of the apprenticeship system gives to furniture history, it takes away with the dispersion of craftsmen. But awareness of the system at least leaves us with the comforting thought that by mentally subtracting the changes in craft techniques wrought by time we can sometimes perceive the solid thread of continuity handed down from master to apprentice.

In any event, it is apparent that the thinking of the furniture historian ought to begin to gravitate away from "the cult of personality," in which association of an object with a maker increases only its monetary value, to the larger picture which reveals the social, cultural, historical, and aesthetic meanings of the object from the point of view of the culture that produced it. Perhaps we shall someday even get away from the pressure to regionalize surviving artifacts and see them as they truly are at one end or the other of a long line of development, which despite the changes that inevitably occurred with the passing years reveals the line of continuity that represents a school of workmanship that persisted over a long period of time—a source of fascination in itself.

Having pieced together what we can about the life of furniture craftsmen from the unflinching testimony of their inventories and having reconstructed as well as we can in a brief survey of the way in which they practiced their crafts and how those crafts were governed (or not governed), the breath of life is still missing from their story. Handicraftsmen emerge from history impersonally, human beings only insofar as they, like the furniture that they made, are relics of the dead past. It is one of the truisms of the study of furniture history that American furniture makers in the seventeenth century lived their lives in the words of the well-known cliché, "beneath the level of documentary scrutiny." None of them was of the gentle class of the time, many of them were illiterate. If they led blameless lives, they did not even find their way into the court records where sins are catalogued for eternity. Aside from a few self-conscious religious diary confessions, a few bills, a few almanacs with notations of the weather written in, none of them left memorials of themselves other than the objects they produced, most of which remain largely anonymous. None of them told us what they thought about their work or what their customers thought of it. As d'Alembert wrote in the eighteenth century, "in a workshop it is the situation that is eloquent, not the craftsman."[72]

The laboring artisan in the seventeenth century had no status, social or intellectual. Forecasting the attitude toward craftsmen expressed by Sprat, in 1610 Rowland Vaughn, an English courtier and husbandman, bade the joiner who was helping build an irrigation system "have patience, [for] the Invention was mine" and as an aside added "I only imploy'd his hand, and not his head." Some seventy years later Moxon wrote, "I See no more Reason, why the Sordidness of some Workmen, should be the cause of contempt upon *Manual Operations*, than that the excellent Invention of a *Mill* should be dispis'd, because a blind Horse draws in it. And tho' the *Mechanicks* be, by some, accounted Ignoble and Scandalous? Yet it is very well known that many Gentlemen in this Nation, of good Rank and high Quality, are conversant in Handy-Works. . . . How pleasant and healthy this their Diversion is, their Minds and Bodies find; and how Harmless and Honest, all sober men may judge?"[73] We cannot help but wonder if Moxon's words represent the beginnings of the romantic conception of the virtues of handwork or if he, who was after all a handicraftsman himself, was trying to induce the gentlemanly class for whom he was writing to find virtue in "handiworks." In either case, the artist remains separated from the gentleman by a social and intellectual gulf that has only rarely been bridged in subsequent centuries.

In the eighteenth century, the writings of Diderot and d'Alembert indicate the winds of social change are stirring. Volumes of comment have been written about the influence of these two men in establishing the intellectual climate in which the French Revolution could come about, and nowhere can the breaking of social barriers be seen more plainly than in d'Alembert's defense of the idea that the superiority of the fine arts over the mechanical arts is "unjust in many respects."

Indeed, he suggests that the latter should be preferred for their "greatly superior utility."[74]

In the same way that the major trends of thought in every age force the historians of that age to reinterpret history, nineteenth-century writers such as John Ruskin and William Morris perceived the end of the handicrafts era in their own time as immoral and urged a revival of handicrafts which, they argued, would result in a revival of morality. Only in a time when reality is too bitter to contemplate—and men are aware of it—could an author write, and furthermore, believe, as Morris did, that "art is the expression of man's pleasure in labour; that it is possible for man to rejoice in his work, for strange as it may seem to us today, there have been times when he did rejoice in it . . . and unless it becomes a pleasure to him again, the token of which change will be that beauty is once again a natural and necessary accompaniment of productive labour, all but the worthless must toil in pain, and therefore live in pain."[75]

After the intellectualizations of centuries of scholars who are writers and not doers, how we long for one single statement from the seventeenth century by a craftsman telling us what he thought about as he worked wood. Did the craftsman really contemplate the beauty his work might result in and strive for it, or did he long for his twelve-hour day to end so that he could rest before beginning another twelve-hour day? Was any craftsman who made a single piece of furniture illustrated in this book truly innovative, or was he bound by his training and by the traditions that relentlessly bore in upon him from the past? The documents are mute on these points. All they tell us is that craftsmen did an uncommon amount of beer drinking after hours, which often landed them in jail. Was the work itself all deadly serious, the Puritan work ethic overwhelming everything? Or was the work like that which occurred in a joiner's shop in a Scottish village in the early twentieth century? Woodworker G. F. Smith recalled his days in that small shop and provided a glimpse of shop life we seldom find in our own colonial records. In the shop, Smith recollected, was "a wooden treadle turning lathe . . . [and it] fell to the function of the youngest apprentice to provide the muscle power. As wont with boys, we passed on our experience of how to gain a rest when the going got too hard. . . . Slight but persistent twitching of the foot on the upward swing of the treadle ultimately broke the cord which formed the belting and so we rested."[76]

Too often we scholars have misinterpreted the past. Well-fed historians who write in modern times have often cited "Puritan piety" as the motivation for keeping the hands of seventeenth-century New Englanders busy. But the local documents of that time and place reveal that there was only one alternative to working with one's hands—starvation. In grander economic terms, it is now well understood that the tiny English colonies in the New World suffered from what we would call an "adverse balance of payments." The goods they imported were of greater value than their exports. Everything that could be made in the colony represented value for which the community would not have to compensate English merchant venturers; therefore, local governments encouraged manufactures because such would keep capital at home.

Although the statutes designed to enforce long apprenticeship periods failed, the apprentice system itself became an important part of the life of colonial craftsmen and indeed persists in some trades today. The New England apprenticeship statutes failed for the same reason that the English Statute of Artificers had, and nowhere is this reason better summarized than in an opinion recorded in the English *Privy Council Register* on October 29, 1669, 106 years after England's statute was passed. The statute "though not repealed yet has been by most of the Judges looked upon as inconvenient to trade and to the increase of inventions."[77]

Few documents detailing the specific relationship between furniture makers and their apprentices in New England have survived from the seventeenth century, but ample evidence demonstrates that apprenticeship was an extremely important ingredient in their lives. Indeed, it was the single most important vehicle by which working techniques, shop practices, and stylistic ideas were spread throughout New England.

NOTES

[1] Davidson, *Life in America*, 1:51.

[2] See Cummings, *Framed Houses of Massachusetts Bay*, figs. 53, 55, 79, 80, 86, 97, 113, et passim.

[3] "Extracts from the Deed Books of the Plymouth Colony," p. 141.

[4] Suffolk Probate, 1:38.

[5] *Proceedings of the Provincial Court [of Maryland]*, pp. 301–2; I am indebted to Arlene Palmer Schwind for this quotation.

[6] *Essex Quarterly Courts*, 2:266.

[7] *OED*, s.v. "joiner," 2; *General Description of All Trades*, p. 124.

[8] *Moxon's Mechanick Exercises*, p. 63.

[9] London Court of Aldermen as cited in Edwards, *Shorter Dictionary*, p. 331.

[10] "Item pd to Thomas Ewen Joyner for all the worke as Byfittes drapery and the dore wh[ich] he made. . . . Item pd to Thomas Ewen Joyner for making xxxiiij yardes drapery there xviij d. per yard" £2.11 (Goodman, "Woodworking Apprentices and their Tools in Bristol, Norwich, Great Yarmouth, and Southampton," p. 379). Wainscotting was paid for by the square yard throughout the seventeenth and eighteenth centuries: "Nov., 1694, This court was called on purpose for wainscotting the hall passage, Stewards roome and Staircase. . . . Ordered that Mr. [Thomas] Poultney should do the Hall at 9 s. p[er] yard: one table at the upper end at [7, erased] s. per foot, Two forms at 2 s. pr. foot and benches at 22 d. per foot" (Company of Joyners, leaf 126 verso). "Wainscotting, the dimensions are taken as in painting, viz., by measuring the height (indenting the string wherever the plain goes, as well as the painters do wherever the brush goes) and then the compass; which multiply the one into the other, dividing the product by 9, and the quotient is the answer in square yards" (Fisher, *Instructor or Young Man's Best Companion*, p. 193.

[11] Contract of 1685, Lidget/Waldron legal papers, Jeffries Family Papers, vol. 6; I am indebted to Joseph W. Hammond for this reference.

[12] Wolsey and Luff, *Furniture in England*, p. 17.

[13] This is a rare instance of a piece of work, executed in England, that portrays a table board, or top, suspended on a pair of trestles, in the French manner.

[14] *Essex Quarterly Courts*, 8:282; F[rothingham], "A Declaration of the Affairs of the English People . . . by Phinehas Pratt," p. 481; *Suffolk Deeds*, 5:533. Savage, *Genealogical Dictionary*, 1:287 notes that Budd was there several years before 1668 but does not indicate the source of his information.

[15] Misterie, from the Latin, *ministerium*, an occupation or trade in this phrase has no overtone of secrecy, as is often imputed to it. *OED*, s.v. "mystery" sb. 2.

[16] Phillips, *Annals of the Worshipful Company of Joiners*, pp. 27–28.

[17] For specific instances see Forman, "Seventeenth-Century Case Furniture of Essex County," pp. 28–36.

[18] Campbell, *London Tradesman*, pp. 171–72.

[19] *Boston Records*, 1:71; "Some letters and an Abstract of Letters," p. 195.

[20] Company of Joyners, leaf 98 verso; Symonds Papers, vol. "A," p. 33, DMMC 75 x 69.18.

[21] Langley, *City and Country Builder's and Workman's Treasury of Designs*, p. iii. The edition of 1750 published by S. Harding, perhaps designed for sale to cabinetmakers, does not have this passage. See Forman, "Continental Furniture Craftsmen in London," pp. 94–103.

[22] Royal Wardrobe Accounts, "From the 22th of June to Mich[aelm]as following 1660" (as cited in Symonds Papers, DMMC 75 x 69.25, pp. 4–5), describe Richard Wearge as "his Ma[jes]ties Coffermaker" and as a "Trunkmaker." Boston had at least one trunkmaker, William Crow, as early as 1691. Crow was still working there in 1700, although no American trunks from this period have been identified (Singleton, *Furniture of Our Forefathers*, 1:176). Cowan, *Members of the Ancient and Honorable Artillery*; Forman, "Urban Aspects of Massachusetts Furniture," esp. pp. 19, 27, and 28.

[23] W. L. Goodman to Forman, October 15, 1976.

[24] *Boston Records*, 2: pt. 1, p. 16; Suffolk Probate, 2:60–62.

[25] *Essex Probate*, 3:24. W. L. Goodman, to whom I am indebted for constant guidance regarding tools and their use, suggests that "revolving plain" is a court clerk's transcription error for "grooving" (plow) planes, essential tools not mentioned elsewhere, and "yoyet irons" are probably "joint irons," a synonym for "joiner's dogs," pieces of iron, bent and pointed at both ends to hold logs steady while they are sawn (Goodman to Forman, October 25, 1972). Transcription errors in inventories of craftsmen's tools are common in court records since the takers of inventories often did not write clearly and court recorders were often unfamiliar with technical terms. See further W. L. Goodman, "Tools and Equipment," pp. 40–51. For inventories see Kane, "Joiners of Seventeenth Century Hartford County," pp. 65–85.

[26] The root sense of the substantive form of "crease," meaning "a fold or wrinkle," carries us back to the concept of "linenfold" and wooden "drapery." The terms "crees," "cress," "cressing," and "creasing plane" are common in seventeenth-century joiners' inventories, but appear less frequently as the eighteenth century progresses. This pattern of decreasing use coincides with the diminished use of so-called shadow molding in New England woodwork, which appears to be a debased descendent of drapery work. The use of the word to describe molding planes likewise reveals a touch of traditionalism.

[27] *Passengers and Ships Prior to 1684*, unpaged addendum entitled "Corrections and Additions"; I am indebted to Jane Rittenhouse Smiley for calling this reference to my attention. See also McElroy, "Furniture of the Philadelphia Area," p. 198. Philadelphia Wills, 1708-113. An olive wood veneered scrutoire of American origin but unidentified provenance, in the Bolles Collection of the Metropolitan Museum of Art, is illustrated in Lockwood's *Colonial Furniture* (2nd ed.), fig. 240, but Lockwood misidentifies the wood as walnut burl. Its white pine drawer linings suggest a New England or perhaps New York origin.

[28] Suffolk Superior Court Files, 95: leaf 48; "Unpublished Letters of Judge Sewall," p. 291; Suffolk Probate, 26:33–34.

[29] "Swash turning" is extremely rare in English seventeenth-century work, and along with "rose turning" is not known on surviving American pieces. For a detailed explanation of the craft, including these techniques, see Holtzapffel and Holtzapffel, *Turning and Mechanical Manipulation*, esp. vol. 2 (1856). Two-axis turning and twist turning are discussed below in the catalogue, under Cromwellian leather chairs, where they first occur on surviving American objects.

[30] Suffolk Probate, 2:12.

[31] "Abstracts of the Earliest Wills," p. 185; Suffolk Probate, 2:27, 28.

[32] Suffolk Probate, 2:28.

[33] Savage, *Genealogical Dictionary*, 4:453; *Essex Probate*, 1:242–43.

[34] Savage, *Genealogical Dictionary*, 1:476, 4:370–71; Perley, *History of Salem*, 2:143. A seventeenth-century chair with a history in the Wickes family of Maine is owned by SPNEA.

[35] Steer, *Farm and Cottage Inventories*, pp. 90, 146, 209. No paints are listed in Wickes's inventory, but the most common green pigment is verdigris, a bluish green shade made by allowing vinegar to work on copper (Salmon, *Polygraphice*, p. 163). Other green pigments were *terra-vert* and *verditer*, both earth colors.

[36] *Essex Probate*, 1:308.

[37] Suffolk Probate, 5:273–74. Adams's son, Nathaniel, was also a turner who specialized in blockmaking (*Suffolk Deeds*, 4:263).

[38] Sewall, *Letter-book*, 1:32, 124; Edwards, *Shorter Dictionary*, p. 170.

[39] Plymouth Inventories, 3: pt. 2, pp. 34–36. These tools are analyzed by W. L. Goodman in "Tools and Equipment."

[40] Savage, *Genealogical Dictionary*, 1:336; Plymouth Inventories, 2: pt. 1, leaves 42–43.

[41] Docket, 6372, Essex Probate Files.

[42] Roubo, *Descriptions des arts et métiers*, sect. 1, ch. 6, p. 133.

[43] MacDonald, *Central New Jersey Chairmaking*, pp. 23–28. I am indebted to Joseph W. Hammond for the attribution of these patterns.

[44] Eaton, *Handicrafts of the Southern Highlands*, p. 156.

[45] Perley, *History of Salem*, 3:334.

[46] *Boston Records*, 10:76; *Suffolk Deeds*, 14:270; James Logan account book (p. 245), as cited in McElroy, "Furniture of the Philadelphia Area," pp. 207–8; Philadelphia Wills, 1739-30.

[47] *General Description of All Trades*, pp. 57–58.

[48] Philadelphia Wills, 1708-111.

[49] Agricola, *De re metallica*, p. 177.

[50] See Cheyney, *Introduction to the Industrial and Social History of England*, pp. 91, 134. Modern scholars now understand that the statute's restrictions had the additional purpose of preventing further migration from the countryside to an increasingly crowded London.

[51] See Stanley-Stone, *Worshipful Company of Turners*, pp. 50–59.

[52] Turners Company Minutes, 1: leaf 74 verso.

[53] *Winthrop's Journal*, 1:112.

[54] Belknap, *Trades and Tradesmen*, p. 10.

[55] *Connecticut Records*, p. 65.

[56] *Massachusetts Records*, 3:132, 4:526.

[57] Banks, *Topographical Dictionary*, pp. xii–xiii. The year 1650 is a reasonable cut-off date for Banks's study, inasmuch as it represents the beginning of the Civil War in England and the

end of "The Great Migration," after which immigration virtually ceased for more than a decade.

[58] Savage, "Gleanings for New England History," pp. 260, 268; Savage, *Genealogical Dictionary*, 3:201; Drake, "Founders of New England," p. 307.

[59] See Forman, "Urban Aspects of Massachusetts Furniture," pp. 15–17; see also the discussion of London artisans working in New Haven, Conn., in Fairbanks and Trent, *New England Begins*, pp. 524–26.

[60] Banks, *Topographical Dictionary*, p. 120; Suffolk Probate, 1:376–77.

[61] Gibbins, *Industry in England*, p. 95; *Massachusetts Records*, 2:87.

[62] *Massachusetts Records*, 2:94.

[63] *Essex Quarterly Courts*, 4:212–13.

[64] The word indenture was used in the seventeenth century to signify any contractual document of which there were two copies, one of which was retained by each party to the agreement. In order to assure that neither document could be falsified in any way, both copies were placed together at the time of execution and one or more edges were cut with a pair of scissors, usually in a fanciful pattern, so that in case of a lawsuit, both copies could be placed together, with their "indented" edges matching up, to confirm their originality.

[65] "Extracts from the Deed Books of the Plymouth Colony," pp. 139–41. Lettice, like many of the seventeenth-century master craftsmen of New England, signed this contract with his mark and therefore may be presumed to be illiterate, a fact which does not appear to have hampered him in the practice of his trade.

[66] *Boston Records*, 2: pt. 1, pp. 156–57. Despite this regulation, the town records contain disappointingly few apprenticeship indentures.

[67] Davies, *Enforcement of English Apprenticeship*, p. 2; on pp. 1–14 Davies provides a complete discussion of the effects of the statute.

[68] The petition is reproduced in the January 1894 *Bulletin of the Public Library of the City of Boston*, pp. 305–6; I am indebted to John E. Alden of the Boston Public Library for calling this document to my attention.

[69] For rural craftsmen see Forman, "The Account Book of John Gould, Weaver," pp. 36–49, and Hempstead, *Diary*. For urban craftsmen see Henretta, "Economic Development and Social Structure in Colonial Boston," p. 76, and Rutman, *Winthrop's Boston*.

[70] Savage, *Genealogical Dictionary*, 1:287.

[71] Various sources; for a complete discussion see Forman, "Seventeenth-Century Case Furniture of Essex County," pp. 42–55.

[72] Diderot and d'Alembert, *Encyclopédie*, "Discours preliminaire des editeurs" (author's translation).

[73] Vaughn, *Most Approved and Long Experienced Water Works* (1610), unpaged (signature L$_3$ verso); an earlier edition exists. *Moxon's Mechanick Exercises*, opening paragraph of Moxon's preface to the 3rd ed.

[74] Diderot and d'Alembert, *Encyclopédie*, "Discours preliminaire des editeurs" (author's translation).

[75] William Morris, preface to Ruskin, *Nature of Gothic*. For an analysis of this book and Ruskin's logic, see Pye, *Nature and Art of Workmanship*, pp. 47–56.

[76] Rose, *Village Carpenter*, p. xi; I am indebted to Christopher G. Gilbert for calling this book to my attention.

[77] Bland, *English Economic History*, pp. 361–62.

CATALOGUE

SEATING FURNITURE MADE BY TURNERS

Turners' chairs of two generally distinguishable types have survived from America's seventeenth century: those in which every element is turned and those in which all the members except the crosspieces of the back (and in some instances the arms) are turned. So little is understood about this handful of chairs in the Anglo-Dutch tradition that we do not even know by what names to look for them in seventeenth-century household inventories. Generations of collectors and antiques dealers have ingeniously filled this verbal void by referring to them as "Pilgrim," "Carver," and "Brewster" chairs, a choice of adjectives that manages to convey a feeling of antiquity-by-association to later and less imaginatively turned chairs of this genre by evoking the image of the hardships endured by the Pilgrims and the names of two of their early leaders. This terminology is ill-chosen because it implies that chairs of this type originated in Plymouth, the sole New England settlement whose records prior to 1640 have not revealed the name of one craftsman who practiced the turned-chair maker's trade and could have made such chairs. It is further misleading because there is and can be only one each of the Carver and Brewster chairs: they are the ones in Pilgrim Hall, Plymouth, associated with Governor John Carver and the Elder William Brewster, and they are not for sale.

The very useful labels "spindle back" and "slat back" have also been applied to these chairs. "Spindle" and "slat" are ancient words in the English language. "*Spindle back*" accurately describes the appearance of the type of chair that we have long assumed was made by the earliest turners working in America, but the word was not used in this way in the seventeenth century. Even when *slat back* begins to occur in the early eighteenth-century records, it is not absolutely clear that *slat* invariably refers to a piece of wood that is horizontally oriented: in most nonfurniture uses, slats are arranged vertically. Moreover, written documents from the period tend to be so vague that they do not confirm or deny the widely held notion that slat-back chairs were not made as early as spindle-back chairs.[1]

The people who sat in turned chairs in the seventeenth century and those who took the inventories of the households in which the chairs were used were much more laconic in recording the chairs than we would like them to have been. In the vast majority of instances, they itemized chairs merely as "chairs." When a qualifying adjective appears in the documents, it generally mentions the material of which the seat is made, or the appearance of that seat as a result of the technique used to make it, or the technique by which the seat was made, or the age of the chair insofar as age might affect its value, or, sometimes, the color.[2] The evidence supports a general rule: the more popular or prevalent a form of furniture is, the better it can be understood by a terse description, thus, the less elaborate or precise any description needs to be in a matter-of-fact document like an inventory.

Letters and craftsman's accounts do not tell us a great deal either. What would we give to know more about the style, wood, and ornament of the chairs Mrs. Margaret Lake of Ipswich, Massachusetts, expected when she ordered "2 armed Cheares with fine rushe bottums" from England in 1645? Were they spindle-back chairs? What was so special about them that they could not have been made by the local turner, Edward Browne, who had lived in Ipswich since 1638?

Browne's inventory tells us nothing about the style in which he was working. At the time of his death in 1659, he had treen ware, unfinished spinning wheels for linen and wool, and 3s. worth of "work done toward chaires" in his shop.[3] The Essex County probate records tell us a little more. In rare instances, they identify chairs as "flag chairs" or "flag-bottomed chairs," occasionally as "bass" (bast) or "bass bottomed chairs," and, least often "twin" or "twine." The more extensive probate records of Suffolk County are slightly more informative. They list a variety of names for these chairs, their values, and on occasion the rooms in which they were found.

1651 "sixe old chairs" valued at 5s.
1652 "4 basse chaires" 6s. (little parlor)
1652 "5 Chares wth Flage bottoms" 8s. (hall)
1653 "2 Sedge Chaires" 3s. (hall)
1658 "Two Rush bottome Chaires" 4s.
    "two base bottomed chaires" 4s. (in the "Chamber over ye Stall"),
    "2 stooles" 3s. (hall)
1659 "7 flagg chaires"
1663 "2 turned matted Chayrs" 4s. 16d. (chamber over the hall)
1663 "4 turned Chayres" 12s.
1669 "3: matted high chayres" 7s. (little parlor)
1674 "ten chairs of turner's work" £1
1676 "10 turned chaires flagg bottoms" £1 (hall)
1678 "one dozn. of turned chair's" £1
1681 "2 green chairs" 4s.
    "6 green chairs & wicker chaire" 12s. (dining room)
1686 "Five new Bass chaires" 10s.
1687 "Three Rush Chaires" 7s.
1690 "7 Green flagg chairs" 14s.
1691 "12 Du[t]ch bass chaires" £1.4
1693 "3 high flagg chairs" 4s. 6d.
    "3 low ditto" 3s.
1693 "6 rush Chaires" 6s. (kitchen)
    "6 rush Chairs" 9s. ("Chamber next the Street")
1696 "[11] matted chairs" 16s. 6d.
1698 "5 Straw bottom chairs & 3 cushions" 9s. (parlor)
1699 "1 great turned chair" (parlor)
    "10 matted chairs" (kitchen)
1711 "9 bass bottom'd Chairs" 20s. (chamber over the dining room)
    "11 bass bottom'd Chairs" 20s. (hall)
1713 "16 Ordinary Chairs" £2
1716 "6 old Flag chairs" 9s.
1729 "[9] Embowed or hollow back Chairs wth fine bass Bottoms" £9[4]

If we were to be consistent with written period terminology, we would have to abandon our fanciful labels and refer to these chairs by the names mentioned in the list—bass or flag or rush or straw or matted bottom or green chairs—or be satisfied to call them turned chairs, after the craft that produced them.

The idea that spindle-back chairs were the earliest type made in New England has long been the starting point for the chronological study of the kinds of turned chairs first made in New England. A corollary of this idea has been that the slat-back chair emerges as a form sometime toward the end of the seventeenth century. A glance at the list of typical inventory references above reveals that neither of these ideas is confirmed (or denied) by the documentary evidence. The chronological precedence of spindle-back chairs seems to be partially based upon the notion that they are more or less the same as chairs illustrated in early medieval European manuscripts and therefore *ought* to be the earliest made here. The rest of the spindle backs' right to precedence comes from their traditional association with first generation immigrants to this country.

If we rely on the written records we cannot then prove the widely accepted idea that spindle-back chairs are the earliest type to be made by turners in this country. Nor can we prove that slat-back chairs were relatively rare in New England before the last quarter of the seventeenth century and enjoyed their greatest popularity in the eighteenth century. Here, we are faced with a clear case in which the furniture must be studied as a document of itself. Even so this approach is fraught with enormous difficulties. No seventeenth-century turner ever intended his products to last for three or more centuries, and few chairs have survived the passage of time without having their posts mutilated or their seats replaced and without losing stretchers, arms, feet, finials, or handgrips.

Indeed, the loss of their seats—the feature by which most chairs were identified in inventories—means that we cannot now even be sure of the vegetable fibers with which these seats were originally made. Today, the leaves of a number of plants are twisted and then woven to make chair seats. "Rush bottomed" was commonly used in the nineteenth century to describe these seats. The word *rush* occasionally occurs in English records of the sixteenth century but in Massachusetts is rarely found in the seventeenth-century inventories of Essex and Suffolk counties and only occasionally appears in those of Middlesex. In New England documents, chairs are most frequently described as "flag bottomed," but because of the scarcity of seventeenth-century chairs with their original seats, the exact plant the word *flag* refers to is not absolutely certain. It is likely that this flag was the sweet sedge or sweet flag (*Acorus calamus*), and that the term was first introduced into New England by migrants from East Anglia, a region that had an abundance of flags in its marshy areas. East Anglian flags had long been exported to London and there used to strew the floors of the homes of wealthy householders and thereby fill the rooms with a sweet scent. The sweet flag is also native to New England and was noticed by John Josselyn—the first careful observer of New England's flora, perhaps as early as 1638, certainly in 1663—when he referred to it as "*Calamus Aromaticus*, or the sweet-smelling reed," which "Flowers in July." Over two centuries later, John Robinson noted that *Acorus* was "abundant" in Essex County.[5]

Despite the infrequent occurrence of *rush* in New England documents, it is probable that rush was used for chair seats in New England at an early date. Although Josselyn does not mention its presence in the seventeenth century, the "great bulrush" (*Scirpus validus*), observed by Robinson in the nineteenth, near "Pleasant Pond, Wenham, growing seven or eight feet high" was an ideal bottoming material. Eighteenth-century New England inventories, particularly those from the north shore of Boston Bay, continue the East Anglian habit of referring to chair bottoming material as "flags," perhaps regardless of botanical accuracy, although we can never be sure. It would take a sophisticated connoisseur of chair bottoms to tell the difference between the twisted leaves of a flag and those of a rush at sight, once they had been installed in a chair. The earliest inventory of an Essex County turner whom we know to have been making chairs is that of Thomas

Wickes of Salem, recorded in 1656. In addition to "made ware as greene Chayres, Wheeles, & Reems [rims]," Wickes's shop also contained £2.10. "in flagges."[6]

Another bottoming material mentioned in the inventories is "twine." John Baldwin of Salem, Massachusetts, had "thre Twin[e] chaiers" valued at 7s. 6d. at the time of his death in 1673.[7] Twine can obviously be made out of any fibrous material although jute and hemp are the usual ones today. Since "twine" describes the result of twisting materials together rather than the materials themselves, we have no way of knowing today what these twine bottoms were made of. Flags may have served for this purpose, but the inner bark of the native lime or linden tree (genus *Tilia*), also known as the bass or basswood tree, is a much more likely candidate and may have constituted what were called "bass bottom," "bassen," "bass," or "bast" chairs in the inventories.[8] This in turn suggests that "bass" and "twine" might be two different words describing the same thing. While the idea that the inner bark of a tree furnished chair-bottoming material to the early settlers of New England may seem far fetched to our generation, a seventeenth-century inventory taker could easily differentiate bast from rush or flag by color or texture. To some extent, it is tempting to believe that this material was not so often used as the inventories might suggest. No New England examples of it that have survived from the seventeenth, eighteenth, or nineteenth century have come to my attention, and, given the sometimes ambiguous terminology inventory takers are accused of using, the word "bass" may merely have represented, in one English regional dialect, a generic term for a vegetable fiber.

Could bass-bottom chairs have a somewhat less abstruse explanation? Could they have been something so simple as what we today call chairs with splint seats? Such bottoms are often found on chairs that look as if they ought to have been made in the seventeenth century, and many of these chairs bear no impressions of earlier flag bottoms on their seat lists. It is well known that the green wood of a number of trees, notably the basket oak (*Quercus prinus*) and the black ash (*Fraxinus nigra*), are capable of being split into long, thin strips that can be woven into chair bottoms. Could the wood of the bass tree similarly be split into bottoming material?

Alas, none of the surviving seats of seventeenth- or eighteenth-century splint-seat chairs in the Winterthur collection has been microanalyzed as basswood, and whatever splint seats were called in seventeenth-century New England still awaits discovery. In Pennsylvania, when such seats do appear in the eighteenth century (they may have been called "checked seats"), they are usually made of ash.[9]

In the same way that "twine bottom" probably refers to a technique of working a material rather than the material itself, "matted bottom" refers to the appearance of a seat rather than to a fiber. Matted bottoms were doubtless made of flags or rush and doubtless resembled those mats that are commonly mentioned in early inventories. Mats were used over the ropes laced between the rails of those bedsteads which did not have a "sacking" (canvas) bottom.[10] The inexpensive ones made in New England could have been woven out of native materials such as the common flag, or perhaps even corn husks.

That the husks, or shucks, from the ears of Indian corn were used to bottom American chairs in the seventeenth century seems too romantic to believe and is even harder to confirm by written documents. A few eighteenth-century chairs actually survive either with the original seat of this material or seat lists with the distinctive, wide impression left by braided husks (see catalogue entry 4). Seventeenth-century American turned chairs with their original seats are virtually nonexistent, so we cannot rule out the possibility of husk seats from that early date. Dried and twisted corn shucks are durable, as strong as flags, and easy to braid into uniform ropes that would be quite satisfactory for chair bottoming. On the negative side, they are short and require considerable splicing, and the thickness of the plaited ropes might require a modification of conventional, English chair-bottoming techniques. Inasmuch as Indian corn (maize) was not naturalized in England until recent times —although it was, along with the pumpkin, the staff of life as well as a medium of exchange for many Americans of the first generation—the use of its shucks for chair bottoms cannot be a tradition brought from Europe and may well be the contribution of coastal Algonkian culture to seventeenth-century furniture. In contrast to continental Europe, New England references to "straw" as a chair-bottoming material are quite rare; the actual use of straw is another question.[11]

That spindle-back chairs were made in Northern Europe earlier than slat-back chairs is an unproved assumption; that spindle-back chairs clearly constituted the majority of turned chairs produced in England during the sixteenth and early seventeenth century is indisputable. If we can believe the drawings in manuscripts, slat-back chairs enjoyed their greatest vogue on the Continent. Inasmuch as English tastes and traditions dominated the furniture production of New England in the seventeenth century, and since virtually every example of the spindle-back chair illustrated in this book is derived from that English tradition, we shall consider this form first.

SPINDLE-BACK CHAIRS

The trade of the turner as chairmaker is relatively straightforward, and turned chairs are represented in manuscript drawings and stone carvings from the ninth through the fifteenth centuries, in paintings of the sixteenth century, and in American inventories of the seventeenth. Indeed, such chairs existed in antiquity, and the style in which they were made, the methods of producing them, and the habit of using them were never completely lost during the Middle Ages. Paul LaCroix published an excellent illustration of one taken from a miniature ninth- or tenth-century drawing in the Bibliothèque Nationale at Paris (fig. 25). This example has the suggestion of ancient classicism with a Byzantine overlay. The form of such chairs or the manner in which they were executed scarcely changed in the following centuries; a beautifully polychromed picture of a similar chair was illustrated in the Speyer Gospel, probably in the year 1197 (fig. 26). Despite their artistic license, these two pictures illustrate one element of the turned-chair maker's art: the turned grooves on the legs of the former

Fig. 25. LEFT. Bishop sitting on a turned chair. Drawing, ninth or tenth century. From LaCroix, *Arts in the Middle Ages and at the Period of the Renaissance,* p. 3.

Fig. 26. RIGHT. Bruchsal, a scene from the Speyer Gospel, 1197. Watercolor and ink. (Bruchsal 1, f.5ʳ, Badische Landes-bibliothek, Karlsruhe, Federal Republic of Germany.) Note the turned chair.

chair and the rings on the legs of the latter one very nearly coincide with the horizontal members which suggests that the artists who executed these pictures, perhaps as much as 400 years apart, were demonstrating that turners in the Middle Ages used the *compas à verge* in the same manner as had the earliest turners in America, to assure that crosspieces would line up squarely with uprights.[12]

Few chairs from the Middle Ages survive in Northern Europe and those that do are subject to conflicting opinions concerning their age. In the absence of carbon dating, the assertion of antiquity for many of these examples is based upon a good deal of faith. Richard D. Ryder's excellent article, "Four-legged Turned Chairs," deals with this problem in a forthright manner and includes not only a fine collection of illustrations from manuscripts of the twelfth through the fourteenth centuries, but also photographs of chairs in this style from England and Scandinavia.[13]

In contrast to the rarity of medieval turned chairs, a large number of triangular, or three-square, chairs with massive elements (fig. 27) can be found in the museums of England and America. These chairs are believed to date from the sixteenth century, but it is likely that the tradition of making such chairs was alive in parts of England in the seventeenth. These elaborately turned and studded chairs are generally reported, by the few courageous authors who have written about them, to have evolved from the triangular stools that were common throughout northern Europe in the Middle Ages. It is possible that the style of turning and studding (bosses?) lavished on these chairs came about in response to some high-style-fashion idea that we cannot any longer associate with the group or a date, but it is equally likely that they were made to display the skills of English turners, or "throwers" as they were sometimes called, and for their owners represented a sixteenth-century artisan's or cottager's gesture toward conspicuous consumption.[14] These chairs have neither flag nor splint bottoms but rather have seats made of flat boards and are perhaps called, strangely enough, "wooden chairs" in inventories.

While we could be tempted to see these triangular chairs as

predecessors of four-legged turned chairs and attempt to find some sort of evolutionary pattern involved here, it is more likely that the three-legged and four-legged traditions marched side by side through English chairmaking history from the time that turning was employed as a furniture-making craft in post-Roman Britain. So little is known about these chairs and their makers that it is still impossible to say whether they represent a rural turning phenomenon or an urban one. Considering that domestic furniture of any sort was uncommon in rural England prior to the middle of the sixteenth century, the idea that this tradition first appeared in urban areas where the accumulation of capital encouraged the creation and sale of furniture does not seem farfetched. If quality of workmanship can separate city work from village work, the surviving examples indicate that craftsmen in both places made these chairs. But the style of these massive chairs is so foreign to the cultivated taste of today that it tempts us to insist that such excesses would never have been committed in the style center that was London. It is likely, however, that the style became popular there, perhaps on rectangular-seat chairs, and was copied in the countryside, perhaps on chairs with triangular seats. This idea may never be proved since any examples that might be found today in the family that originally owned them surely would not be found in London, but rather in an undisturbed village which time has passed by. Indeed in 1761 Horace Walpole hoped to fill his house at Strawberry Hill with "old chairs the seats triangular, the backs, arms, and legs loaded with turnery."[15] He suggested his correspondent look for these in Herefordshire and Cheshire.

Triangular chairs were widely reproduced in the nineteenth

Fig. 27. John Carter, Horace Walpole's great cloister at Strawberry Hill. Circa 1775. Watercolor. (Lewis Walpole Library, Farmington, Conn.) The three-legged chairs were purchased by Walpole at the estate sale of Richard Bateman.

century, and many a prestigious museum, both in America and in England, believes it possesses one of these sixteenth-century rarities but is in actuality displaying a nineteenth-century reproduction or worse. Such is not the case with a famous example of this style made of European wood that has been well known in Massachusetts for almost two centuries as "The Harvard President's chair."[16] Who owned it originally and how it happened to come to Harvard around the middle of the eighteenth century is not known. Its fame has caused it to become symbolic of something more than itself and was the inspiration for an illustration in an 1884 compendium of ideas for Americans entitled *Household Conveniences*. There the rationale for having such a chair and the exhortation to make it one's self, combined with a perception of earlier days as being quaint, "rustic," and hence, crude, was stated thus:

a design of an antique chair which may be easily made. If the pattern is not exactly reproduced, it will suggest the putting together of a chair that will be both useful and ornamental, in the farmer's hall, or "front entry," on the piazza, or, if neatly made, even in the parlor. Those who have the use of a lathe can easily turn the parts, or, in the absence of this, such a chair would be pleasing even if made in rustic work, of such material as the red-cedar, or roots and branches of the mountain laurel.[17]

While many instances of medieval decoration on American case furniture of the seventeenth century exist, there is no firm evidence that chairs of this type were made in America. A very specific reference, however, demonstrates that at least one seventeenth-century Massachusetts household contained one of these chairs, although its place of origin remains conjecture:

the inventory of Richard Jacob of Ipswich, recorded on October 4, 1672, lists "1 3 Square chaire" valued at 4s. This listing was sandwiched between "two flag chaires" worth 4s. 6d. and "fower Lether chaires" worth 32s. total.[18] A chair of English elm (*Ulmus procera*) with a history of ownership in Topsfield, a neighboring town of Ipswich, is in the collection of the Smithsonian Institution. Aside from the two chairs little indisputable evidence can be found which argues that such chairs were present in seventeenth-century New England. None of the earliest seventeenth-century turners' inventories suggests that such chairs were being made in this country, for no three-square chairs appear among the "made ware" in turners' shops, and none of the examples in American collections can be shown to be made of American woods.[19] Of course it is always possible that we cannot recognize these chairs in an inventory because they might not have been called three-square chairs. If they were also known as "buffet" chairs, then John Baldwin of Salem, Massachusetts, possessed three of them, and they were valued at 4s. each when his inventory was filed on November 28, 1673.[20]

The description of a "turned stoole" illustrated in *The Academy of Armory*, written by Randle Holme in the second half of the seventeenth century, further suggests that these three-square chairs may have been known by yet another name. According to Holme, the "Turned stoole . . . [is] so termed because it is made by the Turner, or wheele wright, all of Turned wood, wrought with Knops and rings all ouer the feete [i.e., legs], these [stools] and the chaires, are generally made with three feete, but to distinguish them from the foure feete, you may terme them a three footed turned stoole or

Fig. 28. Dirck Hals, *A Party at Table*. 1626. Oil on wood (oak); H 11″ (28 cm), W 15¼″ (38.8 cm). (Reproduced by permission of the Trustees, The National Gallery, London.)

chaire."[21] The description of a three-legged stool and a three-legged chair, which obviously differ from each other only insofar as the latter possesses a back, makes us wonder if Holme has given us the description for the "back stool," that perplexing and contradictory reference which occasionally appears along with "leather chairs" in the same American inventory.[22]

Although these triangular chairs with their excess of ornament seem hopelessly archaic and provincial beside the Renaissance-inspired forms that we associate with the seventeenth century in England, a reference in the Court Minutes of the Worshipful Company of Turners of London indicates that the taste for overornamentation still had a place in England's style-setting capital. In November 1614, Henry Morris, who had applied to become a member of the company, was ordered to make as his "proof piece" (to demonstrate that he was capable of doing work of master quality) "a great Chaire wth two boards in the back and two rowes of turned pillers: & buttons." Judging from the description, the "buttons" were being applied to a four-square, slat-back chair. There are additional descriptions in these records for a great variety of forms itemized by names that are no longer familiar. How could we begin to find out what was meant by "a du[t]ch arme stoole for a man" (March 1612)? How did it differ from "a woman's armed stoole" (January 1616)? What

were "a duble table" (February 1629) and "a ffrench forme" (August 1637)?[23] Clearly these entries raise serious problems of terminology: how, for example, can a stool have arms? Obviously, in the same way that it can have a back—by no longer being something that we would recognize today as a stool at all. The difference between a man's stool and a woman's might well be one of size, as it was in the nineteenth century, but what constitutes the Dutchness of a "duch stoole?" Can we be sure that "Dutch" did not mean "German?" Perhaps we assume too much when we conclude that by the second quarter of the seventeenth century the taste for triangular chairs had become history. The painting by Dirck Hals illustrated in figure 28 shows a convivial group gathered around a charger of oysters, but are these individuals seated on "three-square chairs," "Dutch stools," or "back stools"?

While triangular-seat chairs appear to have evolved from a stool to which a back was added, no evidence demonstrates that the same craftsmen who made them did not also make four-square chairs. Although it is true that the type of ornamentation associated in England with three-square chairs is rarely found on four-square examples, it did occur at least once, on a child's highchair (fig. 29) now displayed at Hall's Croft, Stratford upon Avon. This chair is an example of the complexity of furniture history that makes it impossible for a

Fig. 29. Turned highchair, England, early seventeenth century. Oak; H 42″ (106.7 cm), W 19″ (48.3 cm). (Shakespeare Birthplace Trust, Stratford-upon-Avon, England. Photo: Symonds Collection, DAPC, Winterthur Library.)

Fig. 30. Turned great chair, possibly New Haven region, Conn., 1670–1700. All turned elements are black ash (*Fraxinus nigra*), seat boards are red oak (*Quercus rubra*); H 41½″ (105.4 cm), W 23″ (58.4 cm), D 16½″ (41.9 cm), SH 17½″ (44.5 cm). (Connecticut Historical Society, Hartford, bequest of Thomas Robbins.)

furniture historian to isolate the ingredients of living craft traditions and package them neatly in mutually exclusive compartments. It would, for example, be very convenient if we could assume that the three-square chair was essentially a rural phenomenon in England, as the Walpole evidence tends to suggest, and that the elaborately decorated, turned, four-square chairs with "buttons" were an urban style, as the London turners company records suggest. But the Hall's Croft chair combines the two traditions with such artistry that it denies those easy assumptions. Until we learn more about the urban turner's craft in England, the differences between rural and urban turned chairs will remain a mystery.[24]

Perhaps the most important feature of the three-square turned chair for the historian of American furniture is not that the chair is three-square or that four-square relatives of it exist in England, but that neither has a rush or flag bottom. A number of American seventeenth-century chairs have board seats, and

it is perhaps through this structural feature rather than stylistic attributes that we can distinguish the small group that constitutes the earliest chairs made in New England from the slightly later rush-bottom examples.

Two chairs with board seats that possess an ingeniously raked back, like that of the Hall's Croft chair, are now owned by the Connecticut Historical Society in Hartford and the Metropolitan Museum of Art in New York, and these may be the earliest chairs made in America. (On the basis of available information we cannot demonstrate that any of the challengers date any earlier.) The chair owned by the historical society (fig. 30) has belonged to that extraordinary institution since the 1840s. It appears in an 1845 daguerreotype, and it was discussed by Benson J. Lossing in a collection of miscellany published in 1851 under the title *Pictorial Field-Book of the Revolution*. Lossing wrote eloquently of the Reverend Thomas Robbins, the librarian of the historical society, and of the room then housed "in a fine edifice called the *Wadsworth Atheneum*." He also wrote about the "many historical curiosities in the library-room," and even sketched a few. Among them was this chair which his illustration shows then lacked the two flanking spindles of the back, subsequently expertly restored. Lossing noted that the chair "was an heir-loom in the family of one of the earlier settlers of New Haven. It is made wholly of turned wood (except the board bottom), fastened together by wooden pegs. . . . The material is ash and its construction ingenious."[25] The records of the historical society from this period in its history are not in good order. Robbins was photographed sitting in the chair. His diary entry for September 19, 1831, notes that he had just obtained the ancient chair which had belonged to his grandfather, a chair that had been imported from England. It has been suggested that Col. James Ward was one of possible donors of this chair. Inasmuch as Ward was a collector of antiquities, we would be hard pressed to demonstrate that the chair was inherited rather than purchased.[26]

Microanalysis of the Connecticut Historical Society chair reveals that its turned members are made of black ash (*Fraxinus nigra*) and its seat board is an oak of the red group (*Quercus rubra*), both American woods. Yet the chair seems so English in character that its American origin would be questioned, were it not for an almost identical chair, slightly more elaborately turned, in the collection of the Metropolitan Museum of Art. Grooves on the inner margin of the seat lists of the museum's chair indicate that it, too, originally had a board seat (which has recently been restored). The chair came to the museum with a history of ownership in the Stryker family of Long Island, and the high quality of turning suggests that it may have been made when the tradition of its turning was somewhat fresher to its maker and that the chair thus dates slightly earlier than its Connecticut cousin.[27] Since much of western Long Island was settled by families from coastal Connecticut, it is possible that the museum's chair originated in Connecticut. (In contrast, evidence of settlement in Connecticut by Long Island families is rare.) However, we need not conclude that both chairs *had* to be made in the same place: all that their resemblance indicates is that both could have been made by the same craftsman or by a master and his apprentice. We must keep in mind that many craftsmen in seventeenth-century America moved about. It is slightly more likely that the historical society example came from coastal Connecticut than Long Island because the style of the turning is related to that on a chair, probably of the next generation, in the Milford Historical Society, Milford, Connecticut, which has a tradition of ownership in the Camp family of Milford.[28] It is possible, too, that the frequent appearance of redundant double arms in turned chairs made later along coastal Connecticut trace their origins back to these two chairs and the locally diffused shop practices of the craftsmen who made them.

The construction of the chairs at the Connecticut Historical Society and the Metropolitan Museum of Art is quite ingenious, as Lossing observed. Their seats are considerably narrower at the back than at the front, which relates them visually, if not linearly, to the three-square style. They are

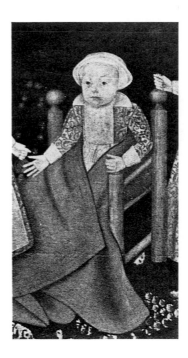

Fig. 31. Dirck Hals, detail from the *Children of Thomas Lucy*. Charlecote Park, Warwickshire, early seventeenth century. (Photo: Benno M. Forman.) Although the cushion covers the seat, this chair appears to have a board rather than a rush bottom, since rush is not indicated on the seat list; moreover, the lists do not protrude through the uprights. Had these details been present in the chairs, it is unlikely that they would have escaped the limner who painted the details of the carpet and costumes so meticulously. The painting also gives lie to the fondly held idea that oriental carpets were so valuable that they were used only on tables.

designed in such a way that the upper posts of the back are no farther apart than the front legs. Indeed, the turner who designed them wished to execute as much as he could upon a lathe. To a technically minded person, the design of these chairs is an exciting and brilliantly rational solution to the problem of making a chair with a canted back. The rear legs and upper back posts radiate like two spokes of a wheel from the horizontal lower back rail, which functions as a hub. In the long view of furniture history, this technique, which introduces a note of comfort into the common man's chair, is innovative, even though the result might look to the modern eye like nothing so much as a chair made with giant Tinker Toy parts. If an English-trained turner wanted to make a chair with a canted back, this must have been the only way he could do it, and the absence of chairs made with two-axis turning among the earliest examples from New England is prima facie evidence of the absence of that technique in those parts of England from which the earliest emigrant turners came. Why then, we may ask, did turned-chair makers not resort to shaping the rear stiles of their chairs in the way that joiners did? The answer is twofold: First, it would then no longer be a turner's chair; and second, at least as far as London was concerned from about 1632 on, turners were prohibited, by an order of the Aldermen's Court, from using any of the tools of the joiners' trade, particularly the "grouffe or plough plaine."[29]

The groove or plow plane is precisely the tool needed to install board seats in turned chairs. The seats are flat boards, sawn or riven, planed smooth, featheredged around the perimeter, and fitted into a groove planed into the inside margin of the seat lists. If a turner elects to use a board seat, the seat lists must all enter the posts at the same level (as opposed to the flag-bottom chairs on which the side lists are slightly higher than the front and rear ones). Some arrangement had to be made to avoid weakening the legs at this juncture. The early seventeenth-century solution was to use thick legs that were considerably more massive than were necessary to support the weight of a sitter. A second problem confronting the maker of turned chairs with board seats was that the weight of the sitter tended to rotate the lists downward, which in turn ejected the boards. This undesirable eventuality was forestalled in the Connecticut Historical Society and Metropolitan Museum chairs by creating large round tenons on the front and rear seat lists which were intersected, inside the legs, by smaller round tenons of the side lists. The small tenons lock the large ones in place so that they cannot rotate. The side lists are further made fast by pins inserted into them through the posts and the front and rear lists.

Auger holes drilled all the way through the uprights are atypical on American turned chairs of the seventeenth century, except on the few early and well-known examples discussed here. This practice is common in northern European chairs and these chairs are sometimes confused with American examples stylistically. If country of origin is important, a museum or collector about to acquire a turned chair with protruding tenons would be well advised to have the wood of which it is made microanalyzed before purchasing it.

The Connecticut Historical Society and Metropolitan Museum chairs as well as the Hall's Croft chair graphically reveal what happened in London early in the seventeenth century: turners were using techniques of the joiner to create a chair that competed in comfort with wainscot and upholstered chairs. In retaliation, the joiners protected themselves by obtaining a court order that prevented the turners from using the crucial tool—the groove plane—without which they could not make a competitive chair. If the American board-seat chairs are derived from London prototypes, it is likely that they were made by turners trained in London prior to 1632, assuming that the Aldermen's Court order was enforced. If the chairs are derived from examples made in rural England, outside the court's jurisdiction, then 1632 is not meaningful in dating the American examples.

The raked back of a chair is important because, like the dog that did not bark in the night in one Sherlock Holmes story, it represents a feature conspicuously absent from the vast majority of English and northern European, provincial, four-square chairs made from the Middle Ages until well into the seventeenth century.

Some evidence that board-seat chairs were made outside of London is suggested by the simple, four-square child's chair illustrated in the early seventeenth-century portrait of the children of Thomas Lucy III of Charlecote Park, Warwickshire (fig. 31).[30] Although the ubiquitous cushion (that all such chairs must have had if a person were to sit in them for a very long time) covers the surface of the seat, the absence of rush on the side seat lists of this meticulously limned picture suggests a seat composed of boards. Moreover, the lists and arms do not protrude through the uprights, which confirms that board-seat chairs did not have to have lists with protruding tenons.

Two board-seat American chairs of the four-square type, like the Lucy chair, do not have a raked back. These two—the Elder Brewster and Governor Bradford chairs—form the touchstone by which all American seventeenth-century chairs have been dated. Because of their association with these two

Fig. 32. Turned chair. From Holme, *Academy of Armory*, 2: bk. 3, ch. 14, facing p. 18, fig. 69. (Winterthur Library.)

early and prominent figures of American history, William Brewster (ca. 1566–1643) and William Bradford (1589–1657), it has been often assumed that they represent the earliest turned chairs made in America. They are virtually identical to each other. Both are owned by the Pilgrim Society of Plymouth, Massachusetts, and are displayed at Pilgrim Hall. Recent microanalyses of the woods confirm the American origin of both. The Brewster chair is made of either American red ash or its subvariety green ash (in either case, *Fraxinus pennsylvanica*), while the Bradford chair is made primarily of American black ash (*Fraxinus nigra*). Both chairs are distinguished by a row of spindles between each arm and seat list, two rows of spindles between the seat lists and the lower stretchers, and two rows of spindles in the back. This last distinguishing feature may be the one described in the London turners company minutes of 1614, as "two rowes of turned pillers."[31] If so, then what we call "spindles" were "pillars" in the early seventeenth century, although the only way to confirm this is to find a turner's estate inventory that was taken by another turner.

The spindles under the seat are another matter and might lead us to suspect that the unknown maker of these chairs had picked up a northern European chairmaking tradition during the twelve years that the Pilgrim fathers spent in Holland. This is an unsafe assumption if it is based purely upon stylistic grounds, since English chairs with this feature are common. Randle Holme illustrated such a chair (fig. 32) in the *Academy of Armory*. Unfortunately, Holme tells us only what we already know: he says that this is a "Turned chaire with Armes."[32]

While the ownership of the Brewster chair cannot be traced back much earlier than 1841, when Alexander Young illustrated it in *Chronicles of the Pilgrim Fathers*, the identity of details of its turning and the placement of the scribe marks on this chair and the Bradford chair (fig. 33) confirm that both came from the same shop. The Bradford chair has a nineteenth-century-paper label glued to its seat which gives a pedigree for it. Assuming that the chair did descend in the paternal line, the successive owners of the chair were William Bradford, his widow Alice Southworth Bradford, Maj. William Bradford, David Bradford, Lydia Bradford Russell, Nathaniel Russell, Jr., and then his sister Catherine E. Russell Hedge. The chair

Fig. 33. Turned great chair, possibly made in Plymouth, Mass., 1630–55. American black ash (*Fraxinus nigra*), red ash (*Fraxinus pennsylvanica*), and a later seat of white pine (*Pinus strobus*); H 45″ (114.3 cm), W 24½″ (62.2 cm), D 18½″ (47 cm), SH 17⅞″ (45.4 cm). (Courtesy, Pilgrim Society of Plymouth, Mass., gift of the heirs of William Hedge. Photo: Jock Gill.) The chair may have belonged to Gov. William Bradford. It is virtually identical to a chair believed to have belonged to William Brewster, also owned by the Pilgrim Society of Plymouth.

remained in the Hedge family until it was given to the Pilgrim Society by Henry R. Hedge in 1953. We can place the Bradford chair in Plymouth at least as early as 1769 when it is said to have been used at a ceremony celebrating the landing of the Pilgrim Fathers.[33] With such a long subsequent association in Plymouth, it is possible that prior to 1769 the chair had not traveled far from the place in which it was originally owned. The pedigree that can be constructed makes the Bradford chair perhaps an even more important document of its time than the better-known but less well preserved chair associated with Elder Brewster.

As is common with furniture said to have been owned by illustrious personages, the Brewster and Bradford inventories neither specifically confirm nor deny the traditions of ownership that accompany these chairs. Elder Brewster had two homes at the time of his death on April 10, 1644. His

Plymouth house contained only "1 chaire," valued at 4s. The house at his farm at Duxbury likewise contained only "1 chaire," and it was valued at the small sum of 1s. When Governor Bradford died in 1657 his inventory specified "2 great wooden Chaires" valued together at 8s. His widow Alice died 13 years later, and the wooden chairs were again listed, this time valued at 6s.[34] Since these "wooden" chairs are not the "carved chairs" (wainscot chairs) listed elsewhere in the inventory and again in his widow's, nor the 5 "leather chairs," and since it is impossible for us to imagine chairs made of anything *but* wood in seventeenth-century Plymouth, then some other reason for characterizing them as "wooden" must have existed. A consistent interpretation is that the takers of these two inventories were following the custom of their times by referring to these two chairs in terms of their bottoming and that these wooden chairs might well be turned chairs with wooden seats, such as the Bradford and Brewster chairs both have. This idea is further enhanced by the 4s. each appraised value—an appropriate value for a turned chair—as opposed to the 12s. each appraised value of his carved, wainscot chairs. Whether the turned chairs owned by Governor Bradford are represented by the Bradford chair in Plymouth cannot be proved, but the inventories seem to demonstrate that he did possess turned chairs with wooden seats (see also catalogue entry 4). To forestall the wild speculation that Bradford owned *both* of the chairs that are today displayed at Pilgrim Hall, it should be noted that this could be argued only feebly: while both were made by the same turner, they do not appear to have been made at the same time and are not a pair. On the basis of the available evidence, neither the Brewster nor the Bradford chair can be accurately dated, which is a pity because they are the most famous of their kind in America.

Study of the Brewster and Bradford chairs produces more confusion than clarification, for one may be tempted to see a northern European influence in their style because these two chairs possess a structural quirk that is common in northern European chairs but rare in English examples. This quirk reveals another solution to the problem of how to put a board seat in a turned chair. In the Brewster and Bradford chairs, the problem was efficiently solved by working rectangular tenons on the ends of the front and rear seat lists and then rectangular mortise holes in the posts (fig. 34). The rectangular tenons are further held fast by the round tenons of the side seat lists, which intersect them and are themselves pinned in place. If nothing else, this technique permits a reduction in the thickness of the posts. It is even more fascinating to speculate on *where* this solution to the problem came from. Since it is first observable on American board-seat chairs of a probable early date from the Plymouth Colony—New England's earliest permanent settlement—and does not appear on the Hall's Croft board-seat highchair nor on the Connecticut Historical Society chair (see figs. 29 and 30), we might be tempted to speculate that an as yet unidentified turner who lived with the Pilgrims in Holland between 1608 and 1620 picked up the technique there and introduced it into New England (see also fig. 52). Unfortunately, this explanation is inadequate; a number of English triangular chairs have rectangular tenons worked on their seat lists, notably an excellent example in the Ashmolean

Museum, Oxford, and two at the Philadelphia Museum of Art. If these three chairs are of English origin, as they seem to be, they illustrate the presence of the technique in England as well as on the Continent. More specifically, they suggest that the rectangular tenon in English chairs may reflect the influence of the many turners who fled northern Europe during the second half of the sixteenth century and settled in the crowded London parishes of St. Botolph's in Bishopsgate, St. Olave's in Southwark, and in Surrey. Turners like John Corborowe, who left Aachen for England at age 22 in 1553, became masters of emigré shops and introduced new construction methods to English-born woodworkers who in turn passed them on.[35] With these facts in mind, we can explore two likely possIbilities. The rectangular tenon came to New England in the mind of an English turner who had trained in a London shop run by an emigrant Dutch or German master, or it arrived in the mind of a turner who trained in Leiden and migrated to Plymouth along with the Pilgrim fathers. If the former is true, we should also find chairs with rectangular tenons in the environs of Boston, where turners from London like Thomas Edsall were active by 1635.

One such chair, known, oddly enough, as the Miles Standish chair, survives in ruinous condition. It has descended through many generations of the Lincoln family of Hingham. Hingham is on the southern shore of Boston harbor, and it supplied timber and foodstuffs to the port city throughout the seventeenth and early eighteenth centuries. The tortuous pedigree of the chair provoked Wallace Nutting to comment, "the expert in evidence will drive a coach and four between some of . . . [its] lines."[36] Nutting brilliantly analyzed the remains of this remarkable chair and pointed out that missing spindles between the arms and seat lists had been replaced with spindles taken from an eighteenth-century pew originally in the Old Ship Meeting House in Hingham. Recent work by John D. Alexander, Jr., also suggests that at one point the chair may have been totally disassembled, its rear posts again turned on a lathe, and then rebuilt. Although this chair has lost its original crest rail, its finials and handgrips, the lower half of each leg (and hence its lower stretchers), the spindles under its arms, and its board seat, and although the spindles of the back have been flattened, probably in the nineteenth century with a view to making it either more comfortable or more stylish in the arrow-back taste, what remains is striking in that the chair does not closely resemble the Brewster and Bradford examples. One feature that sets the Standish chair apart is the baluster shape turned on the front posts between the seat list and armrest and on the rear posts above their juncture with the arms (see catalogue entry 5). In addition, the work lines used by the turner of the Standish chair do not match up with those on the posts of the Bradford and Brewster chairs, strongly suggesting that they came from two distinct shops, both of which used the rectangular tenon.

While the Brewster and Bradford chairs seem to have been made in a Plymouth shop, the Standish chair was most likely produced in either Boston or nearby Charlestown, the latter itself a major woodworking center.[37] The urban origin of the Standish chair is based upon the histories of ownership of an additional three wood-bottom chairs, all of which have sound

Fig. 34. Detail of the rectangular mortise-and-tenon construction of the great chair that is believed to have belonged to William Brewster. Note that the round tenon of the side seat list intersects this joint and is pinned in place. (Courtesy, Pilgrim Society of Plymouth, Mass. Photo: Robert Blair St. George.)

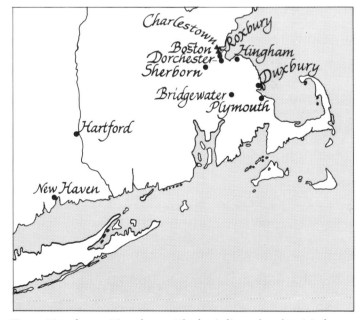

Fig. 35. Map of eastern Massachusetts. The dots indicate where the original owners of board-seat chairs lived; the triangles indicated the major craft centers where documented London-trained first-generation turners worked. (Drawing: Robert Blair St. George and Wade Lawrence.)

histories of ownership and use in Massachusetts' Suffolk County during the seventeenth century: the Mather family highchair, the Eliot chair (now lost), and the Tufts family armchair—the last identified by Nutting as "the most perfect Brewster type." When the locations of all these wood-seat

Fig. 36. Turned highchair, probably Boston or Charlestown, Mass., 1637–63. Poplar (genus *Populus*); H 38⅝″ (98.1 cm), W 18¼″ (46.3 cm), D 14⅝″ (47.2 cm), SH 23¼″ (59.1 cm). (Courtesy, American Antiquarian Society, Worcester, Mass., gift of Hannah Mather Crocker, 1819.) The chair has a history in the Mather family.

chairs are plotted on a map, the two probable centers of production, Boston and Charlestown, emerge (fig. 35).

The Mather family highchair (fig. 36) is a richly evocative artifact because Cotton Mather probably sat in it, no matter how difficult it is for us to imagine that this passionate representative of New England religious rectitude was ever a child. The chair was illustrated in *Furniture of Our Forefathers* (1900) by Esther Singleton who wrote that "it was brought from England by Richard Mather in 1635. It has long remained in the family and was used by Increase, Cotton and Samuel Mather." When Wallace Nutting pictured the chair in the revised edition of *Furniture of the Pilgrim Century* a quarter of a century later, he made no mention of Richard, Increase, Samuel, or the chair's English origin.[38] Whether instinct or experience led Nutting to believe that the chair was made in America, his belief has been confirmed by microanalysis; the chair is made of poplar (*Populus*), wood that we now know

was frequently used with other American woods in the furniture of eastern Massachusetts. Indeed poplar appears in the early chair illustrated in Nutting's *Furniture Treasury* as no. 1801 (now in the collection of the Wadsworth Atheneum, Hartford, Connecticut) and a related chair at Winterthur (catalogue entry 1), and its continued use in the eighteenth century, as is demonstrated by the inventory of John Corning, a turned-chair maker of Beverly, Massachusetts, will be discussed later in this chapter.

If the Mather family highchair was used by Eleazer Mather, the first son of Richard Mather born in Massachusetts, it would date from around 1637, and we could assume it was made in Dorchester. Yet no turners who had trained in London—and thus been exposed to the rectangular tenon—are known to have been working in Dorchester by 1637, or during the rest of the seventeenth century. If, however, this was originally the highchair of Cotton Mather (b. 1663), the later "eccentric . . . never dying author of the *Magnalia*," then it must certainly have been made either in Boston, where his father Increase served as minister of the "new" North Church from 1664 until his death in 1723, or in nearby Charlestown.[39] The dating is further clouded, for, despite the reliance on the rectangular tenon, the chair appears never to have had a board seat.

It is frustrating to be unable to articulate the difference between the stylistic attributes of a chair that could have been made in 1637 and one of 1663, a full generation later. The problem reflects issues revealed by Massachusetts spindle-back chairs in general: the nature of the turner's craft means that there are only so many stylistic attributes by which we judge the date of a chair. The design of a finial and the shape of a baluster are about all there is to go on. The baluster forms on the spindles of the Brewster and Bradford chairs—which may predate the middle of the seventeenth century—if inverted and greatly enlarged would serve nicely as the balusters on any of the court cupboards of Massachusetts with carved dates of the 1680s. In the absence of any dynamic stylistic change in the case furniture of Massachusetts until the very end of the century, we should perhaps not expect to be able to recognize much change in the even more conservative art of turned-chair making.

A highchair that superficially resembles the Mather highchair has a history of ownership in the Sumner family of Massachusetts. Wood analysis revealed that it is made of American silver maple (*Acer saccharinum*).[40] Its finial is similar to that of a chair associated with John Eliot, and like the Eliot chair it has an unusual feature—three upper back rails.

The Eliot chair, perhaps the earliest of the Boston-Charlestown area group, was stolen from the First Congregational Church in Roxbury about twenty years ago. It is known to us today only through an inaccurate copy at the Dedham Historical Society, a woodcut published a century ago in the *Memorial History of Boston*, and a poor photograph that probably dates from the closing years of the nineteenth century (fig. 37). John Eliot, one of the earliest settlers in Boston Bay, came to New England in 1631. After less than a year in Boston, he was appointed minister to the congregation in Roxbury, where he lived for the remainder of his life. The chair bore an inscription that stated it "once belonged to the

Rev. John Eliot, of Roxbury, commonly called the Apostle to the Indians, and was used in his study." It remained in a Roxbury family for many years before being given to the Reverend Thaddeus Mason Harris, who presented it to the church.[41] The chair had a board seat, turned and ornamented spindles between the arms and the seat lists, and two rows of spindles across the upper back and between the front seat list and the bottom front stretcher. Additionally it had three upper back rails, the topmost of which was missing by 1880. If we accept the Roxbury history of ownership—regardless of whether this was John Eliot's chair—and can assume that it is of American origin, then it is likely that the chair was made in Boston or Charlestown, in which case the chair further demonstrates that the style and techniques of manufacture heretofore associated with the Brewster and Bradford chairs were also known and used outside of the Plymouth Colony.

The Eliot chair has characteristics that differentiate it stylistically from the chairs once owned in the Plymouth Colony. First it had three top rails instead of two. Second, the turning of the remaining decorative crest rail is strongly centralized and distinctively different. Third, the compressed balls on the stiles are separated from each other by a disk. Fourth, the finials, although missing their top plume or flame, have more elements than the documentable Plymouth Colony examples.

If the Mather and Eliot chairs are from Boston or Charlestown, then the true place of origin of a number of chairs with characteristics related to them has been obfuscated by the generic term "Brewster Chair" by which they have been identified. Prominent among this group is the handsome Tufts family chair now in the collection of the Metropolitan Museum of Art. It is illustrated in Nutting's *Furniture Treasury* as no. 1799, is made of ash, originally had a board seat (which has recently been restored), and has rectangular tenons on the front and rear seat lists that protrude through the uprights at the side. Nutting described the chair as having been purchased from a Tufts family descendant who lived in Sherborn, a town lying west of Charlestown. The Tufts family was originally from Medford, and if the chair was first owned in Medford, it confirms that wood-seat chairs were made in a central place, the metropolitan center formed by Boston and Charlestown, and then purchased by individuals living in outlying rural centers both north and south. Taken as a group, the Mather, Eliot, and Tufts chairs are the only evidence we have as to what the spindle-back chairs of urban Massachusetts were like during the seventeenth century. It is almost laughable to suggest that these chairs alone can define a Boston area style, but they are the only leads we have. If, however, the argument advanced in my discussion of slat-back chairs with regard to the English family chair (see fig. 42) is cogent, then the logical place of origin for the style in which all of these chairs are made *must* be either Boston or Charlestown, despite the slender evidence that supports it.

As so often happens with research into the history of furniture, the written documents dealing with urban areas are rich and tantalizing but the objects that could illuminate them go unrecognized. Where, for example, are the early seventeenth-century Boston-made turned chairs and tables

Fig. 37. Turned great chair, Boston or Charlestown, Mass. 1630–55. (Photo, late nineteenth-century.) The chair had an Eliot family history; present location of the chair is unknown.

with columnar shapes derived from the London style of turning, as are found on the Boston case furniture with applied half spindles? Have these tables and chairs been misidentified as Connecticut made?[42]

The presumed village or rural origin of the earliest American turned chairs has never been subjected to critical scrutiny. The presence of six turners in Boston prior to 1660 indicates there was a flourishing market for turners there. Further, the trade must have stratified in terms of price, quality, and design, for it supported turners of widely divergent backgrounds. William Betts probably came from a small village in England, while John Wallington and Thomas Edsall came from London, and Robert Winsor, Jr., came from Southwark, London's most celebrated furniture-producing liberty. From this information alone it is easy to surmise that the turner's art was practiced on at least two levels in early Boston: the first was at the standard of English village work, the second must have been equivalent to what was currently being made in London.

According to the first volume of *Suffolk Deeds*, John Wallington "of London, Turner," purchased a farm at "the Rocks goeing to Lin," in 1645. The minutes of the court of the turners company of London show that a John Wallington was elected to the court on October 7, 1605, and to "Master of the company" on June 22, 1613. His son John, Jr., was apprenticed to him in August 1615 and is most likely the man who migrated to New England and died in Newbury after living in this coundry only a decade.[43] Thomas Edsall came to New England in April 1635. He was probably the younger brother of Henry Edsall, a freeman of the London turner company in October 1632 and master of the company from May 23, 1661, until May 28, 1663. Thomas Edsall lived, worked, and apparently prospered in Boston and had at least two sons, Thomas and Henry, who followed him in the trade. He was 47 years old when he came to America. He died in either 1653 or 1676.[44]

The third turner from the London area, Robert Winsor, Jr., we know was living in Boston by 1644. When he wrote his will, on April 24, 1679, he described himself as a "block-maker," a lucrative area of turning in which he specialized, at least in his later years.[45]

In Charlestown, the Larkin family dominated an extremely active turned-chair industry from the seventeenth century until at least the middle of the eighteenth century. The inventory of John Larkin (d. 1678) shows that his well-equipped shop contained all of the tools and materials necessary for the fabrication of chairs, as well as the production of stools, wheels, sieves, and wooden eating utensils:

	£	s.	d.
per turning strings. 6s. [t]wine. 3s. per 12 duz sive bottoms. 3£	3	09	00
per 7 sives. 7s. per bowls. 2£	2	07	00
per 12 doz chareframes. 7£ Lampblacke. 1s.	7	01	00
per sive rims. 10s. per wheel rims. 3£	3	10	00
per trenchers. 3s. wool. 1s. ssheaths. 1s.	0	05	00
per fishing craft. 3s. Leathr. 3s. pease. 6s.	0	12	00
per flaggs. 1£ a parcel of cards. 1s.	1	01	00
per turning strings. 2s. piercing stocks. 3s.	0	05	00
per a skrue & nutt. 10s. wheele. 4s.	0	14	00
per wheel frame. 5s. lumber with a vice. 1£ 10s.	1	15	00
per working tools. 3£. taps & ffasuets. 10s.	3	10	00
per a frame of a stool & lumber	0	11	06
per lumber. 1£. 8 new chairs, 11s.	1	11	00
per bricks. 1£ 4s. 5 doz: chair frames. 3£ 12s.	4	16	00
per 9 doz; ditto. 9£ 11s. lumber. 1£. oars. 11s.	7	02	00
per timber. 4£ 2s. per 1 doz grundlstones. 3£ 12s.	7	14	00[46]

The extent of Larkin's chair production—a total of 312 ready-made chair frames presumably awaiting bottoms made from the "flaggs" he had on hand—demonstrates the market for his wares. The inventory also proves that all these chairs were made on a pole lathe powered by a treadle and "turning strings," and that some of the chairs, if not all, were finished with black coloring made from "Lampblacke" that had been ground and mixed with a medium (probably oil). And Larkin was only one of the many turners working in Charlestown. This large shipbuilding port had also enticed others. Henry Harris, a turner who had apprenticed to Thomas Edsall in Boston, set up shop adjacent to its busy waterside in the late 1660s or early 1670s.[47]

With the web of London tradition spreading with apprenticeship and migration to encompass turners working in Boston and Charlestown, it is impossible to place the board-seat rectangular-tenon chairs with any greater precision than in these two gradually merging, urban centers. As turners working here accelerated their output in response to widening circles of coastal and overland trade, we should expect that some of their chairs will appear with rural New England histories of ownership; we might also expect that, as some of these turners themselves moved to exploit new markets in the countryside, some rural-made chairs will appear to resemble closely the urban-made examples.

Despite assiduous search, the records of nearly every New England town have revealed little about the way in which rural and village turners practiced their trade during the seventeenth century. The public records of Boston, however, are more rewarding. Among the files of the Superior Court of Suffolk County is an instrument that answers one question: How many chair frames could a turner be expected to make in a day in the year 1666? The answer is 2½. The remarkable document that reveals this information was written because an apprentice named Henry Harris, after only two years of training with Boston's Thomas Edsall, decided he had spent long enough learning his trade and decamped for Charlestown and apparently found employment. Edsall sued for the unexpired term of the indenture and the judge decided:

According to a covenent . . . dated the 19th day of March 1666/7, . . . now to end all differences, I judge and order the said Harris either to dwell with & serve the said Edsell eight whole weeks beginning on the 17th Day of this June & to make every of the said weekes fifteen chair frames called ——— [illegible] good & merchantable or else shall make one whole hundred and twenty such frames in the whole 8 week . . . the said Edsell finding & allowing unto him the said Harris sufficient place, tooles & stuff to make them with & so forth.[48]

Although it is important to confirm what numerous surviving chairs suggest—that their makers did not serve a full apprenticeship—the documents concerning the Edsall-Harris controversy do not tell us how much a newly made Boston turned chair in 1666 was worth. Not until the inventory of Nathaniel Adams, Sr., was taken on November 1, 1675, does that information appear, a full generation after Boston was well settled. Two successive entries in Adams's shop inventory reveal that "new Chaires" were appraised at 2s. each while "chaires unbottomed" were valued at 18d. each, thus indicating that a chair bottom was worth 6d.[49] Adams's "flagges" used for the bottoming were of negligible value. Flags were generally itemized as "bundles of flags," and a "bundle," far from being the indefinite quantity that it would appear to modern eyes to be, was in all probability a specific unit of size that was understood by buyer and seller, like a cord of wood is today.[50] A "bundle of flagges" was worth a little more than 3d. in 1734 when the inventory of John Corning was taken at Beverly, Massachusetts.[51] At such a small price, a bundle of flags could not have been a very large quantity, and was perhaps only enough for two chair bottoms. If so, it was equal to about a quarter of the cost of installing it.

Chair bottoming in colonial America was doubtless a profession that was more tedious than artful and very likely quite easy to learn. If the gathering of flags was anything like the gathering of flax, we can assume that it was done by the chairmaker's apprentice or sons and daughters if the shop was near a place where flags grew. If the chairmaker lived in a city, his time and that of his apprentice could be more profitably spent at the lathe, and he likely bought his flags, as did Solomon Fussell of Philadelphia in the eighteenth century.[52]

The art of bottoming as practiced today is the same as it has been for centuries. The leaves of the appropriate aquatic plant are gathered and dried. Before they are woven into the seat, they are wetted to make them supple, and then they are twisted into twine—the larger or thicker end of the leaf twisted with the smaller end of the next to make the twine of uniform thickness. The twines are then wrapped around the seat lists, from the corners toward the center, until the complete, matted bottom is formed. As the dampened flags dry, the bottom shrinks making a tight seat and, by its tension, helps to hold the chair together. At the price of 6d. per seat, allowing ⅓ for flags, ⅓ for the labor, and ⅓ for profit, an efficient bottomer might have been expected to complete perhaps nine seats in a long, seventeenth-century working day. While we may assume that this sort of work could be done by anyone without particular skills, we know that at least in one instance an "old and decayed" turner, Henry Fane of Boston, was bottoming chairs in the year 1672 when he was 83.[53]

Although the seventeenth-century-style spindle-back chair appears to have persisted in England throughout the eighteenth century and well into the nineteenth in only a slightly altered form, the evidence suggests that this was not the case in New England.[54] Either because faster communication between the cities and their hinterland existed here or because economic success in the exploitation of America's natural riches permitted Americans to be more fashion conscious, only a few American spindle-back chairs reveal the stylistic attributes that suggest they were made after the introduction of the William and Mary style. The tendency, especially in New England, was to replace older chairs with ones in the newer fashions: for better use, the banister-back chairs (very much a part of the traditional turner's art), and for slightly more comfort, less expense, and assuredly less fashion, the slat-back chairs.

CONNOISSEURSHIP OF AMERICAN
SPINDLE-BACK CHAIRS

After the table, the chair is the second most anonymous form of furniture. (At least chairs are sometimes remembered, if only apocryphally, because distinguished people sat in them.) The earlier an American chair is in style, the more difficult it has been for historic tradition to keep up with it. No wonder then that the date and place of origin of most American spindle-back chairs have been subject to the roughest kind of conjecture and, as a consequence, that considerable misinformation about the form and the particular examples that embody it has made its way into the lore of furniture collecting. Some of this lore is quaint and harmless enough. Much of it is quite illogical and hinders our ability to conceptualize. Where, for example, are the contemporary oral traditions or later sale catalogues or magazine advertisements touting a turned chair that has an urban provenance? Aside from the Mather family highchair, there is none, which reemphasizes the notion that spindle-back chairs are all of rural or village origin, even though such chairs abound in the inventories of urban estates from an early date.

Many of the ideas that have dominated the collecting of early turned chairs can be traced to the *ex cathedra* statements of Wallace Nutting. The general themes of Nutting's remarks in *Pilgrim Century* are that early chairs are heavy while later chairs are light and that early chairs do not have turnings on the front legs between the seat list and the stretcher while later chairs do.[55] Such generalizations have become a part of the thinking of every person who had to deal with these chairs but had no dated examples to work with and no documentary research to cling to. It is easy to forget that Nutting had no dated examples to work with and, despite his disclaimer to the contrary, clearly illustrated a number of chairs he had never seen. He relied on photographs sent to him by fellow collectors, and he rarely knew where the chairs in these photographs had been acquired or whether they had family histories or even what woods they were made of—a particularly serious error since subsequent examinations revealed that many European chairs made their way into his books.[56] All of this, of course, reveals how unreliable generalizations can be and suggests that emotionally directed connoisseurship wedded to an evolutionary framework will not carry one very far toward accuracy or historical truth if it lacks an objective analysis of materials and some sense of history.

In the matter of ornamental turnings between the seat and front stretcher, for example, Nutting was inconsistent. The Standish chair has them, the Bradford chair does not, yet both have posts of very nearly the same diameter. The Connecticut Historical Society chair has them; the Metropolitan Museum chair from the same shop tradition, and very likely earlier than the historical society chair, does not. These last two chairs are "heavy," and so Nutting's conflicting generalizations suggest that the Connecticut chair is both early and late, which cannot be. It is now clear that the thickness of a piece of wood used in a chair post is more the result of the training of its maker and the extent of his opportunity to practice his trade competitively and hence keep abreast of changing fashions than a feature that can be prima facie wedded to a chronological framework.

The contradictions among closely related chairs can be explained, but the explanation does not answer the question of how to date a seventeenth-century-style spindle-back or slat-back chair within that century. The materials of which a chair is made may very likely someday tell us more about the place and the tradition in which the craftsman is working than anything else.

Turned chairs in the seventeenth-century styles generally appear to be divided into two major categories: those made of ash and those made of closer grained woods such as maple and poplar. While a maple chair may have rails and even spindles of ash, the four legs will always be made of either maple *or* ash, but never both (see, for example, catalogue entry 4). That alone should prompt the connoisseur to approach with caution an early appearing chair that has both woods in its posts. Oak virtually never appears in the posts of American turned chairs, and birch is equally rare. All the examples made of beech that have been microanalyzed in the course of research for this book have been determined to be made of the European and not the American species. The either/or use of ash and maple suggests that two traditions were established by the first chairmakers at work in English North America. In one were men who were trained to make their turned wares out of close-

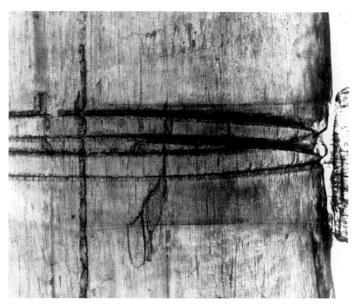

Fig. 38. Detail showing a turned crosspiece with a flared end that was forced into a cylindrical hole drilled in an upright.

grained hardwoods, and in the other were those who preferred ash.

The traditions of chairmaking further are differentiated from each other by the way in which the elements of the chairs are fastened together. One group of makers preferred to turn the crosspieces to a flared end, which was forced into the holes drilled for them in the uprights (fig. 38). Craftsmen working in a second tradition put their reliance in pinning the joints once the chair was assembled. The two traditions are rarely mixed in the spindle-back chairs. The third tradition—the use of glue—will doubtless raise howls of disbelief among the many craftsmen working today who pride themselves on using old and therefore pure techniques of chairmaking. Documentary evidence supports the evidence of the chairs themselves. Glue is often included in the inventories of early turned-chair maker's estates, such as the entry listing "red occur [ocher] and glew" valued at 1s. in the shop of Joseph Carpenter of Rehoboth, Massachusetts, in 1675.[57]

The idea that a chairmaker could turn his posts with much of their original moisture content in them and could dry his crosspieces, or at least their tenons, so that they would absorb moisture from the posts and swell to create a tight finished joint is no longer in dispute. Given the low torque that man-powered lathes were able to attain and the relatively poor quality steel that was available for tool blades and considering the great amount of casting and shrinkage out of round that the posts of these chairs reveal, the point is moot. But, that such chairs can and often do come apart—John Alexander, Jr., describes them as "failure chairs"—indicates that shrinkage techniques were governed by complex factors and, in addition, were not universally used. Nor was the matter of the exact percentage of moisture that was to remain in the tenons always attained. Most seventeenth-century chairs when disassembled reveal that, regardless of the fastening techniques used to assemble them, their makers thought it the better part of valor to glue the joints.

Another notion, undoubtedly popularized by the super-ficial examination of eighteenth-century windsor chairs, is that turners have always used certain woods for certain parts of a chair to make the most of the known characteristics of those woods. While this idea is perpetuated in books dealing with "folk crafts" of a later period, it cannot be confirmed by the early spindle-back chairs examined for this book.[58] The three woods most commonly used for these chairs were maple, poplar, and ash. Usually the entire chair is made of one or the other of these woods. In the instances where two woods are used in the same chair, the uprights are generally maple or poplar, and the crosspieces are ash.

AMERICAN SLAT-BACK CHAIRS PRIOR TO THE WILLIAM AND MARY STYLE

The earliest surviving American slat-back chairs differ from the spindle-back chairs in that they have horizontal slats between the upright rear posts instead of turned spindles and almost invariably have flat outward-flaring arms instead of turned ones. Curiously, the armed versions of these chairs tend to be a little smaller than the spindle-back ones. The slats are usually bowed backward to conform somewhat to the contours of the human body, a nuance that represents a considerable improvement in potential comfort over spindle-back chairs. It is surprising, therefore, that they are not more common.

While the technical difference—spindle versus slat—that distinguishes these two types of chairs is easy to observe and to state, the distinction is not spelled out in the earliest New England inventories, which has given rise to the notion that, because they are not specifically mentioned, slat-back chairs were not made in America as early as the spindle-back variety. Considering that the makers of these two types of chairs used the same ornamental vocabulary of balusters and finials, the argument that they did not make both at the same time requires a somewhat finer analysis than has previously been accorded these chairs.

No surviving Massachusetts slat-back chairs related to the earliest spindle-back chairs are known. This is curious because slat-back chairs appear to be a part of the urban English tradition of chairmaking prior to the time that New England was settled. If we are interpreting them correctly, the Court Minutes of the Worshipful Company of Turners of London refer to slat-back chairs among the "proof pieces." The earliest reference, which seems to combine features of the slat back and the spindle back in the board-seat-chair tradition, occurs in November 1614, when Henry Morris was required to make either "a mans square stoole or a great Chaire wth two boards in the back and two rowes of turned pillers: & buttons." A chair somewhat more closely akin to what we know as a slat back today is described in these records in January 1629. Edmond Browne was ordered "to make a Chaire with a boarded back for a proofe piece."[59] Since such a chair was required as a proof piece in 1629, it is logical to assume that slat-back chairs were an expected part of a London turner's repertoire at that date.

Of the seventeenth-century American slat-back chairs

whose photographs have been previously published in other books, only one has a board seat. That chair, now in the collection of Historic Deerfield, was published by Nutting in the first edition of *Pilgrim Century* shortly after it had been acquired by Chauncey C. Nash, an eminent early collector. This remarkable chair, with conjecturally restored feet and partially missing finials, undoubtedly was made by the same school of turners that was responsible for the Stryker family chair now in the collection of the Metropolitan Museum of Art with which it shares deeply scored, bottom-heavy balusters on its front posts and compressed balls on its rear ones. It is also related to the Connecticut Historical Society chair (see fig. 30). In addition to the three slats between its rear posts, the Deerfield chair has double lower side stretchers and has lost the second side stretcher between the arms and the seat lists. The side seat lists do not protrude through the front and rear posts, although the front and rear seat lists protrude through the sides of the uprights.[60] These protruding tenons are rectangular in shape rather than round, as they are in the spindle-back versions, which, when combined with the absence of the protrusions on the front of the front posts, suggests that the tradition in which the chair is made was refined with the passage of time, which in turn suggests that the Deerfield chair was indeed made later than the spindle-back versions. How much later we cannot begin to estimate.

Insofar as the rest of the slat-back chairs of New England are concerned, conventional wisdom seems to be correct: all the examples from eastern Massachusetts relate, for one reason or another, to the flag-bottom, spindle-back chairs that we now suspect are in the style of the mid seventeenth century, that is, second-generation chairs. The largest group of these, of which perhaps a dozen examples are known, is typified by the example illustrated by Irving W. Lyon in *Colonial Furniture*, no. 57, as long ago as 1891. That chair bears a close resemblance to the spindle-back chair illustrated in catalogue entry 1, which suggests that the slat-back version was either made in Suffolk County, Massachusetts, as the spindle-back version was, or made by a craftsman trained in that place, even though Lyon tells us that the chair was purchased in Killingly, Connecticut. Now in the collection of the Metropolitan Museum of Art, this ash chair (fig. 39) has been overrestored—a not unexpected happenstance since it was owned by Walter Hosmer of Wethersfield, a restorer working for a firm of Hartford woodworkers, Robbins and Winship, famous for its zeal, upon whom most early Connecticut collectors relied. The feet of this chair, excitingly true to our expectations of what the feet of the earliest turned chairs from urban New England ought to have perhaps looked like, were added; we can hardly say restored because we do not know that chairs of this genre had turned feet. The original front stretcher of the chair is missing, and if this chair runs true to the type of the related examples probably from the same shop, its flat, outwardly flaring arms of riven oak have been replaced by turned ones (see catalogue entry 14). The imputed Connecticut origin of this chair is further called into question by a second example, now converted into a rocking chair, owned by descendants of Hingham's Cushing family.[61] Both chairs have balusters that are slightly compressed, in contrast to those on the spindle-

Fig. 39. Turned great chair, slat back, probably Suffolk County, Mass., 1640–75. Ash; H 45½″ (115.6 cm). (Metropolitan Museum of Art, gift of Mrs. Russell Sage, 1909.) Although the chair was found in Connecticut, it was probably not made there.

back type; this feature may represent either an evolution of a design (if they someday prove to be made by the same makers) or the workmanship of a totally different shop.

A third instance of parallels between spindle-back and slat-back chairs occurs when we compare figures 419 and 422 in Lockwood's *Colonial Furniture* with the example in the Shelburne Museum, illustrated as no. 33 (left) in Helen Comstock's *American Furniture*.[62] These chairs appear to have been made by the same school of craftsmen as the chair illustrated in catalogue entry 3 and are stylistically related to examples that may have associations with Plymouth Colony. These chairs vary from the group mentioned above in that their finials are of a different pattern, consisting of fewer elements.

If we momentarily exclude these few groups of chairs, it would be difficult to find a student of New England furniture who would be willing to say that the earliest slat-back chair he had ever handled could have been made as early as the earliest spindle back with which he was familiar. The same feeling occurs when we look at the earliest surviving examples of English turned chairs. In part, this feeling emanates from the construction methods. To use slats in the back of a four-square chair, the maker has to rive them out of a bolt, moisten and clamp each slat, chisel mortises out of the posts by hand, and wedge or pin the bent slats in place. Since this extra labor must raise the price, slat-back chairs must appear in response to some impetus that is independent of cost. While it is difficult to speak with assurance of the relationship of these slat- and spindle-back chairs in Europe, the number of surviving American examples of both types suggests that slat-back chairs did not appear in New England as often in the seventeenth century as spindle backs. When slat backs did begin to appear in quantities or become fairly common, the William and Mary style was in full sway.

While versions of the three-square chair with a slat as its top rail were made in northern Europe in the late Middle Ages (see, for example, Lyon, *Colonial Furniture*, no. 55), it is not easy to determine when slat-back turned chairs were first made in England; indeed, they appear to have escaped the attention of furniture historians there. The famous "Yorkshire" and "Derbyshire" chairs of the seventeenth century resemble the slat-back type, but they are joiners' chairs with the back panel eliminated and the back rails embellished. Illustrations of turned slat-back chairs in early manuscript drawings and paintings suggest that they were far less common in England than in northern Europe. It is quite possible that they were not made in England until the late Middle Ages, perhaps even the sixteenth century, and were introduced either by the emigrant chairmakers from the Continent or at the English fairs and markets in which Dutch, French, and German merchants participated freely during that period. If so, it is further possible that these chairs were first naturalized in those eastern and southern coastal counties of Britain that enjoyed an active trade with the Continent.

Evidence of the widespread use of slat-back chairs in the Germanic countries exists in abundance. A wall painting, believed to date from the end of the fifteenth century, in the Ferdinandeum Museum at Innsbruck, Austria, portrays a continental, slat-back "matted chair" (fig. 40). This richly detailed illustration reveals many of the characteristics that persisted in European turned chairs throughout the following centuries (although the turning on this particular example is confined to the finials, lists, and stretchers). Unlike any of the American examples, the mortise holes for the slats are cut all the way through the rear posts. The turned seat lists and stretchers likewise project through the uprights, a feature that is found only under unusual circumstances on seventeenth-century Anglo-American chairs; the flag or rush seat—usually called "straw" in the continental documents—has the customary and expected cushion that went on such chairs. (Inventories reveal that the use of cushions on matted chairs in New England persisted well into the eighteenth century. This custom accounts for the visually unsettling gap between the lower rail of the back and the seat rail, a gap that is easily noticed on turned chairs displayed without cushions in many museums.) Although the finials atop the back posts are turned, the legs themselves are square in section and, along with the presence of the slat itself, suggest that the saw, drawknife, and chisel were the tools that figured most prominently in the process of making this particular example. Indeed, this chair, and the minimal reliance of its maker on the use of the lathe, represents a chairmaking tradition that is visible on a group of American chairs, which appear quite old but are actually undatable by present techniques, for that tradition persisted in

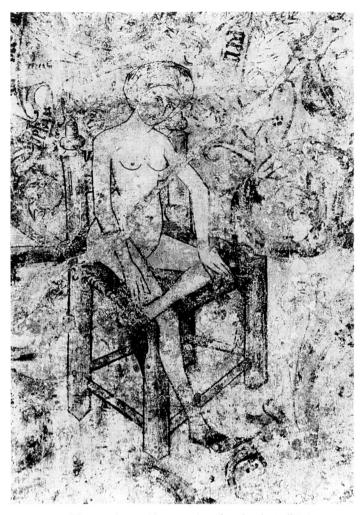

Fig. 40. Detail from *Nachtes Mädchen Sitzend*, attributed to the Hall Painter, Haus Rosengasse, Tirol, Austria, 1480–1500. Fresco; H 55¼" (142 cm), W 38¼" (97.3 cm). (Tiroler Landesmuseum Ferdinandeum, Innsbruck, Austria.) Note the continental slat-back chair.

the Appalachian highlands of the southern United States well into the twentieth century.[63]

Irving P. Lyon, the son of furniture historian Irving W. Lyon, has dealt with the question of early square-post slat-back chairs, a number of which had been found in New England. Although the chairs he illustrates clearly represent several traditions, which suggest that some might have been made by nonprofessional woodworkers, some by carpenters, one by a joiner, and others by persons unknown who possessed lathes, only the Museum of Fine Arts chair, which varies from the rest, has been positively identified by wood analysis as being made of American red oak. It is possible that some of the examples were modeled on a chair remembered by Pilgrims from their sojourn in Holland. If so, these particular forms cannot be dealt with by present research techniques.[64]

The more professional chair from northern Germany illustrated in figure 41 stands in contrast to the slat-back chair from rural Austria. We may presume that this is the type of slat-back chair most familiar to the artist working in Cologne who painted this picture circa 1473. As with the Austrian chair, the mortises for rounds and slats are drilled and cut through the uprights. Although this is a roundabout version of the slat-back chair, it nonetheless well illustrates the bent slats

Fig. 41. Detail from *The Sermon of Johannes Ev*, attributed to the Master of the Life of Mary, Cologne, Germany, ca. 1473. Tempera on board. (Courtesy, Germanisches Nationalmuseum, Nuremberg, Federal Republic of Germany.) Note the slat-back roundabout chair.

Fig. 42. Turned great chair with slat back, possibly made by Samuel Beadle, Jr., Salem area, Mass., ca. 1674. Oak and pine; H 48″ (121.9 cm), W 22¾″ (57.8 cm), D 16″ (40.1 cm), SH 17½″ (44.5 cm). (Essex Institute, Salem Mass. Photo: Richard Merrill.) The chair has a history of ownership in the English family of Salem and later belonged to the Reverend William Bentley who had the date 1692 painted on it. The board seat dates from the nineteenth century.

that are most often found on common chairs of the Continent and common chairs of the Middle Atlantic colonies in America. The slats of chairs in the English tradition are seldom so deeply bowed. The Cologne chair is important for another reason: it is in all probability an urban chair and serves to underline the rarely documentable fact that city dwellers had common chairs for common uses.

Because turned chairs are usually characterized in inventories only by the colors that they are painted or their sizes or the materials with which they are bottomed, it is now almost impossible to tell when they appear in America. The best known example of a New England board-back chair from the seventeenth century is displayed in the collection of the Essex Institute in Salem, Massachusetts (fig. 42). This chair is believed to be an heirloom of the English family of Salem, and like the Essex Institute turkey-work couch (see fig. 112), owes its survival to the Reverend William Bentley. This active minister of Salem received the chair from the great-granddaughter of Philip and Mary English, apparently in the late 1790s. Bentley believed the chair was all that remained of the original furniture of the English household, so he had it painted with the date *1692* to commemorate Mary English who, according to historian James Savage, "suffered very much in the blind ferocity against witchcraft."[65] If this chair is, indeed, a survivor of the plundering of the English house during the witchcraft scare and if it was new when English acquired it, it was made after his arrival at Salem from the Island of Jersey in 1674 and may very well have been purchased then or in 1675 when he married Mary Hollingsworth. If the chair was made in 1674 or later, it is probably the work of Samuel Beadle, Jr. (1643–1706). Beadle lived in Charlestown, Massachusetts, from 1656 to 1661, then moved

to Salem in 1663. After 1683 he was an innkeeper. Attribution of this chair to Beadle, although poorly documented, has a slight basis in probability since we know that he was the only turner working in Salem at that time. It is also possible that English patronized him rather than a Boston craftsman because Beadle's family, like English, came from Jersey. Beadle was about 30 years old in 1674.[66]

The baluster turnings on the rear stiles of the English family chair represent the compressed shapes that appear on early turned chairs found in eastern Massachusetts, particularly in Essex, Suffolk, and Middlesex counties, as opposed to the rather more elongated versions of the same shape that are characteristic of southern Massachusetts. The turnings of the finials are similar to those on the Eliot armchair (see fig. 37) and the Mather family highchair (see fig. 36) as well as the chair illustrated in catalogue entry 1. The turning differs from them in that its topmost element is quite elongated, as opposed to the elliptical rotundity that characterizes the Suffolk County version.

The similarity of the English family Salem chair to the Roxbury/Dorchester/Boston chairs may be accounted for by Beadle's apprenticeship, probably in Charlestown, possibly with members of the Larkin family, Edward (w. 1638, d. 1664), his son John (1640–1675/76), and their descendants. Although Henry Wyckoff Belknap, early historian of Essex County craftsmen, calls Beadle's father a "cabinetmaker," the research of Eleanor Perley has shown that the elder Beadle was, in all probability, a soapboiler at the time of his death. Although wounded in "the Narragansett country" during King Philip's War, the younger Beadle was still working at his trade in March 1678/79, when he was paid £2.1 "p[er] 41 balester for the Towne house" in Salem.[67]

Inventories are frustratingly uninformative concerning the appearance of the slat-back-chair form in New England. No reference seems to be earlier than the "8 chairs wth 5 slatts" valued at 4s. and "Six wth 3 slats" at 2s. 8d. located "in the great lower room" of the impressively furnished inn run by Mercy Oliver of Cambridge, Massachusetts, until her death in 1710. Mrs. Oliver's establishment boasted a wide assortment of other chairs, including "11 cane chairs," "6 Turkey work'd chairs," "6 old chamber chairs" (perhaps the same as the "Close Stool" in the "west great chamber"), "½ doz. Russia [leather] chairs double nail'd," "Six ditto calf," "4 leather chairs single nail'd," and a scattering of other chairs not described explicitly. Those chairs with five slats were undoubtedly in the high-back William and Mary style, but those with three slats might have resembled the earlier style under discussion here. At 4s. apiece, they were not very grand objects, though stylish.[68]

Chairmakers' inventories are somewhat more informative than those of householders, but unfortunately no Essex County inventory that specifies slat-back chairs predates that of a Beverly turner, John Corning (1675–1734, w. ca. 1695). In Corning's shop were:

6 Chair bits & stocks 6s. all & 1 Inch & ¼ at 2s.
1 hand Saw 3s. & 1 old broad ax 3s.
1 frame Saw 1s. 8d.
one Large frame Saw 14s. & 1 ditto very small 1s.
1 Ringed Betle & 1 Iron wedge 4s. & 1 hatchet at 2s. 6d.
1 Nail hamer & 1 lathing hamer 18d. & 1 small gimblit & 1 small hamer at 8d. both
2 Turning chisels at 3s. & 2 Ditto at 18d.
2 Turning Gouges 2s. & 5 Tules for makeing heals [heels] & the Block to them 9s. & 1 old ads at 1s.
1 Shave 2s. & bungborer 1s. & 1 Twibill 1s.
1 Rasp 18d. & 1 Inch auger 1s. & 1 piece of Iron 4d.
2 Rabiting plains & stocks 2s. & 1 three square file & 1 Tapborer 2s. & 1 Chisel 8d. & ½ a cord of popler Timber 10s.
11 two backed New Chairs at 2s. 6d. per
9 two backed new Chairs without bottoms at 18d. per
Rungs and backs for Chairs & stocks & spokes for Spining wheels & other stuff prepared in Shop 15s.
36 bundles of flags for Chairs at 10s. all.[69]

In the never-ending search for period terminology, it is useful to learn from the Corning inventory that the stretchers of chairs were referred to as "rungs" at this date and that what were called "slats" in Philadelphia at this time were called "backs" in Massachusetts. Equally important is that Corning had made-up chairs in stock, which counters our usual conception that chairs were made only to order.

CONCLUSIONS

The chair and its role in the seventeenth-century household has been the vehicle for a number of colorful notions in casual studies of America's social history. The belief that chairs were extremely rare in the colonies during that period has inspired a number of twice-told tales, the validity of which is questionable. The belief is partially inspired by the knowledge that alternative seating existed—forms, stools, joint stools, and benches—and partially by the knowledge that the armchair played a ceremonial role in the hierarchy of order and precedence in those strata of society that were concerned with religious, courtly, and official life throughout the Middle Ages. There is little doubt that this symbolic role of the armchair continued in the colonial period. Occasional references in American documents even support this notion. Samuel Sewall often recorded the perks of rank: December 5, 1716, "Governour [Samuel] Shute comes to my house in his Chariot, with a petition.... Many had Signed it, I signed it in the new Hall; Govr sat in the arm'd Chair."[70]

The inventories of New England reveal that the seat of authority was present in every level of society, from Samuel Sewall, perhaps the most respected if not the wealthiest Puritan of his time, down to the simplest head of a household reading from the scripture to his family in the domain that was his own home. It is also likely that this symbol of deference—honor thy father—was an armchair. It is true that chairs were relatively rare in the Middle Ages, but a further truth that has not received so much publicity is that *all* domestic furniture was rare at that time. In addition, it does not follow that because an armchair might have represented authority in the seventeenth century that no other chairs existed in domestic households in that period. Similarly, the notion that chairs were expensive, when they existed at all, is a half-truth that fails to take into account that two types of chairs were in use during this period—those made by joiners and those made by turners. The former were laboriously sawed out, mortised and tenoned together, and sometimes elaborately carved and molded. The parts of the latter were quickly turned out on a lathe—the tool of mass production—and pinned together and, because they were so inexpensive, were called "common chairs." Common as they were, a dismayingly low rate of survival has made them highly uncommon today—further evidence of their inexpensive nature since objects of negligible value are rarely saved.

Colonial New England abounded in chairs, and the home of the Reverend Nathaniel Rogers of Ipswich, who died in 1655, is a case in point. It contained, in the hall, a round table with 5 joined stools valued at 16s., along with 6 chairs and 5 cushions worth £1; in the parlor, a short table and a "forme," 19s, 6 cushion stools and 2 chairs, £2, and a "great chaire," 6s.; in the chamber, 3 cushion chairs and 2 stools, £2.14 and 2

TABLE 1   SEATING FURNITURE IN ESSEX COUNTY, MASSACHUSETTS

DATES	CHAIRS	ELBOW, GREAT, WAINSCOT/JOINED CHAIRS	STOOLS	JOINED STOOLS	FORMS	BENCHES
1635–64	524	10	115	82	71	10
1665–81	1074	12	174	209	104	1
TOTAL	1598	22	289	291	175	11

Source: Essex Probate, vols. 1–3. The plurals, such as "chairs" and "forms," are counted as two.

TABLE 2   SEATING FURNITURE IN MID ESSEX, ENGLAND

YEARS	CHAIRS	STOOLS	FORMS	BENCH BOARDS [FIXED ?]	BENCHES	NUMBER OF INVENTORIES
1635–39	71	66	33	21	3	21
1658–59[1]	26	25	7	2	0	4
1660–69	176	142	56	5	6	36
1670–79	402	272	109	11	13	52
1680–89	439	301	97	5	5	45
1690–99	264	107	54	3	0	26
1700–09	122	32	20	0	0	12
1712–19[2]	192	30	19	0	0	14
1720–29	239	38	19	0	0	26
1730–31[3]	32	5	0	0	0	2
1743–49[4]	101	5	3	0	0	4
TOTAL	2064	1023	417	47	27	242

Missing: [1]1640–1658, [2]1710–1711, [3]1732–1739, [4]1740–1742
Source: Steer, Farm and Cottage Inventories.

window cushions, £1; in the hall chamber, in a chest with a drawer, 6 cushions, 24s., and a chair (no value); in the garret over the parlor, 1 chair 1s. 2d.; and in the study, a cabinet desk and 2 chairs, £1.5.[71]

Granted that, for a member of the ministerial oligarchy, Rogers's entire estate was larger than the average, oddly enough, the quantity and quality of the seating furniture in his house—upholstered chairs aside—was not grossly atypical. He possessed 16 chairs, 1 of which was a wainscot or great chair, 3 of which were upholstered. The rest appear to have been turned chairs. The house contained enough cushions to go on all of these, and had 2 for the built-in window seats. Most of the important chairs also had footstools with them. In contrast to the chairs were 5 joint stools and 1 form.

The ratio of chairs to other types of seating furniture can easily be determined for one agrarian county in Massachusetts between 1635 and the end of 1681. The tabulations, from the published probate records of Essex County, are shown on table 1. On their face, it is quite clear that the numbers of chairs exceeded all stools, forms, and benches by a considerable margin from the beginning of recordkeeping. Even calculating that forms and benches could accommodate up to 4 sitters, and considering all stools as seating furniture—though surely many were footstools and many joined stools were used as tables—the seating capacity of the chairs still exceeds that of the other types by a 7 to 3 ratio.

Similar tabulations for bodies of English inventories of this sort yield an important control by which we can suggest how life in England varied from life in New England. A recent study of 141 inventories from the parish of Yetminster, Dorset,

from 1576 through 1769, found a total of 274 chairs and 221 stools listed in 112 inventories. In the 56 inventories taken between 1576 and 1677, 84 chairs and 108 stools were listed; although in the next century, 190 chairs but only 113 stools were listed—a dramatic increase in the ratio of chairs to stools.[72] Going back to the sixteenth century we can compare these figures with those found in M. A. Havinden's study of inventories dating from 1550 to 1590. The 257 inventories published by Havinden contain 931 recognizable pieces of seating furniture. Forms, the most prevalent during this period, were mentioned 363 times (39 percent). Next came stools at 241 (25.9 percent); chairs 170 (18.3 percent), benches 118 (12.6 percent), and settles 39 (4.2 percent).[73]

These two English studies suggest that chairs in these areas did not dominate other types of seating furniture until the eighteenth century, which is rather different from the New England picture. It could be argued that it is invalid to compare these English counties with Essex County, Massachusetts, because the economic realities of the areas compared are not taken into consideration. Dorset and Oxford were old and essentially static agrarian counties, while Essex County, Massachusetts, was rapidly growing. Deborah A. Smith, while a student in the Winterthur Program in Early American Culture, undertook to tabulate the frequency of seating furniture in Francis W. Steer's pivotal study of 274 English inventories from the Essex region between 1635 and 1749 (see table 2). Essex, unlike Dorset and Oxfordshire, had profited for more than a century from the wool trade and was thus among the richer counties in England. Moreover, Essex was one of the four areas to furnish large numbers of immigrants to

New England prior to 1650, so we might expect the habits of its natives to be transferred.

Although the surveys of inventories in England and New England are imprecise and not chronologically parallel, they do reveal general trends. In England, chairs became more common as the seventeenth century progressed and by the eighteenth reached a position of dominance. In New England, the ratio of chairs to stools was much higher from the very beginning of settlement, and the great majority of these chairs were doubtless the inexpensive turned chairs, which today survive in much greater numbers than do wainscot chairs and upholstered examples.

We must with effort continually summon back to our consciousness the idea that America in the seventeenth century was in many ways a frontier and that many artifacts which survive from that time were made by men who had an immediate need for those artifacts and often made them themselves: in short, much furniture was probably made by nonprofessional makers or craftsmen who never had the benefit of a formal apprenticeship. The inventories of New England during the first century of settlement reveal that almost every husbandman possessed enough tools to make furniture for his needs. And, of course, wood was plentiful and cheap. When we consider the difficulties in dealing with craftsmen who can be identified from the records, the possibility of dealing intelligently with objects that do not reveal professional workmanship or datable stylistic attributes is remote.

Finally, the multiplicity of surviving chairs that have a variety of stylistic attributes confirms the notion that they were manufactured under a wide variety of circumstances over a long period of time and by craftsmen with varying degrees of ability. The task of trying to determine where and when many of these turned chairs were made is virtually hopeless. The surviving examples do confirm that what is apparent in the documents of the eighteenth and nineteenth centuries was also true in the seventeenth century: a chairmaker lived and worked at every single crossroads in New England.

Unlike pieces of case furniture, which were expensive from the day they were made and were often highly decorated and therefore cherished artifacts of the past, the turned chair was an inexpensive item, more necessary as something to sit on than as a vehicle for "curious" workmanship. To some extent, the simplicity of turned chairs is determined by the nature of the turners' craft itself. Cutting away the unwanted parts of the surface of a cylinder of wood as it revolves in a lathe is a process that limits the type of ornamentation that can be created. Because of the restricted nature of what turning can accomplish decoratively, the craft itself is conservative and the objects produced by it are little subject to stylistic change. In no other form of furniture is the message so intimately conditioned by its medium. Turned chairs made during the first century of settlement in New England are of *only* two styles: those which display massive dimensions and four-square proportions and are decorated with balusters—either elongated or compressed depending perhaps more on where the craftsman was trained than the date at which the chair was made; and second, those that have motifs that take their cue from the chair styles introduced into England following the Stuart restoration.

Documented turned chairs are at least as rare in Europe as they are in America; as a result, few of the examples available for study can with certainty be said to have been made in England and not on the Continent. The fairly free migration of northern European craftsmen to England, especially from the middle of the sixteenth century onward, combined with the contemporary sale of continental furniture at English fairs and markets open to foreigners, make it difficult for us to differentiate the native products of English turners from those of their continental neighbors. The trail is further blurred by subsequent events. Antique furniture has been collected in England since the eighteenth century, and during the nineteenth century many chairs were brought from the Continent to satisfy English collectors; furthermore, when even the continental sources began to run dry, fakes and reproductions filled the marketplace.

The student of furniture who would like to distinguish between English and continental work faces a complicated task. First, no objective technique such as wood analysis aids in distinguishing the furniture of Britain from that of the Continent because the furniture woods of each (with a few exceptions) are the furniture woods of both. Second, the taste of Englishmen of all classes for European fashions guaranteed that continental styles were quickly adopted and copied in England. Third, all English furniture is not homogeneous in characteristics and thus is not recognizable. English furniture making for all the classes below the aristocracy and the merchant class in the sixteenth and seventeenth centuries was highly decentralized, and each region contributed its own variations of style and technique while sticking to the same general stylistic themes. In order to make some order out of this mass of intertwining possibilities, scholars of the future must first learn the regional attributes of the furniture and then isolate objective characteristics, such as details of workmanship or uses of woods, and attempt to track them to their origins. A particular group of chairs that might profitably be studied in this way are those that originally had board bottoms.

It has become fashionable among English scholars in recent years to reattribute most of the chairs now in England to the Continent. Scandinavia appears to be the most popular recipient of these attributions. But it does not follow that because *some* chairs in this style in England today may have been made in northern Europe, *all* were. How, we must ask, could continental examples of three-square chairs find their way into the cottages of Herefordshire in the middle of the eighteenth century? It is certain that the cottagers of that county were not antiques collectors. It must follow then that some triangular-seat chairs were being made in England in rural areas little influenced by London fashions of the day.

It is possible that the surviving chairs themselves give us a clue that will separate—at least roughly—the English examples from the continental ones. For example, can birch ever be found in English turned chairs? And what about construction methods? Is the one strong continental quirk of construction—the round tenons of the seat lists that project completely through the upright posts—invariably present in the four-square chairs in England today? In the case of a number of chairs long believed to be English, these tenons are

Fig. 43. Detail of a three-legged chair showing the rectangular tenon intersected by a round tenon. Europe, sixteenth century. Oak. (Charles F. Williams Collection, Philadelphia Museum of Art, purchased by subscription and museum funds. Photo: Benno M. Forman.)

quite prominent. Stylistically, these chairs often relate to the Dutch chairs illustrated in the Dirck Hals painting *A Party at Table* (see fig. 28), and the turnings suggest they are of seventeenth-century origin. Each seat list of these chairs has a rectangular tenon worked at one end, which goes into a rectangular mortise hole, and a round tenon on the other end, which interlocks with the rectangular tenon of the next seat list, to hold the seat board rigid (fig. 43). The round tenon is often split on its end and wedged with a separate piece of wood. It would be fatuous to state that this technique *never* appears on turned chairs made in England, for not enough examples to prove or disprove this point can be documented. Indeed, a wedged tenon was used on the Hall's Croft highchair (see fig. 29). But the overwhelming popularity of this technique in both earlier and later continental turned work suggests that Germany and the Lowlands are where it was first popular in northern Europe. Perhaps the English chairs that have it should be attributed either to a continental origin or to craftsmen working in England who were trained in continental techniques. A study of English rural documents, particularly those of Norfolk and Devonshire, where large numbers of northern Europeans settled in the sixteenth century, might answer this question. We *know* the answer for London and its liberties: great numbers of Dutch, Flemish, German, and French protestant craftsmen settled there.[74] Since techniques of fastening associated with continental techniques appear in some early New England chairs and since no continental craftsmen appear to have been there to make them, it is likely that these techniques were introduced into Boston and New Haven by turners who came from London, where these techniques were doubtless common, although it would be difficult to illustrate this surmise with a single, documentable London turned chair dating from the early first quarter of the seventeenth century.

A few chairs, historically associated with Plymouth Colony—the Bradford (see fig. 33) and Brewster chairs, for example—exhibit the interlocking round and rectangular tenons associated with the Continental/London/Boston school. In the absence of documentary evidence showing that a professional chairmaker lived in Plymouth, it is perhaps wiser to hold in abeyance the attribution of these chairs to that locality. The vast majority of New England chairs do not reveal these characteristics. While direct continental influences could have found their way into a few communities in New England late in the seventeenth century, evidence of a rural English origin for the majority of early furniture craftsmen there is overwhelming. If through-tenons—round or rectangular— were a commonplace of English rural workmanship, they would certainly appear with regularity, perhaps invariably, in New England furniture. Yet they are virtually unknown. With a few rare exceptions, New England chairs have no projecting tenons at all, round or rectangular, so it must follow that the use of through-tenons was *not* the commonplace method of making chairs in the places that most American turned-chair makers came from.

While no direct evidence reveals that triangular-seat chairs were made in New England, an argument that they were made in England is provided by at least one inventory reference in the 1670s that demonstrates that a first generation English emigrant to America possessed one. Moreover, an example that exhibits known affinities to both English and American examples has been owned in this country for more than two centuries—long before antiques collecting was thought of here.

One feature shared by the spindle-back chairs that are presumed to be among the earliest made in New England is the board seat. Conspicuous among these chairs are the examples, derived from known English prototypes, in the Connecticut Historical Society and Metropolitan Museum of Art. They may have been made in Connecticut and could easily date from the late 1630s. The most famous of all American chairs, the Elder Brewster chair and Governor Bradford chair (see fig. 33), ought to predate 1643 and 1657 (the dates of Brewster's and Bradford's deaths, respectively) if their traditions of ownership are correct. Another chair, the Standish chair, with a reliable family history of ownership by the Thomas Lincoln family of Hingham was perhaps made in the same general place that the Brewster and Bradford chairs were. Massachusetts chairs with board seats that were owned outside of the Plymouth Colony include ones presumably owned by John Eliot (see fig. 37), which could have been made in Roxbury in the early 1640s, and one that belonged to the Mather family (with the rectangular-tenon seat construction but no board seat), which may have been made as early as 1637/38 or as late as 1663 (see fig. 36). All these surviving Massachusetts chairs have rectangular tenons on at least two seat lists. All have or had at one time spindles that extended from either the arms, the lower back rails, or the upper front stretchers to the seat lists. Since these chairs were not made in the Plymouth Colony, it is clear that the style and techniques evident in them were present elsewhere in eastern Massachusetts, which further invalidates the obfuscating terms "Pilgrim" and "Brewster" that have generically been applied to chairs of this type.

The attributes of turned chairs produced in Boston, the metropolis of New England, are difficult to enumerate because few surviving examples can be traced to that place of origin. The presence of London-trained turners there in the first generation of settlement, however, guarantees that the London style was transmitted to America, although we do not yet know for certain what that style was like. Since the Boston style can be suggested only by surmise, it has not been possible to estimate the rate at which the taste for it was disseminated throughout the area that Boston dominated. It follows that the attempt to date this particular group of chairs on a stylistic basis must rest on the shakiest of premises. The presence of the earmarks of the style, however, on the Salem area slat-back chair possibly made by a Charlestown-trained chairmaker for the English family (see fig. 42) suggests that the impact was eventually felt north of Boston. The chairs in the catalogue entries suggest that it was present southward as well.

The majority of the earliest turners in New England did not come from London, and undoubtedly they worked in the styles characteristic of their respective local regions. It is likely that they continued to perpetuate whatever styles they were working in through several generations since turned-chair styles could not have appreciably changed here until the very last decade of the seventeenth century. Thus local traditions burgeoned into regional styles were established and perpetuated in this country. These local traditions can, in a few instances, be recognized, and they are further discussed in the catalogue entries. That they were present in good quantities is demonstrated by the great number of references to rush- and flag-bottom chairs from the earliest documents onward, while board-bottom or "wooden" chairs are rarely mentioned. The infrequent specification of slat-back chairs in household inventories prior to the third quarter of the seventeenth century leaves us no choice but to assume that spindle-back chairs were

the most common form of turned chairs in both the urban and rural households of New England. Turned chairs were not, however, the only type of seating furniture in the inventories. Wainscot or joined chairs appear here and there, and joined stools were common. During the decade of the 1650s, leather- and textile-upholstered chairs appeared with increasing frequency in the more public rooms of wealthy householders. It would be nice if we could state unequivocally that turned chairs were confined to certain rooms in the seventeenth-century house and that they were the chairs of the less well-to-do artisans or husbandmen, as opposed to the mercantile aristocracy, the country gentry, and the ministerial oligarchy. But turned chairs are listed in the household inventories of all classes and in all rooms. In contrast, few men of lesser estate possessed upholstered chairs.

Because of relatively rapid communication between the settled areas of the New England seaboard, as opposed to the slow communication between London and the interior of England, it is possible that changes in style were more quickly adopted by craftsmen in the villages of New England than by their counterparts in England. That might explain why the William and Mary turnings were added to the working vocabulary of common-chair makers soon after the introduction of the style here. These features can be perceived in the chairs dating from the first quarter of the eighteenth century and suggest that spindle-back chairs were not made in New England very often in the eighteenth century, but for this surmise no evidence, pro or con, has been found. As we shall see later, once introduced, the William and Mary style enjoyed an unusually long life since the distinguishing stylistic characteristics of the fashionable "crook foot" style that then followed (with the notable exception of the country cabriole leg) did not lend themselves easily to the turner's method of chairmaking.

NOTES

[1] OED, s.v. "slat," sb. 4. "Slat back" and "banister back" did not find their way into the New England records until the early eighteenth century. The etymology of the word *banister* is considered in the appropriate chapter. The word *splat*, that we use synonymously with *banister*, has not been found used in this sense until well into the reign of George III. The OED does not note the substantive form of *splat* prior to 1833. The word does not appear in Chippendale's *Gentleman and Cabinet-Maker's Director* (1754), Hepplewhite's *Cabinet-Maker and Upholsterer's Guide* (1788), or James Humphreys's, "Prices of Cabinet and Chair Work" (presumably published as a book in Philadelphia in 1772, a manuscript version of this is published in Weil, "Cabinetmaker's Price Book," pp. 175–92, see esp. pp. 182–83); *splat* is used in *The Cabinet-Makers Philadelphia and London Book of Prices of 1796*. We may surmise that the substantive form of this word is derived from the verbal form, which has a hardy pedigree that dates from the fifteenth century and appears to refer to the act of bilaterally splitting a symmetrical object into two symmetrical halves. It is usually used to describe the act of splitting a fish, for example, "Splat that pike" (OED, s.v. "splat").

[2] Turned chairs were generally inexpensive, thus a large number of people owned them. They show up in the inventories in great quantity and are almost always appraised at low values (rarely more than 2s.).

[3] Smith, *Colonial Days and Ways*, p. 72; Savage, *Genealogical Dictionary*, 1:266; *Essex Probate*, 1:306–8.

[4] Suffolk Probate, 2:72, 106, 148, 175; 3:258, 197, 306; 4:154, 172; 5:179; 7:361–62; 5:340; 12:292; 9:63–65, 331; 10:74–75; 8:188, 211; 13:199, 303; 11:153; 14:78–87; 14:88, 91; 17:440–41; 18:209; 19:121; 27:341.

[5] Grieve, *Modern Herbal*, p. 726; Josselyn, *Account of Two Voyages*, p. 77; Josselyn also calls it "Bastard *Calamus aromaticus*" in *New-England Rarities Discovered*, p. 188; Robinson, *Flora of Essex County*, p. 103.

[6] Robinson, *Flora of Essex County*, p. 117; *Essex Probate*, 1:242. A chair owned by SPNEA has descended in the Weeks family of Greenland, N. H. (see fig. 46, below). It is of fine quality

and appears to be of eastern Massachusetts origin and could easily date from the third quarter of the seventeenth century. I am indebted to Brock W. Jobe for calling this chair to my attention.

[7] *Essex Probate*, 2:383. In this reference the final *e* in twine is suppressed, a common happenstance in seventeenth-century orthography.

[8] A lengthy note on the process of making this part of a tree's bark into twine is given in Loudon, *Arboretum et Fruticetum Britannicum*, 1:368–69. The account book of Stephen Whipple, a cabinet- and chair-maker of Salem, Mass., suggests that bark was used in New England for chair bottoms in June 1805. Whipple noted that Stephen Kendall owed him $1 for "bottoming 3 chairs, 2 of them with bark & the other with flags" (I am indebted to Nancy Goyne Evans for this reference). Bottoming with bark may not invariably be twisted bast but splints. Instructions for the method of doing this with the inner bark or cambium of hickory are contained in Alexander, *Make a Chair from a Tree*, pp. 103–13.

[9] Forman, "Delaware Valley 'Crookt Foot' and Slat-Back Chairs," p. 44.

[10] In 1646, "Exported [from Boston] by the Recovery of London John Beanes Master for John Mills Mercht . . . 3 bailes Indian matts" (*Aspinwall Notarial Records*, p. 400). The inventory of Thomas Firman, Ipswich, April 13, 1648, itemizes "In the Chamber: one Bedsted, curtaynes & Vallans" £1.10; "A small fetherbed & boulster & one pillowe," £2; "a Coverlett & Rugg & Matt," £1.10; the inventory of mariner Philip Kirtland, of Salem, April 12, 1661, specifies "a bedstead, 10s., Indean matts 6s." (*Essex Probate*, 1:95, 344).

[11] See, for example, the inventory of Hilliard Veren, Jr., June 24, 1680, "furniture of the house, viz., Parlor . . . 4 straw bottom chaires, 5s" (*Essex Probate*, 3:364).

[12] See Chapter 3 for a discussion of this tool and its alternatives.

[13] Ryder, "Four-legged Turned Chairs," pp. 44–49. Ryder shows a chair in Hereford Cathedral with arches between the front stretcher and the seat rail that are strikingly similar to those of the chair in figure 26 and appear to be original. Their Romanesque character is easily explained: they are semicircles turned on the face of a lathe in the manner of a treenware plate.

[14] The word *thrower*, meaning turner, persists in the German cognate, *dreher*.

[15] Walpole to George Montagu, August 20, 1761, as quoted in Lyon, *Colonial Furniture*, p. 139. According to Lewis, *Horace Walpole's Correspondence*, 1:90, in true collectorly fashion, Walpole outlived his friend and "bought at [Dickey] Bateman's sale, 'eight very ancient Welsh chairs, turned.'" In 1784 the chairs were listed in "The Great Cloyster" (*Description of the Villa of Mr. Horace Walpole*, p. 80); they were sold after Walpole's death. How these chairs were transformed from Herefordshire examples into Welsh chairs is not clear, since a March 9, 1765, entreaty to his correspondent, Hugh Cole, produced no chairs from the "poor cottages in so neighboring a county as Cheshire."

[16] I am indebted to Robert F. Trent whose persistent efforts resulted in the procurement of a specimen from this chair. Wood analysis revealed that the chair was made of European ash (*Fraxinus excelsior*).

[17] *Household Conveniences*, pp. 207–8.

[18] *Essex Probate*, 2:294.

[19] A privately owned chair in this manner was published in Ripley, "An American Triangular Turned Chair?" pp. 104–6. An argument for its American origin was supported by wood analysis, but unfortunately the samples appear to have been taken from replaced portions of the chair. On August 16, 1977, new microanalyses of the chair were undertaken. One of these, from an original leg, proved to be European ash (*Fraxinus excelsior*). I am indebted to S. Dillon Ripley, Anne C. Golovin, Scott Odell, and the Smithsonian Institution for their assistance in making this information available.

[20] *Essex Probate*, 2:383.

[21] Holme, *Academy of Armory*, 2: bk. 3, ch. 14, p. 15, and fig. 73.

[22] This question is further addressed in the introduction to the section of the catalogue on Cromwellian chairs.

[23] Turners Company Minutes, 1 (inverted and from the back): leaves 29 recto, 27 verso, 34 verso, 132 recto; 2: leaf 12 verso.

[24] Insofar as their appearance is concerned, there may have been none. Two orders in the Turners Company Minutes deal with this point. The first, dated September 1, 1609, states "whereas certayne Chaires are brought from Colchester, made there by one ———— [original left blank] for that many of the Seatlists are made of Aspe wch should only be of Ashe accordinge to the orders of this mistery, That the said ———— [blank] who made them shall ether take them home & make them accordinge to the orders, or appoint some in London to doe it for him; or ells that they shall be defaced according to the orders." The second, dated Feb. 20, 1615, ordered, "Chaires that are made at Colchester and other further p[ar]ts from London . . . [be brought] to the Comon hall of this Company . . . that they may be searched according to the orders of the Companie, before they are bought, And then beinge . . . searched to be bought by the m[aste]r & wardens of the Company at theis prices, viz: for plain matted chairs [at 6*s*.] pr dozen; for tourned matted chairs [at 7*s*.] pr dozen. . . . and it is further ordered . . . that the Mr. & Wardens . . . shall devide theis chaires amonge the shopp keepers of the Company" (Turners Company Minutes, 1: leaves 6 recto, 32 recto and verso).

[25] Lossing, *Pictorial Field-Book of the Revolution*, 1:436–38. I am indebted to Philip H. Dunbar for sharing his research about this chair; Dunbar to Forman, May 9, 1977.

[26] *Daily Times* (Hartford) (September 3, 1845); Robbins Diary, 2:236. Later diary references are on August 22, 1833, and September 7, 1833 (2:318, 321). Kane, *Furniture of the New Haven Colony*, pp. 5, 82. Lyon's reference to the chair in *Colonial Furniture* (p. 141) indicates the precise history of the chair has long been in dispute.

[27] The Stryker family chair is illustrated in Comstock, *American Furniture*, no. 19. A related, slat-back version of this chair with straight rear posts, conjecturally restored feet, and partially missing finials, illustrated in Fales, *Furniture of Historic Deerfield*, p. 20, fig. 12, will be discussed later in this essay. I am indebted to Frances Gruber Safford for confirming the presence of the grooves on the lists of the Stryker chair.

[28] Kane, *Furniture of the New Haven Colony*, no. 30.

[29] Phillips, *Annals of the Worshipful Company of Joiners*, p. 28.

[30] Routh and Lees-Milne, *Charlecote Park*. The authors' description of the painting (p. 20) says that it was painted in 1619 and that Richard Lucy, seated, was age 1 year; in the biographical sketch of this same Richard Lucy (p. 11), they give his birth date as 1600.

[31] I am indebted to the Trustees of the Pilgrim Society and to the society's former director, Lawrence D. Geller, for their permission to procure the samples from which the microanalyses were done. Turners Company Minutes, 1 (from back): leaf 29 recto.

[32] Holme, *Academy of Armory*, 2: bk. 3, ch. 14, p. 14.

[33] Young, *Chronicles of the Pilgrim Fathers*, p. 458; Fairbanks, "Four Pilgrim Chairs," p. 2; Comstock, "Pilgrim Chairs," p. 451.

[34] Bowman, "Elder William Brewster's Inventory," pp. 15–21; Bowman, "Governor William Bradford's . . . Inventory," pp. 228–34; Bowman, "Alice (Southworth) Bradford's . . . Inventory," pp. 145–49.

[35] Forman, "Continental Furniture Craftsmen in London," pp. 105–17, esp. p. 108, no. 64. Of the total of 24 turners listed in this appendix, 16 were recent arrivals from Holland and Germany.

[36] Nutting, *Pilgrim Century* (1st ed.), p. 184.

[37] Trent, "Joiners and Joinery of Middlesex County" (conference report), pp. 124–25.

[38] Singleton, *Furniture of Our Forefathers*, p. 182. See also editor's note to "Abstracts of Wills of the Mather Family," p. 340 (I am indebted to Robert F. Trent for this reference). Nutting, *Pilgrim Century* (2d ed.), p. 293 and fig. 303.

[39] Savage, *Genealogical Dictionary*, 3:174.

[40] The chair is illustrated in Comstock, *American Furniture*, no. 17. I am indebted to Milo M. Naeve, Art Institute of Chicago, for providing samples of this chair for analysis.

[41] Winsor, *Memorial History of Boston*, 1:414–15.

[42] See, for example, Forman, "Urban Aspects of Massachusetts Furniture," p. 7, fig. 3; also Kane, *Furniture of the New Haven Colony*, no. 26.

[43] *Suffolk Deeds*, 1:68; Turners Company Minutes, 1: leaves 2, 14 (from front), and 8 (from back); *Essex Quarterly Courts*, 2:4.

[44] Drake, "Founders of New England," p. 307. *Suffolk Deeds*, 7:244; A. C. Stanley-Stone, *Worshipful Company of Turners*, pp. 291–92. The inventory of a Thomas Eddingsell was proved on Feb. 3, 1653 (Suffolk Probate, 2:185); Cowan, *Members of the Ancient and Honorable Artillery Company*, gives the date of his death as 1676. The records reveal that there were at least two men named Thomas Edsall in Boston during the third quarter of the seventeenth century.

[45] Savage, *Genealogical Dictionary*, 4:604; Suffolk Probate 6: pt. 2, p. 282.

[46] Trent, "Joiners and Joinery of Middlesex County" (thesis), pp. 24–25, 136.

[47] Trent, "Joiners and Joinery of Middlesex County" (thesis), p. 25.

[48] Docket 1142, Suffolk Superior Court Files, 12: leaves 48, 50.

[49] Suffolk Probate, 5:273–74.

[50] In Cambridgeshire, England, for example, a "bunch" of reeds consisted of "a bundle 28 inches round"; while in Hampshire, a "bundle of oziers" was "42 inches round the lower band" (Donisthorpe, *System of Measures*, p. 206). According to Hatton (*Merchant's Magazine*, p. 234), a "bundle of bulrushes" was 1/60 part a load, but he does not define a load.

[51] Docket 6372, Essex Probate Files.

[52] See Gould account book, p. 87; Forman, "Delaware Valley 'Crookt Foot' and Slat-Back Chairs," p. 44.

[53] Suffolk Superior Court Files, 12: leaf 50.

[54] See Gilbert, "Regional Traditions in English Vernacular Furniture," p. 70 and fig. 16.

[55] Nutting, *Pilgrim Century* (2d ed.), pp. 282, 293.

[56] For example, Nutting, *Furniture Treasury*, 2:1816, 1821, 1855, 1876, 1888, 1889, 1922, 1980, 1981, 1982, 1984, 1993, 1994, 2003, 2011, 2012, 2020, 2021, 2029–43.

[57] Plymouth Inventories, 3: pt. 2, p. 36.

[58] For example, Eaton, *Handicrafts of the Southern Highlands*, p. 152–54.

[59] Turners Company Minutes, 1 (from back): leaves 29 recto, 131 verso.

[60] Nutting, *Pilgrim Century* (1st ed.), p. 205; Fales, *Furniture of Historic Deerfield*, p. 20, fig. 12. For the Stryker chair see Comstock, *American Furniture*, no. 19.

[61] Lyon, *Colonial Furniture*, p. 143 and fig. 57; Metropolitan Museum of Art, acc. no. 10.125.677; Frances Gruber Safford to Forman, February 17, 1981; I am indebted to Philip Dunbar for information on the Connecticut Historical Society chair and to Robert Blair St. George for calling the Cushing family chair to my attention.

[62] See Lockwood, *Colonial Furniture* (2d ed.) 2:14, 16; the first of these is now in the collection of the Metropolitan Museum of Art, but the whereabouts of the second is presently unknown.

[63] See, for example, Nutting, *Furniture Treasury*, 2: 1786; Eaton, *Handicrafts of the Southern Highlands*, pp. 151–65; and Wigginton, *Foxfire Book*, pp. 128–37.

[64] Irving P. Lyon, "Square-Post Slat Back Chairs," pp. 210–16; with the exception of his chair no. 3, which appears to be joiner-made and executed in the English manner, the rest are in the continental European tradition, as are all of these illustrated in the paintings Lyon found. One example, no. 5, was presented as New England in origin although it was found in Saratoga, N.Y., and could well have been made by a New York craftsman of German or Dutch extraction or, indeed, might be of European origin.

[65] *Diary of William Bentley*, 1:448; Savage, *Genealogical Dictionary*, 2:124; see also Fales, *American Painted Furniture*, p. 14.

[66] George M. Bodge, "Soldiers in King Philip's War," p. 176; *Essex Quarterly Courts*, 8:317–18. Samuel Beadle, Jr., was the father of Lemon Beadle, to whom goes the distinction of executing the earliest documentable piece of free-standing sculpture in Massachusetts, the "handsome wooden soldier" atop the watchtower "in the middle of the street between Mulliken's shop and Stearns and Waldo's brick store . . . [with] Anno Regina in gold letters, 1712" on it (Pickman, "Some Account of Houses," p. 103). Perley, *History of Salem*, 2:385–87; *Essex Probate*, 1:452. For additional information on conflicts between Channel Islanders and native New Englanders, see Konig, "A New Look at the Essex 'French,'" pp. 167–80 (I am indebted to Robert Blair St. George for this reference).

[67] Wyman, *Genealogies and Estates of Charlestown*, 1:70; Belknap, *Trades and Tradesmen*, p. 66; Essex County Deeds, 2: leaf 94; *Salem Records*, 2:279.

[68] Docket 16220, Middlesex Probate (I thank Robert F. Trent for calling this reference to my attention). The total value of Mrs. Oliver's estate was £1,096.19.2.

[69] Docket 6372, Essex Probate Files.

[70] Sewall, *Diary*, 2:839. A ludicrous sidelight on Governor Shute's insistence on maintaining his superiority in regard to being seated is detailed on May 31, 1715 (Sewall Diary, 2:792): "The Govr. comes first to Town," and "was carried from Mr. Dudley's to the Town-House in Cous[in] Dummer's Sedan: but twas too tall for the Staires, so was fain to be taken out near the top of them."

[71] *Essex Probate*, 1:223–25.

[72] Olive, "Furniture in a West Country Parish," pp. 19, 21.

[73] I am indebted to Robert Blair St. George for this count and its statistical tabulation.

[74] See Forman, "Continental Furniture Craftsmen in London," pp. 94–120, esp. pp. 106–20.

TURNED GREAT CHAIR WITH FLAG BOTTOM
Eastern Massachusetts, perhaps Boston, Suffolk County
1650–1675
WOODS: All members with original turned work, a popular (genus *Populus*);
all original seat lists, soft maple
OH 44½″ (112.4 cm)
SH 16¾″ (42.6 cm), SW 24½″ (62.2 cm), SD 21¾″ (52.3 cm)
PROVENANCE: Philip Flayderman; Henry Francis du Pont
58.681

If a chair of this quality were to come on the market today the popular publications that deal with antiques would probably describe it as an "important chair," and quite probably the actual details of what makes it important would be left to each reader's imagination.

Importance, of course, is relative and the appreciation of seventeenth-century turned work is an acquired taste. This chair is no aesthetic marvel to a person whose idea of the consummate American chair is one that was made in Philadelphia two generations later. But when a collector or curator sees such a chair, he knows that a chair of this elaboration is a rare survivor from colonial America, and as such should be preserved for future generations to see. The turner who made it was an artist of consummate mastery, for the chair's design consists of a repetition of the parts that give it its formal qualities, and the decoration has been subtly incised onto the wood within a very small compass. To the person who has visually experienced the earliest furniture produced in colonial New England, the intellectual appreciation of this chair is transformed into an emotional response, as the maker intended.

That a chair which has the particular qualities of this one should have come on the market as late as 1930 represents an antiques collector's dream come true; the early twentieth-century interest in furniture of this period had already put most of the furniture of this class into private collections. The chair was acquired for Winterthur from the collection of Philip Flayderman. Priced catalogues of the sale reveal that its significance and its excellent state of preservation were recognized at the time and that its superior attributes were acknowledged in the bidding for it, which ultimately rose to $4,000—a record price for that era.[1]

The two rows of spindles in the back as well as the rows of spindles beneath its arms give every suggestion that this chair is the product of one of the earliest schools of chairmaking in eastern Massachusetts, although it differs from the Standish, Eliot, Bradford, and Brewster chairs in a number of ways. Unlike those notable examples, it was designed to have a flag rather than a board bottom. It further differs from them in that it has no rectangular tenons nor do its tenons protrude through the upright posts. In addition, it is nowhere pinned. The tenon on the end of each crosspiece is turned to a slightly swelling bulbous shape (see fig. 38). This bulbous tenon takes advantage of the elastic quality of the unseasoned wood used to make the posts. When the rounds are knocked into the posts as the chair is assembled, the posts give slightly to receive them and then clasp them tightly once they are in place. Because the posts will shrink as they expel their natural moisture, the sides of the bulbous tenons that run parallel to the posts have been shaved

off with a knife so that they will not split the posts. Further evidence that the posts were made of uncured wood—if any be required—is the cast (warp) of the left front leg, which was straight when originally turned.

The spindles of this chair differ in style from those of the Bradford and Brewster chairs in that their central element consists of an urn shape rather than a baluster. This shape is mildly suggestive of the upper element of the applied half spindles on a Boston chest of drawers which has doors in the London manner. The top of the finial here is quite round compared with the many other early examples of American turned chairs whose tops are more elongated, which is further suggestive of the topmost knob of the London-derived, Boston-style applied spindles.[2] The top rail of the back has a strongly emphasized central round, flanked by hollows, as opposed to the undifferentiated elements of the analogous rails on the Plymouth-owned examples, and the termini of the horizontal rounds on this chair are somewhat more elongated than the corresponding elements on the Plymouth examples.

The distinctive arrangement of the elements that compose the finial—from top to bottom, a rounded knob above a straight-sided ring over a flaring disk atop a compressed ball—relates this chair to the Tufts family chair. The specific details of that chair's finial and those on the Winterthur example and the nonprotruding tenons on the Winterthur example suggest that the Winterthur chair is a slightly later version of the Tufts chair. The style of the finials on these two chairs may be regarded as the signature of their maker's shop or the school or workmanship that he introduced into this country. The finials and the presence of balusters on the posts further differentiate this school from the one which produced the Governor Bradford and Elder Brewster chairs. These balusters may in this specific instance represent a chronological attribute and for this reason the Winterthur example may be slightly later than the earliest possible date at which such a chair could have been made.

It is too much to hope that the distinctively woven seat of Winterthur's chair is original to it, differing as it does from the usual Anglo-American-style matted bottom we are accustomed to seeing on New England chairs. While the impressions of the flag bottom on the present seat lists are the only ones visible, the front seat list of turned ash is incongruous since the remaining three seat lists are maple. The front stretchers of ash are similarly inconsistent with side and back stretchers of a soft maple. Furthermore, the workmanship of the front list is noticeably different from its fellows and the front stretchers have only the remnants of one coat of black paint instead of the two that cover the rest of the chair. These inconsistencies suggest that the front seat list and front stretchers are not original to the chair. And if only three of the seat lists are original, it is virtually impossible that the seat could be.

As opposed to the Tufts chair, which is made entirely of ash, some of the original parts of the Winterthur chair are made of poplar (*Populus*). It is probable that this wood, a relatively soft and close-grained hardwood, was chosen as a chairmaker's material because it was easy to turn on a man-powered lathe and because it took paint well. Poplar is the same wood that the maker of the Mather family highchair used

cat. 1

(see fig. 36). A closer look at a number of chairs, many previously estimated as being of maple, has revealed that poplar was a much more commonly used wood in the earliest American turned chairs that we have previously suspected. One of these chairs, which varies from the Winterthur example only in that each spindle has an ovoid rather than an urn-shape element at the center, is in the collection of the Concord (Massachusetts) Antiquarian Society. Although it has been restored from the seat lists downward, the remaining parts (not microanalyzed) appear to be poplar. A slat-back version of these chairs, probably from the same shop but not made with the same distances between its cross elements, is in the collection of Historic Deerfield. Wood analysis reveals that it is made of poplar. Other examples of this school, which may be later still, are owned by the Society for the Preservation of New England Antiquities (SPNEA), and the Wadsworth Atheneum. Both are made of poplar.[3]

The Atheneum example was once owned by Wallace Nutting and illustrated in his *Furniture Treasury* as no. 1801. Perhaps it was pride of ownership that caused Nutting to describe it as a "great Carver chair," although in all fairness, he may have been using the word "great" in its seventeenth-century sense, meaning "large." Nutting also observed that the chair has the "Best Back Known." In *Pilgrim Century*, where this chair is illustrated as no. 306, he elaborated on his judgment by stressing "its massiveness, and the [quaint] character of its turnings."[4] Wedded to the notion that massiveness was to be equated with earliness, Nutting could easily rate his chair highly.

Nutting's criteria and attitudes embody one of the quasi-art-historical theories that are often used to date objects that cannot be dated from documentary evidence: early forms are more crude than later ones. Little support for this theory can be found when we compare Nutting's chair with the triangular chairs of the Middle Ages. In the ongoing attempt to refine the techniques of art historical criticism, an equally cogent and more immediate theory has developed: that refined forms "decline" into coarser ones. If we assume that the Winterthur chair closely resembles a European prototype that had shortly before been introduced into this country, then it could be argued that the Nutting example, with its single row of three large spindles in the back instead of two rows of four smaller ones, represents the decline of this tradition because of the observable coarsening of the design. The proliferation of details (substitution of disks for the hollow above the cup of the spindles and addition of disks above the balusters on the posts), and the simplification of the design from its earlier, refined form (elimination of the spindles under the arms and the lower baluster of the back posts, for example) also suggest a decline from an earlier tradition.

While the idea that the spindles and balusters of the Nutting chair are "coarser" than those of the Winterthur example is subjective, Nutting points out one objective feature that is common to both chairs: the rear posts are thicker at the top than they are at the feet. In the Nutting chair, the taper is quite pronounced

and is even visible in the photograph. In the Winterthur chair, it is very delicate, amounting only to $1/8''$ (0.3 cm).

Of course, there is no proof that both chairs were made by the same craftsman or even by the same school of craftsmen. But it cannot be denied that the close similarity of the chairs suggests that one was the model for the other, whether that model was seen in passing or a continuation of one designer's ideas, by his son or an apprentice. Granting that all craftsmen do not have the same abilities or vision, we still have difficulty explaining how a coarse design becomes refined in a relatively short span of time when ample evidence for the opposite direction of change can be found throughout the American colonial decorative arts.

Putting quibbles about aesthetic evaluation aside, Winterthur's chair and related examples, reveal one of the few instances that confirms the idea that the early spindle-back-chair makers of New England also made slat-back chairs. The chair illustrated by Irving W. Lyon as no. 57 in *Colonial Furniture* (see fig. 39) must have come from the same shop as the present example. If the Winterthur example is as early as it appears to be, then it logically follows that slat-back chairs were made here in the first generation of settlement. Comparison of the appearance of the two chairs reveals similarity in details: the compressed balusters are the same, the handgrips are the same, and the horizontal members of both have elongated ovoids at their extremities. Further, both have pairs of vergier marks about $3/16''$ (0.5 cm) apart on the posts at points where double vergier marks are not needed for structural purposes.

A comparison of the vergier marks on the Winterthur chair and on the slat-back version at Deerfield was revealing. It demonstrated that the finials are exactly the same, but that the back of the slat-back chair is taller from the seat rail upwards and the arm is lower. Aside from the incised marks for the finial, no other vergier marks matched up, although the turned balusters on the rear stiles of both chairs are the same size. These indicate that two different vergiers were used for the two chairs, and that the system of spacing the elements on the two chairs proceeded from the same habits of thought—as sure an indication of the continuity of one man's concepts of design as any pattern would be, if we are keen enough to detect it.

N O T E S
[1] *Flayderman Sale*, p. 271, no. 506. To put this price into perspective, a slant-front, ox-bow-front desk with claw feet bearing the label of Benjamin Frothingham in the same sale (pp. 146–47, no. 418) fetched $3,600.
[2] See illustrations of these in Forman, "Urban Aspects of Massachusetts Furniture," pp. 7, 11, 13.
[3] I am indebted to J. Peter Spang III, curator of the Historic Deerfield collections, for providing me with a wood sample for microanalysis and for the exact measurements of the distances between the vergier marks on the back posts. The chair is illustrated in Fales, *Furniture of Historic Deerfield*, fig. 11. Additional examples of the slat-back version are illustrated in Barnes and Meals, *American Furniture in the Western Reserve*, p. 12, and *Garvan Sale*, no. 127. I am indebted to Robert Blair St. George for calling my attention to the SPNEA example and to Phillip M. Johnston, former chief curator of the Wadsworth Atheneum, for providing me with a sample of their chair for microanalysis.
[4] Nutting, *Pilgrim Century* (2d ed.), pp. 299–300.

2.
TURNED GREAT CHAIR WITH RUSH BOTTOM
Eastern Massachusetts, perhaps vicinity of Rowley, Essex County
1640–1680
WOOD: American white or red ash (*Fraxinus americana* or *Fraxinus pennyslvanica*)
OH 47″ (119.4 cm)
SH 18¾″ (47.6 cm), SW 26″ (66.0 cm), SD 18½″ (47.0 cm)
PROVENANCE: Harry Arons; Henry Francis du Pont
58.682

Few chairs of this quality of workmanship, elaborateness of design, and, above all, excellent condition have survived from America's seventeenth century. Because so few of its decorative motifs can be found in exactly this form on other chairs, because its back, arms, and stretchers exhibit very little wear, because the top rail of the back is poorly conceived and executed relative to the rest of the chair and is made to fit tightly by the addition of leather washers, because the handholds have survived on very slender necks, and because the parts exhibit very little warping, several connoisseurs of early furniture have questioned its antiquity. And to their list of reservations may be another: the random arrangement of vergier marks on the stiles at all points where the back and arm crosspiece enter the uprights is serious cause for suspicion.

Indeed, since chairs of such quality have commanded high prices for the past century, it is right and proper to question these points, all of which contradict the cardinal points of connoisseurship of spindle-back chairs. Moreover, it is well known that "Elizabethan" furniture was rediscovered in the third decade of the nineteenth century and the great demand for chairs in that style was gratified by willing craftsmen who still possessed eighteenth-century tools, which were not much different from seventeenth-century ones, and knowledge of the techniques of earlier handicrafts. In the light of this, connoisseurs have every right to be wary, not of the late nineteenth- and early twentieth-century impostures, which usually betray themselves by being modeled too closely on famous examples long ago captured for historical societies and museums, but of the older ones, some of which now have almost a century and a half of wear on them.

John Claudius Loudon documented the beginnings of this phenomenon in England in 1833.

The Style of Finishing and Furniture which prevailed in England during the reigns of Elizabeth and James I. exhibits a mixture of the Italian Architecture with the Gothic; sometimes very rudely composed; and, at other times, in consequence of being in the hands of superior artists, forming harmonious compositions of lines and forms. The remains of furniture in this style are abundant throughout the country; and, as we have before observed, it has of late become fashionable among the metropolitan cabinetmakers to collect it. We shall [illustrate] a few examples, for the sake of showing that this mixed style may be easily applied to all the articles of modern convenience and luxury. . . . The object of these observations is, to show that the present taste for Elizabethan furniture is more that of an antiquary, or of a collector of curiosities, than that of a man of cultivated mind.[1]

It is but a step from the collecting of antiquities to the reproduction of them, and in nineteenth-century America, where British fashions were greatly admired, many reproductions were made. A remarkable extract from a Maine newspaper of 1845 documents an early instance of the taste for antiquities and, more important, the natural consequence of materials in short supply.

There is at present a great rage in some parts of the country for collecting specimens of ancient furniture—a strange freak in the popular taste, which degenerates into a ludicrous one when we find persons who cannot tell what is really ancient, from new things made to look old by order of enterprising manufacturers! In Providence the fever runs high, and is satirized thus in a late number of the Journal of that city. . . .

Fashion, which regulates everything, for a long time held the *Mayflower furniture* in the highest estimation, and it is almost beyond calculating the number of chairs tables and sofas "that came over on the Mayflower," which are scattered through the houses of our city. . . . The Mayflower furniture is beginning to be rather common; and Roger Williams' furniture is at present most in demand. An ingenious mechanic, who had made a great deal of Mayflower furniture, informs us that articles warranted to have been in the family of Roger Williams are decidedly preferred at present. He has made four chairs and one table of this latter description.[2]

This early demand for reproduction furniture in America was not confined to Rhode Island. In the 1840s and 1850s, J. C. Commerford of New York "Made reproductions of Carver, Brewster, and Winslow chairs of seventeenth century from old seasoned oak."[3] It is unlikely that Commerford's chairs would confuse a sophisticated connoisseur today for if they were made of seasoned wood they would not exhibit the shrinkage out of round as do old chairs turned from unseasoned wood. Moreover, the Winslow chair, although made of oak is of joined rather than turned construction, and neither the Brewster nor the Carver chair was made of oak. Indeed, oak is so rarely found in American turned chairs that the presence of this wood in a chair is the first indication that it may be a reproduction.

While all this information is of some help in understanding the hazards of dealing with spindle-back chairs, it is of very little help in understanding Winterthur's chair. This chair exhibits no false leads, except for the vergier marks, and those on other examples have sometimes also proven to be erratic. The chair is made of ash, either American white or American red (*Fraxinus americana* or *Fraxinus pennsylvanica*), both of which are native to the eastern half of the country from Maine to Florida. In addition, this chair closely resembles a chair in the collections of the Smithsonian Institution that is dated 1691 on the rear face of its topmost slat and descended from John Picard of Rowley, Massachusetts (fig. 44). The finials of the two chairs—only portions of which remain on each—are closely related. The turned stretchers of the two chairs have similar elongated termini. And, finally, the locations of the vergier marks are, with few exceptions, similar on both chairs. The marks used at the top of the back posts show that the posts of both chairs were turned with a slat-back chair in mind as the final product. At some point during the production of the Winterthur example, the maker of these two chairs combined back posts meant for a slat-back with details and proportions used on the spindle-back versions.

cat. 2

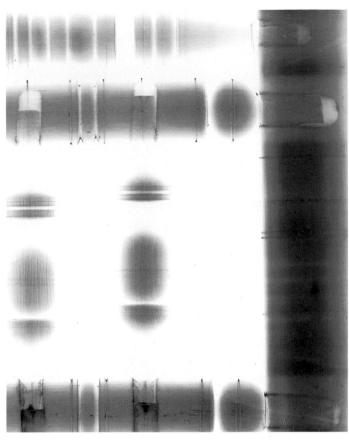

Fig. 45. X-ray photograph of part of the back and one upright of the turned armchair in catalogue entry 2. (Winterthur 58.682.)

Fig. 44. Turned great chair with slat back, possibly Essex County, Mass., 1691. Oak: H 42½″ (108 cm), D.16½″ (41.9 cm). (Greenwood Collection, Smithsonian Institution, Washington, D.C.) The first owner of the chair is believed to have been John Picard of Rowley, Mass.

An X ray of the back portion of Winterthur's chair (fig. 45) clearly reveals the chair is handmade. The auger holes were drilled with a pod (spoon or quill) bit which has a characteristic round shoulder. Furthermore, the dark shadow at the very bottom of the holes clearly shows the little mound of uncut wood that such a bit churns up in cutting but does not remove. The auger holes are of varying depths, as is expected in the case of a hand-powered drill with no stop or other device attached to prevent the holes from being drilled beyond a specific depth. The triangular shadows faintly visible in the center of the end of each horizontal round are graphic evidence that they were turned on a pole lathe with two points on which the wood revolved, rather than a lathe which has the single point at one end and a mandrel on the other. The triangles are also visible on one end of each of the large and small spindles of the back, each pair of which appears to have been turned in one piece and subsequently sawn apart for fitting into the chair back. Both ends of the top rail also exhibit these shadows.

A photograph of this chair taken before Henry Francis du Pont purchased it in the spring of 1947 reveals that the feet were missing from slightly below the bottom stretcher and that the turned plumes of the finials were also missing. The points at which the plumes joined the remaining part of the finials are irregular and well worn indicating that they have long been missing. It would have been a clever forger, indeed, who would make a chair with plumed finials and then remove them. The joints of the chair are held together with glue. There is no evidence that this chair was ever painted. The present finish is brown stain varnish.

NOTES
[1] Loudon, *Encyclopedia of Architecture and Furniture*, pp. 1098–99. There follow invidious comparisons with the designs of Thomas Hope.
[2] Portland *Transcript* (Aug. 2, 1845) as cited in Shettleworth in "Clues and Footnotes," p. 470.
[3] Dreppard, *Handbook of Antique Chairs*, p. 258. Winterthur's Cabinetmaker File in the Decorative Arts Photographic Collection (DAPC) reveals that John C. Commerford, a chairmaker, worked on his own account at various New York City locations between 1831 and 1848. Between 1848 and 1853 he worked in partnership with Edmund Redgate under the firm name Commerford and Redgate, and between 1856 and 1859, with Charles C. Commerford when the firm was known as John Commerford and Company.

TURNED CHAIR WITH RUSH BOTTOM
Eastern New England, probably northern Essex County, Massachusetts, or
southern New Hampshire
1650–1690
WOODS: Spindles and rounds, American black ash (*Fraxinus nigra*), rear legs,
Ohio buckeye (*Aesculus glabra*)
OH 36½″ (92.7 cm)
SH 15⅗″ (40.0 cm), SW 19⅝″ (49.8 cm), SD 13½″ (34.3 cm)
PROVENANCE: Gift of Henry Francis du Pont
58.693

Fig. 46. Turned great chair with spindle back, eastern New England, probably
northern Essex County, Mass., or adjacent Rockingham County, N.H.,
1650–90. Posts are poplar (genus *Populus*), rear seat rail is black ash (*Fraxinus
nigra*); H 40⅝″ (103.2 cm), W at rockers 25½″ (64.8 cm), D 14½″ (36.8 cm),
SH 16¼″ (41.3 cm). (SPNEA, Boston, gift of Mrs. Bertram K. Little. Photo:
J. David Bohl.) The chair has a history of ownership in the Leonard Weeks
family of Sandwich and Greenland, N.H. When the rockers were added, some
years later, the feet were shortened and notched. The finials are a recent
restoration.

Diminutive chairs are often referred to among collectors as
"lady chairs," a term that suggests that they were made for
women. The assumption appears to be based upon the idea
that ladies were invariably smaller than men and that in the
paternalistic society of seventeenth-century New England the
woman of the household was not entitled to an armchair. An
English precedent is the "woman's armed stool" specified as
a proof piece for membership in London's joiner's company
in 1616. In November 1681 Daniel Bartlett of Newbury,
Massachusetts, noted in his accounts a credit to the account of
turner-chair maker Samuel Poore (1653–1727, w. ca. 1674)
for "one chaire for a woman."[1]

That women's chairs were verbally distinguished from
men's chairs suggests the difference was easily recognizable
during the period. The London "woman's stool" had arms,
which implies that the presence or absence of arms was not the
distinguishing feature and essentially leaves only size as the
criterion. Of course we may be reading too much into these
scanty documents: it is quite possible that Bartlett, for
example, was not leaving a design message for posterity but
was merely recording that he was buying a chair for his wife.
Seventeenth-century inventories abound in references to "little
low chairs" and many such chairs are today preserved in
museums and private collections. It could be argued that the
low chairs were the seventeenth-century equivalent of the
nursing chairs or "nurse chairs" referred to in eighteenth-
century documents and plentifully illustrated in nineteenth-
century furniture manufacturers' catalogues and advertisements. The seats of these later chairs are invariably lower than
average, and the chairs rarely have arms, which make them
more convenient for nursing.

Winterthur's chair was catalogued as a Massachusetts chair
in Harvard's tercentenary exhibition.[2] Since the attribution
is not documented, we can only assume that it was then
owned by a Massachusetts family and had a tradition of ownership that was not mentioned, or that it had been found
in Massachusetts. The finials of the chair suggest that the
attribution was correct. To be more precise, the finials are
similar to the Suffolk County type and to others which
originated in eastern Massachusetts. While the vertical
spindles and horizontal rounds of the back are made of
American black ash (*Fraxinus nigra*), the rear legs are made of
the wood of the tree known as the "horse chestnut" or "Ohio
buckeye" (*Aesculus glabra*). The annular rings suggest that the
tree from which the wood was taken was rather small. Buckeye
is an extremely uncommon wood not heretofore known to be
native to Massachusetts; the present natural distribution of the
tree is from western Pennsylvania, west and south to eastern

Kansas and central Texas, and in parts of central Tennessee.[3]
Although the distribution is contrary to the supposed
provenance of the present chair, the chair itself is without
question old and cannot be a reproduction. An armchair by
this same maker (fig. 46), now in the collection of SPNEA,
has poplar (*Populus*) uprights.[4] Like the SPNEA chair,
which has a well-documented history of ownership in the
Weeks family of Sandwich and Greenland, New Hampshire,
this chair was probably made in the area around the southern
border of New Hampshire and the northern part of Essex
County, Massachusetts.

Beyond the irregularities of woods used in the Winterthur
chair, its front legs present their own special problems. They
are made of maple and are repaired; they serve as a textbook
illustration of the type of evidence that is necessary to support
conclusions regarding repairs. (The word "repair" is consistently used rather than "replacement," because it distinguishes work done to prolong the usefulness of an object from
modern work that attempts to reconstruct what the replaced

members may have originally looked like. It is perhaps an unfortunate axiom of furniture connoisseurship that we can often date an object accurately on the basis of its appearance, but only rarely can we date a replacement.) That the front legs of this chair are only $1\frac{5}{8}''$ (4.1 cm) in diameter as opposed to the $2\frac{1}{8}''$ (5.4 cm) diameter of the back legs was immediate cause for suspicion since New England chairs tend to have front and rear legs of the same diameter. Examination of the front legs and their stretchers under a binocular microscope revealed that they have only a single coat of black paint. The rear stiles have three: a thin wash of black next to the wood, a thick coat of tan paint, and the outer coat of black. If the parts of the chair had always been together, each element should at some place reveal that same sequence of paints, if only in the sharpest concave turnings. The rear stiles of the chair are buckeye, while the front legs are a hard maple (probably *Acer saccharum*). Although the rule that the four legs of a chair should be of the same wood cannot be supported by a written document, it is, with only one known exception, the invariable custom on the other seventeenth-century turned chairs examined during the preparation of this book.[5] Furthermore, ornamental turning should be the same on front and back legs. And unlike the back legs, the front legs lack scribe marks indicating where the seat lists and stretchers were to intersect them. Finally, the style of the turnings of the front legs suggests that they are an honest repair made to extend the life of the chair during the eighteenth century.

N O T E S
[1] Daniel Bartlett account book, leaf 32 verso; Belknap, *Trades and Tradesmen*, p. 83; and Belknap, *Artists and Craftsmen*, p. 65.
[2] *Harvard Tercentenary*, p. 48, no. 186, and pl. 29.
[3] Fowells, *Silvics of Forest Trees*, p. 75.
[4] Brock Jobe to Forman, May 25, 1977.
[5] The only recorded exception is a chair attributed to Ephraim Tinkham II (1649–1713) of Plymouth and Middleborough, Mass., now in the collection of the Pilgrim Society, Plymouth, Mass.; the chair has front posts of maple and rear posts of ash. St. George, *Wrought Covenant*, p. 50, no. 46.

4.
TURNED GREAT CHAIR WITH MATTED SEAT
Probably southeastern New England
1640–1680, modified at a later date
WOOD: American ash (probably *Fraxinus americana*)
OH $41\frac{7}{8}''$ (106.4 cm)
SH $17\frac{1}{4}''$ (43.8 cm), SW $24\frac{7}{8}''$ (63.2 cm), SD $21\frac{5}{8}''$ (54.9 cm)
PROVENANCE: Winsor White; Henry Francis du Pont
58.684

The turnings of the finials and rear spindles of this chair relate it to catalogue entry 3. The chair was identified by Winsor White, shortly before his death, as one of the many items he had found for the Winterthur collection.[1] Although the records of Henry Francis du Pont do not show when it was acquired, this chair may be the one that White fondly recalled as an Alden chair when he recounted collecting adventures in 1947: he described it as an "early slatbacked, mushroom arm-chair with the original braided corn-husk seat."[2] Winterthur's chair does not have a slat-back, and we can only attribute that discrepancy to a lapse of memory, faulty reporting, or the number of years that had passed between his discovery of the chair for du Pont and the granting of the interview. The use of the term "Alden chair," in the context of the interview does not seem to indicate that he was attempting to establish another category of chairs to go with the ideas of "Carver," "Brewster," and "Standish" chairs, but rather that he purchased the chair from a family that was related to the Aldens. The style of the finials and spindles is characteristic of the Plymouth Colony and relate this portion of the chair to the Brewster and Bradford chairs. That this chair is more coarsely turned, that it lacks a board seat, that it has one row of spindles in the back instead of two, and that the spindles lack some of the elements found on the Brewster and Bradford chairs (compare with fig. 33) suggests that it was made at a later date. The distinctive feature of the chair is its corn-husk seat which, could it be shown to be of the same period as the back, would be one of the most notable survivals of American seventeenth-century chairmaking.

The chair is a remarkable subject for study and that study still raises more questions than it answers. An old photograph of it in the files at Winterthur reveals that the left spindle of the back had disappeared and the corn-husk seat was sagging badly. The spindle has been masterfully reconstructed, perhaps by Arthur van Reeth, who worked as a restorer for the Winterthur collection before the museum was opened to the public. The spindle is almost indistinguishable from the original ones which, like it, have broken places in the ash and white paint deep in the pores. The replaced spindle was made of well-seasoned wood, which has shrunk no further and, therefore, does not rotate like the older two. The seat has been preserved by the canvas reinforcement attached underneath it. The seat lists are turned and are characteristically flat on their top and inner margins as if they were further shaped with a draw knife or spoke shave. The corn husks have left distinctively wide patterned impressions on the seat lists. There is

Fig. 47. Detail of the front seat rail and plaited corn-husk seating of the chair in catalogue entry 4. (Winterthur 58.684.)

DISTANCE	FRONT LEGS	REAR LEGS
arm to seat list	10¹⁶⁄₃₂″ (26.7 cm)	10¹³⁄₃₂″ (26.4 cm)
seat list to top side stretcher	7¹⁵⁄₃₂″ (19.0 cm)	7¹⁶⁄₃₂″ (19.1 cm)
top side stretcher to top front stretcher	1¹³⁄₃₂″ (3.58 cm)	not scribed
top side stretcher to bottom side stretcher	5²⁶⁄₃₂″ (14.8 cm)	5³⁰⁄₃₂″ (15.1 cm)
bottom side stretcher to bottom front and rear stretchers	1¹²⁄₃₂″ (3.5 cm)	1²⁵⁄₃₂″ (4.5 cm)

no evidence on these lists that this chair was ever bottomed with flag or rush. The finely twisted fibers of the flag bottoms, seldom more than ⅜″ (1 cm) in diameter, leaves a characteristic, narrow impression of the twisted fibers on the lists. Corn husks, in contrast, are twisted together to form a twine and then braided or plaited before being woven into the seat; thus the impression is much broader (fig. 47). If the present seat were replacing a flag seat, the impression of the flag bottom would also be present on the lists. Since there is no flag impression, it is fair to assume that the husk bottom is original to these lists.

Next, the question of whether this seat and these lists are original to the chair must be pursued. The chair itself violates three elementary rules that most seventeenth-century turned chairs follow. First, the turned balusters on the front stiles are not repeated on the rear stiles between the seat and the crest rail. This causes us to suspect that the front legs and the rear structure were not originally made to go together. Confirmation of this suspicion is found in the violation of the second rule: the front and rear posts are not of the same wood. The rear legs are an ash (definitely not the European *Fraxinus excelsior*; perhaps *Fraxinus americana*), the front legs are a soft maple. Measured across the radial plane the front legs are ³⁄₁₆″ (0.5 cm) smaller in diameter than the rear ones. Third, the front legs are covered with a wash of brown paint while the color of the rear legs is a reddish hue and the patterns of *craquelure* also differs. To some extent these last differences can be explained by the characteristics of the woods of which the two sets of legs are made: open-grained ash absorbs the vehicle in which a paint pigment is suspended differently from close-grained maple. Similarly, the variation in the woods might explain away the disparity in the depth of the vergier marks on each set of legs since the same amount of pressure in applying this tool might produce scoring of different depths on woods of different hardness.

The vergier marks, however, offer an explanation for the differences between the front and rear legs that is not based upon any imponderables. On this chair vergier marks, scribed to indicate the placement of all cross rounds that are common to both the front and the rear legs, are not located at the same intervals on all four legs. Those on the rear two are identical to each other, as are those on the front pair. The scribed intervals are as follows:

Although the measurement of vergier marks has not been a part of the recorded data for turned chairs in the past, they are probably more important than any other measurement. Since these marks were executed with a fixed tool, they are the equivalent of patterns and are thus capable of being assessed on an objective rather than subjective basis. The identical intervals between the scribe marks on each pair of legs indicate the validity of the assumption that a vergier was used, while the differences between the marks on front and back legs indicate that the same vergier was not used on *both* sets of legs. That one of the significant scribe markings on the front legs is omitted from the rear ones is particularly damning, since legs made by one craftsman at the same time would be identically inscribed. Closer examination of the marks suggests that they were not made at the same time and were not made by the same craftsman: the deeply scored marks on the rear legs are steadily and firmly incised, the ones on the front legs are much more delicate.

The front legs must have come off another chair. Moreover, that chair has to have been very much like the present one since the placement of arms, lists, and stretchers on the front legs are quite close to those on the rear legs. The top rail of the back is also old but patently too narrow for this chair and too small in diameter to fit the auger holes in the stiles. That the termini of this crosspiece are not of the same size as those of the two below it is inconsistent with the usual practice of the day on related Plymouth Colony chairs and suggests that the top round is also a replacement. The side rounds of the chair, particularly the stretchers, fit the rear legs tolerably well but have tenons too long to fit the front posts properly. Except for the top round, the back seems to be of a piece and the bottom rear stretcher fits perfectly. The arms and side stretchers also seem to belong to this part of the chair. If this is so and the corn-husk seat is original to the lists, they may also be a part of the chair from which the back structure was taken. The question that cannot be answered by examining the chair is how the corn-husk seat could survive the addition of new legs and, even more to the point, if the legs were added in the eighteenth or nineteenth century, what was the reason for preserving the original seat when a more serviceable one could have been put in for a shilling or less?

It seems clear that this chair is made up of elements from three old chairs: the top rail from one chair, the front legs from another, and the rear legs, rounds, spindles, stretchers, and arms from yet another. Each group of elements appears to have been made by a different hand, but oddly enough, all of them seem to be of about the same date: the coarseness of the turning of the back legs puts them in the period of the second generation of South Shore turners, since they are not of the quality and conception of the Brewster and Bradford board-seat chairs, which are assumed to be of the first generation. The front legs have stylistic features that place them also in the second generation. The top rail, which deals in the same motifs as the back spindles, is definitely different from them but does not appear to postdate 1670, at the latest. While it is always possible that these parts were lying around in a family barn and were honestly put together sometime in the past, that three chairs are represented in this one might well suggest the parts came from a dealer's stockpile.

No matter how much we want this seventeenth-century chair to have an original corn-husk bottom, it would be foolish to assert incontrovertibly that its seat was original to it. If a corn-husk seat were to be preserved from the seventeenth century, it is likely that it would be found on a South Shore chair like this one. In the course of examining chairs for this book, several with seats similar to this one—all of them original to their chairs and all woven in the same pattern as this one—have been observed. Two of these chairs were of the slat-back type with William and Mary-style finials and probably did not predate 1740. One of these, privately owned, had no provenance. The other was in an antiques shop in Kingston,

Massachusetts, near Plymouth, circa 1963.[3] A third chair, in the study collection of the Winterthur Museum, has a banister back and is also of southern New England origin. Figure 47 shows a detail of its left seat list. Its style suggests that it was made between 1780 and 1815. To some extent these chairs give evidence as to the long period of time during which corn-husk seats were used in New England chairs. Perhaps some day more positive evidence of the use of corn husks as a bottoming material in the seventeenth century will be forthcoming, but for the moment, it is an idea that is yet to be proved.[4]

N O T E S
[1] Personal Interview by Forman, December 1, 1972.
[2] *Boston Sunday Post* (December 28, 1947), A-10.
[3] *Buxton's Guide to New England Antique Shops*, p. 97.
[4] *Aspinwall Notarial Records*, p. 400, lists "3 bailes Indian matts," among many other items that were not likely to have been made in New England, such as "12 chests of earthenware, 3 Chests glasses, one boxe of belts & girdles." While these items are doubtless being transported through Boston, there are also "200 bush[els of] pease [peas]," and "23 thousand pipe [barrel] staves" that are clearly the produce of New England. Whether the "Indian matts" were of East Indian, West Indian, or New England manufacture can only be surmised. If they were American, they might have been made of corn husks. See also catalogue entry 10.

5.
TURNED GREAT CHAIR WITH FLAG BOTTOM
Perhaps vicinity of Hingham, Massachusetts
1680–1700
WOOD: American ash (not *Fraxinus excelsior*)
OH 43¼″ (109.9 cm)
SH 17¾″ (45.1 cm), SW 33⅝″ (57.5 cm), SD 20⅝″ (52.4 cm)
PROVENANCE: Gift of Henry Francis du Pont
58.521

Although somewhat the worse for wear—the feet have been pieced out 6¾″ (17.1 cm), the three spindles in the back and the bottom stretchers have been replaced, the handholds at the top of the front posts have disappeared, and a layer of upholstery that covered the seat and the back and sides has been removed—this chair is a revealing document of the seventeenth-century chairmaker's art. It appears to have been made in the same shop as the Standish chair.[1]

Stylistically, both chairs are related to the Mather and Eliot chairs (see figs. 36 and 37), which originated in Suffolk County, Massachusetts, and the chair in catalogue entry 4, but all five were not made by the same hand. The balusters on the stiles of Winterthur's flag-bottom chair are more nearly conical in form and meet the upper section of the stiles without flaring outward. The topmost rail of the back is closely related to the Standish chair, although the rail of the latter has an additional element near its termini. These rails are original in both chairs and illustrate that ornamentation differed on top rails and lower rails during the seventeenth century. The finial of Winterthur's chair contrasts with that of the Mather chair; the knob at the top flares outward rather than being ovoid like the one on the Mather chair. Moreover, the disk at its base has

an angular margin slanting inward and downward rather than the sharply flared disk common on Suffolk County examples. When contrasted with the English family chair (see fig. 42), the finial reveals that the examples from the South Shore of Massachusetts Bay are yet another variation of the eastern Massachusetts style, dominated by the Suffolk County—probably Boston—group.

When the Standish chair is set next to its close relative at Winterthur, a startling contrast appears: although both chairs are definitely from the same school of turning, doubtless from the same shop and perhaps by the same turner, the Winterthur chair must have originally been much less expensive than the Standish chair. It never had more than three spindles, and, from the moment it was planned, it was destined to have a rush bottom. It is tempting to believe Winterthur's chair is later than the Standish chair because of these structural differences, but the quality of the turning of the posts is consistently the same in both chairs, and this, if nothing else, should cause us to ponder that facile assumption. What these two chairs represent instead—if what is demonstrably true of the cabinetmakers of the eighteenth century was also true of the turned-chair maker in the seventeenth-century—is that a stripped-down model was available for the customer who desired it, at the same time the deluxe version was being offered to the customer whose pretensions and pocketbook could command it.

N O T E
[1] This chair (discussed in the essay on joined chairs) is now owned by the Pilgrim Society, Plymouth, Mass., and displayed in Pilgrim Hall; see Nutting, *Furniture Treasury*, no. 1814.

cat. 5

6.

TURNED GREAT CHAIR
Probably eastern Massachusetts
1675–1700
WOODS: All American ash (not *Fraxinus excelsior*), except the replaced central
spindle, a maple
OH 41¼″ (104.8 cm)
SH 14⅜″ (36.6 cm), SW 23¾″ (60.3 cm), SD 19¾″ (36.7 cm)
PROVENANCE: Gift of Henry Francis du Pont
58.523

The present appearance of this turned great chair is misleading since only the four posts, the rounds or crosspieces, and two outside spindles of the back may have survived from the seventeenth century. The top front stretcher may also be old, since it betrays no visible attributes of restoration, although how it survived without those earmarks of wear that are the usual guides to antiquity in furniture is a question without an immediate answer. Other aspects of the chair violate our usual criteria: the front legs are of a subtly different color from the back ones and no two sets of vergier marks on any given legs quite match up. As if this were not enough, the appearance of the chair is further affected by the replaced stretchers, which were not turned, as is the custom with most seventeenth-century chairs, but were haphazardly worked with a draw-knife. The result is a chair whose four posts each point to a different spot in heaven.

Despite all of the shortcomings, when judged aesthetically, the chair retains an important feature that guarantees its right to be proudly displayed in any museum of decorative arts: part of the original back feet remain, and that one feature puts this ill-used document of seventeenth-century craft life and design in a class virtually by itself. The vestiges of the feet suggest that they were originally balusters much like the ones further up on the posts, and much like the feet on contemporaneous leather chairs belonging to more affluent citizens of urban New England during this period. If this foot consisted of only a single baluster of the same size as the last one on the rear leg, then the addition of the appropriate portion of that baluster to the leg gives us an original seat height of approximately 16″ (40.6 cm). (This should not be construed to mean that every turned chair had such a foot, or that 16″ [40.6 cm] was the height of every seventeenth-century seat, but it is refreshing that we can be so precise in this one instance.) Doubtless, too, the effective height of the seat was increased by a generously stuffed cushion.

The seat itself is probably not original to the chair for the simple reason that the lists are worked in the same manner as the stretchers and are wedged into the auger holes in the posts. Moreover the wood from which the seat was worked has been microanalyzed as mahogany, and no documentary evidence has been found to suggest that mahogany found its way into a piece of New England furniture in the third quarter of the seventeenth century. Nevertheless, the seat lists do not reveal that a flag seat was ever affixed to them, and so this seat may be considered original to them, although the lists are not original to the chair, thus suggesting that the repairs to the chair were executed in the eighteenth or nineteenth century and were done to prolong its usefulness.

Because the balusters are so abrupt and the finial so attenuated and somewhat removed from the more classic style represented by the chair illustrated in catalogue entry 1, it is easy to jump to the conclusion that this is a provincial chair, but the differences between these two chairs may be the differences of cultural time rather than those of geographic distance. One feature that the two chairs share is that the rear stiles are tapered: in this chair the bottoms of the rear posts are slightly more than ¼″ (0.6 cm) narrower in diameter than the tops. Further the shape of the balusters on the two remaining original spindles suggests the form of the applied half spindles used on non-Boston, eastern Massachusetts case furniture made in the third quarter of the seventeenth century, which gives us the broad date range for the style of this chair. Two other aspects of the turned elements suggest that the chair was made by a well-trained craftsman working in the early style. First, the crest rail motif echoes the form of the balusters, giving a unity to the turning that is not characteristic of provincial chairs. Second, the interstices between the balusters of the rear posts diminish from top to bottom in an orderly manner, and the balusters themselves are graduated from large to small. The measurement from the top of the finial to the top vergier mark for its baluster is 2″ (5.1 cm). The measurements between the vergier marks on the right rear stile are as follows:

MARK	BALUSTER		INTERVAL	
topmost	2 ¹²⁄₁₆″	(7.0 cm)	7⁵⁄₁₆″	(19.2 cm)
second	2″	(5.1 cm)	6⁸⁄₁₆″	(16.5 cm)
third	1¹⁵⁄₁₆″	(4.9 cm)	5¹⁄₁₆″	(12.9 cm)
fourth	1¹⁵⁄₁₆″	(4.9 cm)	4¹⁵⁄₁₆″	(12.5 cm)
fifth	1¹¹⁄₁₆″	(4.3 cm)	3¹²⁄₁₆″	(9.5 cm)
foot at present	⁶⁄₁₆″	(1.0 cm)		
(foot estimated)	(1¹¹⁄₁₆″)	[4.3 cm]		

The diminutions exist and increase the visual effectiveness of the chair.

The central spindle of the back is one of those mysteries that can be solved only with the aid of a crystal ball. It has every earmark of age, but its unique pattern and its soft maple wood preclude its being original to the chair. It appears to have been wedged into place without materially disturbing the other two spindles. The circumstances of its manufacture and installation elude the efforts of connoisseurship.

cat. 6

7.
TURNED GREAT CHAIR
New England, perhaps Massachusetts
1650–1700
WOODS: Stiles, rungs, and arms, American black ash (*Fraxinus nigra*); rear seat list, hickory (genus *Carya*); front seat list, white oak (*Quercus alba*)
OH 44⅛″ (112.1 cm)
SH 16½″ (41.9 cm), SW 24⅛″ (61.3 cm), SD 19⅝″ (49.8 cm)
PROVENANCE: Philip Flayderman; Henry Francis du Pont
58.522

Fig. 48. Detail of the chair in catalogue entry 7 showing the slightly bulbous shape of the swelled-end tenon. The residue of glue is clearly visible at the end of the tenon. (Winterthur 58.522.)

It is embarrassing for a cataloguer to have to be so imprecise in his estimate of the date and place of origin of a piece of furniture, but in the case of a turned, spindle-back chair, the imprecision is excusable because common chairs, such as this one, were made by every village turner in New England, and only in the most extraordinary circumstances is a family history or tradition of ownership—usually unprovable by inventories or other documents—attached to any turned chair.

This turned great chair is something of a monument to collecting fashions and advertising hype in the 1920s. It, along with that in catalogue entry 1, was a part of the Philip Flayderman collection. Both were advertised in the December 1929 issue of *Antiques*, and from this advertisement, we have deduced that the present chair was no. 507 in the sale catalogue of the Flayderman collection. The catalogue is restrained in praise of the chair: it states merely that the chair is "in original condition."[1] The advertisement is considerably more hyperbolic:

CARVER CHAIR (c. 1670). In every respect original, unstained and unpainted, and with finials and turnings intact. The chair is exceptionally distinguished among surviving examples of its type.[2]

When we examine the chair today, we might wonder if we were looking at the same object, so greatly does it differ from its description, and were it not illustrated, we might doubt either our sanity or the level of connoisseurship practiced by the cataloguers of but half a century ago, when most of the great collections of American furniture had already been formed. First, the checked seat is not original, the original probably was flag or rush. Second, the seat lists are replacements, as is clear from the auger holes drilled for them, which are the same size as the holes for arms and rungs but are too large for the present whittled lists and have been plugged to accept them. Third, the scribed lines on the chair still retain traces of a coat of black paint that can be seen with a low-power magnifying glass, and, while that coat of paint might not have been original, it is so deeply soaked into the wood that it remains there today, even though sometime in the past this chair was subjected to a caustic lye solution. Indeed, the corrosive effect of that stripping solution indicates the chair was dipped in it. This method of paint removal created the chair's present weathered and sandblasted appearance, and such ruthless stripping would scarcely have been necessary unless the chair had many coats of paint on it. Last, the turnings are fairly well preserved, but the turned knobs or handholds that once surmounted the front legs are missing. They were probably removed because they were in bad condition. That removal was none too ceremonious; the rough swipes of the saw that accomplished it are clearly visible.

These evidences of use, change, and repair combined with turned ornamentation on the rear legs that matches that of the front legs, a fairly uncommon occurrence among reproduction chairs, suggest that, despite appearances, this is an old chair.

The orientation of the grain of the wood of the stiles in relation to the stretchers and seat lists is orderly and systematic. The side rungs and side lists are perpendicular to the annular rings of the rear legs, which means that the rear legs are slightly rotated in relation to the rear rungs. The front legs are canted inward so that the annular rings are not perfectly oriented to either the side or the front stretchers. The rungs and arms are slightly flared at each end (fig. 48). This would seem to confirm that the maker relied more upon the elasticity of the wood to hold the rungs securely in place than upon shrinkage of the posts to secure the joints. The stiles have indeed shrunk about 1/16″ (0.2 cm) on the tangential line or, as is commonly but ambiguously said, "across the grain." This tiny amount of shrinkage in the stiles, which are about 2 1/16″ (5.2 cm) in diameter suggests that shrinkage of the posts onto the rungs was not a consideration in the maker's mind. Further confirmation of this is the generous amount of dried glue still remaining on the tenon and visible in the illustration. The arms and rungs have shrunk only a minute amount out of round, indicating that they, too, were made from wood that was virtually dry.

The auger hole for the right arm that was drilled in the right rear stile is illustrated in figure 49 and offers graphic evidence of the gentle-shoulder, flat-bottom shape of the pod auger generally used by the seventeenth-century chairmaker. The beginning connoisseur, however, should be warned that the shape of such holes is governed by the shape of the bit that made them and these bits were originally made to no recognizable standard except diameter. In time the worn bits were resharpened many times and the holes that they made may have had many different profiles. Indeed, if a forger chose to make a chair with old tools, his deception would be difficult to recognize from the evidence of tool marks alone.

The chair is made completely of ash, following an English tradition. While the minimal treatment of the turned ornament on this chair suggests that it is of village origin and that might

cat. 7

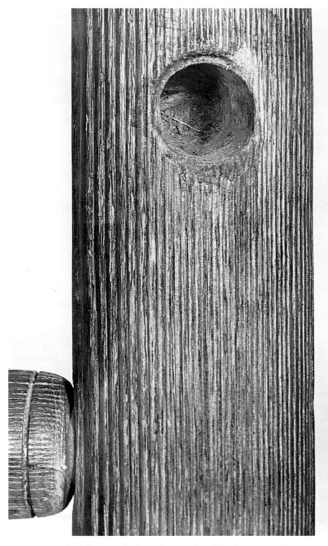

Fig. 49. Detail of the auger hole in the upright of the chair in catalogue entry 7. The configuration of the cut surface indicates that turner used a pod auger. (Winterthur 58.522.)

be defaced according to the orders."[3] And, at least in 1609, there were not many differences in the style of common chairs, for those made in Colchester could find a market in London.

While Winterthur's chair is not of conspicuous aesthetic merit, the rarity of the form itself makes it collectable and a member of a rather small class of chairs that probably does not number more than fifty in all. Inasmuch as the chair came from the Flayderman collection, it would be tempting to attribute it to a Connecticut origin, since that is where Flayderman did most of his collecting. Similarly the ornamentation of each stile (a truncated baluster) might tempt us to dissociate this chair from a Massachusetts origin. However, the design of the finials, albeit rather coarse and four square in outline, is in the Massachusetts manner and makes a tentative attribution to that colony more probable, although far from certain.

The date at which the chair was made is another matter. In a valuable article on English vernacular furniture, Christopher Gilbert illustrates an ash chair made very much in the manner of the present chair, which he dates as circa 1800.[4] His date is perfectly believable, but the question must naturally arise as to why our American chair is dated more than a century earlier than a close English relative. In the absence of firmly dated examples either from England or America, the dating of the two chairs is based upon a number of assumptions. In America, we tend to believe that American furniture makers attempted to reflect current styles in their work. Second, because of New England's relatively sparse settlement, the hinterland relied on the urban settlements along the coast. Third, communication between the settlements—usually by water—was somewhat quicker in New England than was similar communication between the urban centers of England and the countryside. My assumption, therefore, is that in America village-made furniture more quickly reflected the change of styles in subtle ways, by changes of proportion and by the introduction of new stylistic elements.

in turn be derived from an English rural style, the use of ash in English chairs is not necessarily a rural habit. In 1609 the Worshipful Company of Turners of London ordered "whereas certayne Chaires are brought from Colchester, made there by one [blank] ffor that many of the Seatlists are made of Aspe wch should only be of Ashe according to the orders of this mistery, That the said [blank] who made them shall ether take them home & make them according to the orders, or appoint some in London to doe it for him; or ells that they shall

N O T E S
[1] *Flayderman Sale*, p. 270.
[2] Advertisement for Flayderman Sale in *Antiques* 16, no. 6 (December 1929): 453.
[3] Turners Company Mintues 1: leaf 6 recto.
[4] Gilbert, "Regional Traditions in English Vernacular Furniture," p. 70, fig. 16.

8.

TURNED GREAT CHAIR WITH RUSH BOTTOM
Vicinity of Westerly or Kingston, Rhode Island
1670–1710
WOOD: A soft maple
OH 43⅛″ (109.5 cm)
SH 16½″ (41.9 cm), SW 24⅝″ (62.6 cm), SD 18″ (45.7 cm)
PROVENANCE: The Case/Clarke family of Westerly and Kingston, R.I.; on loan to the Museum of the Rhode Island School of Design; Harry Arons; purchased by the museum
56.10.2

This chair has a long family tradition of ownership in the Clarke family of Kingston, Rhode Island, but in many ways seems to be an earlier version of some chairs that were owned in coastal Connecticut. When this chair was added to the Winterthur collection, the following letter from William Case Clarke of West Woodstock, Connecticut, accompanied it:

Nov. 9/'55.

Dear Mr. Arons,

The Old Carver Chair I sold you, came to me by descent from my father William Case Clarke, born in 1842. He did not know who first owned the chair, simply that it had been handed down in the family for a long time. His father, he said, used it daily after becoming partly paralyzed.

Col. George Clinton Clarke, my grandfather was the son of William Case Clarke, a sergeant in the Revolution and known as Judge Clarke. The Judge lived in the Old Homestead at Kingston, R.I. and was a descendant of Joseph Clarke. Joseph . . . arrived in this country about 1638. . . .

The Chair could have been handed down from Joseph, or possibly from [his brother] John, or it could have come into the Clarke family thru marriage. The Joseph Clarke line intermarried with the Anne Hutchinson family, the Dyers, Tillinghasts and others. The . . . father of the Judge . . . [married] Mercy Case. Then the son of the Judge, also married a Case.

. . . Not unlikely the Carver chair was a kitchen piece.

. . . It would seem proper to label the Carver chair as coming from the Judge William Case Clarke family of Kingston, R.I.[1]

Joseph Clarke (1618–1694) born in Bedfordshire, England, came to Newport, Rhode Island, in 1639. He lived "most of his latter years" in Westerly, on the shore of Rhode Island, just over the border from Stonington, Connecticut.[2] It is possible that he or his son Joseph (1643–1727), also of Westerly, was the original owner of this chair, which appears

to date from the middle decades of the seventeenth century (assuming that the chair descended to the last family owner through the paternal line).

Given the elder Joseph Clarke's history of geographic mobility, it would be tempting to associate this chair and two almost identical examples—one in the Hempstead House, New London, and the other in a private collection—with a Newport origin; yet that would be mere conjecture.[3] The spindles of the back are highly reminiscent of the mannerist half spindles common on Essex County case pieces made in the 1670s and 1680s, but the bold elongations of the balusters on the chair along with a distinctive finial design and forward-slanting arms are features that set it apart from the Massachusetts style. The chair more closely resembles other chairs made along the shores of coastal Connecticut, the region to which the south county of Rhode Island was always culturally and economically connected.[4]

Judging from the chair itself, it is probable that in the seventeenth century an owner living in Kingston did not look to Newport for a turned chair but rather bought one from a local turner. Kingston, for example, had two such artisans living and working within its bounds during the last half of the seventeenth century: John Browne and Benjamin Nickols.[5] The finials of this chair and the related examples from this area are based upon a type that is quite different from the *flambeaux* finials used by early Plymouth Colony and Boston area chairmakers, and appear to derive from a much earlier English type. This is also true of the continued use of the slanted arm. Taken together, these features reinforce the notion that this chair in all probability was made by a nonurban turner who, like many of the settlers along the western shore of Rhode Island, had emigrated from the northern or western counties of England.

NOTES
[1] Object file 56.10.2, Registrar's Office, Winterthur.
[2] Austin, *Genealogical Dictionary*, p. 47; Savage, *Genealogical Dictionary*, 1:398.
[3] The example in the Hempstead House is published in Comstock, *American Furniture*, no. 20.
[4] See, for example, Kane, *Furniture of the New Haven Colony*, no. 33.
[5] John Browne had "Turning tooles," "one Crosscut Saw and 1 hand Saw," "one fro," and "Chaires and Sum other Lumber" when he died there in 1716, while his neighbor Benjamin Nickols had "Carpentry tools" as well as "a Lave & A Drill" in the inventory of his estate filed the very next year (North Kingston Probate Records, 5:208, 6:113–14; I am indebted to Robert Blair St. George for these references).

9.

TURNED GREAT CHAIR WITH SPLINT SEAT
American, perhaps New York City
1640–1680
WOODS: American black ash (*Fraxinus nigra*); checked seat, American elm (*Ulmus fulva*)
OH 46½″ (118.0 cm)
SH 17⅜″ (44.1 cm), SW 23⅜″ (59.4 cm), SD 16⅞″ (42.9 cm)
PROVENANCE: B. A. Behrend; Miss C. M. Travers; Henry Francis du Pont
58.680

This chair is closely related to a chair illustrated in Nutting's *Furniture Treasury* as no. 1804. Nutting calls that one a "Transition Brewster," although it is not clear what the chair is in the process of making a transition from or to. Nutting's characterization automatically predisposes the faithful to believe that it was made in the Plymouth Colony at best, or in the Bay Colony at the worst. Nutting presents no grounds for this supposition, and as was often the case, his appraisal of the

cat. 8

cat. 9

chair appears to have been based on a photograph since he added, "present ownership unknown." In actuality, neither Winterthur's chair nor the Nutting example bears much resemblance to the Brewster chair: the Brewster chair has two rows of spindles in the back that reach from crest rail to seat rail, this chair has a lower back rail; in the Brewster chair the spindles under the arms extend to the seat lists, in this chair there is a lower arm rail to accommodate the spindles; the Brewster chair has a board seat, this chair has a splint seat (the flag bottom in the Nutting example appears to be modern); and there are no spindles below the seat lists on either, as there are on the Brewster chair. Every major joint on the Winterthur example is pinned while the Brewster chair has no pins.

The ornamental schemes of the two types of chairs are widely at variance with each other as well. The spindles of the Brewster chair have definite baluster shapes, in the Renaissance-classical manner, while those spindles on the Winterthur and Nutting chairs are in the form of inverted pendant drops, favored by the mannerist designers of northern Europe in the sixteenth century and common on the high-style furniture of the Lowlands in the early decades of the seventeenth century and on English vernacular furniture of the middle quarters of the seventeenth century. Most strikingly divergent from the usual Anglo-American concept of seventeenth-century design, however, is the pattern of the finials. The ball topped by a small knob that usually characterizes a chair in the English manner is not present. Instead, the ball shape is placed high on the finial, is surmounted by two knobs of diminishing size, all mounted on a ringed neck. This type of finial is much more commonly found on Dutch and German turned chairs and suggests that Winterthur's chair and the Nutting example were made by a craftsman who was much more influenced by northern European concepts than English ideas. For the date at which this chair appears to have been made, New York is a much more appropriate guess for a place of origin than New England. This impression is further heightened by the consistent use of pins to hold the crosspieces to the uprights and by the checked seat made of elm (*Ulmus fulva*) splints, a wood not common in New England furniture but sometimes found in the furniture of New York. That such an early chair has a splint seat at all is further indication of the persistence of a northern European tradition, as it is rarely found in early chairs of English and New England origin. When found on New England chairs, splint seats are generally of ash. The present seat appears either to be original to the chair or replaces an earlier splint seat, for there is no trace of the characteristic grooves left by a rush seat on the lists. That the side seat lists enter the uprights above the front and rear lists negates the notion that the lists of checked-bottom chairs invariably enter them on the same level.

No itemized inventories of New York turners from the period in which this chair ought to have been made have survived; however, the names of several turners are in the public records. Among them are David Wessels, called a "chairmaker" when he was admitted a burgher of New York on April 13, 1657, and Jan Hendrickson, referred to as a "chairman" on the next day. Freryck Aarenson is listed as a turner in the Minutes of the Court of New Amsterdam in the

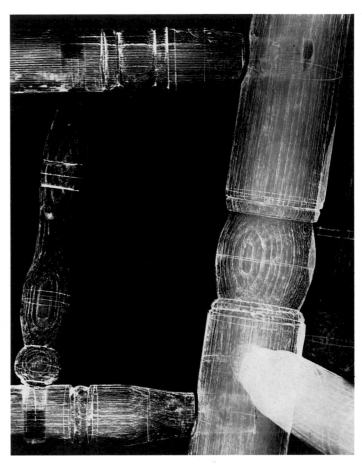

Fig. 50. X-ray photograph showing rear leg and arm lists above the seat on the chair in catalogue entry 9. That the holes were bored at an angle indicates the cant of the back was intentional. (Winterthur 58.680.)

same year and may be the same man mentioned in an account as Frederick Arents in 1686. Later in the century Jacob Blom, "turner" (1698), Johannes Tiebout, "turner" (1699), and Richard Waldron, "blockmaker and turner" (1700), are mentioned.[1]

On Winterthur's chair, black paint covers a layer of red paint that appears to have been the first coat of paint applied to the chair. At present there is no means of scientifically establishing whether the coat of red paint was original since its pigment is an earth color that is still in use. The feet are conjectural restorations; the chair may have had rockers added, probably in the nineteenth century.

The backward rake of the chair is a common feature of surviving seventeenth-century chairs. In contrast to the New England chair discussed in catalogue entry 1, on this chair the backward rake was done for comfort, as an X-ray photograph attests (fig. 50). Had the back been originally made to stand absolutely upright, the auger hold in the rear stile would be perpendicular to the post, instead it has been drilled at an angle. The X ray of the arm, lower arm rail, and spindles shows that the holes in these rails are also perpendicular; so the arm spindles, being turned to a small diameter, are bent to conform to the rake of the chair. Thus, the X ray offers further confirmation that unseasoned wood was generally used by seventeenth-century turners.

The front stretchers have the same sequence of paints on them as the stiles. Moreover, they and the seat lists are turned in the same manner at their termini. These factors suggest that the stretchers are original (the same applies to those of the Nutting example). Given this, the stretchers are a rare instance of survival. Most front stretchers were generally worn through by generations of sitters who tended to hook their feet on them and lean back, and here perhaps the rake of the chair circumvented that necessity.[2]

NOTES
[1] *Burghers . . . and Freemen*, pp. 20, 21, 22, 63, 72, 590; *New Amsterdam Court Minutes*, 7:68, 151; New York Probate, Liber 19B:259.
[2] The American habit of leaning back in a chair was noted, more than a century after this chair was made, by Dr. Benjamin Silliman (1779–1864): "As I was sitting in a chair," "Mr._____ [from England] told me that he should have recognized me as a New Englander had he not known me. Upon my inquiring for the pecularity which marked my origin, he told me that no one except a man educated in New-England ever leaned back in his chair, so as to make it stand upon the two hinder feet only" (quoted in Leibundguth, "Clues and Footnotes," p. 1158).

10.

TURNED GREAT CHAIR WITH FLAG BOTTOM
Long Island, New York
1690–1750
WOODS: Posts, a maple; rounds and spindles, hickory (genus *Carya*)
OH 54¼″ (137.8 cm)
SH 17″ (43.2 cm), SW 33⅜″ (84.8 cm), SD 25⅛″ (63.8 cm)
PROVENANCE: Horton family of Southold, N.Y.; Charles Wolsey Lyon; Henry Francis du Pont
57.598

At the time this chair was added to the Winterthur collection in 1937, it was accompanied by a lengthy typescript detailing its long history in the Horton family of Southold, Long Island, New York. The typescript, dated November 8, 1937, was prepared by Wayland Jefferson, then "Official Historian of the Town of Southold," probably at the behest of Charles W. Lyon, from whom the chair was purchased for the Winterthur collection.

The typescript gives a detailed line of descent to the last family owner and states that the chair was originally made for Jonathan Horton (1647–1707) by his brother Joshua, a carpenter. The chair was believed to have been the one referred to in Joshua Horton's account book as "a great chair" to be made of hickory and willow. In that account book, "a grate bed" was also mentioned. The bed was charged to Jonathan at £10 and the chair at £3. The chair bottom was to be of rush "woven by Indian squa[w] Hanna." In the inventory of Jonathan Horton, two "grate beds" were listed, as was "a Grate Chaire and Stoole," valued at £3.[1]

Fascinating as the story is, and exciting as it would be to have a chair by a known maker dating from 1672 whose original seat was woven by an Indian squaw, numerous problems arise when we compare the chair with these details. In the first place, the chair is made of only two woods: the uprights are of a maple, which is now so badly riddled with wormholes that its exact species cannot be determined, and the rounds are made of hickory (*Carya*). No willow is to be found in it. Second, the adjective "great," which merely means large and often the presence of arms in seventeenth-century parlance, could as easily refer to a chair of joined construction as it could to one that was made by a turner. Turned examples were much less expensive than their joined counterparts; the 1689 inventory of Anthony deMill of New York City, for example,

contained "2 great cheers" valued at 4s.—a clear indication that they were too inexpensive to be anything but turned.[2] Thus, the selling price of £3 for a turned chair seems unusually high—it would be thirty times the value of either of the chairs in deMill's estate.

Despite these inconsistencies, the tradition of ownership in the Horton family is very strong. It is possible that this chair dates from 1672 since there is no stylistic impediment to its having been made that early. It is more likely, however, to have found its way into the family at a later date. If it were made for Jonathan Horton's son, James (b. 1694), it might well be the "great arm chair" listed in 1768 in the "west room" of the house he had inherited from his father. It is impossible to state with any certainty whether James's chair was a turned example or a very out-of-fashion wainscot chair inasmuch as it was valued at only 4s. Possibly it was a turned chair, but that same room had "two rush bottom chairs" appraised at the somewhat higher valuation of £1.5 (12s. 6d. each); thus we must ask why a "rush bottom" was not specified for the armchair when it was listed as it was for the two more valuable examples that were probably in a later style.[3]

Although the Horton family underwent various vicissitudes during the revolutionary period, "one great arm chair" valued at 6s. was found in the home of James's son, Barnabas, when the inventory of his estate was taken in 1787. Forty-four years later, the inventory of his son, Benjamin (1755–1831), contained "1 Great Arm Chair" valued at $2.50. The chair remained in the old Horton homestead during the time of Benjamin's son, David Austin Horton (1804–1893), "in the corner of the front parlor, where it rested for forty odd years." Wayland Jefferson, as "a very small boy, was told by David A. Horton, that the chair had belonged to Capt. Barnabas Horton, his grandfather." Upon the death of David Horton's widow in 1902, the chair was bequeathed to Silas Austin Horton Dayton, a grandnephew, from whom it passed to the last family owner, Miss Mary L. Dayton, in 1928.[4]

Oddly enough, the documentary evidence adduced by Mr. Jefferson is as good as any that decorative arts historians have to go on in the matter of establishing family traditions, but we cannot wholeheartedly accept the original ownership because of the discrepancies in the early pages of its history. The tradition of family ownership is sufficiently supported by

cat. 10

documents from the middle of the eighteenth century onward, but not by the earlier ones. However, on its own evidence, the chair does not appear to be the work of a carpenter (although Joshua Horton, indeed, may have been a very versatile seventeenth-century one) but rather looks like the product of a professional turner; the shape of the large baluster and its prominent collar is a common feature on New York furniture.

The chair betrays no false notes that would tempt a careful connoisseur to doubt its early origin, and its stylistic attributes do not discourage the idea that it may well have been made in the quarter century that straddles the year 1700. Its large size, often a source of speculation, can be assumed to indicate only that it was made for a large person, since its seat height is conventional. A related chair is in the collection of the Bowne House, Flushing, Long Island, New York.[5]

NOTES
[1] Wayland Jefferson typescript, pp. 1, 2, in object file 57.598, Registrar's Office, Winterthur. Horton's account book, then said to be in the New-York Historical Society or the New York Public Library is, unfortunately, currently not in either place and must be assumed lost.
[2] New York Probate, Liber 3: leaf 143. See also catalogue entry 17, below.
[3] Jefferson typescript, p. 3, in object file 57.598, Registrar's Office, Winterthur.
[4] Jefferson typescript, pp. 8–10, in object file 57.598, Registrar's Office, Winterthur.
[5] See Failey, *Long Island Is My Nation*, fig. 17.

11.
TURNED CHAIR WITH RUSH BOTTOM
New York or northern New Jersey
1690–1740
WOODS: Stiles, rungs, and spindles, American black cherry (*Prunus serotina*); seat lists, white oak (*Quercus alba*)
OH 34⅞" (88.6 cm)
SH 16½" (41.9 cm), SW 17¾" (45.1 cm), SD 15¼" (38.7 cm)
PROVENANCE: J. Stodgell Stokes; Henry Francis du Pont
54.525

This chair and its near mate (see catalogue entry 12), introduce yet another strand into the complex fabric of American furniture history. Recognizably unlike New England spindle-back chairs of the seventeenth century that are derived from an ancient tradition of turned chairs, this chair represents the turner's response to the style made popular by the leather-upholstered Cromwellian chair of the early seventeenth century. Turner's examples of this style were undoubtedly made in Antwerp (an elaborate one is in the Plantin-Moretus Museum), in Amsterdam (a related and immaculately turned example in walnut with a pierced and highly ornamented board crest rail is displayed in the Rijksmuseum), and in the countryside surrounding Amsterdam. The style reached a high point of elaboration among the turners living in the area of Germany known as the Altes Land, in the vicinity of Hamburg—the collection of the German National Folk Museum in Nuremburg is rich in examples of them.[1] Which one of these strains the American examples are most closely related to is a matter of opinion and will remain so until better regional studies, both American and European, are undertaken.

The American examples have been attributed to Bergen County, New Jersey, on the basis of the nineteenth-century occurrence there of slat-back chairs with a similar finial.[2] And, in truth, the design of the side and rear stretchers on Winterthur's chair appear often on New Jersey chairs of a later style. Yet, given the absence of better documentation, we can honestly say only that these chairs could have been made in any place where chairmakers from the Netherlands set up shop in this country. The earliest published spindle-back examples in this style are the two illustrated as 2085 and 2086 in Nutting's *Furniture Treasury*, with a caption that states, "This page is an interlude, to show a series of distinctive chairs found in New Jersey." Both chairs were the property of J. Stodgell Stokes, a Philadelphia collector who formed an extraordinary collection of early Pennsylvania and New Jersey furniture. The present whereabouts of chair 2085 is not known, but 2086, a superlative example, is in the Mabel Brady Garvan Collection at Yale University. One of its stretchers is of hickory (*Carya*), a native American wood, which in the absence of any evidence that it is a replacement, may substantiate the chair's American origin.

A number of chairs related to the Winterthur example are known. The sole examples that have ever been attributed to a craftsman are a pair of chairs said to have been made by Hendryk Glaever of Crosswicks Creek, New Jersey.[3] The attribution appears to have been made on the basis of the initials H.G. carved on the rear stiles. The Granville, Massachusetts, antiques dealers who sold the chairs to the New Jersey State Museum provided the information for the attribution; however, no documents supporting the attribution or citing a provenance for the chairs appear among the records of the museum. The probate records and deeds in the New Jersey State Archives which might confirm this attribution do not contain any references to Hendryk Glaever, which prevents us from verifying his occupation.[4] The Glaever attribution is weakened by the existence of an identical pair of chairs, privately owned in Michigan, that have the carved initials H H conjoined in the Dutch manner on their rear stiles. The existence of different initials on two sets of identical chairs suggests the possibility that they are not the maker's initials.

A final chair, which varies slightly from the Winterthur example in the articulation of its rear spindles, was illustrated in 1886 in the *Catalogue of the Albany Bicentennial Loan Exhibition*, and indeed, the possibility that some or all of these chairs were manufactured in New York cannot be overlooked.[5] At least three chairs in the collection of the Huguenot Historical

cat. 11

Society at New Paltz, New York, are closely related slat-back versions of these chairs and have virtually identical finials. Two of these chairs are in the Hugo Freer House and have histories of ownership in the Wright family of New Paltz.[6] It should also be noted that the chair in the next catalogue entry, closely related to this example, was purchased in Sheffield, Massachusetts, a town close to the New York line.

It is perhaps evidence of old-fashioned or illogical thinking on our part to believe that related objects invariably proceed from the same source: there are sufficient differences between the present chair and the following example to suggest that two different craftsmen made them, and if the evidence of two hands is apparent in the objects, then it is an easy step to assume as well that they may have been made at two different times and thus in two different places, especially when the evidence indicates that the form was made over a long period of time. It is also problematic whether the American examples are derived from Dutch or German antecedents. In truth, the only thing that can be safely stated about these chairs is that the craftsman who brought this style of chairmaking to America was trained to make it in northern Europe, and northern European chairmakers migrated to New York as well as New Jersey.

If the span of time in which we assume their northern German counterparts were made is correct, then the American chairs could have been made at anytime between 1660 and 1825 and still have looked very much as they do. It would be tempting to go along with the German furniture historians who prefer to date their examples of these chairs in the nineteenth century. Bernward Deneke illustrates a classic example of the form, complete with the repetitively turned ovoid stretchers, in his thoughtful book, *Bauernmöbel*.[7] The neoclassical urn atop its rear stiles—a motif virtually unknown in New England furniture until the late decade of the eighteenth century—suggests this date. However, experience has shown us that all the styles of historical furniture are international in character and that the accidents of taste and the migration of craftsmen mean that some attributes of a local version of the style are transmitted while others are not. If we look, for example, at the painting *The Bloodletting* (fig. 51) by Quiryn Brekelenkam who worked in Leyden, Holland, between 1648 and his death in 1668 or 1669, it is apparent that urn finials were present on furniture in Leyden around the middle of the seventeenth century. Indeed, it is this very articulation of the finial and to some extent the shape of the feet that suggest that Winterthur's American chair was made earlier rather than later. We can well understand the conservatism of European scholars who date chairs in this manner so late, for numerous examples with a board crest rail on which dates have been carved show that these chairs were being made with little decline in the vigor of their turning late in the eighteenth century. Deneke has illustrated an armchair made of ash and dated 1795.

A similar chair (fig. 52), owned by a dealer who found it in northern New Jersey, was brought to Winterthur Museum for examination in the spring of 1977 by clock specialist Edward F. LaFond. Microanalysis revealed that it also is made of European ash (*Fraxinus grandifolia*). How or when it came to

Fig. 51. Quiryn Brekelenkam, *The Bloodletting*. Leyden, Holland, ca. 1660. (Foundation Johan Maurits van Nassau, Royal Picture Gallery, Mauritshuis, The Hague, Netherlands.)

this country is not known. Although it clearly stems from a seventeenth-century chairmaking tradition, its resemblance to the late eighteenth-century German examples suggests that it cannot be considered the inspiration for the American example.[8]

A comparison of the two chairs is enlightening. The seat of the American chair is of rush, the German chair has a board seat. This means that the task of constructing the American chair was simpler—the seat lists did not have to be grooved, and the seat boards did not need to be sawed out, feathered, and smoothed. The seat lists on the European chair all enter the legs at the same level, and the front and rear lists have rectangular mortise-and-tenon joints on them to prevent the lists from rotating downward and ejecting the seat board when the chair is sat upon. The side lists have round tenons which pierce both the legs and the tenons of the front and rear seat lists, further rendering the structure rigid. As if this were not enough, the lists are additionally pinned to the legs, in that typical overstructuring often found in objects of wood made in the seventeenth-century manner. Conversely, the seat lists of the American chair enter the uprights at different levels, as is customary with chairs that are designed to have rush bottoms. This means that the juncture of seat lists and legs will be stronger than is customary with board-seat turned chairs. Theoretically, this also means that the turner who makes his chairs with rush bottoms could make the legs lighter. In the

Fig. 52. Turned chair with spindle back and board seat, probably late eighteenth or nineteenth century. European ash (*Fraxinus excelsior*). (Private collection in 1977. Photo: Benno M. Forman.) The chair is similar to late eighteenth-century German examples and to the chair in catalogue entry 11

Fig. 53. Turned chair with slat back, probably Bergen County, N.J., 1790–1835. Maple and ash; H 37″ (94 cm), W 18″ (45.7 cm), D 14″ (35.6 cm), SH 16¼″ (41.3 cm). (Winterthur 71.135.)

case of the Winterthur chair, the maker did not make the stiles lighter for either of two reasons which spring immediately to mind: one physical, the other aesthetic. He may have felt that he should not lighten the stiles because he believed the cherry wood (*Prunus serotina*) was more likely to split than was the more commonly used ash. Or, he may have felt that to lighten the stiles would spoil the appearance of the chair; that is, habit and training made it unthinkable to him that the chair could be lighter.

Aesthetically, the two chairs are similar in detail but different in overall appearance—a principle that is demonstrably true in other forms of furniture and at other times in history. The top and bottom rails of the backs of both chairs are virtually identical. The same may be said of the upright spindles in the backs except that in the American chair, the upper rondel, baluster, and column shape are not present. It does not so much seem that the shape has been eliminated from the American chair as it seems to have been added to the German chair. The former has a low back, which suggests that it stems from the tradition of Dutch, urban, high-style turned chairs of the first half of the seventeenth century. The latter chair, with its attenuated elements requiring a taller back, appears to have undergone a process of elaboration as often happens when urban styles are subjected to a rural taste over a long period of time. Thus, in no sense does the German chair stand as the prototype of the American example but rather

demonstrates that both have gone their separate ways from a common ancestor.

While it is a well-known principle of furniture history that styles tend to persist in agrarian or isolated cultures, thereby causing the furniture made in such a context to appear much older than it really is, the tell-tale signs of such lateness are usually visible in the object itself: ornamental shapes tend to lose their early vigor or attain a nonacademic and often bizarre exuberance instead; workmanship tends to become muddy; or newer stylistic elements become incorporated into the vocabulary of ornament. Such signs do not appear in Winterthur's chair; thus in the absence of documentary evidence to the contrary, an early date of manufacture for this chair can be safely assumed. Indeed, a related three-slat chair of unknown provenance (fig. 53) in Winterthur's study collection has many attributes of nineteenth-century manufacture—notably the style of the front feet and the lightness of the stiles—and suggests what the continuation of this tradition in nineteenth-century America was like.

NOTES
[1] I examined the Plantin-Moretus example in 1969 on a visit to Antwerp; see also Vogelsang, *Le meuble Hollandaise*, pl. 56, no. 158; Deneke, *Bauernmöbel*, figs. 13, 16, passim; Kirk, "Sources of Some American Regional Furniture, Part I," p. 798.
[2] See Lynes, "Slat-Back Chairs of New England and the Middle Atlantic States," pp. 104–7.

[3] The chairs are illustrated in *An Exhibition of . . . the New Jersey State Museum*, no. 2 (accession no. 68.117).
[4] When the dealers were contacted recently in regard to this matter, they could no longer remember the name of the antiquarian from whom the information was originally acquired (dealers to Forman, April 25, 1977); Barbara Colesar to Forman, May 9, 1977.

[5] *Catalogue of the Albany Bicentennial*, facing p. 136. I am indebted to Charles F. Montgomery for this information.
[6] Kenneth E. Hasbrouck to Forman, June 8, 1977.
[7] Deneke, *Bauernmöbel*, fig. 16.
[8] Compare the details with Deneke, *Bauernmöbel*, fig. 13.

12.

TURNED CHAIR WITH RUSH BOTTOM
New York or northern New Jersey
1690–1760
WOODS: All turned elements, American black cherry (*Prunus serotina*); seat lists, American black ash (*Fraxinus nigra*)
OH 34⅜" (87.3 cm)
SH 16¾" (42.6 cm), SW 18¾" (47.6 cm), SD 16⅛" (40.9 cm)
PROVENANCE: The 1750 House, Inc., Sheffield, Mass.; Henry Francis du Pont
54.526

This chair and the previous example are closely related in form. Both are made of cherry and have stretchers of the same design. But when we come to examine the details of their ornamentation, there are more differences than similarities.

Chair no. 11 has no turned elements below the lower back rail and has a ring flanked by balusters on the upper back stile; in contrast, chair no. 12 has three bold single ring turnings on the lower stile and three joined rings topped by a baluster on the upper stile. The back rails are also distinct. Rings separate the oblong turnings on chair no. 11 but do not on no. 12. The front legs are also different. Chair no. 11 has baluster feet with a thick neck and a single turned ring above and below the front stretcher. The other chair has baluster feet with a slimmer neck accentuated by a thin ring, two rings below the stretchers, and a ring topped by a baluster above the upper stretcher.

The most striking variation between the two chairs is the way in which the finials are articulated (fig. 54). On chair no. 11, the finial is robust and clearly derived from the form of a classical urn; that on chair no. 12 is highly attenuated. Could the man who conceived an urn finial which looked like the one on the former chair have possibly tolerated the form of the latter one? These differences represent the kind of change that leads art historians to talk about the "decline in the traditions" among craftsmen. Of course, neither of the chairs is precisely datable, and to speak of the change in terms of a *decline* is a two-fold assumption that chair no. 12 is later than its mate, and that both are made by the same craftsman or closely related craftsmen like a father and a son or a master and his apprentice.

The concept of "decline" implies a value judgment, which in this case is justified by the seventeenth-century "academic" form of the finial, as it appeared in Leyden in the middle of the seventeenth century, being established by the Brekelenkam painting (see fig. 51). By that standard, chair no. 12 does not conform to the academic norm and is inferior in design. Declension, however, does not explain how the tradition was reinvigorated by the time that the slat-back chair in figure 53 was made.

Fig. 54. Detail showing the profiles of the finials on the turned chairs in catalogue entries 11 (left) and 12 (right). (Winterthur 54.525, 54.526.)

Leaving aside conventional prejudices as to what a chair should look like, my appraisal of chair no. 12 revealed that it actually has some features that are closer to the European tradition than those of no. 11, notably that its front legs have an overhanging lip or ring at the top. Moreover, the thin neck of the feet is very much in the manner of numerous European chairs illustrated in Deneke's *Bauernmöbel*. Likewise on no. 12 the repeated ball turnings on the spindles of the back (of which there are four between the baluster shapes as opposed to the two of the other example) are closer in conception to the seventeenth-century example in the Rijksmuseum than the elongated version on chair no. 11.

Thus, when the stylistic evidence of the two chairs is weighed, it is, in the final analysis, very difficult to assert which chair is the earlier; but, at the very least, if they are both reasonably contemporary with each other, it is unlikely that they were both made by the same craftsman.

13.

TURNED GREAT CHAIR WITH RUSH BOTTOM
England, perhaps Dorset
1620–1650
WOODS: Stiles, back, and arms, European field maple (*Acer campestre*); stretchers (replaced), American hickory (genus *Carya*)
OH 41¾″ (106.1 cm)
SH 16⅝″ (42.2 cm), SW 24½″ (62.2 cm), SD 18¾″ (47.6 cm)
PROVENANCE: Waterman Family of Cranston, R.I.; Cushing's Antique Shop, Providence, R.I.; Israel Sack, Inc.; Henry Francis du Pont
58.683

Winterthur has a sole example of a piece of furniture made in an early seventeenth-century style, made of English wood, yet possessing a long history of ownership in an American family. This example, whose stiles are of European field maple (*Acer campestre*), has replaced stretchers of American hickory (*Carya*), both woods that are native to their particular hemispheres and easily identified by microanalysis.

Family ownership of this chair dates back to the late eighteenth century, long before American collectors began to decorate their homes with English antiques. It first came to the notice of furniture collectors when it appeared in an advertisement by Cushing's Antique Shop of Providence, Rhode Island, in 1927.[1] The advertisement stated that the "chair [had] belonged to Dr. George Waterman, of Cranston, whose brother, Zuriel Waterman, signed the Rhode Island Declaration of Independence." The last family owner wrote:

Rehoboth, Mass
Dec. 7, 1926
The Carver Chair sold to Nathan Cushing belonged to Dr. George Waterman of Cranston Rhode Island whose brother Zuriel Waterman was one of the signers of the Declaration of Independence. The chair was inherited by his mother Feeby Waterman Allen. Willed by her to me, Mrs. Clara B. Allen, wife of George W. Allen of Rehoboth Mass. (Dr. Waterman died in 1829)
CLARA B. ALLEN
My age 75 years[2]

Although we do not know much about Zuriel Waterman, the association of this chair with the Waterman family and the chair's distinctive character, which set it apart from the recognizable chairs of New England, suggest that this may be one of the earliest identifiable pieces of furniture owned in Rhode Island. If the chair did come down to the last family owner through the paternal lines of the Waterman family, it might have originally been brought from England by Richard Waterman, who sailed to Salem, Massachusetts, with John Endicott in 1628 and went with Roger Williams to Rhode Island a decade later. Waterman became a large landowner in the vicinity of Providence and died there in 1670. His son, Nathaniel (1637–1712), inherited the family lands. Nathaniel's son, also named Nathaniel (d. 1725), resided on this property, between Warwick and Cranston, and had a son

Zuriel (b. ca. 1701) from whom the later Zuriel and Dr. George were descended.[3] Unfortunately no inventory of Richard Waterman survives, and those of his sons and grandsons, although they contain chairs, are not sufficiently specific to enable us to identify this chair among them.

While it would be tempting to assume that this chair originated in the vicinity of Dorchester or Weymouth, Dorsetshire, inasmuch as Richard Waterman sailed from there with John Endicott in 1628, Roger Peers of the Dorchester Museum has advised that Waterman is a name that appears in the records of Dorsetshire only once in the sixteenth century and not at all in the seventeenth. Gabriel Olive, a distinguished antiquarian and scholar, is of the opinion that the style of the present chair is more akin to those of Herefordshire than Dorset.[4]

It would be tempting to make invidious comparisons between this chair and some of the more flamboyant turned chairs that were made in the seventeenth century. Quite clearly it is a restrained example. In this case the restraint is attributed to a certain timidity or conservatism on the part of the maker's design concept. It is quite different in spirit from three-square turned chairs mentioned in the Introduction to this section. Certainly its restraint did not come about because of the nature of the material, since field maple, rarely found in English chairs, can be turned to a very small compass and still retain great strength. The character of the turning is, in many ways, suggestive of much of the nonurban turning of New England, such as, for example, the applied spindles on numerous chests and cupboards from the New Haven Colony.[5] This resemblance, however, is not one of cause and effect, and neither turning is indebted to the other in any demonstrable way. Both, however, share one historical feature—they were executed in villages in the seventeenth century where common furniture was not strongly influenced by the design currents that were in vogue in urban style centers.

Chairs such as this one should be judged on their own merits because, like the two delightful balusters on each of the back spindles, they are full of the sort of novelty that is rarely recognized in the work of urban academicians but often appears in the work of village turners, where a different view of life emerges.

NOTES
[1] Advertisement, *Antiques* 11, no. 4 (April 1927): 305.
[2] Object file 58.683, Registrar's Office, Winterthur. The quotation is also in *Cushing Sale*, p. 54, lot 173.
[3] Austin, *Genealogical Dictionary*, pp. 408–11; Savage, *Genealogical Dictionary*, 2: 120, 4:432.
[4] Gabriel Olive to Forman, July 28, 1977. A midlands attribution may be more appropriate given the resemblance of the Winterthur example to another chair in the collection of Rhode Island School of Design (RISD) that descended in the Carpenter and Gardiner families of Dighton, Mass., and Warwick and Providence, R.I. If the RISD chair was originally owned in the Carpenter family, it was undoubtedly made in Hampshire or Wiltshire, the counties from which they emigrated to America (see St. George, *Wrought Covenant*, pp. 77–78). I am indebted to Thomas Michie for information about the RISD chair.
[5] Kane, *Furniture of the New Haven Colony*, nos. 12, 13, 23, 24.

14.
TURNED GREAT CHAIR WITH RUSH BOTTOM
Boston or Charlestown
1650–1700
WOODS: All turned members, a poplar (genus *Populus*); arms (replaced), a white oak (*Quercus alba*)
OH 43¼″ (109.9 cm)
SH 16″ (40.6 cm), SW 22½″ (57.1 cm), SD 16⅜″ (41.6 cm)
PROVENANCE: The Smith's American Antiques, Townsend Village, Vt.; purchased by the museum
78.110

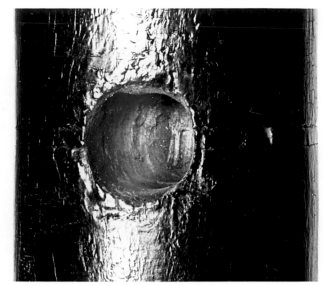

Fig. 55. Detail of post on the chair in catalogue entry 14. Note the chisel-cut square hole that is designed to accept the tenon of the flat arms. (Winterthur 78.110.)

This chair is one of eight related examples distinguished from other surviving early New England chairs by their combination of flat, draw-shaven arms, three back slats elegantly graduated in height from bottom to top, and impressive, well-executed *flambeaux* finials comprised of a ball, a reel, one or two flattened disks, and an ovoid knob. Although the eight are strikingly similar in appearance, subtle differences in their overall design and in the location of scribed work lines on their posts suggest that these chairs actually fall into two distinct groups. Group 1, comprised of the present example and an almost exact duplicate in the collection of the Shelburne Museum, Shelburne, Vermont, was likely the output of one of the large turneries in Boston or nearby Charlestown; the shops of Nathaniel Adams, Edmund Larkin, or Stephen Fosdick are high on the list of possible makers.[1] These two chairs are distinguished by the use of poplar, as opposed to maple, in the principal posts, which suggests that they are products of artisans who also made other surviving examples of chairs with turned arms which also have poplar posts. Poplar is slightly softer than maple—its fibers show the imprint of a fingernail easily—yet it turns to almost as precise an edge as does maple, making it an ideal material for a large urban shop, like that of Larkin, who was accustomed to stockpiling large numbers of completed chairs in anticipation of exportation.

Six chairs are in group 2. One has a history in the Clarke family of Ipswich, one in the Howe family of Concord, one in the Balch family of Beverly, and one in the English family of Salem (see fig. 42); the other two have no known histories. These six chairs all have maple posts and share a finial design which has a more elongated knob than either the Winterthur or Shelburne examples.[2] That three chairs have North Shore histories suggests that they were probably made there, especially when we consider that almost all towns had turners working within their limits. In Essex County, the most logical choice for a center of local turning production on any large level is Salem. Both the English and the Balch family chairs come from the immediate area, and Salem was the only town in Massachusetts outside Boston and Charlestown that supported the large-scale production of frames for upholstered chairs.[3] Yet how was the Boston–Charlestown-type chair transmitted to Essex County?

While it remains difficult to state for sure, Samuel Beadle seems to have had a fundamental role in introducing the urban Boston–Charlestown style of turning to the Salem area. As mentioned earlier, Beadle was a turner who was trained in Charlestown—perhaps in one of the leading shops—prior to 1661 and then set up shop in Salem, where he worked until his death in the early eighteenth century. Beadle, along with Samuel and James Symonds, must have been among the more active of Salem's woodworking artisans during the seventeenth century, and perhaps Beadle made some of the split spindles that the Symonds shop used on its elaborately decorated case furniture.[4]

When Winterthur acquired this chair its arms were formed by two cut-down turned legs taken from a late Victorian rocking chair. The question then arose: did it originally have turned arms like those on many surviving chairs, or the more unusual flat arms? The answer appeared once the Victorian replacements were removed. Still visible in the posts, despite the distorting effect of the round holes bored to accept the rocker legs, are squared holes cut with a chisel to accept the originally flat arms (fig. 55). Like those on the Shelburne chair, which is the only other flat-arm chair with poplar posts to survive intact, the now restored arms for Winterthur's chair are of white oak.

From available evidence, most of these chairs were originally colored black.

NOTES
[1] The Shelburne example is illustrated in Comstock, *American Furniture*, no. 33. Trent, "Joiners and Joinery of Middlesex County" (thesis), pp. 6–7, 24–29.
[2] See the catalogue entry on the Clarke family chair from Ipswich in Fairbanks and Trent, *New England Begins*, 2:216–17. One of the chairs with no history is illustrated in Dean Fales, *Furniture of Historic Deerfield*, p. 20, fig. 11; the other is illustrated in Ginny Caputo, "Concord, N.H.," p. 24C (collection of Lillian Cogan). The wood used in the posts of the Clarke family chair has not been microanalyzed and is currently hidden by later coats of paint.
[3] See Trent, "Two Seventeenth-Century Salem Upholstered Chairs," pp. 34–40.
[4] See Forman, "Seventeenth-Century Case Furniture of Essex County," pp. 41–55.

15.
TURNED GREAT CHAIR WITH RUSH BOTTOM
Norwich or Lebanon, New London County, Connecticut
1660–1715
Woods: Posts and arms, a soft maple; slats, rounds, and lists, American black
ash (*Fraxinus nigra*)
OH 43⅜″ (109.3 cm)
SH 15½″ (39.4 cm), SW 24¾″ (62.4 cm), SD 23″ (58.0 cm)
PROVENANCE: I. Winick, N.Y.; Henry Francis du Pont
58.691

16.
TURNED GREAT CHAIR WITH RUSH BOTTOM
Norwich or Lebanon, New London County, Connecticut
1660–1715
WOODS: Left rear stile, a soft maple (genus *Acer*); top rear stretcher, an oak of the
white oak group; top slat, red maple (*Acer rubrum*)
OH 45⅜″ (115.3 cm)
SH 18⅛″ (46.1 cm), SW 22″ (55.9 cm), SD 16⅜″ (41.6 cm)
PROVENANCE: Mrs. Harry Horton Benkard; Mrs. Reginald P. Rose; given to the
museum by Mr. and Mrs. Reginald P. Rose in memory of her mother, Mrs. Harry
Horton Benkard
74.40

These two chairs are members of what is possibly the largest group of surviving seventeenth-century American chairs. The authors of the catalogue of *New London County Furniture*, assert that approximately a dozen chairs of this type have been found in the Norwich–Lebanon, Connecticut, area. They illustrate a privately owned chair which was found in that neighborhood —long a happy hunting ground for antiques collectors—as recently as 1971. Irving W. Lyon first illustrated one in 1891 and explained, "it was bought in Lebanon, Conn., in 1878, from a family in which it had been for several generations." Another example, in the Blair Collection at the Metropolitan Museum of Art, was illustrated by Nutting in *Pilgrim Century* as no. 358 and in *Furniture Treasury* as no. 1887. In the former book he estimated its date of manufacture as between 1680 and 1690 and stated that it differs slightly from the Lyon example; however, the minute differences are as much attributable to the interval between the making of the two chairs as they are evidence of two makers. Yet another example is in the Leffingwell Inn, Norwich; the Brooklyn Museum owns one; two others are in private collections in Milwaukee. All these examples have maple uprights. An additional chair, which varies from the group only in that the spool under the finial is a ball and the uprights are made of ash, is in the Bayou Bend Collection, Houston.[1]

Although slat-back chairs are a great rarity in the seventeenth-century Anglo-American tradition, these twelve chairs are the happy exception. Furthermore, no chairmakers with obvious continental backgrounds have been found in the Norwich–Lebanon area. A closely related English chair was pictured by Peter H. Ditchfield, an English minister who wrote a great many books, including a little volume entitled *Country Folk* (1923). The book was illustrated with photographs (taken by a Mr. Manley as early as 1861) of citizens of a small village in Berkshire, known as Titsey (fig. 56).

While the exact date of the English chair or its American relatives cannot accurately be assessed, there is no good reason why they cannot date from the middle of the seventeenth century since they are not related to identified and dated examples from elsewhere and consequently cannot be tied to any tight scheme of the transfer of stylistic ideas. Indeed, the

Fig. 56. Dame Frances Bowra, Titsey, Berkshire, England. Photograph by Mr. Manley taken sometime between 1861 and 1875. From Ditchfield, *Country Folk*, p. 94.

American examples have no features that can be associated with any other area of New England.

If the American chairs were made in Norwich, they could date as early as the 1660s. If they were made in Lebanon, they probably date from about 1700, when that township was first settled. The vigor with which these chairs are turned and the style of the finials suggest the earlier date is quite possible, for reasons which will appear below, and if this is so, it effectively eliminates the possibility that the chairs were made in Lebanon.

The thorough research of Houghton Bulkeley, Ethel Hall Bjerkoe, and Phyllis Kihn reveal several craftsmen in seventeenth-century Norwich who could have made these chairs. Among them, is John Baldwin, a turner, who was working in Norwich in 1662. Thomas Tracy (1610–1685), a shop carpenter, housebuilder, and joiner was in Salem in 1637 and worked in Norwich from 1662 until his death. And Benjamin Burham died in 1737 leaving an inventory of 45 dozen chair rounds.[2] It is impossible on the basis of the scant information available to suggest which, if any, of these craftsmen could have made this chair, but the chair illustrated as no. 4 in *New London County Furniture* appears to be of a later date than the Winterthur and related examples. This suggests that the continuity of styling exemplified by these chairs was passed on to a later generation of chairmakers who were influenced by the style of chairs from eastern Massachusetts and who modified the basic style of these chairs to suit the eighteenth-century taste for compressed balusters and rounded slats.

Chairs of this type are notable in several respects. Most obviously, the oversized handgrips that crown the front posts are one of two turner's conceits (the other is illustrated in catalogue entry 17) that were executed in America in the seventeenth century. This conceit requires the woodworker to start with a very large piece of wood and turn it very little for the handhold and considerably more for the legs. In the case of chair no. 15 the handhold is slightly larger than 3½″ (8.9 cm) and the legs are 2″ (5.1 cm) in diameter; thus the effect is one of novelty. While a ratio of 1 to 1.75 is apparent on the front legs, it does not appear to be a scheme of proportions that is consistently repeated throughout the chair.

As has been pointed out many times, only those handgrips which are turned with the leg from one piece of wood may be considered original. Handgrips such as those on no. 16 have often been characterized by the picturesque adjective "mushroom," although the period name by which they were called, if it was anything other than "great pommels," has not been discovered. The handgrips have been so desirable to collectors that they have often been added to chairs that did not originally possess them. Undoubtedly the quality of uniqueness and individuality that distinguishes these chairs in the eyes of collectors was a feature that appealed to the original owners as well. In addition, the profligate use of wood in this way suggests that turners readily exploited the plentiful supply of it in New England. That the maker chose curled maple—a hard and ungrateful wood to turn—suggests that these chairs were relatively laborious to make and therefore relatively expensive in their time.

The legs of the two chairs reveal quite well the circular lines around the outside of the legs left by the turner's gouge and the mark from the point of the lathe on the top surface of the handgrips. These latter marks are common on seventeenth-century armchairs and have often been accentuated by having been dug out to the point where they are no longer recognizable as the mark of the point on which the leg revolved while being turned in a lathe. It has often been suggested that the further digging out of this mark has been caused by the habit of hanging a grease lamp, usually called a "Betty lamp," from the handgrips to permit nocturnal reading. While the documents of the period present no evidence either to confirm or deny this notion, the mention of standing candlesticks and of stands with candlesticks in many seventeenth-century inventories suggests that this practice would have been redundant, if not positively dangerous as well as futile, since the attachment of grease lamps at this point drops them down too low to be of much use in reading a book held on the reader's lap.

Although chairs of this type have been said in the past to be made of maple and hickory, that assertion is only half correct. Wood analysis of no. 15 shows that its arms and its four posts are a soft maple, but the slats, stretchers or rounds, and seat lists are black ash (*Fraxinus nigra*). It would be remarkable to find hickory in a New England turned chair of this early period, although it appears in eighteenth-century examples. In addition to its recognized quality of hardness even before it is cured—a singular feature that mitigates against its being used

on a man-powered lathe—hickory is also noted for its elasticity and tendency to "whip" in the lathe; it will bow away from the cutting tool when pressure is applied to it. On turned chairs, hickory is much more commonly found in seat lists and is generally worked with a draw knife or spokeshave.

Another unusual feature of this group of chairs is the outline of their slats. By far the most common way of treating a slat is to make it flat on the bottom edge and crescent-shape on its top edge; on these chairs the slats are flat on both edges and have an ogee bracket worked at each end of the top surface. These brackets are of a form commonly seen on East Anglian furniture and as pendant forms in architecture. This particular style of bracket is commonly found in Connecticut furniture, rarely in that of eastern Massachusetts, and may be most vividly seen on the board chest displayed at the Hempstead House in New London and illustrated as no. 6 in the *New London County Furniture* catalogue.

That these both are slat-back chairs reminds us that they combined the art of turning with some simple joinery: the slats were sawed out, moistened, and bowed backward in a clamp; when they dried, they retained their bowed shape. They were then inserted into mortise holes already chiselled into the uprights. Their top slats and both ends of their arms were pinned into the posts. The rectangular mortise holes in their rear posts depart from the usual turner's vocabulary of techniques and suggest that these chairs were made by a craftsman who was more than a mere turned-chair maker. Moreover, these mortises were not drilled before being chiselled (compare with fig. 34).

These chairs are difficult to evaluate aesthetically. The massive arms, with their definite downward slant, do not relate to the known traditions of turning in eastern Massachusetts. The treatment of the arms is similar to that on some chairs from England's West Country and from Wales (see for example, fig. 29), a tradition that was quite old by the time this chair was made. The same may be said of the finials, which are not in the usual finial style of New England spindle-back chairs. There are no spindle-back chairs related to this group, although a rare side chair with two slats identical to this one is illustrated in Nutting's *Pilgrim Century* as no. 308, which was purchased in New Bedford in 1922.

The character of the finials can be explained in two ways. Either they represent the transportation of an English regional type that has not yet been published, or they are the invention of the maker of this chair, who was more accustomed to doing turning as an adjunct to joinery than making chairs, and did not choose typical turned chair finials as his model when he decided to make a chair. Indeed, the shape of this unique group of finials is much more like those of the upholstered scroll chairs, common in the homes of wealthy householders in England at the end of the sixteenth and beginning of the seventeenth centuries (discussed below).

One last feature of one of the Winterthur chairs (no. 15) not generally shared by the group as a whole is that it was converted to a rocking chair while the feet were still relatively intact, thus preserving them to a remarkable extent. The second Winterthur example (no. 16) was not so fortunate; its front legs have been pieced out 6⅞″ (17.5 cm) at the feet, and its rear legs

cat. 15

cat. 16

a remarkable 8⅞″ (22.5 cm). As a result, its lower left side stretcher is new, and the lower members were taken from another old chair.

X rays indicate that the backward slant of the rear posts on both chairs was the original intent of the maker.

NOTES
[1] Lyman Allyn Museum, *New London County Furniture*, p. 15; Lyon, *Colonial Furniture*, p. 144, fig. 58; Johnson, "Leffingwell Inn," p. 568; Warren, *Bayou Bend*, no. 1.
[2] Lyman Allyn Museum, *New London County Furniture*, pp. 109, 111, 128.

17.
TURNED GREAT CHAIR WITH MATTED SEAT
New York
1640–1700
WOODS: Posts, slats, rounds, and lists, soft maple; right arm, an oak; left arm, hickory (genus *Carya*)
OH 46″ (115.9 cm)
SH 16⅞″ (42.9 cm), SW 26⅜″ (66.5 cm), SD 21¼″ (53.6 cm)
PROVENANCE: Dwight Blaney; Israel Sack, Inc.; Henry Francis du Pont
58.690

This chair is related to several others, one of which has been associated with a New York family and is now owned by the Museum of the City of New York. That chair has uprights, front and side stretchers, and an under arm rail that are turned in a pattern identical to this one. Although the New York chair has lost its handgrips and finials, judging on the basis of what remains, they were of the same pattern as those on the Winterthur example. The chair now in New York has been said to have been originally owned by Abraham Riker, who was born in New Amsterdam in 1655 and died on his farm at Newtown, Long Island, in the eighteenth century. Although the records do not reveal that it had a tradition of family ownership, it was purchased from a member of the Riker family in 1940. A third chair, in the collection of the Art Institute of Chicago, formerly belonged to B. A. Behrend, and is pictured as no. 8 in the catalogue *Furniture by New York Cabinetmakers*. Like the Winterthur and Museum of the City of New York chairs, it has an elaborately turned lower arm and ring-turned uprights, but the turning of these elements as well as that of the front stretchers and the finials suggests that it was made at a later date. A fourth chair, with finials identical to the Winterthur example but with rounded slats like the other three chairs, is in the Museum of Fine Arts, Boston.[1] All four chairs possess outward-flaring flat arms, which have square tenons at their ends and are pinned through the uprights in square mortise holes.

If massive size, bold articulation, and elaborate finials are indicators of age, then the Winterthur chair is the earliest of the three. It has no history of ownership, and its documentary relationship to New York is nonexistent; nothing is known about it prior to its publication as no. 318 in Nutting's *Pilgrim Century* when it was in the collection of Dwight Blaney of Boston.[2] No history of ownership or place of origin was mentioned when Nutting republished it in the *Furniture Treasury* as no. 1822. Although he compared it to the Carver chair and pronounced this example as being later (which it indubitably is) on the questionable evidence that it has "no turnings below the seat," Nutting's praiseworthy instinct led him to compare it with two other examples in *Pilgrim Century*, nos. 305 and 324, which are Massachusetts chairs and the least characteristic Anglo-American type. On the Winterthur chair Nutting particularly noted the "winged" slats, of which there are four in contrast to the usual three on the New England examples, the outward-flaring arms, which also occur on some Massachusetts slat-back chairs (see figs. 42, 44, and catalogue entry 14, above), the lower arm rail, which is common on triangular-seat chairs, the elaborately turned front stretchers, and the finials, which, he said, are "very boldly and handsomely turned."[3] Nutting probably did not have a chance to examine the chair himself, since he does not mention one additional characteristic—the uprights taper from their tops to the feet, an attribute that he had previously noted on the "great Carver chair" (*Furniture Treasury* no. 1801, *Pilgrim Century* no. 306) which he once owned. He also did not mention the flattened handgrips (rare on New England chairs), or the outward-flaring base of the finial, both of which are common features on northern European, particularly Scandinavian, chairs. Of course, Nutting did not know that this was *not* a New England chair; thus his inability to fit it coherently into the context of "Pilgrim" furniture is understandable. The very factors that he remarks upon, however, are those that suggest the chair is made in the northern European manner.

Chairs such as Winterthur's can be as confusing today as they were in Nutting's time, because northern European style influenced English vernacular furniture as well as the more pretentious style in the seventeenth century. A case in point is the remarkable turned armchair (fig. 57) at Strangers' Hall, Norwich, which John T. Kirk called to the attention of American students of furniture in his pioneering article, "Sources of Some American Regional Furniture."[4] That chair and Winterthur's chair are articulated in the same ways: four slats, the topmost of which is sculpted and all of which are bowed backward for comfort, bold finials with a vase-shape

cat. 17

Fig. 57. Turned great chair with slat back, possibly English-made but of a Dutch type, mid seventeenth century. The original posts and slats are ash; H 43¼″ (109.9 cm). (Strangers' Hall Museum, Norfolk Museums Service, Norwich, England. Photo: John T. Kirk.)

base, turnings on the downward tapering posts between each slat, and flat arms with an additional turned rail below them. The Stranger's Hall chair is so different from the few other surviving English slat-back chairs of its period that we ask: Is it an English chair? Subsequent investigation does not solve the problem: the chair has no history or provenance and was purchased for the Norwich City Museum in 1927.[5]

If we can someday prove that the Stranger's Hall chair was indeed made in England, it was probably made by a craftsman who had emigrated from the Lowlands. And if this, in turn, is so, then there is no more likely place for it to have been made than Norwich, since the town was the center of the Anglian textile weaving industry and the neighborhood was heavily settled by Walloon, Dutch, and Flemish craftsmen from the mid sixteenth century onward. One of the rationalizations for allowing foreign craftsmen to emigrate to England from the fifteenth century onward was to improve the crafts in England. A statute of the first year of the reign of Richard III (1483) stated that foreign-born craftsmen could take only apprentices who were of English birth. This ordinance, restated in 1523, 1524, and 1530, was apparently still in force as late as August

31, 1640, when "Thomas Spillinge [was] ap[p]r[enticed] to a Dutch Chayermaker."[6]

Although it staggers the imagination to believe that a piece of furniture made in the tradition of the first generation of settlers of New Amsterdam could survive and still be identified today, the Riker chair clearly suggests such a possibility. And if that chair is of New Amsterdam origin, then Winterthur's chair may well be from the same place.

The study of seventeenth-century furniture is now sufficiently mature for us to be able to acknowledge that common, turned chairs are as often listed in urban inventories as they are in rural ones, although the vast majority of these chairs that are found today turn up at country auctions. There is no impediment to believing that this chair could be the product of an early turner working in New Amsterdam since we might expect a slat-back chair in the northern European manner to be made in a Dutch colony early in the century. Unfortunately, the earliest surviving probate records of New York City are scarcely more informative about turned chairs than are those of New England. The 1686 inventory of Cornelis Stenwyck lists "3 old matt chayers" valued at 8s. Mathew Taylor, whose name suggests that he is of English extraction, had "14 rush chaires" worth 15s. the next year. In 1701, James Graham of "Morrisiana," now in the Bronx, possessed an "elbo chair and cushing" valued at 6s., and in December of the next year Peter Jacobsen Marius owned "1 blew elbow cheare [and] one matted ditto," but no evaluation was placed upon them. Marius, a wealthy merchant, also had "6 Turkey Leather chears" in the same room. In 1709, Dr. John Briges possessed, in addition to much fine furniture, "6 matted chairs and two Armed ditto" valued at £4.2.[7] The use of the term "elbo" or "elbow" to denote an armchair is fairly common in New England prior to this time and should not be construed as being of particular significance in New York, except insofar as it denotes that the inventory was taken by someone who spoke English.

While there is no proof that this chair was made in New Amsterdam or early New York, the earliest records of the colony abound in turners whose names indicate that they were of northern European extraction. The earliest are on the Burgher List of 1657, "burgher" being the Dutch equivalent of the English word "freeman." Among them are to be found the names of David Wessels, called a "chairmaker," Jan Hendricksen, called a "chairman"—which may or may not mean a chairmaker—and Freryck Arentzen. Arentzen may be Frederick Arents of Steenwyck mentioned in an inventory of 1686. Because of the fragmentary nature of the New York records, the lists between 1657 and the mid 1690s are lost. However, in February 1698/99, Johannes Tiebout and Johannes Byvanck of Staten Island, both turners, were made freemen of New York. Tiebout, who may have been of Huguenot origin, died in 1711. In July of 1698, Jacob Blom, a turner, was made a freeman, and the following September, Arent Bloom, perhaps a relative, was identified as a "blockmaker," although he is simply called a turner at the time of his death in 1709.[8]

Names in the New York records are fascinating. Byvanck and Blom are Dutch, van Gelder suggests that the bearer of the name came from the southern Netherlands, Tiebout may have been French, and Aarensen and Hendricksen, the earliest of all, could well have been Scandinavians, a group whose presence in New Amsterdam prior to the arrival of the Dutch is all but forgotten by decorative arts historians. It is perhaps a coincidence, but the only other turner's conceit known in seventeenth-century American chairs, in addition to the "mushroom" handgrips discussed in the previous entry, survives on the two chairs related to this one—and were once present here, too—and on two Swedish chairs. The conceit consists of a ring that hangs from a turning whose circumference is too large for the ring to have been slipped over its end (fig. 58). This free ring is easy to turn with the small gouge called a "hook," which has a cutting edge on its side rather than on its point. Joseph Moxon illustrated this tool in his *Mechanick Exercises* and explained that it "is used when the Work stands on the right or left side [of] the *Workman*. . . . It is more difficult for a *Workman* to use than a *Gouge*, because it is made thinner and slendered than a *Gouge*, that its edge . . . may easier come to the Stuff it works upon . . . [and it] is more difficult for the *Workman* to guide it, because it is . . . more subject to tremble." Doubtless the nicety required in using the hook precluded the appearance of this ring on much turned furniture, and its survival on the two American chairs and the two Swedish examples in the churches at Baldishol and Herrestad—the latter believed to date from the twelfth or thirteenth century—is remarkable.[9]

One additional bit of proof that turned chairs with this elaborate form of finial with multiple flange turnings represent a specifically Dutch tradition, as opposed to a more general Anglo-Dutch one, is *The Pancake Maker*, a seventeenth-century painting by Rembrandt pupil Nicolaes Maes. Shown in a room of distinctly humble status, that chair has the same distinctive finial and a shaped upper slat that is much wider than those below it.[10]

Fig. 58. Detail showing the free ring on the arm list of a turned great chair. (Art Institute of Chicago.)

NOTES

[1] Dilliard, *Album of New Netherlands*, fig. 94; Margaret Stern to Forman, April 29, 1974; Miller, *Furniture by New York Cabinetmakers*, pp. 14–15; Randall, *American Furniture*, p. 159, no. 121.

[2] Mrs. Blaney's daughter remembers the chair in their Boston home but does not know where her father acquired it; interview by Forman, June 20, 1972.

[3] Nutting, *Furniture Treasury*, p. 306 and no. 318.

[4] Kirk, "Sources of Some Regional Furniture, Part 1," p. 796. Another English chair with loose turned rings, now in the collection of Temple Newsam House in Leeds, is illustrated in Wolsey and Luff, *Furniture in England*, fig. 88.

[5] Michael Day to Forman, April 19, 1977. The chair has since been deaccessioned (A. J. Tibbles to Catherine E. Hutchins, January 24, 1986).

[6] See Moens, *Walloons and Their Church at Norwich*; *Statutes of the Realm*, 3:765–66 (the statute, addressed to the weaving trade, encompassed all others as well); Millican, *Register of the Freemen of Norwich, 1548–1713* (Norwich, 1934), as quoted in the Symonds Papers, DMMC 75 × 69.33.

[7] New York Probate, Libers 19B:222; 14A:21; 2:182, 174 (fol. 1); and 6:193.

[8] *New Amsterdam Court Minutes*, 7:151–53, 68; *Burghers . . . and Freemen*, pp. 20, 21, 22, 72, 63, 70; New York Probate, Libers 19B:265; 2:88; 3:30.

[9] *Moxon's Mechanick Exercises*, pl. 16, fig. D, and p. 186; Ryder, "Four-Legged Turned Chairs," pp. 44–49, figs. 1, 5.

[10] I wish to thank Robert F. Trent for bringing this painting, now at the Museum of Fine Arts, Boston, to my attention.

SEATING FURNITURE MADE BY JOINERS

WAINSCOT CHAIRS

While seventeenth-century turners were busy designing and building spindle-back and slat-back chairs, joiners and carpenters were making a wider array of seating furniture which relied for its sturdiness on mortise-and-tenon joints and on board-and-nail construction. Predictably the frequent and hard use given to much of the joiner-made seating furniture means that what actually survives is of a generally high quality, and includes joined and carved wainscot chairs, joined or "joint" stools, joined forms (elongated stools used for more than one sitter), and joined settles. Examples of these furniture forms made from boards and fastened together with nails are nowadays extremely rare and, more frustratingly, often difficult to date because of their relatively simple workmanship and their lack of decoration (see catalogue entry 42).

Among the surviving forms of American seventeenth-century joined seating furniture, none exists in greater number or is more impressive than the great, joined, wainscot chairs whose commanding appearance betrays their origin in the era of boldly turned, decoratively carved, and polychromed oak. It has always been assumed that the European ancestors of these chairs were first used in churches and found their way into the homes of the aristocracy during the Middle Ages. This easy assumption is doubtless based upon illuminated manuscripts which abound in pictures of princes seated on wooden thrones and princes of the church seated on hooded or canopied cathedra, both far more ornately carved than their linear descendants of the seventeenth century. What seems obvious from the pictures is less clear when we come to examine the few

wooden chairs that have survived from the sixteenth century and earlier: it is virtually impossible to say which examples may have been made for churches, or if they were made at an earlier date than the others, which may have been made for domestic use, inasmuch as all furniture of this period shares the same techniques of manufacture and decoration. It is possible that nonportable, wooden chairs appear in both domestic and secular contexts in northern Europe at about the same time.

The few published inventories of fifteenth- and sixteenth-century English churches make little mention of nonfixed furniture of any sort. For example, the inventory of Saint Mary at Hill, London, in 1431 reveals but a single piece of case furniture: a chest containing church documents ("evydens that longeth to the chirche"). An inventory of the church's goods in 1496/97 is rich with textiles and metals, but notes only three pieces of movable furniture—2 "cheyres of Iron for Rector Coris." An early domestic inventory, dating from sometime between 1524 and 1531, filed among the papers of the church reveals that in the hall of the house owned by John Porth, of London, "layt the kynges seruant," was "a closse chare of wanskott," but the bulk of the seating furniture in that room consisted of four joined stools, a "stakyd" form (a slab bench with four stake feet), "two tornyd chares," and a "chayre of spaynysche makyng" valued at 16d. and another "close chare." Thomas, Lord Wharton of Healaugh, Yorkshire, possessed "one Chare of wanescot with a bull head on it" in 1568, the bull head being his coat of arms.[1]

Wherever the precedent for using them came from, joined chairs, usually of rather slight value, are listed in a few Oxfordshire inventories of the 1570s and 1580s. "One Joyned

Bedstede A Trokle Bedd A Cubberd A Table a Joyned Chere and one Joyned Stole" valued together at £1 were itemized in the parlor of William Wyse, a yeoman of Banbury, in March 1577/78. "A Joyned Cheyre" viewed the following May in the hall of Ralph Newbery, a husbandman, of Cropredy, was valued with a table and a joined stool at only 1s. 8d. Leonard Dalton of Witney possessed "a Joyned chayre" worth 5s. in August 1581, and Thomas Taylor, the elder, yeoman of Witney—a man whose household goods were worth £162—possessed one appraised along with nine joined stools in his "new parlor" at 14s. in October 1583.[2] The rarity of the form is emphasized by the four references to joined chairs, which are all that can be found among the 222 inventories published in Oxfordshire.

The extraordinary inventory of the sumptuous furnishings at Hardwick Hall, taken in 1601, reveals its owners' clear preference for seating furniture whose woodwork was covered with textiles. About a half dozen "wood chares" are listed in minor rooms, and since no values are given, it is not absolutely clear that they were the products of the joiner's rather than the turner's art. "A great Chare trymmed with Crimson velvett imbrodered with golde and with a golde frenge" in the "Best Bed Chamber" is also listed, but from this description it is unlikely that much of its woodwork showed.[3]

Two "wainscott" chairs, each with "an old cushion" were in separate bedchambers at Stondon House, in Wiltshire, the home of Ralph Sadlier in 1623. "One seald [ceiled] cheare," valued at 7s. along with two buffet stools and a little table, was listed among the effects of Henry Robinson, a gentleman of Swinsty, Yorkshire, in December 1639. At Tart Hall, the London home of the Earl of Arundel in 1641, "in the Roome ioyning to [the footman's] Hall" were "Two great wood chayers with Armes & Backs" and "Another of the like fashion but lesser," and "Another chayre of the same wood without Armes."[4] These chairs do not appear to have been in a room frequented by the masters of the house, because in those rooms the vast majority of the chairs were upholstered (this will be discussed later).

Scanty as the citations may be, they are informative in two ways. First, they show that chairs of any sort were rather rare in the homes of the middling sort in England in the generations immediately prior to the settlement of America, and second, they give us an insight into the way the words *wainscot, joined, ceiled, great,* and *wood* were used in England to identify what we generally refer to today as "wainscot chairs."

The etymology of the noun *wainscot* is unclear. In the early Middle Ages, it referred to oak wood of a particularly fine quality. Eventually, it came to refer to woodwork made out of oak, as in the phrase "wainscotting about the walls," and to oak wood itself, regardless of its quality.[5] It was also used as an adjective to refer to furniture made of oak, and this appears to have been its common meaning by the seventeenth century. When used to describe a chair, it seems clear that it generally referred to a framed chair in the joiner's manner with a wooden seat.

Ceiled, or *seiled,* was a synonym for *joined.* It described the joiner's panel-and-frame woodwork and survives today in the word *ceiling,* a concept transferred in an age when ceilings were still made of panels of wood in a joined frame. Furniture is rarely described as "ceiled" in seventeenth-century American documents. *Ceiled* may have been almost archaic by the second quarter of the seventeenth century; however, it was occasionally used, as is demonstrated by the May 1644 inventory of John Jenny of Plymouth, Massachusetts, who possessed "i seeled chest" valued at 6s. 8d.[6]

Wood seems a curious adjective by which to identify a chair, since there was no other material for chairs to have been made of in the seventeenth century. This specification seems less strange when we bear in mind that chairs were almost always identified in inventories by the material with which they were upholstered, and a reference to a "wood chair" strongly suggests that the chair had no textile or fiber upholstery. On occasion references in Pennsylvania inventories are unmistakably clear, such as the mention on June 5, 1736, of "11 walnut wood bottomed chairs" valued at 40s. in the inventory of Nehemiah Allen of Philadelphia.[7]

Additional adjectives used by inventory takers are "armed" and "great," but these terms also apply to turned chairs, which often had arms or "elbos" just as joined chairs did and which were often "great" meaning "large" in seventeenth-century English. It is probable that by the eighteenth century, "great" had lost the connotation of size and was used to refer merely to an armchair, as in the coastal Connecticut inventory of Elizabeth Wells, recorded August 11, 1729, which lists "Great chair" 5s., "4 Low great chairs" £1.6.[8]

By the time Englishmen began to migrate to North America, the great, joined, wainscot chairs made totally of wood and fitted with separate cushions were no longer fashionable in the homes of the English aristocracy—if they ever had been—and were found almost exclusively among the yeomanry. Indeed, when we look critically at the photographs of wainscot chairs in the numerous books that illustrate them, only a very few of those examples that escaped being "improved" in the nineteenth century have earmarks of London design or fine urban workmanship, or appear to have been made in the sixteenth century.

"Towe Joynd Chaires" valued at 5s. appear in the first major inventory recorded in Essex County, Massachusetts—a list of the estate of John Dillingham of Ipswich, possessed by his widow Sarah in 1636. Dillingham had come to New England in 1630 from Leicestershire, and his chairs may have been made in England, inasmuch as no joiners working in Ipswich at this date have been identified. Such chairs, however, were certainly within the competence of any carpenter, of whom several were at work by the time Dillingham immigrated. An "ould Joyne chayre with a couer" valued at 4s. appears in the December 1650 inventory of John Cross of Ipswich, and two others appear in Newbury inventories in 1654 and 1655, valued at 5s. and 3s. 6d. respectively. On March 28, 1663, Mary Smith of Marblehead willed to her granddaughter, Mary Ebron, "my littell Joynt Chare," but unfortunately this chair cannot be identified in her inventory.[9] That three of the six earliest joined chairs mentioned in the Essex County inventories were owned by women is notable. With the death of their spouses, these women inherited the rights of respect associated with such chairs.

Not until the inventory of Thomas Gardner of Salem was taken in February 1674 was the phrase "wenscott chair" used in an Essex County inventory. Gardner, whose chair was valued at 5s., had come to Cape Ann in 1624 or 1625, probably from Sherborne in northern Dorsetshire, as part of a project to establish a fishery in New England.[10]

No references to joined or wainscot chairs in the Suffolk County Probate Records predate those in the Essex County records. A survey of the more descriptive Suffolk County records, however, illustrates that general statements cannot be made about preferences for wainscot chairs in urban, as opposed to rural, homes or in homes whose contents are of higher rather than lower value. Nor does the presence of such chairs necessarily denote social status. Thomas Lamb of Roxbury, whose estate amounted to £112, had "two joyned chaires and one other in the parlour" valued at 10s. in 1646. They were furnished with "2 Turkie cushions & one auld cushion" worth 12s. In the same year, Captain Joseph Weld, of Roxbury, whose estate was valued at £2,028 had a "wooden chair" worth 5s. in his "best chamber." In all, he had 5 chairs and 5 joined stools in his home. In the hall, or main room, of Reverend John Cotton's Boston home in 1652 were "1 Joyned chaire and 2 basse chaires" valued at 19s., while in his "great Parlour" were 7 leather chairs of unspecified value and "1 Great chaire and forme" worth 8s. As late as 1663, David Evans, a wealthy Boston merchant whose estate amounted to over £1,400, possessed 2 "joint chayres" in addition to his leather and turkey-work examples.[11] It is clear that in the 1660s, upholstered chairs were more important in the homes of well-to-do Bostonians than were the old-style wainscot chairs.

In the Plymouth Colony, the 1657 inventory of William Bradford contained "2 great Carved Chaires" valued at the very high price of £1.4. When the inventory of his widow, Alice, was taken thirteen years later, these chairs were listed again at the same valuation.[12]

The earliest datable example of an American wainscot chair may rightly be called a "ceiled" chair and may have been referred to as a "close chair" in the sixteenth century. The chair was originally made for Michael Metcalf of Dedham, Massachusetts, and in 1902 was given to the Dedham Historical Society by Louisa E. Harris, a direct descendant of the original owner (fig. 59).[13] Metcalf's initials and the believable date 1652 are carved into its back panel. It may well be the "joyned chair" valued at 6s. in the 1664 inventory of Metcalf's estate. Additional chairs of this type known to have been made in New England have not been identified (see, however, catalogue entry 29). Although made of white oak, the Metcalf chair is recognizably of American origin, and may have been made in Dedham by a joiner from East Anglia. A closely related English chair of more conventional form, but almost identical carving, is illustrated in *Chats on Cottage and Farmhouse Furniture*.[14] A related American chest is in the Lee House, owned by the Old Lyme Historical Society, Old Lyme, Connecticut.

In light of the Mainwaring/Corbet family example at Higher Peover, Cheshire, it would be tempting to consider the 1652 Metcalf chair an anachronism which must date from the

Fig. 59. Joined great chair with enclosed bottom, eastern Massachusetts, 1652. White oak; H 46¼" (117.5 cm), W 22½" (57.2 cm), D 17½" (44.5 cm), SH 16⅜" (41.6 cm). (Dedham Historical Society, Dedham, Mass., gift of Louisa E. Harris. Photo: Benno M. Forman.) The chair was made for Michael Metcalf of Dedham.

middle of the sixteenth century, but in an agrarian society, furniture forms tend to persist long after they have become outmoded in the social circles that set the fashions for a culture. An even later example from Limburg, Netherlands, bears the date 1764 on the crest rail (fig. 60).[15]

A chair of totally different character, made by a craftsman trained in a very different part of England, was given to Bowdoin College, Brunswick, Maine, by E. Wilder Farley in 1872. This chair (fig. 61) has been attributed to the hand of Thomas Dennis of Ipswich, Massachusetts, a direct ancestor of the chair's donor. Thomas Dennis's title to the authorship of this chair, however, is ambiguous because of one of those curious quirks that often blur the search for positive historical facts. Dennis married Grace Searle, the widow of William Searle, a joiner (b. Ottery St. Mary, Devonshire, 1611; married Grace Cole, 1659; emigrated ca. 1663; d. ca. 1667) who was Dennis's predecessor in Ipswich. Searle bequeathed all of his possessions to his wife, and it is likely that this fine chair, and other examples of Searle's work, passed into the Dennis family upon Grace Searle's marriage to Thomas Dennis, thirteen months later.[16] A similar but less well articulated chair is in the collection of Essex Institute. The

Fig. 61. Joined great chair, attributed to William Searle, Ipswich, Mass., 1663–67. Oak; H 48″ (121.9 cm), W 25½″ (54.8 cm), D 17½″ (44.4 cm), SH 17½″ (44.4 cm). (Bowdoin College Museum of Art, Bowdoin, Maine, gift of E. Wilder Farley, 1872. Photo: Richard Cheek.)

carving of the atlantes and the design of the panel of the Essex Institute chair are perceptibly different from that on the Bowdoin College example, as is the turning of the front legs. These differences could represent the decline of a craftsman's abilities over a period of time, or they could indicate the two chairs, despite their overall similarity, were made by two different craftsmen.

The latter idea, suggested by the details of the chairs themselves, is borne out by surviving documents. The inventory of William Searle included only one notable chair, which must have been of unusual character, since it was valued at the remarkably high amount of £1. When the estate of John, the only son who survived Thomas Dennis, was inventoried in 1757, it listed not one but "2 wooden Great Chairs Carved" valued at 2s. John Dennis was the grandfather of Sarah Dennis, through whose descendants the chairs found their way into the Farley and Brookhouse families and thence, by gift, to the institutions that now own them.[17]

Compelling visual evidence has survived to suggest that Searle was the craftsman who brought the particular florid style of carving and the iconography embodied in the chair in figure 61 to New England. The chest in figure 62 bears the carved inscription on its left frame MF 1671 EC, perhaps commemorating a marriage, which cannot now be identified. The chest illustrates the style in which Searle was trained and in which he must have trained an apprentice, since Searle left his native village eight years before the date inscribed on the chest. The practice of polychroming carved woodwork, very much alive in Ottery St. Mary at the time this chest was made, was also brought to New England, as a surviving chest (fig. 63) dated 1676 with an Ipswich history vividly demonstrates.[18]

The English chest, the American chair and chest, and related chests in the Ipswich Historical Society, the Wadsworth Atheneum, the Metropolitan Museum, the

Museum of Fine Arts, Boston, and private collections in New Hampshire, New York, and North Carolina illustrate an important point in regard to the treatment of a given iconographic motif in one place over a period of time. The motif—a jug with flowers emanating from its mouth—on the back of the chair in figure 61 was very probably inspired by the decoration on a pew end dating from 1526 in Saint Mary's Church, Ottery St. Mary (fig. 64).[19] Searle, and doubtless his master and his master's master, saw that pew every single Sunday, and they perpetuated its motif in their own work. The process of abstraction that resulted in the change of pattern is a well-understood principle of art history, but rarely is it so well documented.

William Searle and his Massachusetts apprentices were not the only joiners producing chairs; three important wainscot chairs have Connecticut origins. One chair descended through the family of Gov. William Leete and is presently displayed at the Henry Whitfield House, Guilford. It was probably the "on[e] Great joyners: Chair" valued at 8s. in the governor's 1683 inventory. Another chair, originally owned by Thomas Robinson of Guilford, was identified in his inventory in 1712 as "1 Great Joynery Chair." A third wainscot armchair, owned by Robert Treat of Milford, was described in 1710 as "an old wooden chair" and valued at 4s. "Old" in this third instance may well mean that the chair was

Fig. 62. LEFT. Joined chest, Ottery St. Mary, Devonshire, England, 1671. (Private collection. Photo: William N. Hosley, Jr.)

Fig. 63. BELOW, LEFT. Joined chest, attributed to William Searle or, more probably, the shop of Thomas Dennis, Ipswich, Mass., 1676. White oak; H 31¹¹⁄₁₆″ (80.5 cm), W 49⅝″ (126.1 cm), D 22⅝″ (57.5 cm). (Winterthur 82.276.)

Fig. 64. BELOW, RIGHT. Detail of carving on a pew end in Saint Mary's Church, Ottery St. Mary, Devonshire, England, 1526. (Photo: Benno M. Forman.)

then fifty years old. The reference is further important because it contains a strong hint that the chair was also considered somewhat old fashioned; it was appraised at less than half the value accorded his "6 common sort of chairs," perhaps indicating that wainscot chairs were not being made in the colony in 1710.[20]

It is difficult to state with certainty when wainscot chairs were no longer being made in New England: no single date could intelligently encompass all of the possible customers' attitudes toward fashion, nor take into account that craftsmen who had been trained in the joiner's tradition continued to work into the eighteenth century. In 1690, "one great chair" in

the inventory of Moses Paine of Boston was appraised at only 2s. in an estate worth £113.[21] By the mid 1690s, many Boston inventories listed cane chairs in the William and Mary style (although many households furnished earlier contained mostly leather chairs, probably in the Cromwellian style), but references to wainscot chairs are scarce.

What is true for a merchant in Boston, however, may not be true for a farmer in Freehold, New Jersey. It is clear that anybody in Freehold who wanted one could have purchased a wainscot chair in 1695. An unusual example with this date carved on its back panel is owned by the Monmouth County Historical Association. This atypical chair has the

Fig. 65. Robert Rhea, joined great chair with carved back. Freehold, N.J., 1695. White oak with a back of yellow pine; H 42¾″ (108.6 cm), W 25¾″ (65.4 cm), D 27¾″ (70.5 cm), SH 16⅝″ (42.2 cm). (Courtesy, Monmouth County Historical Association, Freehold, N.J. Photo: Helga Studio.)

Fig. 66. H. G. (probably H. Guthrie), joined great chair with carved back. Aberdeen, Scotland, 1600–1650. (Hall of the Combined Guilds of Aberdeen, Trinity Hall College, Aberdeen, Scotland: Photo, courtesy Robert Logan.) The chair was made for the barbers and wigmakers' guild.

carved initials of its maker, Robert Rhea, conjoined with those of his wife, Janet (fig. 65). The chair was made by Rhea, a joiner, after his arrival from Scotland in 1685 and represents yet another strain of British regional furniture in America.[22] A chair from the extraordinary collection of Trinity Hall College, Aberdeen, Scotland (fig. 66), shows Rhea's roots as a craftsman in the style of this wainscot chair, his system of proportional relationships, the design of his specific motifs, and such details as the unusual curved "elbos."[23] And another of the Scottish examples is dated 1690—five years after Rhea emigrated to America. It is clear that Rhea had not only learned the techniques of his trade in Scotland, but the idea of what a grand chair should look like as well. We know that Rhea lived near Freehold, New Jersey, for a decade prior to the creation of this chair, yet, the chair itself does not reveal that he was exposed to other alternatives of what a chair could look like. Other than that the carved panel of the back is made of American yellow pine, all other parts are made of oak, in the traditional British joiner's manner. Indeed, it is very likely that Rhea was a joiner, who could do turning of good quality and conception in addition to carving, and not merely a carpenter, as others have implied.[24] We cannot help wondering if the conjoining of his wife's initial with his own indicates that she was

welcome to sit in this chair as well as the lord and master of the household.

By far the largest group of surviving wainscot chairs in America is that type generally referred to by collectors as "Chester County chairs," because they have been found in large numbers throughout Chester County and southeastern Pennsylvania over the years.[25] With a few notable exceptions, very little is known about them: only two chairs and one settle have inlaid dates and initials, indicating when they were made; a few others have family histories. But the vast majority are made of black walnut, while a few rare examples are made of oak.

The popularity of black walnut in the middle colonies gives all the wainscot chairs made there a generic similarity of appearance, but when they are examined individually, as they are in the catalogue that follows, at least two British and two continental cultural strains can be discerned in the details of design and construction. The vast majority of these chairs are modeled on a distinctive type found in southeastern

Fig. 67. Joined chair (legs missing), Wakefield, Bucks County, Penn., 1714. Black walnut (*Juglans nigra*); inlay wood unknown. (Private collection. Photo: Benno M. Forman.) The maker of the chair may have trained in Wales. The chair has a history of ownership in the Hoopes family.

Fig. 68. Joined chair, probably made in Cheshire, England, late seventeenth century. (Private collection. Photo: Benno M. Forman.)

Lancashire and neighboring Cheshire. Closely associated with that strain and easily confused with it are chairs with Welsh details. A third strain is related to Germanic styles and a fourth—represented by a solitary chair in the Winterthur collection—has affinities to Swedish workmanship. If these superficial resemblances ultimately prove that some of these chairs were made by craftsmen of Swedish and German extraction, then it must follow that the chairs were made across a large geographic area, since craftsmen of Swedish and German backgrounds have not been identified among the earliest seventeenth-century furniture makers in Chester County. Indeed, it is possible that the Swedish and Germanic strains predate the arrival of the British in Pennsylvania.

Stylistically the American chairs related to the British examples are of three general types. The first and most obvious is the armchair modeled on a type of wainscot armchair that was made in rural England during the second half of the seventeenth century, although the conception of the chair is somewhat older. The second is a smaller, generally high-back side chair constructed in the joiner's manner but stylistically related to the leather or turkey-work upholstered chairs popular in urban England during the second quarter of the seventeenth century. A third type, a provincial version of the cane chair

with a wooden seat, became popular in England during the last quarter of the seventeenth century and was somewhat more common there than in America.

The earliest dated American example of these British-style chairs is aesthetically marred by the loss of its legs but retains great historical significance. It is made of black walnut (*Juglans nigra*) and is inlaid with the initials I·H and the date 1714 (subsequently changed to 1704) (fig. 67). It has survived in the hands of a direct descendant of the original owner, Joshua Hoopes (d. 1724), a Yorkshireman, who settled in Wakefield, Bucks County, Pennsylvania. His choice of this particular type of chair was perhaps not so much based on what he remembered from his home county, where the style was probably not being made when he emigrated, but on what was available to him when he decided to buy this chair some thirty-one years later. His descendants moved the chair to Chester County. The chair is remarkable not only because it is dated and its provenance is identifiable, but because it is one of few American examples that have pyramidal finials, or "tops," in the manner of an English chair (fig. 68). Another chair, almost identical but undated, was owned in 1924 by C. Watts Mercur. The Mercurs were a Bucks County family, which adds additional weight to the possible Bucks County origin of both chairs. The Hoopes family chair is the earliest datable example of Pennsylvania furniture with vine-and-berry inlay that was probably introduced into America by a craftsman from southern Wales.[26]

The vast majority of the so-called Chester County chairs and related settees have rounded finials, in contrast to those on the Hoopes chair and the one in Cheshire, England; however, the English example and the most striking examples of the Chester County chairs do share one feature—a pierced and scalloped crest rail. This piercing, which generally takes the shape of a pair of inverted single quotation marks, has enabled us to trace the style to southern Lancashire and Cheshire, where numerous related examples survive, although the precise village in which chairs with this feature may have originated has not yet been discovered. Most of the chairs of this type are made of black walnut, but a few rare examples, such as the chair in figure 69, are made of oak. The side stretchers of this oak chair are not original and probably replaced rectilinear stretchers like that on the back. The front feet have been restored; the original board bottom (doubtless recessed like that on figure 82) has also been replaced. The chair, recently owned by David Stockwell, Inc., of Wilmington, Delaware, was once owned by T. van C. Phillips and later by Walter Jeffords and has a tradition of ownership by the Pennock family.[27] It exhibits three features that suggest it is of an early date. First, the inside margin of each stile is chamfered rather than molded or having moldings applied to set off the back panel; second, the back panel is flat rather than fielded; and third, the chair is made of red oak rather than the more common black walnut. Obviously any of these could be explained in a number of ways, but, in the absence of more positive evidence, together they argue for the idea that the chair was made by a craftsman who had recently arrived in Pennsylvania and was working in the manner and with the material most familiar to him. An additional example of the Chester County chair in oak, owned by the Chester County Historical Society (see fig. 82), is not recognizably related to the Stockwell chair in any detail of its construction or design, and is believed to have been owned by Aaron James of Westtown Township, Chester County, who came to Pennsylvania with William Penn.[28] The James chair has overtones of Welsh workmanship and style and does not relate stylistically to the majority of Chester County chairs. A walnut example of the chair, also owned by the historical society, is mature in the conception of its turnings and distinguished by two back panels oriented horizontally; it was owned by the Bonsall family of Upper Darby, Delaware County, near Philadelphia.

The Chester County Historical Society also owns a side chair of somewhat different character, and made of walnut, that is identical to the Winterthur example illustrated in catalogue entry 25. This variation seems to draw its inspiration from a rural type of English wainscot chair modeled on the popular Cromwellian-style upholstered chairs. An English example, in the parish church at Ormskirk, Lancashire, is illustrated in

Fig. 69. Joined great chair, probably southeastern Pennsylvania, late seventeenth or early eighteenth century. Red oak. (Private collection.) The maker had emigrated recently from southern Lancashire or Cheshire. The chair has a history of ownership in the Pennock family of Chester County, Penn.

figure 70. Like most of the American examples, it has rounded finials that project above the crest rails. Additional examples, some of which are illustrated in the catalogue, are in Saint Oswald's Church, Lower Peover, Cheshire, about 16 miles south-southwest of Manchester, and in the parish church at Delamere, Cheshire (see figs. 81 and 86).

Documentary evidence supports the notion that the resemblance of Chester County chairs to those in Cheshire, England, is more than a coincidence. The evidence illustrates one of the axioms of American decorative arts history: furniture made in rural towns follows a contemporary or even slightly earlier fashion of a nearby urban area. As early as 1935, William Macpherson Hornor, Jr., identified two joiners from Cheshire who came to Philadelphia in 1683. The first, Richard Clone from Nantwich, arrived on the *Endeavour*.[29] The presence of Clone in Philadelphia suggests that the earliest examples of these wainscot chairs in the English manner were very likely made in that town. How long Clone lived and worked in Philadelphia is not known; no inventory of his estate was probated. The idea that wainscot chairs were present in the town is supported by an inventory taken in 1688, only five years after the original settlement by Englishmen. Anna Salter had owned "2 wooden large Chaires" valued at 6s. as well as "4 smaller ditto," both lots valued at 6s. each. She also possessed "4 turkey worke cushons" to distribute among them.

Fig. 70. Joined chair, Ormskirk, Lancashire, England, 1660–1700. (Church of Saints Peter and Paul, Ormskirk, Lancashire, England. Photo: Benno M. Forman.) This is a rural type of chair modeled on the Cromwellian upholstered chair.

chairs were described only as "walnut," 37 more were described as of "black walnut," and 26 were specified as "oak."[32]

The earliest unambiguous reference that indicates the presence of joined chairs in Chester County occurs in the 1708 inventory of Ralph Fishbourne of Chester who had been living in Pennsylvania at least since 1692. Fishbourne's "outward room" contained "½ doz of oaken Chaires" valued at £2.10. These chairs are referred to as "6 Wainscot chairs" in the inventory of his widow, Elizabeth, taken the following year. They were not the least valuable set of chairs that Fishbourne possessed, nor were they in the best room; that honor belonged to the "½ doz. of Caine chairs" valued at £3.12. in "the Inward Chamber." The "Seald arme chear" in the large room of John Hoskins's home in Chester in 1716 was also a wainscot chair. It was valued at 10s.[33]

Evidence of how late the chairs continued to be made as opposed to merely being used because they were there can never be definitively answered by inventory descriptions. A settle with the inlaid date 1758 and the initials of its original owners, Isaac and Elizabeth (née Darlington) Pyle, of Birmingham Township, is in the collection of the Chester County Historical Society. The settle is attributed to Elizabeth Pyle's brother, Abraham Darlington. Darlington was the son of a saddler from Waverham, Cheshire, and is believed to have been a carpenter. The 1791–1810 account book of Darlington's nephew Amos, a cabinetmaker, has survived but it contains no evidence that Amos made furniture even remotely related to chairs and settles.[34] If the rhythms of life among the primarily British settlers of agrarian Chester County were similar to those of the relatives they left behind, we could assume that such furniture continued to be made until the 1770s, about the same time as a high-back joined armchair, with 1777 and neoclassical paterae carved into its back, was made in England.[35]

While distressingly little can be found out about the British furniture makers of the late seventeenth century working in southeastern Pennsylvania, even less is known about those from Sweden and Germany who preceded them. The records of these settlers are so scanty, their settlements so distant from each other, and their subsequent assimilation into the dominant culture so complete that only glimpses of their presence can be seen in surviving furniture. The same is true in middle-colonies architecture, where little that is distinctively Swedish can be found, although the Swedes settled in Delaware in the late 1630s.

Horace Burr, who translated the early records of Wilmington's Old Swedes Church in 1890, remarked that the "mechanical skill [of the Swedish colonists] seems to have been only adequate to building their plain log houses, and making log canoes, carts, sleds, etc.," an opinion that has generally been adopted by subsequent writers who dealt with the history of colonial Delaware. But when the first census of the United States was taken, citizens of Swedish origin still constituted 3.9 percent of the population of New Jersey, 0.8 percent of Pennsylvania, and 8.9 percent of Delaware, and it is almost inconceivable that this group could have been so completely assimilated that no vestige of their arts could be

Further, the research of Ruth Matzkin into the earliest probate records of Philadelphia County between 1683 and 1710 reveals that many wainscot chairs were present in the outlying area as well. Among the 1608 chairs owned by residents of English extraction, 130 were referred to as "wooden" without any further elaboration except that 4 were oak and 60 were walnut.[30]

The second joiner who is identified in contemporary documents to be "from Cheshire" was John Maddock. Maddock also arrived in Philadelphia on the *Endeavour* in 1683 and was married there in 1690. He is mentioned in the records of Ridley in 1698 and Nether Providence in 1698. Both were townships in Chester County, but it is not clear that he was then living in either one since the notices show only that he bought and sold land there.[31] That Maddock is first known in Philadelphia and later had Chester County associations may account for the transference of the taste for this style from Philadelphia into the adjoining county before the seventeenth century had run its course.

Whatever the circumstances of dissemination into Chester County, an inventory survey by Margaret B. Schiffer reveals that a great number of chairs described variously as "oak," "walnut," "joined," and "framed" were owned by county residents throughout the eighteenth century and well into the nineteenth. Among the inventories that Schiffer tabulated, 209 found.[36] Indeed, a joined chair at Winterthur (catalogue entry 32) confirms their presence here.

While New Sweden was established chiefly to trade with the Indians, the rich agricultural lands and moderate climate of the Delaware River valley prompted many to turn to agriculture, and by the time of William Penn, a second generation was living on large, prosperous, and well-furnished farms. Although their urban settlements were small and scattered, notable among them was the settlement at New Castle, Delaware, which supported a few craftsmen prior to 1700, although they have not been easy for us to identify (see also catalogue entry 73). Often the evidence that they were craftsmen is circumstantial. The early probate records of Philadelphia County, where a few estates of residents of what is now Delaware were proved, have revealed the name of at least one craftsman of Swedish origin who could have made a chair such as the one illustrated in catalogue entry 32. His name was Broer Sinnexen (also spelled Brewer Sencke, Senex, and Senecar). Sinnexen's inventory reveals that, like many of his fellow Swedes, he was a craftsman as well as a farmer. At the time of his death in 1708, his tools included 1 hammer, 6 gimlets, 6 chisels, 2 saws, 2 plane irons, "3 plaine irons with Stocks," 6 augers, "one square of iron," 1 froe, 1 "drawing knife," 1 adz, and miscellaneous axes and hatchets. He is mentioned many times in the court records of New Castle, Delaware, between 1683, when he was naturalized as an English subject, and 1696. These records reveal that at one time Sinnexen owned 770 acres of land in the area north of Christina Creek. He also contributed significantly in food and money toward the construction of the Swedish church at Wilmington, although the church records do not reveal that he performed any work on the structure, which was at some distance from his home and was mainly built by English craftsmen from Philadelphia.[37]

Sinnexen's inventory reveals that his home was far from a crude log cabin containing few amenities. His estate, appraised at £173, contained a "couch" valued at 10s., "one black wallnut Table and Chaires" worth £1.10. and a "chest of drawers" valued at £1. The presence of a chest of drawers in Sinnexen's inventory is an informative comment upon the matter of cultural assimilation: it is unlikely that this would have been found in his home had he remained in Sweden. At the turn of the eighteenth century, chests of drawers were common in England but almost unknown in northern Europe where chests and cupboards were generally used for the storage of textiles.

Wainscot chairs were used by emigrants from northwestern Germany who settled in Germantown, seven miles northwest of Philadelphia, in 1682. Unlike the Swedes, many of the earliest Germans in Pennsylvania were oriented toward an urban environment, doubtless because many were craftsmen by training. One walnut chair in the Winterthur collection (catalogue entry 31) exhibits several northern Germanic stylistic touches. (The early eighteenth-century northwestern German influence is distinctively different from that of the later southern German influence and is more obvious in turned work than in joined pieces. It will be more fully discussed in the introduction to carved-top crook-back leather chairs.)

Fig. 71. Detail of ovoid holes and the pegs to fit them. The holes and pegs indicate the chair was made by a craftsman who trained in northern Europe. (Photo: Benno M. Forman.)

One feature of northern European workmanship on the walnut wainscot chairs distinguishes it from the work executed in the Lancashire/Cheshire and Welsh manners: the pins that hold the tenons in the mortises are made in a distinctive manner. As was earlier noted, in both the middle colonies wainscot chairs derived from English West Country types and the English-inspired joined furniture of seventeenth-century New England, the pins are generally rectangular in shape and generally protrude a scant fraction of an inch above the surface of the wood into which they are driven. They retain their rectangular look today, even though they were driven into round holes drilled by round bits. The pins used in the furniture with northern European attributes are distinctively different. Their heads often (but not invariably) have an ovoid profile—shaped much like a lemon—with two rounded sides opposite each other and two pointed sides between them (fig. 71). Only two facts can account for this feature: either the pin shapes the hole or the hole shapes the pin. When we first observed this characteristic, we assumed that it was unlikely that a round bit could drill a hole that was ovoid in profile, and that the pin was, therefore, the agent responsible for this phenomenon. After investigating this possibility by going through contortions no self-respecting craftsman could use and still make a living, we discarded the idea and proceeded to examine the possibility that the hole somehow shaped the pin. Thanks to the pragmatic demonstrations of John D. Alexander, Jr., we now know that this is often what happens.

Alexander noted that the points of these holes always appeared at the corners where the long grain of the wood gave way to the cross grain. He also knew that the piercer bits used in the seventeenth and eighteenth centuries to drill pin holes tend to cut wood best across the grain and tend to push the wood aside where the long grain meets the bit, especially if the wood is not completely dry. In a short time, Alexander was able to produce in various kinds of wood a number of holes that were essentially lemon-shape in section. Half of the puzzle had been solved.

The other piece of the puzzle fell into place when a field trip to Germany enabled us to examine a large quantity of German furniture. We found that, contrary to English seventeenth-century joinery practices in which pins are generally left square, German joiners either chamfered them along opposite edges, giving them an elliptical profile which fit into a nonround hole more snugly, or chamfered their pins to an octagonal section. Even when the pins are octagonal and are driven into the nonround hole tightly, they are compressed into the nonround parts of the hole, filling it rather neatly. Because surface contact between the pin and the wood surrounding it and the additional wedge effect that is gained by using an elliptical pin is great, such a pegging system is extremely efficient. While these ovoid pins and holes are not found in every joint in the furniture suspected of being made by a craftsman trained in the Germanic tradition, at least one or more such pins can be found in each of the chairs in the Winterthur collection that cannot be stylistically related to the Lancashire/Cheshire style.

It cannot be argued that this technique invariably identifies the work of a late seventeenth- or early eighteenth-century crafts-man of northern European extraction since the apprentice-ship system guarantees that dissemination of a construction technique begins within a decade of its introduction. Nor can it be said that this is a characteristic of all Germanic workmanship, since it does not invariably appear on joined work in the styles practiced by those craftsmen from Germany who came to Pennsylvania after 1725. Yet, when it appears on a piece of middle colonies furniture made in the seventeenth-century style, it cannot be ignored and must make us pause and reflect upon the possibility that the piece of furniture may have attributes that are not traceable to the dominant English influence.

OTHER JOINED SEATING FURNITURE

Although they have not survived in such quantity, other types of seating furniture made during the seventeenth and early eighteenth centuries seem to have been more universally owned and used. Seventeenth-century inventories of the gentry, the rural yeomanry, and the urban middling sort in both England and America reveal that the most common pieces of seating furniture prior to the reign of William and Mary were the joint stool, the buffet stool, and the form. Yet despite their presence in almost every household until the end of the seventeenth century, and intermittently after that, they were often of such slight construction and of so little monetary value that they were not deemed worth preserving. Stools of joined con-struction were relatively lightweight and when subjected to hard use proved fragile; even more transient and, alas, more typical from an historical point of view were stools of turned or stick-and-slab construction. Only one rush-bottom turned stool from the early eighteenth century in America survives, and no early "countrey stools" or "crickets," as Randle Holme called them when he illustrated them in 1681, are known.[38]

Holme included a stool in his *Academy of Armory* and described it as "a Joynt stoole . . . so called because [it is] all

Fig. 72. "Joynt Stoole." From Holme, *Academy of Armory*, 2: bk. 3, ch. 14, facing p. 18, fig. 72. (Winterthur Library.)

Fig. 73. Buffet stool. From Holme, *Academy of Armory*, 2: bk. 3, ch. 14, facing p. 18, fig. 71. (Winterthur Library.)

made and finished by the Joyner, hauing a wood couer" (fig. 72). "In most places in Cheshire," he continued, "it is termed a Buffit stool." Cheshire was a predominantly agrarian county during the seventeenth century with little widespread regard for the intricacies of London style, so it is no wonder that joint stools with wooden seats were seen as being the same as buffet stools, which were usually upholstered and covered with sumptuous fabric and fringe, like the "eight highe stooles of tawny velvet with cases" listed in the winter dining chamber at Northampton House when it was inventoried in 1614. Holme himself illustrated one saying it was properly called a "stool (or stool frame) . . . covered and Fringed   studed or garnished of gold colored Nails" (fig. 73).[39]

Although only one buffet stool made in seventeenth-century America survives (and it sadly lacks what may have been its original covering), references in the probate records of the period suggest not only their presence but also their being recognized as different from joint stools. When the Reverend Thomas Shepard of Cambridge died in 1649, he owned "one red plush stoole" that he kept in the hall chamber of his large house. In 1670/71 Thomas Bishop, a local merchant, of Ipswich left "two buffed stooles, [and] two joynd stools"; his neighbor Samuel Jacobs had "fower stooles with Cloth and fringes" when he died the next year. These latter stools could have been fully upholstered or, more likely, they could have been joint stools each of which had a "wooden cover" actually fitted into grooves along the upper inside face of the top rails providing a surface into which a cushion could be set and not move. Such an arrangement may have been the type of "cushion stoole" mentioned in the 1655 inventory of the Reverend Nathaniel Rogers of Ipswich. The extra workman-ship on the stool to afford this kind of textile appointment meant that it must have been more expensive than a regular stool; the "cushin stool" owned by Richard Jacobs of Ipswich at his death in 1672 was valued at 2s. 6d., a sum that was equal to what many chests and turned chairs warranted when appraised.[40]

None of these New England references, of course, suggests the high degree of attention afforded stools in the courtly circles of English taste during the period. Aristocrats intent on

Fig. 74. Francisco de Zurbarán, *The Young Virgin*. Spain, probably 1620s. Oil on canvas; H 46″ (116.8 cm), W 36″ (94 cm). (Metropolitan Museum of Art, New York, Fletcher Fund, 1927.)

furnishing their newly built country houses with suites of matching objects saw stools as integral to their grand designs. Yards of expensive textiles were lavished upon stools and their cushions. The inventory of the countess of Leicester, taken in 1634/35, cites an impressive array of turkey-work cushions, cushions covered with "stamells carsey," "1 longe cusheon of crimson trimd with gould," "fower silk coveringes frindged, for 4 lowe stooles," "a long needleworke cusheon stufte with feathers," and, finally, "six joyned stooles with needle work, seats covered with yealowe cotton frindged."[41] The presence of fringe suggests that these stools were covered to match existing sets of back stools (as will be discussed in the section on Cromwellian furniture). However, in both America and England, the many stools that survive with wooden seats were not in any way designed specifically for upholstery but often were used with a cushion.

Joint stools often are cited in impressive numbers even in colonial households, although none can rival the 175 walnut and oak stools in the houses of Lord Lumley when he died in England in 1590. When enumerated in colonial inventories, they usually occur in groups of 6 or 12 and almost always in conjunction with the table around which they were placed during use. Richard Lumpkyn of Ipswich, for example, had "one table with six ioyned stooles" worth £1.5 in 1642.[42]

Most joint stools that survive from the seventeenth and early eighteenth centuries had an average original seat height of about 22″ (55.9 cm), thus making it possible for the sitter to rest his feet on the stretcher of the table, away from the convection drafts that ran along the floor and up the chimney. Stools intended for work areas like the kitchen or rear lean-to were about 3″ to 4″ (7.6 cm to 10.2 cm) shorter and enabled the user to rest his feet on the ground; these stools must have been called "low joynt stools" during the period. Still other stools that survive in many of America's museums and historic houses are a bit too tall for sitting and, coupled with their thinner legs and rails, and tops that overhang their frame beyond the point of being able to support a human's weight, must have been designed as tables; in 1667 Elizabeth Giggles of Salem owned "a stoole table" worth 3s., and as late as 1751 Lettice Bedgood of Suffolk County owned "1 Joynt Stool Table."[43] In many instances, these small tables probably were used for small work like needlepoint or to hold books in between readings (fig. 74). The confusion between joint stools and joint stool tables has led many historians of the decorative arts to misidentify examples, a problem compounded by instances in which a

Fig. 75. Form or bench. From Holme, *Academy of Armory*, 2: bk. 3, ch. 14, facing p. 18, fig. 77. (Winterthur Library.)

Fig. 76. Settle. From Holme, *Academy of Armory*, 2: bk. 3, ch. 14, facing p. 18, fig. 70. (Winterthur Library.)

table has received sufficient wear on its feet to make its current height comfortable for sitting.

"Joynt formes" were also often used as tables. Holme described them in detail: "Some are made with turned feete, 4 or 6, according to its length, hauing railes or Barres both aboue, for the seate to be fixed vpon, and below, to hold the feete firme and stiddy."[44] In contemporary records "form" is used interchangeably with "bench." Holme used the terms synonymously, and the form he illustrated we now would call a bench (fig. 75). As in Holme's example, benches usually had planked ends and no intermediate stretchers or rails. More typically, a bench was built into the wall, often underneath a window, so that a table pulled over against it could receive adequate natural illumination. For example, in 1659 William Averill, an Ipswich, Massachusetts, carpenter, contracted to build for Richard Jacobs "a table and frame of 12 or 14 foot Long and a joyned form of 4 foot Long and a binch Behind the table." No built-in benches survive in American houses constructed before 1730, although early in this century Wallace Nutting claimed one did in a house of Wrentham, Massachusetts, and published a blurry photograph of it in the second edition of *Pilgrim Century*.[45]

During the seventeenth century, forms were used in both houses and public buildings. By the third quarter of that century, they were not sufficiently individualized to remain acceptable in the public rooms of a New England house. In 1677, for example, a form was used in the kitchen of William Hollingworth's house in Salem, while chairs graced his "best roome." This is fully consistent with the frequent use of forms as seating furniture for women and children in a culture that regarded chairs as icons of patriarchal authority; a seventeenth-century print shows a mother and her children huddled together on a form as they listen to the counsel of the husband/father who sits on a chair. Forms were also used for group seating by the less affluent in many New England meetinghouses and courthouses. On June 15, 1686, the deacons of King's Chapel in Boston agreed "that Mr. [William] Smith the Joyner do make 12 formes, for the service of the church, for each of which he shall be paid 4s. 8d." Here the forms commissioned represented an investment on the part of the parish to provide seating. Previously indi-

viduals had carried stools or crickets to and from service. John Ruddock of Marlborough, Massachusetts, owned "a Crickett Chaire Much Carried 5s." when he died in 1692/93; doubtless it had been used just for such weekly sabbath-day journeys.[46]

Finally, seventeenth-century individuals relied on local joiners and carpenters for the production of settles, large pieces of furniture that were designed specifically to control drafts in small houses and to shield the farm family from the chilly air sweeping up the chimney. For this purpose, settles were enclosed in some manner below the seat and had a high back. They also always had arms. Holme described the settle he illustrated (fig. 76) as "the old way of makeing the chaire." "Some term it a settle chaire, being so weighty that it cannot be moued from place to place, but still abideth in it[s] owne station, hauing a kind of box or cubbert in the seate of it." While the Metcalf family chair illustrated in figure 59 meets the last of Holme's requirements, it is not a settle; it is too narrow to perform the function of a draft stopper. To stop drafts, settles need to be wide enough to serve as a room divider, a kind of temporary wall, and hence are often between 4′ and 7′ (1.1 and 2.1 m) wide. English examples are often much longer (up to 9′ [2.8 m] in England's western counties) and combine the function of a settle bed with that of a storage chest.[47]

Settles were fashioned from both joined and nailed construction. If nailed, they were often embellished by elaborate cutwork on their arm supports (see catalogue entry 44). English settles can be regionalized on the basis of these arm designs, with the plain and the bacon settles of Dorset and Devonshire being perhaps the most recognizable.[48] Until students of American furniture history pay more attention to these ingenious forms, they will continue to be misunderstood and misidentified. Although many English examples survive which, like that illustrated by Holme, have rounded backs, all the American examples I have seen have straight backs, although the particular rake of the back and how it is braced for stability may provide clues for their more precise classification in the future.

SUMMARY

In the second edition of *Pilgrim Century*, Wallace Nutting stated that, as of 1924, "some six or eight American wainscot chairs have come to light." He did not illustrate any examples from New England other than those found in Connecticut, and, perhaps construing the word "wainscot" literally to mean oak chairs, virtually ignored the walnut examples from Pennsylvania and environs. He further stated that he was "unconvinced" that any of the carved examples that he knew could have been of American origin.[49] The number he cited could perhaps be doubled today in the light of subsequent research, and if the middle colonies examples are included, that number would be increased perhaps tenfold. Even at that, this group of chairs represents an extremely rare type of seating furniture, only slightly less rare than the surviving forms and joined stools. This rarity of survival, and indeed the scarcity of documentary references to joiner's chairs, enhances the oft-cited generalization that chairs were uncommon in seventeenth-century America. We now know that chairs were available, although wainscot chairs, at least in New England, were owned by only a few. In Essex County, Massachussetts, among the 2,053 wills, inventories, guardianships, and administrations of estates recorded from 1635 through 1681, only 22 "wainscot," "great," "joined," and "elbow" chairs are listed; however, there are 1,598 listings of other types of chairs, and stools are mentioned 289 times, joined stools 291, forms 175, and benches 11.[50] It therefore follows that what was rare then is rare now.

The twenty-two "wainscot," "great," "joined," and "elbow" chairs in these inventories were owned by only ten people, two of whom owned ten of the chairs: Thomas Woodbridge (d. 1681) of Newbury owned "7 great chaires with armes," and John Paine (d. 1677) of Ipswich and Boston owned "3 elbo chayers." Paine's household goods in Ipswich amounted to only £138, but this gives a faulty picture of his family status or habits of life, since his father, William, who had come from London, had been a merchant adventurer of considerable means and had left an estate worth more than £3,300. Woodbridge was the son and grandson of ministers from Wiltshire. His father was an Oxford graduate and politically active in England during the 1650s and '60s, and his uncle was Thomas Parker, the influential minister of Newbury. Among the other owners was Sarah, widow of

John Dillingham, "a man of respectable condition" from Leicestershire, who had died shortly after he had emigrated. She may have been related to two of the more substantial members of the Massachusetts Bay Colony, Samuel Appleton and Richard Saltonstall. Her inventory amounted to £385. Rebecca Bacon of Salem, who died in 1655, was the daughter of a former mayor of Coventry, and had come to this country with her husband, William, from Dublin. Her estate amounted to £195. Adam Hawkes of Lynn, who possessed a joined chair at the time of his death in 1671/72, had the largest estate in Essex County of any person in the group: it amounted to £817. He may have come to New England as a young man in the party of John Winthrop, but little else is known of him. Thomas Gardner of Salem, who had originally migrated in 1624 or 1625 to establish a fishery, left an estate valued at £274.16 in 1674. With the exception of Henry Fay, all of the owners of these joined chairs were of the gentry, the early merchant aristocracy, or the privileged ministerial class. Fay was a weaver of Newbury, who owned a joined chair worth 3s. 6d. at the time of his death in 1655. His estate totaled only £18.[51] Aside from Fay, the documentary evidence reveals that the average yeoman or husbandman did not own such chairs, and that those wealthier people who did own them generally had emigrated from rural areas far away from the stylish circles of London. Some of the lord-of-the-manor status that was associated with such chairs in provincial England was doubtless transferred to the colonies.

NOTES

[1] Littlehales, *Medieval Records of a London City Church*, pt. 1, pp. 27, 31, 33, 37. "Table" here is meant in the sense of a "tablet" (cf. *OED*, s.v. "table" sb. 2a). See *OED*, s.v. "stake" 2b, and "staked"; Brears, *Yorkshire Probate Inventories*, p. 31.

[2] Havinden, *Household and Farm Inventories in Oxfordshire*, pp. 84–85, 92, 128–29, 152.

[3] Thornton, "A Short Commentary," pp. 23, 25, 30, et passim.

[4] Heal, "A Great Country House in 1623," pp. 113–14. Brears, *Yorkshire Probate Inventories*, p. 92; Cust, "Notes on the Collections Formed by Thomas Howard," pt. 2, p. 98.

[5] *OED*, s.v. "wainscot."

[6] *OED*, s.v. "ceiled," sb. 1 and 2. John Jenny inventory, p. 171.

[7] Philadelphia Wills, 1736-450. I am indebted to Cynthia Baldwin for this reference; it was obtained from the document at City Hall Annex, Philadelphia, Penn., rather than the microfilm edition.

[8] Fairfield Probate, 7:208.

[9] *Essex Probate*, 1:4, 127, 188, 216, 411; see also Savage, *Genealogical Dictionary*, 2:50.

[10] *Essex Probate*, 2:425; Savage, *Genealogical Dictionary*, 2:230.

[11] Suffolk Probate, 2:48, 52–57, 2:107; 4:154.

[12] Bowman, "Governor William Bradford's . . . Inventory," p. 230; Bowman, "Alice (Southworth) Bradford's . . . Inventory," p. 148.

[13] Suffolk Probate, 4:214; see also "Metcalf Family Treasures," pp. 1–2.

[14] Hayden, *Chats on Cottage and Farmhouse Furniture*, p. 191. For a detailed discussion of East Anglia joiners in Massachusetts, see St. George, "Style and Structure," pp. 1–46.

[15] See Jourdain, *English Decoration and Furniture*, p. 242 (this book is the most reliable survey of English furniture of this period). Many of the inhabitants of Limburg belonged to the Roman Catholic Church and often decorated their household furniture with religious symbols, and such chairs remained in use with the rural population of Limburg until the end of the nineteenth century (J. deKleyn, curator of the Nederlands Openluchtmuseum, Arnhem, to Forman, May 4, 1972).

[16] Irving P. Lyon, "Oak Furniture of Ipswich," pp. 230–33; *Essex Probate*, 2:96; I am indebted to W. F. Bennett, clerk of the Ottery St. Mary Urban District Council, for information from his research in the church records about Searle.

[17] *Essex Probate*, 2:96; Fales, *Essex County Furniture*, fig. 7; Lyon, "Oak Furniture of Ipswich," p. 233.

[18] I am indebted to Abbott Lowell Cummings for calling this chest to my attention; it was first discovered by Katharine Simonds Thompson and published by Helen Park, ("Thomas Dennis, Ipswich Joiner," p. 42), and since then we have learned that Searle was born in 1611 not 1634. This chest was described in St. George, "Staniford Family Chest," 16B-18B.

[19] W. F. Bennett to Benno M. Forman, October 14, 1970.

[20] Kane, *Furniture of the New Haven Colony*, pp. 21, 63, 67.

[21] Suffolk Probate, 8:179.

[22] For a full discussion of the chair and the history of ownership see Lyle and Zimmerman, "Furniture of the Monmouth County Historical Association," p. 187; and Monmouth County Historical Association, *New Jersey Arts and Crafts*, p. 6.

[23] I am deeply indebted to Robert Logan of Aberdeen, Scotland, for his generous permission to use this photograph and for his help in locating it (Logan to Forman, November 22, 1975). All of the Trinity Hall chairs are illustrated and interpreted in Learmont, "The Trinity Hall Chairs, Aberdeen," pp. 1–8.

[24] Monmouth County Historical Association, *New Jersey Arts and Crafts*, p. 6.

[25] Schiffer, *Furniture . . . of Chester County*, p. 266.

[26] Virkus, ed., *The Compendium of American Genealogy*, 6:783; [Keyes], "Some Pennsylvania Furniture," pp. 222–25, fig. 2c. The present location of Mercur's chair is unknown. Twiston-Davies and Lloyd-Johnes, *Welsh Furniture*, fig. 120; and Edwards, *Shorter Dictionary*, p. 205, fig. 25.

[27] See [Keyes], "Some Pennsylvania Furniture," p. 225, fig. 4c.

[28] Cope, *Historic Homes*, 2:82.

[29] Hornor, *Blue Book*, p. 3, suggested that Clone's name may have been confused with that of Richard Gove, also working in Philadelphia at the time. However, the research of Cathryn McElroy effectively removes any ground for error; she demonstrates conclusively that Gove came from Plymouth, England, two years later than Clone (McElroy, "Furniture of the Philadelphia Area," pp. 184–85). Inquiries made in the vicinity of Nantwich have so far failed to turn up wainscot chairs of any type from the seventeenth century.

[30] McElroy, "Furniture of the Philadelphia Area," p. 34; Matzkin, "Inventories of Estates in Philadelphia County," p. 24.

[31] Hornor, *Blue Book*, p. 4; McElroy, "Furniture of the Philadelphia Area," p. 195; Schiffer, *Furniture . . . of Chester County*, p. 153.

[32] Schiffer, *Chester County . . . Inventories*, p. 104. On p. 105 Schiffer cites a "framed Chair" in Concord, 1717; "2 Joynted Chares" in Chester, 1717; "eighteen framed wooden Chairs" in Kennett, 1743; and "three old Square Joynt Chairs" in Londonderry as late as 1816.

[33] "Letters of William Penn," p. 426; Schiffer, *Chester County . . . Inventories*, pp. 107, 301; Philadelphia Wills, 1708-102.

[34] Schiffer, *Furniture . . . of Chester County*, fig. 21 and pp. 63–64. Amos Darlington account book, Chester County Historical Society, West Chester, Pa. The saddler's trade involves a thorough knowledge of joinery.

[35] Hayden, *Chats on Cottage and Farmhouse Furniture*, p. 201.

[36] Burr, *Records of Holy Trinity (Old Swedes) Church*, p. 4; *Historical Statistics of the United States*, 2:1168 (I am indebted to Ellen M. Rosenthal for the latter reference).

[37] Philadelphia Wills, 1708-112; *Records of the Court of New Castle*, 2:19, 37, 83, 102, 170, 202, et passim; Burr, *Records of Holy Trinity (Old Swedes) Church*, pp. 44, 50–51, et passim.

[38] See Wadsworth Atheneum, *Connecticut Furniture*, p. 78, fig. 132; the stool has a history in the Sikes family of Suffield. See Holme, *Academy of Armory*, 2:bk. 3, ch. 14, facing p. 18.

[39] Holme, *Academy of Armory*, 2:bk. 3, ch. 14, pp. 14–15; Edwards, *Shorter Dictionary*, pp. 500, 502.

[40] The stool which was originally upholstered is illustrated and discussed in Kane, *Furniture of the New Haven Colony*, no. 26. Docket 20289, Middlesex Probate; I am indebted to Robert F. Trent for this reference. *Essex Probate*, 2:213, 281; 1:224; 2:294.

[41] As quoted in Halliwell, *Ancient Inventories*, pp. 12, 34, 10, 43, 79, 10, and 80. I am indebted to Linda R. Baumgarten for these references.

[42] Edwards, *Shorter Dictionary*, p. 502; *Essex Probate*, 1:43.

[43] See the "lowe joyned stooles" cited in a 1661 inventory from Taunton, Mass., in Plymouth Inventories, 2:73. *Essex Probate*, 2:94; Suffolk Probate, 45:362; I am indebted to Linda R. Baumgarten for the latter reference.

[44] Holme, *Academy of Armory*, 2:bk. 3, ch. 14, p. 15; see also the inventory of Kenelm Winslow of Plymouth, Mass., taken in 1672: "1 long table and a forme" (Plymouth Inventories, 3:pt. 1, bk. 1, p. 57).

[45] As quoted in Cummings, *Architecture in Colonial Massachusetts*, pp. 213–14. Nutting, *Pilgrim Century* (2d ed.), nos. 601–2.

[46] *Essex Probate*, 3:192; Axtell, *School Upon a Hill*: cover illustration; deacons as quoted in Greenwood, *History of King's Chapel in Boston*, p. 24; Middlesex Probate, 8:141; I am indebted to Robert F. Trent for this last reference.

[47] Holme, *Academy of Armory*, 3:bk. 3, ch. 14, p. 14; see Olive, "West Country Settles," pp. 20–22.

[48] Olive, "West Country Settles," pls. 30–39.

[49] Nutting, *Pilgrim Century* (2d ed.), p. 281.

[50] *Essex Probate*, vols. 1–3 were part of this survey. While it is true that the inventories represent only those people for whom inventories were filed, they nonetheless represent a unit that has a beginning and an end and can be subjected to statistical analysis. The analysis does discriminate between the same chairs which might appear in a husband's inventory and later in that of his widow, or those mentioned in wills and listed in an inventory, too, although these instances are exceedingly rare.

[51] *Essex Probate*, 3:424, 177; 1:5, 23, 216–17; 2:254, 425; Savage, *Genealogical Dictionary*, 3:333, 337–8; 4:631–33; 2:50, 380; 1:92.

18.
JOINED GREAT CHAIR
Essex County, Massachusetts
1640–1685
WOODS: Left rear stile and front stretcher, red oak (*Quercus rubra*); crest rail, an oak of the white group
OH 36½" (92.7 cm)
SH 16⅝" (42.2 cm), SW 22¼" (56.6 cm), SD 21" (53.3 cm)
PROVENANCE: Mrs. William B. Church; Ginsburg and Levy; purchased by the museum
54.73

Although this chair, with the initials N.N. incised on its crest rail, surfaced in New York sometime prior to 1938, it is one of six surviving chairs by the same joiner, and three of the six were collected in Essex County, Massachusetts, in the nineteenth century. The chair with the strongest tradition of Essex County ownership was given to the Danvers Historical Society by descendants of William Nichols of Topsfield (emig. by 1638, d. 1696). Although his farm was within the bounds of Topsfield Township in 1696, the land was within the bounds of Salem when Nichols purchased it in 1652.[1] A second chair, formerly owned by Henry F. Waters of Salem and now in the collection of the Museum of Fine Arts, Boston, was "picked up in Essex County," according to Dr. Irving W. Lyon's notes of 1883.[2] A third chair, now in a private collection in Massachusetts, was acquired from dealer James T. Moulton of Lynn, Massachusetts, on August 21, 1875, for the sum of $26.50.[3] The fourth chair, an heirloom of the Batchelder family of Hampton, New Hampshire, is in the collections of the New Hampshire Historical Society, Concord.[4] A fifth chair, with no reliable history of ownership, is in Pilgrim Hall, Plymouth, Massachusetts. All six chairs have identical crest rails and identical scrolls on the stiles above the arms, and all share the distinctive leaf pattern within interlaced semicircles, although it is found on different members of each chair. The Pilgrim Society chair and the Winterthur example are identical.

In "Dennis or a Lesser Light?" written at the very moment when Thomas Dennis was the most popular figure in American decorative arts history, Homer Eaton Keyes concluded, after an acute analysis of the style and iconography and an even more perceptive study of the construction of the Winterthur chair and some of the related examples, that they were indeed made by a "lesser light."[5] Today's judgment would be somewhat more moderate: we would merely say a "different light," since we now know that at least forty joiners lived and worked in Essex County during the seventeenth century. Keyes did note the telling point that, more than anything else, disqualifies Thomas Dennis as the possible maker: the front legs and arm supports of the chairs are square in section and were worked with saw, drawknife, and plane or carver's gouge; they were not turned in the manner of those on the Dennis family chair owned by the Essex Institute. Whether the joiner who made the six chairs did not do turning or, more likely, preferred not to ornament the front posts with turning, cannot now be known.

The flat crest rail that overhangs the sides of the stiles, the absence of brackets beneath the crest rail, and the interlocking semicircles with abstract leaf-carving suggest the form and decorative vocabulary style of East Anglia furniture, although no exact prototype of the carving has been identified. Similar carving is on an unidentified chest whose present whereabouts are unknown, a photograph of which is item B-2594 in the archives of the Furniture and Woodwork Department of the Victoria and Albert Museum, London. This chest has a motif of S scrolls in the medieval manner attached by a classical ligature that suggestively resembles the scrolls on the Winterthur chair. Many motifs found on furniture believed to have been made by craftsmen who migrated from East Anglia to Connecticut and perpetuated the decorative traits of that area in Connecticut are also visible. Notable among them are the scrolls themselves, which also appear on a small box from Guilford, Connecticut (fig. 77). The presence of similar motifs in seventeenth-century furniture from two widely separated places in New England does not necessarily mean that the craftsmen were in contact with each other or that a craftsman emigrated from Massachusetts to Connecticut; the similarities can be equally well explained by migration patterns. Craftsmen from neighboring areas or even the same one in England settled in different places in America. For in every case, while the motifs are similar, the details of execution are different.

Fig. 77. Box or desk, probably made in Guilford, Conn., 1670–1700. Oak and pine; H 9" (22.9 cm), W 29⅜" (74.6 cm), D 19" (48.3 cm). (Museum of Fine Arts, Boston, bequest of Charles Hitchcock Tyler.)

The various identified Essex County wainscot chairs are either completely undecorated or are decorated with carving. None has a back ornamented with applied geometrical moldings or half spindles.[6] This suggests that Winterthur's chair and its relatives were all made either fairly early in the history of seventeenth-century American joinery, or by first generation craftsmen, trained in the earliest style that appears in this country. The arcades carved into the crest rail of Winterthur's chair suggest similar arcades applied to the front of a chest of drawers owned by SPNEA and presently displayed in the Cooper-Frost-Austin House, Cambridge, Massachusetts. The applied turnings on that chest of drawers, which appear to date from early in the fourth quarter of the seventeenth century, are a distinctive type associated with Salem, Massachusetts.[7] In the absence of better evidence, it is likely that this chair and its mates originated among the joiner-carvers of Salem, whose early work, prior to the applied-molding style, has not been otherwise identified.

NOTES

[1] Keyes, "Dennis or a Lesser Light?" pp. 296–300; Savage, *Genealogical Dictionary*, 3:283. No inventory for Nichols was recorded.

[2] Irving W. Lyon as quoted by Keyes in "Dennis or a Lesser Light?" p. 296, fig. 1.

[3] Illustrated in *The Georgian Period, Part II*, pl. 2; letter from current owner to Forman.

[4] See New Hampshire Historical Society, *Decorative Arts of New Hampshire*, fig. 18.

[5] Keyes, "Dennis or a Lesser Light?" pp. 296, 300.

[6] An outstanding exception is the privately owned chair of Plymouth Colony origin related to no. 1787 in Nutting, *Furniture Treasury*.

[7] Virtually identical turnings appear on a cabinet from Salem, Mass. (Winterthur 58.526).

19.
JOINED GREAT CHAIR
Northern colonies, New York through New England
1640–1700
WOODS: Framing members, white oak (*Quercus alba*); seat, American white pine (*Pinus strobus*)
OH 38¼" (97.2 cm)
SH 17½" (44.5 cm), SW 23¾" (60.3 cm), SD 15½" (39.4 cm)
PROVENANCE: Gift of Henry Francis du Pont
58.692

Although the back stiles have been broken and shortened at some time in this chair's history, and the crest rail, which has no groove on its inner perimeter to hold the back panel, may have been replaced, and the oak back panel itself replaces a pine panel that was present when the chair was acquired for the Winterthur collection, the remaining parts of this rare example are of unusual interest.

First, the seat of white pine (*Pinus strobus*) is original, thereby establishing the chair's American origin.[1] It further suggests that the chair did not originate south of New York. The seat has a serrated perimeter that was cut with a square-nose chisel rather than the usual crescent-shape gouge. Second, the turned feet are in extraordinarily good condition and their state of preservation is unusual among American wainscot chairs. Last, each arm is doubly indented on its under surface, a feature that is only occasionally found in English furniture of the sixteenth and seventeenth centuries but is quite common in northern European work.

Although the proportions of the chair are spoiled by its lowered crest rail, the quality of the original joinery is above the average. Not only are all of the seat-frame members and the stretchers carefully molded on their outer surfaces, but the backs of the rear stiles are similarly treated. The turning is not of an equally high level of workmanship; the pieces have occasional sharp ridges instead of more generally rounded shapes. Moreover, the arrangement of baluster forms is inverted by English and New England standards but similar to that found on continental balusters of the early eighteenth century. In this chair, the classical origins of the concept were likely forgotten. The spool was likely the first element turned by the craftsman who was probably using a pole lathe. The spool would offer a satisfactory place around which to wrap the thong or rope that extended from treadle to pole and provided the power to turn the wood in the lathe. All this suggests that the joiner who made this chair had a provincial training and did his own turning.

The rear panel of the present chair was replaced in June 1941 by Morris Schwartz. The crest rail bearing the carved date 1668 appears to be an old replacement, and at that time the rear stiles were shortened to accommodate it.

NOTE

[1] Removal of the seat in May 1970 revealed that no other seat had ever been on the chair.

20.
JOINED GREAT CHAIR
New York City or Dutch Long Island
1640–1700
WOODS: Red oak (*Quercus rubra*), except front seat board of white oak
OH 43″ (109.2 cm)
SH 18⅜″ (46.7 cm), SW 21⅝″ (54.9 cm), SD 17⅜″ (44.1 cm)
PROVENANCE: Found in Southampton, L.I., N.Y., in 1875 by Edwin J. Hoyt, Brentwood, L.I., N.Y.; Henry Francis du Pont
53.104

This chair is an outstanding example of furniture made in colonial America, not only because of the artistry of its execution, but also because it represents the earliest type of joinery practiced by the Dutch furniture craftsmen of New York prior to the introduction of English styles and craftsmen in 1664, although the chair itself may well have been made after that date.

The problem of attributing furniture on the basis of stylistic interpretation is underlined by this example: virtually every motif present here can be found on English wainscot chairs of the sixteenth and seventeenth centuries, especially in London work or work from other areas that had some contact with the Lowlands. And yet, the whole appearance of the chair would prompt a British furniture historian to say: "not English." Details of decoration, such as the bold double undercut (bowed downward in the center) under each arm is more vigorously rendered than on most English and New England examples. The leaf-decorated scrolls on the crest rail are closer to Italian prototypes and are much more academic in character than those on the average English or New England wainscot-chair crest rail. The scrolled brackets, which create an aesthetic transition from the rear stiles to the crest rail, retain much of the architectural character that such supports would have, were they functional rather than ornamental.

Although the same techniques were used in making joined furniture throughout northern Europe, one discernible difference distinguishes many chairs made in the English tradition from those made in the Lowlands. On New England wainscot chairs, the seat is invariably formed by placing a board horizontally upon the seat rails, and molding the protruding edges with a fillet and quarter round, sometimes called a "thumbnail molding." On numerous Dutch chairs of this type the seat boards are flush with the outside edge of the rails, and a separate piece of molding has been nailed onto them, a practice that can be observed on Winterthur's chair. Similarly, the particular articulation of the columns with rounded bottoms on the front stiles are totally different from the more self-consciously academic columns that dominate the English tradition in America.[1]

It is not clear from the few surviving seventeenth-century inventories of New York if the wainscot chair was common among the Dutch settlers. A rare reference to what may possibly be this type of chair occurs in a 1682 inventory: Joseph Taylor, definitely a settler of English extraction, possessed "A worked Great Chayre 12s."[2]

NOTES
[1] Kane, *Furniture of the New Haven Colony*, nos. 25, 27, 28.
[2] New York Probate, Liber 2.290. While "worked" can mean "carved," it is equally possible that it refers to needlework.

21.

JOINED GREAT CHAIR or WALNUT CHAIR
Southeastern Pennsylvania
1683–1710
WOOD: Black walnut (*Juglans nigra*)
OH 47¾″ (121.3 cm)
SH 18¼″ (46.4 cm), SW 22⅝″ (57.5 cm), SD 16¾″ (42.5 cm)
PROVENANCE: Bequest of Henry Francis du Pont
61.1143

The absence of a fielded panel in the back and the presence of bold indentation on the underside of the arms of this chair may be attributes that indicate an early date of manufacture. The top of the crest rail, too, seems to capture the vitality of outline of seventeenth-century chairs made in the western counties of England, suggesting that the tradition was fresh at the time this example was made in America. The rounded tops of the stiles here do not automatically represent a decline in vigor or, alternatively, carelessness on the part of the maker of this chair, although those features on other examples are more elaborate. The rounded finials of this chair conform to one of the several local variations of the English models, such as the chair in figure 78 from the church of Saints Peter and Paul, Ormskirk, Lancashire. The symmetrical ball turning, rather than the more common baluster shape for the arm support, is also visible on the legs of the English example. The overall lightness of the turning and the double side stretchers of the Winterthur chair suggest that its maker was influenced by the style of Cromwellian leather chairs which are marked by the first use of double side stretchers in English furniture.

The seat is a replacement.

Fig. 78. Joined chair, Ormskirk, Lancashire, England, 1660–1700. (Church of Saints Peter and Paul, Ormskirk, Lancashire, England. Photo: Benno M. Forman.)

cat. 21

22.
JOINED GREAT CHAIR or WALNUT CHAIR
Southeastern Pennsylvania
1683–1720
WOOD: Black walnut (*Juglans nigra*)
OH 48″ (121.9 cm)
SH 18⅝″ (47.3 cm), SW 21¼″ (54.6 cm), SD 17½″ (44.5 cm)
PROVENANCE: Bequest of Henry Francis du Pont
61.1154

Fig. 79. Joined chair. Lancashire, England, 1660–1700. (Church of Saints Peter and Paul, Ormskirk, Lancashire, England. Photo: Benno M. Forman.)

Although we know the date at which several of the wainscot chairs were purchased for Winterthur, we do not know their family histories or a specific place of origin. The shape of their arms and the use of quarter round moldings run on their framing members relates the present chair and the next example to the 1758 settle attributed to Abraham Darlington.[1] The careful articulation of the turnings on Winterthur's chair, the robust crest rail, the deeply undercut arms, and the extra quarter round on the upper surface of arms near the stiles suggest a first generation craftsman—perhaps Darlington's master—who lived somewhat closer in time to the date at which this style was introduced into Pennsylvania. The rounded finials are similar to those on a chair in the church of Saints Peter and Paul, Ormskirk, Lancashire (fig. 79), although it is doubtful that the English chair has always been in the church. Indeed many such chairs were considered "appropriate" to a church in the nineteenth century, and were acquired, usually locally, for the parish church.[2]

The treatment of the crest rail is somewhat simpler than that of the oak example in figure 69, which very likely preceded this one of walnut in date of manufacture. The crest rail, with its angularly cut upper perimeter and its smooth transition to the stiles suggests that the West Country manner was modified over time in Pennsylvania.

The seat boards and their retaining strips are replacements.

NOTES
[1] Schiffer, *Furniture . . . of Chester County*, fig. 21. The settle is in the collection of Chester County Historical Society, West Chester, Penn.
[2] See, for example, Roe, *Ancient Church Chests and Chairs*, p. 55; and Temple Newsam House, *Oak Furniture from Yorkshire Churches*, p. 5.

cat. 22

cat. 23

23.
JOINED GREAT CHAIR or WALNUT CHAIR
Southeastern Pennsylvania
1695–1730
WOOD: Black walnut (*Juglans nigra*)
OH 45⅛″ (114.6 cm)
SH 17⅛″ (43.5 cm), SW 22½″ (57.1 cm), SD 17⅝″ (44.8 cm)
PROVENANCE: Bequest of Henry Francis du Pont
67.1170

The subtle differences between this chair and the two preceding examples cannot be assumed to indicate differences which might be expected to occur in chairs made by the same craftsman over a period of time, but rather represent the hands of two different makers. The major differences between this chair and the earlier two are the substitution of a fillet and hollow quarter round for the deep cut on the underside of the arm and the addition of opposed baluster forms at the center of the front stretcher. The balusters of the arm supports are somewhat more attenuated than those on the previous examples, and may be assumed—in the absence of documentation—to reflect a slightly later style. In addition, the upper end of these balusters is less elaborately articulated than the corresponding elements on the previous chair.

The seat is an incorrect replacement. The original seat boards fit into a groove in the seat frame near its upper margin much like the English example illustrated in figure 68. Replaced seats are common in most Pennsylvania wainscot chairs since the original seat boards had relatively delicate featheredges which broke easily.

cat. 24

24.
JOINED CHAIR or WALNUT CHAIR
Southeastern Pennsylvania
1700–1730
WOOD: Black walnut (*Juglans nigra*)
OH 43″ (109.2 cm)
SH 17⅝″ (44.8 cm), SW 17⅞″ (45.4 cm), SD 14¾″ (37.4 cm)
PROVENANCE: J. Stodgell Stokes; Henry Francis du Pont
61.1150

When this side chair was acquired at the sale of the J. Stodgell Stokes estate in 1948 no provenance accompanied it. Probably du Pont bought it to make a pair with another chair now known to be of a later date, which was in his collection as early as 1935.[1] Stokes also possessed an armchair which matches the present chair and, according to the catalogue, was "apparently made to accompany it." This assertion presents a distinct possibility and tends to confirm inventory references which list "walnut chairs" as a group, probably referring to side chairs, as opposed to "walnut armchairs," usually listed singly and invariably valued at a higher rate, because the workmanship and materials for those chairs are proportionally greater.

The seat on this chair is not original. Applied moldings were once glued to the inside perimeter of the real panel which suggests a slightly later date of manufacture for it than the previous examples.

NOTE
[1] *Stokes Sale*, p. 23; see du Pont, Accession book, 1:509 June 5, 1935, Registrar's Office, Winterthur, noting a "wainscot side chair" purchased from Frank P. Ewing of Concord, Penn.; Forman, interview with Mr. Ewing, June 29, 1975. The chair (Winterthur 61.1155) is not included because it is of a later date.

25.
JOINED CHAIR or WALNUT CHAIR
Southeastern Pennsylvania
1705–1735
WOODS: Black walnut (*Juglans nigra*); stringing, a maple
OH 43″ (109.2 cm)
SH 17¾″ (45.1 cm), SW 18⅛″ (46.0 cm), SD 16¼″ (41.2 cm)
PROVENANCE: Bequest of Henry Francis du Pont
64.1780

Fig. 80. Detail of stringing on the bottom section of an oak cupboard, England, 1675–1725. (Private collection. Photo: Benno M. Forman.)

Although this chair has the same symmetrical turnings as the armchair illustrated as catalogue entry 24, the possibility of a later date of manufacture is suggested by the inlaid maple stringing on the back panel. The stringing technique cannot be documented by a surviving piece of Chester County furniture made any earlier than 1706, when a chest of drawers with the initials I B, was made. This chest of drawers is important because it was listed in the 1799 inventory of John Worrall of Nether Providence as a "Little Old Bureau Markt I B 1706," and Nether Providence is a township in which one of the immigrant joiners from Cheshire, John Maddock, is known to have owned land in the 1680s and '90s.[1] An identical walnut chair is owned by the Chester County Historical Society.[2]

Stringing, as an inlay or as an accent to veneer, is found on good but not extraordinary English furniture in the late Stuart style and persists well into the eighteenth century in the British provinces. An example of such stringing on an English oak cupboard bottom of unknown provenance is illustrated in figure 80. That pattern was laid out with a compass, and the center points of the arcs are visible in the photograph. Such stringing and the identical method of laying it out are often found on Pennsylvania furniture, dated examples of which span the years 1706 to 1788 (see also catalogue entry 29). The presence of the tulip motif on the oak cupboard indicates that such decoration is as likely to be found on British furniture as on that of northern Europe. A chest with a drawer on a frame with related stringing and a tulip-bud inlay is in the collection of the National Museum of Wales. It is dated 1734.[3] The question of whether such stringing, when found on a piece of Pennsylvania furniture, betokens a Welsh origin for its maker cannot be answered on the basis of present evidence. If this technique were introduced into Pennsylvania by Welsh craftsmen, it probably was adopted by other craftsmen in a very short time.

The pins used on the Winterthur chair are of the squarish, British type. An evolutionary touch can be noted in the unusual but unquestionably original angular brace that joins the rear legs to the seat frame and functions structurally as a second side stretcher, a common feature in American chairs of this style but somewhat rarer on the English examples of the same date.

The seat of this chair and its rear feet are modern restorations.

NOTES
[1] Schiffer, *Furniture . . . of Chester County*, figs. 118, 119; Schiffer also lists (p. 103) a John "Haddock" joiner, who sold a tract of land and a house in Nether Providence Township to William Simpson in 1692. Six years later Simpson bought land from joiner John Maddock. Since no other mention of John Haddock is found in the Chester County records, it is possible that the name "Haddock" was recorded instead of Maddock.
[2] Schiffer, *Furniture . . . of Chester County*, fig. 124.
[3] This chest with drawer on frame is illustrated in Edwards, *Shorter Dictionary*, p. 205, fig. 25. There is some question as to whether the frame is contemporary with the chest.

26.
JOINED CHAIR or WALNUT CHAIR
Southeastern Pennsylvania
1710–1735
WOOD: Black walnut (*Juglans nigra*)
OH 42¼″ (107.3 cm)
SH 18¼″ (46.4 cm), SW 18⅜″ (46.7 cm), SD 13¾″ (34.9 cm)
PROVENANCE: J. Stodgell Stokes; purchased by Henry Francis du Pont
61.1151

This chair was also purchased at the Stokes sale, and also had no history of ownership.[1] The undulating crest rail sets it apart from the rest of the Pennsylvania chairs in this section and suggests that it may be a rather late example. The opposed baluster, or "double pear" shape, of the front stretcher also suggests a late date. A decorative molding is planed on the interior horizontal edge of each back rail. The overall appearance of the chair is suggestive of a similar chair in Saint Peter's Church, Delamere, Cheshire, England (fig. 81).

The seat boards are modern.

NOTE
[1] *Stokes Sale*, p. 48.

Fig. 81. Joined chair, Delamere, Cheshire, England, 1660–1700. (Saint Peter's Church, Delamere, Cheshire, England. Photo: Benno M. Forman.)

cat. 26

JOINED GREAT CHAIR or WALNUT CHAIR
Southeastern Pennsylvania
1700–1730
WOOD: Black walnut (*Juglans nigra*)
OH 45¾" (116.2 cm)
SH 16⅜" (41.6 cm), SW 20⅞" (53.0 cm), SD 17" (43.2 cm)
PROVENANCE: Bequest of Henry Francis du Pont
65.2249

Fig. 82. Joined great chair, southeastern Pennsylvania, 1710–40. Oak. (Chester County Historical Society, West Chester, Penn.) The chair is believed to have been made for Aaron James, Westtown, Chester County, Penn.

Although the crest rail of this chair is stylistically related to that of the previous example, the overall configuration is generally similar to an oak chair believed to have been owned by Aaron James of Westtown, Chester County, Pennsylvania (fig. 82). With these two chairs yet another strain of old world craftsmanship in Pennsylvania furniture emerges.

The type of arm on the two chairs is essentially a simplified version of a joined arm that is found on English provincial chairs of north and west country origin. The profile of the arm, however, is identical to that on a Welsh chair. In both cases the arms are cut from a narrow board. The back, composed of vertical slats or "staves," and the undulating crest rail are similar in appearance to the corresponding parts of an eighteenth-century couch, or daybed, from Penyth, Glamorganshire, owned by the National Museum of Wales.[1]

The back and seat of Winterthur's chair represent a departure from the usual treatment. Although the present seat lists are not original to the chair, round auger holes in the legs and stiles show that the original seat supports consisted of rounded, shaved, and turned lists that accommodated either the splint or checked type as it now has or a rush bottom rather than the typical framed seat and the usual board bottom.

The possibilities of Welsh influences in the James chair, the Hoopes chair (see fig. 67), and the present example have not been explored by American scholars, but the appearance of these pieces suggests such influences. Welsh craftsmen lived in southeastern Pennsylvania, although none of them as yet can be associated with the chairs in the Winterthur collection. Among them was Humphrey Bate, Bristol Township, Philadelphia County, who died in 1727. His inventory indicates that coopering was his primary trade, since he possessed "a coopers Joynter." Bate, however, also possessed "11 Plains, 8 augers, one rabet . . . 2 lathes & 2 crooked tools for a Turnnor" in addition to "a Welsh bible" and "the whole duty of man in Welsh."[2] (Inasmuch as furniture tends to be collected more frequently than barrels, the trade of the cooper has been given little attention by furniture historians. However, the skill necessary to taper a barrel stave and miter it so that it fits perfectly against the adjacent stave requires easily as much training and judgment as the tasks of a furniture maker.) Winterthur's chair is sufficiently different from the usual professional chair of middle-colonies origin to suggest that it may not have been made by a man who produced many chairs.

The James family chair was, on the other hand, produced by a professional joiner. A Welsh joiner named Llewellin Phillips was working in Chester County in 1699 and in Philadelphia in 1704. Another joiner, William Lewis, owned property in Aston Township and may have been the son of the

William Lewis, trade unknown, who arrived in Philadelphia from the parish of Illan, Glamorganshire, Wales, with a wife, a daughter, and four sons in 1686. Griffith Lewis, perhaps the son of William Lewis, Jr., died in 1737. Lewis called himself a carpenter in his will but left both carpenter's and "joyners" tools to his sons, William and Samuel. Five years earlier Lewis had received "Joyners and Turners Tools & Instruments" worth £4.7 as a bequest from his brother-in-law, James Booarman, who lived in Philadelphia County. Booarman's will states that Lewis lived in "the Great Valley in the County of Chester & province [of Pennsylvania]." Members of the Lewis family continued to practice the trade of furniture making into the nineteenth century; Abel Lewis, a joiner, possessed both cabinetmaker's and turner's tools in Tredyffrin, Chester County, at the time of his death in 1835.[3]

Of course, it is impossible to associate the James chair or the Winterthur chair with any member of the Lewis family, but the biographical facts show that at least one family of craftsmen from Wales lived and worked in southeastern Pennsylvania over a long period of time. That these craftsmen in all likelihood passed on their techniques and designs from one generation to the next also illustrates the difficulty of accurately

cat. 27

dating a solitary piece of furniture that could have been made at any time by any of them.

All four feet of the Winterthur chair have been pieced out approximately 2⅜″ (6 cm), and the seat and seat lists are modern.

NOTES
[1] Twistor-Davies and Lloyd-Johnes, *Welsh Furniture*, pls. 28, 7. Temple Newsam House, see *Oak Furniture from Yorkshire Churches*, et passim.
[2] Philadelphia Wills, 1727-65. I am indebted to Ellen M. Rosenthal for calling this reference to my attention.
[3] Schiffer, *Furniture . . . of Chester County*, pp. 196, 144, 143; Cope, *Historic Homes*, 1:487; McElroy, "Furniture of the Philadelphia Area," p. 166.

28.
JOINED GREAT CHAIR or WALNUT CHAIR
Southeastern Pennsylvania
1700–1735
WOOD: Black walnut (*Juglans nigra*)
OH 43½″ (110.5 cm)
SH 16⅝″ (42.2 cm), SW 23″ (58.4 cm), SD 16½″ (41.9 cm)
PROVENANCE: Bequest of Henry Francis du Pont
61.1153

Similar to the previous chair in organization, this chair, with its unusually graceful and well-proportioned turnings, retains its original single, featheredged seat board. A great deal of wear on the inside upper margin of the front seat rail shows that this chair was used over a considerable period of time without a cushion. The balusters of the arm supports are a departure from the usual forms found on most Pennsylvania walnut chairs and suggest either that they were derived from the type that appear on Philadelphia-made, turned armchairs (see catalogue entry 29) or that the Philadelphia type was derived from examples like this one. If the former is the case, this chair might have been made in the 1730s.

The balusters of the arm support and the design of the front stretcher hint that the craftsman who ornamented these elements may have been familiar with the "plain" version of the carved-top leather chairs popular in Boston during the first twenty years of the eighteenth century. The absence of a scored line around the middle of the baluster on the arm support further heightens this impression. The double pinning of the crest rail and front stretcher is unusual, but the pins are of the square-head type rather than the lemon-shape variety, which suggests that this chair is in the Anglo-American rather than the northern European tradition.

cat. 28

29.
CLOSE STOOL *or* **CLOSE CHAIR**
Southeastern Pennsylvania
1756
WOODS: Frame and panels, black walnut (*Juglans nigra*); rear seat rail, a conifer; inlaid stringing, a maple; inlaid berries, initials, and date, probably chestnut (not microanalyzed)
OH 44¼″ (112.4 cm)
SH 16″ (40.6 cm), SW 22¼″ (56.5 cm), SD 16¼″ (41.2 cm)
PROVENANCE: Bequest of Henry Francis du Pont
67.1172

Fig. 83. Detail of inlay design in the crest rail of the chair in catalogue entry 29. (Winterthur 67.1172.)

The variety of descriptions in many sources often leads to confusion when we try to put an exact name to furniture that is no longer in common use. The present chair is in that category. Careful examination of the structure beneath the present board seat reveals that it was originally used as "chair of ease" or a "necessary" and once contained a chamber pot. The usual designation for such chairs in seventeenth-century American inventories is "close stool," but given an inventory taker of delicate sensibilities, such a chair could very well have been described merely as an armchair. Chairs of this type were usually confined to the more private rooms of a home. For example, in 1731 David Lloyd of Chester had one armchair in his dining room and one in his "lodging room."[1] The second armchair could easily have been a close chair. Since close stools are often inventoried in bedrooms, or "chambers" as such rooms were called, "chamber pots" or "chamber stools" often are used to describe these as well.

"Close stool" is an old phrase. It was found by the editors of the *OED* as early as the year 1410. It is not certain that all joined chairs with an enclosed section, such as the Metcalf chair (see fig. 59), were used for this purpose when they were originally made, but there can be no question that Winterthur's chair was. While at least one inventory taker in London used the term "close chare," the usual term in the colonies was "Close stool"; however, the high valuation placed on them generally suggests that they were chairs rather than what we think of today as "stools."[2]

An example valued at 6*s*. was listed in the hall chamber of William Clarke of Salem, Massachusetts, on June 25, 1647. Caspar Wistar of Pennsbury Township, Chester County, Pennsylvania, possessed a "Mahogany Close Stool Chair" at the time of his death in 1811.[3] Chairs made specifically to hold chamber pots are fairly common in collections of American furniture, but there are also many examples that were converted from regular armchairs as tastes and fashions changed.

It is virtually impossible to say to whom an object with only two initials belonged when no history of family ownership is known for that object. The date of manufacture inlaid in the crest rail of this chair makes it one of the most important documents of its type in the Winterthur collection. The implication that a joiner's chair was made in Pennsylvania and still found acceptance by a customer in 1756 has important cultural ramifications. While we are accustomed to examples of furniture made to an archaic taste among the subcultural groups of northern European extraction in Pennsylvania and New York, it is rare to be able to cite an irrefutable example made by a craftsman working in a style that had long been superseded by others in style-conscious Philadelphia. If such

chairs were made in America in the mid 1750s, there is no reason to assume that they could not have been made even later, confirming to some extent the practice suggested by the existence of an English wainscot chair dated 1777.[4]

If such chairs continued to be made in rural areas long after they had become unfashionable in more urban centers, something about them ought to reveal that they were made later than those examples created when the style was relatively new and fresh. In the case of this chair, such later features are the rounded crest rail and the ball atop the baluster on the arm supports.

The crest rail does not necessarily allude to a later style. The arm support, with a rounded ball over a long-necked baluster, repeats a treatment used on the arm supports of rush-bottom armchairs made between 1730 and 1750 in the Philadelphia shops of Solomon Fussell and his onetime apprentice, William Savery.[5]

The chair is an excellent example of the method used by some Pennsylvania craftsmen to lay out a design to be inlaid. Almost all the larger elements of the design are segments of circles that were scribed onto the board before being gouged out and inlaid with a light-color wood. The points that served as the center of these circles can be clearly seen in figure 83. This plan was used on several chests of drawers, a desk, and an elaborate clock case in the Winterthur collection. The clock, containing the face plate with the inscription "Jacob Godshalk Philadelphia," is of particular interest, as the case may have been made late in the eighteenth century. Godshalk worked in Philadelphia from 1768 until about 1780.[6]

The seat boards and bottom stretchers of Winterthur's chair are not original, and some of its decorative maple stringing is missing. A series of symmetrically arranged holes, now plugged, suggests that at one point in the nineteenth century it boasted tufted upholstery.

NOTES
[1] Schiffer, *Chester County . . . Inventories*, p. 108.
[2] *OED*, s.v. "close-stool"; Littlehales, *Medieval Records of a London City Church*, p. 37.
[3] *Essex Probate*, 1:66; Schiffer, *Chester County . . . Inventories*, p. 105.
[4] Hayden, *Chats on Cottage and Farmhouse Furniture*, p. 201, lower right.
[5] See Forman, "Delaware Valley 'Crookt Foot' and Slat-Back Chairs," pp. 41, 64.
[6] Object file 57.971, Registrar's Office, Winterthur.

30.
JOINED GREAT CHAIR, WALNUT CHAIR, or RAKED-BACK CHAIR
Southeastern Pennsylvania
1715–1740
WOOD: Black walnut (*Juglans nigra*)
OH 42⅛″ (107.0 cm)
SH 17¼″ (43.8 cm), SW 22¼″ (56.5 cm), SD 17″ (43.2 cm)
PROVENANCE: Bequest of Henry Francis du Pont
67.1176

Fig. 84. Detail of the grooves cut to hold the seat board of the joined chair in catalogue entry 30. (Winterthur 67.1176.)

Fig. 85. Detail of the scribed line on the arm and handgrip of the joined chair in catalogue entry 30. (Winterthur 67.1176.)

Pennsylvania inventories usually describe chairs in terms of the material with which they are upholstered or the wood of which they are made; collectors' terminology today refers to this type as a "banister-back chair." The term "slat-back" might be equally applicable since early eighteenth-century definitions of the word reveal that slats were pieces of wood as often oriented vertically as horizontally. This chair varies from the usual banister-back chair in that it is made by a joiner and has turned ornamentation rather than being a turned-chair maker's chair. Since the upper rear stiles cant backwards, perhaps the only period term we can safely use to describe it is "raked back"—a phrase that occurs in an entry for January 1739 in the account book of Solomon Fussell, a Philadelphia maker of turned chairs.[1]

The highly figured walnut crest rail of the chair suggests that it was made by a craftsman who was familiar with the method of decorating crest rails by piercing them, a method that is also commonly found on chairs made in Cheshire, England (see fig. 68), and possibly in neighboring Wales. Its form is derived from wooden or leather-upholstered chairs, made in provincial areas in the cane-chair style; it lacks the backward-raking rear feet, or "great heels," common in urban examples.

The chair originally had a board seat, framed by the seat rails on four sides and fitted into a groove near the upper edge of the inner perimeter of the frame, in the manner of the chair in catalogue entry 28. The upper part of this groove was removed in modern times to permit the installation of a modern stuffed leather seat (fig. 84). The original seat was sunk slightly below the seat frame, perhaps to hold in place the separate cushion that we assume was invariably used on board-bottom chairs. It has been suggested that the two small holes in the crest rail were used to attach a back cushion, but this notion is at variance with a crest rail made of a decoratively grained piece of walnut. Furthermore, the edges of the holes do not reveal any wear. A related chair with its original seat has a long tradition of ownership in the Pennock family of Primative Hall, near Philadelphia. It is illustrated as plate 10 in Hornor's *Blue Book*.

The pin holding the tenon of the lower back in place in a mortise cut into the right rear stile is clearly visible in figure 84. This pin is rectangular in shape and is typical of pins in the English manner found in New England furniture of the seventeenth century and in the Middle Atlantic colonies furniture inspired by West Country English traditions (compare with the next entry).

A scribed line on the inside of each arm and a circle with a clearly visible center point on the handgrip (fig. 85) show how each arm was laid out with a rule, dividers, and scribe prior to being shaped. Another scribed line along the middle of the upper surface of the arm defines the apex of the arc of the upper surface of the arm. Arms in this style are rare on Pennsylvania wainscot chairs and probably do not predate the first decade of the eighteenth century. A related arm appears on the banister-back chair with board seat (see catalogue entry 72) and on a slat-back rush-bottom chair of a later date (Winterthur 67.1725).

The slats of this chair have elaborate moldings, symmetrically arranged, consisting of a fillet, swelled half round, fillet, hollow half round, fillet, swelled half round, and fillet. The upper outer edge of the seat rail retains its original bead. The unusual placement of the rear stretcher below the side stretchers gives the chair an uncluttered appearance.

The seat of this chair is modern, and the entire chair has been bleached and refinished.

NOTE
[1] Fussell, account book, p. 13.

31.
JOINED CHAIR or *WALNUT CHAIR*
Southeastern Pennsylvania, possibly Germantown
1720–1750
WOOD: Black walnut (*Juglans nigra*)
OH 42¼″ (107.3 cm)
SH 17½″ (44.5 cm), SW 18¼″ (46.4 cm), SD 14⅝″ (37.1 cm)
PROVENANCE: Bequest of Henry Francis du Pont
66.698

Fig. 86. Joined chair, probably the West Country of England, 1680–1720. (Saint Oswald's Church, Lower Peover, Cheshire, England. Photo: Benno M. Forman.)

This walnut chair illustrates the difficulty of tracing the origins of stylistic attributes in the absence of a reasonably firm idea of when the object in question was made. Superficially, the chair appears to be a version of the Pennsylvania, Cromwellian-style, square-back wainscot chair which has responded to the challenge of the stylistic attributes of the early eighteenth-century cane-chair style as practiced in England and America. And its most impressive feature—the carefully executed, vertically oriented fielded panel that composes its back—can be found in English West Country chairs, such as a particularly fine example in Saint Oswald's Church, Lower Peover, Cheshire (fig. 86); this same treatment is common in the better rural chairs of northern Europe. Lest we forget, the so-called Cromwellian style, of which this chair is reminiscent, is historically derived from continental prototypes which persisted over a long period of time.

Non-English features are as prevalent in this Pennsylvania chair as are English ones. Front legs turned on their upper ends are uncommon on English chairs of the early eighteenth century. The manner in which the vertical muntins that support the rear panel are molded is not common in West Country English chairs related to this example, although this and other unusual quirks of design could as well be an innovation of the craftsman who made the chair as it could be evidence of a continental tradition at work. The simple columnar shapes of the front stretcher and the rear stiles are not particularly rural English characteristics. The finials, likewise, do not suggest the type of finial that we associate with English provincial furniture, and the prominently articulated ring between the base and the flared crown seems closely related to those of the slat-back chairs of Germanic origin. The side and back seat rails are much narrower than the West Country English type (see catalogue entry 28) and are rounded on their upper edges. A noteworthy feature, not expected in the usual middle colonies wooden chair, is the curious hollow-corner crest rail. (The lower back rail is the mirror image of the crest rail.)[1] If paintings and drawings are accurate, such crest rails appeared on northern European chairs from the Middle Ages onward. The style survived into the nineteenth century as chairs in Frilandsmuseet, Copenhagen, demonstrate (fig. 87).[2] One final feature of Winterthur's Pennsylvania chair that does not appear in the seventeenth-century English prototypes is the double-ogee sculpting of the lower edge of the front seat rail. It is tempting to see this as a northern European trait, but it is equally possible that this idea was borrowed from the front seat casing of the Pennsylvania slat-back chairs made in Germantown and Philadelphia also during the early eighteenth century (fig. 88), some touches of which appear to owe their origin to ideas and chairs imported from New England in the intercoastal trade. If this skirt treatment is

Fig. 87. Joined great chair with slat back and turned decoration, Europe, nineteenth century. (Courtesy Frilandsmuseet, Copenhagen, Denmark.)

Fig. 88. Joined chair with slat back and turned decoration, Germantown or Philadelphia, Penn., 1710–40. Maple; H 45⅛″ (114.6 cm), W 25½″ (64.8 cm), D 21¼″ (54 cm), SH 15¾″ (40 cm). (Winterthur 52.236.)

derived from New England ideas, then it suggests a late date of manufacture for this chair, perhaps toward the end of the first quarter of the eighteenth century. The turning and the backward rake of the upper rear stiles are features that do not appear on any of the Pennsylvania chairs derived from English West Country traditions.

The process of turning rear stiles so that they are at an angle to the legs cannot be easily accomplished with a pole lathe. This implies that the craftsman who made the chair had a wheel or "great" lathe and a "round-collar," or a similar device, to permit such off-axis turning.[3] Although American chairs of this type are rare and the major turnings on this chair contain allusions to columnar rather than baluster shapes, clearly the work was executed by a craftsman who was well versed in the turner's techniques. On the basis of present knowledge, it is unlikely that all these features would be embodied in an early wainscot chair made in a Philadelphia shop. All of this suggests that the chair was probably made in one of the major shops of an outlying area. A card tacked under the seat board bears the following inscription in ink:

This chair when fitted up in 1851 was 105 yrs old: it belonged to Grandmother Reaver.

In another hand, the following has been added:

1886   140 yrs   1746.

The fitting up mentioned in the card could have referred to casters on the feet and some sort of upholstery that a series of tack holes around the upper perimeter of the seat frame shows was added to the seat later, embellishments that subsequently have been removed.

The earliest reference to a Reaver family is that to magistrate Jacob Reaver, who lived at the corner of Germantown Avenue and Harvey Street in 1809.[4] A virtually identical chair, with a history of ownership in the Ashe and Davis families of Germantown, and later by the Twaddell family in outlying Pennsylvania, is now in a private collection in Wisconsin. These histories of ownership along with the stylistic attributes of two chairs in question suggest that we might well look to Germantown as their place of origin.

Probably the leading turner in Germantown was Jacob Shoemaker, who left all his "Turning tools and all other Tiber Materials Utensils & Tools belonging to the Trades of Turning and Wheel Making" to his son, Jacob, in 1722. Shoemaker, who probably came from Kriegsheim, in the Palatinate, arrived in Pennsylvania with Daniel Pastorius in 1682. He was living in Germantown by 1688 and moved to Philadelphia in 1715.[5]

It is fatuous to argue that this chair represents a pure and early strain of the Germanic tradition in Pennsylvania, since the strain is obviously not pure. Many touches such as the stretcher arrangement and the shapes of the turnings of the front legs suggest that the maker was influenced by Anglo-American furniture or craft traditions. That this chair reveals the act of accommodation in progress makes it a valuable document of eastern Pennsylvania culture of its time. It stands in contrast to the numerous examples of furniture made in Pennsylvania by craftsmen from southern Germany who arrived in the colony later, settled in primarily agrarian areas, and made furniture that is stylistically indistinguishable from what they made in their homeland. The furniture made by the earliest immigrant German craftsmen almost always manifests the characteristics of the dominant English taste and as such shows that the popular nineteenth-century concept of the American "melting pot" reflected a condition that was at work much earlier and resulted in objects of unusual character which could not have been made elsewhere.

NOTES
[1] This hollow-corner treatment is visible on the Pennsylvania leather-upholstered chair illustrated in fig. 168.
[2] I am indebted to Mary Hammond Sullivan for calling this chair to my attention and to Margit Baad of the Frilandsmuseet for this photograph. The chair was purchased by the musuem in 1958. It has no provenance. For a similar crest rail, see fig. 39.
[3] Moxon's Mechanick Exercises, p. 193 and pl. 13, fig. H.
[4] See Shoemaker, "Inhabitants of Germantown and Chestnut Hill," p. 476.
[5] Shoemaker will as cited in McElroy, "Furniture of the Philadelphia Area," p. 205; and Philadelphia Wills 1722-272A.

32.
JOINED CHAIR or WALNUT CHAIR
Southeastern Pennsylvania, Delaware, or neighboring New Jersey
1680–1730
WOOD: Black walnut (*Juglans nigra*)
OH 40¾" (103.5 cm)
SH 17⅜" (44.1 cm), SW 15⅞" (40.3 cm), SD 14⅛" (35.9 cm)
PROVENANCE: Bequest of Henry Francis du Pont
67.1166

Although this chair superficially resembles French chairs in appearance, numerous attributes suggest that it properly belongs with the chairs made in the vicinity of Philadelphia. Unlike French or French Canadian examples, it is made totally of black walnut (*Juglans nigra*), a native American wood that is not known to have found its way to France, where the European variety *Juglans regia* is native, and a wood that does not grow as far north as Canada, where birch (*Betula*) was the common wood for joiners' chairs. Furthermore, on early Canadian examples a medial stretcher connects the low side stretchers while this chair has stretchers extending from leg to leg around its perimeter. This chair also lacks the double pinning of the crest rail and stretcher common in the Canadian type, and the pins are ovoid in shape, rather than the square Canadian type.[1]

The attributes that distinguish this wooden chair from other walnut chairs of this type produced in Pennsylvania are its high back and rounded crest rail. Rounded crest rails are found in English chairs, but not with such high and narrow backs. And one New England wainscot armchair with a rounded top is displayed at the Henry Whitfield House, Guilford, Connecticut.[2]

Habitual as it is for students of American furniture to look to England for prototypes, English wainscot chairs of the seventeenth century are merely one variation of a joiner's tradition that was widespread throughout northern Europe. An arched crest rail, very much in the manner of a chair at the Whitfield House, for example, appears on a Swedish-made wainscot chair dated 1672 in Göteborg's history.[3] That chair exhibits most of the attributes common to northern European wainscot chairs, including those of England, and, since it probably came from western Sweden, which traded with England in the seventeenth century, may even reflect some English influences. But the chair, like all furniture in the seventeenth and eighteenth centuries, also exhibits distinctively national characteristics in its design: rather top-heavy turned balusters on the front legs and arm supports; a single row of low stretchers; and thin vertically oriented arms which bow gracefully downward between the handgrip and the rear stiles. Another example illustrated in Erixon's *Möbler* (pl. 683) came from West Gotland and has the narrow back and a carved rounded crest rail joined into the upper ends of the rear stiles with a single pin in each joint, like the American example. It bears the carved date 1680. Numerous other Swedish chairs in Erixon's book exhibit the rounded crest rail (pls. 658, 661,

693, 694, and 707), and a few even possess cutout handgrips on their backs to make them more portable (pls. 381–83), although these last chairs are of the sgabello type. Other chairs have paneled backs such as are seen on the English West Country chairs (pls. 657, 658, 659, 660, and 666), and some combine narrow high backs with a solid deep crest rail that is rounded on the upper margin and sculpted on the lower edge (pls. 645, 663, and 664).

While the stretcher arrangement of Winterthur's chair is of the conventional Anglo-Pennsylvania type, narrow back, high-arch crest rail, and back panel with a sculpted lower margin suggest that the appearance of this chair owes a greater debt to Swedish ideas of design than to English ones. Further evidence of this is furnished by the elongated vase-shape turnings on the front stretcher, a feature common on Swedish chairs and on American chairs made in the Swedish manner.

It cannot be denied that Winterthur's chair combines Anglo-American and Swedish-American features and is thus not a pure representation of either culture. But we may conclude from its appearance that its maker, if not Swedish by birth and influenced by the English tastes of the dominant cultural group surrounding him, either learned his craft and the basic tenets of the style in which he practiced it from a craftsman of Swedish origin or made this chair specifically to suit the tastes of a customer of Swedish background. Since this chair is made of the ubiquitous black walnut of Pennsylvania wooden chairs, it requires a little effort to see it as basically reflecting northern European rather than English traits. Northern European traits also appear in several other chairs in this catalogue, notably those discussed in catalogue entries 72, 73, and 74; the illustrations here and in those entries present the full range of Swedish characteristics exhibited by chairs in America.

References to Swedish furniture makers are rarely encountered in the colonial probate records, but evidence of their presence in this country is slowly accumulating as more furniture that previously had been dismissed as "Scandinavian" is now being subjected to microanalysis. While no name can at present be suggested for the maker of this chair, it is unlikely that Broer Sinnexen, mentioned earlier, could have made it; his inventory does not reveal that he possessed the lathe and gouges necessary to execute the turned elements here. It is more likely that this chair was produced by a second- or third-generation craftsman who had begun to absorb the Anglo-American culture around him.

The center seat board of this example has been replaced.

NOTES
[1] See Palardy, *Early Furniture of French Canada*, p. 213, figs. 265–74.
[2] This remarkable chair is illustrated in Kane, *Furniture of the New Haven Colony*, no. 29. It is made of white oak and is one of the few examples believed to be of American origin that has a double cut under the arms. It further possesses rear stiles whose upper ends are sculpted into "ears" suggesting that the craftsman who made it was trained in the Yorkshire-Derbyshire joiners' tradition, where such ears are a usual feature (see Temple Newsam House, *Oak Furniture from Yorkshire Churches*, figs. 16, 17).
[3] See Erixon, *Möbler*, pl. 680.

33.
JOINED CHAIR or WALNUT CHAIR
Southeastern Pennsylvania
1720–1750
WOOD: Black walnut (*Juglans nigra*)
OH 42½″ (108.0 cm)
SH 17¼″ (43.8 cm), SW 17⅝″ (44.8 cm), SD 12⅞″ (32.7 cm)
PROVENANCE: Bequest of Henry Francis du Pont
61.1152

Although this chair is superficially suggestive of English North Country and West Country chairs in the seventeenth-century style, its sculpted skirt suggests a date of manufacture in the 1720s at the earliest. Indeed, its overall form is probably derived from the small upholstered chairs without arms, produced in Boston and other urban centers from the mid 1720s onward.[1]

The boldly fielded panel, which has an extra hollow bead around its uppermost surface, and the molded upper and lower margins of the side stretchers, which have a quarter round flanked by fillets, suggest unusual care on the part of the joiner who made this chair. The replaced lower rear stretcher is molded on its front surface and undoubtedly is an exact copy of the original. (This is confirmed by the mortise holes in the rear stiles into which the stretcher is fastened, which were hollowed out on their front surfaces to accept a molded stretcher.)

The relatively simple turned elements do not compare favorably in workmanship or conception with the details of joinery that lift this chair above the ordinary. The turnings are, however, scored lightly in a decorative manner, a technique reminiscent of northern European habits of workmanship rather than English ones. The pins in this chair are round rather than rectangular.

The seat board on this chair replaces a similar original seat, and the feet and lower stretchers are modern.

NOTE
[1] See the introduction to easy and low chairs and catalogue entry 85.

34.
JOINED GREAT CHAIR
Lancashire, England
1670
WOOD: Oak
OH 37¼″ (94.6 cm)
SH 15¼″ (38.7 cm), SW 22¾″ (57.8 cm), SD 15″ (38.1 cm)
PROVENANCE: Gift of Mr. and Mrs. Howard Moss in memory of Louis Moss
81.290

This chair is one of a very few chairs from the Lancashire/ Lake District in the northwest of England that is in American collections. Despite its fragile condition, it is an important document of the transferal of specific English regional construction techniques to the New World by emigrant artisans. Specific features of this chair, notably its use of mitered tenons on the rear stiles and its use of through-tenons at the intersection of the arms and the rear stiles, also appear in the joined furniture of the upper Connecticut River valley be-ginning with the influx of northern English artisans into that area in the late 1670s.[1]

This chair has lost both of its side stretchers, its rear stretcher, and at least half of its original front stretcher. In addition, its small turned feet are gone. In all likelihood, its handgrips were probably much longer than at present, and its crest rail was probably also supported at its ends by small applied brackets that provided a smooth visual transition between the rear stiles and the narrow crest rail. The stock in this chair is uniformly thinner than that on American examples of the period and was sawn rather than riven prior to fabrication.

NOTE
[1] The use of mitered tenons in joined woodwork from the Lake District of Lancashire and the West Riding of Yorkshire has been discussed in Forman, "Note," 519; and Gilbert, "Regional Traditions in English Vernacular Furniture," pp. 53, 75. Its relevance to furniture produced in the Hadley area of western Massachusetts is asserted in Kane, "Seventeenth-Century Furniture of the Connecticut Valley," p. 92, and, most recently, in Kirk, *American Furniture and the British Tradition*, ch. 4.

cat. 35

35.
JOINT STOOL
Attributed to Stephen Jaques, Newbury, Massachusetts
1680–1710
WOOD: Red oak (*Quercus rubra*)
OH 20½″ (52.1 cm), OW 17¼″ (43.8 cm), OD 13⅝″ (34.7 cm)
PROVENANCE: Rudel family of Newbury, Mass.; Malcolm A. Norton; Henry
Francis du Pont
57.537

36.
JOINT STOOL
Possibly Essex County, Massachusetts
1680–1710
WOODS: One side rail, red oak (*Quercus rubra*); other side rail and top, white oak
(*Quercus alba*)
OH 21⅞″ (55.6 cm), OW 16⅞″ (42.9 cm), OD 11⅞″ (30.2 cm)
PROVENANCE: Gift of Henry Francis du Pont
57.538

These two stools are in remarkable condition, considering the extraordinary amount of wear that seventeenth-century stools must have received. Number 35 is attributed to Stephen Jaques

(b. 1661) who was the son of a Newbury, Massachusetts, carpenter, Henry Jaques (w. 1640s). Stephen was probably working by 1680, and is believed to have made a table along with "a new pulpitt" for the second Newbury meetinghouse shortly after he completed building that structure in 1698/99. The table, now in the collection of the Historical Society of Old Newbury (first illustrated and attributed to Jaques by Mabel Munson Swan in 1945), was still in place in the mid eighteenth century. For in 1806, the Reverend John Popkin recalled the meetinghouse of his youth: "The body of the house was filled with long seats. Contiguous to the wall were twenty pews. The spaces for the pews were granted to particular persons, who appear to have been principals. Before the pulpit and deacon's seat was a large pew containing a table, where sat the chiefs of the fathers." According to Swan, Stephen Jaques had worked in Boston in 1680, which may explain why the table made for the meetinghouse nineteen years later seems closely related to Boston prototypes.[1]

The Jaques table and its well-documented provenance are

cat. 36

important to the stool in the Winterthur collection because of their close visual similarity. The turnings on the stool are identical to those on the table, and, according to its last private owner, Malcolm A. Norton, "This little stool . . . was, for many generations, in the Rudel family of old Newbury, Massachusetts, until it came into my possession."[2] The other stool (no. 36) has turnings closely related to those on the stool and table attributed to Jaques; each leg has a baluster whose shoulders break sharply as they move upward to a small collar or ring. The shoulders on the legs of the Jaques stool break less subtly than do those on the second Winterthur example; the latter has a much more deeply scored line turned in the mid section of the baluster itself, and a shorter columnar section at the top. The stool no. 36 is a singular survival of an American joint stool with almost all its original height; its feet suggest what other stools, whose legs are now worn down to either a single ball or their lower stretchers, must have looked like when first made. The extra height boosts the seat height of this example to almost a full 22″ (55.8 cm) and would have per-mitted its user to sit comfortably at a dining table with his or her feet resting on the table's stretcher, an inference that is confirmed by relative absence of excessive wear on the top side of the stretchers on these two stools.

Both stools were constructed of riven stock, as the slightly wedged-shape sections of their top rails indicates. Marks left by the joiner's hatchet on the inside surfaces of these rails show that the material was worked quickly. The tops of these two stools are original and are formed by a single oak board secured to the frame with wooden pegs. The Jaques stool has a peg driven through the top into each of its four posts, plus one driven down into the middle of each of its side rails; stool no. 36 only has pegs driven into the corner posts, although sometime later nails were added to hold the top firmly to its rails.

NOTES
[1] Swan, "Newburyport Furnituremakers," pp. 222–25. The pulpit contract is quoted in Currier, *History of Newbury*, p. 334. Popkin is quoted in Currier, *History of Newbury*, p. 335. For a related Boston table, see the example now in the collections of the Wadsworth Atheneum illustrated in Comstock, *American Furniture*, no. 113.
[2] Norton, "Joint Stool and Candlestick," p. 227.

37.
JOINT STOOL
Probably New Haven, Connecticut
1640–1680
WOOD: One leg, post oak (*Quercus stellata*)
OH of frame 19½" (49.5 cm), OW of frame 15" (38.1 cm), OD of frame 13"
(33.0 cm)
PROVENANCE: Winsor White; Henry Francis du Pont
65.2004

38.
JOINT STOOL, LOW STOOL
Probably Guilford, Connecticut
1660–1700
WOODS: Frame, American silver or red maple (*Acer saccharinum* or *Acer rubrum*);
seat, northeastern white pine (*Pinus strobus*)
OH 13½" (34.4 cm), OW 11¼" (28.6 cm), OD 11¼" (28.6 cm)
PROVENANCE: Bequest of Henry Francis du Pont
70.1349

These two stools relate closely to several examples of joined furniture with histories of ownership in coastal Connecticut that are illustrated in Patricia E. Kane's outstanding regional study. The turnings on the legs of no. 37 are well executed columnar forms with distinctive round cushions at the base and a sharply delineated collar at the top. They resemble the turnings on a joint stool now in the collections of the Wadsworth Atheneum that Kane attributes to New Haven. Kane's attribution is based on the stool's similarity to the Yale College president's chair, which Kane suggests may be the work of Lawrence Ward, a turner working in New Haven and nearby Branford from 1639 until shortly after 1666. The beautifully articulated columnar form of the turning on the chair and two stools are correct by pattern-book standards, and probably represent the work of London-trained turners. Working in the New Haven area, these artisans probably produced the London-style split turnings that are applied to

cat. 38

the case furniture made by joiners William Russell (1612–1648/49) and William Gibbons (emig. by 1640–d. 1689), who came from the parish of St. Stephen, Coleman Street, London, and were active in New Haven during the first generation of settlement.[1]

The smaller stool (no. 38), used as a foot stool and called a "low stool" during the period, has turnings that closely resemble those on the Thomas Robinson chair at the Wadsworth Atheneum and a chair-table now at the Smithsonian Institution. Kane attributes these two objects to Guilford, Connecticut.[2]

Both of Winterthur's Connecticut stools were originally painted red. The taller of the two (no. 37) has a newer top, the large overhang of which was stabilized by three pine cross-braces. The middle of these braces has been let into the top edges of the side rails. The side rails show extensive evidence on their inner faces of being reduced from bolts with a joiner's

hatchet. The top probably dates from the late eighteenth century. When it was added, it and the frame, still red, were given a coat of gray paint; since then the entire object has been colored a muddy brown. The low stool (no. 38) still has its original top pegged in place. The top was reinforced by cut nails at some point during the nineteenth century. Like the stool itself, the top is exactly square. Stereoscopic microscopy has revealed that beneath a later layer of blue casein paint are a coat of Prussian blue, a color not invented until 1704, and, next to the wood, a layer of red earthen color.[3] Both stools retain portions of their original turned feet.

NOTES
[1] Kane, *Furniture of the New Haven Colony*, nos. 25–28, pp. 82, 81, 84; see also the attribution of furniture to Russell and Gibbons in Fairbanks and Trent, *New England Begins*, 3:482–83.
[2] Kane, *Furniture of the New Haven Colony*, nos. 27, 28.
[3] See "Report of Examination," September 1976, object file 70.1349, Registrar's Office, Winterthur.

cat. 39

39.
JOINT STOOL
Boston, Massachusetts
1690–1720
WOODS: Top and leg, black walnut (*Juglans nigra*); end rail, walnut
OH 22⅝″ (57.5 cm), OW 17⅞″ (45.4 cm), OD 14⅛″ (35.9 cm)
PROVENANCE: Found in Boston by Roland B. Hammond; purchased by the
museum
60.189

Unlike the stools in the previous entries, the present example, which still has its original finish intact, was made in an urban context and made from walnut, a wood prized by turners of the William and Mary period for its smooth regularity in cutting and for the brilliant luster it attained when properly finished. In his *Mechanick Exercises*, Moxon detailed the manner in which turners brought the completed piece of turned work to such a smooth finish. After bringing the stock to the final desired profile, he explained,

they smoothen the work with the Edge of a piece of a Blade of a broken Knife, basil'd away, by following the Work with it: That is,

holding the basil'd Edge of the Knife close against the Work while it comes about: For then its sharp Edge scrapes or shaves off the little roughness the grosser Tools left upon the Work.

Lastly, they hold either a piece of Seal-skin or *Dutch* Reeds (whose outer Skin or Filme somewhat finely cuts) pretty hard against the Work, and so make it Smooth enough to polish.

Hard Wood they polish with *Bees-wax, viz.* by holding *Bees-wax* against it, till it have sufficiently toucht it all over; and press it hard into it by holding hard the edge of a Flat piece of hard Wood made sizable and Suitable to the Work they work upon, as the Work is going about. Then they set a Gloss on it with a very dry Woollen Rag, lightly smear'd with Sallad Oyl.[1]

The turners and cabinetmakers using walnut in Boston during the seventeenth and early eighteenth centuries undoubtedly used a similar series of steps, although we know from several inventories that New England craftsmen substituted shark skin for the "Seal-skin or *Dutch* Reeds" as their principal abrasive during fine finishing.

The turnings on the legs of this stool resemble in a general way many of the turnings on cane and leather chairs made in

Boston during the last decade of the seventeenth century and the first three decades of the eighteenth century. Yet in their particular profile they appear very similar to the turned legs and stretchers on a walnut table now in the collection of the Historic Winslow House Association in Marshfield, Massachusetts, and on the Boston easy-chair frame (see fig. 186). Notably, the turnings on the legs of each of these three pieces consist of a full baluster surmounted by a deeply undercut disk that appears on no other object known to this author.

The stool is, with the exception of replaced feet, in excellent condition. It has never had its original finish altered. The original top is fastened by four walnut pegs driven down through the top into the four posts. The slight wear on its stretchers suggests that it was most frequently used at table.

NOTE
[1] Moxon's, *Mechanick Exercises*, p. 213.

40.
JOINED FORM
Scituate or Marshfield, Massachusetts
1650–1700
WOODS: Leg, a soft maple; side rails and side stretchers, American black ash (*Fraxinus nigra*); seat, northeastern white pine (*Pinus strobus*)
OH 20¼″ (51.4 cm), OW of seat 81¼″ (206.4 cm), OW of frame 58⅝″ (149.9 cm), OD of seat 11⅜″ (28.9 cm), OD at feet 11⅝″ (29.5 cm)
PROVENANCE: Mrs. Gustav Radeke; Rhode Island School of Design; Maxwell Turner; Harry Arons; Henry Francis du Pont
56.94.6

This form is an extremely rare survival of what, along with stools, was the most common type of seating furniture used in seventeenth-century America. In design, forms were simply elongated stools. Because of their greater length, joiners charged extra for them. Indeed, in 1694, the company of joiners in London ordered that one of its members "should [make] . . . two forms at 2s. pr. foot," indicating that artisans charged by the running foot for anything over the minimum size—probably the dimensions of a square stool.[1]

The turnings on Winterthur's example place it firmly within a group of closely related objects documented as coming from what must have been large and active woodworking shops in Scituate and Marshfield, two towns along the southern shore of Massachusetts Bay to which many artisans migrated from nearby Plymouth. While the distinctive barrel-and-vase turning on this form is also seen on a wide range of cupboards, stools, joined chairs, joined tables, and cradles from the south shore region, the presence of hollow-quarter-round elements at the top of the barrel and at the bottom of the vase links this most precisely to two pieces: a joined stool with a history in the Totman family of Scituate (fig. 89), now in the Scituate Historical Society, and a table with drawer (fig. 90) now in the Smithsonian Institution. That stool and table, however, demonstrate the difficulty of separating the products of the Scituate and Marshfield shops, shops which were geographically close and linked through kinship ties throughout the seventeenth century. While the

Fig. 89. Detail of the turnings on a joined stool, Scituate, Mass., 1650–1700. Black ash (*Fraxinus nigra*) and white oak (*Quercus alba*). (Scituate Historical Society, on display in the Cudworth House, Scituate, Mass. Photo: Robert Blair St. George.) The stool has a history of ownership in the Totman family of Scituate.

Fig. 90. Joined table with drawer, probably Marshfield, Mass., 1650–1700. Oak, ash, pine; H 23″ (58.4 cm), W of frame 34¼″ (87 cm), D of frame 18″ (45.7 cm). (Greenwood Collection, Smithsonian Institution, Washington, D.C.)

Totman family stool has always been in Scituate, the table in the Smithsonian has carving on its drawer front that is exactly like that on a board chest with drawer that descended in the White family of Marshfield.[2]

Woodworkers in the two towns throve on the active shipbuilding activity that by the early 1690s marked the yards on the North River as the most productive in all of New England. The principal woodworkers included three first-generation craftsmen: William Ford (1604–76) from the parish of St. Olave's, Southwark, Thomas Little (I) (emig. 1630, d. 1672) from Surrey, and Kenelm Winslow (1599–1672) from Worcestershire. A multitude of second and third generation artisans continued working in the area. Joseph Waterman (1649–1710/11) set up shop and was joined by his sons Anthony and Joseph. (The 1716 inventory of Ichabod Bartlett of nearby Duxbury specified "one Chest & box & trunk at Watermans 12d [and] one Trunk at the [same] place 5d," furniture that he had contracted for that had not yet been delivered.) Other artisans included Isaac Little, a grandson of Thomas Little (I), whose estate in Marshfield included "a joyn worke Cupboard not finished" worth £1 in the west lean-to of his house in 1699, and Joseph Tilden of Scituate, from whom came a board chest with incised decoration still owned in Scituate.[3]

When Wallace Nutting first illustrated Winterthur's form in his *Furniture Treasury* (no. 2710) in 1928, he marveled at its projecting seat board, saying "The wide overhang would seem to have invited disaster." And the overhang does seem greater than that on most known English examples and than that on a possibly Pennsylvania form once in the collection of J. Stodgell Stokes and now owned by the Philadelphia Museum of Art. Yet the top on the Winterthur form is original. Unlike most seventeenth-century New England joint stools, whose seat boards are pegged to their framing members (see catalogue entries 35, 36, 38), the seat on this form is secured with large T-head nails—essentially rose-head nails whose heads are bent down on two sides during their production to form a clench—that are driven flush with the board's surface.

In his caption to the Winterthur form, Nutting also noted that it was then in the collection of the Rhode Island School of Design. It was given to that institution by Mrs. Gustav Radeke in 1920, and sold to Maxwell Turner on November 26, 1956. He must have quickly sold it to Harry Arons, from whom Henry Francis du Pont purchased it in December of that same year.[4]

NOTES
[1] November 27, 1694, Company of Joyners, leaf 128 recto.
[2] St. George, *Wrought Covenant*, figs. 5–7, 13, 16, 28–30, 33, 37–39, 40.
[3] Plymouth Inventories, 4:5–51, 1:315–16 (I am indebted to Robert Blair St. George for these references). St. George, *Wrought Covenant*, fig. 24.
[4] Carol C. Sanderson to Forman, March 24, 1972.

41.
SLAB FORM or SLAB BENCH
Eastern United States, possibly southeastern Pennsylvania
1720–1850
WOOD: Oak
OH 22″ (55.9 cm), OW 70¾″ (179.7 cm), OD at feet 21″ (53.3 cm),
OD at seat 10⅜″ (26.4 cm)
PROVENANCE: Bequest of Henry Francis du Pont
65.2833

This slab form warrants our attention because it represents a typical kind of seventeenth-century seating furniture that survives only in a very few artifacts (see catalogue entry 44), all of which are nearly impossible to date. It is made from a single slab, the outer round "bark edge" of a tree that is left after the marketable boards have been sawn.[1] This slab form, while fully in stride with the kind of technology used to make such objects in the early years of English settlement in America, could just as easily date from the middle of the nineteenth century or even later. To make a form, four roughly worked pieces of oak stock ("stake feet") were inserted into holes bored into or through the slab of wood. In his memoirs, Samuel Griswold Goodrich recollected his youth in what is now Ridgefield, Connecticut: "I was about six years old [in 1799] when I first went to school . . . we were all seated upon benches, made of what were called *slabs*—that is, boards having the exterior or rounded part of the log on one side: as they were useless for other purposes, these were converted into school-

benches, the rounded part down. They had each four supports, consisting of straddling wooden legs, set into auger holes."[2]

The stake feet on the Winterthur example were intended not to penetrate all the way through the slab, although one has, probably because the holes had been drilled a bit too deep into the underside of the slab. Prior to its restoration in 1981, the top ends of the legs had never been wedged, indicating that the maker did not use blind wedges in order to tighten the joint.[3] At its thickest point, this slab measures 4¼″ (10.8 cm).

The marks on the surface of the slab also indicate that a knife or other edge tool was used repeatedly here, which suggests that it may have been less often used as a bench for sitting than as a work horse for a butcher or slaughterer. In basic design, it resembles closely the horses or workbenches known through early engravings to have been used by many different kinds of artisans. Randle Holme compared slab forms or benches to a "countrey stoole, or a planke, or Block stoole" (fig. 91); they both "being onely a thick peece of wood, with either 3 or 4 peece of wood fastned in it for feet. Note that if these be made long, then they are termed, either a Bench, a Forme, or a Tressell."[4]

Winterthur's example was found on the porch of the Kershner House in Wernersville, Pennsylvania. It no longer retains its bark on the rounded side and at some time received a coat of brown coloring. Similar examples are in the collections

Fig. 91. Country stool. From Holme, *Academy of Armory*, 2: bk. 3, ch. 14, facing p. 18, fig. 74. (Winterthur Library.)

of the Museum of Fine Arts, Boston, and the Plymouth Antiquarian Society. The former example, known to have been used as a slaughterer's horse, is close to the Winterthur example in construction. The Plymouth bench varies in that its seat is actually fashioned from a milled plank which is supported by two battens into which the stake feet are secured.

NOTES

[1] William Porton's inventory (1693) specified "nine plank, [and] one slabb: 20 foot long, one foot broad" (Lower Norfolk County, Va., Deeds, 5:197a–99a; I am indebted to Patrick Henry Butler III for this reference).

[2] Parley, *Reminiscences of a Lifetime*, p. 364. His term "straddling" refers to the fact that the legs had to be set quite far apart and flare outwards for stability.

[3] Conservation report, object file 65.2833, Registrar's Office, Winterthur.

[4] Holme, *Academy of Armory*, 2:bk. 3, ch. 14, p. 15.

cat. 42

42.
JOINED SETTLE or SETTLE BENCH
Southeastern Pennsylvania
1720–1770
WOOD: Black walnut (*Juglans nigra*)
OH 50⅞″ (129.2 cm)
SH 16⅜″ (41.6 cm), SW 71⅞″ (182.6 cm), SD 22½″ (57.1 cm)
PROVENANCE: Bequest of Henry Francis du Pont
64.1781

This impressive settle, with graceful, sloping arms, well-executed balusters on the arm supports, and the distinctive knob finials at the top of its rear stiles, closely resembles joined chairs made of black walnut produced in Pennsylvania by joiners who emigrated from Wales and northwestern England in the early eighteenth century (see catalogue entries 22–25). Except for some wear to the bottom of its front feet and rear posts, the frame is in good condition. The leather covering and its upholstered foundations were replaced in this century; unfortunately, none of the original seating material survives,

nor does any evidence of the original upholstery techniques. The presence of original leather covering on the settle in the next entry suggests what might well have been a typical practice in southeastern Pennsylvania while yet another example with a joined frame and leather seat and back demonstrates that settles may often have been upholstered.[1]

Unlike settles made with board-construction techniques, joined settles are too heavy to be moved frequently. Thus, it seems likely that massive settles such as Winterthur's were used to subdivide a room. In southeastern Pennsylvania, where many houses had front doors that opened directly into the "hall" (the main living space of the house), the settle also would have deflected the cold air and, if placed at a right angle to the door, would have formed a small inner hallway that functioned as a lobby entrance to the house itself.

NOTE
[1] Nutting, *Furniture Treasury*, no. 1634.

43.
JOINED SETTLE, SETTLE BENCH, or LEATHER BENCH
Southeastern Pennsylvania
1720–1770
WOODS: Frame and skirt board, black walnut (*Juglans nigra*); seat boards and internal support cleats, white oak (*Quercus alba*)
OH 49½″ (125.7 cm)
SH 17½″ (44.5 cm), SW 72⅛″ (183.2 cm), SD 21⅞″ (55.6 cm)
PROVENANCE: Gift of Henry Francis du Pont
58.551

Made of walnut and white oak, this unusual settle with its one-piece ox-hide upholstery was found in Pennsylvania. On the basis of the turnings and the joined construction, it is difficult to date precisely. This piece may have been produced by the craftsman or master of the craftsman who made another settle dated 1758 with the initials of Isaac and Elizabeth Pyle. The latter settle, preserved in the Chester County Historical Society, is attributed to Elizabeth Pyle's brother, Abraham Darlington, a West Goshen Township carpenter.[1] The Winterthur settle has some features in common with the Pyle family example, notably fielded (what Moxon called "tabled") panels in the tripartite skirt; virtually identical arms and turned arm supports; and the rounded finials or knobs of the type common on joined chairs made in Cheshire, England.[2] Unfortunately, it cannot be demonstrated that Abraham Darlington learned any of his father's trade. We do know that the elder Darlington was apprenticed to a saddler in Waverham, Cheshire, England, in 1701, and probably emigrated to Pennsylvania prior to the completion of his term. In a letter dated 1716 he is referred to as a "sadlor in Chester in Pensilvane."[3] Given these circumstances, Abraham Darlington may have been taught the skills necessary to perform the rudimentary upholstery on this object.

The ox hide was too small to cover the large settle frame entirely, and where the hide stopped short—at those places where the head and the shoulders of the beast had been—the maker pieced in other parts of the hide that were remnants. In so doing, he sewed the pieces together with heavy linen thread of the sort commonly used by saddlers in assembling leather harnesses and tack. The precision of the work suggests the hand of a trained leatherworker, for the well-regulated hand-punched holes are equidistant from one another. Furthermore, because the back and seat are formed by a single piece of leather, and any pressure exerted on either place would put inordinate stress on the tack-and-trim strip holding the leather to the rear seat rail at the "crease" of the seat, the artisan adroitly placed a total of eleven large tacks with heads ½″ (1.3 cm) in diameter intermittently along the crease to augment the row of smaller tacks. Only two of these larger tacks have pulled loose, whereas many of the smaller tacks, whose heads average about ³⁄₁₆″ (0.5 cm) in diameter, have been pulled completely through the leather.

Whereas most Cromwellian chairs have girt webbing, sack cloth, and grass stuffing, the leather seat on this settle is supported by the boards which rest on a white oak cleat nailed to the inside faces of the front and rear stiles (one of these cleats has been replaced). There is approximately 1¼″ (3.2 cm) of space between the leather and the upper surface of these support boards, a gap that has never been filled with grass or hair stuffing to increase the sitters' comfort.

Many of the leather trim strips on this settle are missing or are in fragmentary condition. Their original location was as follows: one strip along the top edge of the top back rail; two strips down the front face of each rear stile, from finial to arm and from arm to seat; one strip along the crease at the rear of the seat; one along the outside face of each side seat rail; and one along the outside face of the front seat rail. Based on surviving sections, these trim strips averaged about ½″ (1.3 cm) in width. All of the tacks used were iron, and none, including the large tacks along the seat crease, had brass heads like those used on seventeenth-century upholstered chairs and couches.

NOTES
[1] Schiffer, *Furniture . . . of Chester County*, p. 63; Cope, *Genealogy of the Darlington Family*, p. 84.
[2] *Moxon's Mechanick Exercises*, p. 109.
[3] Cope, *Historic Homes*, 1:30.

cat. 43

44.
SETTLE or SETTLE BENCH
Probably southeastern Pennsylvania
1725–1860
WOOD: Northeastern white pine (*Pinus strobus*)
OH 62⅝" (159.1 cm)
SH 16⅝" (42.2 cm), SW 72" (182.9 cm), SD 19⅝" (49.9 cm)
PROVENANCE: Bequest of Henry Francis du Pont
60.743

Although this settle may date as late as the middle of the nineteenth century, it is significant to the study of early American furniture history because it aptly illustrates the design of the large, board-sided settles that were commonly used in the seventeenth century near the hearth. In 1667, for example, the inventory of Richard Engleden of Boston recorded "one pine settle to sett before the fyar."[1] The lightweight construction and rear boarding that extended all the way down to the floor made these large settles both easily movable and protective against drafts that must have plagued seventeenth- and eighteenth-century householders. Only a few examples of this type of hooded settle, with a board across the tops of the side boards, survive; one illustrated as no. 1628 in Nutting's *Furniture Treasury* and another advertised for sale in March 1977 are the closest in overall design and in construction to the Winterthur example.[2]

The Winterthur settle has three important construction details that suggest a southeastern Pennsylvania origin. First, the wooden pins that secure the framed construction of its rear stiles and muntins are offset diagonally from one another, rather than being driven in equidistant from the shoulders of the tenon they hold in place. The example in the *Furniture Treasury*, now in the collections of RISD, shares this Germanic construction detail. Second, both the RISD and the Winterthur settles have a half dovetail cut at either end of the front seat rail at its junction with the side boards. Finally, the ends of the seat board on the Winterthur example are cut so that two small tenons protrude; these tenons are set into corresponding mortises in the side boards, and are con-

sequently visible from the side of the object. These details also suggest the presence of an artisan trained in a Germanic tradition.

These last two details are shared by a small "bench table," which Margaret Schiffer attributes to the shop of Joseph Sheneman (1805–1875) of West Pikeland Township, Chester County, Pennsylvania.[3] The Sheneman bench table also has the same double-ogee-cutwork design at the bottom of its side boards that appears on Winterthur's example, and its seat width—an even 72" (182.9 cm)—is the same as well. Schiffer's attribution to Sheneman is suggestive in light of the Germanic quality of both the through-tenons and the use of offset pegging, the latter of which is often seen in the construction of Pennsylvania German doors. And, although no data exist to argue either pro or con, Sheneman was likely of German extraction, since the name is certainly not among those of Chester County's early English and Welsh settlers. In addition, the half dovetails and seat rails held in place with wooden pins rather than nails (nails being more the custom with board settles in the English tradition), suggest a German maker for the Winterthur settle. The moldings on the fielded panels in the settle's back cannot be dated with precision. Moreover, while the through-tenons and the offset pegging appear on Sheneman's nineteenth-century work, they are techniques which had long been in use among Pennsylvania German woodworkers; hence, this settle could date as early as the second quarter of the eighteenth century.

The lower rear right corner of the right side board has been pieced out approximately 2" (5.1 cm) with a piece of white oak. At that time the outside cleats, which are cut to the same profile as the cutwork still present at the bottom of the side boards, were added to provide additional support at the feet. The rear boards below the level of the seat have been replaced.

NOTES
[1] Suffolk Probate, 5:117–19.
[2] Advertisement of Gary C. Cole, *Antiques* 91, no. 3 (March 1977): 447.
[3] Schiffer, *Furniture . . . of Chester County*, pl. 92. A 1669 inventory from New Haven calls this a "settle table" (as cited in Kane, *Furniture of the New Haven Colony*, p. 65).

cat. 44

CROMWELLIAN-STYLE UPHOLSTERED CHAIRS AND COUCHES

ORIGINS OF THE CROMWELLIAN LEATHER-CHAIR STYLE

Since the late nineteenth century, the upholstered chair and couch with a relatively low back panel and a high seat frame that is square rather than trapezoidal in plan has been identified with Oliver Cromwell, leading general of the English Revolution and lord protector of England from 1653 until his death in 1658. It seems that Victorian aesthetes and romantic historians were convinced that the religious enthusiasms of the English Civil War led to iconoclastic destruction of any religious imagery that smacked of popery and to widespread secular asceticism whose expression in terms of decorative arts was a severe undecorated style. Thus, historians of English silver concocted the terms "Puritan" spoon and "Puritan" porringer to refer to plain forms thought to have been popular about the middle of the seventeenth century, and historians of furniture began calling the many plain leather and turkey-work chairs "Cromwellian" chairs. The implicit irony of the term "Cromwellian" is that the style was popular *throughout* the seventeenth century. Furthermore these chairs were upholstered in sumptuous silks, velvets, cloths with gold threads, and needlework designs, in short with textiles that are by no definition austere.

Despite its ahistorical origins, the term "Cromwellian" is used in this catalogue, partly because it has become so prevalent, and partly because it is convenient in distinguishing between the earlier seventeenth-century upholstered chairs, some of which had low backs and some of which had high ones, and the late seventeenth-century upholstered chairs that had high backs and were influenced by the cane-chair style. As the following discussion will make clear, the nineteenth-century concept of the "Cromwellian" style has little to do with the historical reality of the origins of this style of seating furniture. In the early decades of the seventeenth century, joined furniture with an upholstered seat was by no means common among the yeomen and husbandmen of England and New England. Joined stools, joined forms, and turned chairs remained the prevailing types of seating furniture, and on them stuffed cushions were commonly placed to soften the contact of the body with unyielding board and flag seats.

Richly covered wood chair frames that had hide or fabric seats and S-curve legs that crossed in front (perhaps similar to the "Scrowle chairs" in the Earl of Northampton's dining chamber in 1614) represent a fixed version of collapsible, portable chairs, often of metal, that were in common use by the military throughout the Middle Ages.[1] In Europe such fixed chairs appeared in the households of wealthy aristocrats and princes of the church during the fifteenth and sixteenth centuries and appeared as "chairs of state" throughout the seventeenth century. At the courts of Louis XIII and Louis XIV, they may also have influenced the use of the *pliant*, or folding stool, with its quasi-military or feudal associations. When made of wood, chairs of state were expensive because of the labor required to saw out the compass shapes, the waste of wood implied by large scantlings upon which the shapes had to be laid out, the expense of fine upholstery materials and garnishings used on them, and finally the labor of fitting the fabric to the frame.

Countless inventory descriptions make these rich chairs

195

vivid to the mind's eye and clearly reveal that the fabric was by far the most important component of the chair. An extraordinary bill among the British Royal Household accounts describes one set of eight chairs commissioned for the coronation of James I in 1603. For this set the "tymber work" cost only £1 per chair; the textiles on them and labor needed to upholster them brought the cost of each chair to just over £67.14; the entire set cost £541.12.3.

	£ s. d.
53 yards cloth of gold	202.10.00
13 yards of crimson damask for the backs	20.10.00
lace of gold and silver as a garnish	202.02.00
fringe of gold and silver	52.10.06
silk fringe	20.03.11
silk thread	1.04.06
fustian for the seats	4.00.00
down stuffing	4.00.00
bullion nails	2.10.00
gilt nails	10.13.04
black tacks	no charge
iron stays	1.00.00
sackcloth, girtweb, canvas, and buckram	2.08.00
workmanship at 25s. per chair	10.00.00[2]

The 1603 bill is not difficult to follow because much of the shop parlance and many of the materials are similar to those used in the upholstery trade today. The hammer-driven hardware was divided into two categories: brass nails and iron (black) tacks. Nails were regarded as embellishments, while iron tacks functioned as the hidden or at least inconspicuous fasteners that held the textile components on the wooden frames. The standard foundation components—girt web, sackcloth, and down-proof canvas and buckram—were adopted from the saddlemaker's repertoire of materials and techniques during the Middle Ages as an ideal flexible way of suspending textiles from an open wooden framework. While the covers and trims of the coronation chairs of state obviously were the grandest the society had to offer, it is nevertheless astonishing to see how expensive they were; gold tissue, solid silver, and gold lace (made of drawn wire) were extravagant, especially when one realizes that these chairs could not last more than twenty or thirty years because of the fragility of the cloth of gold and damask. Undoubtedly when the chairs were discarded, the precious trim was melted down for sale. Indeed, the only chairs of state that survive are far less grand, although covered in sumptuous silks.

Rare inventory descriptions and memoranda of bills are notoriously prone to subjective interpretation. For the modern reader they remain most ambiguous on the points that were most clearly understood at the time they were written: the style the object was made in and the object's name. In the absence of documented and datable examples, we can infer only that at some point in the sixteenth century, most likely in Italy but perhaps in Spain, a modified version of the chair of state was introduced and the style was quickly copied. The new form combined the leather seat of the portable X-frame stool of antiquity with a rectilinear frame (fig. 92). The chair could be made cheaply, or it could be elaborated with all the ornamentation a furniture-maker's shop could muster or hire—turning, carving, veneering, and gilding among them.

Fig. 92. Joined chair with leather seat, Italy, late sixteenth century. (Location unknown.)

From the craftsman's point of view, it offered woodworkers an opportunity to encroach upon the trade of the mercer/upholder who had until then covered the woodwork of chairs of state with fabric and thereby reaped the greatest part of the profit.

Different cultures at different times have given different names to this type of chair. F. M. Atkinson justifiably translates *chaise à vertugidan* from the French of Roger de Félice as "a farthingale chair." It seems fairly clear from the inventory of Gabrielle d'Estrees (1599), which lists "Neuf chaises de bois de noyer doré, cinq à vertugadin et quatre à bras" (nine gilt walnut chairs, five farthingale and four with arms), that the distinguishing feature of farthingale chairs is the absence of arms. The phrase "farthingale chairs" has not been encountered in contemporary English or American inventories; however, "back stool" and "back chair" are frequently specified in English inventories. Peter K. Thornton has convincingly argued that these phrases also refer to the new style of upholstered chair. That both "farthingale chair" and "back chair" referred to a side chair is supported by numerous inventory references. For example, that of Lady Dorothy Shirley, of Faringdon, taken in 1620, listed in the blue bed chamber "two chayers and one back chaier," and in the yellow bed chamber, "one chair, one back chaier, one lowe stoole," and in a third room "one Turkey-worke stoole wth a backe." To her inventory takers a "back stoole" was not the same as a "back chair."[3]

Fig. 93. Joined chair with leather seat, Spain, 1580–1610. Walnut with leather. H 35″ (88.9 cm), W 16⅞″ (42.5 cm), D 14½″ (36.8 cm). (Trinity College, Hartford, on display at the Wadsworth Atheneum.) The chair has a history of ownership in the Wanton family of Rhode Island.

Among a group of notes taken by R. W. Symonds from an uncited manuscript in the British Museum collection is a "Bill for goods deliver'd" on April 9, 1646, which lists "2 Elbow chayres and a back stoole of Irish Stich" for 10s. This reference seems to demonstrate conclusively that a back stool was an upholstered chair, and it is particularly gratifying to find that one of them was upholstered with Irish stitch, a type of embroidery better known today as Florentine stitch, or flame stitch, and commonly associated with the eighteenth century. Among the Royal Household accounts for the period between Michaelmas (September 29) 1660 and Michaelmas 1661, Symonds found that Robert Morris, an upholsterer, was paid £2.6 for "one great Chaire, & six backchaire frames turned & culloured" that were designated for "Mr. Oneale, one of ye Grooms of his Ma[jes]ties Beddchamber." Additional evidence suggests that the phrase "backchair" continued in use in the eighteenth century, although the form of the chair thus referred to had undoubtedly changed. In an undated manuscript mentioning the "Counte de Harcourte, The French Ambassador" (probably Simon Harcourt, ambassador at Paris from 1768 to 1772, "two doz of Turkey woorke back stooles" were rented for 18 weeks at a cost of 48s.[4]

The October 1665 inventory of Thomas Roper's inn, parish of St. Dionis Backchurch, London, listed "3 high back stooles covered with leather." Whether these were high backstools or highback stools is not clear. The phrase "back stool" appears only twice in Massachusetts inventories, those of William Tyng and William Franklin of Boston in 1653 and 1658, respectively, and because of its rarity must be interpreted as a localism of speech in seventeenth-century New England; the vast majority of American inventories refer to this form of furniture as a "leather chair."[5]

A fascinating reference that adds yet another term to our list occurs in the correspondence of Jeremias van Rensselaer, who in 1660 asked his brother, Jan, in Holland to send "8 Spanish chairs for the gentlemen, to be used when we hold council, for at present we use only pine benches."[6] A remarkable Spanish chair with a history of ownership in the prominent Wanton family of Rhode Island (fig. 93) may be of the type ordered by van Rensselaer. As the Dutch retained a taste for Hispanic artifacts long after they became independent of Spain in 1609, it is interesting to note that the Wanton chair, like its sixteenth-century prototypes, lacks stuffing under its heavy leather sling seat and back. Most chairs shown in Dutch paintings dating from 1600 have quilted foundations in their seats. In all probability fashionable chairs like the Wanton chair were provided with cushions. It is also noteworthy that on these chairs the elimination of the stay (lower back) rail permitted the back to conform to the sitter's body.

While the identification of the Spanish chair must be supported by argument and logic, abundant references to "leather chairs" in seventeenth-century French, English, and American inventories appear to identify the form quite clearly. Indeed, the phrase "leather chair" came to serve as the generic name by which this style of chair can now be easily recognized in documents of the seventeenth century. Henry Havard noted that among the furniture given by Henri IV to Robert Remy in 1582 were "six grandes chères couvertes de cuyr rouge, jaune, orange, garnies de clouz doréz" (six great chairs covered with red, yellow, and orange leather, garnished with gilt nails).[7]

That the probable style may be inferred from the leather upholstery does not mean that similar chairs were not upholstered in rich silk and woolen materials. Within a scant six years of Henri IV's gift, "six leather chayres" appear among the "household stuff" at Kenilworth Castle, following the death of Robert, earl of Leicester. While the entry does not tell us if the seats were stuffed, it does tell us that the custom of using cushions continued, for listed on the same line in the inventory are "twelve cushions of stamell." It is not perfectly clear that the "two great chayers with backs of leather," listed in February 1610 among the items in his house at Cockesden by the next earl of Leicester, had leather seats, too, but the mention of "two leather framed chairs" valued at 5s. each in the 1620 inventory of Christopher Trenchfield, parish of St. Dunstan's in the East, London, is more encouraging. The unusually detailed household inventory (1641) of Tart Hall, owned by the countess of Arundel, widow of a well-known art collector of the early Stuart period, reveals that the "greate Room or Hall" contained "Nyne great Italian Chayres of Walnutt tree with Armes: the Seates & Backes covered wth red leather, sett with brasse Nailes gilt and Tops aboue of brasse gilt."[8]

The scarcity of London inventories of the 1630s and 1640s hinders research about the less aristocratic strata of English society in an urban context, where stylistic innovations are usually first noticed; but by the time the estate of James White of St. Mary le Bow, London, was viewed on August 12, 1643, "eight leather chairs," in a room whose contents indicate that it was used for dining, posed no descriptive problem for the inventory takers. White was a man of moderate means, sufficiently well-off to possess considerable "cheny" ware and have his other seating furniture, hangings, and furnishings upholstered en suite in "perpetuana." It is probable that by that time the joiners of London, working for a mercantile clientele, had allied with upholsterers to offer the novel innovation—a chair with a permanent cushion built into its seat (fig. 94).[9]

On the Continent, chairs in this general style continued to proliferate. Chairs such as the one used by Peter Paul Rubens (1577–1640) in his Antwerp atelier—and still preserved there—are somewhat narrower than Italian examples, perhaps because they were derived from Spanish prototypes. Rubens's chairs were probably made later than the leather chairs mentioned in the earl of Leicester's 1610 inventory. Another version with an embossed-leather seat, preserved in the Rijksmuseum of Amsterdam, must predate the year 1637 when an almost identical chair upholstered in cloth was depicted in a painting of Willem van Heythuszen by Franz Hals (now in the Musées Royaux des Beaux-Arts de Belgique, Brussels).[10]

L'Hyver (fig. 95), by Abraham Bosse, a popular Parisian engraver, shows that the fully developed style in France (circa 1635) included stuffed seats and backs. Bosse reveals more than the mere style of the chairs; he portrays them in a dining parlor, virtually identical to many described in English and American inventories of a slightly later date. The chairs are arranged in a row against the wall and brought to the table for use. The hangings on the walls, the leaded casement windows in the Dutch manner, the wide-frame looking glass hung flush against the wall, the crisply creased tablecloth so obviously just removed from the linen press, a carpet underneath the tablecloth and on top of the table, and the multipurpose nature of the dining parlor with a fully furnished bed for sleeping and the wafer iron (*beignet*) for cooking, all convey the customs of refined seventeenth-century life. A wicker hand-screen, used to shield the face from the flames of the fireplace, clarifies the otherwise incomprehensible inventory entry of Boston's Henry Webb who had "3 hand screnes" in his parlor.[11] Another Bosse engraving, *La Benediction de la table* (fig. 96), shows chairs with columnar front legs. By combining the two images we get a composite picture of the chairs with fringe running around the perimeters of the seat and back, and stiles between seat and back sheathed with a textile and embellished with brass nailing, all conventions of the style prior to the mid seventeenth century. The simplicity of these French chairs, as opposed to the Italian-Hispanic-influenced Flemish chairs whose frames were enlivened with turned and planed ornament and whose seats and backs were relatively lower, suggests that English joiners selectively combined elements from both French and Dutch prototypes. The avowedly French-looking chair depicted in a rare allegorical print by English dilettante engraver, Sir Edmond Marmion (fig. 97), may be evidence of French influence or further proof that Marmion borrowed

Fig. 94. Joined chair with leather seat, England, 1630–60. Oak; H 53″ (134.6 cm), W 19″ (48.3 cm). (Location unknown.) Only the best chairs had turnings on the front legs, stretcher, and (although not on this chair) between the seat and the lower back rail.

liberally from Bosse's engravings. The gallant sits on an upholstered chair that has vasiform turnings that are more Dutch than French, yet the rest of the frame resembles the plain, rectilinear French chairs seen in Bosse's engravings.

An unusual representation of the chair (fig. 98), accompanied by a complete description, was published by Randle Holme in his extraordinary catalogue of seventeenth-century-English thought, artifacts, trades, and customs. Holme's engraving shows the familiar form that the upholstered joined chair had taken in England by the middle of the century. While Holme does not specifically mention that chairs of this type were often upholstered in leather, he unmistakably defines their character:

This is a Chaire made up by an Imbrautherer, which being all of one colour, needs noe more termes; but if it be of contrary colours, as when it is made up of needle, or turkey worke then the fringe is diurse coloured; a chaire . . . covered with Turkey work (or the seate and back of Needlework) proper ffringed answerable there to, garnished (or set with Nayles), of [Golden color]. Some will [call it] onley, a Turkey worke Chaire. Some [call it] a stoole-chaire, or back-stoole. If the chaire be made all of Joyners worke, as back and seate, then it is termed a Joynt chaire or a Buffit chaire. Those which have stayes on each side are called Arme chairs or chaires of ease.[12]

Holme's tiny engraving is richly detailed, even to the fringe used on all cloth-upholstered chairs in the seventeenth century.

Fig. 95. Abraham Bosse, *L'hyver*. Paris, France, ca. 1635. Engraving. (Metropolitan Museum of Art, New York, Harris Brisbane Dick Fund, 1926.)

Fig. 96. Abraham Bosse, *La Benediction de la table*. Paris, France, ca. 1635. Engraving. (Metropolitan Museum of Art, New York, Harris Brisbane Dick Fund, 1926.)

The pommels surmounting the stiles are not found on surviving English chairs in this style and, in all probability, are a carryover from the previous type. They are present on a chair in a circa 1605 painting attributed to the studio of John de Critz. Another name for this feature may have been "tops." The 1641 inventory of the countess of Arundel listed "Three Armed Chayers of walnutt Tree, the Backes & seats Couered with Red lether Furnished wth guilt nayles & tops of Brasse guilt." Her inventory is often quite specific, and since a continental origin is not specified for these chairs but is for other items, they may have been made in London.[13]

What little we know about the dissemination of the style into the English countryside suggests that, as with any new style, the pattern of dispersion reflected lines of social and economic status rather than geographical proximity to a center of fashion. In 1621, William Goodwin, dean of Christ Church, Oxford, had "one great chair covered wth redd leather & six other chaires of the same leather" in his parlor. The inventory of a wealthy and distinguished Bristol merchant, John Whiston, taken June 1, 1629, records in the "little parlor" of his town house "two Chayers with leather backes," in addition to joined stools and forms. Leather chairs first appear among the published inventories of the yeoman class of Essex County in January 1660, when John Sapsford of Writtle left "Fower Russia lather Chairs & one green Chair, [worth] 18s." in his parlor.[14]

That such chairs were being purchased for provincial homes between 1656 and 1667 is skillfully pointed out by Peter

Fig. 97. LEFT. Edmond Marmion, *The Five Senses: Hearing*. England, 1640–55. Engraving; H 5″ (12.6 cm), w 6⅞″ (17.5 cm). (Pepys Library, Magdalene College, Cambridge, by permission of the Master and Fellows. Photo: Edward Leigh.)

Fig. 98. ABOVE. Upholstered chair. From Holme, *Academy of Armory*, 2: bk. 3, ch. 14, facing p. 18, fig. 68. (Winterthur Library.)

C. D. Brears in his book on Yorkshire inventories. Brears notes that consecutive inventories of the same house, taken by the same men, show that William Richardson, Esq., who died in 1667, had made significant changes in the furnishings of the house he had inherited from his father, Richard, eleven years earlier. The room listed as the "parlour" in 1656 had become the "Dineng Roome" in 1667, and an expensive bed and its furniture, along with the "five chaires & nine stooles great & small' worth £1.1.6, had been replaced with "one Dozen of Rushy leather chaires," valued at £4 and "two greate chaires, of the same work," £1.[15]

We know that leather chairs were available in London in the 1620s, during the reign of James I, but at the moment no means exist to permit us to estimate how common they became during the reign of Oliver Cromwell. Furthermore, the same style, with perhaps a few innovations in proportions, upholstery materials, and ornamentation of its wooden members, continued to be the usual form of an upholstered chair throughout the reigns of Charles II and James II.[16]

Such were the conditions of life in New England during the first decades of its existence and so scanty are the surviving records of household furnishings that no evidence of upholstered furniture of any kind can be found in New England earlier than the "3 leather chaires and 3 smaler leather chaires" worth £1.10 listed in the hall of John Atwood's home at Plymouth, on February 23, 1643/44. Atwood had come to Plymouth from London in 1636 and was a respected and valuable settler. In 1641 he became a member of the Court of Assistants of the Company and served until his death three years later.[17] Atwood was not unsympathetic to the religious beliefs of the community, but he was not himself a "Pilgrim." He was a man of means who had come to New England as a representative of the London investors in the company.

Considering his social standing and his London connections, and that no indications of a craftsman capable of making leather chairs have been found in early Plymouth records, Atwood's chairs probably were imported from London.

An extremely significant upholstered great chair traditionally owned by the Winslow family of Plymouth Colony may resemble the kind of chairs Atwood owned (fig. 99). The chair has broad French-style proportions, columnar turned ornament on the stiles, and heavy rolled arms like those of a contemporary wainscot armchair. It also resembles the upholstered armchair in the de Critz painting. Because its frame is made of beech, the chair is unquestionably English. It may have been brought to the New World as early as the 1630s. At some point, the frame was altered by the addition of four heavy iron brackets, two on each side just below the seat, so that rectangular poles could be passed through the brackets and the chair could be hoisted aloft by two or more bearers, presumably as an invalid's chair rather than as a grander sedan chair. The chair has suffered repairs and alterations in the nineteenth and twentieth centuries but has recently been restored to its original appearance. Tacking and nailing evidence on it and on a related chair at the Victoria and Albert Museum suggests that it was covered with a textile, fringes, and brass nailing when new.

In the relatively more urban setting of Boston, leather chairs were undoubtedly present earlier than 1645, but they were not recorded until the inventory of Thomas Coytmore was taken in that year. Coytmore lived in Charlestown, Massachusetts, as early as 1636 and "was master of good est[ate], an enterpriz[ing] merch[ant], went in several voyages to distant l[an]ds and was lost on a voyage to Malaga by shipwr[eck], 27 Dec[ember] 1645, on the coast of Spain." He left "12 lether chaires" valued at 2s. 6d. each and "11 Cushions" worth

Fig. 99. Leather chair, probably London, England, prior to 1635. European beech (*Fagus sylvatica*); H 41⅝" (105.6 cm), W 25¾" (65.4 cm), D 18" (45.7 cm), SH 16" (40.1 cm). (Pilgrim Society, Pilgrim Hall, Plymouth, Mass., bequest of Anna Nightingale Warren Hobbs, 1957. Photo: Courtesy Connecticut Historical Society, Robert J. Biondi.) The chair has a tradition of ownership in the Winslow family of Plymouth County.

1s. 8d. each. Since we know of no craftsman in the region who could have made these chairs, we must infer that they were imported, as doubtless were his "Spruce Chest, wicker chaire," and a clock that was valued at £1.18. William Aspinwall, clerk of the writs in Boston between 1643 and his abrupt return to England sometime shortly before 1653, noted in 1650 that "12 russia leather chaires," shipped aboard the *Speedwell* from London, were received on August 2, 1650, by one Thomas Leacock, a Boston merchant.[18]

Among the probate records of Suffolk County, Massachusetts, no leather chairs are listed prior to 1652 when "7 leather Chaires" valued at slightly more than 8s. 6d. each were itemized in the "great Parlour" of the Reverend John Cotton. Cotton's chairs cannot be dated, but we can calculate that the "one Leather chayre & one Cushan stoole" valued together at 9s. in the 1653 inventory of Simon Eyre, Jr., probably had not been in Boston long, inasmuch as Eyre had been married only a few years before his sudden death at the age of 29. In the hall of William Paddy were "11 Rushia Leather chaires" valued at 11s. each. Paddy was a wealthy Boston merchant whose household goods and real estate amounted to £537.12 in a total estate of £2,221.6.1½. In the "closet" of Capt. Edward Hutchinson of Boston on August 24, 1675, were "6 Lether chairs and 1 armed Chaire" valued at £1.13. That "8 cushens" are listed next in the captain's inventory suggests the cushions were sometimes used on leather chairs; the pairing "5 leather chares & 5 cushings old" valued at £1.10 in the 1701

inventory of William Teller of New York confirms the notion. A final listing in the Suffolk County probate records is "One Elbow Leather Chair" valued at 6s., in the July 9, 1688, inventory of Giles Master, Boston.[19]

The first leather chairs in the probate records of nearby Essex County, Massachusetts, were listed in the hall (great room) of Salem's William Clarke who possessed "3 red Leather chairs" valued at 13s. 4d. on June 25, 1647. The red suggests they were upholstered in russia leather, which often had this characteristic hue. Surprisingly, leather chairs are not mentioned again in Essex County until the inventory of Nathaniel Grafton of Salem was taken on July 26, 1671. Grafton was married in 1665, at the age of 23, to Elizabeth, daughter of Moses Maverick of Marblehead. When Grafton died, "one duzzen of leather Chaires" valued at 6s. 8d. each were listed in his "west chamber."[20] Such a large set of chairs was probably purchased during the six years of his married life rather than inherited from either side of the family. Moreover, since there were craftsmen in Boston capable of making such chairs after 1660, it is likely that they were of American origin.

Because of its durability, leather continued to be the most popular upholstery material in colonial America. Doubtless it was this quality that motivated the Corporation of Harvard College to vote on April 8, 1695, "that six leather chairs be forthwith provided for the use of the library & six more before the commencement, in case the Treasury will allow of it." A note dated December 22, 1697, advises that six russia-leather chairs were indeed purchased for 15s. each from Thomas Fitch, a 28-year-old Boston upholder (upholsterer) and son of a cordwainer.[21] The price per chair is twice the usual value assigned in the inventories for a leather chair, so it is possible that Fitch made them in the high-back, carved-crest style inspired by the cane chairs introduced in the 1690s; however, this remains speculative since none of these chairs survives.

We cannot use the phrase "high back" to distinguish between Cromwellian and cane-chair styles because some American chairs in the Cromwellian style had high backs, as an extremely early reference to "6 high back chaires and 2 lowe backe chaires" in the 1652 inventory of William Tyng of Boston demonstrates. In 1652 the cane-chair style did not yet exist in England. As the following discussions of turkey-work chairs and couches suggest, Cromwellian-style chairs probably continued to be made in New England into the first few decades of the eighteenth century. Indeed, the style may even have persisted in London long after the introduction of several newer styles; the Royal Household accounts show that between 1734 and 1740 Sarah Gilbert supplied sets of "Turkey work" chairs to the "House of Peers."[22]

CROMWELLIAN TURKEY-WORK CHAIRS

Countless authors have misidentified turkey work as a form of needlework. Examination of surviving examples proves that it was a loom-woven, hand-knotted textile similar in structure to rugs and carpets woven in the Near East. A detail of the reverse side of a turkey-work-chair back dating from between 1640 and 1700 reveals the structure of the weave and incidentally

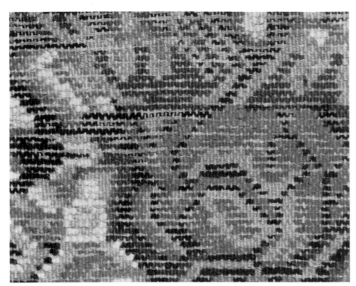

Fig. 100. Turkey-work seat cover, England, perhaps Norwich, 1640–1700. Ca. 19″ × 12″ (48.3 cm × 30.5 cm). (Museum of Fine Arts, Boston, Mass.)

shows how vivid and varied the colors were when new (fig. 100). The warp (the vertical cords strung in the loom) was single strands. The weft (the horizontal cords interlaced with the warp cords) was arranged in pairs. The hard, twisted linen cords of which the warp and weft were fashioned were extremely durable. The weaver began by stringing all the warp cords on the loom. The double weft cords were then passed between the warp cords with a shuttle. As each row of weft cords was inserted, the woolen yarns of which the pile was made were knotted over the warp cords, and each successive row was beaten into place to insure a tight weave. The double weft cords passed under and over the individual warp cords, alternating across the entire width of the piece being woven, and the over-and-under pattern was reversed with foot pedals between each row of weft cords. On all turkey work, the yarns were knotted with turkish knots. In the sample illustrated, there are twelve knots per running inch in the weft and six rows of knots per running inch in the warp direction, making a total of seventy-two knots per square inch (6.5 sq. cm), a dense weave by the standards of European carpet weaving. Once the entire field of the piece was completed, usually with striped or checkered borders of red, white, and black, it was removed from the loom and the edges were woven into a tight selvedge about half an inch wide. The ends of the yarn on the front side were then clipped, and the piece was washed to produce the soft pile of the finished product.

Turkey work, with its colorful and deeply tufted, or thrummy, pile, was not considered very fashionable among the English upper classes in the first half of the seventeenth century, perhaps because a wide selection of far richer and more obviously expensive textiles, often silk and fabrics worked with gold and silver thread, were available for conspicuous decorating. Yet among the otherwise rather backward-looking furnishings in the "Great Dyninge Chamber" of Stondon House, near Ware, Hertfordshire, the home of Ralph Sadleir in 1623, were "Six newe stooles of Turkie worke." "Sixteene stooles" furnished with "Sixteene Cushions of Turkie worke" were sat upon at a "longe Table wth a Carpett of Turkie

worke," and an additional table in the same room was furnished with a "Carpett of Turkie worke."[23]

Anne, viscountess of Dorchester, had a few turkey-work chairs and stools scattered about Gosfield Hall, Gosfield, Essex, when she died in 1638; the countess of Arundel had none at all at Tart Hall, London, in 1641. Edward Sackville, the fourth earl of Dorset, had "12 high stolles of Turkey worke" in his great hall and "18 backstooles of Turkey woorke" in the great dining room but nothing else covered in that fabric at Knole, Sevenoaks, in 1645. Perhaps the material had little appeal to noble households by the 1630s because it had become popular among the great merchants of London and was considered bourgeois. Richard Astell, a merchant tailor of London, for example, had in 1658, "14 turky work chairs & stooles" worth £3.12 in his dining room.[24]

If the petition of the English woolen manufacturers of 1683 is accurate, before cane chairs became popular in the 1680s, "five thousand dozen of Setwork (commonly called Turkey-work Chairs, though made in England,)" were "yearly made and Vended in the Kingdom . . . . [And] Great Quantities of these Chairs were also vended and sent yearly beyond the seas."[25]

What may have occasionally been the work of the ladies of the English upper classes in the middle of the sixteenth century, when turkey work was a novelty, must have become a cottage industry by the end of the century and throughout the seventeenth. A provocative entry in the earl of Leicester's 1584 inventory specifies "a Turquoy carpett of Norwiche work," 2 yards long and 1¼ yards wide (182.9 cm by 114.3 cm), among the many oriental and recognizably Middle Eastern "turkey" carpets at Kenilworth Castle. This suggests that one such center of the industry was among the Flemish and Walloon textile workers of Norfolk, and indeed, many of the early examples preserved in various English collections have East Anglian associations. Other settlements, such as East Smithfield and Southwark, both liberties of London, ought not to be discounted. Toward the end of the seventeenth century, turkey work was done at Bradford, in the West Riding of Yorkshire.[26]

In New England, turkey work first appears as an upholstery fabric on cushions rather than on chairs. In 1646, Thomas Lamb of Roxbury possessed "2 Turkie cushions," valued at around 4s. each, and probably used them on the "joyned chaires" in his parlor. The next year Elizabeth Goodale of Newbury, who had perhaps come to New England from Great Yarmouth, Norfolk, in 1638 or 1639, left "2 turky cushions" valued at 5s. each, and Adam Winthrop, son of the governor, possessed "5 turkey worke quishins not made up," £1.2.6, or 4s. 6d. each, at the time of his death in 1652. The first reference to turkey work firmly affixed to a piece of furniture is the "2 high turkey worke" stools in the "parloure" of William Tyng, a wealthy Bostonian, who died in 1652. When Gov. John Haynes of the Connecticut Colony died in 1654, his "Parlour" contained "3 turkey wrought Chaires" valued at 8s. each—the earliest appearance of that form in a New England inventory.[27]

Twenty-one years after the first leather chairs were listed comes the first Suffolk County listing for "6 turkey worke

Chayers," valued at 12s. each, in the hall chamber of Boston merchant David Evans, who died in August 1663. (Indicative of the changing fashions are "14 Leather Chayres" valued at only 5s. each that Evans had in the relatively more public room below.) "Six Turkeye worked Chaires & 6 Cushins" were listed in the inventory of another Boston merchant, Robert Nanny, one month later.[28]

The portrait of Mrs. Elizabeth Freake and her daughter Mary (Worcester Art Museum, Worcester, Massachusetts), first painted in 1671 and altered in 1674 (when Mary was added to the original composition), portrays a turkey-work chair. There is little question that the chair was one of the "14 Turkie workt chaires" listed in John Freake's inventory after his death in 1675. The chair in the picture has rear stiles ornamented with turned columns, and since no known American-made upholstered-chair frames of this period have similar ornament, the inference is strong that the Freakes' chairs were imported from England.[29]

When the estate of Edmund Downes of Boston was appraised on July 13, 1669, "4 tables wth Cloath Carpett, 18 Turkey worke Chayers" were listed in his "dyning Roome" (the earliest use of this room terminology in New England inventories; the second use occurs in the inventory of the equally wealthy Antipas Boyce of Boston a few months later). Turkey-work chairs were more expensive to buy and were also more perishable than their leather counterparts, as is confirmed by inventory entries specifying slipcovers, such as the "one dozen of turkey work chaires wth covers" valued at £7.4 in the February 15, 1675, inventory of Jonathan Getlines (Getlives) of Boston.[30]

Two extremely important references from probate inventories demonstrate that two New Englanders were making turkey work much like that which was mass-produced in England. The 1693 inventory of Samuel Rogers of Ipswich, Massachusetts, who had distinguished relatives but was not himself very wealthy, specifies "A Turkiwork Loom"; so too does the 1709 inventory of prosperous widow Sarah Bidwell of Hartford.[31] Undoubtedly Bidwell and Rogers or more probably his wife were making chair seats, chair backs, and cushion fabric. If the looms were big enough, the weavers may even have attempted to make table carpets.

Inventory takers readily distinguished genuine hand-knotted turkey work from embroidered needlework pieces. For example, the 1659 inventory of Jacob Sheafe of Boston specified "6 Turkie 2 Cuishons & 3 wrought" valued at £2.5. The wrought cushions were probably crewelwork, as is implied by an item in the 1660 inventory of Henry Webb: "6 needle work Cushions wrought [and] 4 drawn to work." Whether the designs had been drawn in Boston or in England is not clear in Webb's case, but in a letter dated March 26, 1687, to Daniel Allen in England, Samuel Sewall conveyed a message from his wife to Allen's wife. Mrs. Allen was directed to buy for Mrs. Sewall "white Fustian drawn, enough for curtins, wallen counterpane for a bed, and half a duz. chairs, with four threeded green worsted to work it."[32]

The extraordinarily fashionable Boston household of Capt. Thomas Berry (d. 1696), contained "1 dozn. Turkey worke Chairs" valued at an astounding 30s. apiece.[33] These contrast

Fig. 101. Turkey-work chair, London, England, 1680–1700. Beech, original turkey-work back with remains of polychrome worsted galloon; H 48¾" (123.2 cm), W 21⅞" (55.6 cm), D 17⅝" (44.8 cm), SH 17⅝" (44.8 cm). (Museum of Fine Arts, Boston, Mass., gift of Mrs. Winthrop Sargent.)

markedly in value with his two other sets of six turkey-work chairs; one valued at 9s. per chair, the other set at 10s. each, and one of which was described as "old-fashioned." As will be discussed below in connection with couches, these last references bring up an important question: Were the expensive and newly made sets of turkey-work chairs that appear in inventories of the mid 1690s, and later, in the so-called Cromwellian style, or were they high-back cane-chair frames covered with turkey work? An English chair with a history of ownership in the Winthrop family of New England points to the second possibility (fig. 101). The frame of the chair is made of beech, and the style of the frame suggests a date in the 1680s or 1690s. The seat of the chair had long since perished when the chair was donated to the Museum of Fine Arts, Boston, in 1917, but still attached to the frame, despite the loss of its sackcloth backing and most of its marsh-grass stuffing, was the original turkey-work back panel. The back was affixed with brass nails driven into braided, multicolored woolen galloon that is identical to the heading of the original fringe used on a turkey-work couch in the Essex Institute (see fig. 112). Because the back was oriented vertically, in contrast to the older style of frame which was oriented horizontally, one might presume that this fabric was a stopgap measure, specially made for a colonial gentry family who wished to have turkey work placed on frames designed for caning. Another possibility might be that an upholsterer was sent new chair frames while his fabric supplier was still making fabric to suit the old-style frames. Because New England merchants were often at the whim of London distributors, an occasional shipment of outdated textiles demanded that the recipient resourcefully adapt it to popular furniture forms. In 1704, for example, Thomas Fitch of Boston wrote that he had received from London a shipment "with the bottm & back of Irish stitch." In order to make the best of what was apparently a bad situation, Fitch reoriented the covers so they fit William and Mary chairs: "I frequently put those Fashion Backs length ways to make new Fash[ion] backs, and very few discern the difference: and If they do 'tis accounted good husbandry."[34] In the instance of the Winthrop family chair, however, an examination of the warp and weft and knotted pile of the back demonstrated that it was woven with the pile vertically oriented. The conclusion is inescapable: designers in the production centers of turkey work in England altered their designs to weave turkey-work fabrics that suited the new-fashioned cane-chair frames.

Since there is only one cane-chair-style frame in England or America that retains an original turkey-work cover it is likely that after 1695 most owners of turkey-work chairs believed that high-back chairs made in the Cromwellian style (and perhaps ornamented with twist turning) were more compatible with either cane or leather upholstery. Two documented groups of furniture provide the evidence for this. First, the above-mentioned inventory of Captain Berry itemized an expensive set of 12 new turkey-work chairs valued at £18 (30s. apiece) and more than three times the individual value of the chairs in two older sets. The 1724 inventory of Harvard College president John Leverett, who married Berry's widow in 1697, lists the same sets of chairs. The two older sets from the 1696 Berry inventory were lumped together as "12 Small Turky Chairs," while the expensive set of twelve is grouped with the couch and identified as "12 Large Turky Chairs & Couch."[35] The implication is that the newer, expensive chairs in Berry's 1696 estate were high-back chairs in the Cromwellian style, intended to be en suite with the couch. They may have resembled the high-back Boston example illustrated as figure 64 in Irving W. Lyon's *Colonial Furniture* and now in the collections of the Metropolitan Museum of Art.

Another case where the distinction between low-back and high-back turkey-work chairs in the Cromwellian style can be isolated with precision is in several sets of chairs purchased for the Holyroodhouse Palace of Edinburgh, Scotland. As brilliantly demonstrated by Margaret Swain, at least 36 turkey-work chairs in the low-back Cromwellian style were purchased in London for Holyroodhouse in 1668. Of the surviving examples, 1 has a frame ornamented with ball turnings much like those of the standard Boston upholstered chair frame, while 2 have frames ornamented with balusters related to that of an American frame perhaps made in New York (now in the collection of Pocumtuck Valley Memorial Association, Deerfield, Massachusetts). Documents relating to the purchase suggest that those in charge of buying the chairs in London were shopping around for the cheapest chairs available and were not too concerned whether or not the frames

of all 36 chairs matched. In 1685, an additional 48 chairs were purchased, and 3 surviving examples from that consignment have high-back frames in the Cromwellian style with twist turnings. That the design difference between low and high backs had stylistic significance is proven by an inventory of Holyroodhouse taken in 1714, when the cane-chair style certainly was at its height of fashionability in England. The inventory takers recorded "twenty eight Carpet Chairs, whereof nine are laigh back'd the other 19 newer fashioned."[36] This evidence, in combination with the survival of the Winthrop chair with a cane-chair-style frame and turkey-work covers, suggests that New Englanders had the option of ordering either Cromwellian-style or cane-chair-style frames with turkey-work covers well into the first two decades of the eighteenth century. It is impossible, however, to conclude on the basis of the laconic inventory references which type of frame was more popular.

THE CRAFT OF MAKING UPHOLSTERED CHAIRS

Although surviving American upholstered chairs have varying amounts of turning ornamenting their members, they are all joiner-made. Their seats are invariably framed with a mortise-and-tenon joint, as opposed to a round tenon fitted into an auger hole which serves as the usual joint on turner-made chairs. Likewise, the stretchers are all invariably joined into the legs by a mortise and tenon, in the same manner that joiners made wainscot chairs before upholstered seats and backs were introduced. The turnings of the front legs and stretcher that consist of ball turnings and disks tend to be monotonous visually. The turning of the rear stiles that appears on some examples, although stylistically insignificant, represents a technological departure of some magnitude when compared with the turning practiced by the turned-chair makers of the period. The turned-spindle and the slat-back chairs of Boston appear never to have been made in any manner except "traditional straight turning." In contrast, the rear stiles of leather-upholstered and turkey-work chairs cant backward both above and below the seat rail and are ornamented with turnings that cannot be achieved by traditional straight turning techniques. Although this type of turning appears to be difficult, it is in reality simple to execute. In the absence of a contemporary craftsman's term, the phrase "off-axis turning" is used to describe its appearance, and "two-axis turning" is used to describe the way in which it is achieved.

Two-axis turning may be used to ornament only the upper part of the stile or only the lower, or both, depending upon the taste of the maker. The device used to attain it may be as complex as the "round Collar," which Joseph Moxon illustrated in plate 13 of "Turner's Work" but did not clearly explain in his text. A much simpler method that can be used on even so elementary a device as a pole lathe is schematically illustrated in an ingenious drawing by Stuart King of High Wycombe, Buckinghamshire (fig. 102). He described this device as a "buckle . . . for a chair bodger's pole lathe . . . for turning off centre."[37] As shown in his illustration, the upper

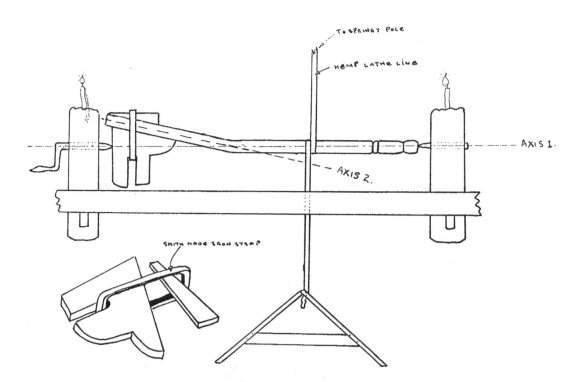

part of the chair stile has already been turned on axis 1. The craftsman has but to loosen the buckle and wedge, reverse the stile end for end, refasten the wedge, and turn whatever shapes he pleases on the lower part of the leg. In other words, the axis marked 2 is placed on the lathe so that it will occupy the same position as the axis now numbered 1 in the illustration. It should be pointed out that there are various other ways of accomplishing this, and doubtless some of the "mandrels" itemized in the inventories of American turners in the early eighteenth century were designed to achieve this end. King's solution is illustrated not as a document of the seventeenth century, but as one ingenious craftsman's solution to a technological feat that is not explained by period documents yet is proved by numerous chairs.

The spindle-back chairs of New England are all straight turned. The turners of the first generation who made them may not have possessed the technique of two-axis turning, and the second generation trained by the first may consciously have rejected it. If this is so, then it is possible that the earliest New England leather chairs were fabricated with unturned rear stiles as was the Endicott leather armchair (Museum of Fine Arts, Boston), a chair that is believed to have been owned originally by physician Zerubbabel Endicott (1633?–1684) of Salem. It is possible that some chair-frame shops in Boston never adopted the two-axis-turning technique and others did; however, the uniformity of Boston frames also suggests that many shops could and did produce plain or turned rear stiles to suit the upholsterer's or the customer's wishes. Certainly the three surviving upholstered-chair frames made in Salem, two of which were constructed in different shops but all of which were turned in the same shop, illustrate this; one chair has two-axis turning while the others do not.[38]

Since two-axis turning is not manifest in the work of eastern Massachusetts' earliest turned-chair makers, it is likely that the technique was introduced by a craftsman who arrived a little later. Such a craftsman may well have been a man like joiner David Saywell, son of "Reinold [Reginald] Saywell of Salisbury, Old England." David Saywell has the distinction of being the last English-trained joiner to come to Boston before the second generation of native-born and trained joiners began to work. He had arrived long enough before August 15, 1660, to have married Abigail Buttolph. When his estate inventory was taken on October 16, 1672, he had considerable "new worke" made up in his shop, among it "6 chaire frames" valued at about 5s. apiece—too expensive to be turned chairs, too cheap to be wainscot chairs, and therefore probably upholstered-chair frames. He also owned "24 paire of iron screws and nuts" worth 48s. These last are rarely mentioned in inventories and may have been used for bedsteads or to hold the fall mechanism in place on couches like that at the Essex Institute (see fig. 112). Although joiner Saywell died too early to have made the Essex couch, his shop could produce turned work, as the inventory listing "a lave & benches in the Shop" indicates.[39]

Among the native-born joiners who could have made such chair frames is John Scottow (1644–1678, w. 1665), the "only sonne of the late Thomas Scottow," also a Boston joiner. In 1661 Thomas left his son a lathe for turning. Among the younger Scottow's personal furniture at the time of his death were 9 leather chairs, perhaps of his own making, valued at 9s. 5d. each. At the time of his death in 1692, George Nicholson, a joiner whose estate was valued at £646, possessed 13 leather chairs worth 6s. each and a leather couch valued at 12s. The 1696 inventory of Boston joiner Henry Allen listed "3 chests, 7 frames for chairs, 18 frames for stools" worth £2.8," "Web," and "new cloth 46 yds." not valued individually.[40]

Leather chairs undoubtedly were made in other urban areas of colonial America at this time. Three frames by two different joinery shops have been documented to Salem.[41] Four other examples, three of which retain their original upholstery foundations and leather coverings, differ in every respect from the standard Boston product and probably originated in New York despite their New England histories of ownership. A leather chair made of American black ash (*Fraxinus nigra*) was collected on Long Island in the late nineteenth century. (It now belongs to the Society for the Preservation of Long Island Antiquities, Setauket, New York.) The example mentioned earlier that has baluster ornament and a high, narrow, Dutch-style frame (Pocumtuck Valley Memorial Association, Deerfield, Massachusetts), and one with a similar frame and ornament made of maple (Wadsworth Atheneum, Hartford, Connecticut) were probably made by a New York joiner. The makers need not have been of Dutch extraction; English joiners influenced by Dutch-style frames could easily have made them, as the Dutch-style chairs made for Holyroodhouse in 1668 suggest. Finally, the so-called Lady Fenwick chair (fig. 103), while proportioned much like Boston chairs, has an entirely different vocabulary of combined ball-and-baluster turnings that is unlike those on any Boston chair.[42] It, too, is probably a New York product. On a different level, a chair whose frame and upholstery are entirely in the Swedish style but whose frame is made of American red oak may be a New York or, more probably, a Philadelphia product (see fig. 111).

Evidence of the shipment of upholstered chairs from Boston prior to 1700 is scanty. In the absence of newspapers and intercoastal shipping records, only court records that note items in litigation provide additional facts. One such event was adjudicated on July 20, 1699, in the Suffolk County Court of Common Pleas: "Jonathan Everard of Boston, upholsterer," won a suit against "Maj. John March of Newbury, merchant and defendant . . . for not paying the sum of Seven pounds thirteen shillings justly due . . . for twelve chaires alias Leather Chairs sold and delivered to the Def[endan]t in December 1696, as per book may appear."[43] Again, it cannot be stated with certainty that these references from the 1690s incontrovertibly refer to leather chairs in the Cromwellian style; they may equally refer to plain-top high-back leather chairs made in the cane-chair style.

Upholstered chairs are found in American inventories prior to the date at which upholsterers are known to have been working here, and quantities of upholstery and drapery wares were likewise being imported into Boston and disseminated throughout New England and southward through the intercoastal trade. The vagueness of the references, such as £200 "worth [of] upholstrie," imported by Joshua Huse of Boston on the *Chapman* from London, July 21, 1648, do not reveal what upholstery materials were. On July 26, 1650, "one Turkie paragon"—a coarse camlet—was delivered from the *Swallow* to Boston merchant Elias Roberts. Richard Hutchins received "30 Russia Hydes" on the same ship. The "4 dozen calve skins in a hogshead" for one Mr. Creswick arrived on the *Mary* of Bristol on June 24, 1651, and may well have been destined for chairs. They may have been installed by a "saddler," "mercer," or "tailor," since in those years no upholder appears in the records.[44] On the other hand, these types of pliable and durable leather were also used for other items such as boots, gloves, saddles, bellows, and book covers.

Fig. 103. Joined chair with sealskin seat, probably New York, 1665–1700. Oak, maple, sealskin; H 36¾″ (93.3 cm), W 18¾″ (47.6 cm), D 15½″ (39.4 cm), SH 20″ (50.8 cm). (Old Saybrook Historical Society, Saybrook, Conn.)

Russia leather was made by tawing ordinary hides in an oil extracted from birch bark rather than in milk of lime. This process made the leather supple and less subject to rot, mold, and decay, and it is this type of leather that is found on virtually every surviving seventeenth-century and early eighteenth-century American leather chair. The leather has a characteristic crosshatching, often still visible (fig. 104), which is not a decorative feature but is a direct result of the method used to process the leather. The surface of the partially tawed skin was manually broken, perhaps with a sharp-edge board, perhaps with a metal or a bone scoring tool, to enable birch oil to penetrate the hide thoroughly.[45] The uniformity and fineness of the crosshatching on russia leather clearly contrasts with the coarse, deeply scored crosshatching on ordinary calf marked in imitation of russia leather that can be found on some English chairs.

The 1653 inventory of Robert Turner, a shoemaker of Boston, contained "17£ of Russia leather at 20d pr £ . . . 14:05:00," although no leather chairs were listed in his personal estate worth a total of £384.4.11. As yet, research has not revealed that the tawing of russia leather was being carried on in Boston, or anywhere in New England, at that time. For example, John Glover, a prominent Boston tanner, had the following items in his inventory:

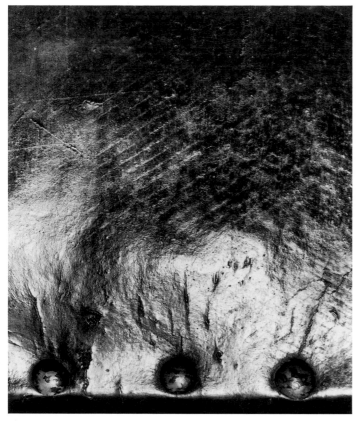

Fig. 104. Detail of distinctive cross-hatching pattern on the russia-leather upholstery on the chair in catalogue entry 45. (Winterthur 58.694.)

	[£ s. d.]
In dry leather	102.00.00
415 hydes in the Barke	600.00.00
45 hydes in the Lyme at 15sp hyde	33.15.00
313 west India hydes	187.00.00
15 hydes in the Lyme	11.05.00[46]

Conspicuously absent are russia-leather hides.

The sole surviving American example with another sort of upholstery leather is the Lady Fenwick chair (see fig. 103). This covering is sealskin (often spelled phonetically in inventories as "Soyle" skin). Properly speaking, sealskin is akin to a vellum and is not a tawed leather. It is cured by rubbing alum on the inner side of the hide and drying it to a stiff cardboardlike texture. During this period and on into the nineteenth century, sealskin was widely used to cover trunks and coffers. When stretched and affixed to the flat surfaces of such containers, sealskin was adequately supported. While references to sealskin chairs in inventories are not common, they occur frequently enough to suggest that some people liked the velvety texture of the hair which was left on the surface of the hides when they were cured. Yet it is perplexing to find this inflexible and brittle material being used on chairs, since chairs required flexible, yielding fabrics.

Although two essential components of chair upholstery are not itemized among Aspinwall's notes or merchants' inventories prior to the 1660s—girt web and brass nails—even more important for us is the absence of a craftsman identified as an upholsterer. The craft of the upholsterer was threefold in the colonial period. In one capacity, he was an importer, retailer, and wholesaler of English and European textiles that were used for the elaborate furniture associated with bedsteads, the upholsterer's main stock-in-trade. Considerable capital or credit was required to establish such a business, and the pertinent inventories suggest that this drapery or mercery trade made the upholsterer's craft equivalent to those of the goldsmith and the tanner in the hierarchy of profitable careers. Consistent with this, the documents reveal that a socially well placed group of second-generation New Englanders, such as Edward Tyng, Jr., and Ebenezer Savage, engaged in the business.

In his second role, the upholsterer was very much involved in the furnishing of drapery for funerals: renting funeral palls and other fixtures; supplying escutcheons or hatchments; arranging for such additional niceties as gloves, often from his own stock, memento mori rings from a goldsmith, and clothing for the relatives of the deceased; having the grave dug; arranging through a joiner or carpenter for the coffin; and supplying biers on which to lay the coffin during the period of watching the deceased.

The third role, the upholstering of chair frames made by another craftsman, was almost a sideline of small proportions and profit, and an aspect of the trade that cannot be documented in New England earlier than the appearance of William Allen in Boston in 1662—forty years after the settlement at Plymouth, thirty-three years after the establishment of the "Old Planters" at Naumkeag (Salem), and twenty-seven years after the settlement of Boston on the Shawmut peninsula.[47]

Randle Holme's *Academy of Armory* gives the clearest contemporary picture of how an upholsterered chair was made. Holme catalogued the "terms of Art" used by upholsterers "about their work in [making] a Stool or chair" as follows:

Girth it, is to bottom it with Girth Webb [i.e., saddler's girt web] stret drawn and crossed [interlaced].
Canvice it, is to nail the Canvice on the top of the Stool or Chair Frame, over the Girth Webb ["sacking" or "crocus," a loosely woven linen cloth, was also used].
Rowle it, is to put Rowls on the top edges [of the seat frame, usually marsh grass held by being whipped with a reed or other flexible shoot, if rolls or fox edges were used at all].
Stuffing, is to stuff it with Hay, Wool, Flocks or Feathers [marsh grass was the universal New England stuffing before horsehair was introduced about 1700].
Fringing, is to Nail the Fringe about the Stool seat at the sides [on leather chairs, strips of leather were used].
The Seat, is that place sitten upon.
Backing, is to Nail the Back on a Chair suitable to the Seat ["suitable to" means en suite].
Garnishing, is the finishing it with Brass Nails.[48]

The drapery and funerary aspects of the upholder's trade were obviously carried on in New England long before upholstered chairs were made. As the inventories and deeds of rural Massachusetts do not reveal the presence of upholsterers in the smaller villages, we must assume that this function was carried out as a sideline by local craftsmen and tradesmen for the most part. And when a member of the gentry died, his or her funeral was handled by Boston tradesmen.

Salem, the most important town in Essex County and the second largest in Massachusetts, did not have an upholsterer working until George Herrick arrived from England in February 1685/86. At the time of his death in 1695 Herrick possessed "6 lether" chairs of unstated values. No upholsterers other than Herrick have been found in the records of Salem or elsewhere in Essex County in the seventeenth century. Aside from John Wolfinden, who emigrated from England in 1683 and moved to Roxbury, where he may have worked for Joshua Lamb, we know of no other upholsterers who worked outside of Boston during the seventeenth century. That twelve upholsterers can be identified as working in Boston prior to 1700 further emphasizes the urban nature of the craft and points to Boston as the center of manufacture for upholstered chairs. This is further confirmed by the generic similarity of the fifty or more chairs attributed to Boston.[49]

Boston's first upholsterer was English-born William Allen (1637?–1674). By 1662, he was a young tradesman living in Boston. Allen was employed for the remaining twelve years of his life by Edward Tyng, Sr., a prominent brewer, merchant, and importer, and Allen probably taught the upholsterer's trade to Tyng's son, Edward, Jr. (b. 1649), who was identified as an "upholster" in a deed dated December 12, 1681. The elder Tyng was familiar with textiles and mercery ware, for on June 3, 1648, he attempted to pay a debt of £500 with "good woollen & linnen cloth & stuffs &c fresh & merchantable to the value of a thousand pounds" that he had in his possession in Boston at that date.[50] Allen was probably brought to New England to help satisfy the growing demand for upholstered furniture, which Tyng may well have been importing prior to Allen's arrival.

The younger Tyng may have in turn trained Ebenezer Savage in the upholsterer's trade. Savage (1660–1684) was the eighth son of the distinguished Thomas Savage, captain of the Ancient and Honorable Artillery Company of Boston. Because he was not likely to inherit much of his father's estate, the younger Savage saw in the upholsterer's trade an opportunity that he could not ignore. Savage saw opportunity as well in his marriage to Martha Allen, daughter of Capt. Bozoan Allen, wealthy Boston tanner, importer, selectman and representative.[51] Although his estate amounted to only £93.15.6 when he died at the age of 24, Savage's inventory is one of the great documents of seventeenth-century New England artisanal life. The items pertaining to his trade give by far the richest insight into the upholsterer's trade of that date and are quoted here in full.

INVENTORY OF THE GOODS OF EBENEZER SAVAGE, DECD:

	£ s. d.
Impr. 6 p[iece]s. darnix at 48s. 4d. p ps	14:10:00
It[em] 370 lb. Lizbon Feathers at 6d. p lb	9:05:00
It. 5 pa[ir] small stripd. curtains 17s. p pa., 3 pa. large Curtains 20s. p pa	7:05:00
It. 1 pa. faided green Curtains 21s., 13 cradle Ruggs at 34s. p ps.	3:04:00
It. 5 yd. red shaded cushion stuffe 3s. p yd	:15:00
It. 2 remnants cushion stuffe 11 yd. at 2s p yd., 2½ yd strip 't ditto 3s. p yd	1:09:00
It. 2 coverlets 15s., four yds. of Canvis in Remnants 3s.	:18:00

It. 12 guilt calves skins at 2s. 6d. p ps., four red calves skins & peices 6s.	1:16:00
It. 1 ps. girt web 2s. two cushion covers 18d.	:03:06
It. 2 m. brass nailes no. 6 at 8s. p m. 4 m. ditto no. 7 at 7s. p m.	2:04:00
It. 2 m. ditto no. 8 at 5[s.] 6[d.] p m., 7 m. burnisht nailes in small papers 12s.	1:03:00
It. 2 m. more brass nailes no. 7 at 7s. p m	:14:00
It. 2 fine silke button fringes 40s. p ps	4:00:00
It. 2 silke fringes with double x. 40s. p ps	4:00:00
It. one silke fringe 40s. 3¾ lb. silke fringe at 20s. p lb	5:15:00
It. Curtain rods 2[s.] 6[d.] 7¼ lb. worsted Fringe at 5[s.] 6[d.] p lb.	2:02:00
It. 4 small remnants of Ticken and one of buckram	:03:00
It. 2 damnified small Ruggs	:02:00
It. one beame and scales & one halfe hundred weight	1:00:00
It. one square Table 15s. three low leather chaires 15s	1:10:00
. . . It. 2 bu malt 7s three hamers, a pa. pincers 2 pa. Sheers 7s	:07:00
. . . It. one old trunke 3s. one Leather chest of drawers 15s	:18:00
. . . It. one old chest 2s. five yd. printed woolsey 13[s.] 4[d.].	:13:04[52]

During the 1680s and 1690s many upholsterers left the trade. Edward Tyng, Jr., inherited part of his father's vast mercantile empire in 1681 but probably worked very little at his trade. He began to dabble in politics and became successful on the eve of his death in 1701 en route to his new post as Governor of Nova Scotia. In 1684, Ebenezer Savage died. In 1693, Edward Shippen—who had made his fortune in real estate—moved to Philadelphia, where he became the first mayor. This left Jonathan Everard (w. 1688–1705) and Thomas Fitch (w. 1689?–1736) as the sole American-born upholsterers in the town. William Downes joined them around 1695. Downes (b. 1675) followed the pattern of the old mercer/upholsterers and was interested primarily in trade. He accumulated an estate amounting to £6,761, Old Tenor, by the time of his death in 1747.[53]

The gap was filled by immigrant upholsterers who are infrequently mentioned in the records of the affairs of the town; it can be concluded that they were merely skilled craftsmen whose impact on the community could be measured only in terms of good workmanship. In 1685, Alexander More was admitted a resident; in 1688, Joseph Juet appears, perhaps associated with Jonathan Everard; Harry Clarke worked there between 1688 and 1692; John Cutter or Cutler, perhaps a freeman of the London company of joiners, arrived in 1700, as did George Baker, also of London. After that, the record is silent, neither mentioning these men again nor advising of new arrivals until Ruppert Lord, who advertised "Cannopie Beds lately come from England" in 1714.[54]

CROMWELLIAN COUCHES

"Couch" is an ancient word in the English language. Chaucer used it in its classic sense in *The Legend of the Good Women* to signify a form of furniture upon which to recline or sleep, and indeed the English word implies its French origin in *coucher*, meaning "to lie down." Less than a century later the

Fig. 105. Edmond Marmion, *The Five Senses: Taste*. England, 1640–55. Engraving; H 5″ (12.6 cm), W 6⅝″ (16.9 cm). (Pepys Library, Magdalene College, Cambridge, by permission of the Master and Fellows. Photo: Edward Leigh.)

author of *Merlin, or the Early History of King Arthur, a Prose Romance* (circa 1450) used the word in such a way as to indicate that this type of furniture was also sat upon, so that the dual use of this form, as we find it throughout the seventeenth century, has precedents in England that date back for a considerable time.[55] Scattered references throughout sixteenth-century manuscripts and printed texts also refer to this form, or to something very much like it, as a "daybed," but this word virtually disappears in the texts of the seventeenth century and does not reemerge in common use until the nineteenth century. The labels "chaise longue" and "fainting couch" do not appear before the 1830s.

As is true with most words in a living language, the names of forms of furniture tend to remain constant through time while the forms they are used to describe undergo changes according to the dictates of fashion and the ingenuity of the craftsmen who made them. Some idea of the form of the couch in England in the generation prior to the settlement of America is given by an unusually informative warrant for payment found by R. W. Symonds among the British Royal Household accounts for the year 1585. The Royal Treasurer was directed to pay

To William Jasper for timber work of one couch of curled ash painted lutecolour and varnished, bottomed with girthwebb, and ironwork to the same, the price of the timberwork . . . £6.
To George Gower for painting and varnishing of the same £16
To Thomas Grene for bottoming of the same with girthwebb £1-6-8
To Gilbert Polson for iron work for the said couch . . . £2-3-4
To Edward Baker for making a mattrass, etc. [no amount given].[56]

The warrant reveals that several crafts were necessary to produce this couch and illustrates the division of labor among specialists in an urban area at that time. Foremost among these craftsmen was Jasper, who undoubtedly designed the couch, perhaps in collaboration with the upholsterers Grene and Baker. The frame was made completely of joined work, since

the turner's craft is not mentioned in the bill nor is it likely that the turners company of London would have permitted a turner to work in a joiner's shop at this point in its history. Jasper functioned as the "primary contractor" and was likely responsible for integrating the work of the other craftsmen into the finished product. That the frame was bottomed with girt web reveals the couch was designed to have an upholstered bottom. Grene clearly was an upholder, and so may Baker have been, but it is also possible that Baker was a mattress maker exclusively. Judging from contemporary upholsterers' bills, it is fair to bet Baker's "et cetera" may have cost considerably more than the total of the goods and services billed by the other craftsmen mentioned in the warrant. That the painter-stainer was to receive £6 for his portion of the job suggests that the frame had considerable woodwork, probably paneled ends like those on a couch in Hardwick Hall in Derbyshire.[57] The choice of ash for the frame instead of oak is uncommon for the period and may have been made because its relatively finer grain would permit the paint to adhere better than would oak, without sacrificing structural strength. The word *lutecolor* mentioned in the bill does not appear in the *OED* but the root word, *lute*, was a clay used by chemists and distillers to seal containers and by pipelayers to seal joints between ceramic pipes. Perhaps the lute was an earth pigment or a bole used to seal the grain of the ash prior to embellishing it with figures of some kind. The significance of the payment to Polson, the blacksmith, for "ironwork" is considered below.

The stylistic development of the couch in the seventeenth century can be reconstructed to some extent from engravings, surviving examples, and inventory references. It seems fairly certain that during the early years of the century the stylistic emphasis shifted from having a great deal of painted, joined paneling to being almost completely covered with textiles. A couch that bears evidence of this trend appears in a somewhat anachronistic engraving (fig. 105) by Sir Edmond Marmion, who flourished during the period of Charles I, Oliver Cromwell, and Charles II. The couch has the rigidly fixed, canted ends of earlier couches, more in the manner of a bedstead than a piece of seating furniture. It also has no back, as if it were intended to be used for sleeping, but it is curiously small in size and in the engraving is obviously being used for sitting. Moreover, it is being used in a room where food is being served. It is not easy to tell exactly what Marmion's sources were or whether the furniture that he illustrates represents contemporary English furniture or not. Marmion relied heavily on the engravings of Abraham Bosse for his inspiration, and many of the stools and andirons in his engravings are more French than English.

As furniture historian Peter Thornton has pointed out, some of the ambivalence surrounding the appearance and use of the couch may stem from its relationship to beds on the one hand and to chairs of state on the other.[58] In royal and aristocratic households, all three were used under canopies, or "sparvers," and were marks of extremely high station. Beds, couches, and chairs of state were often further dignified by a pair of flanking stools that were used only by court favorites. Thus it was possible for the connotations and actual use of beds to carry over into the use of the couch, whether it was the single-end style favored in France (the *couchette*) or the double-end version seen in the Marmion engraving. Monarchs, nobles, and princes of the church reinforced their status through the ceremony of receiving state visitors while in bed, lying propped up with bulky pillows, and certainly couches, with their canted ends, may have been used in this manner.

Inventory references from the third decade of the seventeenth century confirm the emphasis upon textiles in association with couches in the home of the English aristocracy. In 1620, the parlor of Lady Dorothy Shirley of Faringdon, Berkshire, contained "one silke couch or double chaire embroydred." The inventory of the household goods of the countess of Leicester, taken October 6, 1626, reveals that two couches had been added to the furnishings of Kenilworth Castle since the previous inventory of 1610. In the great parlor was "1 fayre cowch chaire of black feegured sattin, covered with yealowe cotton fringed," while in the "Dyeinge Chamber" was "1 fayre orrice worke couchchaire, covered with yealowe bayes."[59] The terms "couch chair" and "double chair" underscore the difficulty people had in distinguishing between a couch to lie upon and a couch to sit upon. They also point to the strong resemblance between frames of couches and those of armchairs in the Cromwellian style.

The famous couch at Knole, Sevenoaks, is illustrated in the *Shorter Dictionary* and suggests the high point of the completely upholstered couch.[60] In its original state (1625–45), the Knole couch probably had a heavy "bed," or "case," a mattress laid on the seat that brought the seat almost level with the tops of the arms. It probably also had thick bolsters and cushions, such as those attached to the falls on the arms. Additional features seen in that example are an extra fly of material under the back to fill in the gaps between the back panel and seat, rather like the valance on a bed, and similar flies or bases extending from the seat to the floor, again like those of a bed. These sumptuous fixtures, which even in American inventories sometimes are referred to as the "furniture" of the couch, confirm the idea that the couch was the single most expensive form of seating

furniture (except for beds) throughout the seventeenth century.

Show wood reappeared on the couch form—if it ever entirely disappeared from less costly examples—by 1641. The drawing chamber on the second floor of the new wing of Tart Hall in the earl of Arundel and Dorset's London palace contained a "Couch of painted wood on some partes thereof, thereon a Couch bed [heavy cushion or mattress] of red Damaske & two Long Cushions & Basis [bases] of ye same, the last fringed with Crimson silke & gold, the Couch and Cushions Couered & a foote Carpett of read Leather."[61] Despite the painted portions, this couch probably resembled the Knole couch in many respects.

By 1660, a notation in the Royal Household accounts shows that the couch had unmistakably taken on the shape that is illustrated by the relatively inexpensive example now at Rufford Old Hall, Rufford, Lancashire (fig. 106). The accounts record the payment of £1.13.4 to upholsterer John Younge for a "Couch Frame turned & with best Ironworke to it." Two further references in these accounts specify that John Whitby, a London joiner, supplied "for ye Drawing Room [at] Whitehall, 1 Large Couch frame with Iron worke."[62] The documented references to "ironwork" in English bills spanning 75 years become clear with this last quotation: this ironwork was the ratchet-and-keeper mechanism that allowed the great wings, or falls, mounted on the arms to be raised, lowered, or fixed in any of several intermediate positions between the horizontal and the vertical, as shown on the Rufford example (fig. 107). Evidence of the removal of similar iron work can be seen on the backs of couches in Essex Institute and Winterthur. The purpose of these upholstered falls remains unclear. Their iron supports and hinges were not strong enough to have borne much weight. Their adjustability may have been an effort to make them function as screens to block drafts. Alternatively, the falls may have been a holdover from the earlier form of the couch whose ends raised and lowered from a point near the side seat rails and permitted reclining when the couch was used for sleeping. Hinged at the arms, as they are on the Knole, Rufford, and related American examples, the falls will not admit of this use, unless heavy mattresses and pillows raised the back of a reclining person closer to the vortex of the angle of the upright arm and hinged fall.

No references to couches are recorded among the scanty probate files of the Prerogative Court of Canterbury, prior to an entry dated August 1, 1666, listing the property of Sir Thomas Corbett, baronet, of Wood Bostwick, Norfolk. In his drawing room were "two couch chayers one covered with Dornick"; another "couch-chayer" was located in the parlor chamber.[63] Before that date, however, couches had begun to appear in American inventories. One of the earliest references is in 1648: Peter Makakil left his heirs a "Cowtch," equivalent in worth to 40 pounds of tobacco, in his Maryland home. Others are mentioned in Maryland inventories of 1656 and 1657, the first in an estate that amounted to the value of 27,864 pounds of tobacco.[64]

Early references to couches are likewise found in Virginia inventories. Indeed, there are more of them relative to the number of inventories proved than are found in New England.

Fig. 106. Couch, England, 1640–60. Oak with leather upholstery; H 40½" (102.9 cm), W excluding wings 72¾" (185 cm), D 26¾" (68 cm). (Rufford Old Hall, Rufford, Lancashire, England. Photo: John A. Harrison, Southport, Lancashire, and the National Trust of England.)

Fig. 107. Detail showing curved ratchet-and-keeper mechanism on the couch in figure 106. (Rufford Old Hall, Rufford, Lancashire. Photo: John A. Harrison, Southport, Lancashire, and the National Trust of England.)

A couch is listed in the inventory of Elias Edmonds in 1654, another in the estate of Abraham Noone in 1656, and a third in that of Francis Cole in 1659. None of these is described or assigned monetary value, but the other furnishings of each house are fairly conventional for their time. There were "two couch beds" and "1 couch" in the 1663 inventories of Oliver Segar and Humphrey Owen. In 1675, the home of William Notlan of Lancaster County contained a "couch flock bed etc." valued at 300 pounds of tobacco while in the next year, the estate of Henry King had "1 couch bed & covering & furn[iture]" worth 250 pounds of tobacco. Some idea of what constituted "couch furniture" is conveyed by the 1679 inventories of William Smith of York County, which listed "1 couch & couch bedd, rug, blankett & pillow," and of Capt. John Underhill, which contained "1 old Couch, 1 old fether

bed, couch, 2 new fether billows [pillows]" valued at £1 sterling.[65] Other inventories indicate that such "furniture" was the usual accompaniment to couches. The conclusion is inescapable; many planters were using couches as beds, perhaps for guests, perhaps to escape from the heat of their great beds during the summer months. But these "couches" are ambivalent references. It is difficult to tell if the term refers to a wooden frame or to the heavy mattress or bed upon which the sleeper rested. It is even more difficult to divine from such references whether the use of couches for sleeping was derived from the elevated English practice of reclining upon couches in state or form a more mundane use of them as mere sleeping quarters.

So little is known about the furniture produced in the South before 1650 that it is difficult to say whether any of these couches were made in this country. Some of the less expensive examples may have been, but the better ones were undoubtedly imported from England where the tobacco raised by the planters was sold and where planters had credit with which to purchase goods. Similarly, the first couches mentioned in New England records came from England, and little evidence survives to suggest that the upholstery trade was a growing concern in New England before the 1650s. When the estate of Boston merchant William Tyng was appraised in October 1652, his hall contained "1 greene Couch laid wth a case" valued at £2.10. The couch was slipcovered en suite with a great chair, eight leather chairs with cases, and "1 old green Elboe chaire," valued together at £6. Elsewhere in Tyng's home was "1 great Quishion for a Couch" appraised at £1.

When the worldly goods of the Reverend John Cotton of Boston were listed in December 1652, his "studdy" contained a couch valued at 20*s*. On August 16, 1655, the hall chamber of the Reverend Nathaniel Rogers of Rowley, Massachusetts, contained "a couch & an old coverlet" valued at 7*s*., in addition to a completely furnished bedstead.[66] The richest of all the early couches recorded in New England inventories, unfortunately not described in detail, was valued at an impressive £7 and stood in the parlor of Henry Webb, a Boston merchant who died in 1660. Unlike the couches that appear in rooms that clearly were not regularly used for sleeping, and hence could be pressed into nocturnal service should an unexpected visitor arrive, Webb's couch was in the same room as his best bed and bedstead, and was doubtless used only in the daytime. When the inventory of Jonathan Mitchell, poet-minister of Cambridge, was taken on July 9, 1668, his parlor contained "1 couch to sleep on" worth 10*s*. The estate of respected magistrate Samuel Symonds of Ipswich, appraised in 1678, contained a "Couch chaire, leather Chaire & a Stoole" valued at £1 in the parlor chamber, while in the following year the inventory of his son, William, contained a "coutch chayer"—perhaps the same one—valued at 15*s*.[67]

A turkey-work couch, described as "1 Turkey wrought couch" valued at £1.5 en suite with "13 Turkey wrought chairs" worth £3.5 turns up in the 1682 inventory of the Honorable William Calvert of Calvert's Rest, St. Mary's County, Maryland. No reference specifying this rare form of furniture has been noted in a Massachusetts inventory prior to a listing of "a Couch & 8 turkie work chaires" in the study of the wealthy Reverend John Oxenbridge of Boston on January 5, 1674.[68]

An ingenious and tightly argued article by Robert F. Trent demonstrates that the extraordinary turkey-work couch made of American soft maple and now in the Essex Institute in Salem, Massachusetts, dates from after 1697. The covers of the couch were listed in the fashionable household of Capt. Thomas Berry, who was killed in 1696. At his death, his Boston home contained three different sets of turkey-work chairs and some "Turky Work for a Couch," valued at 16*s*., stored in a trunk in the "Dineing Room Chamber." The following year Berry's widow, Margaret, married John Leverett, at that time a young Harvard College graduate who was part of the liberal theological faction that was soon to found the Brattle Street church and to wrest control of Harvard College from the grip of the Mathers. In 1707, Leverett became the president of the college and with his wife removed to Cambridge. He died in 1724, and his inventory lists all the sets of chairs itemized in Berry's inventory, including "12 Large Turky Chairs & Couch" valued at £9. One of the executor's of Leverett's estate was his nephew, the Reverend Nathaniel Appleton of Cambridge. Appleton apparently kept the couch as a memento; it is next listed in a 1784 inventory in his "Great Room," identified as "A turkey wrought Settee," and valued at £1.10. This extremely rare and well-documented set of inventories tracing the descent of the couch suggests that Leverett had a couch frame made after his marriage to the

widow Berry in 1697. The descriptive terms in the Leverett inventory and the construction of the couch suggest that such high-back seating furniture was still fashionable in the late 1690s despite the introduction, several years earlier, of high-back upholstered chairs in the cane-chair style.[69]

The couch next passed from Nathaniel Appleton to his son Nathaniel, Jr., and was sold at a vendue, or estate auction, in 1819. The purchaser was Essex County antiquarian the Reverend William Bentley of Salem, who recorded his purchase in his diary:

This day I was at a Vendue where I received from the family of Appleton a settle which was formerly in the family of Dr. Appleton. Dr. Holyoke, now living aet. 91, & son of President Holyoke, near neighbor to Dr. Appleton at Cambridge, recollects the Settle for 80 years, & it is an antient part of the furniture of the family at Ipswich. It is not far from the form of those now used in our houses being stuffed in the back & seat as our Settees & Sophias are only open between the seat & Back. It appears to be worn, but not the parts seperated. The flowers are raised upon the ground not unlike our carpets. It is 5 feet long & 4 high & above 2 feet wide, in the frame. It has six feet, two in the middle, strongly framed together with rounds across & in front. The work is nowhere depressed by use but has its proper swell in the back & seat & it is nowhere rent or injuried by the want of any part. The sacking in the back & under the seat is sound. I was not a little pleased with the possession & I found no rival claims. All were willing to dispose of to a friend of the family what they feared to destroy & dared not disgrace.[70]

After Bentley's death late in 1819, the couch was repurchased by members of the Appleton family and donated to the historical society from which the Essex Institute was later formed.

According to Margaret Swain of Edinburgh, the most assiduous student of English turkey work, no other examples of couches with their original covers in place exist. The much-published couch at Aston Hall, Birmingham, apparently is a twentieth-century marriage of turkey work from a large carpet and a period couch frame.[71] Other turkey-work couches in collections like the Burrell collection in Glasgow also appear to be twentieth-century connoisseurs' wish fulfillment. The Essex Institute example is, therefore, quite important.

As was true of leather- and cloth-upholstered chairs made in seventeenth-century New England, the two earliest American couches were the work of urban craftsmen. The style of the turning with which they are ornamented is identical to that of the largest surviving group of leather chairs that, for the reasons discussed earlier in this section, appear to have originated in one shop or series of shops, and that shop had to have been located in a place where the clientele insisted on up-to-date furniture and high standards of workmanship. That the couches required the services of three separate crafts for their manufacture—those of the joiner, the turner, and the upholsterer—points to Boston as the only community to support all of those trades at one time between 1660 and 1700. Salem is the exception to this rule, and the three known upholstered-chair frames from that town are from a different shop tradition.

1 Shirley, "Inventory of the Effects of Henry Howard," p. 354.

2 Add. ms. 34,321 manuscripts department, British Museum, as copied in the Symonds Papers, DMMC 75 × 69.28, p. 75.

3 de Félice, *French Furniture in the Middle Ages*, p. 81; Havard, *Dictionnaire de l'ameublement*, 1:638; Thornton, "Back Stools and Chaises à Demoiselles," p. 103; Nichols, *Unton Inventories*, pp. 21–22.

4 Symonds Papers, DMMC 75 × 69.26, n.p., and 75 × 69.18, p. 8.

5 Arches Wills, no. 1669; Suffolk Probate, 2:139, 3:196.

6 Jeremias van Rensselaer to Jan van Rennsselaer, September 14, 1660. *Correspondence of Jeremias van Rensselaer*, p. 238; I am deeply indebted to Arlene Palmer Schwind for this reference.

7 Havard, *Dictionnaire de l'ameublement*, 1:636.

8 Halliwell, *Ancient Inventories*, pp. 141, 73; Arches Wills, no. 1979; Cust, "Notes on the Collections Formed by Thomas Howard," pt. 2, p. 98.

9 Arches Wills, no. 2112; for late, provincial versions of this style, see Agius, "Late Sixteenth and Seventeenth Century Furniture in Oxford," p. 77 and pl. 24B.

10 See Lyon, *Colonial Furniture*, fig. 60; Rijksmuseum (acc. no. 5837; cat. no. 189). I am indebted to T. H. Lunsingh Scheurleer for pointing out this relationship to me.

11 Suffolk Probate, 4:52.

12 Holme, *Academy of Armory*, 2: bk. 3, ch. 14, p. 14.

13 Cust, "Notes on the Collections Formed by Thomas Howard," pt. 3, p. 234. For the de Critz studio painting see Sotheby, Parke, Bernet, *Sale no. 3366: Fine Americana*; chair with "two gilte pomellis" is in the 1536 inventory of Catherine of Aragon as cited in Symonds Papers, DMMC 75 × 69.28, p. 92.

14 Agius, "Late Sixteenth and Seventeenth Century Furniture in Oxford," p. 77; McGrath, *Merchants and Merchandize in Seventeenth-Century Bristol*, p. 80; and Steer, *Farm and Cottage Inventories*, p. 90.

15 Brears, *Yorkshire Probate Inventories*, pp. 100–101, 124–25.

16 See Thornton, "Back Stools and Chaises à Demoiselles," p. 101, fig. 5, for an example at Knole which is believed to date from ca. 1625, although the furnishings of that house were sold in 1645; see Phillips, *History of the Sackville Family*, p. 355.

17 Atwood inventory, p. 153; Savage, *Genealogical Dictionary*, 1:77, says that he was "treasurer"; but see Willison, *Saints and Strangers*, p. 309, where he is called an "assistant governor."

18 Savage, *Genealogical Dictionary*, 1:467; Suffolk Probate, 2:51; *Aspinwall Notarial Records*, p. 416.

19 Suffolk Probate, 2:106, 136; 4:195; 5:288; New York Probate, Liber 2:152; Suffolk Probate, 10:412.

20 *Essex Probate*, 1:65, 2:226; Savage, *Genealogical Dictionary*, 2:289.

21 Harvard College Book, No. 5, citing Thomas Brattle's Journal, 1693–1713, p. 50; "Account-books of Treasurers of Harvard," p. 353 (I am indebted to Richard H. Saunders for pointing out this reference to me); Savage, *Genealogical Dictionary*, 2:169.

22 Suffolk Probate, 2:137–47; Symonds, "Turkey Work, Beech and Japanned Chairs," p. 224.

23 Heal, "Great Country House in 1623," p. 112. The entries suggest a room richly furnished with textiles en suite.

24 Steer, "Inventory of Anne, Viscountess of Dorchester"; Phillips, *History of the Sackville Family*, pp. 353–54; Prerogative Court of Canterbury, probate 2, no. 438.

25 As quoted in Symonds, "English Cane Chairs," pt. 1, p. 12.

26 Tattersall, *History of British Carpets*, pp. 37, 40–41, 51–52, 28; Halliwell, *Ancient Inventories*, p. 147; Symonds, "English Cane Chairs," pt. 1, pp. 14, 15.

27 Suffolk Probate, 2:48, 104, 141; *Essex Probate*, 2:448; Inventory of Governor John Haynes, June 31, 1654, Probate Files, Connecticut State Library.

28 Suffolk Probate, 4:151, 161.

29 See the catalogue entry by Joy Cattanach on the Freake portrait in Fairbanks and Trent, *New England Begins*, 3:460–61; Savage, *Genealogical Dictionary*, 2:202; Suffolk Probate, 5:294.

30 Suffolk Probate, 5:172, 12:48.

31 Hartford County Probate, 8:9–11; docket 24062, Essex Probate Files.

32 Suffolk Probate, 3:293, 4:54; Sewall, *Letter-book*, 1:44.

33 Suffolk Probate, 8:139.

34 Thomas Fitch to Benjamin Newberry, May 29, 1704, Fitch letterbook, AAS; I am indebted to Robert Blair St. George for this reference.

35 Docket 14045, Middlesex Probate; I am indebted to Robert F. Trent for this reference.

36 Swain, "Furnishing of Holyroodhouse," pp. 122–30, esp. p. 129.

37 King to Forman, February 4, 1976; I am indebted to William L. Goodman for putting me in touch with Mr. King.

38 See Trent, "Endicott Chair," pp. 103–19. Trent, "Two Seventeenth-Century Salem Upholstered Chairs," pp. 34–40.

39 Suffolk Probate, 7:255, 263; Savage, *Genealogical Dictionary*, 4:33.

40 Savage, *Genealogical Dictionary*, 4:39–40; *Suffolk Deeds*, 4:307; Suffolk Probate, 4:60–62, 12:286–87, 13:47–48, 11:163–64.

41 Trent, "Two Seventeenth-Century Salem Upholstered Chairs," pp. 34–40.

42 I am indebted to Robert F. Trent for calling my attention to this chair.

43 Suffolk Common Pleas, 2: leaf 5 verso.

44 Huse also may have been spelled Hewes, see Savage, *Genealogical Dictionary*, 2:407–8; *Aspinwall Notarial Records*, pp. 406–7, 414, 415, 430. Saddlers, in particular may have functioned as upholsterers since their familiarity with working with leather girt webbing and such provided them with the materials and skills most necessary for furniture upholstery.

45 A description of this process is in Beman, *Mysteries of Trade*, p. 108: "Calf skins being steeped in a weak bath of carbonate of potass and water, are well cleaned and scraped to have the hair, &c., removed. They are now immersed in another bath, containing dog and pigeon dung in water. Being thus freed from the alkali, they are thrown into a mixture of oatmeal and water to undergo a slight fermentation. To tan these hides, it is necessary to use birch bark instead of oak bark; and during the operation they are to be frequently handled or agitated. When tanned, and perfectly dry, they are made pliable by oil and much friction; they are then to be rubbed over gently with birch tar, which gives them that agreeable odour, peculiar to this kind of leather, and which secures them against the attacks of moths and worms. This odour the leather will preserve for many years; and on account of it, Russia leather is much used in binding handsome and costly books." See also Davis, *Manufacture of Leather*, pp. 574–81; and Johns, *Forest Trees of Britain*, p. 212.

46 Suffolk Probate, 2:74, 3:3–4; Savage, *Genealogical Dictionary*, 4:348.

47 *Suffolk Deeds*, 4:71.

48 Holme, *Academy of Armory*, 1: bk. 3, ch. 3, p. 97.

49 Belknap, *Trades and Tradesmen*, p. 85; docket 13126, Essex Probate Files; Perley, *History of Salem*, 3: 200; Boston Records, 10:73.

50 *Suffolk Deeds*, 4:71, 225; Savage, *Genealogical Dictionary*, 1:37; Boston Records, 14:3, 17; 10:30; *Aspinwall Notarial Records*, p. 131.

51 See Davidson, *Life in America*, 1:57; and Savage, *Genealogical Dictionary*, 1:29, 4:23.

52 Suffolk Probate, 9:264–65.

53 Savage, *Genealogical Dictionary*, 4:357, 87; 2:65; Boston Records, 9:138; Suffolk Probate, 40:441.

54 Boston Records, 10:61, 1:142; Suffolk Probate, 10:142; Suffolk Common Pleas, 1: leaf 18, 2: leaves 104, 108 verso; Company of Joyners, leaf 153 recto; Suffolk Common Pleas, 2: leaf 61 verso; Dow, *Arts and Crafts in New England*, p. 106.

55 *OED*, s.v. "couch."

56 Symonds Papers, DMMC, 75 × 69.28, p. 122. (Symonds's citation is "L.C. 9, 73." The instrument is dated December 28, 1582.)

57 This couch is illustrated in Edwards, *Shorter Dictionary*, p. 264, fig. 1.

58 Thornton, *Seventeenth-Century Interior Decoration*, pp. 172–74.

59 Nichols, *The Unton Inventories*, p. 18; Halliwell, *Ancient Inventories*, pp. 88, 91.

60 See Edwards, *Shorter Dictionary*, p. 264, fig. 2. According to an inventory in Phillips, *History of the Sackville Family*, pp. 353–70, the furnishings of Knole were sold at vendue late in 1645. The present couch may well have been brought to Knole from some other Sackville family house, or may postdate 1645. In the inventory of the house dated September 30, 1645, "1 Guilt Couch," with "1 Damaske Cover" is in the withdrawing chamber between the "Great Dyning Roome" and the "Queenes Chambr." It is the only couch in the major rooms used by the family.

61 Cust, "Notes on the Collections Formed by Thomas Howard," pt. 2, p. 99. "Basis," according to Randle Holme, were "the lower Valens at the seat of the Bed, which reacheth to the ground, and fringed for state as the vper Valens, either with Inch fring, caul fring, Tufted fring, snailing fring, Gimpe fring with Tufts and Buttons, Vellem fring, &c." (*Academy of Armory*, 2: bk. 3, ch. 14, p. 16.)

62 Symonds Papers, 75 × 69.18, p. 10; Symonds, "Charles II. Couches, Chairs and Stools," pt. 1, pp. 19–20.

63 Prerogative Court of Canterbury, probate 5, no. 1872.

64 *Maryland Archives*, 51:386–87, 100–102, 81. I am indebted to Arlene Palmer Schwind for the first of these references.

65 Lancaster County, Va., Deeds, 1:2–4, 28, 68, 271; Lancaster County, Va., Wills, 5:15–16, 13–14; York County, Va., Wills, 5:138, 437–38; I am indebted to Patrick Henry Butler III for these references. It should be noted that the currency referred to in most estates is a colonial currency (Mass., N.Y., Pa., etc.) rather than the more highly valued pound sterling.

66 Suffolk Probate, 2:138, 140, 108; *Essex Probate*, 1:225.

67 Suffolk Probate, 4:53; Middlesex Probate, 5:284 (I am indebted to Robert F. Trent for this reference); *Essex Probate*, 3:269, 304.

68 Maryland Probate, Liber 2:206 (I am indebted to Arlene Palmer Schwind for this reference and to Cary Carson for pinpointing the exact location of Calvert's Rest); Suffolk Probate, 5:225.

69 Trent, "History for the Essex Institute Turkey Work Couch," pp. 29–37.

70 Bentley, *Diary*, 4:595.

71 Swain to Forman, May 29, 1977; Woodall, "Furniture at Aston Hall," pp. 59–64.

45.
LEATHER CHAIR, RUSSIA- or RED-LEATHER CHAIR, or
LOW-BACK CHAIR
Boston, Massachusetts
1665–1695
WOODS: Legs and stretchers, red maple (*Acer rubrum*); seat frame and back rails,
red oak (*Quercus rubra*)
OH 36″ (91.4 cm)
SH 21″ (53.3 cm), SW 18″ (45.7 cm), SD 15¼″ (38.7 cm)
PROVENANCE: Found by Harry Arons between Salem and Boston, Mass.;
Charles Montgomery; Henry Francis du Pont
58.694

Fig. 108. Detail of original sackcloth bottom and girt web of the leather chair in
catalogue entry 45. (Winterthur 58.694.)

Little seventeenth-century furniture survived the eighteenth and nineteenth centuries without repairs, or the twentieth century without restoration. The present chair is a remarkable exception inasmuch as its frame has undergone no restoration and, except for the replacement of parts of the trim strip around the seat and a subtle coat of green lacquer over the leather, it is a remarkably pristine example of what such chairs looked like between 1660 and 1695 when they were popular in most urban centers and used throughout New England. Only three other chairs from this shop tradition retain their original upholstery foundations and leather covers: the Endicott great chair (Museum of Fine Arts, Boston); a chair with no known history that was found in New Brunswick, New Jersey (Museum of Fine Arts, Boston); and a chair with a history of ownership in Connecticut (Wadsworth Atheneum, Hartford). Two other examples (Newport Historical Society, Rhode Island; Henry Ford Museum and Greenfield Village, Dearborn, Michigan) retain fragments of their webbing, sackcloth, and grass stuffing. The same sort of green lacquer, apparently a nineteenth-century attempt to preserve leather, is on a New York-made William and Mary armchair (Museum of Fine Arts, Boston).

The legs and stretchers of Winterthur's chair are made of red maple (*Acer rubrum*), a close-grained wood generally preferred to beech by the turners and joiners of Massachusetts for its soundness in the unworked state, the beauty of its surface, which required relatively little smoothing beyond that received from the gouges used to shape it on the lathe, and the uniformity of its grain, which permitted even staining. The seat rails, back rails, and adjacent stay rail are of red oak (*Quercus rubra*), a wood whose extra strength recommended it for those parts of a piece of furniture where thin tenons had to sustain major stresses. Oak was slightly less expensive than maple, and its rather open-grain structure was not objectionable since these rails were to be covered by the upholstery. Occasionally upholstered-chair frames from this shop tradition are all maple, and far more often the side and rear stretchers are made of oak.

The use of oak for seat rails, stretchers, and back rails persisted in the Boston and New York upholstered-chair traditions well into the eighteenth century. The earliest Boston upholstered chairs represent the first major instance in which colonial furniture makers departed from the habitual European practice of using oak as a primary or "show" wood. English joiners tended to use oak or beech, and their most expensive chairs were either walnut or painted-and-gilded beech. While one American example which may have been made in New York is made entirely of oak (Pocumtuck

Valley Memorial Association, Deerfield, Massachusetts), a Salem example (Museum of Fine Arts, Boston), and another New York example (Society for the Preservation of Long Island Antiquities, Setauket, New York) are made in whole or in part of ash.

Many leather chairs also possess a feature that was not used on wainscot or turned chairs previously made in New England: turned ornament on the rear stiles between the seat and the back panel. The ornament is on a part of the stiles that cants 14 degrees from the vertical, and thus required a special lathe to execute it. (This is more fully discussed at catalogue entry 52.) The English chair illustrated in figure 94 does not have this extra touch, although numerous other contemporary English examples do. Nor was it used on the Endicott great chair (Museum of Fine Arts, Boston) and a number of other chairs from that shop tradition that, instead of turnings, have chamfers on the inner surface of the stiles. Whether the presence or absence of this extra turning is of chronological significance cannot be judged on the basis of known documented examples. And it does not necessarily follow that chairs with this type of turning cost more, since the extra labor was offset by the need to cover the stiles with leather at analogous points on plain examples.

The characteristic surface appearance of the russia leather on Winterthur's chair is shown in detail in figure 104. The original sackcloth or crocus bottom and girt web are intact; the stitches in the center of these go through the marsh-grass stuffing and were intended to inhibit shifting (fig. 108). A single row of original brass nails along the top edge of the trim around the seat, balanced by corresponding iron tacks along the bottom edge of the trim, is the original treatment. No brass nails garnish the trim strip on the rear of the seat frame. These nails are shallow in profile, and in addition to the usual copper and zinc found in seventeenth-century brass, they contain a surprisingly low 0.01 percent of silver, 0.5 percent tin, 0.5 percent lead, and a trace of antimony as impurities. A red stain, containing traces of iron, appears to have been the original finish of the wood; however, these chairs may have been among

the first American forms to have received walnut-colored varnishes. (Such varnishes are often found on this type of frame and are too uniform in character to have been added later by various repairmen.)

In the seventeenth century, russia leather was usually red, the dye being worked into the leather as it was tawed. And when "red" leather is specified in the inventories, it is almost certain that the chairs were covered in russia leather. The leather of Winterthur's chair is permeated with red, but this is covered by the green lacquer. That the lacquer covers the heads of the brass nails as well as worn or broken places in the leather itself indicates the lacquer is not original. Furthermore no references to painted leather chairs have been found among the pro-

bate records of Suffolk County, although among the possessions that an otherwise unidentified "Mr. Allen of Barbadoes [left] at Mehitabel Munnings" in Boston were "2 painted Leather Quishons and Carpitt" valued at 10s. on March 6, 1659/60.[1]

In 1596 an English translation of a Dutch book gave instructions for dyeing leather: "To dye red felles [hides] ye shall seeth Lacke [probably madder lake, a red pigment] in bene straw and a cursy [curtsy – a small quantity of] pisse. . . . Then put therein so much as two great beanes, and then take in ounce of brasill water [another red dye extracted from brazilwood] and so let them seeth together."[2]

Most of the painted or gilded leathers found in inventories

were of Dutch or Spanish manufacture. Characteristically both painted and gilded leathers received sealer coats of gamboge, an organic resin from Cambodia, which yields a yellow pigment. In fact, gilded leathers were not really gilded; they were silver-leafed and became golden in hue after the application of gamboge.[3] Such must have been the gilded calfskins listed in Ebenezer Savage's inventory (see p. 208).

Finally, Winterthur's chair also has a light canvas with a green-glazed surface attached to the rear surface of the back panel to conceal the sackcloth inside the panel's frame. While the manner in which this canvas or dressed duck is attached suggests that it is a later addition, another chair frame with

original upholstery made in Boston (Museum of Fine Arts, Boston) has an original lining of this same green duck. And a frame with twist ornament and original upholstery (North Andover Historical Society, Massachusetts) has a green glaze applied directly to the sackcloth on the rear of the back panel.

NOTES
[1] Suffolk Probate, 3:380.
[2] *A Booke of Secrets*, folios 4–42.
[3] For an excellent analysis of seventeenth-century colors, see Jonathan L. Fairbanks, "Portrait Painting in Seventeenth-Century Boston," in Fairbanks and Trent, *New England Begins*, 3: 449–53.

46.
LEATHER CHAIR or LOW-BACK CHAIR
Boston, Massachusetts
1665–1695
WOODS: Stiles and stretchers, red maple (*Acer rubrum*); seat frame and back rails, red oak (*Quercus rubra*)
OH 34⅝″ (87.9 cm)
SH 19½″ (49.5 cm), SW 18″ (45.7), SD 15″ (38.1 cm)
PROVENANCE: Henry V. Weil; Henry Francis du Pont
54.524

This chair and the chairs in the preceding and the following entry are extremely uniform, a characteristic of the standard, Boston, upholstered-chair frame; however, certain variations can be observed among the fifty or more Boston examples known to survive. Some have higher backs, and others have lower seats—the latter achieved by eliminating one ball from each pair of ball turnings on the front stiles. (The variations in seat height may have been related to rituals of seating precedence, with the higher seats indicating higher status.) Some frames lack turnings between the seat rails and the back panel. Others have one stretcher on each side instead of two. Occasionally the two central-ball turnings and reeded disk of the front stretcher are eliminated in favor of an unpunctuated series of ball turnings. The shape of the turned foot can be stubby, or, as on one frame (Wadsworth Atheneum, Hartford), elongated fully 2″ (5.1 cm) more. And, of course, other woods can be used.

That the workmen who were producing the frames were not infallible is demonstrated by mistakes visible on some frames. Defective stretchers were used, with large knots and checks. Often the blanks from which the stiles or front stretcher were fashioned have an imperfect grain structure or were squared up too small to accommodate a full turning; in such cases, the resulting flattened or irregular face was simply positioned in so that it did not show on the completed frame. One frame (Museum of Fine Arts, Boston) was fashioned with a front seat rail cut too long for the frame, but the joiner used it anyway and, as a result, the front legs are out of line. Apparently the purchaser did not object, and the chair has survived three centuries of use.

An old photograph of this chair and the chair in catalogue entry 47 in the object files at Winterthur shows that both chairs were in poor condition, having suffered much from water damage, but were an identical pair that had survived together. The old photograph also reveals that the upholstery of the backs had already been restored once. The present hide on the back is unusually thick and is not russia leather, so it probably is not original. This chair does retain its original girt web, sackcloth, and seat cover. The trim around the seat is a restoration and is incorrectly attached, double nailed instead of single nailed as on the preceding example.

CROMWELLIAN-STYLE UPHOLSTERED CHAIRS AND COUCHES 217

47.
TURKEY-WORK CHAIR, LEATHER CHAIR, or
LOW-BACK CHAIR
Probably Boston, Massachusetts
1670–1695
WOOD: Right rear seat rail, soft maple (genus *Acer*)
OH 35¼″ (89.4 cm)
SH 19″ (48.3 cm), SW 18⅜″ (46.7 cm), SD 17⅜″ (44.1 cm)
PROVENANCE: History of ownership in Bradford family of Duxbury and
Kingston, Mass.; Henry V. Weil; Henry Francis du Pont
58.695

The seventeenth-century inventories of urban New England abound in chairs of this style upholstered with cloth fabrics. After turkey work and leather came green serge as a poor third in popularity. Other fabrics were red serge and blue serge, yellow damask (often a woolen textile rather than silk one), velvet (again, often wool as well as silk), camlet, plush, printed woolsey, wrought, needlework, Irish stitch, and "striped worked."

The present example was reupholstered about 1948 with two fragments of turkey work that had belonged to the Bradford family of Duxbury and Kingston, Massachusetts. No turkey work appears in the inventories of either Gov. William Bradford (d. 1657) or his widow Alice (d. 1670), but this is a matter of indifference, since it is probable these pieces were nineteenth-century reproductions following period patterns.

A turkey-work–chair back (Museum of Fine Arts, Boston)

as well as original covers on three Boston chair frames (two at the Metropolitan Museum of Art, one at the New York State Department of Education, Albany) demonstrate that chair seats and backs were woven with a flowered field surrounded by either a narrow red, white, and black striped border or occasionally a checkered or chevron border. Beyond this border was a half-inch wide finished selvedge pile. On chair frames the turkey work was invariably trimmed with a multicolored fringe woven of the same woolen crewel as the woven panels. The ½″ (1.3 cm) head, or braided part, of the fringe was nailed over the fabric selvedge at 2½″ (6.4 cm) intervals. Some of the brass nails on the Essex Institute turkey-work couch (see fig. 112) still retain fragments of the heading of the fringe that ran around the edges of the seat, back, and arms.

The use of fringes also accounts for a number of other design features. On all known examples of these frames, the turned ornament of the front stiles beneath the seat rails and of the rear stiles below the lower rail of the back panel always begins about 1½″ (3.8 cm) *below* the juncture of stiles and rails. Fringes including the heading were 2″ (5.1 cm) wide. The fringe hung down to the beginning of the turned ornament. Some idea of the appearance of a suite of green serge upholstered and fringed furniture can be gained from a couch, armchair, six chairs, and two stools produced by Douglas Campbell, Andrew Passeri, Constance LaLena, and Robert F. Trent in 1980–81 (fig. 109).

Fig. 109. Douglas Campbell, Andrew Passeri, Constance LaLena, and Robert F. Trent, reproductions of late seventeenth-century Cromwellian-style upholstered furniture, 1980–81. (Courtesy Saugus Iron Works, National Historic Site, Saugus, Mass.) The furniture is displayed in the parlor chamber of the iron works house.

CROMWELLIAN-STYLE UPHOLSTERED CHAIRS AND COUCHES   219

48.
*WALNUT CHAIR, WOODEN-BOTTOM CHAIR, or
LOW-BACK CHAIR*
Probably Philadelphia, Pennsylvania
1683–1705
WOODS: Seat, white oak (*Quercus alba*); remainder of chair, black walnut
(*Juglans nigra*)
OH 39¼″ (99.7 cm)
SH 17⅝″ (44.8 cm), SW 18⅞″ (47.9 cm), SD 19⅜″ (49.2 cm)
PROVENANCE: Descendants of Robert Pearson, Crosswick's Creek, N.J.;
J. Stodgell Stokes; Joe Kindig, Jr.; Henry Francis du Pont
57.1389

The British Royal Household accounts for 1672 contain a bill from Richard Price, a London joiner, for "back Chair frames turned all over wth the twisted turne." The description aptly fits the present chair. (Regrettably no similarly detailed description has been found in a contemporary American inventory.) Thanks to the incomparable research of R. W. Symonds, it is possible to be even more precise about the contemporary English names and names for the type of turning. Twist turning is first mentioned in the Royal Household accounts in 1671, and is variously referred to by different furniture craftsmen. Richard Price built chairs that were "French turned all over." Twelve years later, in 1683, he furnished chairs "turned of the Dutch turning." While Dutch turning and French turned may be synonymous they may equally well be different. French turned may have signified a single spiral of the type that is common on French furniture and is occasionally found in England, while Dutch turning may have referred to the double type, which is much more common on Netherlandish chairs. Whether this idea is correct or not, the type of turning on Winterthur's chair is also referred to by Price as "twisted double" in a bill dated 1678.[1]

Winterthur's chair is one of the rarest survivals of the American framed-chair maker's art and was undoubtedly equally rare in its time because of the large amount of labor required to make it. It is one of two side chairs found in New Jersey. The other example (Philadelphia Museum of Art) was found prior to 1925 in "a forgotten attic of one of the oldest houses in the neighborhood of Hamilton Square, New Jersey." The Winterthur chair was purchased on March 20, 1948, at the sale of the J. Stodgell Stokes collection. A small piece of ruled notebook paper pasted under the seat of the chair may be the "family records" mentioned by Wallace Nutting when this chair was illustrated as no. 2087 in the *Furniture Treasury*. The label, now faded and completely illegible, was transcribed in 1925: "This chair belonged originally to the first Robert Pearson. He immigrated to America in A.D. 1680, settled on Crosswicks Creek. The chair was manufactured A.D. 1699, the same date as the old chest. Robert Pearson died A.D. 1704."[2]

While this statement has the ring of authority to it, the inventory of "the Goods, Chatteles and Credits of Robert Pearson of Nottingham in the Country [County] of Burlington, yeoman," recorded on May 4, 1704, does not incontrovertibly confirm it. Only a few chairs are in the inventory. "Sum old Chairs 2 tables A box of Drawers" are valued at £3.18. If, as the label states, the chair was made in 1699, it is not likely that the chair would be considered "old"

only 5 years later. Nor could this chair and five more like it be worth so slight a sum as the 18*s*. that "4 old boxes and 6 chairs" were assessed—a maximum of 3*s*. per chair, if the boxes had no value at all. Moreover, the absence of any mention of cushions for chairs such as this one, which was specifically designed to have a cushion, casts serious doubt as to whether Pearson's inventory lists this particular chair.[3] Furthermore, research has failed to reveal the existence of a chairmaker at Crosswick's Creek in the last quarter of the seventeenth century. Indeed, this chair so closely follows its English prototypes and is of such high quality in conception and workmanship itself that it suggests the hand of a highly trained urban craftsman rather than a rural joiner. It forms a striking contrast to the straight-turned examples illustrated by Symonds in his articles, although he does illustrate two examples very much like it, one of which is noteworthy for its twist-turned elbows, or arms, in the French manner.

While for classification purposes this chair could be said to be in the Cromwellian style, its size as well as its ornamentation show that it is a later example and probably was made during the period of the Stuart restoration. It partakes of the new concepts of design that made their way into English furniture after 1660. Generally, such chairs have slightly higher backs than the Dutch-inspired New England chairs (see catalogue entries 45–47), which belong to an earlier phase of the style. (Compare also with the Italian chair of the mid seventeenth century illustrated as fig. 121.) The high-back style, however, *did* exist in New England leather and turkey-work chairs which similarly date after 1675 or so.

A comparison of the measurements of the present chair with those of the classic Boston leather chair illustrated in catalogue entry 45 dramatizes this difference. The width of both seats is about the same. Every other dimension, however, is quite different and gives the Pearson chair a different look despite its generic similarity to the others: the back is 3″ (7.6 cm) taller, the seat is 4″ (10.2 cm) deeper, and the seat itself is 3½″ (8.9 cm) closer to the floor. (The last dimension may indicate that the seat was designed to accommodate a cushion.)

Several pieces of furniture with the "twisted turne" can be identified in Massachusetts work. A leather-upholstered chair made of American beech (*Fagus grandifolia*)—a rare, early use of that wood—has no history of ownership but exhibits good quality twist turning and is doubtless of Boston origin (North Andover Historical Society, North Andover, Massachusetts). A related example from the same shop also survives (Congregational Library, Boston), as does a pair of extraordinary upholstered-chair frames, probably covered with leather originally, that have the same stretcher ornament and upholstered seats and backs but are made of American silver maple (*Acer saccharinum*) (Historic Winslow House Association, Marshfield, Massachusetts). A table with similar twist ornament and "falling leaves" was owned by Charles R. Waters of Salem and is illustrated in Esther Singleton's *Furniture of our Forefathers* (p. 200); its present whereabouts are unknown. None of these examples, with the possible exception of the Marshfield chairs, displays the bold turning of the Pearson chair.

To cut a spiral or a double twist demands careful workmanship on the part of the turner. That this technique

Fig. 110. Detail of double-twist turning on the chair in catalogue entry 48. (Winterthur 57.1389.) Note the marks left by the rasp.

Fig. 111. Leather-upholstered chair with twist turning; Swedish style; probably made in Philadelphia, but possibly in New York, 1685–1720. American red oak (*Quercus rubra*); fragments of the original foundation and leather cover still remain; H 38″ (96.5 cm), W 19″ (48.3 cm), D 17¼″ (43.8 cm). (Yale University Art Gallery, New Haven, Conn., anonymous gift.)

was not common in the English colonies in the seventeenth century is indicated by the survival of so few objects with it. Lathes to cut screws are mentioned in the technological literature of Europe as early as the *Mittealterlichen Handbuch* of about 1480. In this book, a handmade lead screw engages a movable tool rest that cuts a spiral as the lead screw and the work attached to it turn together. A similar arrangement was illustrated by Jacques Besson in *Theatrum instrumentorum et machaninarum* (1563; pl. 13). This is essentially the same principle used by Henry Maudsley when he reinvented this type of screw lathe in the late eighteenth century. Another type, in which the work rather than the cutting tool moved, was illustrated by Jacob Leupold in *Theatri machinarum*. Yet evidence of such labor-saving devices has not been found in an American craftsman's inventory prior to 1756.

Except in the instance of an undatable and unusual candlestand at the Essex Institute, the double-twist-turned elements on American furniture were shaped rather slowly and laboriously with a handheld rasp. The rasp produced a rough, irregular surface. The cut was made with short strokes that left easily recognized marks in contrast to the smooth, continuous cut produced by a traversing gouge that could run the entire length of the piece in one movement (fig. 110).

Crosswick's Creek was a short and convenient boat ride from Philadelphia, and so perhaps Philadelphia was the place of origin of the Pearson chair. If the cane chair of English walnut (*Juglans regia*) illustrated by Esther Singleton was owned by William Penn, as tradition holds, or by one of his contemporaries, a taste of twist turning was present in the community. Even more persuasive proof is provided by a singularly important leather chair in the Swedish style; it is made of red oak (*Quercus rubra*) and retains fragments of its original, Swedish-style foundation and leather covers (fig. 111). While it may have been made in New York, it is far more likely that this chair was made in Philadelphia sometime between 1685 and 1720 by a Swedish craftsman. Its large size, French-inspired single-twist turnings and high back parallel a number of Swedish examples, and the chair forms a counterpoint to the English-looking Pearson chair.

Because of their resemblance, the Swedish-style example in figure 111 superficially appears to be the prototype upon which the Pearson chair was based. Closer study of the two raises a more likely explanation: both chairs are from the same set and were made by an immigrant chairmaker who had been accustomed to making this kind of chair in England. This

craftsman probably came from London, where such chairs were being made in the 1670s and 1680s. Further evidence of a Pennsylvania origin is furnished by the manner in which the seat is executed. The two tongue-and-groove boards of white oak which compose the bottom are fitted into a plowed groove ½″ (1.3 cm) below the upper rim of the seat frame, perhaps to permit the more convenient use of a cushion that then could be fitted in the recess and would not have to be tied to the rear stiles to remain firmly in place. This type of recessed seat bottom is common in Pennsylvania walnut chairs of the wainscot type.

Among the many Philadelphia craftsmen who could have made the Pearson chair, John Fellows and Richard Gove are likely candidates. Fellows had come to Philadelphia in 1682 and was listed as a "Cabenett Maker" at that time, although Abraham Hooper, the joiner who took his inventory on October 12, 1694, calls him a "joyner." Among the items in Fellows's shop were "6½ of Round wall-nutt Loggs" worth £6.10, "219 foot wall-nutt-plank" worth £1.15, "240 foot wall-nutt-boards" £1.8.6, "350 foot of oak boards" £1.8, "3 turning chisells and one leathe" £2, "a parcell turning tooles" 7s., "file[,] chisells" 6s., "one leathe, one drawing knife, one rasp nippers" £4.6, "one dozen Chair frames" worth £4.4, along with considerable unfinished case furniture, and all the usual joiner's tools such as planes, bits, augers, saws, and so forth.[4] Gove, from Plymouth, England, had settled in Philadelphia by 1687, made his will in 1707, and died before 1710, when the will was proved. Gove, in addition to walnut "Stuffe," possessed joiner's tools, "carving tools, 1 dozen of files and rasps, two turning lathes [one with a great wheel]," and other tools.[5]

NOTES
[1] As cited in Symonds, "Charles II. Couches, Chairs, and Stools," pt. 2, pp. 86–87, 90; and in Symonds, "Cane Chairs of the Late 17th and Early 18th Centuries," pp. 177–78.
[2] Object file 57.1389, Registrar's Office, Winterthur.
[3] New Jersey Probate, 1:305–8.
[4] Philadelphia Wills, 1694-104.
[5] Philadelphia Wills, 1688-53, 1710-181.

49.
COUCH
Boston, Massachusetts
1660–1700
WOOD: Maple (genus *Acer*)
OH 42⅛" (107.0 cm)
SH 16¼" (41.2 cm), SW 65½" (166.4 cm), SD 25⅛" (63.8 cm)
PROVENANCE: Joe Kindig, Jr.; Henry Francis du Pont
58.698

The many affinities between Winterthur's couch frame and that in the Essex Institute (fig. 112) indicate that both were made by the same Boston shop. While some of the difference in the height of the back may be accounted for by the splice that joins the tops of the rear posts with the crest, the overall differences between the two may stem from problems posed in the initial effort of making a frame to fit the dimensions of an

cat. 49

Fig. 112. Couch with turkey-work covering. Frame: Boston, oak and maple; textile: probably Norwich, England, wool and linen. H 45¼" (115.6 cm), W 59⅝" (151.5 cm), D 28⅛" (71.4 cm), SH 15¼" (38.7 cm). (Essex Institute, Salem, Mass.)

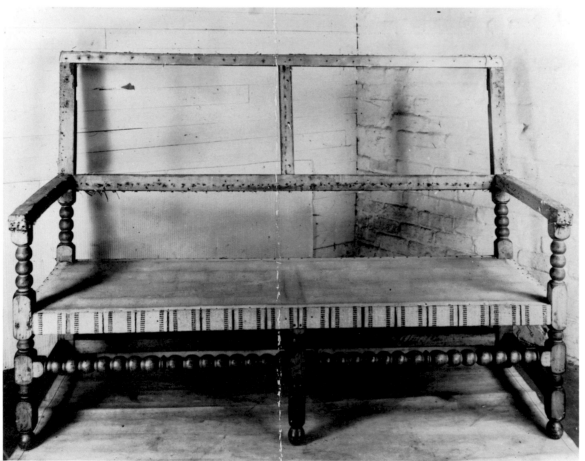

Fig. 113. Old photograph of the couch in catalogue entry 49. (Winterthur 58.698.)

Fig. 114. Detail showing where the dovetail hinge fit on the back and arms of the couch in catalogue entry 49. (Winterthur 58.698.)

existing set of turkey-work covers. The history of the Essex Institute couch suggests that its seat and back covers were purchased *before* the frame was made, and the present state of the covers indicates that both the upholsterer and the joiner did, indeed, meet with difficulties. The ends of the back cover are wrapped far around the rear stiles in an unconventional manner. Similarly, the rear edge of the seat cover is trimmed back, an indication that the seat was made too shallow. The inference is very strong that the Winterthur frame was made slightly later and that it was far closer to the appropriate dimensions for a set of turkey-work covers.[1]

Part of the difficulties that the joiner who made the Essex Institute example experienced can be attributed to the special upholstery requirements of a couch frame and to the infrequency with which a joiner made couch frames. Because of their extraordinary length, couch frames had to be provided with a strut running from the central front leg to the rear seat rail; otherwise the rails might bow in when the upholsterer stretched webbing tautly across them. In various forms of eighteenth-century seating furniture where such struts were introduced, their upper surfaces were hollowed out to prevent the sitter from hitting the strut as the webbing yielded under his or her weight. Not so with the frames of either the Essex Institute or Winterthur Museum couches; their central struts have straight upper surfaces with sharp edges. In order to lessen the possibility of a sitter dropping down onto an uncomfortable hard edge, the upholsterer of the Essex Institute couch used twice as much grass stuffing on the seat. This unusual treatment required two equally unusual rows of stitches along the front edge of the seat to prevent the thick stuffing from shifting away from the front seat rail over time. This double stitching is different in form but alike in principle to the stitching seen at the center of the seats of chairs from the same shops.

X rays reveal that the top few inches of each of the rear stiles and the medial brace of the Winterthur couch were broken and reworked with new tenons. Since the juncture of crest rail and stiles is one of the weakest points in seating furniture, these joints are often found to have been repaired. Judging from the surface condition of the paint on both parts, the repair was made in the nineteenth century, at which time the upholstery appears to have been replaced. A photograph of the couch taken before it received its present upholstery (fig. 113) reveals rows of rusted tack holes on the front surfaces of the stiles, medial brace, crest rail, and stay rail, which prove that the couch had a sackcloth back tacked beneath the stuffing and cover.

Notches in the rear stiles are likewise visible on both couches. They held the stationary iron keeper that permitted the falls to be raised or lowered to various angles by a toothed ratchet. The notches are flanked by two holes in which bolts with nuts were affixed. The bolts on the Essex Institute couch have been sawed off flush with the back of the stiles; the holes where such bolts once were affixed on the Winterthur couch are plainly visible in the photograph of the stripped frame. Evidence of the dovetail hinges that formed the base of the falls mechanism is visible on the arms (fig. 114).

NOTE
[1] For a fuller discussion of this see Trent, "History for the Essex Institute Turkey Work Couch," pp. 29–37; see also Trent and Fairbanks, *New England Begins* 3:533–34, pl. 31.

50.

COUCH

Possibly Rhode Island

1700–1730

WOODS: Legs and stretchers, sugar maple (*Acer saccharum*); seat rails, a maple of the soft group.

OH 42⅛″ (107.0 cm)

SH 19¾″ (50.2 cm), SW 74⅜″ (188.9 cm), SD 25⅛″ (63.8 cm)

PROVENANCE: Found in Providence, R.I.; Winsor White; Henry Francis du Pont

58.547

When this couch was purchased for the Winterthur collection on January 10, 1945, the following information accompanied it: "Early 18th centy settee with turned legs and stretchered base; upholstered back & seat[.] Originally made for and the property of the first Huguenot Minister of the State of Rhode Island, who went there from Mass. late in the 17th cety."[1] The association of this couch with a Huguenot may have been inspired by partially erroneous information about the turkey-work couch at the Essex Institute.[2] But if the tradition of ownership is correct, the first owner was Ezekiel Carré, who settled with about twenty-five families of émigré Frenchmen in 1686 in what is now known as the Frenchtown area of East Greenwich, Rhode Island. Carré was a native of the Island of Ré, a few miles off the French coast due west of La Rochelle. Unfortunately, no inventory exists for Carré's estate. He disappears from the Rhode Island records in 1691 when his colony was disbanded, and presumably he left Rhode Island at that time.[3]

In any case, the turned ornament of the front stretcher suggests that the couch dates somewhat later than 1691. It sufficiently resembles the stairway balusters of the Benjamin Cushing house (ca. 1737) now to warrant an attribution to a craftsman working in Providence early in the eighteenth century.[4] This form of turning, based on the bilaterally symmetrical baluster of classical antiquity, was denominated a *double poire* (double pear) by Charles Augustin d'Aviler (fig. 115) and is an attenuated and elaborated form of the baluster turning commonly found on New England table legs in the latter decades of the seventeenth century and on through the first half of the eighteenth.

A couch without arms or falls is virtually unknown in England, and its appearance in Rhode Island might be construed as a provincial variation of the older couch or couch-chair form, updated with turned ornament from the newer cane-chair style. However, an extraordinary couch frame of this exact form, in a small public collection in eastern Massachussets, demonstrates that this variation must have been current in England about 1690 to 1720 (fig. 116). That example, made of beech and chestnut and undoubtedly English, retains its original upholstery foundation and leather covers garnished with staggered double brass nails. Scribed lines for mortises at the bottom of the stiles indicate that the frame has been cut down in height considerably, perhaps as much as 6″ (15.2 cm). The vasiform turnings on the front stiles, as well as the elongated baluster turnings on the two front stretchers, form perfect analogues for the ornament of the Winterthur example. It therefore appears that in both England and America, a version of the older couch chair without arms continued to be made long after the period of fashionability for the Cromwellian-style upholstered chair had ended.

With the introduction of the cane-chair–style couch into New England in the 1680s, the role, function, and even the name of the older style couch appears to have been transferred to the daybed in fashion-conscious urban centers (see "Cane Couches"). American inventories fail to reveal that the form of the present example might have been referred to as a "settee," a

Fig. 115. Double pear, detail of "Balusteres d'apui . . . balustres extraordinaires." From (d'Aviler), *Cours d'architecture* (1710), 1:319, pl. 94.

Fig. 116. Couch without arms, England, 1690–1720. European beech (*Fagus sylvatica*) and chestnut; original upholstery and foundation; H 31″ (78.7 cm), W 70″ (177.8 cm), D 20½″ (52.1 cm), SH 14¼″ (36.2 cm). (Photo: Robert Blair St. George.) The couch has a history of ownership in the Kingsley and Mason families in eastern Massachusetts.

term that the *OED* does not note prior to 1716.[5] Indeed settees are not specifically referred to in America before the early 1730s, about the time the cabriole leg appeared. The precedent for the settee was the easy chair and *its* antecedents, invalid chairs made for European aristocrats during the seventeenth century. In other words, the easy chair was not a Cromwellian armchair augmented with padded wings and rolled arms, nor was the settee a similarly augmented Cromwellian couch.

The rear stiles, back rails, and upholstery of the Winterthur example are modern.

NOTES
[1] du Pont, Accession book 3:681, Registrar's Office, Winterthur. Forman, interview with Winsor White, December 1, 1972.
[2] Singleton, *Furniture of Our Forefathers*, p. 196.
[3] Baird, *History of the Huguenot Emigration to America*, 2:295, 297, 303–4, 310.
[4] The house is now located at 38 1/2 North Court Street in Providence. Downing, *Early Homes of Rhode Island*, pp. 142, 170, drawing 39b.
[5] See *OED*, s.v. "settee."

cat. 51

51.
STOOL
England or possibly Philadelphia, Pennsylvania
1680–1720
WOOD: Black walnut (*Juglans nigra*)
OH 13¼″ (33.7 cm), OW 12¼″ (31.1 cm), OD 12¼″ (31.1 cm)
PROVENANCE: John C. Millcy; muscum purchasc
64.152

It is impossible to state whether Winterthur's low stool fashioned of American black walnut was made in England or in Philadelphia. Its frame is far lighter than those of oak joined stools with wooden tops made before 1700, but otherwise the stool is squarely in the seventeenth-century–design tradition. The exquisitely turned Doric columns of the posts, embellished with fine echinus rings and enlivened by a subtle entasis, strongly imply that the stool is the product of an urban joiner or turner.

While it is shown without upholstery here, the stool was upholstered originally. Both high and low stools covered with red silk velvet and gold fringe survive at Knole, Sevenoaks, and two unquestionably American examples with similar square plans and low seats are also known.[1] In all these examples, the intention was to drape the fringe so that it hung down to just above the capitals of the columns.

The function of such low upholstered stools is not clear, although it is probable that they did not function as footstools. Inventories often list both high and low stools, sometimes in the same room with high- and low-back upholstered chairs, and undoubtedly such groupings bore some relationship to rituals of seating precedence.

NOTE
[1] See catalogue entry 38, and Kane, *Furniture of the New Haven Colony*, no. 26.

CANE CHAIRS AND COUCHES

The Cane-chair-makers not only make the Sort, (now almost out of Use) but the better Sort of matted, Leather-bottomed, and Wooden Chairs, of which there is great Variety of Goodness, Workmanship and Price; and some of the Makers, who are also Shop-keepers, are very considerable Dealers, employing from 300 to upwards of 500£. in the Trade. The Work is pretty smart, the Hours from six to nine; and a Journeyman's Wages 12s. a week.

A General Description of All Trades

The introduction of chairs with cane bottoms and backs in northern Europe and America is one of the high points in the story of the seventeenth-century decorative arts as an international phenomenon. In no other form of furniture and at no other time do so many crosscurrents of political and commercial history and the history of taste come together to create so vividly a new style. While many of the details remain to be documented, the broad outlines of the story may be inferred from surviving furniture, written documents, and engravings.

It is perhaps artificial to treat the cane chair as if it emerged in a vacuum, independent of other types of chairs, which influenced its styling and which, in turn, were influenced by it, but contemporary inventories treat cane furniture as a specific entity, suggesting that, in its time, it was thought of in just that way. For furniture specialists today to lump it in with other types of upholstered chairs neither reveals the rich complexity of the history of this influential form, nor permits us to perceive its impact upon the chairmaking industry—for an industry it was—in England and America.

Several aspects of the cane-chair phenomenon graphically reveal the birth of a number of ideas and innovations. For one, these chairs were literally mass-produced and in consequence brought fashionable urban-style chairs within the economic reach of great numbers of people throughout the western world. For another, they freed the craftsman's imagination to ponder new ideas about the design possibilities of the chair, a form that had remained essentially static for centuries. Third, the popular demand for these chairs encouraged their production in both joiners' and turners' shops and tended to blur the distinctive character of each shop, causing the emergence of a new craftsman, the chairmaker. Last, the chairs introduced a totally new and exotic type of upholstery fiber—cane—which became a standard material that has been used in western cultures ever since. For the American furniture historian, the cane chair is especially important since its appearance in American inventories documents the beginnings of the so-called William and Mary style in this country.

Cane had found its way to England by the first decade of the seventeenth century and was promptly taxed at the rate of 66s. 8d. per thousand, a sum that undoubtedly guaranteed that little would be imported, although some probably was by the East India Company of London. It was not the cane itself (*Calamus rotang*) that was used to upholster chairs, but its suckers, which grow to enormous length. These suckers, called rattan, were undoubtedly brought into western Europe for use as a type of twine long before they were used to bottom or upholster chairs. The *OED* does not note the presence of rattan prior to 1681, but a somewhat earlier reference is in an account by Athanasius Kircher, a Jesuit missionary who visited China in 1655. "Amongst . . . various sorts of Reeds, may be comprehended another kind that grows upon some Mountains in China in great abundance, and is called by the Indians Rotang; but in Europe *Rotting* or Japan Canes. . . . This sort of Reed is very tough, and being green, is made use of instead of Cords to tye or bind anything withal." Although Kircher does not tell us so, rattan had for some time been used in the Orient to make chair seats. It was brought to Europe by Dutch traders who for generations maintained a monopoly on trade with China.[1]

The cane chair is a type of furniture that can be treated as a distinct entity, but the motifs used on various cane chairs emerged in four distinct phases in northern Europe before 1700.

Since early in the twentieth century, scholars have generally believed that the earliest English examples of the cane-chair form were simply late versions of the Cromwellian-style chair, with a twist-turned frame, on which cane upholstery was added (fig. 117).[2] That cane was added to a frame which was originally designed to be upholstered with textile or leather has been difficult to demonstrate but seemed obvious because a far greater number of surviving late Cromwellian twist-turned chairs have textile upholstery or board seats rather than cane. But given the lack of datable evidence, it is equally valid to postulate that this rather broad and somewhat squatty twist-turned frame was introduced into England early in the period of the Stuart restoration and that it was originally designed to be upholstered in cane. If this hypothesis is correct, then textile upholstery was substituted for cane and not the reverse. Some support for this argument is provided by the proportions of this chair frame, which are recognizably different from those of the earlier Cromwellian chairs, and several features that are European, not English. Double-twist turning was common on chairs made on the Continent, particularly in Holland. Flat, outward bowing horizontal arms are a northern European shape whereas vertically oriented arms are characteristically an early seventeenth-century English style (see catalogue entry 48). Two additional features—the medial stretcher and the raised rear stretcher—are also found on continental chairs. All four ornamental elements can be traced back through Europe.

Twist work is one of the ancient turner's conceits of the western world. An excellent example of the technique survives on a column built by the Romans in Jerusalem and is believed to have been Bernini's inspiration in 1623 for the columns that support the altar covering of the papal throne at the Vatican. Evidence that the motif, in a more purely classical form, may have been submerged during the Middle Ages is furnished by an illustration of Saint Luke that is found in the Gundohinus Gospels dating from A.D. 754. The motif, found occasionally in Islamic arts, was popularized in Spain and Portugal during the sixteenth century by craftsmen and designers working in a Italianate manner.[3] Twist work was used on the legs of ebony chairs with cane bottoms—the so-called Braganza chairs—made in India for Portuguese royalty (fig. 118) and may represent the first evidence of the Europe-to-the-Orient-and-back-again transfer of ideas that became common in eighteenth-century decorative arts.

The first European chairs with cane seats were indeed merely an old form with a new upholstery material. But new motifs were soon added and they, in most cases, may be traced to post-Renaissance architectural devices created by the artists and artisans of sixteenth-century Italy.

The most striking new motif was the high back, which probably came into use in France shortly before the middle of

Fig. 117. Phase 1 cane chair: low-back, twist-turned frame, cane seat and back. England, 1660–90. (Photo: Symonds Collection, DAPC, Winterthur Library.)

the seventeenth century. Its antecedents were high-back immovable chairs, such as thrones, used in Europe during the Middle Ages. The high back on the cane chair is simply a design concept. It was probably reintroduced for no better reason than to differentiate it from those with low backs that were so ubiquitous during the first half of the seventeenth century.

Perhaps the decorative features which most clearly distinguish the cane chairs of the late seventeenth century from their predecessors are the prominently carved scrolls. Such scrolls are common on the best quality chairs made in Italy during the late sixteenth and early seventeenth centuries. The scrollwork is often combined with floral motifs or abstract leaves and architectural elements, such as egg-and-dart moldings that are worked into the seats and backs, and architectonic motifs worked into the crest rails. The scrolls are often C shapes with volutes at their termini, or they are long S shapes, as on the legs of a *sgabello* (fig. 119). The abruptly reversed scroll, well illustrated in the crest rail of the same chair, had for many years before been used as an architecural device on Italian churches, on sgabelli, and on leather-upholstered chairs (see fig. 92). Chairmakers of northern Europe favored this to such a degree that it has become

Fig. 118. Braganza chair, India, 1500–1600. Ebony with ivory inlay; H 39¾″ (100.3 cm), W 21½″ (54.6 cm), D 18¾″ (47.6 cm), SH 19¾″ (50.2 cm). (Hinwick House, near Wellingborough, Northamptonshire, England.) This is one of four such chairs; an armchair of the same type is also on display at Hinwick House.

Fig. 119. Sgabello, Venice, Italy, 1500–1600. (Photo: Benno M. Forman.)

commonly known as the "Flemish scroll." Wooden chairs with scrolled motifs were made in Germany, especially in the south, well into the nineteenth century. A solitary pair of chairs in this style was made in London at the beginning of the second quarter of the seventeenth century.[4]

The chairs were probably made in London for Sir Henry Rich and may have been designed by Francis Cleyn (d. 1658). Although Cleyn spent most of his adult life in England, he was born in Rostock, Mecklenburg-Schwerin, Germany, and studied in Rome, where he learned *grottesco* painting, and Venice, where he met Sir Henry. Horace Walpole espied the chairs in the early 1760s in "a beautiful chamber adorned by [Cleyn] at Holland-house, with a ceiling in grotesque," and decided that these "two chairs, carved and gilt, with large shells for backs were undoubtedly from [Cleyn's] designs; and are evidence of his taste."[5] Although these chairs were made in England, the designs are Italianate in every detail except the flat, laterally bowed arms. What is significant about all this is that ornament on Italian chairs inspired northern European craftsmen for more than a century.

The third features, the gracefully curved arms of the cane chair and its textile-upholstered relatives, are distinctive elements that are easier to trace, although it is a moot question whether they developed in France, where they are found on low-back chairs, or in Italy. An extraordinary chair from Italy, which we can happily date to the year 1652 (fig. 120), displays the curved arm in its fully developed form and, in the absence of datable French examples, is evidence that Italy once again was the source of inspiration for the design.[6] The graceful sweep of the arms and handgrips is a far cry from the flat arms on Italian chairs made earlier in the century and quite distant from the thick arms of joiner-made upholstered chairs. The new-style arms are carefully molded, enriched with carved foliage, and terminate in volutes—a harmonious integration of architectural and decorative ideas. The arm supports and the legs are decorated with exquisite turned balusters, above which are little spindles suggesting the columnar shapes that became ubiquitous later in the century. Indeed all these features were quickly adopted in the north. This Italian chair is further remarkable in that it retains its original polychromed and fancifully tooled leather upholstery; gilded and tooled leather work had been a common feature of Italian chairs since the sixteenth century.[7]

While we are often hard put to show how Italian ideas about furniture got to northern Europe, it is clearer how Spanish ones got there, since much of the Netherlands was dominated by Spain in the seventeenth century. The Italian chair in figure 120 is important in the history of furniture because it reveals the inspiration of many motifs used on leather-upholstered chairs made on the Iberian peninsula. Yet

Fig. 120. Armchair with leather upholstery, probably made in Lombardy, Italy, 1652. (Private collection.) The chair bears the heraldic crest of Ranato Borromeo who married Giulia Arese in 1652.

Fig. 121. Armchair, Italy, possibly seventeenth century. Walnut and leather; H 44⅞" (114 cm), W 25⅝" (65 cm), D 18⅛" (46 cm), SH 18⅞" (48 cm). (Courtesy Museu Municipal, Portalegre, Portugal.)

despite assiduous efforts, our attempts to find dated or otherwise documented examples of the famous Portuguese and Spanish leather chairs that relate to this specific Italian example have met with no success. It seems clear that the ideas for the Hispanic versions came from Italy about the middle of the seventeenth century.

We do not yet know whether the Portuguese or the Spanish first made their chairs in the Italian manner. The late Robert C. Smith, an ardent advocate of the arts of Portugal, found a rare Italianate example in the collection of the Museu Municipal, Portalegre, Portugal (fig. 121). This unusual chair has a square back, curved and molded arms and voluted handgrips, turnings similar to the Italian example in figure 120, and a fully developed front stretcher of boldly intertwined, reversed scrolls.[8]

Perhaps the palm should go to the Portuguese for introducing the style to Iberia, but tradition has long accorded the attribution to Spain on the merits of chairs like that in figure 122. Indeed, the Spanish attribution is logical. Spain brought this type of leather upholstery to perfection, and the leather finishers of Cordova had gained an international reputation before the middle of the seventeenth century. The backs of many Spanish chairs are decorated with the coats of arms of distinguished families, which ought to enable a scholar to date them someday; others are embossed with antic or grotesque figures, putti, flowers, and rinceaux. (All of these classical motifs, literally recreated by the Italian designers working in the Renaissance or modern manner, are suggestively similar to

carved designs on the northern European examples.) The bold arched top of the Spanish chairs may derive from the rounded top of that recognizably Spanish chair on which a piece of leather is stretched in a graceful swag from the crest to the front rail—in the manner of a twentieth-century canvas deck chair.[9]

Before the end of the seventeenth century many of the same attributes of the Spanish chair began to appear in the furniture of northern Europe, especially that of the Lowlands. The leather chair from Spain, when translated into the different medium—the turned, molded, and carved wooden chair with cane seat and back of the Netherlands—cannot help but exert a strange fascination on students of decorative arts. This brilliant Netherlandish adaptation repeats, note for note, the themes of the earlier Spanish chair: the outline of the crest and bottom rails of both gently undulate, sometimes complementing, sometimes echoing each other; the castiron and gilt or brass finials atop the stiles are replaced by turned wooden ones; both chairs have turned, ogival balusters on their legs and massive, carved stretchers rich in shape and ornament; the "great heels" of the back legs are likewise common to both; so, too, are the strongly molded arms terminating in architectural volutes and the famous "Spanish foot." And the molded arms on the Spanish chairs may indeed have suggested the treatment for the exposed parts of the back frame and seat of the cane chair.

The Spanish foot, whose origin no scholar has yet found a document to explain, perhaps represents nothing more

Fig. 122. Armchair with leather upholstery, Spain, mid seventeenth century. From Jacquemart, *History of Furniture*, facing p. 190.

Fig. 123. Architectural bracket. From Marot, *Recueil de plusieurs portes* (ca. 1680), 2: pl. 4. (Winterthur Library.)

Fig. 124. Varguenno, Spain, 1565–1600. Walnut; H 57″ (144.8 cm), W 40⅞″ (103.2 cm), D 15½″ (39.4 cm). (Saint Louis Art Museum, St. Louis, Mo.)

romantic than an architectural bracket of the type often illustrated in the engravings of such designers as Jean Le Pautre and Jean Marot (fig. 123), or a refinement of the earlier termination, sometimes treated animalistically and sometimes as a floriate scroll, already ubiquitous in trestle-foot Italian furniture and Spanish furniture made in the Italian idiom (fig. 124). In all probability this foot does not appear in northern Europe until late in the seventeenth century or early in the eighteenth when the idea of a back whose crest rail symmetrically echoes the bottom back rail, as in the Spanish chair, becomes popular as well.[10]

Although research in Europe has failed to reveal the period nomenclature for this foot, two American documents may do so. The first reference occurs in a letter dated "20th 12mo 1712/3" from James Logan of Philadelphia to James Askew, his London factor. Logan ordered "2 finest Virginia Walnut Chairs . . . wth Paws at ye feet." Considering that Logan ordered these at a time when chairmakers of London were still making William and Mary-style chairs, we find it logical to believe that Logan was referring to chairs with Spanish feet (of course, the terminology may be of his own coinage and not represent the lingo of the chairmakers of the time). A second reference also uses animalistic imagery. On March 8, 1732/33, Samuel Grant, a Boston upholsterer, noted the sale of "4 doz Leather Chairs claw feet @ 27[s.] . . . £64.16.00" in his journal.[11] The date is rather late in the history of the style and the statement not incontrovertibly a reference to this type of foot.

To point out a few of the motifs and sources for the ideas of the cane chair does not explain the ingenuity with which they were organized, developed, and combined into a distinctive and fresh style by talented northern European turners, joiners, and carvers. Nor does it explain why or how it became immensely popular. In Portugal, the Italian manner may have first been adopted for no better reason than that people who could afford to indulge a taste for exoticism did so. And the leather-upholstered Spanish versions of these chairs are handsome, showy, and, since they required a great deal of labor, probably quite costly. Their dissemination into the Lowlands is easier to explain; Spain still ruled much of the region, and furniture was easily transported even within a warring empire.

Finally, numerous authors over the years have asserted that cane chairs were transported from France to England by Charles II, when the monarchy was restored in 1660. The story goes that Charles and his court, who had sojourned in France (his mother's native country), brought to England new French forms and a taste for the luxury associated with them. None of the surviving documents or chairs substantiates this assertion. Furthermore, the few documents that mention the cane chairs show that they enjoyed their initial popularity among the upper-middle classes not the royalty and the aristocracy, both of whom continued to manifest a preference for upholstered furniture. It is nonetheless possible that the so-called Braganza chairs, like the example illustrated in figure 118, were brought to England by the king's wife, Catherine of Braganza, whom he married in 1662; but such chairs were a novelty, not a product of the industrial arts, and were Indo-Portuguese, rather than French, in taste. Stylistically their twist turning seems to be new, but if Luke Vincent Lockwood and other writers are correct, that technique was already popular in English furniture before the Stuarts again assumed the throne.

THE PHASES OF THE CANE CHAIR IN ENGLAND AND AMERICA

In 1934 and 1951, Robert W. Symonds published an extraordinary series of five articles in which he meticulously documented the transformation of the cane-chair styles in England from the 1660s through the early eighteenth century.[12] These brilliant articles, which stand as the definitive study of the subject, deal with the documents and contain illustrations of a great variety of surviving examples. Careful examination of the illustrations reveals that, while the chairs vary in their ornamental motifs, certain types of decoration recur and that the chairs with similar ornamentation are generally related in size and proportions as well. The observable differences between the related groups tempt us to believe that they may form a succession of styles that can be equated with the verbal documents to reveal—perhaps in rather rough terms—the chronological sequence in which the various styles appeared in England and hence may be expected to have been imported into or made in America. The exercise is not without its problems, but, as will be revealed in the following pages, it illustrates two principles of furniture history: first, as we come closer to modern times, the sequence of styles succeed each other with greater frequency, and, second, the types of objects men make fall into two categories—those which "evolve" from their beginnings and those which are influenced by outside impulses—and these categories are not mutually exclusive.

Among the documents unearthed by Symonds is a remarkable petition to Parliament by the woolen manufacturers of England that gives us our only clue to the date at which cane chairs were introduced into England. The petition was written in 1688. It states that "about the Year 1664, Cane-Chairs, &c. came into use in *England*" and proposes the manufacture of cane chairs be prohibited because of the deleterious effects on the manufacture of cloth for upholstery. Assuming that the authors of this petition correctly dated an event that had occurred almost a quarter of a century earlier, we must construct any hypotheses concerning the development of English cane chairs using 1664 as a firm beginning date. The petition further informs us that at first these chairs were rather plain in nature but "in time they came to be carved."[13] Symonds thus suggests, as did Lockwood, that the earliest cane chairs made in England were most likely those few surviving examples of the type illustrated in figure 117. This inference is given reasonable support by the large caning pattern of the chairs, a result of the wide spacing of the holes in the seat and back frame—as if the chairmakers of London (where these chairs were doubtless first made in England) were not sufficiently familiar with cane to work it with finesse—and by the rather massive seat lists, which became considerably lighter as the style evolved.

Insofar as the middling sort of people are concerned, a survey of 49 itemized inventories in London probate records from 1664 to 1683 uncovered a mention of cane chairs in only 3 inventories. The earliest of these is October 3, 1674, in the inventory of Robert Mannynge, a gentleman of Cambridge who resided in the parish of St. Andrew, Holborn. His parlor contained "2 elboe chairs canne botham" and 6 turkey-work chairs. The inventory of Capt. Francis Digby, endorsed on January 15, 1676/77, included "12 cane chairs wth 12 cushions and backes of Damask" valued at £5 and "one couch and squab of the same" worth £3.10. His dining room contained "12 cane chairs and table" worth £6.2.[14] Not until 1683 do cane chairs begin to appear with frequency, and then not in every inventory nor according to any discernible pattern.

The Digby reference reveals that cushions were used on the backs and seats of cane chairs and that the chairs even at this early date were purchased in sets of a dozen; yet it is frustrating to us that the London inventories do not more often list the separate values of objects. Such a listing would help clarify when the early style of cane chairs, in the late Cromwellian manner (see fig. 117), was abandoned for the second phase of the style—those with higher backs, and floriate crest rails in the manner of the Braganza chair (see fig. 118) and with molded, flowing arms ending in volute handgrips, in the manner of the chair in figure 120. Symonds asserts that chairs with carved elements ought to have been made in England around 1680, and, indeed, a "Caned Chaire" described in the Royal Household accounts may have been a high-back example (but it was also a special-purpose chair that reclined).[15] Since no cane chairs in the late Cromwellian style with carved decoration have survived, the reference in the accounts seems to demonstrate that by 1680 the style in England had already moved into a new phase.

The development of a cane chair with a high back could have occurred spontaneously among the craftsmen of London, but it is more likely that the high-back version is the high-style version, made in response to stylistic attributes that already had been adopted on the Continent in the third quarter of the seventeenth century. Indeed, in the Netherlands numerous cane chairs were made about this same time, and they have high backs, scroll front legs, fluent carving, and twist-turned rear stiles.[16] In the case of many English shops where similar chairs were made, it is possible that specific designs represent the grafting of some new fashionable features onto chair frames that still retained a rather low back and the twist turning associated with it, but it is equally possible that these low-back versions with twist stiles were cheaper models and thus were made *after* the phase two high-back chairs were introduced into England and not before.

The most characteristic feature of English chairs in the second phase is that the crest rail and front stretcher—which are generally of the same design—are carved with floral motifs in relatively low relief, are decidedly rectilinear in appearance, and have margins that are not very deeply indented. Some of the examples of this type have columnar rear stiles, a feature that may represent either a later variation of this phase or merely a less expensive one.

No chairs in the manner of the first phase of the English cane-chair style are known to have been made in America, and it is doubtful that any in the second phase were made here either. However, it is clear from the American records dating from the mid 1680s that cane chairs were present in the colonies. In the absence of documentation that American craftsmen were making them, we must presume that these cane chairs were imported. One low-back second-phase chair (fig. 125), owned by the Corporation of Harvard University and presently stored in the Houghton Library, illustrates this point. The chair has a history of ownership by Judah Monis (probably born in Italy, 1683; lived in New York, 1716–20, and Boston, 1720–60; d., Northampton, 1764), the first instructor ever appointed by Harvard College. He served the college as professor of Hebrew from 1720 until 1760. Monis must have bought the chair secondhand if he acquired it in America. Presumptive evidence would suggest that he purchased the chair in Boston, where he ran a small shop to supplement his stipend as a college professor, but the documented presence of a closely related chair in New York suggests that he acquired it during his sojourn as rabbi at Jamaica, Long Island.[17] The New York chair is of European beech (*Fagus sylvatica*). No particular quirk of the turning on either chair can be seen in the later American cane and leather chairs. In contrast to the quality of its turning, the quality of the carving on the Monis chair is so shockingly poor that possibly no British scholar will want to claim it as a product of that island. It is equally possible that this chair was not executed in London, if indeed it is a British chair, for the history of American commerce shows that these colonies did not rely totally upon London for their imports. But appearance alone is insufficient proof that this is a rural chair, because by the late seventeenth century many London chairmakers were doing their own carving, rather than sending parts out to specialists.

Fig. 125. Phase 2 cane chair: floriate crest rail and front stretcher, low back, twist-turned stiles. 1675–1700. Beech (microanalysis as to whether European or American was inconclusive). (Corporation of Harvard University, Cambridge, Mass.) The chair may have been owned by Judah Monis.

Additionally we must recognize that the date 1680 which seems to refer to the second phase of the cane chair in the Royal Household accounts is deceptively late. The style represented by the Monis chair—which has twist-turned stiles and other features in common with the earliest cane chairs—was introduced somewhat earlier, perhaps in the opening years of the 1670s. Supporting evidence for this is also contained in the royal household accounts: on November 6, 1677, a walnut armchair (not necessarily cane upholstered) "wrought with scrowles" and costing £3 was furnished for His Majesty's bedchamber. In the same bill, joiner Richard Price also supplied chairs "of walnuttree twisted" for the royal yacht. These entries indicate that twist turning and scrolled carving were both being made at that date, but the entries for the next few years do not mention twist work and suggest that this type of turning, which had been popular for more than a decade, was on the wane and that scroll carving was the newest fashion.[18]

Nowhere in the accounts does Price refer to these chairs as having "Flemish scrolls," and we must therefore interpret that phrase as a modern coinage, but large numbers of surviving chairs with the motif suggest that Price's 1677/78 delivery of one "Elbowe Chaire of wallnutt Cutt with scrowles all over" made for Charles II marked the emergence of a third phase of the cane-chair style.[19]

The advent of the Flemish scroll as a motif in English cane chairs was accompanied by a further development: turning is deemphasized on the front legs, and carving becomes a major method of ornamentation. The carving is generally a large reverse-curve scroll, topped by a turned element where the leg enters the seat list; a ball turning is often at the base and serves as the foot. On most surviving examples the ball foot has often completely been worn down or has rotted away. An excellent English chair of this type made of European beech (*Fagus sylvatica*) and now in the Winterthur collection reportedly came from a family who "had a pair which they said came from some branch of the Penn tribe in Pennsylvania."[20]

Even though the crest rail and front stretcher of the Flemish-scrolled chairs are rather rectilinear (see fig. 160), these chairs are sufficiently different from their predecessors to show that cane-chair making in England had taken a new turn. Floral carving becomes secondary to scroll carving. The rear stiles are no longer twist turned but consist of a series of baluster forms with various degrees of attenuation that are interspersed with balls, rings, and small, sometimes architectonic, columns. This change in style also occurs on continental chairs, a typical example of which is the child's highchair of Dutch origin (see fig. 163).

It would be very convenient if we could equate the introduction of scroll carving and baluster stiles in England to the arrival of Dutch designers and craftsmen in the wake of the accession of Mary, the daughter of James II, and William of Orange, her consort, to the English throne in 1689, but the records indicate that the style preceded that political moment by several years. Chairs in this style were imported into America, and notable examples with sound histories of ownership in colonial America but made of European beech (*Fagus sylvatica*) are in the collections of Essex Institute, Connecticut Historical Society, Wadsworth Atheneum, and Pennsylvania Historical and Museum Commission. Yet another belongs to SPNEA, but it was much altered when it was converted into a rocking chair in the nineteenth century and has new parts of American maple.

At least two chairs in the third phase—stylistically the earliest so far identified—were made in New England. One with a tradition of ownership in the Winthrop family is in the collection of Massachusetts Historical Society, and the other, from the Morse family, is at Winterthur (catalogue entry 52). It is possible that both of these chairs were made before 1690, for the baluster shapes of the rear stiles are of the phase-three type. Presumptive evidence that these two chairs were made before 1690 is also suggested by the chair illustrated in figure 126 that, while it has similar phase-three–type front legs, has phase-four rear stiles and crest rail. Microanalysis reveals that it is made of American beech (*Fagus grandifolia*). It is now in a private collection and was believed by its last family owner to have

Fig. 126. Phase 4 cane chair: high back, scroll-carved crest rail, turned stiles, C scrolls on front legs. Boston, ca. 1689. American beech (*Fagus grandifolia*); H 53½" (135.9 cm), W 23⅜" (52.4 cm), D 18¾" (47.6 cm), SH 16⅞" (42.9 cm). (Private collection.) The chair was probably owned by Stephen Minot.

belonged to Stephen Minot (1662–1732) of Boston. If Minot purchased his chair at the time of his marriage in 1689, then that is the approximate date at which the manufacture of cane chairs in the fourth phase began in the colonies.[21]

Symonds was able to document a variation in the decoration of scrolled chairs relatively soon after the introduction of the third phase. On March 5, 1685/86, Elizabeth, widow of Richard Price, furnished the royal household with a number of cane chairs for the "Service of the Office of his Ma[jes]t[ie]s Great Wardrobe." Eight were of "Wallnuttree Carved with Boyes & Crownes att 12s [each]."[22] A number of beechwood chairs with this motif have survived both in England and on the Continent. Notable examples are in the King's Chamber at Knole. They reveal that a giant step forward in the conception and ornamentation of chairs had taken place in the eight short years since the third phase was introduced, yet these chairs are not sufficiently different in proportions or ornamentation to be classified a distinct phase. No American examples with this type of decoration are known.

The fourth phase of the English cane chair dominated the last decade of the seventeenth century and represents the most mature and most distinctively English version of the style. In this phase, the crest rail and front stretcher break out of the rectilinear bounds that had conventionally confined them, and C scrolls are commonly worked into the designs: foliage tends to replace decorative flowers on these elements, carving becomes bolder and more three-dimensional, and the rinceaux become heavier and more redolent of baroque ideas. At the same time, the rear stiles become almost exclusively architectonic columns in the classical manner: the finest examples are enriched with carved floral motifs or vines in relief, the less expensive versions have fluted columns, and the inexpensive types are plain.

That the front legs on some of these chairs are perpendicular to the front seat list and on others are splayed outward at a 45-degree angle has been interpreted to be of chronological significance. This idea seems logical, considering that the chairs ornamented with Flemish scrolls usually have legs that are perpendicular to the front of the chair, but no dated or documented chairs that might demonstrate this chronology have come to light. Thus it is likely that the variation in the orientation of the front legs on fourth-phase chairs is a matter of personal innovation among the many shops that made chairs in this style and that both types are nearly contemporaneous.

This fourth phase of the English cane chair is of great importance to students of American furniture because the manufacture of this important furniture form begins in America during the same period. The features of most of the chairs made in America during the last decade of the seventeenth century strongly imply that they were created by English craftsmen who had immigrated to these shores. That suggestion is further strengthened by a crucial piece of evidence. Virtually all these chairs—especially the New England examples—are made of American beech, a curious choice of material since two generations of New England chairmakers had preferred maple to beech for upholstered chairs.

It may be illusory to believe that a sketch of the seventeenth-century phases of the cane-chair style gives us a base from which to date undated examples, be they English or American. The study of decorative arts history shows repeatedly that styles do not replace each other abruptly, but that stylistic attributes tend to persist in certain shops once they are established and therefore may show up on pieces of furniture made much later. Every successive phase tended to accumulate some of the characteristics of earlier ones, and in virtually every phase simpler, less expensive versions were available, often reflecting the exigencies of economical production as much as the taste of the times.

In the middle of the last decade of the seventeenth century another idea about the styling of chairs begins to appear in England. Cane chairs made in response to this idea were inspired by the engravings of such men as Daniel Marot (1663–1752), a Parisian designer who fled to Holland at about the time of the revocation of the Edict of Nantes, found employment with William of Orange, and by 1694 had moved to England. Chairs in what might be called the "Marot style" established a new fashion in England, a classic example of which is an upholstered easy chair made for the duke of Devonshire by Thomas Roberts of London around 1700 (see fig. 150). Attributes of the new style dominated American chairmaking during the first quarter of the eighteenth century, the same period in which cane chairs reached their height of popularity and were extensively manufactured in New England.

In England, the most expensive of the upholstered chairs had legs made in the form of classical pedestals for busts or terms. These legs were usually rectilinear in section and were either carved, if made of expensive woods, or gessoed and gilded. In the finest English cane chairs, the legs may have been turned and carved, and, in a slightly less expensive version, the carving was dispensed with. The term shape is often retained, and when rendered on the lathe—marking the return of turning as a major technique of ornamenting the front legs—this shape appears as an inverted baluster, often quite bulbous (see catalogue entry 57) and suggestive of a northern European mannerist approach.[23] In the least expensive versions of these chairs, the front legs are ornamented with small turned balusters or colonnettes, and the stretchers are also usually turned. The backs are also quite different from anything seen on earlier cane chairs. The crest rail is usually symmetrical with the bottom back rail—on the less expensive versions, sometimes only approximately so. In many fine versions, the upright back supports disappear and the caning extends to the stiles. On the least expensive, the bottom back rail is straight. In either case the portion of the back that outlines the caning is molded with a plane or simply carved. The turned finial disappears. Generally these chairs are shorter and broader than their predecessors. All in all, these characteristics are sufficiently different from their predecessors to constitute the beginnings of a fifth phase. An inexpensive English example from the first quarter of the eighteenth century that conservatively retains the vertical back supports is illustrated in figure 127. This chair appears to have furnished the general plan and the details for the craftsmen who designed the largest group of surviving American cane chairs early in the eighteenth century (see catalogue entry 54), most of which were made after George I became the king of England in 1714.

A final, sixth phase of the cane chair's development in America emerged when Chinese furniture appeared in western markets in the beginning of the eighteenth century. While the overall shape of the cane chair changed little, American craftsmen had by the late 1720s and early 1730s selectively updated existing forms with the addition of a curved crest, a single solid vasiform rear banister, and a coat of lacquer. The cabriole leg also first appeared during this sixth phase.

SUMMARY OF THE CHRONOLOGY OF CANE-CHAIR STYLES IN ENGLAND AND AMERICA

Connoisseurs of furniture wish to be as precise as possible about the date at which objects were made, since any

Fig. 127. Phase 5 cane chair: turned legs, molded stiles and crest rail. England, 1700–1725. (Present location unknown; formerly owned by Speke Hall, Liverpool, England. Photo: Benno M. Forman.)

generalizations about chronology are reliable only if the basic facts are correct. Unhappily, it is not always possible to be precise. In the case of cane chairs, as with all other forms, we find ourselves dealing with a great number of examples, made by a great number of craftsmen in different shops, each of which had its own personality, problems, and techniques. We cannot help but admire Symonds's boldness in attempting to deal with myriad variations. It is clear from the observation of furniture, particularly those forms being produced in great numbers over a relatively short period of time, that designs are continually being modified in response to many stimuli and that basic forms are continually updated by the addition of newer motifs. Moreover, just because someone is making a newer type of chair somewhere does not mean that the older type is not still being made in another shop. Consequently furniture tends to combine the old and new in such a way that it is virtually impossible to date a piece accurately. Each student of furniture, therefore, will have his own ideas of how

forms "developed," and each student will be partially right and partially wrong in his conclusions, which must have a large measure of subjectivity in them.

Nevertheless, the documents and objects surveyed for this book suggest a chronology of English cane-chair styles that affected the appearance of American examples (table 3).

THE INFLUENCE OF THE ENGLISH CANE CHAIR IN EUROPE AND AMERICA

However tentative its beginnings, the English cane chair became extremely popular. Richly carved examples were made in walnut and other fine woods for the gentry, and simpler versions in beech—often stained brown to imitate walnut or painted black to suggest ebony—were made for other customers. By the last decade of the seventeenth century, cane chairs were filling the need among all classes in England for a handsome and serviceable chair. Indeed, the cane chair appears to have quickly supplanted the better-quality turned chair as an inexpensive chair and endured until the windsor chair replaced it two generations later.

The reasons for the popularity of cane upholstery are stated by the representatives of the London cane-chair makers in their lengthy response to the woolen manufacturers' petition of 1688. "Cane-Chairs," they explained, "gave . . . much satisfaction to all the Nobility, Gentry, and Commonality of this Kingdom, (for their Durableness, Lightness, and Cleanness from Dust, Worms and Moths, which inseparably attended Turkey-work, Serge, and other Stuff-Chairs and Couches, to the spoiling of them and all Furniture near them)."[24]

That cane-chair making had become an industry in England by the last decade of the seventeenth century is suggested by the minutes of a court held on December 30, 1689, at Joyner's Hall in London:

upon request of divers members of this Company who are Cane stoole Squabb and Couch makers and others depending upon the said trades alleging that the Company of Upholsterers London have appeared before th hon[ora]ble house of Commons with others to procure the passing of a bill to prohoibite and hinder the making of Cane chairs & that this Court would be pleased to present a peticion to the honble house of Commons on behalfe of themselves and some thousands concerned in making the said chaires & that the said bill might not pass to prevent their utter ruine and disstruccion and that they would be pleased to Countenance the same by their appearance before the said house and that they would be pleased to affix their common seale thereunto which this Court taking the same into consideration doe consent thereunto.[25]

A comment in the actual petition confirms this in rich detail. Cane chairs, it states, "came to be much used in *England*, and sent to all parts of the World; which occasioned the Chair-Frame Makers and Turners to take many Apprentices; and Cane Chairs, &c. coming in time to be Carved, many Carvers took Apprentices, and brought them up to Carving of Cane-Chairs, Stools, Couches, and Squobs only: And there

TABLE 3   CHARACTERISTICS OF CANE CHAIRS

PHASE	CHARACTERISTICS	MADE IN ENGLAND	MADE IN AMERICA	ILLUSTRATED
1	Late Cromwellian style with cane bottom and back; double-twist turning; low back; broad seat	beginning in 1664, still being made in mid 1670s	none known	fig. 117
2	Twist-turned stiles and legs; floral-carved rectilinear crest rail and stretcher; turned (usually ball) finial; high back; broad seat	possibly being made in the late 1670s, definitely so by 1680	none known	
	A. High-back version			fig. 142
	B. Low-back version			fig. 125
3	High back; narrower seat; baluster-shape stiles (occasionally with small columnar shapes, rings, balls); urn-shape finials; higher relief carving (primarily foliage)		one pair with foliage carving known	cat. no. 52
	A. Flemish-scroll crest; stretcher and legs generally perpendicular to front of seat; crest rail still essentially rectilinear	definitely made in late 1670s	many imported examples known	fig. 126, legs
	B. "Boyes and crowns" or related foliate carving	made for royalty in 1685	none known	
4	Higher and often narrower back and seat; often ebonized; carving of crest rail has scrolls (usually C shape) worked in with foliage; crest rails and stretchers break out of rectilinear mold; front legs have carved C scrolls (turned legs in cheaper versions) and are perpendicular to front of seat or are set at 45-degree angle to seat, facing outward	possibly made in mid 1680s, certainly made in 1690s; continues into reign of Queen Anne; datable English example in Sweden after 1697; dated English example 1703	large group made in Boston	fig. 126 stiles & crest rail; figs. 128, 129, 151; cat. no. 53 stiles & crest rail
5	Molded stiles, crest rail, and bottom seat rail; back often completely caned with no vertical back rails; turned front legs are generally bulbous, inverted balusters, often enriched with carving; first appearance of Spanish feet	the "Marot" style, perhaps made from the mid 1690s into reign of George I	earliest examples probably made in Philadelphia; numerous Boston examples made between 1717 and 1730	figs. 127, 148; cat. nos. 54, 55, 56, 57
6	Curved crest rail; crook (cabriole) legs; vase-shape banister, solid back (splat); cane bottom only; often lacquered	about 1715 at earliest, into early 1740s	rarely found; a few Boston examples known	

were many Apprentices bound only to learn to Split the Canes, and Cane those chairs, &c." According to the petition, by 1688 "Six thousand Dozens of Cane-Chairs, Stools, Couches, and Squobs," were made in England—mostly in London—yearly and "above Two thousand Dozens [were] yearly Transported into almost all the Hot Parts of the World, where the Heat renders Turky-work, Serge, *Kidderminster*, and other Stuffed Chairs and Couches useless."[26]

Chairs in museums throughout the western world confirm the influence of England's export trade. These chairs came to be referred to as chairs "in the English manner." For the first time in decorative arts history an English style was widely copied in Europe. A chair whose crest rail is carved with the monogram of King Charles XII of Sweden (reigned 1697–1718), in the collection of the Nordiska Museet, Stockholm, if not made by an English craftsman, owes every detail of its appearance to English cane-chair design. A chair, with every attribute of the English cane-chair idiom in the Schloss Charlottenburg, Berlin, with a few nuances of carved and turned shapes that set it apart, is illustrated by Heinrich Kreisel in *Die Kunst des deutschen Möbels*. Inquiries about this chair revealed that a guild of English chairmakers existed in Berlin around 1700. To complete the circle, a remarkable walnut chair in the English manner, but clearly the work of an Italian craftsman, has an Italian provenance and is in the Civiche Raccolte Artische, Milan.[27]

The English colonies in North America offered a ready market for English cane chairs. Large quantities found their way to New England and the middle colonies during the last two decades of the seventeenth century, and probably earlier to Virginia, Maryland, and the Carolinas. The extent of this trade has been well documented by Symonds.[28] At port of embarkation value, £4,898 worth of chairs were shipped to America from England between 1697 and 1704 (excluding 1698). Since the Colonial Office Records, from which this information was abstracted, do not itemize the entries, it is not clear what portion of these were cane chairs, but considering the overwhelming popularity of the style during this period, it is likely that at least three quarters of them were. Allowing 5s. as the wholesale cost of each chair at London, the astounding number of over 14,600, or "twelve hundred dozen," cane chairs, most of them in the phase-four style, were sent to the colonies during this seven-year period. Symonds's tables can be rendered into percentages, and they reveal that approximately 42 percent of these chairs were shipped to Virginia and Maryland and about 6 percent to Carolina, or a total of 48 percent to the South, where little fine furniture is known to have been produced prior to 1750. It is even more surprising that 38 percent went to New England, where chairmaking had flourished for three generations; 10 percent went to New York and just under 4 percent to Pennsylvania. That 52 percent of the chairs found their way to colonies that had a thriving furniture industry and only 38 percent went to those which were essentially agrarian is an important comment on the desire that Americans had for these chairs. Numerous English cane chairs have been found along the Atlantic seaboard in modern times, and until microanalysis of wood came to the aid of the

Fig. 128. Phase 4 cane chair: high back, turned stiles, scroll-carved crest rail and stretcher, C-scroll front legs. Scandinavia, probably Sweden, ca. 1700. Beech; H 55⅛" (140 cm), W 19¼" (48.9 cm), D 20⅞" (53 cm), SH 19" (48.3 cm). (Winterthur 58.539.)

Fig. 129. Phase 4 cane chair: high back, scroll-carved crest rail, C-scroll front legs. Scandinavia, probably Sweden, ca. 1700. Beech; H 55⅛" (140 cm), W 19¼" (48.9 cm), D 20⅞" (53 cm), SH 19" (48.3 cm). (Winterthur 58.540.)

American furniture historian, most of the chairs were believed to have been made here. The books of Luke Vincent Lockwood, Esther Singleton, and even so keen an observer as Wallace Nutting are profusely illustrated with cane chairs now known to be made of European woods, usually beech (*Fagus sylvatica*), covered by layers of stain, paint, and grime and easily confused with maple, the traditional wood used in New England.

The general rule of thumb among early collectors of American furniture was that simple cane chairs were probably American and elaborately turned and carved ones were English.[29] Microanalysis and close examination of many examples in public museums and in private collections has generally confirmed the half of the rule: elaborate chairs are usually English. But most of the simple ones are English, too. To confuse the issue further, some chairs that recently have been identified as Philadelphia made are very close to excellent and showy English prototypes. But, carving alone is no indicator of origin or, indeed, of authenticity. Cane chairs were much reproduced in the nineteenth century, particularly in

England. Some seventeenth-century American chairs have carving of exquisite workmanship while many seventeenth-century English chairs are roughly executed (historically consistent with the demand for them and the mass-production atmosphere in which they were made), and the nineteenth-century reproductions have the best carving of all.[30]

Another rough-and-ready guide stated that a fine caning pattern with small holes indicated English workmanship and that coarse caning was American. However, chairs made in both hemispheres display both types of caning, depending upon the standards established by the masters of the shops involved. In almost all cases, the caning on the identified American examples is quite fine, a result of their having been made rather late in the history of the style.

It is quite likely that most of the English cane chairs with long histories of ownership in American families have been here since the year they were made. Typical of the fine quality chairs that were exported to America during the early years of the eighteenth century is the pair made of English beech illustrated in the second edition of *Furniture Treasury* (nos.

2033, 2034) and now in the Winterthur collection (figs. 128, 129). These chairs were sold to du Pont in 1940 by Edward C. Wheeler, Jr., of Boston who had owned them "a good many years. . . . One of them was found in Newton and the other in the home of an old sea captain on Cape Cod."[31] The chairs are identical to a pair at Pilgrim Hall, Plymouth, that have a local history of ownership in the White family. The four chairs are doubtless from the same set, and the evidence of a Massachusetts provenance places them among the few examples of English furniture that can be identified as having been owned in colonial New England. A similar story could be told of dozens of chairs and should be told, for only by understanding this furniture can we understand an important link in the chain of events that shaped the taste of a generation of New Englanders who wanted furniture in a new and exciting style.

Cane chairs appeared in a number of places in the colonies before they appeared in Boston. Christopher Taylor of Philadelphia possessed "five cane chairs" valued at 9s. each at the time of his death in 1685. Cane chairs are also listed in the 1687 inventory of Pennsbury, William Penn's manor house on the Delaware. Similar chairs doubtless appeared early in the manor houses of wealthy Virginia planters whose natural trade route ran to England and who had credit in London, yet they do not show up in a Virginia inventory prior to the "6 cane chairs and 1 couch" listed on December 18, 1689, in the "chamber" of Rowland Jones, a minister of York County. Jones also possessed "6 Caine Chairs" valued at £1.16 and "1 caine Couch" worth £1 and kept them in his "Study."[32]

Undoubtedly, stylishly fashionable English furniture was among the "considerable quantity of Goods for the Governour" which arrived in Boston some days before Sir Edmund Andros himself appeared in late 1686. If cane chairs were among these goods, they were probably the first to be seen on the Shawmut Peninsula. According to the estate inventories cane began to appear in the 1680s. The earliest reference to cane chairs in a Boston inventory occurs on July 9, 1688; "six cane chairs" valued at £2.8 were listed in the estate of Giles Master, "the King's attorney." Master could not have lived in Boston more than a few years prior to his death and was not likely to have been popular in a society that despised lawyers on principle. He possessed a hatchment that suggests he at least had some connection or pretensions to family status, despite the slight amount of £36.14 at which his propertyless estate was appraised. Three years later John Ragland of Boston, who was probably a mariner, left an estate with "six cane back chairs" and "6 bass bottomed chairs" jointly appraised at £3.10. We know nothing about Ragland, except that he owned a house worth £250 near the town dock. He does not appear on the tax list of 1687, nor does his widow Mary appear on the list of 1695. The total value of his estate was £313.[33]

Cane chairs do not occur again in the probate records of Boston until "six cane chaires," worth £5.2 are listed in "the Lower Room" of Dr. Thomas Pemberton's home on November 30, 1693. Pemberton also possessed other pieces of furniture in the "new style," including "a chest of drawers and a table," valued at £8.[34] A "chirurgeon," a native of Massachusetts, and a son of one of the founders of Old South

Church, Pemberton was also an intimate of Sir William Phips, the native-born, royal governor who replaced Andros, much to the relief of many New Englanders in 1692, and had accompanied Phips on an abortive expedition to capture Quebec in 1690.

When Governor Phips sailed to England in the fall of 1694, he left in the "Hall" of his Boston home "12 cane chairs and 1 couch . . . £7" and much additional furniture in the new style. By that date, cane chairs are listed in inventories with increasing frequency. Furthermore, they are found in the estates of people on lower rungs of the social and economic ladder. William Gross, whose total estate amounted to only £50, had "a dozen of Cain chaires" worth £3.10 in September 1694. Five months later Capt. John Ware possessed "1 doz. of caine chaires" valued at £1 each. In 1695, the lavishly furnished home of Capt. Andrew Cratey at Marblehead contained, in addition to "one doz of caine chears" valued at £7.4 in "the great Hall," a dozen, conspicuous, "Lackered Cane chears" valued at £12, and a "ditto couch . . . £3," a "Japan case of drawers" £10, "1 ditto case for Plate" £10, and 350 ounces of silver to go in it. The "1 old Cain chaire" valued along with "2 Flagg [rush-bottom] chairs" at only 8s. in the December 28, 1697, inventory of Joseph Eldridge, a Boston mariner whose estate amounted to £1,281.5.10, indicates that a few isolated cane chairs may have been in use prior to 1688, as does another reference in the 1712 inventory of John Raynesford, a mariner, who possessed "6 very old cain chaires" at 5s. for the lot. In 1714 John Warton, perhaps the grandson of John Winthrop on his mother's side, had "10 cain chairs a Cain Couch and Cott—all very much worn" worth £4 along with 10 obviously newer cane chairs valued at £5, in an estate that totaled £1,118.13.6.[35] Additional references to "old" cane chairs occur in 1716 and 1717. Cane chairs, however, are so often mentioned in the Boston inventories after 1700 that it is clear they remained the most popular chairs in urban New England for at least twenty years.

Cane as an upholstery material continued to be used in England and America into the 1730s. Many of the earlier English furniture historians attempted to confine the cane-chair styles to the seventeenth century or the earliest years of the eighteenth, but many surviving English examples, as well as account books, letters, and newspaper advertisements, reveal that these chairs continued to be made and sold throughout the reigns of Queen Anne and King George I. Numerous references to cane chairs in eighteenth-century American inventories likewise suggest that some cane chairs were made in the so-called Queen Anne style. Indeed, an advertisement in the Charleston, South Carolina, *Gazette* for December 23–30, 1732, lists among the "Goods lately imported, and to be Sold, by Yeomans and Escott, . . . dozens of cane Chairs, elbow Chairs & Couches" which, at that date, could be in no style other than the compass-seat, crook-back, crook-leg variety. The researches of Christopher G. Gilbert have revealed that the shop of the elegant London cabinetmaker, Giles Grendy, produced cane-bottom, Queen Anne-style chairs, albeit for export to Spain, between 1735 and 1741, which was well into the reign of George II.[36]

No seventeenth-century English or American observer described the art of cane-chair making in the way that Randle Holme described the art of upholstering chairs. Fortunately, chair caning came back into vogue during the third quarter of the eighteenth century in France—perhaps it had really never been out—and A. J. Roubo meticulously recorded every aspect of the process.[37] Surviving early eighteenth-century chairs reveal that the method had not basically changed in the intervening years. According to Roubo, the technique for caning chairs came to France from Holland, and it is clear from the surviving English cane chairs that they too are stylistically indebted to the Dutch.

English cane chairs of the fourth phase—the first in which English chairs are not wholly derived from Netherlands prototypes—fall into two distinctive categories. In one, the crest rails sit between the rear stiles; in the other, the crest rail perches atop the stiles. These variations have been construed to be of chronological significance, and indeed, it is obvious that some of these chairs must be later than others, but which are which? That these cane chairs are assembled in two different ways does not offer the desired clue. Their divergent appearance can with better reason be traced to the very beginnings of cane chair manufacture in England. The chairs reflect the habitual attitudes of craftsmen who thought in very different ways when they designed their chairs, considering not only how they would ultimately look, but also, as a practical matter, how they could be manufactured. It is apparent from the surviving examples of the first and second phases that shops that had specialized in upholstered chairs as well as shops that had made turned chairs both began to produce cane chairs when they first became popular. The earliest English examples of the phase-one style are clearly derived from a chair made to be upholstered, but even in these examples, the method by which the seat frame is installed varies from that of the traditional upholstered chair. The seat rails, instead of being oriented vertically to support leather or textile upholstery, are oriented horizontally to be drilled for the cane. The chairs are a hybrid in another way, for the stiles, legs, and stretchers are ornamented totally by turning, and the twist turning that is used on them is not the easiest type to execute. This continued in phase two; the joiners thought as joiners think and, wherever they could, used rectangular mortise-and-tenon joints, while the turners thought in "turnerly" terms and used turned tenons, completed on the lathe, and fitted them into round auger holes. These techniques give a better clue to the significance of the difference between those chairs in which the crest rails are perched atop the stiles in the turnerly fashion and those chairs in which the crest rails are set between them in the joinerly manner.

By the time cane chairs reached their third phase, the records clearly show that the demand—especially for the cheaper versions—had outstripped the capacities of the old established shops to produce them and that many craftsmen, perhaps with little experience, had set up shop to make cane chairs. These third-phase chairs exhibit features of both the joiner and the turner.

In the same way that the cane chairs combine the stylistic attributes of both crafts, they also combine the techniques once exclusively reserved for the separate crafts of joiner and turner in London. Because turning is so much a part of the look of cane chairs prior to about 1710, many of the joints that appear to be a turned tenon entering a round auger hole in reality have a rectangular tenon cut on the end of a turned element and a rectangular mortise cut in the element into which it fits, where it is held in place by a pin (fig. 130). This particular illustration is taken from an American chair, but the same techniques are found on English and Dutch chairs and graphically illustrate the blending of turning and joining techniques by a new breed of craftsmen who were neither turners nor joiners but called themselves "chairmakers."

The method of framing the seat offers a good clue by which connoisseurs can often determine whether a particular chair is old or not, for the staggered rows of holes drilled to hold the cane are often broken in old chairs (fig. 131). Generally the upper interior top edge of the seat frame was chamfered so that no sharp edge would cut the cane as a person sat down on it. These chairs are almost never found today with their original cane in the seats, although the back caning is often intact. Judging from late nineteenth-century chairs with their original cane seats fragile but intact, a cane bottom was expected to endure 35 or 40 years of use before having to be replaced. To some extent both of these ideas are supported by inventory references such as that of Thomas Steele of Boston who had "6 old-fashioned cane chairs wth bass bottoms" at 5s. in March 1735/36.[38] These chairs are not a special form which combined rush bottoms with cane backs; the cane backs were probably original, and the seat had been replaced with another material (see catalogue entry 54).

Perhaps the durability of cane explains why we find so few advertisements offering to rebottom cane chairs prior to the one in the Boston *Gazette* in the summer of 1730, in which "John Lane, from London," advertised that he "Canes and Bottoms both New and Old Chairs, after the best manner, [in a shop] over against Dr. Cooke's in School Street, Boston."[39] In 1734 Nicholas Gates, whose shop was "next to the sign of the Pewter Platter in Front Street, Philadelphia," offered "Cane Chairs of all Sorts made after the best & newest Fashion: old Chairs caned or Holes mended (if not gone too far) at reasonable rates."[40]

Then as now, caning was charged on the basis of the number of holes across the front of the seat frame, as a letter from Thomas Fitch, a Boston upholsterer, entrepreneur, and importer, to his London factor, Silas Hooper, in 1725, makes clear: "Capt. Lithered bot for Mr. H[enr]y Deering Some Cane Chiars of 46 holes in front of Seat wholly Walnutt frames, the fore feet of the same fashion [at 13s. as] those Charg'd [me at] 21[s.], [of which] 14 have but 37 holes and part of them not Walnutt but only culler'd over, so that the maker ought . . . to make you a further considerable allowance [the chairs] being so much over Charg'd."[41] Since the number of holes in the seat frame governs the fineness or coarseness of the caning pattern, this note from 1725 further refutes the notion that the caning pattern is an indicator of the date of manufacture of a chair.

Fig. 130. LEFT. Detail of the cane chair in catalogue entry 54 showing a joiner's rectangular tenon and mortise hole used in combination with turned decoration. (Winterthur 74.120.)

Fig. 131. RIGHT. Detail of the cane chair in catalogue entry 54 showing the holes drilled for the caning of the chair seat. (Winterthur 74.120.)

WHO MADE THE NEW ENGLAND CANE CHAIRS?

That American-made cane chairs exist is extremely important. The earliest chairs are stylistically ambitious and like their English predecessors are made of beech. Indeed, without microanalysis they could easily be mistaken for European chairs and often have been; American beech (*Fagus grandifolia*) and European beech (*Fagus sylvatica*) look alike to the naked eye.

Cane chairs are among the greatest rarities of all the forms made in colonial America and are all the rarer since only one or two possible examples that might prove to be of nonurban origin have been identified.[42] Numerous advertisements in the Boston newspapers from 1714 onward offered cane chairs from England for sale. These advertisements confirm what the inventories of Boston suggest: English cane chairs found a ready market in Boston, which accounts, to a great extent, for the scarcity of American examples. American craftsmen had to compete with the twofold advantages of a fashionable and serviceable London product that could be imported and sold more cheaply than it could be produced here.

In the last quarter of the seventeenth century, the craft designation "chairmaker" emerges in urban American documents, just as it does in English ones. The term first appears in the New England records on a deed dated October 27, 1684, identifying Thomas Stapleford as a "chayre maker" of Boston. Stapleford had resided in Boston at least since 1678. By the 1690s he was living in Philadelphia where he was known as a "chair fframe maker." Stapleford left his Boston property "neer the Forthill" "in the tenure of Thomas ffitch," a Boston upholsterer. If Fitch rented Stapleford's property when the latter left Boston, then Stapleford knew both Fitch and Edward Shippen, Boston's leading upholsterer of the period, with whom Fitch served an apprenticeship. Moreover, it is likely that Stapleford left for Philadelphia at the encouragement of Shippen, who had moved there in 1693, and that all three remained in touch with each other in the succeeding years.[43]

From the bare-bones designations of Stapleford's craft as that of chairmaker and chair-frame maker, the assumption might follow that Stapleford's chair frames were turner's work, but the research of Cathryn J. McElroy reveals that Stapleford

was a joiner whose shop produced tables, boxes, coffins, and bedsteads.[44] While there is no documentary evidence that Stapleford produced cane-chair frames, his name must be mentioned in this study because he was an active craftsman during the period in which the first cane chairs appear in Boston.

Evidence of who made the first cane chairs in Massachusetts is highly circumstantial. The chairs may have been made around 1696 at the behest of John Brocas, the first documented English cabinetmaker to work in Boston. The 1698/99 inventory of Ralph Carter contains the earliest references to cane chairs in a furniture craftsman's estate: "12 cane chaires" worth 5s. each "[i]n the great chamber over the shop." Since Carter's entire estate was valued at only £72.17, it seems fair to assume that he made his own furniture and, thus, these chairs. Even if they were new chairs, their slight value does not necessarily mean that they were imported. Although Carter is called a "joyner" in his inventory, the "Sundry Turning Tooles[,] plains[,] augurs & all" assessed at £5 in his shop reveal that he was also a turner. And he was capable of doing turning in a big way: he possessed a great lathe, one of the earliest thus far noted in American inventories. Biographical information about Carter is scanty. He was definitely practicing his trade when he signed the petition dated May 23, 1677, to the General Court praying that all craftsmen who would be permitted to work in Boston would have to serve an apprenticeship. He was a contemporary of Richard Knight and Edward Budd, both of whom were carvers, but we do not know if they carved any of his furniture.[45]

It is increasingly clear that all the work done on a cane or leather chair was not done in a single shop. Evidence from the decade of the 1720s survives to indicate that, as had happened in London, specialists worked as jobbers for Boston's chairmakers. The eighteenth-century account books of upholsterers Thomas Fitch and Samuel Grant show that chair frames were sent to them on contract. It is logical to assume that carvers made a similar arrangement with chairmakers. Presumptive evidence for this is found in the records of the Suffolk County Court of Common Pleas. The varied lawsuits involving Samuel Mattocks, Sr., and Samuel Mattocks, Jr., suggest that they jobbed out work to specialists and on

Fig. 132. Chippendale-style chairs, Boston, 1760–80. Mahogany; H 36⅝" (93 cm), W 32½" (59.7 cm), D 21¼" (54 cm), SH 16¾" (42.5 cm). (Winterthur 59.2639, 59.2640.) Note the profile of the rear stretcher on each of these chairs.

occasion also served as jobbers and furnished chairs or parts of chairs to another chairmaker.

Samuel Mattocks, Sr., appears to have been the son of a tailor also named Samuel Mattocks and the brother of James Mattocks, a Boston cabinetmaker, and the father of Samuel, Jr. (b. December 17, 1688). The father and son are identified jointly as "chairmakers" in a lawsuit filed in the Court of Common Pleas in October 1720. Next, the younger Mattocks, who had done work for Charlestown joiner John Davis, sued Davis for nonpayment of account in the amount of £4.19.1. During 1723 one of the Mattockses brought suit against John Lincoln, a Boston carver, who had contracted by promissory note to execute £4 worth of carving but had defaulted. The following year one of the Mattockses sued Edmond Perkins, joiner, for debt, which suggests that they had supplied Perkins with chair parts or other turned work.[46]

The sole documentary reference that reveals that cane chairs were made in Boston does not occur until relatively late in the period covered by this book and involved this same Edmond Perkins. Upholsterer Thomas Fitch noted in his book among "Sundry Accounts Debtor to Cash in December 1724 . . . Edmond Perkins lent him to buy Cane 12th Instant . . . £25."[47] Perkins (1683–1761) may have been one of the two most important chairmakers in Boston during the first half of the eighteenth century. He was the son of Edmond Perkins of Boston and probably began his training around 1696 with a Boston joiner, whose identity cannot be determined. Perkins was old enough to have begun working on his own account in 1704 and was certainly doing so by the time he married widow Mary Ferris in 1709. Their son William (1716–1769) became a chairmaker. In 1722, one L. Edmund Perkins, widower,

married Esther Frothingham, daughter of Boston shipwright Peter Frothingham. This marriage produced a number of children, at least two of whom, Henry (d. 1783) and John, became chairmakers. A third, Edmond, Jr., was probably also engaged in the family trade. In 1760, the Perkins house "in Mackrel Lane" and "several chair-maker's shops" were consumed by the great fire that devastated Boston's North End. Losses in the fire undoubtedly account for the paucity of information contained in probate records. Perkins's estate amounted to only £40 in 1761, which obscures his importance as a furniture maker.[48]

Perkins, identified as a "joiner" in documents dated 1711 and 1724, was called a "chairmaker" when his inventory was proved in 1762. He was an important supplier of chair frames, bedstead "cornishes," and other woodwork to upholsterer Grant, whose account with Perkins for £88.6 was settled on August 8, 1729. Some idea of the quantity of goods Perkins supplied to Grant can be deduced from the records. On February 19, 1730/31—nineteen months later—accounts were again reckoned, and Grant owed Perkins an additional £152.[49] Assuming that Perkins was supplying Grant with leather-chair frames, and given that Grant was selling leather chairs for 26s. and 27s. each, of which 8s. represented the leather upholstery billed by Grant, and allowing an advance of one-third for profit, chair frames may have cost Grant 12s. each. If so, £152 represents roughly 250 chair frames, a sizable number by any standard.

The careers of Edmond Perkins and his sons spanned the eighteenth century; thus, there is an outside chance that we may identify his and their work. Only one group of related William and Mary–, Queen Anne–, and Chippendale-style chairs, some with cane seats and others with upholstered seats, is readily apparent in the Winterthur collection, and they may well be from the Perkins shop. Because characteristic features are common to all, these chairs when viewed as a group suggest the persistence of learned craft practices in a single school of chairmakers—perhaps even one family (compare the chairs in catalogue entries 54, 57, 76, and 90 and figs. 132, 170).[50] Although the style in which this school of craftsmen worked was continually updated to conform with the changing tastes of their customers and the changing fashions of the times, all their chairs retain familial characteristics which identify them as the lengthened shadow of a group of cane chairs made in the William and Mary style. Among these characteristics are the chamfers on the rear legs above the stretcher; the backward rake of the rear feet, which suggests the great heels of the earlier period; thin, almost parsimonious seat rails that are only thick enough for a small tenon to fit into the equally small mortise hole in the legs, which made it necessary to retain stretchers, a jarring note for chairs in the Chippendale style. The stretchers further demonstrate the evolution of the thinking of the designers of these chairs—the configuration and design of the stretchers in figure 132 are identical to those on the William and Mary cane chair identified by the punched initial in catalogue entry 54. Although the significance of the initial remains undiscovered, many of these chairs were made by either the Perkins family or some other family whose working manner persisted over a great span of time.

CANE CHAIRS IN PENNSYLVANIA

Few Philadelphia cane chairs have been identified with certainty. The two chairs attributed to Philadelphia in this catalogue suggest that in the production of cane chairs the town made up in quality what it lacked in quantity. William Macpherson Hornor's search of the Philadelphia records has revealed furniture makers actively working from the earliest date of settlement.

Given that Philadelphia was established during the era in which the cane chair was rapidly becoming the most popular chair form in England and that most of the craftsmen who settled in Pennsylvania came directly from England, it follows that the earliest furniture made in Philadelphia was probably closely related to stylish English furniture of the time. It also follows that the principles of connoisseurship which have enabled us to piece together the story of cane chairs in Boston will be of little assistance in understanding the cane chairs made in Philadelphia.

As discussed above in the chapter on woods, black walnut was the wood of choice in the middle colonies, even in the opening years of English settlement. On his first trip to Pennsylvania in 1684, William Penn listed "the Trees of Most Note" growing in his colony. First among them was "the black *Walnut*," followed by "*Cedar, Cyprus, Chestnut, Poplar, Gumwood, Hickery, Sassafrax, Ash, Beech* and *Oak* of divers sorts, as *red, white* and *black, Spanish Chestnut* and *Swamp,* the most durable of all: Of all which there is plenty."[51] Most of these woods quickly found their way into furniture. On

October 12, 1694, the first detailed inventory of a Philadelphia furniture maker was taken. The late John Fellows, a joiner, left in his shop "6½ of Round wall-nutt Loggs" valued at £6.10 as well as "219 foot wall-nutt-plank . . . 240 foot wall-nutt-boards" and "60 foot wallnutt Scantling." The plank was valued at 2d. per board foot, the boards at 1½d., while the "pyne" boards listed in his inventory were valued at a little less than 1d. a foot, an unusually slight differential in price.[52] Since pine is softer than walnut and can be sawn in less time, the price is usually lower. That it is so little lower in Fellows's case indicates that the difference was probably based on sawing time and that the woods themselves must have been equally available at that date.

The capacity for mill sawing in Pennsylvania existed from an early date. On July 29, 1684, James Claypoole, newly arrived in Philadelphia from London, wrote Edward Haistwell that the settlers "have a corne mill going, and are setting up a saw mill and glass house." Seven years later, C. Pickering reported "several *Saw-Mills* are *Built that go by Water and more are Building* . . . in many places of the Country." The 1699 inventory of joiner James Chick lists "Sundry parcells of Wallnutt planke and Boards at Brandywine Creeke [near Wilmington, Delaware; doubtless the boards were mill sawn], supposed to be worth £15."[53] These scattered references reveal that walnut was already popular among the woodworkers of Philadelphia in the late seventeenth century.

The idea that furniture of American black walnut was made in America depends upon our being able to show that black walnut was not shipped in any quantity from the colonies to England. Evidence on either side of this question is scarce. It is unlikely that New England exported walnut to Europe because the wood was not common in New England to begin with. Indeed, much of the walnut used in New England appears to have been imported from the South. At the beginning of the eighteenth century, Pennsylvania was exporting many goods to the West Indies; little evidence of shipment from Pennsylvania to England has been found.[54] Most of the writers who have commented upon woods suggest that the furniture makers of London preferred wood from northern Europe because it could be purchased and processed more cheaply than wood from America. On a purely economic basis, it is clear why this was so. The shipping costs to England doubled the price of any wood, and thus American would only have been used profitably by craftsmen who had customers willing to purchase items made of expensive wood. Furthermore, in England the figure of American walnut was considered inferior to that of French walnut. Nonetheless, some American black walnut was shipped to England from Virginia and by the mid seventeenth century was known as "Virginia walnut." According to William Strachey, "yt is well bought up to make waynscott, tables, cubbordes, chairs and stooles of a delicate grayne and cullour like ebonie." Thirty-four years later John Evelyn echoed Strachey's comments. Yet, as mentioned earlier, there is little evidence of its use. At the end of the seventeenth century William Fitzhugh, a Virginia planter, had difficulty selling two lots of black walnut in England. Undoubtedly other planters in the southern colonies were shipping black walnut to England throughout much of the seventeenth century, but the evidence of this or black walnut's use is scanty.[55]

In contrast, furniture of black walnut was widely admired in America, and in at least one instance such furniture was commissioned in London by an American. On February 20, 1712/13, James Logan of Philadelphia instructed his London factor, John Askew, to purchase "2 finest Virginia Walnut Chairs at 9s or 9s 6." July 1 Logan augmented the order: "I would have ye two black walnut chairs I wrote for made up half a Dozen besides an Armed one, to suit those I have."[56] Despite the American admiration for it, black walnut does not appear to have found its way into much English furniture. It does, however, become a wood of preference for cane chairs that have a history in the Middle Atlantic colonies.

In Philadelphia cane chairs began to appear early on, but until 1699 they were luxury items that appeared only in estates with value of £300 or more. In an overall survey of chair forms mentioned in inventories of the 1682–1710 era, Ruth Matzkin found 331 references to chairs that could be identified by type, of which 143 leather chairs constituted the largest group. Next, in order of popularity were cane chairs (97 listings). Given this taste for cane chairs, it is illogical to argue that the local chairmakers did not satisfy at least some of the demand for them. Initially, the chairs were probably of English origins. The first reference to "five cane chairs" valued at 9s. each is in the 1685 inventory of Christopher Taylor, a merchant and register of wills. This comes only two years after Penn's colonists settled in the city and three years before another set of cane chairs (valued at 8s. each) were itemized in a Boston inventory. Two years later "2 gre[a]t Cane Chayers" were in the "Paller," and "2 small Ceane Chayres" were in the "Paller Chamber" at Pennsbury, William Penn's residence on the Delaware River.[57]

While no trace of Taylor's cane chairs can be found today, numerous examples in widely varying styles have been associated with original ownership by William Penn, including one illustrated in Nutting's *Furniture Treasury* (no. 2043) and now at Winterthur (58.54). Wood analysis reveals that few of these chairs are of American origin. Microanalysis of Winterthur's chair has revealed that it is made of European beech (*Fagus sylvatica*). A cane armchair of similar style, but not from the same set, was once owned by Howard Reifsnyder until his collection was dispersed in 1929. According to the sale catalogue, Penn brought the chair from England about 1699. During the eighteenth century it was presented to Henry Babcock, whose great-granddaughter gave it to Herbert Stokes in 1846, and it remained in the Stokes family until Reifsnyder acquired it.[58]

An earlier style cane chair, now in the library of the Pennsylvania Hospital, is also said to have been owned by Penn. It is a twist-turned armchair made of European walnut (*Juglans regia*).[59] Another cane chair, which belonged to the heirs of James Logan who reportedly acquired it from Pennsbury, is owned by the National Park Service.[60] Although the particular manner in which the feet are articulated is similar to those of the example in catalogue entry 57, which suggests that it might be of American origin, microanalysis reveals that the chair is made of English walnut.

Only one of the "William Penn chairs" has been positively identified as having been made of American wood and is almost certainly of American origin. It is an armchair made of American beech (*Fagus grandifolia*), a wood that never made its way into the export trade. The chair belongs to the Historical Society of Pennsylvania in Philadelphia.[61]

References to cane chairs in Philadelphia's probate records occur with increasing frequency after 1700. In 1708, John Hunt possessed "11 cane chairs" worth 25s. each, "1 black Ditto" worth 24s., and "1 elbow Ditto broke" at £1.5. The next year, widow Elizabeth Fishbourne of Chester had "6 cane chairs" valued at £1.16 "in the Chamber over the Parlor," and Mary Jeffs of Philadelphia had "6 cain Chairs partly broaken" valued at £1.10 or 5s. each.[62] As far as documentary evidence is concerned, cane chairs reach their apogee in Philadelphia in 1722 when the inventory of the exquisitely furnished home of Jonathan Dickinson was recorded. Dickinson, who owned a plantation on Jamaica as well as a mansion in Philadelphia, left an account book which reveals that he imported mahogany as early as 1699 and had furniture made from it. The descriptions of his cane chairs show that they were lavish, and the valuations suggest that they were among the most expensive examples of their type in America. Among them were:

In the best Parlour	
6 Elbow Cane Chairs at 20[s.]	£6
8 common ditto at 16[s.]	6. 8.
Front Chamber	
2 Elbow Cane Chairs with blew Harateen cushions	2.10.
[en suite with the bed hangings]	
Best Chamber	
Cane Couch	2.10.
12 Elbow Cane chairs at 22[s.]	13. 4.
2 Cane Stools	1
Chamber over Upper Kitchen	
Cane Couch and blew silk Squab	2.15.
6 Elbow Chairs D[itt]o with blew Cushions at 24[s.]	7. 4.[63]

In Philadelphia, as in Boston, the popularity of the cane chair apparently outlived the William and Mary style. On March 12, 1740/41, Solomon Fussell, a Philadelphia chairmaker and merchant, billed "½ Duz: Cane chairs . . . to William fisher" at £6, but more than a year earlier Fussell had also begun billing customers for newly fashionable chairs with "crook'd feet," that is, chairs with cabriole legs in the Queen Anne style.[64]

Several chairmakers were working in Philadelphia by 1700. Any or all of them could have been making cane chair frames, but the research of Cathryn McElroy has associated the name of only one craftsman—Thomas Stapleford—with cane chairs (see catalogue entry 57). Stapleford, the "Chair fframe maker" from Boston, had moved to Philadelphia a year or so after the death of John Fellows in 1694. While the detailed inventory of Fellows's shop contains no mention of cane or of cane chairs, the presence of two lathes, a considerable quantity of turning tools, and "one dozen of Chair frames" valued at £4.4 reveals that he made chairs as well as case furniture.[65]

Fig. 133. Stool, Pennsylvania, probably Philadelphia, 1700–1720. Black walnut; H 19¼″ (48.9 cm), W 16⅛″ (41 cm), D 13¾″ (34.9 cm). (Historical Society of Pennsylvania, Philadelphia, gift of Maria Dickinson Logan, 1939.) The stool is believed to have been among the furnishings of James Logan's home, Stenton. The top was probably caned.

As the first identifiable chair-frame maker on the scene in colonial Philadelphia, Stapleford was in a position to command the cane-chair-making trade from its beginnings. Indeed, his working career spanned the entire time that the style was popular.

Another craftsman who appears to have made cane chairs in Philadelphia prior to 1700 is Charles Plumley. Plumley had arrived by 1698. When he died a decade later, his shop contained "6 Carved Maple Chairs ntt finished" valued at £3 (10s. each) as well as "2 black Carved Chair frames" at 9s. each (see Appendix 1). His home contained "6 black caine chairs" valued at 10s. each, perhaps japanned to go en suite with his "black screetore" appraised at £3.10.⁶⁶ Although Plumley had unfinished case furniture in his shop, he also had among his tools a center bit (the earliest such reference yet found in an American inventory), which indicates that he gave due attention to the making of chairs. It is possible that his "2 black Carved Chair frames" were black walnut chairs, although this cannot be maintained with any vehemence; chairs in Philadelphia inventories of the early eighteenth century are described by either the adjectives *cane* or *walnut* but never both.

The one piece of caned walnut furniture of indisputable Philadelphia origin is a footstool (fig. 133). It was given to the Historical Society of Pennsylvania by Maria Dickinson Logan in 1939 and is believed to have been part of the furnishings at James Logan's home, Stenton, built in 1717.⁶⁷ The original frame at the top was undoubtedly caned. This is indicated by the legs. Rather than being mortised and tenoned

into the upper rail, the turned tenons fit into auger holes on the underside of the top, which is also a typical treatment for caned chairs. The caned top has been replaced with the present upholstered one. The bulbous legs of the stool are similar in design to those on two chairs in the catalogue (nos. 57 and 58) and have numerous counterparts in English furniture, but the feet are Germanic in style, which suggests that this stool was turned by a Philadelphia turner of German descent. The footstool's medial stretcher has the same abruptly narrowed turning on either side of the central ball as is found on the Thomas Lloyd chair (catalogue entry 57). The legs have swelled balusters each with a ridge at the top, which is typical of later Philadelphia turnings, and columnar elements in the English manner, like those on the arm supports of a cane chair made in the William and Mary style and recently owned by David Stockwell, Inc., of Wilmington, Delaware. The broadest part of the turning on the footstool has an incised groove in the manner of that done by Philadelphia's Germanic school. Unlike the larger balusters on the chairs in catalogue entries 57 and 58, the diminutive ones on this footstool were made of wood that was glued together to provide a piece of walnut sufficiently large for bold turning.

Most of these turned attributes are found in what may be the sole easy chair of Philadelphia manufacture during the early eighteenth century, illustrated in Nutting's *Furniture Treasury* as no. 2048. It was then owned by an eminent Philadelphia collector, J. Stodgell Stokes.

CANE COUCHES

The early eighteenth-century date for the manufacture of the Essex Institute's turkey-work couch (see fig. 112) is indeed curious when we stop to consider that one-ended cane couches with double-twist-turned uprights in the Dutch manner had been introduced into London by the 1670s. An early example of the London version of this new style of couch with a cane bottom is illustrated by Ralph Edwards in *The Shorter Dictionary* (p. 265, fig. 4). Superficially, this type of couch represents an evolved version of the older style English couch with one of the ends removed. Yet the one-ended couch had long found favor in France, at times in the guise of the royal form of bed known as a *couchette* and at other times in the form of an upholstered daybed with a heavy bolster at one end called a *lit de repos* (literally, "bed of ease"), an example of which was upholstered in "satin with a pearl-gray ground and flowers and panels of pale red, green and beige, decorated with a very rich fringe of gold and silver." Less elevated versions are depicted in French engravings throughout the seventeenth century, including those by Abraham Bosse. The *Memoirs* of Mademoiselle de Monpensier fortuitously tell us that Henriette Marie, widow of Charles I and mother of the exiled Charles II, was "seated upon a *lit de repos*" and surrounded by "all the princesses and duchesses of Paris" when they stayed at the Chateau de Chilly in 1656.⁶⁸ Thus there is good reason to believe that this form of couch was introduced into England, as were many other French ideas and tastes, with the restoration of the Stuarts to the English throne in 1660.

Unfortunately, the English did not translate the lit de repos form as "daybed" or "bed of ease," but simply applied the older term *couch* to the new furniture form. This occurred even though the new form was one-ended, sat rather low to the floor, and was designed primarily for reclining. Stylistically, the form is related to cane chairs, and conceptually it is a side chair with an elongated seat frame. That cane couches are itemized in both English and American inventories offers clear evidence that the increasing affluence in the upper reaches of society permitted the uses of the couch to be divided between two distinct pieces of furniture: the couch, represented by numerous cane or upholstered examples, was for reclining; the settee, in essence a double easy chair that had evolved from the easy chair and *not* from the Cromwellian-style couch, was for sitting. And by the 1730s, Englishmen were also enjoying a third piece, the sofa, which was wider than the settee and also was derived from the easy chair.

The first cane couch appears in the London home of well-to-do Capt. Francis Digby in January 1676/77. In a room that must have been used as a parlor, Digby had "12 cane chairs wth 12 cushions and backes of Damask" valued at £5 and "one couch and Squab of the same" worth £3.10.[69] Among the subsequent inventories in the Public Records Office, entries for couches with cane bottoms are no more frequent than those covered with textiles.

Assuming that the older style couch was never upholstered with cane, we can document the appearance in America of the new-style couch with reasonable accuracy, yet the search for couches among the estates of men who possessed the first cane chairs here is not immediately gratifying. Christopher Taylor of Philadelphia, who died in 1685, had no couch in his inventory, nor was one listed in the 1687 inventory of William Penn's Pennsbury (but there was one in the "Best Parlour" by December 1701). The first mention of a cane couch in the colonies is in the September 9, 1688, inventory of Francis Richardson, a New York merchant whose estate was valued at £1,860.7. Curiously enough, no mention is made of cane chairs, which almost always accompany cane couches. Fifteen months later a "caine couch" valued at £1 and "6 caine chairs" valued at £1.16. (6s. each) were inventoried in the study of the Reverend Rowland Jones of York County, Virginia. These were probably of English manufacture. Jones also possessed two additional couches. One, very likely of the earlier type, was described as "old" and demoted to his kitchen, and another, not described, was in his bedchamber.[70] It is impossible to estimate how recently Mr. Jones's cane couch had been acquired or to explain the laggard appearance of the form in America since it had appeared at least twenty-five years earlier in London.

References to cane couches are equally rare in New England. Neither Giles Master, nor John Ragland, nor Dr. Thomas Pemberton—the earliest owners of cane chairs in Boston—had a cane couch. Indeed, the first cane couch inventoried in Massachusetts appears not in Boston but in Marblehead, then a humble village with only one conspicuously wealthy citizen, merchant prince and trader Andrew Cratey, formerly of London. Captain Cratey purchased land in Marblehead on August 3, 1689, and built a lavish mansion house which, with its acre of land, was valued six years later at £700. Among the many expensive olivewood veneered, inlaid, japanned, and gilt pieces of furniture in this house were "1 doz. of lackered Cane chears" valued at £12 and "1 ditto couch" valued at £3, at Cratey's demise, age 44, in 1695. We must assume that his furniture was all brought from London, probably around 1690. In that same year Sir William Phips was appointed sheriff of New England. Either then or two years later when Phips was appointed royal governor, he furnished his elegant Boston home. Phips was recalled to London in 1694 and died there a few months later. The inventory lists, in addition to a dozen cane chairs and a couch in the hall, "14 chairs 1 Couch & Squabb" valued at £7.12 in the dining room. The squab for the couch in the hall was then in the hall chamber. In the ensuing decade, the verbal formula "cane couch and squab" occurs with increasing frequency. In 1699 Peter Butler of Boston had one valued at £3 as well as a dozen turkey-work side chairs and a turkey-work "elbow" chair in his parlor. Shortly thereafter Sarah Harris also had a cane couch and squab matching the seven cane chairs.[71]

The word *squab* is etymologically unusual, coming from a Scandinavian origin, and meaning, when applied to a person, fat and flabby. The *OED* notices it in use in 1664 and again near the end of the century when it was found in a description of a squab made of cloth of silver. Peter Thornton has shown that a squab at this period can be an overstuffed footstool, but the context in which it generally appears in late seventeenth-century New England inventories almost certainly indicates that a squab is a generously stuffed mattress or cushion used on a couch. Samuel Shrimpton, a Boston merchant, pewterer, and brazier, owned a cane couch at the time of his death in 1705, and Boston goldsmith David Jessee had one with a quilt on it in 1706. Cane couches abound in the Boston inventories of the first quarter of the eighteenth century and, moreover, are valued at a wide range of prices, from a low of £1.10 to a high of £4.10; in both instances the couch had a pillow, and the latter had a squab. Even Cotton Mather meditated upon the sins of this world on a cane couch valued at £2.4 in 1728. In the same year, Joseph Allen of Boston left a "black cane couch and Six Chairs Ditto" valued at £7.[72]

CONCLUSIONS

For the first time in the history of western decorative arts, a combination of events created a popular fashion. A large laboring force in an urban center (London)—not fully employed since the middle of the sixteenth century—began making chairs that required diversified skills: turning, joining, carving, caning, and varnishing or staining. The traditional separation of crafts in London suggests that initially these specialities were contracted out. But the chairs had to meet a number of requirements. If made, conceived of, and sold in sets of at least six, the chairs within each set had to have a certain uniformity, had to have the same quality, and had to be produced economically in order to compete in the export trade with the products of the places to which they were shipped.

This suggests a concentration on a special part of the chair by a worker who did nothing else. Follow, for example, a rear stile through the process of fabrication. It was first rough sawn out of a plank to the approximate shape, then sent to the turner, then to the carver, and then came back to the chairmaker so the chair could be assembled and stained. Finally the chair was caned. Such a pattern of manufacture can occur only in an urban setting where the various specialties are readily available, and, because each craftsman does what he does best, the result is a chair of professional finish. It is almost an axiom that a craftsman usually excels in *one* skill, rarely in all of them.

Considerable advantages accrue to both maker and customer when this method of division of labor is followed. If the work is subcontracted, the entrepreneur or master who is producing cane chairs does not have to maintain workers in his shop when there is no work to do or no orders to be filled. Competition for subcontracting work and the efficient production of the specialized parts must ultimately lower the sale price and thus make these chairs available to more people, which in turn enables what is the fad among the elite to become a fashion for the commonality.

Such a method of craft organization suggests as well that patterns were used extensively to guarantee the uniformity of parts. If this is so, the attribution of an actual chair to any given shop is not only a virtual impossibility at this late date but is a pointless exercise, for many hands must have been engaged in its production. This concept of the jobbing of parts, with slight variations, gives us the first feasible explanation for the stamped, punched, and carved initials that are common on English cane chairs. In his study of the shop of London cabinetmaker Giles Grendy, Christopher Gilbert convincingly demonstrates that the various initials stamped on chairs that Grendy sold between 1737 and 1741 to the duke of Infantado, Lazcarno, Spain, correspond to the names of craftsmen who are known to have worked for him during that period.[73] Therefore, the stamped initials do not represent the initials of jobbers or specialists in separate shops, but rather the initials of journeymen or "day workers," working in Grendy's own shop. Why? Pride of workmanship and the desire for immortality—theories that have often been advanced to explain these initials—seem rather too sentimental. It is quite likely that a more practical reason existed. If Grendy's shop was organized like those of London and Philadelphia later in the eighteenth century, it is probable that his workers were paid on a piecework basis; thus the stamp indicates the chairs or the parts that each individual craftsman made.[74]

Cane-chair making in America, as in England, appears to have been an urban phenomenon: village craftsmen here do not seem to have essayed the style. Sufficient cane chairs and documentary records from only one colonial urban center have survived on the basis of which generalizations, however tentative, can be made. That place is Boston. When we compare the list of known Boston chairmakers with that of Boston cabinetmakers, an important difference becomes immediately apparent. The introduction of cabinetmaking techniques into Boston can be traced to the immigration of one man, John Brocas from England. In contrast, the earliest possible cane-chair makers—Thomas Stapleford, Ralph Carter, the two Samuel Mattockses, and Edmond Perkins—were either native-born Bostonians or were already working in Boston before cane chairs were made in England. It is probable, therefore, either that we have missed identifying a chairmaking equivalent of Brocas or that Brocas himself was instrumental in introducing cane-chair making into New England.

But when the few documentary facts are compared with the surviving chairs, another idea becomes clear. The design and construction techniques of Boston's earliest veneered case furniture in the cabinetmaker's style shows that the maker or makers were working in an academic tradition, learned through apprenticeship. The earliest style of Boston cane chair (see catalogue entry 52), on the other hand, displays a conservatism, a novel attitude toward proportion and the combination of elements, and a general weakness of carving that suggests its design either was derived from an imported English example—of which there were a great number in the province—rather than conceived of by a craftsman who had learned his trade in an English shop, or was made by an emigrant craftsman who had been bred a turner and knew nothing of carving. The later style—with molded rear stiles, made after about 1717—is derived from known English prototypes. In marked contrast, the Philadelphia examples in the catalogue are so English in conception, design, and execution that there is no question that they were made by craftsmen who had been in this country only a short time.

Whatever further research reveals about the place of origin and the regional origins of American cane chairs, as more examples are identified by microanalysis, it is clear from the data now in hand that chairmaking in colonial America was a totally different story after the introduction of the cane chair from what it had been before that time. While the old separation of crafts had to be broken down in urban England, strict separation had never been practiced in New England, and so the freedom of design that the new style introduced found a receptive audience of practitioners here who capitalized upon that freedom by producing fascinating chair designs throughout the balance of the eighteenth century.

NOTES

[1] *Rates of Merchandizes* (London, 1609) as cited in *English Experience*, no. 165; Kircher, *An Embassage . . . to . . . the Emperor of China*, app. 2, p. 253; "Menusier," in Roubo, *Description des arts et métiers*, pt. 3, sect. 2, ch. 5, p. 622.

[2] Lockwood, *Colonial Furniture* (2d ed.), 2:33.

[3] Hamlin, *History of Ornament*, p. 161, and fig. 43; Panofsky, *Renaissance and Renascences*, fig. 10. The entire Gundohinus manuscript in the Bibliothèque Municipale, Autun, France. For Islamic antecedents, see the columnar form with spiral fluting above the entrance to the Bibi Khanum mosque, Samarkand (construction of which began in 1399), illustrated in Hill and Grabar, *Islamic Architecture*, figs. 47, 48. I am indebted to Paula N. Reiss for this reference.

Spanish examples are presented in Doménech and Bueno, *Antique Spanish Furniture*, pl. 28, fig. 45; see also fig. 124.

[4] One of this pair is in the Victoria and Albert Museum, London, and is illustrated in Edwards, *Shorter Dictionary*, p. 118, fig. 12.

[5] Walpole, *Anecdotes of Painting in England*, 2:227.

[6] See also Alberici, *Il mobile Lombardo*, p. 90. I am indebted to Ms. Alberici for generously providing a photograph of this remarkable chair to me and for permission to illustrate it here.

[7] See Jacquemart, *History of Furniture*, p. 190.

[8] The identical turnings and front stretcher appear on a later seventeenth-century chair

illustrated in Smith, *Art of Portugal*, fig. 247.
9 Hamlin, *History of Ornament*, p. 153; Doménech and Bueno, *Antique Spanish Furniture*, pl. 39. Chairs in this style were known in America in the early nineteenth century when one of them was referred to as a "Campeachy chair," after the Mexican province of Campeche where Spanish colonial examples were still being made; see also Montgomery, *American Furniture*, fig. 120.
10 For illustrations of this bracket form in several architectural contexts, see Smith, *Art of Portugal*, pls. 42, 43, 45, and especially 68.
11 Logan to Askew, February 20, 1712/13, correspondence book, James Logan Papers, HSP (I am indebted to Bradford L. Rauschenberg for this reference); Grant daybook, March 8, 1732/33.
12 Symonds: "Charles II. Couches, Chairs, and Stools," pt. 1, pp. 15–23; "Charles II. Couches, Chairs, and Stools," pt. 2, pp. 86–95; "Cane Chairs of the Late 17th and Early 18th Centuries," pp. 173–81; "English Cane Chairs," pt. 1, pp. 8–15; "English Cane Chairs," pt. 2, pp. 83–91.
13 Symonds, "English Cane Chairs," pt. 1, pp. 13–14.
14 Prerogative Court of Canterbury, Probate 5, nos. 482, and 514.
15 Symonds, "Cane Chairs of the Late 17th and Early 18th Centuries," pp. 173, 174. The bill is dated November 2, 1680, and was for "a Caned Chaire with Eares and Elbowes to move with Joynts [hinges] and a Footstole with Iron worke to fold." A chair of this type is privately owned in Leeds. An upholstered example is among the furniture at Ham House.
16 See Vogelsang, *Le meuble Hollandais*, pl. 51, fig. 144.
17 Microanalysis of a good specimen from Harvard's chair was inconclusive; it displayed a slight preponderance of factors associated with American beech (*Fagus grandifolia*), but it also had other features associated with the European variety (*Fagus sylvatica*). In the light of this curious situation, we have hesitated to say that it is made of American beech. Improved microanalytical techniques may someday positively identify this chair as being of American origin. I am indebted to Margo Scott of the Fogg Art Museum, Harvard University, for calling this chair to my attention. A detailed biography of Monis is included in *Sibley's Harvard Graduates, 1722–1725*, 7:639–46. For the New York chair see Failey, *Long Island Is My Nation*, fig. 19. I am indebted to Dean Failey for providing samples of the chair for microanalysis.
18 Symonds, "Charles II. Couches, Chairs, and Stools," pt. 2, p. 90; see, in contrast, Edwards, *Shorter Dictionary*, p. 124, fig. 32.
19 Symonds, "Charles II. Couches, Chairs, and Stools," pt. 2, p. 90.
20 Edward C. Wheeler to du Pont, November 12, 1940, object file 58.541, Registrar's Office, Winterthur. On the basis of this slim evidence, Nutting published the chair twice in his *Furniture Treasury*, once giving William Penn as the original owner, and once with no owner designated (nos. 1994 and 2043). The second chair is now owned by the Pennsylvania Historical and Museum Commission. For further discussion of chairs said to have been owned by Penn, see catalogue entry 57.
21 Savage, *Genealogical Dictionary*, 3:217–18. The Minot chair originally had arms. It is also one of a sizable group of related chairs, a few of which have eastern Massachusetts associations. One side chair has a history of ownership in the White family of Weymouth, a second is in the Cambridge Historical Society (see Comstock, "Pilgrim Chairs," p. 450); others in the group are armchair and side chair, Salisbury House, Worcester; side chair, John Hancock Insurance Company, Boston; couch, owned in Hingham, and illustrated in Nutting, *Furniture Treasury*, as no. 1588. I am indebted to Gilbert T. Vincent for the last two of these references.
22 Symonds, "Cane Chairs of the Late 17th and Early 18th Centuries," p. 175.
23 See Edwards, *Shorter Dictionary*, p. 670, fig. 1.
24 Symonds, "English Cane Chairs," pt. 1, p. 13.
25 Company of Joyners, leaf 47 verso.
26 Symonds, "English Cane Chairs," pt. 1, pp. 13–14. A survey of Virginia inventories of the late seventeenth century shows, however, that cane chairs were rare in that colony (see Singleton, *Furniture of Our Forefathers*, p. 46 ff). The London origins of the cane-chair industry are cited in Defoe, *Complete English Tradesman*, 1:266: "The chairs, if of cane, are made at London; the ordinary matted chairs, perhaps in the place where they live."
27 See Wallin, *Nordiska museets möbler*, 1:176, fig. 309; Kreisel, *Die Kunst des deutschen Möbels*, 1:634; Dr. W. Baer, Schloss Charlottenburg to Forman, July 21, 1972; Sordelli, *Il mobile antico*, p. 150, fig. 1. Another cane chair, probably of Italian origin, is illustrated in Cescinsky and Gribble, *Early English Furniture and Woodwork*, 2:223, fig. 317.
28 Symonds, "Export Trade," pp. 152–63.
29 Fowler, *A Dictionary of Modern English Usage*, p. 717, suggests that the user hopes a rule of thumb "will take him right more often than it takes him wrong." Fowler insists that the user of this dubious aid does so to save himself "the troubles of working out his problems separately."
30 The private chapel of one of the stateliest homes in England has a dozen remarkable cane chairs of which only one—the simplest—is old.
31 Edward C. Wheeler, Jr., to du Pont September 4, 1940, object file 58.539, Registrar's Office, Winterthur.
32 Matzkin, "Inventories of Estates in Philadelphia County," p. 20; Cummings, "Account of Goods at Pennsbury Manor," p. 408; York County, Va., Probate, 8: 362–63 (I am very much indebted to Patrick Henry Butler III for this last reference).
33 Sewall, *Diary*, 1:127. Edward Cranfield, royal governor of New Hampshire, may have had cane chairs some years earlier. Since both Cranfield and Andros left New England prior to their deaths no inventories confirm these conjectures. Savage, *Genealogical Dictionary*, 3:170; Suffolk Probate, 10:412, 8:179.
34 Suffolk Probate, 13:304–5.
35 Phips died shortly after arriving in London and an inventory of his Boston home occurred in 1694/95, Suffolk Probate, 11:200–202. Suffolk Probate, 13:492, 683; Essex Probate Files, 305:86–88; Suffolk Probate, 8:167, 18:52,392; Savage, *Genealogical Dictionary*, 4:495.
36 I am indebted to Susan B. Swan for the S.C. quotation; Christopher G. Gilbert, "Furniture by Giles Grendy," pp. 544–50.
37 See "Menusier," in Roubo, *Description des arts et métiers*, pt. 3, sect. 2, ch. 5, pp. 622–34. A translation of the section dealing with chair-caning technique appears in Appendix 2. A paraphrase of Roubo's information is given in *Encyclopédie méthodique*, 4:682–85.
38 Suffolk Probate, 32:434–36.
39 Advertisement, Boston *Gazette*, August 31-September 7, 1730; I am indebted to Brock W. Jobe for this reference. The mention of "new" cane chairs at this date suggests that cane chairs in the Queen Anne style were being made in Boston. A rare example, made of soft maple and beech, is illustrated in Downs, *American Furniture*, no. 12.
40 Advertisement, *Pennsylvania Gazetteer*, June 27, 1734; I am indebted to Malcolm Smith for this item, which does not appear in Hornor, *Blue Book*. Prime, *Colonial Craftsmen of Philadelphia*, p. 167, shows the name as "Gale." No further mention of Gates or Gale has been found in the records.
41 Fitch to Hooper, October 6, 1725, Fitch Letterbook, MHS.
42 A set of chairs that do not relate to identified urban types but are believed by their owner to be of American origin have been microanalyzed, and are illustrated in Reynolds, "Towns of Glastonbury, Rocky Hill, and Newington," p. 519.
43 *Boston Records*, 10:76, 9:146; *Suffolk Deeds*, 14:270. Fitch and Shippen are discussed at greater length in the next section of the catalogue.
44 McElroy, "Furniture of the Philadelphia Area," p. 208.
45 Suffolk Probate, 14:87. The 1677 petition to the General Court is reprinted in January 1894 *Bulletin of the Public Library of the City of Boston*, pp. 305–6. Savage, *Genealogical Dictionary*, 3:39; *Boston Records*, 7:161–62.
46 Suffolk Probate, 15:304; Savage, *Genealogical Dictionary*, 3:177; *Boston Records*, 9:188; Suffolk Common Pleas, 9:199, 353; 10:346; 11:65.
47 December 1724, Fitch Account book, p. 308, MHS.
48 Savage, *Genealogical Dictionary*, 3:394; Suffolk Probate, 60:318, 82:657; see also Kaye, "Eighteenth-Century Boston Furniture Craftsmen," pp. 291–92. Vose, "Great Boston Fire of 1760," p. 291.
49 Suffolk Probate, 17:301, 61:437–40; Suffolk Common Pleas, 11:446. Grant daybook, August 8, 1729, February 19, 1730/31.
50 See also Downs, *American Furniture*, nos. 96, 156.
51 Penn as quoted in Crouch, *English Empire in America*, p. 99.
52 Philadelphia Wills, 1694-104.
53 "Extracts from the Letter-Booke of James Claypoole," p. 411; "Some Letters and an Abstract of Letters from Pennsylvania," p. 197; Philadelphia Wills, 1699-228.
54 On the importation of walnut into Boston, see Jobe, "Boston Furniture Industry" (conference report), pp. 3–48. The main exports from America to England were codfish and white pine, the latter of which was used for ship masts (see Albion, *Forests and Sea Power*).
55 Strachey as quoted in Helen Lowenthal, "History in Houses (Dyrham Park)," p. 868 (I am indebted to Bradford L. Rauschenberg for calling this reference to my attention); Evelyn, *Sylva*, pp. 58, 59; Davis, *William Fitzhugh and His Chesapeake World*, pp. 339, 361, 367 (I am indebted to Arlene Palmer Schwind for this reference); Symonds, "Turkey Work, Beech and Japanned Chairs," p. 222.
56 Logan to Askew, February 20, 1712/13, July 1, 1713, Correspondence book, Logan Papers, HSP.
57 Matzkin, "Inventories of Estates in Philadelphia County," pp. 20, 104. Cummings, "An Account of Goods at Pennsbury Manor," pp. 408, 411.
58 Wheeler to du Pont, November 12, 1940, object file 58.54, Registrar's Office, Winterthur; it is also illustrated in Nutting, *Furniture Treasury*, no. 1994, with no mention of the Penn family provenance. The Reifsnyder chair is illustrated in Keyes, "Editor's Attic," p. 275; *Reifsnyder Sale*, pp. 239–40.
59 An early reference to it is in Quynn, *Diary of Jacob Engelbrecht*, May 10, 1821 (I am indebted to Arlene Palmer Schwind for this reference). It is illustrated in Singleton, *Furniture of Our Forefathers*, p. 135, and in Naeve, "English Furniture in Colonial America," p. 552. I am indebted to Raymond V. Shepherd, Jr., and Caroline Morris for their assistance in obtaining wood samples for microanalysis.
60 This chair is illustrated in Iverson, *American Chair*, fig. 28.
61 Illustrated in Gowans, *Images of American Living*, p. 81. The skirt board does not appear to be original to the chair.
62 Philadelphia Wills, 1708-108, 1709-141, 1709-152.
63 As quoted in Gillingham, "Estate of Jonathan Dickinson," pp. 420, 422–25.
64 An American cane chair with crooked legs from New England is illustrated as no. 12 in Downs, *American Furniture*. This chair's legs are beech, and the seat frame is made of an American soft maple (*Acer pennsylvanicum*). Chair no. 11 in Downs's book is made of European walnut (*Juglans regia*) and is probably of English origin. Fussell account book, pp. 3, 34.
65 *Suffolk Deeds*, 14:270; Savage, *Genealogical Dictionary*, 4:87; Philadelphia Wills, 1694-104.
66 McElroy, "Furniture of the Philadelphia Area," p. 198; Philadelphia Wills, 1708-111.
67 Shepherd, "James Logan's Stenton," fig. 25. I am indebted to Raymond V. Shepherd, Jr., for calling this stool to my attention and to Peter J. Parker of the Historical Society of Pennsylvania for permission to examine and sample the stool.
68 Havard, *Dictionnaire de l'ameublement*, 3:428.
69 Prerogative Court of Canterbury, Probate 5, no. 514.
70 Logan Papers, cash book, APS; New York Probate, Liber 14:43; York County, Va., Probate, 6:362–63 (I am indebted to Patrick H. Butler III, for the Virginia reference).
71 Perley, "Marblehead in the Year 1700," p. 83; Essex Probate Files, 305:86–88; Savage, *Genealogical Dictionary*, 3:421; Suffolk Probate, 11:200–202; 14:146; 15:132.
72 Early in the eighteenth century Robinson Crusoe eased the rigors of his life with "a Squab or Couch, [made] with the Skins of the Creatures I had kill'd, and with other soft Things" (as cited in *OED*, s.v. "squab"). Suffolk Probate, 15:492–93; 16:143, 561; 21:475–76; 26:376–77, 367–70.
73 Gilbert, "Furniture by Giles Grendy," pp. 554, 549.
74 See Montgomery, *American Furniture*, p. 19 ff.; and Gillingham, "Benjamin Lehman, a Germantown Cabinetmaker," pp. 289–306, in which each entry shows the price of the item in question, and the amount paid to the journeyman for the work.

52.
CANE CHAIR WITH CARVED TOP
Boston, Massachusetts
1689–1705
WOOD: American beech (*Fagus grandifolia*)
OH 51⅞″ (131.8 cm)
SH 19″ (48.3 cm), SW 18¼″ (46.4 cm), SD 15¼″ (38.7 cm)
PROVENANCE: South Shore of Boston; family of Samuel F. B. Morse; Roland B. Hammond; museum purchase
73.382

Although it is a crude production by comparison with contemporary English examples, this chair of American beech (*Fagus grandifolia*) is stylistically one of the earliest examples of the cane chair made in New England and is an important document of American craft and cultural life. (An exact mate to it, if not from the same set then assuredly by the same craftsmen, has been in the collection of the Massachusetts Historical Society since 1924.)[1]

When the chair was added to the Winterthur collection, a label glued to the right rear back panel contained the following information:

Flemish 1660
Sam. Morse
Sarah Morse Carver
John Carver Beale.

If the chair descended through the Morse family until such time as it came into the Carver family and then to the Beale family, that would suggest a south of Boston history. The Minot chair (see fig. 126) also has a south of Boston history of ownership. Even though both chairs turned up in the same area, we cannot conclude that they were made there, especially since we have no documentary evidence that cane chairs were made elsewhere in New England outside Boston. Aside from the resemblance of the medial and rear stretchers to the rear stretcher of the Minot family chair no other single characteristic relates to identifiable traits on other American cane chairs. The design of the front legs is common on both American and English chairs. Indeed the legs are similar to those on the Minot chair, but a close comparison of the two chairs in 1973 revealed that they were not cut from the same pattern. The seat of the Winterthur example is approximately 2″ (5.1 cm) higher than that of the Minot chair.

The mate at Massachusetts Historical Society was a gift of Clara B. Winthrop of Boston and, according to Winthrop family tradition, it was imported from England about 1684. However, in the absence of contemporary evidence that beech was ever exported from America to England prior to the nineteenth century, it is fair to presume that both the Winthrop chair and the Winterthur example were made in New England. Ownership of the historical society's example by a Boston family reinforces the presumption that Boston is the place where both chairs were made. The date of 1660 on the label of the Winterthur example is far too early for its date of manufacture. The date 1684 associated with the Winthrop example is much more realistic and is close to the first mention of cane chairs in a New England inventory (1688). The style of the front leg—whether facing forward as in these examples or

canting outward at a 45-degree angle as in the leather chairs in catalogue entries 61 and 62 below—represents a form that was made in England during the last decade of the seventeenth century and places this group of American chairs among the earliest of their type made in New England. The seat frame of this chair has a molding run on its upper surface, a touch which seems to have no precedent in English cane chairs, and contrasts with the typical manner of molding the outer margin of the seat during the 1690s.

As a craftsman's product, the chair itself is highly provocative. The simple joinery is as well done as that usually found in English or American cane chairs of good but not extraordinary quality. It is clear that the conception and workmanship of the turning is assured, but the turning suffers when compared with that of the 1690–1710 period. The finials have an uncommonly long base and an unusually flat back. The design and workmanship of the individual elements on the rest of the stiles also lack the finesse that we have come to expect on professionally made turned chairs of the time. On each stile the uppermost ball is less round than it might have been; the neck of the baluster below is rather elongated while the bottom too suddenly bulges outward. The ring at the top of the lower baluster is quite thin, and the neck of the lower baluster is thicker than the upper one. The turning between the lower back rail and the seat is rather awkwardly set on the block below it. On the medial and rear rails the point at which the two balusters meet is abrupt and weak (later the intervening ball became the common solution to this problem; see fig. 126).

The design and execution of the carved work on the chair has its problems as well. The crest rail, with an incongruous upward bow between the cane and the molding, is filled in with punch work, as if to disguise an error in design. The symmetrical curled fronds of the crest suggest an inexperienced hand working with an unfamiliar vocabulary of design. Further evidence of inexperience is found in the carving; the outline of the vertical rails that support the cane of the back is not symmetrical from top to bottom and the right back rail is an inverted version of the left one. The design motif on the back supports is echoed on the front legs. The joiner's work, which consists of making and molding the seat frame and cutting the 18 mortises and tenons for one chair (216 in all for a set of a dozen), was more laborious than artful and tells us little about the maker.

Although the chair admirably captures the exuberance of the cane-chair style, the flatness of the carving, as well as the lack of logic in the design of the crest rail, and the error in creating the patterns from which the vertical rails of the back were cut suggest two possible interpretations of how this chair came to be made. One is that it is an early effort by an American craftsman who was not trained to make cane chairs and either could not or would not employ the services of a professional carver. The other possibility is that it was made by an immigrant craftsman who was familiar only with the turning and assembly aspects of chair-frame making and had previously worked in a London shop that had relied upon a specialist to execute carved work.

Physical evidence supports the idea that this chair was

cat. 52

commissioned by someone other than the final customer. The capital letter I, representing either an I or a J, and the monogram "IP" are stamped twice on the back of the left rear stile at its junction with the rear seat list (figs. 134 and 135). These initials are made in two very different ways: the single I is chased, or punched, with a round-face punch that was hammered into the wood sixteen times to produce the letter. The IP was stamped into the wood with a single stroke, and it was done twice, since the first impression was not successful. Such stamps and indeed initialing itself are not common on American furniture prior to the introduction of the cane-chair style. The records do not reveal an immigrant English turner with the initials I.P. who might have made these turnings on a piecework basis for a Boston joiner in the last decade of the seventeenth century; however, the possible identity of the man *behind* this production does not elude us. During the last decade of the seventeenth century, only one new immigrant of importance known to have been working in the William and Mary style arrived in Boston from England. That man is John Brocas, a cabinetmaker who is first noted in Boston when Samuel Sewall mentions in his diary on November 20, 1696, that among his dinner guests that day were "Mr. Woodbridge and his Kinsman Brockherst."[2]

That the Winterthur chair and the Winthrop family chair have so many new features in common further suggests that Brocas commissioned both, especially since we know that the chairmakers' trade was a specialty apart from that of the cabinetmakers (moreover, Brocas's inventory of 1740 does not indicate that he engaged either in turning or chairmaking).[3] Furthermore, Waitstill Winthrop, the probable buyer of the Winthrop family chair, most likely patronized the town's most fashionable furniture craftsman at his time, John Brocas.

Stylistic considerations aside, the chair itself betrays three additional features that are uncommon on earlier upholstered chairs made in New England. First, the choice of beech rather than maple is out of character for a New England-trained chairmaker. Second, the one pair of joints on this chair that are made with a round mortise and tenon—at the junctions of the front legs with the seat list—reveal that its maker used a center bit (fig. 136) rather than the quill, or "spoon," bit commonly used on American chairs made prior to this. (The hole that this tool makes is distinctive; it leaves a sharp edge around the perimeter at the base, cuts a generally flat bottom, and leaves a characteristic conical indentation at the center. The advantage of using this tool is that in a relatively thin piece of wood it produces a mortise hole that has a maximum surface area into which the largest possible tenon can be fitted for the best possible retention and adhesion.)[4] Third, the turning of the lower rear legs between the seat and the feet was common on English chairs of the early Stuart restoration period, but not on American chairs. Considering the amount of evidence that points to English thinking in this chair, combined with the crudities of the execution, it is impossible to believe that it is totally the creation of an American-trained craftsman.

The lower lobes and upper right lobe of the back frame of this chair have been restored. The caning is modern. A coat of brown paint covers a coat of black paint that may be original.

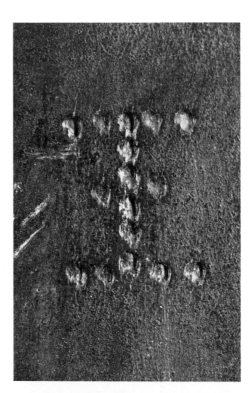

Fig. 134. LEFT. Detail of punched I on the back of the stile of the cane chair in catalogue entry 52. (Winterthur 73.382.)

Fig. 135. BELOW. Detail of stamped IP on the back of the stile of the cane chair in catalogue entry 52. (Winterthur 73.382.)

Fig. 136. BOTTOM. Detail of the front leg in the cane chair in catalogue entry 52 showing the mortise hole made with a center bit. (Winterthur 73.382.)

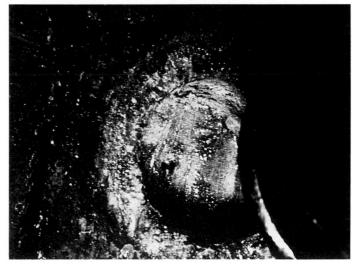

NOTES
[1] See Kane, "Furniture Owned by the Massachusetts Historical Society," fig. 2.
[2] Sewall, *Diary*, 1:360.
[3] Suffolk Probate, 35:239.
[4] The center bit is further discussed in catalogue entry 53. Documentary evidence of the presence of this tool in America appears in the 1708 inventory of Charles Plumley of Philadelphia; see Appendix 1.

53

CANE CHAIR WITH CARVED TOP
Probably Boston, Massachusetts
1700–1710
WOOD: American beech (*Fagus grandifolia*)
OH 49⅝″ (126.0 cm)
SH 18½″ (47.0 cm), SW 18″ (45.7 cm), SD 18⅜″ (46.7 cm)
PROVENANCE: Bequest of Henry Francis du Pont
58.964

The turned rear stiles, or backs, of this chair of American beech (*Fagus grandifolia*) evoke the style of excellent, but not extraordinary, cane chairs made in London around the year 1700. That the chair was made by a craftsman newly emigrated from an urban chairmaking center in England, such as London, and from a shop that took pains with its work is made clear by the delicacy of the turning, by the skill with which the stiles are designed and executed, and by the molding around the caning of the back, which forms a continuous frame. This type of frame was rarely executed because the molding on the top rail and on the lower back rail had to be hand carved and had to match the profiles of the vertical members, which were run with a plane. This nicety is not often observed on American chairs even of high quality (see catalogue entry 57) or on English chairs of a quality that might cause them to be confused with ordinary American examples.[1]

Much of the natural presence of this chair may be attributed to its carved crest rail of ambitious design and unusual height. Although the carving is quite flat, flat-carved crest rails are a characteristic of all these chairs. By English standards this chair would be considered rather ordinary, but by American standards it is an extremely ambitious design expressed in workmanship of unusual quality. The high quality of workmanship and design suggest that the chair is an early product of its type although, if it is of Boston manufacture, it is unlikely to predate the arrival of cabinetmaker John Brocas (1696) and probably was not made prior to 1700. It may well be the first use in New England of pure columnar stiles, ogee balusters on the front legs, and scrolled feet. It also demonstrates the early use of two-axis turning of the rear legs and stiles.

The impression that this chair was designed by a craftsman who thought in terms of turned rather than joined chairmaking is heightened by the crest rail that literally crowns the chair by appearing to perch on the turned stiles although it is actually held in place by rectangular tenons fitted into mortise holes in the crest rail. Overlapping seat lists are fastened together by a round tenon turned on the upper end of each front leg, a turner's solution. Cane chairs are the earliest type of chair made in America to have the "great heels" with their dynamic backward cant, although such heels are mentioned in the Royal Household accounts in 1672/73 when joiner Richard Price billed Charles II 18s. for "a great Elbowe chair ye frame turned all over[,] wth great heeles."[2] That these heels do not appear earlier on upholstered American chairs suggests the particular version of the leather or the turkey-work chairs being made in the colonies was established prior to the introduction of great heels in England (1670s), and that the American cane chairs with great heels postdate the mid 1670s.

While microanalysis of woods tells us which hemisphere of the globe a chair might have been made in, it does not precisely indicate where in that hemisphere it was made. Because American cane chairs of any type with turned rear stiles are rare in this country, the decorative features that might permit us to be precise in our attributions of the place in which they were made are not well understood. The problem is particularly acute with any early urban example of a new style. This difficulty plagues the attribution of the present chair; its striking novelty prevents us from drawing upon our familiarity with recognizable techniques or design features already practiced in that community at an earlier date.

Much of the design vocabulary of Winterthur's chair can be associated with New England work in the William and Mary style. The inverted baluster high on the rear stile is not common in American chairs, but it can be seen, although not so well articulated as here, on the legs of a high chest of Boston origin in the Winterthur collection (66.1306) and indeed in the turned work on numerous other examples of Boston case furniture in American collections. Unrelated to Boston turning in any way, however, are delicately articulated collarinoes and perfectly tapered architectonic columns that constitute the rest of the stiles. These feature a much closer resemblance to the Philadelphia chair illustrated in the next entry than they do to the Boston high-back leather-upholstered chairs that appeared early in the eighteenth century.

The ring above each scroll foot is a feature found on a maple armchair of eastern Massachusetts origin and a walnut chair made in Pennsylvania (see fig. 168). Since that particular Pennsylvania chair had already absorbed a New England front-stretcher design, we may assume that it likewise absorbed the design idea for the collar above the foot. The design of the medial, rear, and side stretchers is found on other Boston chairs in this catalogue, notably the leather chair illustrated in catalogue entry 64, which may be roughly contemporary with this example, and the cane chair in catalogue entry 55, which was probably made a decade later. These stretchers also appear on a cane armchair of similar design but slightly less careful workmanship, now in the collection of the Wadsworth Atheneum. That chair is also American beech (*Fagus grandifolia*).[3] The bilobe front stretcher also appears on the upholstered chair illustrated in catalogue entry 85.

While the aesthetic merits place Winterthur's chair in a special class, the chair serves as an important and object lesson in connoisseurship for this vital period of American furniture making. In the first place, a generation ago the most knowing connoisseur would have summarily dismissed a chair such as this as an English example simply because it is made of beech. But in 1952 Gordon Saltar of Winterthur Museum devised the beech test (subsequently confirmed by the Royal Forestry Commission at Prince's Risborough, England), and scholars have been able to separate American beech *Fagus grandifolia* from its visually identical European counterpart, *Fagus sylvatica*. (The tandem rays and crystals present in the American variety but absent from the European counterpart can be seen only by microscopic examination.)

In the second place, that the mortise holes (fig. 137) for the front stretcher were drilled with a center bit would have been grounds for suspecting that this chair was a nineteenth-century forgery. However, the discovery of center bits in the 1708

cat. 53

inventory of Charles Plumley of Philadelphia offers documentary evidence that such a tool was in use among sophisticated furniture makers almost a century before the tool appears in the pages of tool catalogues published by manufacturers in Sheffield and Birmingham, England. Figure 137 reveals the profile left by the center bit used on this chair: a shallow conical depression in the center (without the gimlet threads left by the nineteenth-century hand-driven version of the tool), and a clean-cut indentation around the perimeter caused by a spur at the edge of the bit. The flat bottom of the hole suggests that this bit was a refined version of the button bit used by horners in the seventeenth century to cut buttons that were then covered with cloth. Such bits were commonly used by seventeenth-century London craftsmen who made chests of drawers with doors that had inlaid design. The center bit drilled the holes into which bone was inlaid, while the button bit was used to cut the inlay itself (fig. 138). The presence of such a tool in a chairmaker's kit would be unusually helpful since the auger hole at the front corners of a cane chair seat, through which the round tenon on the upper end of the front leg must pass (fig. 139), had to be executed with great care in order to avoid piercing the upper surface of the seat frame. A pod auger or spoon bit makes this difficult to do neatly, quickly, and with maximum effectiveness, while a center bit makes it easy. The evidence that this rarely documented tool was used on this chair reinforces the impression given by its design: it is the work of an urban English chairmaker who had brought a tool he had been accustomed to using at home to this country when he immigrated. Considering that London was the center of the cane-chair industry in England during the last decades of the seventeenth century, we would be surprised if evidence of this tool did not turn up on a great deal of English furniture.

The age of this chair is further confirmed by the turner's gouge marks that, in typical early eighteenth-century fashion, were never smoothed away before the chair left the shop in which it was made. That the original cane seat was replaced with rush and that the bottom rails are naturally oxidized everywhere except where the cane passed from hole to hole on the underside further enhances the credibility of the chair's age. The craftsman who made this chair retained many of the habits of English chairmaking, yet he was working in America. It is understandable that he used unseasoned wood, since American lathes developed no more torque than did their English counterparts. (Evidence that the wood was unseasoned is plainly visible on the warped rear stiles, particularly the right one, and the inward-bowed back panels, both caused by shrinkage of the cane as it dried out.) The rough carving on the back of the crest rail is typical of both English and American cane chairs of this period—in a professional shop extra time was not wasted on niceties—and is not typical of reproductions. Most surprising of all is that the craftsman who made this chair used beech with the bark still on it, a custom followed by English chairmakers of the period. (The bark is still visible on the underside of the medial and rear stretchers.) One would think that in a place where wood was plentiful this would not have been done. This evidence further emphasizes the probabilities that this chair was made by an urban craftsman who had to import his wood from outside

Fig. 137. LEFT. Detail of the front leg of the cane chair in catalogue entry 53 showing the mortise hole made with a center bit. (Winterthur 58.964.)

Fig. 138. BELOW. Detail showing the shallow cut made with a center bit for the circular piece of inlay decoration on a chest of drawers from London, England, ca. 1660. (Winterthur 70.428.)

his community rather than procure it from a nearby forest.

The chair presently has a coat of black paint, which is not original, over a coat of red stain, which may not be original either. There is no evidence that this chair was originally intended not to be stained, unlike the chair in catalogue entry 54. Yet it should be pointed out that inventory references to stained or painted cane chairs are rare.

Urban chairs made in this style with turned legs commonly have additional wood glued to the front and outside of each

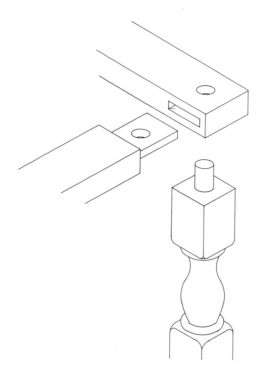

Fig. 139. Mortise-and-tenon joint (for a chair seat) bisected on the underside by the tenon (of the leg). (Drawing: Wade Lawrence.)

been removed and the caning has been reinstalled. At that time it was decided not to replace the seat lists since the original seat lists tell much of the story of the chair and offer evidence of age.

According to estate inventories and upholsterers' account books, cushions were commonly placed on cane chairs. The cushion that is presently displayed on this chair was modeled on one engraved on the 1736 billhead of Boston upholsterer Samuel Grant. The volume of the cushion was determined pragmatically: Grant noted that Nathaniel Green's 8 cushions required 12 pounds (5.5 k) of feathers, thus each cushion contained 1½ pounds (0.7 k) of feathers.[4] The presence of a well-stuffed cushion on such a chair as this adds a new dimension to our thinking about the desire of our forefathers for comfort, as well as visually unifying the seat and back of the chair because the cushion fills the wide gap between them.

The cane on the back of the chair appears to be original; that of the seat is a modern replacement. The toes were restored by Nicholas Quinn in January 1976.

foot to offer sufficient wood for the carver to execute the toes. This practice caused little extra labor for the turner since it also allowed him to turn a slenderer piece of wood for the rest of the leg (in contrast see fig. 145). Moreover, because the turner had considerably less wood to cut away, he realized a saving in labor and, hence, cost. On most chairs, these glued-on portions have fallen off in time, and this chair is no exception: the toes are a restoration. In recent years the later flag seat has

NOTES
[1] See, for example, the chair said to be of maple, and thus presumed to be of American origin, but actually of European beech (*Fagus sylvatica*) illustrated in Garrett, "Furniture Owned by the American Antiquarian Society," p. 407. I am indebted to Georgia Baumgardner of the AAS for providing samples for microanalysis.
[2] Symonds, "Charles II. Couches, Chairs, and Stools," pt. 2, p. 86.
[3] The eastern Massachusetts chair is illustrated in Warren, *Bayou Bend*, no. 13. The collar is a common feature on English chairs as well. It is present on the English chair that appears to have been imported into Philadelphia and illustrated in Hornor, *Blue Book*, pl. 8, and on a chair in the Wadsworth Atheneum (acc. no. 26.443) illustrated in Nutting, *Furniture Treasury*, no. 1985.
[4] The billhead is illustrated in Jobe, "Boston Furniture Industry" (conference report), p. 33; December 15, 1729, Grant daybook.

CANE CHAIR WITH CARVED AND MOLDED TOP
Boston, Massachusetts
1717–1730, perhaps 1721
WOOD: A maple of the soft group
OH 45⅞" (116.5 cm)
SH 18⅞" (48.0 cm), SW 17" (43.2 cm), SD 14½" (36.8 cm)
PROVENANCE: Family of Daniel Perkins, Bridgewater, Mass.; Philip W.
Adams; Calvin Williams; Mrs. Daniel H. Baker; Ronald Bourgeault;
purchased by the museum.
74.120

Fig. 140. Detail of punched I on the rear stile of the cane chair in catalogue entry 54. (Winterthur 74.120.)

When the present chair was added to the Winterthur collection in 1974, a letter and a statement of provenance accompanied it. Both were written by Mrs. Daniel H. Baker of Falmouth, Massachusetts: "This chair belonged to John Hancock, first Governor of Massachusetts. It was presented to me in 1854 by Mr. Calvin Williams of West Bridgewater. The Rev. Daniel Perkins of Bridgewater was stepfather to Governor Hancock. Mr. Williams was related to the Perkins family and the chair came from them to him, and from him to me in its present condition. It originally had a cane seat like the back."[1]

As is true with most traditions of ownership, the germ of truth must be sifted from the wishful thinking. It is clear to modern students of furniture that while John Hancock (b. 1737) conceivably could have owned this chair, he was not the original purchaser, since the style in which the chair was made had long been out of fashion in Boston by the year Hancock attained his majority (1758). If this chair has any historical association with the Hancock family, a better candidate for the original owner is Hancock's stepfather, the Reverend Daniel Perkins (b. 1697). Perkins was graduated from Harvard College in 1717 and in 1721 became the minister of Bridgewater, where he lived until his death in 1782. He married Ann Foster of Charlestown on November 6, 1721, and easily could have purchased the chair and others like it in celebration of the doubly auspicious occasion of setting up housekeeping and attaining his first pulpit. Reverend Perkins subsequently took (ca. 1751) Mary Hawke Thaxter Hancock as his second wife, which doubtless gave rise to the tradition mentioned in Mrs. Baker's statement. Mr. Perkins was Mrs. Hancock's third husband.[2]

The Perkins family chair is one of at least twenty-six related early eighteenth-century cane chairs that have survived into the twentieth century. These chairs form the largest group of cane chairs of American origin. Three are known only from photographs; nineteen of the remaining chairs, including this example and that in catalogue entry 52, are marked either on a rear stile or on the bottom rail of the back with the punched capital letter "I" with a cross-serif (fig. 140). Twenty-six of the chairs are listed in table 4, and it is to this list that the numbers in the following discussion refer.[3] With a single striking exception made of American walnut (no. 20), all of the examples of this group that have been examined during the course of preparing this book are made of maple; however, no. 26 (not examined) is reported to have parts made of beech and a birch apron. Except for the chair illustrated in catalogue entry 52, all of the marked chairs have *some* stylistic and construction features in common, but they vary in the design of

their crest rails and the design and arrangement of their stretchers. All have a rectilinear seat with flat outside edges, all have straight and rather stiff rear stiles that could have been cut from the same patterns, and all (except nos. 24 and 26 which have crook legs) have Spanish, or claw, feet of the same design and carved in the same way: the foot is surmounted by a long block with chamfered corners, a short baluster, a small block with chamfered corners, a longer baluster, and a block with squared corners (the analogous block on the rear legs is generally chamfered). All except no. 17 have turned cylinders on their rear legs and all have great heels. All except nos. 24 and 26 have a tripartite front stretcher that is smaller in scale than the analogous element on the Boston leather chairs of the period (see catalogue entry 76). The front stretcher is invariably composed of a central disk flanked by two round balls, with horizontally oriented columnar shapes leading to a terminus at each end. The termini generally consist of a fillet, a half round, a groove (and sometimes two), and a more or less tapered cone that terminates in a round tenon, invisible when the chair is intact, that enters an auger hole in the front legs. The sharp-edge blocks on the legs immediately under the front seat rail show that every chair in this group originally had a double-ogee skirtboard, or apron, such as remains on nos. 9, 10, 12, and 13. When this board is in place, it forms a smooth and handsome line with the legs and reinforces the chinoiserie effect suggested by the *ju i* that forms the central motif of the crest rail on no. 19.[4] When the apron is missing—as it is in the majority of cases where the original cane seat has been replaced with flag or splint and then ultimately restored in the twentieth century with cane—the chairs appear cruder and less professionally finished than they did when they were new.

Two basic differences among the twenty-six chairs are generally obvious. First, the crest rails are of nine distinct types, even though the essential form of the chair remains constant; second, the lower stretcher assembly is arranged in two ways. In what appears to be the earliest stylistic arrangement, the side stretchers are bilaterally symmetrical, and the medial stretcher is located directly under the middle of the seat. In the second group, the design of the side stretchers is asymmetrical, so the medial stretcher is moved toward the front of the chair. The

idea that the latter type of stretcher arrangement is historically later than the symmetrical arrangement is strengthened when we observe the persistence of virtually identical side and rear stretchers on fine urban Massachusetts chairs that cannot have been made prior to the middle of the third quarter of the eighteenth century (see fig. 132). A more subtle variation among the chairs appears in the style in which these lower stretchers are turned. The side stretchers of the symmetrical type consist of a central block flanked by two horizontally oriented columns, each of which is in turn flanked by a ring. The stretchers have a conical terminus at the front and a square block at the rear. On the chair in catalogue entry 53, the medial stretcher terminates in a square block that has a rectangular tenon cut on it and fits into a rectangular mortise in each side

stretcher, but on the chairs of the I group the medial stretchers have round tenons that are fitted into auger holes in the blocks of the side stretchers. Those on which the side stretchers are not symmetrically arranged are generally of the type found on catalogue entry 54. Beginning at the front leg, their elements consist of a small baluster, a ring, the block for the medial stretcher, a deeply scored groove, a columnar shape that tapers to a ring, followed by a block at the rear leg. The single exception is chair no. 8, which has laterally arranged rectangular stretchers in the manner of a crook-back leather chair, such as the example illustrated in catalogue entry 76.

Inasmuch as none of these chairs bears physical evidence of where or when it was made or what the meaning of the punched I may be, it is conceivable that arranging the entire

TABLE 4	I CHAIRS			CREST		STRETCHERS		
NUMBER	LOCATION	PROVENANCE	MARK	TYPE	STYLE	TERMINI	REMARKS	REFERENCES, COMMENTS
I-GROUP CHAIRS WITH SYMMETRICALLY ARRANGED SIDE STRETCHERS								
1 side chair	private collection	found in Michigan	I	A	ogee, fillet, scroll	hollow turned	gentle swell in center	*American Folk Arts, Keene Coll.,* Detroit Institute of Arts (1960), p. 21.
2 side chair	Wenham Hist. Society, Wenham, Mass.	unknown	I	A	same as no. 1	front: missing; rear: same as no. 1	side stretchers replaced	Unpublished.
3 side chair	Henry Ford Museum, Dearborn, Mich.	unknown	none	A	same as no. 1	same as no. 1		Comstock, *American Furniture,* no. 37. Front skirtboard original, side ones possibly not.
4 side chair	Harvard College, Cambridge, Mass.	E. A. Holyoke	I	B	molded, exterior bumps	tapered cone	sharp medial apex	Unpublished.
5 side chair	Connecticut Hist. Soc., Hartford	unknown	I	B	same as no. 4	same as no. 4		*Chairs in . . . Connecticut Historical Society* (1956), p. 13.
6, 7 side chairs (a pair)	unknown	F. H. Bigelow, Cambridge, Mass.	?	B	same as no. 4	front: slight taper, fillet; rear: no taper, preceded by half round	groove at apex	Nutting, *Furniture Treasury* (2d ed.), nos. 2044 & 2045.
8 side chair	Smithsonian Institution, Washington, D.C.	unknown	I	C	similar to no. 4 but 2 bumps near top	side and rear stretchers are rectangular	arranged like leather-chair type	Unpublished. A unique example.
9, 10 side chairs (a pair)	American Antiquarian Soc., Worcester, Mass.	unknown	I	D	flattened ogees and top knot, long sprays	conical, no grooves on termini	gently swelled in center	Singleton, *Furniture of Our Forefathers,* p. 188. These chairs have never been painted or stained.
11 side chair	Museum of Fine Arts, Boston	Dwight Blaney collection	none	D′	flattened ogees, crescent top knot, no sprays	front: same as no. 9; rear: unusually short, no grooves, tapered cone		*Hudson-Fulton Celebration Catalogue* (1909), no. 104. Catalogue says "birch"; microanalysis says "maple."
12, 13 side chairs	National Park Service: Derby House, Salem, Mass.	found at Salem, Mass.	I	D	same as nos. 9, 10	no. 12 close to no. 9; no. 13 half round just before conical terminus		Nutting, *Furniture Treasury* (2d ed.), nos. 2046 & 2047. Ball feet.
14 armchair	private collection	unknown	I	D″	highly arched ogees, long sprays	straight tapered cone		Unpublished. Arm supports—baluster with single ring at neck—tenoned to seat rail ⅓ depth from front.
15 armchair	private collection	unknown	I	D″	same as no. 14	ring and groove		Unpublished. Ogee skirtboard.
16 side chair	Trent House, Trenton, N.J.	unknown	I	D′″	same as no. 18, highly arched ogees, short sprays	same as no. 14		Halsey, *Handbook of the American Wing* (1924), fig. 25; except for symmetrical side stretchers, identical to no. 19; proper skirtboard.

group so that their collective attributes and distinctions can be tabulated will yield additional information. A roughly chronological arrangement based upon stylistic attributes is shown in table 4.

The first and most obvious fact that emerges from this enumeration of the chairs is that the punched I cannot represent the mark of an owner, since it appears on chairs with eleven different styles of crest rails (including the four variations of the D type and the chair illustrated in catalogue entry 52) and three more that have a different stretcher arrangement—a total of fourteen variations. Cane chairs were made in sets and purchased in increments of half dozens, not including armchairs, which are always itemized separately. Each one of the fourteen variations is representative of a set of six or twelve chairs. If

the I were an owner's mark, then that one owner must have possessed at least eighty-four chairs in eleven different styles, an idea that not only staggers the imagination but is nowhere confirmed by any of the inventories of New England—even the richest households rarely had more than two sets of cane chairs. Similarly, since no punched initial other than I has been found on any of the cane chairs in this style, it cannot be assumed that each set of chairs was coincidentally owned by a person whose name began with I.

The second idea that emerges from the list is that Massachusetts was very likely the place in which these chairs originated. One (no. 17) was owned in Boston, and another (no. 25) may have originally been owned there or in Quincy. A third (no. 11) was by 1909 owned by a famous Boston

TABLE 4   I CHAIRS *continued*

NUMBER	LOCATION	PROVENANCE	MARK	CREST TYPE	CREST STYLE	STRETCHERS TERMINI	STRETCHERS REMARKS	REFERENCES, COMMENTS
				I-GROUP CHAIRS WITH SYMMETRICALLY ARRANGED SIDE STRETCHERS				
17 side chair	Museum of Fine Arts, Boston	Edes family, Boston, Mass.	I	E	double round corners, round piercing	unknown		Randall, *American Furniture*, no. 127. Rear legs are chamfered rather than turned—a unique and perhaps late feature.
18 armchair	Bayou Bend, Houston, Texas	unknown	I	F	ogee ends, hollowed (scooped) center	similar to no. 14		David Warren, *Bayou Bend*, no. 15. Arm supports similar to no. 13 in style but are part of front leg, into which seat rails are tenoned; cf. no. 24.
				I GROUP CHAIRS WITH ASYMMETRICALLY ARRANGED SIDE STRETCHERS				
19 side chair	Winterthur Museum	Perkins family	I	D′″	same as no. 16	same as no. 14	fat ring, fillet, thin ring, taper	Illustrated as catalogue entry 54 here. Since stretcher arrangement differs from no. 16 and crest rail differs from no. 14, implication is 3 different sets whose crests are variations of D theme.
20 side chair	Wadsworth Atheneum, Hartford, Conn.	unknown	I	D′″	same as no. 16	similar to no. 14		Unpublished. Retains original apron; columnar side stretchers. Only known example of group made of American walnut (*Juglans nigra*). Crook back and toes restored.
21 side chair	Historic Deerfield, Deerfield, Mass.	Ashley family	I	D′″	same as no. 16	similar to no. 14		Fales, *Furniture of Historic Deerfield*, no. 28. Ends of crest rail less pointed than no. 19 here.
22 side chair	Pilgrim Society. Plymouth, Mass.	Alden family	I	F	same as no. 18	similar to no. 14		Unpublished. Since stretcher arrangement differs from no. 18, not from same set of chairs as no. 18.
23 side chair	Unknown	Stoddard family, Northampton, Mass.	?	G	high double ogee, carved sprays, pierced ground	similar to no. 14		Sack, *Opportunities in Antiques 15*, item 919.
24 side chair	Monmouth Co. Historical Assn., Freehold, N.J.	unknown	I	H	double ogee to flat top, volutes atop ogees	front: replaced; rear: same as no. 11	side stretchers are balusters	Unpublished. Retains original apron; earliest example, stylistically, with crook or horsebone leg.
25 armchair	Winterthur Museum, Winterthur, Del.	Hancock (?), Quincy (?), and Sheafe families	none	G	same as no. 23	similar to no. 14	ring, groove straight taper	Illustrated as catalogue entry 56 here.
26 armchair	Longfellow House, Cambridge, Mass.	Wadsworth, Longfellow families	I	G	same as no. 23	similar to no. 14	ring turning on rear stretcher	Unpublished. Crook legs; arm supports stylistically related to those of no. 14; legs similar to fig. 170.

collector. A fourth (no. 19) may have been purchased in Boston prior to the owner's removal to Bridgewater. One (no. 4) was owned in Cambridge, and two others (nos. 6 and 7) of the same type may have been found there. A pair were found in Salem (nos. 12 and 13), and another (no. 2) appears to have associations with Wenham. Two may have come from the Duxbury area (nos. 22 and 24). Two relatively late examples of the style (nos. 21 and 23) were owned in western Massachusetts, but at least one of these families (the owners of no. 23) had Boston associations. The straggler found in Michigan (no. 1) was purchased for only a few dollars in a junk shop by its singularly perceptive present owner and may be presumed to have made its way westward with a migrating family.

It is perhaps too easy to assume, in the absence of documentary evidence indicating that cane chairs were made prior to 1735 anywhere else in Massachusetts, that all of these chairs originated in Boston, especially since the chairs within the group vary considerably among themselves. Considering that they are all tied together by the mysterious I mark, we could argue that all the chairs bearing the mark must originate from the same locale. This assumption is supported by the fact that some of the chairs appear to have been owned originally in Boston: while Boston-made chairs are known to have been shipped from that metropolis, no furniture from Northampton, Deerfield, Duxbury, Salem, or Wenham is known to have been shipped to customers in Boston. Yet it is always dangerous to invoke the concepts of familial relationship of design and workmanship as proof that an entire group of objects originated in the same place (see catalogue entry 80 for example). In this case, however, the assumption may be warranted because most of the related examples bear the same mark and the differences among them are primarily in the form (but not the quality) of the crest rails, which indicates that they are the products of an industry rather than isolated copies by a number of craftsmen widely scattered over a large area. Further, the arm supports of the armchairs of the group are in many cases the same in design and execution as the analogous elements on the better understood, Boston-made, leather-upholstered armchairs.

The third idea that emerges from the list is that there were more stylistic variations among these chairs than there were chairmakers' shops in Boston in the 1720s. Given that not every shop in Boston was making cane chairs, the numerous differences could be explained as either variations developed by one shop to satisfy a number of customers, or the interdependence of shops—a documentable fact in Boston. The latter could explain the introduction of a number of combinations of variations well in excess of the actual number of shops involved. The presence of symmetrical stretchers on most of the armchairs, for example, cannot be construed as a quirk of the armchair form, since armchairs nos. 25 and 26 have asymmetrical stretchers. The Bayou Bend Collection armchair (no. 18) has symmetrically arranged side stretchers, while the Alden family side chair with the same crest rail design (no. 22) has asymmetrically arranged stretchers. These observations mean one of two things: either the symmetrical/asymmetrical arrangement has no chronological significance, or the chairs

were being made in more than one shop. Confusing the matter further are the Perkins, Ashley and Wadsworth examples (nos. 19, 20, and 21), with D'" crest rails and asymmetrical stretchers and the Trent House example (no. 16) with the same crest rail but symmetrical stretchers.

If the progression from symmetrical to asymmetrical stretchers is roughly chronological (although if the chairs are made in different shops the styles might overlap) then perhaps the designs of the crest rails represent a roughly chronological progression as well. Following the tenets of the style as practiced in England, it is easy to imagine that the Keene, Wenham Historical Society, and Henry Ford Museum/ Greenfield Village side chairs (nos. 1, 2, and 3), which have symmetrical stretchers and upward projecting and outwardly curving crest rails, are among the earliest examples in the group. Yet as other combinations of the elements illustrate, the chairs are in perfect chronological order. The Edes family chair (no. 17) has symmetrically arranged stretchers but is a prime candidate for a late date of manufacture for two reasons: first, the double-round-corner crest rail is a feature of late, crook-back leather chairs (see catalogue entry 81) and is found on a Boston cane chair with horsebone or "cabriole" legs (Downs, *American Furniture*, no. 12) that could hardly predate 1730; second, that the rear legs are chamfered, in the manner of Boston Queen Anne chairs, suggests the chair was made at about the time that this feature was being incorporated into chairs with leather seats upholstered over the rail or with newer cushion (slip) seats, which appeared in Boston around 1730. Thus, some Boston chairmakers must have been making chairs with symmetrical stretchers at the same time that others were making asymmetrical ones. The Wadsworth-Longfellow example at the Longfellow House, Cambridge (no. 26), is related to a fascinating chair once owned by the shop of Israel Sack, which like no. 26 has cabriole legs with claw feet similar to the later leather chair illustrated in figure 170.[5] The Sack chair also has chamfered rear legs, a crook back with stiles molded on the front surfaces, a baluster-shape splat, and a modified D'" crest rail with short sprays. As with the later-leather example in figure 170, the ogee skirtboard is no longer a separate piece of wood but has been integrated into the front rail of the seat frame, which has been designed to accept a cushion seat. This chair cannot easily predate the early 1730s, and its features suggest that the I-group chairs with variations of the D-type crest rail are a style perhaps dating, like catalogue entry 54 (no. 19 on the table), from the decade of the 1720s.

When the earliest of the I-group chairs was made cannot be accurately pinpointed. In the introduction to the next section of the catalogue we shall see that leather-upholstered chairs with crook backs and molded, rather than turned, stiles do not appear in the accounts of Boston upholsterer Thomas Fitch until February 27, 1722.[6] Inasmuch as crook-back chairs are not identifiable in Boston inventories prior to this date, we have no choice—based on present knowledge—but to assume that this feature does not long predate 1722 in Boston. Since I-group cane chairs have molded stiles, like the crook-back leather chairs, they ought not to predate this fashion by a great deal. If it can someday be shown that the crook back of the

Boston leather chairs with molded stiles descended from a Boston straight-back version, such as the present group of cane chairs represents, then it is likely that some of the I-group chairs predate their leather counterparts. The date might even be pushed back to 1717 if the chair owned by Edward Holyoke, president of Harvard, was acquired at about the time of his marriage to Elizabeth Browne in Marblehead.[7] That this might be so is suggested by the inventory references which demonstrate that cane chairs were the most popular chairs throughout the first quarter of the eighteenth century and doubtless were considered the most fashionable to own. It is possible, therefore, that the Keene, Henry Ford, and Wenham examples predate the Holyoke type by a few years.

These suppositions may seem unduly conservative, for they suggest that the cane chairs of the I group enjoyed a relatively short period of popularity, perhaps only from around 1715 to 1730. The features that they share with the crook-back, leather-upholstered chairs—the tripartite stretcher and the double-hollow-corner crest rails (neither of which is found on leather chairs with turned stiles)—indicate that this short time span is a real possibility and that it is perhaps wiser to look only at the very earliest examples of these chairs as possible forerunners of the leather-upholstered examples with molded stiles, and the rest as an alternative to them.

The stiffness of the rear stiles in the entire I group superficially suggests that the purchasers of this type of chair were not willing to spend the extra money that was necessary to buy the same model with a crook back. Actually, caning across the wide expanse of a crook back presents such great technical difficulties that crook-back cane chairs are virtually unknown, even in Europe.[8]

The meaning of the punched I on the back of the chairs is not self-evident. A comparison of the auger holes in the present chair with those of the similarly marked chair in catalogue entry 52 reveals a startling fact. The auger holes in the stylistically earlier chair were drilled with a center bit while those in the legs, stretchers, and seat of the stylistically later chair were drilled with the more familiar and older style tool known as a pod auger (fig. 141). If the punched I represents the initial of the maker, we must presume that both of these chairs were made in the same shop, but that presumption does not fit with the evidence that the center bit was not used on the stylistically later chair. The center bit is a superior tool that is useful for drilling wood that has lost much of its original moisture content, such as an urban chairmaker might have to deal with. It enables the user to drill a hole with great precision and ease and would not cheerfully be dispensed with by any craftsman who had ever used one. The evidence of the variation in the auger holes in these chairs demands that we explore the possibility that they were being made in more than one shop.

That the crest rails of the I-group chairs are of different designs is not evidence of more than one shop, for variations of this sort are the lifeblood of craftsmen/designers who are working in a competitive urban context and are mining the same stylistic vein. Nor are the variations on the interior carving of crest rails of the same pattern an indication that they were made in several shops, since it is always possible, indeed probable, that some of the crest rails were executed on contract

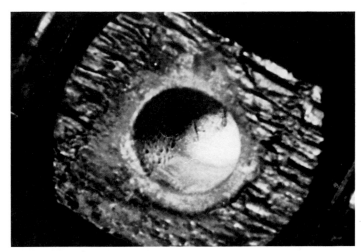

Fig. 141. Detail of a hole cut by the pod auger on the chair in catalogue entry 54. (Winterthur 74.120.)

by one or more specialist carvers, working in their own shops, shops that were independent of the shops in which the chair frames were made. But that crest rails of the same design (D, D′, D″, and D‴) were obviously laid out with four different patterns is virtually impossible to explain as the work of one shop. The chairs in the American Antiquarian Society (nos. 9 and 10), for example, have crests of the D type that consist of flattened ogees, a flared element with long sprays that reach down to the upper edge of the crest rail. The D″ crest rail is similar, but the ogees arch upward much more boldly. These two crest rails could not have been cut from the same pattern. The D′″ crest rail is closely related to the D″ type, except that the sprays are visibly shorter. They, too, would require yet another pattern, and logic tells us that while a shop might have different patterns for the crests of side and arm chairs because they differ in width, no shop should have three different patterns for the crest rail of a side chair since a set of chairs made from these different patterns would not be uniform, hence would not look like a set.

The same problem appears when we compare the medial and rear stretchers of these chairs, for they form yet another series of variations on the same theme. The rear stretchers of the Keene, Wenham, and Henry Ford Museum chairs (nos. 1, 2, and 3) have hollow-turned termini, like the front stretcher of the leather chair illustrated in catalogue entry 66. They swell gently to the center. The Holyoke and Connecticut Historical Society chairs (nos. 4 and 5) swell abruptly to a sharp central apex. The American Antiquarian and Blaney chairs (nos. 9, 10, and 11) have very short termini with soft shoulders and a gentle, rounded swell. The Winterthur and Deerfield examples (nos. 19 and 21) have one type of terminus on the medial stretcher and another on the rear. In short, the group displays a basic similarity in overall appearance, but the details of execution reveal many hands at work and many ideas of what a turned stretcher should look like.

If these chairs were made in several shops, then how can the punched initial that ties them all together be explained? In 1965, Richard Randall interpreted the monogram on the Museum of Fine Arts example as a "double E," possibly that of some member of the Edes family, from whom the chair came to the museum. Chairs were occasionally marked with their intended owners' initials, but perhaps only if they were being shipped a long distance. In 1705, for example, Thomas Fitch billed Mrs. Judith Pease in New York "for Six Rushia leather Chairs, and . . . for six more of the same sort all marked Ᵽ with chalk on the ba[ck]."[9] Now, more than a decade and a half later, many more chairs with the initial are known and the possibility that all of them were associated with the Edes family makes Randall's theory untenable. Indeed, the mark is less like a cypher based on the letter "E" and more like a capital "I" with a cross-serif—the common way of printing this letter in the seventeenth and early eighteenth centuries. This does not clear up the mystery, however, for the letter could equally well represent the letter "J," which was interchangeable with "I" until the nineteenth century.

The most obvious alternative explanation to its being an owner's mark is that the monogram is somehow related to the process of making the chair. If this is so, numerous possibilities suggest themselves. The mark could well represent the initial of a journeyman (as was the practice in Giles Grendy's London shop) who wished to identify the work he would be paid for. This would explain why some chairs are marked and others of identical character are not. But if this were the case, then "I" or "J," whoever he is, would have been the only journeyman in Boston, and, moreover, he must have remained a journeyman for at least fifteen or more years, an unlikely coincidence of circumstances at best.

Conversely, the initial could be that of a master craftsman who thus identified his frames before they went out to a specialist's shop for carving or upholstering. This is an attractive theory but has shortcomings in that the leading chairmakers of Boston in this period were named Edmond Perkins, John Leach, Samuel Mattocks, and possibly Anthony Underwood. Only John Leach's first name could be represented by I, which forces us to conclude that Perkins and Mattocks made few cane chairs, even though Perkins is the sole Boston craftsman we can document as having purchased cane for chairs, and his shop and the Mattocks shop were in operation prior to the arrival of Leach in Boston.

A third possibility is that the initial is that of a craftsman who made some frames on contract for another shop, in which case it would identify the work for which he, like a journeyman, would be paid. This could also explain why some chairs of a certain pattern are marked and others of the same pattern are not. But even this, the least objectionable theory, has its shortcomings. For one thing, the way in which the I is punched on the chairs varies from one chair to the other. The I on the Keene chair is quite small—only ⅞″ (2.2 cm) high. The one on the Massachusetts Historical Society chair (mentioned in catalogue entry 52) is larger than the one on the Winterthur example of the same type and has more strokes on the cross-serif. Both differ from that on the chair in this catalogue entry. The punched monogram is also located in different places on different chairs, sometimes on the back of a rear stile, sometimes on the lower rail of the back. Since the monogram is punched by hand, there is no good reason why it should be uniform from chair to chair, and since the chairs were made over a period of time, the variations of placement and style of punching may have little significance.

Fourth, the initial could be that of someone only peripherally associated with the chairmaker's business, who bought chairs from all the makers of Boston and shipped them out in the export trade. If such a man existed, he has escaped our attention and, as in the case of the journeyman, would have to be the only cane-chair exporter in Boston, an unlikely situation.

It would be a happy event if the mark could be shown to represent the initial of the framemaker since that would make this group of chairs the earliest "signed" chairs made in America. No craftsman so far identified with chairmaking in Boston in this period has a name that begins with an I. If the letter is construed as a J, a marvelous candidate would be John Jackson, a joiner who emigrated from London to Boston on July 18, 1716—a date that very nearly coincides with the date at which these chairs could have first been made. But, Jackson appears only twice in Boston records, first when he arrived and second a month later, when he was warned by the selectmen to depart the town.[10] Whether Jackson heeded the warning or not is unrecorded, but this name cannot be identified with the chairmaking trade in the later public records of the town. In any event, Jackson seems a poor choice as the craftsman identified by the I mark, since 1716 would be a surprisingly late date for the I-marked chair in catalogue entry 52 or another stylistically early chair—no. 1985 in Nutting's *Furniture Treasury* which is also marked on the rear of its back seat rail— to have been made, assuming that the marks are contemporary with the chairs. Fyfield Jackson, a joiner and cabinetmaker (1702–1728, w. 1724) who died insolvent, is another possibility, but he did not live long enough to have made the marked examples with crook legs (nos. 24 and 26). It is more likely that the I chairs were made in the shops of craftsmen who specialized in chairs, were capable of doing turned work, and were called "chairmakers." One craftsman who might fit this description was James Johnson, who is referred to by that occupational label in the daybook of Samuel Grant on January 29, 1732/33, and again on September 16, 1733. Johnson purchased sundries from Grant, perhaps to be credited against his account for services rendered.[11] Because the name "James Johnson" was common in Boston, it has not been possible to discover further details about him. Thus how long he may have been working in Boston prior to these recorded dates or for whom he may have worked remains unknown.

With these three names, the known possibilities are exhausted. None of them seems to fill the bill because an explanation which attempts to identify these frames with a single shop ignores the knowledge that we now have of the interdependence of craftsmen in Boston; that is, we cannot prove than *any* of the urban chairs were made by one man or necessarily in one shop. Indeed, the evidence of the variations in crest-rail patterns of this group and the use of center bits on some and pod augers on others suggests that the I chairs were not made in a single shop. This probability is further supported by the variations in the medial and rear stretcher combinations, which is an instance in cane-chair making that parallels the situation with the stylistically similar leather-upholstered Boston chairs discussed in catalogue entries 75, 76,

Fig. 142. Phase 2 and 3 cane armchair: carved top and stretcher, twist-turned stiles, wide seat. Probably England, ca. 1695. European beech (*Fagus sylvatica*). (Private collection.)

Fig. 143. Detail of the stamped initials MI or MP on the back of the stile of the cane chair in figure 142. (Private collection.)

Fig. 144. Detail of the punched I on the back stile of the cane chair in figure 142. (Private collection.)

and 77, all three of which were made in different shops. Indeed, aside from their generic similarity, the only attribute that all the I chairs have in common is that they are caned. This, far from being the simple-mindedly obvious point that it seems to be, suggests one further possibility for the identity of I, that it is the punched mark of the person or shop in which the caning was done. Even today caners identify their work with initials, and this could explain why some of the chairs are marked and others are not. In addition, it would explain why no punched initials have been found on Boston leather chairs of the same date as the cane chairs, an especially telling point since at least some of these leather chairs had to have been made in the same shops as their caned cousins.

A piece of circumstantial evidence that supports this proposition is illustrated by a cane chair (fig. 142) that microanalysis reveals is made of European beech (*Fagus sylvatica*), therefore, it is presumed to be of English origin. This chair bears stamped initials (fig. 143) which are commonly found on English cane chairs but are rare on American ones; it also bears the punched I (fig. 144), no examples of which have been observed on the cane chairs in the major museums of England. It seems likely that this chair, which had by the

twentieth century found its way to Exeter, New Hampshire, was originally made and caned in England about 1695 and was recaned in Boston some thirty or thirty-five years later, at which time the Boston caner added his mark.[12] While it is always possible that an English craftsman punched this monogram, its presence in New England suggests that the chair on which it appears was worked on in America, and the possibility that best explains this is that it was recaned here. If this is indeed the case, it is possible that the I mark on any one of the American examples need not necessarily be exactly contemporary with the date at which it was manufactured but could have been added when it was recaned at a later date. This could explain, for example, why some chairs have the punched I and others of the same model, from the same shop, possibly from the same set, do not.

Although the records of Thomas Fitch and Samuel Grant have led us to the discovery of the names of numerous Boston chairmakers, they are not sufficiently detailed to inform us about the subcontractors who worked for these makers. It is possible that journeymen caners worked both independently in their own shops and in upholsterers' shops as well, in the same manner that journeymen upholsterers, seamsters, and seamstresses did, depending on seasonal demands. Their names are never mentioned, and the work that they did is merely debited "to Shop" in the Fitch and Grant documents. Only two Boston professionals who specialized in caning—the husband and wife team of John and Sarah Lane—have emerged from obscurity, but their names appear too late for them to have been the original caners of most of the chairs of the I group. The earliest reference to them occurs in the August 31–September 7, 1730, edition of the *Boston Gazette*, when "John Lane, from London" advertised that he "Canes and Bottoms both New and Old Chairs, after the best manner, [in a shop] over against Dr. Cooke's, in School Street, Boston." A subsequent advertisement in the *New England Journal* for June 14, 1737, advised that "Sarah Lane, widow of John Lane, carries on the Business of Caning Chairs," and a final one in the *Gazette* of June 23–30, 1740, informs us that the widow had remarried, but was still living in School Street, and that "Sarah Goodwin . . . Canes Chairs, Couches, and Stools, with the utmost Fidelity and Dispatch."[13]

It is a matter of great frustration that with so much evidence at our command, we are still not capable of positively identifying the shop in which Winterthur's chair frame was made. The best clues—and they are weak ones—are offered to us by the accounts of Thomas Fitch and Samuel Grant and suggest that the shops of Edmond Perkins and John Leach were the most productive ones in Boston. However, it is doubtful that the basic design of the style originated with either of them. Of the two, Leach (d. 1748; followed in the trade by a son named James) may be eliminated because of the details of his turnings (compare the termini of the medial and rear stretchers of the chairs in fig. 156 and catalogue entry 77 with those on catalogue entry 54). The line of continuity between the turnings of the chair in entry 54, the example in the Queen Anne style illustrated as no. 23 in Joseph Downs, *American Furniture* (attributed by Downs to a Connecticut origin, but now understood to have been made in Boston), and those on the Chippendale style chair illustrated in figure 132 make a far more persuasive case for its manufacture in the Perkins shop. Perkins, who continued to work into the 1760s and had four sons who were chairmakers working long past the middle of the eighteenth century, provides the sort of biographical data that makes the later chairs attributable to his shop as well as this one.[14]

Despite our inability to discover beyond a reasonable doubt the name of the maker of Winterthur's I chair or the meaning of the punched letter, the chair stands in its own right as an important document of the decorative arts that contributes to our knowledge of early eighteenth-century eastern Massachusetts style. When the chair came onto the market in 1974, it had a stuffed, textile-upholstered seat cover. Upon removal of the modern cover, a woven splint seat of American black ash (*Fraxinus nigra*) was found beneath it. This seat, somewhat broken and fragile in nature, had been added to the chair after the original cane seat had broken out. That cane seats were quite quickly replaced in Boston is documentarily revealed as early as February 18, 1718/19, when the inventory of the chamber of Thomas Gilbert of Boston listed "3 cane back chairs with bass bottoms" valued at 9s.[15] Assuming that Gilbert acquired his chairs as early as 1690, the original cane bottoms lasted only about twenty-five or thirty years. The splint seat on Winterthur's chair, by the same token, may well date from the middle of the eighteenth century and is among the earliest examples of its type in the Winterthur collection.

After the splint seat was added, the chair received a coat of black paint, which covered the front corners of the seat frame not protected by the seating material. Close examination of the unpainted portion under the splint seat reveals that this chair originally had been neither painted nor stained.[16] This discovery proves beyond doubt that the pair of I chairs in the collection of the American Antiquarian Society, which betray no evidence of having been painted or stained, have indeed miraculously escaped that fate for two and a half centuries. These chairs and the Winterthur example, therefore, indicate that, contrary to popular belief, high-style maple or beech cane chairs in the William and Mary style were not invariably ebonized with black or stained to imitate walnut when they were new. These chairs and doubtless many others yet to be discovered form a special class of light-color chairs comparable to the light-color, marquetry case furniture popular in England during the last decade of the seventeenth century and their burl maple veneered equivalents made in Boston between 1696 and 1730. Documentary support for this idea may well be alluded to in the 1723 inventory of Thomas Smith, a Boston barber whose home contained "6 cane chairs Varnished" worth 10s. apiece.[17]

Winterthur's chair has remarkably retained three of the four glue blocks that had been added to the front feet prior to carving. Figure 145 shows the appearance of the front of the left foot prior to restoration. The dried glue that overlays the surface of the wood is cracked and readily visible. The wood under the glue was roughened so that the glue would not be completely pressed out when the block for the toes was clamped onto the leg. The tool used to accomplish this roughing is called a "tooth plane" today, as it was in 1717 when one was itemized in the inventory of William Howell, Boston cabinetmaker.[18] Howell probably used his primarily for veneering case furniture.

Equally worthy of notice is that the feet of the chair have received surprisingly little wear, with the result that the little platform which extends about ⅛″ (0.3 cm) of an inch high below the foot (fig. 146) has been preserved. This kind of platform was undoubtedly ubiquitous on the feet of urban

Fig. 145. Detail of the cane chair in catalogue entry 54 showing the front left foot with the glued-on block missing. (Winterthur 74.120.)

Fig. 146. Detail of the cane chair in catalogue entry 54 showing the right front foot and pad intact. (Winterthur 74.120.)

chairs with this style of foot during the first quarter of the eighteenth century. It was designed to put the weight of the chair onto the leg and not onto the foot, thus protecting the glued-on toes. Such platforms, however, had the opposite effect since any accidental pressure on the lower part of the projecting glued-on portions would work like a lever, making it easy to break them off.[19] That the feet on this example are in such a good state of preservation indicates that the present seat height, 18⅝″, is very nearly what the maker intended it to be.

Nail holes in the underside of the front seat rail reveal that a sculpted skirtboard (apron) was removed from between the front legs at the time the splint seat was added. The pair of chairs illustrated in Nutting's *Furniture Treasury*, nos. 2046 and 2047, show what such a skirtboard originally looked like. The influence of this skirtboard is reflected in the chairs made by the Gaines family chairmakers of Ipswich, Massachusetts, and Portsmouth, New Hampshire, and is a commonplace on Boston easy and upholstered chairs of the period (see catalogue entries 85 and 87) and the earliest cushion-seat and banister-back Queen Anne examples of the 1730s.

NOTES

[1] Object file 74.120, Registrar's Office, Winterthur. The statement is undated, but it must have been written shortly after a companion letter, which is postmarked August 4, 1907. We may assume, from the existence of the letter and its contents, that the chair was sold about that time to the addressee, Philip W. Adams of Falmouth Heights.

[2] Wyman, *Genealogies and Estates of Charlestown*, 1:362; Savage, *Genealogical Dictionary*, 3:397; Cary, "Some Notices of the Family of Perkins in America," pp. 211–16. No close relationship between this branch of the Perkins family and Edmond Perkins, the Boston chairmaker who is discussed later in this entry, can be established. The chair could have been part of the household goods of the Reverend John Hancock, Sr. (1702–1744), Mrs. Hancock's second husband, whom she married in 1733. Or it may have originally belonged to her and been part of the furniture acquired at the time of her first marriage (1729/30), to Samuel Thaxter (1695–1732) (see *Sibley's Harvard Graduates, 1713–1721*, 6:208–10, 316–19, 71). No matter who owned it first, the chair must have been made between 1721 and 1729.

[3] The chair with punched I illustrated in catalogue entry 52 is not included in this table because it is stylistically distinct from the other I chairs.

[4] The *ju i* is a stylized mushroom and was perceived by the Chinese to be a symbol of authority. See Williams, *Outlines of Chinese Symbolism and Art Motives*; I am indebted to Colin M. Streeter for calling this motif and its meaning to my attention.

[5] Israel Sack, *Opportunities in American Antiques 4*, no. 184.

[6] February 27, 1722/23, Fitch account book 1719–1732, MHS.

[7] *Sibley's Harvard Graduates, 1701–1712*, 5:268.

[8] A cane chair that had a crook back invariably had a solid, rectilinear splat, flanked by small panels of cane. At least one example was made in America, probably in Philadelphia. See Margaret B. Schiffer, *Furniture . . . of Chester County*, pl. 66.

[9] Fitch to Pease, May 8, 1705, Fitch letterbook, AAS; I am indebted to Robert Blair St. George for this reference.

[10] *Boston Records*, 29:239, 13:10. Savage, *Genealogical Dictionary*, 2:530; Suffolk Probate, 15:407; Suffolk Common Pleas, 9:73.

[11] January 29, 1732/33, September 16, 1733, Grant daybook.

[12] I am indebted to Dr. Edward T. Fogg for directing my attention to this chair and to the owner for his permission to examine, analyze, photograph, and publish this chair.

[13] I am indebted to Brock W. Jobe for the two references from the *Boston Gazette*. The *Journal* advertisement is from Dow, *Arts and Crafts of New England*, p. 106.

[14] If the quirks of stretcher termini may someday be proved to be an index to the attribution of Boston chairs, an example in the "Chippendale" style that may well have been made by Leach's son, James, may have survived into the twentieth century. This chair was owned in the third quarter of the eighteenth century by Benjamin Edes of Boston and was illustrated and discussed by Homer Eaton Keyes in, "Another Tea Chair," p. 355. The stretchers of this chair are executed in the same manner as those of the Edes family chair (Randall, *American Furniture*, no. 127), and the idea that a later generation of the Edes family may have patronized the same family of chairmakers as their ancestors did makes an intriguing possibility to speculate upon and forms a fascinating footnote to decorative arts history.

[15] Suffolk Probate, 21:561–62.

[16] Wax is the only finish on the unpainted portions of the chair. I am indebted to Winterthur conservator Mervin Martin for the determination of this.

[17] Suffolk Probate, 23:65–66.

[18] Suffolk Probate, 26:33.

[19] Just such a loss was suffered by the left front toe of this chair; it was restored by Winterthur conservator Nicholas Quinn in 1974.

55.
CANE ARMCHAIR WITH CARVED AND MOLDED TOP
Boston, Massachusetts
1715–1720
WOOD: American beech (*Fagus grandifolia*)
OH 47⅞" (121.6 cm)
SH 16½" (41.9 cm), SW 25⅞" (65.7 cm), SD 24¾" (62.9 cm)
PROVENANCE: Bequest of Henry Francis du Pont
54.527

This chair, made totally of American beech (*Fagus grandifolia*), appears to be from the same school of craftsmanship as the previous example but varies from it in a number of ways. The turned columnar shapes on the legs (between the front stretcher and the seat) and the design treatment on the side, medial, and back stretchers are not like those on chair no. 54. The turning of this front stretcher is much gentler in aspect and the balls flanking the central disk are not nearly so round as those on the previous chair. The bottom of the blocks at the seat rail are surprisingly flat on their bottom edge, and filled-in tenons on their inside faces indicate that this chair once had a sculpted apron beneath the front seat list. All of these features, combined with the design of the medial and rear stretcher, suggest that this chair is stylistically earlier than the preceding one; however, the crest rail suggests a later style. The rear legs are somewhat stiffer on this chair, but this feature probably has no chronological significance and represents rather the taste or the technological limitations of the equipment of the shop in which it was made. Unlike the previous chair, this one has no punched initial on its back side.

Many of the quirks of turning on this chair relate it to the somewhat earlier armchair with turned stiles and elaborately carved crest in the collection of the Wadsworth Atheneum, illustrated in Nutting's *Furniture Treasury* as no. 1985, and microanalyzed as American beech.[1] The style of the turning, particularly of the medial and side stretchers and the arm supports, combined with arms that are pinned into the stiles rather than wedged in the manner of the Boston leather chairs of a slightly later type, suggests that the Wadsworth example is closely related to English cane chairs with turned stiles and is probably an early example of the embowed-back cane-chair style made in America.

The Winterthur example appears never to have been painted. The bottom 2¹⁵⁄₁₆" (7.5 cm) of the feet are restorations. The front seat list was originally rounded, as the side ones still are, but has been squared off, perhaps at the time that a flag bottom was put on this chair. The marks of that flag bottom are visible on the upper front edge of this list. The cane of the seat is modern. The triangular braces at the junction of the arms and rear stiles are not original.

NOTE
[1] I am indebted to Phillip Johnston for samples of this chair.

56.
CANE ARMCHAIR WITH CARVED AND MOLDED TOP
Boston, Massachusetts
1720–1730
WOOD: American maple (*Acer pennsylvanicum*)
OH 49⅞" (126.7 cm)
SH 16½" (41.9 cm), SW 24¼" (61.5 cm), SD 21" (53.3 cm)
PROVENANCE: History of ownership in the Hancock family; Philip Flayderman; Henry Francis du Pont
54.528

This cane armchair was acquired at the sale of the furniture and silver of Philip Flayderman on January 4, 1930.[1] A notarized statement dated August 8, 1929, and signed by Lucy Cushing Richardson accompanied the chair and averred that this chair and two others had "always remained within the exclusive care and possession of the immediate family of John Hancock and his wife, Dorothy Quincy Hancock." The document continued: "the 'Spanish Toe Armchair' with the

cat. 55

cat. 56

carved top is the original and identical chair in which John Hancock was inaugurated Governor of Massachusetts. This chair has been handed down from generation to generation with this history, legend and tradition as a part of the heritage. This chair was my mother's prized possession and was always with her even when she went to Phila[delphia]. . . . I am a descendant of Dorothy Quincy Hancock whose sister Mary Quincy was my great grandmother by virtue of her marriage to Jacob Sheafe."[2]

While the family tradition of ownership is strong, and it undoubtedly descended through the Hancock and Sheafe family as believed, this chair seems a curious choice for John Hancock to have made as an inauguration chair in 1780, considering that it was then fifty or sixty years old. If the tradition is true, that giant of American politics consciously used the chair to publicly commemorate the past generations of his distinguished family, for it is likely that this chair was made at least a decade before he was born. If this chair did indeed come from the Hancock family, it is likely that it was made for his father, Ebenezer, or his uncle, Thomas, whose estate he inherited. It is equally possible that the chair came into the Hancock family through Hancock's marriage to Dorothy, daughter of Edmund Quincy of Braintree, or into the line of the last family owner through the marriage of her great-grandmother, Mary Quincy, to Jacob Sheafe. All these families trace their origins to the vicinity of Boston. It is unlikely that this chair was owned by Daniel Perkins, who is the probable owner of the other chair with Hancock family associations illustrated in catalogue entry 54, since this would imply that the Reverend Perkins possessed two sets of cane chairs of approximately the same date but in slightly different styles.

A side chair that matches this armchair descended in the family of John Stoddard (1682–1748) of Northampton, Massachusetts. Another side chair with a Stoddard history is at the Northampton Historical Society. Israel Sack attributed a side chair from the same set to Connecticut. The ascription seemed logical considering Northampton's proximity to Connecticut but was made before scholars learned the true extent of the export trade from Boston. According to Sack, the inventory of John Stoddard's estate mentions "nine cain chairs" valued at 34s. or about 3s. 9d. each. Assuming that the Sack chair was one of this group, it would have been about twenty-five years old at the time the inventory was taken, and 3s. 9d. seems a fair value.[3]

The most marked variation between this chair and the example illustrated in catalogue entry 54 is the design of the crest rail. With respect to the style and arrangement of the stretchers, the articulation of the arm supports, the large chamfer on the back stiles at the junction of the seat lists, the style of the arms themselves, and the profile of the moldings run on the side and bottom rails of the back, the chair can be traced to the Boston school. The armchair does have a lower seat than a side chair and does not have the characteristic elongated baluster between the front stretcher and the seat. The turnings on the front stretcher are also slightly bolder in profile than those of the side chairs. The crest rail is less cramped because the armchair is wider than the side chair, and its design

suggests a date of manufacture in the mid to late 1720s. These differences serve to illustrate the idea that several shops were producing nearly identical versions of the current styles to meet the orders of upholsterers or other merchants who ultimately sold them to retail customers (see the introduction to the next section of the catalogue). Accordingly, it is almost an impossible task to correlate the surviving chairs with any of the makers found in the Boston documents of the period.

The records of the Court of Common Pleas of Suffolk County underline the interdependence of Boston's furniture craftsmen and suggest that the conception of the lone craftsman with his sons or apprentices working in his own shop producing his distinctive brand of furniture is incorrect, although that ideal might hold true in a rural village. The court records offer evidence that John Lincoln, a carver, did specialty work for the Mattocks family of chairmakers (and if so, perhaps also for cabinetmaker John Mattocks), augmenting evidence in the Fitch and Grant account books. Other interrelationships also emerge. In 1714, Benjamin Davis and Thomas Odell, both called chairmakers, worked in partnership, perhaps until Davis's death in 1718. The records also show that Edmond Edes, a joiner, possibly one who specialized in ship work, sued John Bushnell, another joiner, for debt in 1713 and 1715; that Thomas Webb, a joiner, sued John Lincoln, the carver, in 1723; that John Pillet, a joiner, sued John Goodwin and Thomas Wharton, carpenters, in 1714; and that William Sutton, a joiner, sued William Whetcomb, an upholsterer, for debt in 1715.[4]

The difficulty in dating the chairs is equally great. In addition to the style of the arms and arm supports that appear on Boston leather-upholstered armchairs with turned stiles that were made in the first decade of the century and on the embowed-back models made between 1723 and 1740, the turned rear legs of this chair (as opposed to those that are chamfered) appear on Boston maple chairs with slip, or cushion, seats made in the early 1730s as well. The point of these observations is that a chair such as this one can, under the best of circumstances, be viewed as a product made at a specific moment of time, but it is also a part of a continued development of Boston chairs over a longer period of time, which is especially noticeable in an urban context where the details of even basic models are continually being changed.

The toes on the front feet of this chair are replaced. The original apron is missing, and the chair has been upholstered several times. The cane has been restored.

NOTES
[1] *Flayderman Sale*, p. 202, item 459. It was also advertised in *Antiques* 19, no. 6 (December 1929):450.
[2] Object file 54.528, Registrar's Office, Winterthur.
[3] Theus, *Savannah Furniture*, fig. 16, pp. 75–85, sets out the history of the first Stoddard family chair; I am indebted to Kevin Sweeney for bringing the historical society chair to my attention. Israel Sack, *Opportunities in American Antiques 16*, p. 367, fig. 919. I am indebted to Albert Sack for lending me a photograph of the chair for study. That chair appears to possess its original seat apron.
[4] Suffolk Common Pleas, 6:140, 5:211, 10:232, 6:245.

57.
CANE ARMCHAIR WITH CARVED AND MOLDED TOP
Probably Philadelphia, Pennsylvania
1700–1720
WOODS: Black walnut (*Juglans nigra*)
OH 44⅛″ (112.1 cm)
SH 16⅜″ (41.6 cm), SW 22⅞″ (58.1 cm), SD 16¼″ (41.2 cm)
PROVENANCE: Gift of David Stockwell
55.130

An oval brass plate, engraved in the manner common in the 1790–1820 period, is attached to the rear of the crest rail of this chair. It reads

CHAIR
OF
THOMAS LLOYD
Governor of Pennsylvania
1684 to 1693.

If Thomas Lloyd was the original owner, the chair must have been made prior to January 8, 1694/95, when Lloyd's will was submitted for probate by his widow, Patience.[1]

Chairs with molded stiles, as opposed to turned ones, are usually thought to have become popular in England around 1700, but the documentary evidence is ambiguous. Although chairs such as this one were likely made in Philadelphia prior to Lloyd's death in 1694, it is difficult to demonstrate. The possibility that the family tradition is incorrect is given some support by the records of the province of Pennsylvania, which do not reveal that Thomas Lloyd was ever governor. And if the tradition is wrong in this respect, it is possible that it is faulty in other respects as well. Perhaps this chair was originally owned by one of Thomas Lloyd's two sons, Mordecai and Thomas, and that the family tradition represents the understandable error of one generation. No inventory was filed for the elder Lloyd, but according to his will, his Patience retained their joint household goods while their children inherited shares in the real estate and tenements. If Patience kept the chair upon her death, it could have passed to her sons or have gone into the Hill, Moore, or Story families through her daughters.[2]

Despite the difficulty of confirming its provenance, the chair itself offers ample evidence of a Pennsylvania origin. It is made of black walnut (*Juglans nigra*), the most common wood of better Philadelphia furniture made prior to the time that mahogany became more fashionable. As discussed earlier, although black walnut is not prima facie evidence of the American origin of a piece of furniture (see also catalogue entry 68), the Lloyd chair shares a number of traits with other pieces of early eighteenth-century furniture found and probably made in Pennsylvania. The carved feet abruptly butt into the leg, without rounded shoulders to provide transition to the block above them, which is unlike the feet on the best chairs of England and New England. This is difficult to explain, but the same technique can be noted on a leather chair made on the Iberian peninsula (Metropolitan Museum of Art), and an English-made cane couch (catalogue entry 60). Its appearance here may be caused by technical considerations rather than aesthetic ones, but the same treatment occurs on the American cane chairs believed to have been owned by William Penn,

which also suggests that this is a characteristic quirk of the Philadelphia region.[3]

Less characteristic of American workmanship are the bulbous balusters on the legs, arm supports, and front stretchers that were made by gluing blocks of walnut to a narrower core of wood prior to turning (fig. 147). There were a few cogent reasons for doing this. The man who made this frame could have consciously chosen this technique to avoid the checking or cracking of the wood that often occurs when a large piece of unseasoned wood is turned. It is even more likely that the maker used the technique to save on labor and materials; it allowed him to turn substantially narrower pieces of wood for the legs. Chairmakers of London, who bought wood at considerable expense, often used this technique. That it was resorted to on a piece of furniture made in America, where wood was plentiful, comes as a surprise to students who are primarily familiar with New England chairs on which a much less bold style of turning was practiced. However, as we have seen, gluing up was used in every Boston cane chair that has Spanish feet.

In addition to being less boldly turned, Boston high-style cane chairs vary from this Philadelphia chair in another way: they are almost always made of maple or beech rather than walnut. This emphasizes the idea that regional differences in techniques and materials tend to impress such a strong regional identity upon the furniture made in the colonial period that broad generalizations about attributes are difficult to make. One distinctive feature of this chair that can be found on slightly later pieces of Pennsylvania furniture is the multireeded scroll foot, such as that on the leather chair illustrated as figure 168, and the numerous examples of the dressing-table form usually said to be of New Jersey origin, the best examples of which were probably made in Philadelphia or Germantown.[4]

Two chairs related to the present example were once owned by Howard Reifsnyder, who collected an extraordinary group of high-style Philadelphia furniture during the early twentieth century. The first of these chairs was illustrated in the catalogue of the Reifsnyder sale in 1929 as no. 619. Because the

chair was made of walnut, it was sold for $475—a fair price if it was English, and a bargain if it turned out to be American. The chair is now in a private collection, and microanalysis revealed none of the factors needed to identify it as American walnut and thus it is assumed to be European walnut (*Juglans regia*). The chair has an elaborately carved crest rail and beautifully articulated Spanish feet. The European attribution comes as no surprise. Considering that Reifsnyder was extremely discriminating in his tastes and formed his collection for the most part in Philadelphia, it is probable that the chair was imported to that colonial center when the style was first in vogue.

A second chair, similar in appearance but different in almost every detail, was also owned by Reifsnyder and was pictured as no. 376 in the catalogue of his sale (fig. 148). Because that chair was made of beech and the collector's rule of thumb in the early twentieth century cautioned that "beech cane chairs are English," it brought the somewhat smaller sum of $275. Two priced catalogues of the sale provide conflicting information about its fate. One of them, privately owned, says that the item was bought by S. Sarota, a New York antiques dealer who specialized in ceramics and also had a shop in Portland, Maine. The other priced copy, in the files of Sotheby Parke Bernet, New York, successors to the American Art Association, state that the chair was "unclaimed" after the sale and was returned to the estate. The whereabouts of this chair are unknown, but its close visual relationship to Winterthur's chair virtually confirms the American origin. The 1927 photograph reveals that, despite the elaborate crest rail, the chair probably originated in the same shop or shops as the Winterthur example: the articulation of the rear stiles, the molding of the seat, the turning of all the stretchers, and the abruptly squared bottom edge of the block above the feet are identical on both chairs.[5] The unusually long great heels and unusually scrolled front feet suggest that the Reifsnyder example was somewhat over-restored. The arms of both chairs appear closely related as well, but arms on similarly priced chairs from Holland, England, New England, and Pennsylvania in that period are practically indistinguishable. The photograph of the Reifsnyder chair makes it appear as if it varies from the Winterthur example in one important respect: the blocks on the legs into which the front stretcher is fastened are square rather than bulbous. But the unusually long tenons on the ends of the front stretcher are evidence that the turnings on the legs were once glued-up bulbous shapes that had come unglued and been discarded. This notion is further confirmed by the upper and lower edges of the blocks. They are gently curved—as if to continue the parabola of the bulbous turning—while the analogous portions of the blocks at the feet and seat rail, which were always intended to be blocks, are much longer. The turning of the stretcher is identical to that of the Winterthur example. The variations in details between the two chairs indicate that they could not originally have belonged to the same set. For example, the arm supports of the Reifsnyder chair differ significantly from those of the Winterthur example; they are somewhat more like those on the leather chair, illustrated in catalogue entry 80. The flat-bottom, caplike turning between the elongated baluster and the arm is

Fig. 148. Phase 5 cane armchair: turned legs, crest rail that matches molded stiles. Probably Philadelphia, 1700–1720. From *Reifsnyder Sale*, no. 376.

similar to the element that appears on either side of the central ball on the medial stretcher of the Logan footstool (see fig. 133) as are the bulbous turnings of the legs. That the medial and rear stretchers of the Winterthur chair are not identical, which is not characteristic of English chairs of this period and of this quality, further supports the idea that this chair originated in America. The variations in the outlines of the crest rails further emphasize the differences between the two chairs.

The possible presence in Philadelphia of three stylistically related sets of chair is provocative. We know that one of these was English and made of European walnut, a second was made of beech, and a third was made of black walnut.

The existence of the Reifsnyder European walnut chair is significant when we consider how the design for the Reifsnyder beech chair and the Winterthur walnut example from the same shop made its way to Philadelphia. In such instances we usually assume that an immigrant craftsman brought the style with him, a notion that is superficially supported by the bulbous elements of the front stretcher and front legs of the Winterthur example, which are glued up rather than turned from the solid. Although we could see this as the importation of an English technique, an alternative explanation—ease of execution—is conceivable, which makes the presence of an immigrant craftsman unessential since the English walnut chair could have served as a prototype. This idea is supported by the early eighteenth-century Philadelphia records. A search through them failed to reveal an immigrant cane-chair maker who could have been responsible for this chair.

Indeed, when we consider the research of Cathryn J. McElroy into the craftsmen working in Philadelphia at this time, we do not find that a great many of them are making cane chairs. Only Thomas Stapleford can be associated with cane-chair making by documentary references. The first reference to Stapleford's chairmaking activities occurs relatively late in the history of the style. In 1721 he purchased "Merch[andize] from Britain: for 3 Doz Cane for Chairs" from John Reynell. The second reference to caning occurs in Stapleford's will, which was proved in 1739. He left to his "daughter Elizabeth . . . half a dozen Cane Chairs to be finished at the Charge of my Estate by my Executors." Stapleford had come to Philadelphia from Boston in the mid 1690s.[6] If Stapleford, like upholsterer Edward Shippen, kept up his Boston connections, his shop is a poor place to look for the origin of this chair; the chair exhibits no recognizable quirk of New England design in the articulation of the arms or the shape of the stretchers. Conversely, no New England chair displays the particular articulation of the feet nor the extraordinary balusters on the legs and arm supports that occur on this chair, the single feature that places it and the examples related to it in the exclusive

group of furniture masterpieces made in America during its first century of northern European colonization.

The seat and back of Winterthur's chair have been over-upholstered at one time; the cane is modern. The right side stretcher is replaced, and the lost sides of the two arm supports were restored by Nicholas Quinn in 1976.

NOTES
[1] Philadelphia Wills, 1694-105.
[2] Philadelphia Wills, 1724-312. The inventories of Lloyd's sons are not on file.
[3] Comstock, "Spanish-foot Furniture," p. 58; one of the Penn chairs belongs to the Historical Society of Pennsylvania, Philadelphia, and the other, now on loan to Pennsbury Manor, belongs to the William Penn Memorial Museum, Harrisburg.
[4] See the examples illustrated in Downs, *American Furniture*, no. 322, and in Hornor, *Blue Book*, pl. 17.
[5] I am indebted to David Stockwell and William Stahl for the sales data; Keyes, "Editor's Attic," p. 275.
[6] John Reynell Ledger and Philadelphia Wills 1739-30 as quoted in McElroy, "Furniture of the Philadelphia Area," pp. 207–9. Stapleford, whose role in Philadelphia chairmaking is discussed later, is variously identified in the records as a chairmaker and a chair-frame maker. He probably presided over an extensive shop engaged both in chairmaking and in joiner's work.

58.
CANE CHAIR WITH CARVED AND MOLDED TOP
London, England, or possibly Philadelphia, Pennsylvania
1685–1710
WOOD: Black walnut (*Juglans nigra*)
OH 50⅜" (127.9 cm)
SH 17¾" (45.1 cm), SW 17⅝" (44.8 cm), SD 14¾" (37.4 cm)
PROVENANCE: James Sorber; museum purchase.
77.60

This black walnut chair accentuates the difficulty of distinguishing a well-executed Philadelphia cane chair from London examples made from the same wood at approximately the same date. Like the Lloyd family chair and the now unlocated example from the Reifsnyder collection discussed in the previous entry, this chair relies on glued-up turnings for the dramatic contours of its front posts. Yet the turnings on the Lloyd chair are pale by comparison, all of which suggests that this chair is the product of one of the large London shops that employed the best turners of the period. Such shops fabricated chairs that were then exported across the western world. This chair has beautifully articulated columnar turnings above the balusters on the front posts. The seat rails are molded, as they are on most London-made chairs (in contrast the rails on the Lloyd and Reifsnyder chairs are unadorned). The transition from the bottom of the front post to the foot of this chair is visually eased by chamfers. In addition, the baluster turnings on the front stretcher of this chair are graceful throughout and contrast markedly with the less subtle breaking of the shoulders on the balusters of the Lloyd chair. The stretchers are finely executed and replete with precisely cut fillets in contrast to the softer turnings on the corresponding points of the Philadelphia examples. Finally, the carving on the crest rail is unmatched by any of the well-documented Philadelphia examples but resembles known English examples closely (fig. 149).

Still, the attribution of this chair to a Philadelphia artisan must be considered in light of the black walnut stock used in its fabrication. (A chair now in the collections of Sturbridge Village and another privately owned in North Carolina are also made of black walnut.) Certainly an as yet undocumented chairmaker from London could have been working in Philadelphia. There is no reason why an artisan recently arrived from London could not have made chairs exactly like those he had made before emigrating, and the prime wood in the Philadelphia area for the production of chair frames was black walnut. Yet until additional work has been done and

Fig. 149. Phase 4 and 5 cane chair: top carved to match molded back panel, turned stiles, Spanish feet. London, England, 1685–1710. (Photo: Symonds Collection, DAPC, Winterthur Library.) Compare the crest rail on this chair with that on the chair in catalogue entry 58.

until additional examples of walnut chairs of this quality turn up with good histories of ownership in Pennsylvania area families, the attribution of this chair must remain uncertain.

Portions of the front feet on this chair are missing. The cane seat is a modern replacement. The crest rail and the front seat rail have split and been reglued, and there is a patch in the top surface of the left seat rail.

cat. 58

59.
CANE COUCH
London, England
1720–1730
WOOD: Left front foot, European beech (*Fagus sylvatica*)
OH 41⅛″ (104.4 cm)
SH 15¾″ (40.0 cm), SW 20⅞″ (53.0 cm), SD 59⅜″ (150.8 cm)
PROVENANCE: Bequest of Henry Francis du Pont
58.578

The dealer who sold this couch to Henry Francis du Pont in 1924 stated that he had purchased it in Hampton, New Hampshire, and that it was made of maple.[1] Microanalysis of the wood proves it to be beech and further suggests that the couch is English in origin. Like the example in the next entry, this frame has bipartite turnings on the stretchers between the legs and a strongly undercut form of foot with applied toes (some of which are missing). The back posts and crest are molded, a style that came into use in Boston about 1722. The back is hinged and has chains to lower it; the chains are modern.

NOTE
[1] du Pont, Accession book 1, Registrar's Office, Winterthur.

60.
CANE COUCH
London, England
1700–1720
WOODS: Right rear leg, rear medial brace, left seat rail, second left foot, European beech (*Fagus sylvatica*); crest and right finial (both replaced), American maple (*Acer pennsylvania*)
OH 41¾″ (106.0 cm)
SH 15⅝″ (39.7 cm), SW 22″ (55.9 cm), SD 60¼″ (153.0 cm)
PROVENANCE: Martin Gay, Hingham, Mass.; Winsor White; Henry Francis du Pont
66.1312

In 1924 Wallace Nutting identified the wood of which this couch is made as walnut. Wood samples taken at Winterthur prior to 1966 indicated that the frame was made of American maple; however, later examination revealed that all the samples had been taken from the elaborate scrolled crest, which is a replacement.[1] Samples subsequently taken from elsewhere on the frame reveal that it is made of European beech, and there is little question that the couch was made in England and brought to this country in the eighteenth century. Although the back is now stationary, it originally was hinged at the bottom and provided with chains in the manner characteristic of most urban couch frames in this style; it is thus understandable that the original crest was broken and replaced, as were the finials. Whether these replacements represent an eighteenth- or a twentieth-century repair is difficult to determine from examination of the refinished frame.

Wallace Nutting was eager to have the couch be an American example because "We have never elsewhere seen anything like the two additional longitudinal sets [of stretchers] which are mortised into the cross members below."[2] The side stretchers are remarkable in number and in their distinctive profiles: two pairs of intermediate side stretchers with plain swelled turnings, one pair with tripartite turnings, and three pairs of outer side stretchers with bipartite turnings. That all these appear on a single artifact strongly suggests that this couch was made in a large London shop that had different but interchangeable turned elements prepared, stockpiled, and ready for use.

The form of foot—deeply undercut at the top, pieced out at the bottom, and carved with two rounded grooves and pronounced toes—is characteristic of London chairs but not colonial ones. That the carving of the feet was "very well done," was another reason Nutting wanted to believe the couch was American.[3]

A series of holes on the sides of the seat rails, visible in the photograph in *Pilgrim Century* but since filled, indicate that the couch was upholstered at some point. In addition, the holes for caning have been redrilled. The crest and finials are replacements.

NOTES
[1] Wallace Nutting, *Pilgrim Century* (2d ed.), 2:402, 424, fig. 582; object file 66.1312, Registrar's Office, Winterthur.
[2] Nutting, *Pilgrim Century* (2d ed.), 2:402.
[3] Nutting, *Pilgrim Century* (2d ed.), 2:402.

CARVED TOPP'D, PLAIN TOPP'D, AND CROOK'D-BACK LEATHER CHAIRS

The household inventories of colonial America make no distinction between the leather-upholstered chairs popular when New England was first settled and those with higher backs and more slender proportions that replaced them toward the end of the seventeenth century. Both are referred to with an economy of words as "leather chairs." Even inventory values do not always reveal when one style is in the process of being replaced by another, for simpler versions of a new style were often appraised at the same level as elaborate examples of a waning style.

A few surviving letters and bills of upholsterers Thomas Fitch and Samuel Grant reveal what the surviving chairs suggest: in Boston the high-back leather chairs of the late seventeenth century and the first third of the eighteenth were made in two distinct phases. The earlier phase of the style, identified in the Fitch bills and letters from 1704 onward as being either "carved topp'd" or "plain topp'd" (referring to the decoration of the crest rail), also had turned rear stiles and baluster-shape front feet. The later phase of the style had a "crook'd" back with an essentially geometrical crest rail and concave rear stiles that were molded on their front surfaces, and, usually, carved Spanish (claw) feet. These later chairs were made in Boston beginning in 1722. The phase appears to have been designed to exploit the popular characteristics of contemporary English cane chairs. The later version likewise had English cane counterparts but also drew much of its spirit from upholstered chairs. Why the second version made a laggard appearance in Boston is difficult to explain, especially since it probably was already in use in Philadelphia. Indeed the technique of molding stiles was used on the best English upholstered chairs at the turn of the eighteenth century. Ironically, many of the English upholstered chairs of this period reflect the attributes of continental cane chairs, while less expensive English cane chairs—of the type that generally found their way into the export trade to the colonies—reflect the attributes of better cane chairs and upholstered examples.

The exact sources of the American leather chairs of this period are difficult to unravel, so confused are we about their lineage. One idea, however, emerges when we compare the European and American examples: the invariable choice of leather in contrast to textile upholstery or, indeed, the choice of leather in preference to cane cannot be explained as obvious conservatism, expressed by a preference for a durable material over a perishable one, nor as provincialism. The russia leather used to upholster the majority of the New England chairs was imported and quite expensive, and the chair frames cost roughly twice as much as competitive cane chairs imported from England.

The earliest New England William and Mary leather chairs were made with a number of variations, and the Winterthur collection is unusually rich in examples of them. By the middle of the first decade of the eighteenth century, however, one style had captured the imagination of Americans, and this particular chair, produced in at least two shops, became what we will refer to here as the "standardized Boston leather chair." This chair was made in great quantities for use throughout New England and for the export trade southward and prompted imitation throughout the colonies. Many of the early variations can be related to English prototypes, but the standardized Boston leather chair represents the strain that unquestionably had the most far-reaching impact on the history of American chairmaking and thus is the strain that can be pursued most profitably in this introduction.

The expensive and elaborate English chair illustrated in figure 150 has many features which can be seen in the American versions and captures the essence of the best London chairs of circa 1700. Probably made by Thomas Roberts for either Devonshire House in London or Chatsworth, the chair has a cluster of floriated scrolls on the crest rail, suggestive of the manner of the published designs of Daniel Marot and thus northern Europe.[1] It also exhibits most of the chair vocabulary of the period: molded seat rail and stiles; molded, flowing arms with compound downward, then upward, and outward lines ending in a voluted handgrip; an artfully conceived stretcher with a useless but visually indispensable finial; and baluster shapes on the front legs and arm supports (scarcely recognizable in this carved version as forms that would be executed by turners when the style descended on the social and economic scale).

The presumed date of the Roberts chair is given some credence by the description of a suite of lesser seating furniture advertised for "Sale by Auction, Fryday the 2d of July next 1703 in Chesil St. in the Strand." The set, accompanied by a black card table at £9, consisted of "4 Damask Chairs with Moulding, 2 Elbow, 2 round Stools, 2 Square Stools," in addition to "3 Moulding Stools covered with Green Velvet and Laced with Gold Lace, £4."[2]

Assuming the Roberts chair was made around 1700, then the cane chair illustrated in figure 151 with the believable date 1703 carved on the stiles shows how quickly stylistic ideas could find their way into a far less expensive chair. The crest rail was probably created by a London craftsman familiar with the types of ornament used on examples like the Roberts chair, since cane-chair making in England, as in America, was an urban craft and every maker in the city knew what every other maker was doing. The use of beech instead of walnut, of cane instead of silk, and turned elements instead of carved ones represents normal economies that permit popularization. Finally, the crest rails of both these chairs suggest a basic motif that is found on the largest surviving group of American carved-top leather chairs.

BOSTON LEATHER CHAIRS WITH PLAIN AND CARVED TOPS

Recent research confirms that Boston was the center for the manufacture of leather-upholstered chairs in New England prior to the end of the seventeenth century. On April 8, 1695, the trustees of Harvard College voted "that six leather Chairs be forthwith provided for ye use of ye Library, & six more before ye Commencement, in Case ye Treasury will allow of it." In the "Harvard College Book," kept by Thomas Brattle, we find that the treasury did indeed permit the purchase of six additional chairs: on December 22, 1697, Brattle entered into it a memorandum of "Cash pd Mr Tho. Fitch for 6 Russia chairs had of him last Commencement for ye Colledg Library, as [per] his mans recpt on his ——— [note?]

Fig. 150. Thomas Roberts, carved-top chair in the Daniel Marot style. London, England, 1700. (National Trust, on display at Hardwick Hall. Photo: courtesy Country Life.) The chair was made for the duke of Devonshire.

Fig. 151. Phase 4 cane chair: high back, turned stiles, molded back panel, scroll-carved crest rail and C scrolls on front legs. London, England, 1703. (Dealer owned in 1974.) Feet and finials are conjectural restorations. The chair possesses simplified versions of the motifs used on the chair made by Thomas Roberts illustrated as figure 150.

£4:10." At 15s. each, these chairs were twice as valuable as the Cromwellian type listed in the inventories, and, assuming that russia leather was slightly less expensive than turkey work, we may conclude that these were high-back chairs, thus part of their value must have been stylistic novelty.[3] Why they cost more than the examples that he was shortly thereafter shipping to New York is not clear.

Fitch's surviving letter- and account books suggest that the

Fig. 152. Plain-top leather chair, Boston, 1690–1710. Maple, oak, tulip; H 45¼″ (114.9 cm), W 18½″ (47 cm), D 15¾″ (40 cm), SH 18¼″ (46.4 cm). (Wallace Nutting Collection, Wadsworth Atheneum, Hartford, Conn., gift of J. P. Morgan.) The front stretcher indicates the chair was probably made in the same shop as the chair in catalogue entry 66. A New York version of the stretcher is on the chair in catalogue entry 70.

chairs furnished to the college might have been very much like the one illustrated in figure 152. In letters written to customers outside of Boston over the next few years, Fitch refers to leather chairs with either carved or plain tops. On May 8, 1705, he wrote to Judith Pease, who perhaps lived in Rhode Island, that he was sending her "six Rushia Leath Chairs . . . & six more of the same sort all marked ℗ with chalk on the ba[ck]. The price is 13/6 a ps. which is less by 6d. a pcs than I have sold any for many years past." In November he shipped six of the same to Mrs. Elizabeth Carr in New York: "the Lowest price of them is 13/6d apcs and I have not sold them under this [in] many years." It is possible that these leather chairs were in the Cromwellian style, but in 1709 in the last of a series of letters in regard to thirty unsold chairs of the same description that he had sent to Benjamin Faneuil of New York on speculation more than two years earlier, Fitch wrote: "I wonder the chairs did not sell; I have sold a pretty many of that sort to Yorkers since, and tho some are carv'd yet I make Six plain to one carv'd; and can't make the plain so fast as they are bespoke, so yo may assure [them] that are customers that they are not out of fashion here."[4]

Such a chronological series of letters about a group of related chairs, some carved and some uncarved, clearly cannot refer to American Cromwellian chairs because Cromwellian chairs had no carved elements.[5] But American examples of leather chairs have survived in good numbers, and the plainer ones are characterized by a turned front stretcher and a crest rail— usually of oak—that is chamfered on the upper front edge,

while the carved versions have a carved stretcher and a carved crest. The finials, the columnar stiles, the scored lines on the stiles between the seat and lower back rails, and the use of materials in the example illustrated in figure 152 compare in every detail with analogous parts of the carved examples that were made by Boston craftsmen and prove that plain-top chairs were made in the same shops as carved ones (see catalogue entry 66).

The plain crest rail and turned stretcher were misleading features years ago when most information about American furniture was passed on by word of mouth. They caused many students to assume that because they were plainer and were therefore less expensive than the carved type they must either have originated in another place or have been made by a less skilled chairmaker. In addition, the picture was further blurred by a group of leather chairs with plain crest rails but elaborately turned stiles (see catalogue entries 69, 70, and 71) that differed markedly from the examples with carved crest rails whose details of design show that they clearly did come from another place. These types ultimately became known as "Piscataqua chairs" among dealers and collectors because numerous examples of the plain leather chairs, which we now know were made in Boston, were found in the Piscataqua River valley, near Portsmouth, New Hampshire, in the early days of collecting. This name was given further legitimacy by the oblique mention of the genre in a pioneering article, in 1963, written long before the full extent of the eighteenth-century trade in Boston chairs throughout New England had been identified. Since no evidence has subsequently been introduced to demonstrate that a major chairmaking industry actually existed on the banks of the Piscataqua until 1770— long after these chairs were popular—the term "Piscataqua chair" must be considered merely a handy dealer-collector phrase that has been used to identify a high-back, leather-upholstered chair with turned stiles, turned front stretcher, and a flat crest rail chamfered on the upper front edge.[6] In short, this terminology cannot be construed to indicate in any way the place in which these chairs were made.

The standardized Boston leather side chair with turned stiles has survived in fairly large quantities. It was made in a number of variations, the most expensive of which, with carved crest rail and carved stretcher, is represented by catalogue entry 65, and a slightly less expensive version of which, with a turned front stretcher, is represented by catalogue entry 66. The banister-back chair with flag seat in figure 153 could easily have come from the same shop as the chair in catalogue entry 65—a surmise that is prompted by the high quality of the workmanship and materials, as well as the proportions of the front legs which are similar to those found on the more expensive leather-bottom examples. It also has nearly identical measurements, the characteristic finials, and the expected grooves on the rear stiles between the seat and the bottom rail of the back. Such a chair was without doubt similar to one of the "18 carved flag chairs" sold by Edmond Perkins of Boston to Timothy Woodbridge of Newbury for 10s. each in 1722, and it has remained unrecognized because of the unwarranted assumption that banister-back chairs were prima facie country furniture.[7]

Fig. 153. Carved-top chair with banister back and flag seat, probably Boston, 1690–1725. Soft maple, with seat rails of red oak; H 47⅞" (121.6 cm), W 17⁵⁄₁₆" (44 cm), D 14" (35.6 cm), SH 17¼" (43.8 cm). (Mabel Brady Garvan Collection, Yale University Art Gallery, New Haven, Conn.) This chair probably came from the same shop as the chair in catalogue entry 65.

The leather-upholstered carved-top Boston chair must have been considered the tour de force of this style and clearly served as the paradigm for flag-bottom banister-back chairs made throughout New England, from the Housatonic to the Piscataqua and points inland, where chairmakers from different shop traditions executed countless variations.

Ironically, the presence of Boston-made leather chairs in some quantity in New York state is the sole clue to their Boston origin: none of the surviving examples have Boston histories, although they occasionally turn up in Massachusetts families. It is also no surprise that these chairs have long been believed to have been of New York origin; they have been there since a week or two after they were made. A classic example of such a group of Boston chairs owned in a New York family are the set of four now at Washington's Headquarters, Newburgh, New York, but formerly in the Dutch Reformed Church at Fishkill. These chairs are stamped P. v. P., believed to be the initials of Philip ver Planck, and are mates to the Boston

example illustrated in catalogue entry 65. An armchair of the same group, believed to have been owned by Capt. Peter Schuyler of Albany, is in the collection of the Henry Ford Museum in Dearborn, Michigan, and another, which descended through the Church family from Gen. Phillip Schuyler of Albany via his daughter, Angelica, is now at the Munson-Williams-Proctor Institute, Utica, New York (see fig. 180).[8]

While there is almost no written evidence that these chairs were made in New York, documentary references to the shipment of leather chairs from Boston to both New York City and Albany do exist. On October 22, 1701, the "Sloop Rachell from Boston: Ben. ffunnel [Faneuil]" brought "12 leather chaires . . . [from] Boston where the above goods were made."[9] On April 22, 1707, Thomas Fitch sent Captain Faneuil "2 doz Russia Leather Chairs . . . p[er Capt. Dierk] Adolph at 16s [a]ps.," and advised him that "Russhia Leath[er] Elbow chairs will be 28s. aps." The armchairs were sent on June 23. From the lengthy correspondence between Fitch and Faneuil, it appears that these slightly more expensive chairs had been specifically ordered by Faneuil (as opposed to a half dozen chairs, double nailed "made here" at 14s. each that Fitch sent on speculation). On April 16, June 21, and July 19, Fitch shipped more: "they sell very readily here and [I] doubt not of yor ease to sell them there." On March 28, 1709, he filled the order of Albany's Abram Wendell for "Twelve Russhia Chairs & one Arm[chair]." Wendell must have complained about the price, for Fitch's next letter is full of salesmanship: "the chairs are extraordinary Leather & at the lowest price: I refused ready money for them at the same price meerly to sute ye."[10] The sale must have stuck, Wendell does not mention them again.

While we can only surmise that the russia chairs mentioned in the foregoing correspondence had carved tops, while the side chairs priced at 14s. did *not*, there can be no doubt that those Fitch shipped to Nicholas Tienhoven in New York City, on October 30, 1710, *did*. Fitch wrote: "This serves to Inclose yo a receipt for six Russhia carv'd chairs sent pr. [Capt.] Direck Adolph, they are very good and will doubtless be to yor content."[11]

Although none of Fitch's ledgers prior to 1719 survives, another of his letterbooks, for the years 1714–17, does. Fitch continued to ship leather chairs to New York and elsewhere during that period and on April 14, 1717, billed "1 doz. Rushia Leather carved chairs" to Theodore Atkinson, probably of Portsmouth, New Hampshire, for £13.4, or 22s. each. The letterbook also reveals that Fitch procured his russia leather from England inasmuch as he wrote to John Crouch of London on November 23, 1715, that he was "pleased you did not attempt to send me any Rushia Leather it being high. Never send me any but when cheap else t'won't answer [my needs]." A few days later, he wrote to Samuel Arnold, also of London, that "I'm pleased you defer sending any Rushia leather until cheap otherways t'will not answer for it never rises [in price] here."[12]

A hiatus in the surviving Fitch correspondence between the end of 1717 and the spring of 1724 interrupts the story. However, the customs ledgers of Massachusetts and the "New

York Treasurer's Accounts" preserved among the Colonial Office Papers in the Public Records Office, London, reveal that the shipment of chairs to New York continued through the second decade of the century, although details concerning them are not specific. Chairs were shipped from Massachusetts on November 16, 1714, aboard "the sloop 'Success' Jonathan Sayr, master, 20 tons for N.Y." and again on September 29, 1715. On May 10, 1716, "19 Chairs" were imported into New York on board "The Dolphin of N.Y., Jacob Waldron, M[aste]r."[13] In contrast, no instances of chair shipments from New York to Boston have been found.

The last recorded chairs of this early phase shipped from Boston to New York went to Robert Livingston of Livingston Manor and were sent by Boston merchant, Edmund Knight, a relative of Livingston's daughter-in-law. A letter and invoice in the Livingston correspondence reveal that on July 10, 1721, Knight billed Livingston for "2 doz Russia leather chairs & 3 elbow chairs" at £42.0.6, or roughly 16s. per side chair. In a letter of November 10, 1722, Knight, who acted as a factor for Livingston in Boston, wrote: "Your couch is now sent by [Arnout] Schermerhorn & put into Mr. Van Horns bill of lading & you have enclosed Mr. [William] Down[es] note for making it. . . . PS Since the above [was written,] Mr. Downs has brought the [easy?] chair and put it on board Schermerhorn with some pieces of leather left on board the sloop Speedwell Arnout Schermerhorn master. . . . [The] couch the making of which amounts to as p[er] note of particular[s] inclosed [is] £3.05.00."[14]

THE SECOND PHASE OF THE BOSTON LEATHER CHAIR

It is a pity that the documentary records from the beginning of the third decade of the eighteenth century are in such disarray and are so fragmentary, because the Boston leather chair took on a new form during these years. The first evidence that indicates this change appears on February 27, 1722, when Fitch billed Edmund Knight for "1 doz crook'd back chairs" at £16.4, or 27s. each.[15] It is doubtful that crook'd back can refer to Queen Anne style chairs at this early date, since the other attributes of that style, such as slip seats and crook legs, are not mentioned at this time in his accounts.

When the Fitch letters resume, among the first is one dated March 20, 1723/24, to Adam Powell in New York, stating his intent "next week to send you Dozen of Rushia newest fashion'd chairs," which did in fact go out on April 4, and were billed as "12 Rushia new fashion'd chairs" at 27s. each or a total of £16.4.[16] Fitch's letters reveal a preoccupation with fashion. Since fashion is what sells merchandise, it is possible that he was using the phrase to make his merchandise appear more attractive. On the other hand, it could equally well mean that the chairs in question were of a recognizably new type, and that the variety with crook backs, molded stiles, and carved double-hollow-corner crest rails that we have come to associate with "Boston chairs," had emerged in Boston around 1722 (see catalogue entry 76). A set of eight such chairs with a solid history of ownership has long been in the possession of the

Fig. 154. Set of four leather chairs with molded stiles and tops, England, 1710–25. Oak. From the advertisement of William Lee, *Antique Dealer & Collector's Guide*, new ser., 2, no. 11 (June 1948): 57.

van Rensselaer family of Albany. Many of them are stamped with the initials of Philip van Rensselaer (1747–1798), and one has the initials of his father-in-law, Robert Saunders (1705–1765), from whom the chairs were probably inherited.[17]

These chairs differ from the earlier version in several ways. First, instead of having turned, columnar stiles, their stiles are sawn from a thick plank and molded with a plane on the front surface. Second, while the crest rails are executed by a carver, the carving is not floral but merely repeats the profile of the stiles around the perimeter of the top. Last, when viewed from the side, the stiles and back supports have a gentle curve backward and upward into the crook shape we now fancifully term "spooned."

Molded, or planed, rear stiles are a feature found on the finest upholstered chairs made in England by the very end of the seventeenth century, on good quality London-made cane chairs shortly thereafter, and probably on average quality cane chairs by 1710.[18] (An English chair of this last type [fig. 127] bears more than a passing resemblance to the American examples.) The fashion had certainly found its way into English leather-upholstered chairs made for the wider market by the second decade of the eighteenth century, as the four chairs illustrated in figure 154 suggest. Those four leather-upholstered chairs also have a high rear stretcher and turned medial stretchers connected to solitary side stretchers which reveal their relationship to contemporary cane chairs.

The molded stiles, molded crest rail, double-baluster front stretcher, baluster-decorated front legs, Spanish feet, tripartite front stretcher, and swelled medial and rear stretchers of the chair in figure 127 are features of English leather and cane chairs that Boston cane-chair makers adopted as early as 1715. Whether this transferal of motifs came about by an intentional copying of an imported English chair or by the emigration of an English-trained craftsman, such as John Jackson, who lived briefly in Boston in 1716, is not presently known.

It might be helpful if we were able to attach a contemporary term or description to this type of crook'd and molded rear stile. It is tempting to believe that this was the kind of chair occasionally singled out in inventories as one with an "embowed back." Although the *OED* gives "arched" as the meaning for *embowed*, embowing planes are a fairly common item in joiners' and carpenters' inventories. On November 14,

1717, Joshua Hempstead of New London, Connecticut, "worked at Jno. Coits Emboing Waals for 1d. pr. foot . . . [and] did 48 foot"; this is unintelligible if "embowing" is "arching."[19] The sense of embowing as running a decorative molding with a plane is made clear in a Portsmouth, New Hampshire, house contract, dated April 6, 1698; it specifies that the carpenter is to "in boe all the Summers, girts and beames" and to plane all the parts of the framing members "which is to be Seen after the finishing of the house."[20] Yet we also have embowed used in a different sense in other records. The detailed inventory of Royal Governor William Burnet, dated October 13, 1729, specifies that the governor's mansion in Boston contained "1 Dozen leather chairs with embowed backs" valued at 24s. each, and "nine embowed or hollow back chairs with fine bass bottoms" worth £1 each.[21] Although the word *embowed* may be ambiguous in the first of these two inventory references, in the second one the meaning of the alternative word, *hollow*, is clearly used to designate a spooned or concave shape. Thus the chairs referred to very likely had crook backs of the type illustrated in catalogue entry 76. This conflicting evidence on the use of the term *embowed* is yet another instance of words serving a dual function.

While they were called "Boston chairs" elsewhere, the daybook of Samuel Grant, a Boston upholsterer, merchant, and importer, confirms the idea conveyed by the Fitch manuscripts: in Boston the chairs were merely called "leather chairs."[22] Grant's accounts record in meticulous detail an almost incredible amount of information about leather-chair making and shop practices in Boston. Grant, whose shop was located "at the Crown and Cushion in Union Street near the Town Dock," sold numerous leather chairs—with frames made by other craftsmen such as Edmond Perkins, John Leach, and James Johnson. The frames were upholstered to his customers' specifications either in his own shop or on a piecework basis by independent craftsmen such as "Thomas Baxter . . . Boston upholdster."[23] Chairs were sold to private individuals; "Rufus Green . . . Goldsmth at soth End" purchased "6 Leather chairs" at 26s. each. Merchants John and Jacob Wendell purchased in quantity, and for them and others who were shipping these chairs from Boston, Grant added two charges, one for "porterages," the other for coarse cloths like crocus, oznabrigs, and russia linen to pack the chairs in prior to exportation aboard ship. Many chairs were sent to fill a specific order. Others Grant sent on speculation: February 4, 1728/29, "Voyage to New York p the sloop Swallow . . . sundry consign'd to mr. William Clear on my accot, . . . Vizt: 24 Leather chairs @ 26[s.] . . . £31:4." The price of 26s. per chair prevailed until May 19, 1733, when 24 were billed to James Allen at 27s. each, although on the following September 24, Caleb Richardson of Boston bought a half dozen at 26s. each. It is likely that the chairs shipped at the higher price had "claw feet," as did the "4 doz: Leathr chairs claw feet" billed 27s. each on March 8, 1732/33, to Peter Faneuil of Boston, while those billed at 26s. had turned feet.[24] These entries further help us to chart the rate of inflation in Boston, or more properly, the decline in value of Massachusetts currency: in 1705 Fitch priced equivalent chairs at 13s. 6d. to 14s.[25]

Elbow, or arm, chairs are rarely mentioned in Grant's accounts, but when they are, the price is 48s.[26] At 22s. more expensive than the side chair, today's casual logician might wonder if the term "elbow chair" did not, in fact, describe something more elaborate than the usual Boston armchair, but if we calculate the extra work and materials required to construct and embellish an armchair, the price seems less excessive. Armchairs are invariably larger than side chairs, so more materials of every type must be used. An armchair requires a longer piece of wood for the front legs whose extensions support the arms, and these elements must be turned or otherwise shaped, which adds to the cost. Two additional mortises and tenons must be cut, and two additional holes must be bored in order to fasten the arms to the supports and the rear stiles. The stiles must be planed at the junction with the arm to assure a tight fit, and the arms must be drilled and pinned to the arm supports. Finally the carefully sculpted arms, small works of art in themselves, must be cut into compass shapes, molded deeply on their upper surfaces, and their terminal volutes—imaginatively called "ram's horns" today—had to be laid out and carved.

For the historian of taste, the most exciting aspect of Grant's journal is the detailed insight that it gives into the decline of the William and Mary style in the most fashionable furniture made in Boston. After nine months of accounts listing forms we have come to associate with the William and Mary style, on October 14, 1729, Grant sent one chair of "red Chainey" with "New fashion round seat" to merchant Arnout Schermerhoorn in New York. Exciting for us, the "round seat"—a characteristic heretofore unmentioned in the Fitch and Grant manuscripts—is identified as a "new fashion"; in 1729 the only "new fashion" that could be emerging in Boston is what we now call "Queen Anne" style. Thirteen months later, a second characteristic of the new style is noted: Grant billed Nathaniel Green £2.12 for "1 Couch frame horsebone feet."[27] Later entries begin to flesh out the image. On October 8, 1731, Grant billed Edward Andrews for "6 Leathr Chairs Cushn Seats," 28s. each. These chairs cost 2s. more than his usual leather chairs, and the description and additional cost suggest that the "cushion seats" are what we today call "slip seats." The additional cost—amounting to 14 percent of the value of the chair—represents the added labor of making the seat frame itself (4 mortise-and-tenon joints) and rabbeting the seat rails (which must be of prime quality wood because they show) to receive the cushion seat. On January 22, 1731/32, Grant billed Messrs. Clark and Kilby £12 for "6 Leathr Chairs Maple frames horbone round feet & cush Seats @ 40[s.]." This entry shows that horsebone feet can be round, that the chairs have cushion seats, and that each chair cost 14s. more than Grant's former staple, the leather chair. That he billed James Allen two weeks later for "12 leather chairs @ 26[s.]," shows that Grant was still selling the old style chairs, as indeed he continued to do for a decade longer (see catalogue entry 80). Incidentally, in the same 1731/32 order, Allen purchased "1 horbone feet Couch fram wth Squab & pillo . . . £6:11."[28] Grant sold numerous couches and chairs with horsebone feet over the next few months and finally on September 8, 1732, billed John Fairweather for "8 Black

Wallnutt chairs cushns of Leathr" at 30s. each and "6 Maple Chairs cushn Seats of green cks" at 37s. each, an entry that dispels any idea that furniture historians could identify the place of origin of surviving chairs solely on the basis of woods or upholstery materials and also dispels any doubt that the "new fashion" by 1732 could be anything but a full-blown, Queen Anne-style chair.[29]

Through the following months, the entries settle down into less descriptive language, but the prices of these chairs are consistently high: on the average, 37s. for side chairs and 48s. for elbow chairs in walnut. The old-style leather chairs were still being sold on March 30, 1737, for Grant billed six of them to Ralph Hart for £9, or 30s. each.[30] Entries in Grant's journal between 1733 and 1737 reveal that what had been exceptional items from his shop in 1729 had become a part of the normal production of 1733 and were accepted as the current style and listed at the new prices. No further description was necessary for either himself or his customers.

The sequence of events seems to provide an airtight answer to one of the nagging questions of American decorative arts history: When does the Queen Anne style appear in Boston? Even though Grant's ledger for the years prior to January 1728/29 does not survive, Fitch's 1719–32 accounts do. And no entries in Fitch's accounts indicate that the Queen Anne style developed before 1729. Whether the Grant accounts explain the beginnings of the end of the William and Mary style in all of New England is practically immaterial. It is enough to know that it occurred in an important Boston shop over a specific period of time. It is the ramifications of the change that are most significant.

Between October 14, 1729, and September 8, 1732, those craftsmen who made chairs for Samuel Grant and those customers who bought the chairs had adopted a new fashion that is today called the Queen Anne style. Our own unfamiliarity with early eighteenth-century shop jargon makes the terse phrases that Grant used to describe this style seem strange to us. "Horsebone round foot" grates on our ears. Since documentation of artisans in general and furniture style more specifically is so scarce, one might even be tempted to conclude that horsebone foot was a phrase that Grant coined to describe a new fashion he could not otherwise name, a fashion being made in early Georgian Boston that he certainly would never have thought to name after Queen Anne, who after all had been dead fifteen years. Yet the term "horsebone" was not new in 1729. Forty years earlier a bill for the furnishings of Hampton Court Palace specified a stool "of walnuttree carved all horsebone with leaves & figures holding up the Crowne in the fore raile." In 1927 F. J. Rutherford associated the description with a surviving scroll-leg stool. In 1701/2 Thomas Roberts submitted a bill for a set of stools with "the foreparts carved horsebone, French feet," a matching chair of which has survived at Hampton Court (fig. 155).[31] Although Roberts's work was done a year before Queen Anne came to the throne, and although the exact manner of articulating his carved and gilt horsebone foreparts with their acknowledged debt to French design may not have crossed the ocean, the phrase did. There are then three questions we must ask: Is the twenty-eight years it took the term to travel from England's

Fig. 155. LEFT. Upholstered chair with horsebone feet, attributed to Thomas Roberts, London, England, 1701/2. (Hampton Court, Collection of Her Majesty the Queen.)

Fig. 156. BELOW. Crook-back chair with compass seat, leather cushion, horsebone round feet, attributed to the shop of John Leach, Boston, ca. 1732. Walnut; H 40¼" (102 cm), W 22" (55.9 cm), D 20⅛" (51.1 cm), SH 18" (56.1 cm). (Winterthur 54.523.)

Hampton Court to Boston's North End a long time? How much longer did it take it to travel the Hudson River valley? And, can the Boston chair in figure 156 dated circa 1732 be described as 1 walnut, crook-back, compass-seat chair with leather cushion seat and horsebone round feet priced at 40s.?

Aside from the details of nomenclature and the indications of the sequence of styles in Boston furniture, the Fitch and

Grant records make clear by implication a much more significant fact: the urban chairmaker was not his own master but derived much of his business from the commissions of local upholsterers or fellow craftsmen, rather than from the ultimate purchaser.

If we assume that the Fitch manuscripts are representative of the dealings of Boston entrepreneurs with their New York counterparts, then a large part of the demand for leather chairs in New York was satisfied by chairs made in and exported from Boston. We can thus see how early students of eighteenth-century decorative arts mistook Boston chairs with New York histories of ownership for New York chairs. Nevertheless, we cannot avoid asking ourselves what the chair-frame makers, carvers, and upholsterers of New York were producing to earn their living. Obviously they were making chairs whose identity has, in the main, escaped the attention of collectors and scholars.

The attributes of a style in any period are various combinations of the same general design elements. The problem of identifying regional variations is particularly acute for students of early eighteenth-century chairs because chairmakers used a relatively restricted vocabulary of ornament. The elements of this vocabulary consisted of ogee balusters, columnar stiles, C scrolls, and leaf carving—and the same elements were used in Holland, England, and the colonies. Since the records reveal that Boston's leather chairs dominated the coastal American marketplace, we may assume that the stylistic elements associated with Boston examples found their way into chairs made in other towns. The finial on the stile of the Boston-made chair illustrated in catalogue entry 65 is a classic case in point. It consists of a compressed ball which is separated from the urn- or vase-shape base by an unconventional hollow. By the normal tenets of connoisseurship, each time we see this distinctive finial on an American chair, we would conclude that the chair was made in Boston. But this turning also appears on a remarkable armchair with a New York history of ownership (fig. 157), which tells us that the normal tenets of connoisseurship are not sufficiently refined to be accurate.[32]

Although generically related to the Boston type, the New York armchair, formerly in the collection of Mrs. Charles L. Bybee and the late Mr. Bybee, differs from the Boston examples in enough ways to be recognizable as a distinctive creation. The arm supports and the finials are of the Boston type, as is the general order of the elements on the stiles, but they are handled differently. The column on the rear stile of the chair has a collarino near the top that is lower than that on the Boston chairs and a ring at the base of the column—the latter is a feature found only on the Boston's earliest leather chairs (see catalogue entries 61, 62, and 64). The compressed baluster beneath the column is virtually identical on chairs from both Boston and New York. At this point in its construction, the Bybee chair asserts its own character with an unexpected elaboration. The next elements moving down the stile are a

Fig. 157. Carved-top leather chair, New York City, 1690–1710. Maple, oak; H 53¾″ (136.5 cm), W 22⅞″ (58.1 cm), D 16⅜″ (41.6 cm). (Museum of Fine Arts, Boston, gift of Mrs. Charles L. Bybee. Photo: Edward A. Bourdon, Houston, Texas.) According to an unsigned statement dated 1906 in the files of Israel Sack, Inc., this chair "was given to the Rev. John Chester of Albany by one of his parishoners. John Chester gave it to his Sister, Elizabeth Chester, who gave it to her old nurse, after whose death it was hunted up and secured by Letitia C. Backus, wife of John Chester Backus. At her death it was left to her Grandson John Chester Backus Pendleton." This chair is also sometimes erroneously referred to as the "Synod of Dort Chair" because of a persistent legend that it was used at that convocation in 1612. Part of the legend attached to it also asserts that it "was brought over to this country by one of the old Dutch families." The chair was damaged in a fire early in the 1970s before it was given to the museum.

flat-bottom cap, an elongated baluster, then a ring and ball, all of which is much more reflective of an Anglo-Dutch cane chair than anything done in New England. The exuberance of these turnings is echoed by the carving of the crest rail and front stretcher. Although the central motif—symmetrical foliage—is suggestive of Boston, the C scrolls that flank it are a distinctive feature, as are the rosettes between the terminal volutes and second scrolls on the stretcher. In addition, the Bybee chair is set apart from the Boston chairs by its flat lower margin on the crest rail and hence rectangular rather than arched upholstery on its back. The crest is slit and the original upholstery was pulled through and nailed to the back of the

Fig. 158. Carved-top leather chair, New York, 1690–1710. American striped maple (*Acer pennsylvanicum*); H 47½″ (120.7 cm), W 25½″ (64.8 cm), D 27″ (68.6 cm). (Sleepy Hollow Restorations, Tarrytown, N.Y., on display at Cortlandt Manor, Croton-on-Hudson, N.Y.) The chair has a history of ownership in the van Cortlandt family.

rail. A single row of tack holes on the back of the crest rail shows that the slit was used only once.

Another closely related armchair with most of these features is privately owned in Virginia. It was illustrated as a New York chair by Israel Sack in 1959.[33] That chair, perhaps not from the same frame shop as the Bybee chair, also has the slit in the crest rail through which the upholstery was originally pulled and tacked. It differs from the Bybee chair primarily in the design of the arm support; it has an urn-shape element beneath the baluster. This shape is a common motif in New York furniture and is prominently executed on the great folding-leaf table formerly owned by Sir William Johnson and now in the collection of the Albany Institute of History and Art.[34]

Of course the history of ownership of the Bybee chair in the Chester family of New York gives us no more license to assume that it was made in New York than do the histories of ownership of numerous Boston chairs found there. And indeed, a New York origin for the Bybee chair and the one

illustrated by the Sack brochure could not be argued effectively if additional chairs did not support the attributions. A third chair with similar carved elements (fig. 158) was first published by Luke Vincent Lockwood in *Colonial Furniture*. This chair, presently displayed at van Cortlandt Manor, Croton-on-Hudson, New York, has a long history of ownership in the van Cortlandt family, and is made totally of American soft maple (*Acer pennsylvanicum*). Its turnings are so distinctive in style it is doubtful that the chair could have been made in the same shop as the other two examples.[35] A flag-bottom, arch-top chair with almost identical stiles, illustrated in Esther Singleton's *Furniture of Our Forefathers*, has a history of ownership in the Pruyn family of New York. This simple and inexpensive chair is not likely to have been made for the coastal trade and probably had not traveled far from the place it was made by the time Singleton published it. An additional example with the hollow crest rail common to New York chairs is illustrated in Nutting's *Furniture Treasury*. One of unknown provenance is illustrated in Fales's *Furniture of Historic Deerfield*.[36] The most distinctive feature of the van Cortlandt chair is the shape of the arms, which are recognizably northern European in design and actually quite French in character (see catalogue entries 69 and 70). It differs from the rest of the New York leather chairs with carved tops in that there is no slit in the crest rail through which the leather is pulled and fastened.

Yet another chair in the Museum of Fine Arts, Boston (fig. 159), is also related to the group. This example, of enviable character and presence, retains its original double-nailed russia-leather upholstery. It shares with the Bybee chair the same pattern of rear stiles, although on this chair it is much more rotundly articulated and, because the back is shorter, is more compressed; the two chairs also share the ring-barrel-ring turning on the rear stiles between the lower back rail and the seat rail. The arm supports on figure 159 consist of bold balusters in the double-pear shape on either side of a central ring and are unlike those on Boston leather chairs but like those on the van Cortlandt chair and on a Dutch armchair which surfaced in a New York collection and is now in the Rijksmuseum, Amsterdam.[37] The turned front stretcher—which we may assume is a convention on plain-crest, high-back leather chairs regardless of their place of origin—is the same pattern as that used for the rear and medial stretchers on the Bybee chair. Similar stretchers, finials, and rear stiles on Winterthur chairs are discussed in catalogue entries 69, 70, and 71.

The arms of the plain-top leather chair set it apart from all the chairs made in colonial America. Instead of the conventionalized form, the arms are enriched with foliate carving both at the volutes and at the juncture with the rear stiles. Although this treatment can be found on English cane chairs that appear to be derived from Dutch prototypes or were perhaps even made by Dutch craftsmen working in London, it is tempting to see in its presence on this chair a strong northern European—perhaps Dutch—influence on the craftsman. An almost identical treatment, executed in somewhat higher relief, appears on three chairs in a slightly earlier style at the Rijksmuseum. An arm with a closely related profile but

Fig. 159. Plain-top leather armchair, New York, 1700–1725. Maple, oak; H 47″ (119.4 cm), W 20½″ (52.1 cm), D 17½″ (44.5 cm), SH 14⅜″ (36.5 cm). (Museum of Fine Arts, Boston, Arthur Tracy Cabot Fund.)

these chairs could be accepted easily as the sort of variation of a basic style, in the aggregate they represent a well-defined school of chairmaking that has only been hinted at by the attributions of a few perceptive dealers in antique furniture, notably Benjamin Ginsburg, Albert Sack, and Fred J. Johnston. That many of these chairs can be associated with New York families and *none* with New England families strongly suggests that New York is their place of origin. Furthermore, because they are urban expressions of their form, we can be even more precise and say that they originated in New York City.

From this group of chairs we can abstract in a general way the characteristics that we should expect to find in a New York leather chair. New York chairs have complex, turned stiles with a short column, and either balls or short balusters atop long balusters. Flat-bottom caps (half round turnings) above the balusters are common. On chairs that have barrel-like turnings on the stile between the seat rail and the lower back rail, the barrels have fat rings at their tops and bottoms. The rear feet go straight down to the floor on the back side and are chamfered on the forward side. Some chairs have double side stretchers, often of oak, and these are thicker than those on the Boston examples. When the side and rear stretchers are rectangular in section rather than turned, the rear stretcher enters the rear legs at the same point that the side stretchers do. When the front stretcher of a New York chair is turned, its ends terminate in blocks, which are joined to blocks on the front legs by mortise-and-tenon joints (see fig. 159). In order to get a sufficiently bold turning on such stretchers, a piece of wood thicker than the legs is used. Upon final assembly, the front stretcher is fitted flush with the front of the front legs and thus overhangs in the back, often more than a ¼″ (0.6 cm). The stretcher is pinned from the front, not the back.

The details of New York chairs contrast markedly with those on Boston chairs. The Boston type has a long column above one small baluster on the stile, cylindrical turnings between the seat and the lower back rail that are invariably scored about ⅜″ (1 cm) from their ends; rear feet that rake backward on both back and front surfaces; single side stretchers, and a rear stretcher that is positioned higher than the side ones. The stretchers are made of maple or red oak.

The chairs from the two cities also exhibit similarities. Both Boston and New York chairs may have a finial whose vasiform base is separated from the ball above it by a hollow. The plain-top versions of both Boston and New York chairs may have turned front stretchers in the same style: two central balls flanked by balusters, with the neck of each baluster leading to a ring, and then a block.

The difficulty of separating the chairs of Boston from those of New York is illustrated by an example in the Mabel Brady Garvan Collection at Yale University Art Gallery and its mate, illustrated in Lyon's *Colonial Furniture*, both of which were found in Connecticut.[39] Each is a Boston chair in style but a New York chair in execution, so both must be classified as New York chairs. Connecticut traded heavily with New York in the eighteenth century, and New York-made furniture was as likely to find its way into that colony as Boston-made items when something other than a local product was wanted.

without the foliate carving also appears on an upholstered easy chair found in New York, which further ties this entire group of chairs to New York.[38] While the Dutch influence on the craftsman who made the chair in figure 159 cannot be supported by documentary evidence because his identity is unknown, the assumption is nevertheless warranted on the basis of the possible preferences of the customer who originally ordered this chair since a chairmaker in New York, of all places in colonial America, could expect to have customers with a taste for things Dutch. Perhaps the most significant aspect of the carved arm on the chair is that it is a stylistic feature derived from an early cane-chair prototype, which suggests that it may have been made earlier than the Boston examples of the standardized chair.

THE ATTRIBUTES OF
NEW YORK LEATHER CHAIRS

The quirks of design among the New York leather chairs are distinctive and numerous. The differences suggest that the frames are the products of a number of shops. While any one of

The summary of characteristics of New York leather chairs may seem tedious to the general reader, but close attention to the details of these chairs is absolutely necessary. At least one of the shops producing leather chairs in New York made what is essentially a copy of the standardized Boston leather chair with carved crest rail and turned stiles that is recognizable only because the chair exhibits a few quirks of the New York school. A surviving chair from this shop (fig. 160) is owned by the Albany Institute of History and Art and is presently displayed in the Van Alen House, Kinderhook, New York. The top ball of the finial is only slightly separated from the vase beneath it and is rounder than its Boston counterpart, a fillet is turned on the under side of the collarino, a ring rather than incised grooves appears at the base of the column, a compressed ball is turned beneath the baluster under the column, and no grooves are incised on the barrel-like shapes between the seat and lower back rail. The side stretchers are slightly thicker than those on the Boston examples, and the rear stretcher enters the legs at the same level as the side stretchers in the New York manner. The carved element between the C scrolls on the front stretcher and crest rail is floral, in the manner of the van Cortlandt and Bybee chairs, rather than foliate as on the New England examples. The sprays that spring from the center of the carving on both crest and stretcher are longer and more acutely bent than those of Boston. Both stretcher and crest are severely chamfered on their rear, upper, outer corners (not visible in the photograph) and the front stretcher is pinned to the legs from the front rather than the back. Most significant of all is the treatment of the top line of the upholstery on the back. On this chair it is straight, with the characteristic slit through which the upholstery is pulled and tacked; on the usual Boston chairs, it is a rounded arch (see catalogue entries 65 and 66) that echoes the arch on the bottom edge of the front stretcher. Since the russia-leather upholstery of the back is original, there is no possibility that this treatment is a subsequent sophistication.

Recognition of the New York origin of the Van Alen House chair does not automatically smooth out all of the problems with chairs copied from the Boston style. A case in point is the chair which Joseph Downs in 1934 attributed to a New York origin on the basis of its similarity to the set of chairs stamped P. v. P. (mentioned earlier), which we now know are of Boston origin.[40] Judging as well as we can from the published photograph, the chair Downs was dealing with (its present whereabouts are unknown) has two features of the Van Alen House chair—a crest rail with a flat bottom and a turned ring at the bottom of the column on the stile—that suggest a New York origin, but in every other respect the chair is closer to the Boston type. The differences may represent a transitional stage in the process of standardization that the Boston chairs underwent—for it appears that these chairs were made in Boston over a period of twenty-five or more years—or they may indicate that the taste for these chairs in New York was satisfied by a craftsman who had trained in Boston and had opened up a shop in New York, or by a New York craftsman who did not choose to tamper significantly with the successful Boston model.

Two other versions of the New York–style chair have survived. One (now in a private collection) which has a

Fig. 160. New York version of the standardized Boston carved-top leather chair, New York, 1710–30. (Albany Institute of History and Art, Albany, N.Y., on display at the Van Alen House, Kinderhook, N.Y.)

carved top and is related to the Van Alen House chair, lacks the typical New York rosettes, but has elongated sprays flanking the central leaf carving at the apex of the crest rail, in the manner of the Bybee and van Cortlandt chairs.[41] If the crest rail were not related to the one on the Van Alen House chair, it would be difficult to identify this chair as being of New York origin, so closely is it modeled upon the Boston examples. Its rear stretcher is above the side ones, and the scored lines on the turnings between the seat rail and the lower back rail—totally absent on the Van Alen House chair—are rather closer to the ends of the turned cylinder than are the Boston type. Its baluster-ring-ball-and-ring front stretcher is similar to that on the New York chairs illustrated in catalogue entries 69 and 70. This type of stretcher, which is unknown on Boston chairs with carved tops, also appears on a second version of the chair, now in the Wallace Nutting Collection at the Wadsworth Atheneum, Hartford. The photograph of this chair as initially published by Nutting is somewhat misleading inasmuch as the chair had a Boston-type carved top; however, examination of the chair itself in 1977 revealed a row of tack holes on the back of the crest rail beneath a glue joint that secures the carved section.[42] The Wadsworth chair is a plain-top New York chair whose crest rail was copied from a Boston example (consistent with Nutting's good taste) and added in modern times under the guise of restoration. The carved crest has subsequently been removed. That the rear stretcher enters the legs at the same level as the side stretchers confirms its New York origin.

The Wadsworth chair illustrates that while it is easy enough to discriminate between carved-top chairs made in the two cities, the plain-top chairs, with their fewer tabulable details of design and workmanship, pose greater problems. It is not clear, for example, that the type of turned front stretcher that consists of elongated balusters flanking two smaller ones, such as the one that appears on the New York chair illustrated in catalogue entry 71, does not also appear on plain-top leather chairs made in Boston. Among the chairs that fall into this diagnostic limbo are two in the Clarke House at Strawbery Banke, Portsmouth, New Hampshire, a pair owned by Sleepy Hollow Restorations and displayed in Philipsburg Manor, North Tarrytown, New York, and one in the Cape Ann Historical Association, Gloucester, Massachusetts. On the basis of present knowledge, all could be from either New York or Boston.

These last chairs raise a significant question: How can we identify the products of an urban center if they are nearly exact copies of those of another center? If documentary evidence revealed that chairs were being imported from Boston into New York solely by merchants, it would be speculative to assume they could have found their way into the hands of craftsmen who copied them. But in this instance, the letters of Thomas Fitch eliminate guesswork. Boston-based Fitch sold at least one set of carved-top turned-stile leather chairs to New York City upholsterer Richard Lott.[43] With Boston frames in his shop it would have been but a simple step for upholsterer Lott to have them copied by a New York chairmaker, and, if that craftsman made more exact copies than did the maker of the Van Alen House chair, it would be virtually impossible to distinguish them from the Boston examples, which were made in a number of different shops and vary slightly among themselves anyway (compare catalogue entries 65 and 66 with 75, 76, and 77).

An armchair in the Winterthur collection (catalogue entry 64) appears to be one of the earliest examples of Boston-made leather chairs. In materials, construction, and workmanship, it is closely akin to the standardized Boston leather chair, but its crest rail and front stretcher are of a novel design that we have not so far been able to document as being executed by Boston's chairmakers. Its arm is pinned to the rear stile in the cane-chair manner, and indeed its side, medial, and rear stretchers relate it more to cane than leather chairs. It has the ring turned at the base of the column, as on the chair illustrated by Downs, rather than the scored lines of the standard Boston type. Its provenance does not enable us to say without question that it was made in Boston; an identical chair has a history of ownership in the Smith family of Smithtown, New York.[44] In short, the attribution of this or any undocumented chair requires considerable detailed analysis of the larger group of which it is a part.

If the attribution of some chairs to New York is correct,

then it follows that the different types of chairs available to customers in New York offer objective confirmation of the makeup of New York society at that period. The purely Anglo-Boston chairs were imported by merchants of all cultural backgrounds —Englishman Richard Lott, Huguenot Benjamin Faneuil, Englishmen Robert Livingston at Livingston Manor and Abram Wendell in Albany, Hollanders Nicholas Tienhoven, Arnout Schermerhorn and Adam Powell in Manhattan, along with Mesdames Hooglandt and Rosevelt, representing Dutch families of unknown political leanings. The quantities of chairs that many of these customers ordered from Thomas Fitch were too large for them to have been for personal use, and so we may assume that the chairs were bought to be resold to people who wanted Anglo-Boston chairs.

Second, the presence of numerous variants of these chairs suggests that New York chairmakers were capable of satisfying the assorted tastes of their culturally diverse community. While we cannot be certain that the Downs example mentioned earlier was not made in Boston, the variants with unique overtones, such as the Van Alen House chair, were assuredly made in New York. Related to them are plain-top high-back leather chairs with turned front stretchers and elaborate stiles that are rather stiff in their stance but have wonderfully elaborate turnings and are the most distinctively baroque in character (see catalogue entries 69, 70, and 71). Perhaps the quibble over the relative Dutchness or Englishness of the New York chairs may never be settled, but we cannot avoid noting that their design indicates that a taste existed in New York for an elaborately turned leather chair of a type not found in New England and that the decorative schemes used to satisfy that taste make the chairs distinct from the New England examples.

THE ORIGINS OF THE NEW YORK STYLE

Three possible sources for the New York style of leather chair can be conceived of, but, given the complex interrelationships, it is virtually impossible to state whether any one of them, or indeed all of them to some degree, account for the way these chairs look. This is the perennial problem when we deal with New York, for influences on furniture made there could come directly from Holland, or France, or from England which had been influenced by Holland, or from Boston, which had been influenced by England, which had been influenced by Holland.

We know that Boston dominated the coastal trade of colonial America in the first quarter of the eighteenth century. And we suspect that Cromwellian-style chairs were exported from Boston prior to 1700. Is it cause and effect that the form of the Anglo-Boston Cromwellian chair is similar to the New York leather chair? The similarity between the two is graphically illustrated by figure 161. The stiff rear leg with only its front surface chamfered to suggest a heel is the same; the double side stretchers are the same; the angle of the back to the rear legs is the same; the flat crest rail, chamfered on its front upper edge, and the narrow seat are the same. That the back is

Fig. 161. Profiles of a New York plain-top leather chair dating from 1710–25 and a Boston low-back leather chair dating from 1665–95. The chair on the left is catalogue entry 71, the one on the right is catalogue entry 45. (Winterthur 58.570, 58.694.)

Fig. 162. Carved-top leather chair with a slit at the crest rail through which the leather is pulled; probably England but possibly the Netherlands, 1680–1700. (Photo: Symonds Collection, DAPC, Winterthur Library.) The balusters of the stiles are unusually bottom-heavy for an English chair. The "boyes and crowns" of the crest rail and stretcher, executed in a sketchy manner, suggest that this chair, if English, was made after 1685, when that motif was carved on cane chairs for the British Royal Household.

higher and that balusters and columns have been substituted for the compressed-ball turnings of the earlier Boston chair betray the New York chair as an object in the baroque taste. Are these details evidence that the New York makers were familiar with earlier Boston products?

The Boston–New York similarities may be mere coincidence. It is possible that the New York chair was derived from a European, perhaps English, type (fig. 162) that itself reflects the development of a high-back chair from the low-back Cromwellian style. Such a chair would have been made in a European shop that was obviously catering to customers who could not afford expensive chairs. The finial of this European chair is closer to the New York type than to the Boston type. The apparently original double-nailed russia-leather upholstery is pulled through a slit in the crest rail, in the manner of the Bybee, van Cortlandt, Van Alen House, and Sack chairs. The horizontal rails of the back are slightly concave as are those on the chair illustrated in catalogue entry 69. It shares with the New York leather chairs a flat-bottom half round, or cap, above the elongated baluster on its stiles, a flat-top finial, and straight rear feet chamfered only on their front edges. The rear stretcher enters the rear legs on the same level as the side stretchers, in the New York manner. This chair also illustrates another aspect of the European leather chair: its seat is relatively narrow and not unusually far from the floor, as if the ubiquitous footstools that we see in Dutch genre painting were not intended to play a part in the way it was to be used. If this

European chair is English, then the style of the New York chairs is English, and the New York high-back leather chairs took their inspiration from a part of the English tradition that was unknown or less influential in Boston. If, on the other hand, this European chair is continental, then the New York chairs are northern European in inspiration.

A child's highchair in the Rijksmuseum (fig. 163) makes a strong case for a Dutch influence on the ornamentation of New York leather chairs. The turnings of that chair have the flat-bottom caps that we find on New York work. In addition, its conventionalized stiles consist of a column upon balusters. The Dutch highchair also has a finial almost identical to that on the Bybee chair. Were these attributes brought to New York by an emigrant craftsman from Holland? The picture is further complicated by a version of the finial of the Dutch highchair and the Bybee chair that is also common on Boston-made chairs in this period. How did that come about? Did this

Fig. 163. LEFT. Highchair with scroll-carved legs and a cane seat and back, North Netherlands, 1675–1700. European beech (*Fagus sylvatica*); H 46¹⁄₁₆″ (117 cm), W 15″ (38 cm), D 11″ (28 cm), SH 23⁷⁄₈″ (58 cm). (Rijksmuseum, Amsterdam, Netherlands.)

Fig. 164. RIGHT. Carved top chair stamped with the initials IB. London, England, 1675–1700. Mahogany, nineteenth-century textile upholstery. (Nordiska Museets, Stockholm, Sweden.) An identical chair in the same museum is stamped AB.

particular form of the finial make its way from Holland to England and thence to Boston and New York? The chair in figure 164 possesses this finial, is unequivocally of London make, and is stamped with the maker's initials, I B.[45] Were the chairmakers of Boston merely inspired to make this Dutch-looking finial because so many more of their chairs were destined to be exported to New York, where such a finial was known and preferred?

Correspondence between Thomas Fitch in Boston and Benjamin Faneuil in New York makes it woefully apparent that the New York merchant was able to give his Boston colleague no pointers on fashion. Fitch repeatedly corrects Faneuil's notions of what to order: plain-top leather chairs are "not out of fashion here" (1709); leather couches are "as much out of wear as Steeple crown'd hats" (1707); "wee don't furbelow any [couches] of late. If you will [insist on having] it done I will send it to be tack'd on per next [ship]" (1715/16).[46]

Finally, in contrast to the New York chairs made in the Boston style, a number of other leather chairs made in New York can be more easily dealt with. These chairs are, by any standards, conservative in form, despite the exuberance of their ornamentation. This conservatism, amounting to a look backward in time, is similarly reflected in the silver, painting, and architecture preferred by a large segment of the population

of New York. These chairs indicate, as other arts do, that a segment of the populace of New York preferred to ignore the English presence there. Indeed, their actions are an axiom of anthropology: the cultural group that seeks to retain cultural identity first ignores the mainstream of the life surrounding it, then enshrines and perpetuates the forms of the past, and ultimately becomes static.

LEATHER CHAIRS IN PHILADELPHIA

The student of Philadelphia furniture who searches for illustrations of carved-top leather chairs in the early eighteenth-century style in that earliest and best-known furniture compendium, the *Blue Book*, is in for a shock: not one is included. The surviving inventories of the period are likewise silent. Yet there is reason to believe that such chairs did exist. Over 140 leather chairs of varying descriptions were specified in Philadelphia County inventories prior to 1710.[47] An entry in the 1708 inventory of John Jones, a Philadelphia merchant, lists "12 Russia chairs" valued at 10s. each and immediately below is "5 walnut ditto" at 6s. each. The value of the latter is unusually low for new and fashionable chairs, but that they were made of walnut, a very popular wood in Pennsylvania and rare in New England, suggests that they may at least have been of Philadelphia origin. More encouraging is the rich 1708 inventory of Ralph Fishbourne of Chester whose home contained "½ dozen of Leather Chaires" valued at 10s. each, in contrast to "½ doz. old Turke work chairs" in the same room and patently in the older manner that were worth only 6s. each. The possibility that new leather chairs lurked somewhere in the Fishbourne household at the time of his death is heightened by a reference in the inventory of his widow, Elizabeth, the following year: "4 high leather Chairs" valued with "2 old low ditto" at £2. But these references are atypical. Indeed, it would seem from the 1722 inventory of Jonathan Dickinson that cane chairs—the only type that appear in his remarkable estate—remained the most suitable type of chair among the fashionable merchants of Penn's great town.[48]

The inventories of Philadelphia's craftsmen are not much more informative. The list of household goods owned by Charles Plumley, the sole Philadelphia woodworker of his time who can with assurance be called a cabinetmaker, contained "6 leather Chairs" valued at £2.10, or 8s. 2d. each. They were doubtless in the new style if they were like the "2 black Carved Chair frames" valued at 9s. each among the unfinished work in his shop.[49] The details of any of these chairs remain anybody's guess. It is fair to assume that they were not appreciably different from the types being produced in England at the time. It is also possible that they exhibited traits of Boston chairs, inasmuch as two important craftsmen involved in chairmaking emigrated from Boston to Philadelphia before the end of the seventeenth century.

The first and ultimately the most influential of these former Bostonians was Edward Shippen, the progenitor of a long line of prominent Philadelphians. Shippen came to America from England around the year 1669, settled in Boston, and married Elizabeth Lybrand, a Quaker. There is some doubt that Shippen was a Quaker prior to this marriage, since he was a member of the prestigious Ancient and Honorable Artillery Company of Boston, a clubby militia organization unlikely to select members from religious groups that were not socially acceptable. Shippen is called an "upholder" in a deed of 1677 and an "upholsterer" in another deed, two years later, and since he was then nearing 40 years of age he was probably a master of his trade. In 1693 he moved his family to Philadelphia, "on invitation of Penn, and became the first mayor under the charter of 1701." Shippen's Boston ties are not merely of academic interest. Thomas Fitch's letterbook reveals that Fitch had learned the upholsterer's trade from Shippen, managed Shippen's properties in Boston, and on occasion acted as his factor from 1693 until Shippen's death in 1715.[50] Unfortunately Fitch's account books prior to 1719 no longer survive, so any early shipments of Boston chairs to Philadelphia by Fitch are unrecorded.

Another Boston furniture and chair-frame maker, Thomas Stapleford, moved to Philadelphia in the 1690s, probably at the behest of Shippen. It is likely that some of the characteristics of Stapleford's manner as taught to his apprentices persisted in Boston. It is also likely that whatever chair style Stapleford made in Boston in the early 1690s he made in Philadelphia later on in that decade. Thus both Stapleford's and Shippen's early Philadelphia carved-top chairs may be indistinguishable

Fig. 165. Leather chair with molded stiles, probably Philadelphia, 1695–1710. Soft maple (genus *Acer*); H 41" (104.1 cm), W 18¼" (46.4 cm), D 14¾" (37.5 cm). (Newtown Library Company, on display at Pennsbury Manor, Bucks County, Penn.)

from their Boston counterparts. Stapleford's migration to Philadelphia, like Shippen's, is of more than academic interest inasmuch as a Boston deed of 1696 informs us that Stapleford's former shop in Boston was "in the Tenure . . . of Thomas ffitch," which confirms that Fitch, Shippen, and Stapleford were well acquainted with each other and probably remained in touch through the following years.[51]

While we have no inkling of what type of upholstered chairs this pair of transplanted Boston craftsmen initially produced, we do have some evidence about the later versions, those with molded stiles and Spanish feet. A maple chair displayed at Pennsbury Manor is one of these (fig. 165). It is part of a set of three chairs and retains its original and quite fragile, walnut-color varnish that is perhaps ⁄64" (0.04 cm) thick. These three chairs, according to a century-old tradition, were presented to the "Judges of the Court at Newtown" by William Penn. Indeed, it is likely that they were made in Philadelphia during Penn's lifetime.[52] These chairs with low backs bear a superficial resemblance to the seventeenth-century leather chairs of Boston: the straight rear legs are chamfered on the front surfaces and the chairs have double side stretchers. The rear stretcher is placed considerably higher than those on the Boston-made Cromwellian chairs, which suggests that this chair postdates the mid 1690s.

Pleasant as it may be for us to believe that we can see echoes of the early Boston style as it might have been brought to Philadelphia by migrating craftsmen, there are details of design that give the chair its distinctive appearance. These details therefore may be considered characteristic of the place in which the chair was produced and may owe no more to the Boston school of chairmaking than they do to contemporary English designs. Likewise, no basis exists for the assumption that details of styling—such as molded stiles or baluster-turned legs and claw feet—were introduced into both Boston and Philadelphia at the same time, or from the same source. The thinness of the seat rails is unlike the Boston type. The distinctive outward flare of the crest rail is unknown in New England, although the double-ogee design of the molded top is slightly reminiscent of the crest rails that appear on some of the Boston cane chairs (see the discussion at catalogue entry 54). The distinctive, decorative gouge marks on the front of the crest, the short chamfer of the rear stiles at the seat rail (which causes the grooves in the stiles to terminate asymmetrically), the grooved balusters on either side of the central spool on the front stretcher, and the flat-bottom block immediately above the claw feet are all features that can be associated with other Philadelphia chairs.

Perhaps the most important aspect of the chair is that it retains much of its original upholstery (fig. 166), although most of the leather on the back panel has been removed. In contrast to the seats on the New England chairs, the stuffing, which consists of marsh grass, is quite sparse, and perhaps was never much more than ¾″ (1.9 cm) thick. The narrow girt web, a type used both by saddlers and upholsterers, was tacked to the outer upper edge of the seat rails with two tacks near the margins of the web, then folded back over and tacked once. It is loosely woven in the manner that we have come to associate with English upholstery techniques. A piece of linen canvas was laid over the web and tacked to the rail. Above this came the stuffing, which was basted with linen thread that went through web, canvas, and stuffing in a rectangular pattern that is visible at the center of figure 166. The stitching kept the stuffing from shifting. The identical method was also used in Boston. The leather was then stretched over the seat and tacked to the sides of the rail. A band of leather as wide as the seat rail and about ⅛″ (0.3 cm) thick was then placed around the perimeter of the rail and fastened with two rows of ornamental brass tacks across the front and along the sides. Plain iron tacks were used across the rear of the seat. The chair also has a mark on the rear of its crest rail (fig. 167) that is too deliberate to be an accident, although its meaning is at the moment obscure. The survival of the varnish, leather upholstery, and stuffing are little short of miraculous.

At least two additional chairs from the same shop are also known. One, a walnut-stained maple armchair with cane bottom and cane back, is privately owned in Virginia. It has

Fig. 166. Detail of the underside of the upholstered seat of the leather chair in figure 165. (Newtown Library Company, on display at Pennsbury Manor, Bucks County, Penn.)

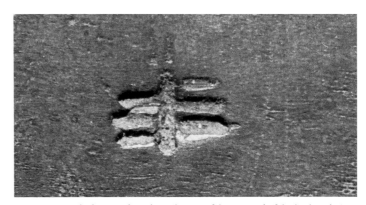

Fig. 167. Detail of stamped mark on the rear of the crest rail of the leather chair in figure 165. (Newtown Library Company, on display at Pennsbury Manor, Bucks County, Penn.)

an arched, molded crest rail with flaring corners like those of the Newtown chair at Pennsbury Manor and a related though longer stretcher. The medial and rear stretchers are turned. (That the cane chair has turned stretchers while the leather chair has rectilinear ones does not necessarily imply a chronological relationship between the two chairs, but may equally well represent conventional, contemporary criteria of appropriateness as determined by the type of upholstery with which a chair is covered.) Another chair, perhaps made in the early 1720s, was in the collection of the Chester County Historical Society, West Chester, until it was stolen in 1980. In addition to the arched, molded, and flared crest rail, this armchair has a leather bottom and a crook back with a solid "splat" that is rectilinear in shape and suggestive of the Chinese manner of early Queen Anne style English chairs. Its front stretcher is identical to that on the Virginia chair. Like other Philadelphia examples, the volutes of the handholds

Fig. 168. Leather armchair with molded stiles and crest rail, possibly Philadelphia, 1710–30. Walnut; H 42¼″ (107.3 cm), W 24¼″ (61.6 cm), D 24½″ (62.2 cm), SH 17⅛″ (43.5 cm). (Private collection.) The chair was formerly in the collection of Titus Geesey. The Pennsylvania chair varies considerably from the New England prototype in that the seat is not stuffed, the volutes of the arms are distinctly different, and the tripartite front stretcher has a characteristic middle-colonies hollow taper at its extremities. In addition, the overall proportions of the chair are squatter than the New England version.

have more carved spirals than do New England examples.[53]

Two other chairs that display familial characteristics of the Philadelphia group, but with distinct variations of their own, have survived. One of them, now privately owned in Delaware but formerly in the extraordinary collection formed by Titus Geesey, could easily date from the decade of the 1720s (fig. 168). The upholstered seat, straight rear stiles with asymmetrically terminating grooves, and stretcher arrangement are the same as those of the Newtown chair. An unexpected and compressed baluster softens the transition to each front foot, and the crest rail is not flared. Two features from the Boston school of chairmaking have been incorporated in it: a hollow-corner crest rail, very similar in feeling to the one on a chair in the Museum of Fine Arts, Boston, with a history of ownership in the Edes family of Boston and South Dartmouth, Massachusetts, and a tripartite front stretcher, clearly modeled on those of the post-1717 Boston cane chairs with straight backs and molded stiles (see catalogue entry 54) and the crook-back leather chairs made at a slightly later date. A side chair illustrated in Hornor's *Blue Book* has thick seat

rails that suggest it originally had leather upholstery and a typical stretcher of the type that appears on Philadelphia cane chairs but is otherwise closely related to this armchair. It is reported to have been owned by Thomas Masters, but if we have dated it properly was more likely the property of Thomas Masters, Jr.[54]

The single-hollow-corner crest rail is not found on Boston chairs until the time of the crook leg. If Philadelphia was influenced by Boston styles, the Geesey collection chair cannot predate 1730. The tripartite front stretcher, on the other hand, is ubiquitous in Pennsylvania. The distinctive articulation of this pattern in the Geesey collection chair displays the characteristics that separate it from others made in Boston and elsewhere in New England: hollow-turned termini and incised grooves around the circumference of each of the large balls (see catalogue entry 76 and fig. 178).

While the differences in the detailing of stretchers seem negligible on Philadelphia's leather chairs, they are unmistakably important on later slat-back chairs in Philadelphia and are characteristic of chairs made throughout Pennsylvania and New Jersey for more than a century. The presence of this stretcher on a Pennsylvania chair that has all the earmarks of workmanship dating from 1715 to 1720 suggests that some attributes of Boston leather chairs of this period were sufficiently well known in Philadelphia to be paid the sincerest form of flattery: imitation. While we cannot prove that the design of this chair was in any way the result of the Shippen-Stapleford-Fitch relationship, the chair offers strong evidence that Boston leather chairs were being imported into Philadelphia long before specific references to "Boston chairs" and "New England leather chairs" appear in the documents of Pennsylvania and Maryland during the late 1730s.[55] Indeed, the wording of many of the inventory references suggests that much of the demand for leather chairs in Philadelphia was satisfied, as in New York, not by local chairmakers but by local merchants who imported chairs from Boston.

The trade in Boston chairs is painfully reflected in the oft-quoted and rather plaintive advertisements of Philadelphia upholsterer Plunkett Fleeson. These advertisements, republished in 1929, first gave the name "Boston chairs" to the public. Fleeson's most famous notice appeared in the *Pennsylvania Gazette* for September 23, 1742. In it he announced that he "made and sold . . . at the Easy Chair, in Chestnut Street . . . black and red Leather Chairs, finished cheaper than any made here, or imported from Boston, and in Case of any defects, the Buyer shall have them made good; an Advantage not to be had in the buying Boston Chairs, besides the Damage they receive by the Sea."[56] A chair such as Fleeson was describing may very well have been like the one illustrated below in catalogue entry 80. It is a facsimile of a Boston chair, with recognizable Philadelphia characteristics, and it could well have been made in 1742 or even later. This chair coupled with Fleeson's advertisements tends to explain the presence of what must have been easily recognized as "Boston" and "New England" leather chairs in Pennsylvania and Maryland inventories of the 1760s.

While the Geesey collection chair and the related side chair illustrated by Hornor might have been considered fashionable in 1725, neither they nor the type described by Fleeson could have been considered to be the most fashionable chairs among Philadelphia's merchant aristocracy in 1744. By then, the cabriole leg had appeared. Hornor found a 1742 reference to it, which must have come from the account book of Solomon Fussell.[57] Inexplicably, Hornor missed a March 11, 1739/40, reference on the same page of Fussell's accounts, "1/2 Duz: Crookt feet Chairs" which places the cabriole leg in Philadelphia two years earlier. But Fussell was making inexpensive, rush-bottom chairs in 1740; if "crookt feet" appeared on his chairs they had probably graced better quality high-style Philadelphia chairs for some years, possibly since the early 1730s (about the same time they appeared in New England), although the evidence that could confirm this assertion has so far eluded researchers.

Those students of American furniture who may be offended by the notion that such behind-the-times chairs as William and Mary–style standardized Boston leather chairs could be vended successfully in Philadelphia in the 1740s may perhaps be mollified by the observation that the chairs were not being sold in direct competition with the elaborate early Georgian chairs for which Philadelphia is justly famous. We cannot insist that the taste of all Pennsylvanians was the same, or that the Boston leather chair did not appeal to a conservative group within the society who continued to use them. Indeed similar conservative English families continued to use and have joiners make wainscot chairs and settles in the seventeenth-century manner until the middle of the eighteenth century. Thus, we have every reason to believe that these comfortable, durable, and handsome Boston leather chairs and their local imitations enjoyed a long period of popularity in Philadelphia, its environs, and Maryland, where they fitted neatly into the intermediate price range between the turned, slat-back, rush-bottom, maple chair at the low end of the price scale and the early Georgian, carved, crook-leg, cushion-seat, walnut chair at the other.

LATER LEATHER COUCHES

Couches upholstered in materials other than cane are also listed in colonial American inventories, but given the persistence of examples in the Cromwellian style (discussed earlier), it is often difficult to know whether the "couch" in a 1720 inventory reference, for example, is of the old style or the new style. In 1693 widow Margaret Thatcher of Boston possessed a couch upholstered in "Irish Stitch"—the type of needlework more commonly known to us today by the nonperiod terms "Florentine stitch" or "bargello"—valued at 35s. But what did her couch frame look like? The same problem occurs when we consider the appearance of the "leather couch" valued at 30s. in the 1707 inventory of Jacob Melyn of Boston.[58] The year 1707 is crucial in establishing a rough chronology of upholstered couches in the new style, since that is when Thomas Fitch informed his factor in New York that leather couches were no longer stylish and that "cane couches or others we make like them wth a quilted pad are cheaper, more fasho[nable], easie & usefull; ye price of [those]

we make wth pad is about [£]3.15." Fifteen years later Fitch was producing and shipping "crook back'd," claw-foot leather chairs with double-hollow-corner crest rails, and it is likely that he was sending couches that matched. And, of course, he was also busy selling couches to Bostonians: on June 11, 1723, Fitch billed Jacob Wendell, a Boston merchant, for "1 Couch fraim and Squob of red Chainy," at £4.14.4; on August 17, 1724, he shipped Richard Wybird of Portsmouth, New Hampshire, "1 couch fraim & Squob" priced at £4.19.9.[59]

Although Fitch is often garrulous in his letters, almost no specific details concerning couches and squabs can be gleaned from his terse billings. The accounts of his former apprentice, Samuel Grant, are happily much more specific. On October 4, 1729, Grant charged Nathaniel Green 42s. for a couch frame, 12s. for "bottomg," probably with canvas, and 12s. for a "tick" to hold 15½ pounds (6.8 k) of feathers at 3s. 6d. per pound.[60] The following May, Grant billed Capt. John Morke £5.16 for a "Couch & Squob of red Chainy," and 3s. 6d. for "1 pr. Chains for ditto" that permitted the head of the couch to be lowered and raised. In August of 1730, while leather chairs in the crook-back manner were still being billed in his accounts and before the cabriole-leg style had completely emerged in Boston, Grant presented James Davenport with an itemized £5.13.10 bill for a couch. The bill specified:

	[£	s.	d.]
1 Couch fframe	1:	12:	
5 yd. Green chainy @ 5/4d	1:	6:	8
12 yd. binding [@] 7d		7:	
9¾ yd. wool @ 16d		18:	
cardg do		6:	8
slevesilk 2/ brass nails 1/ girt & canv: forhd. 1/		4:	
bottom and bottoming		12:	
makg squob & pillow. fill & quilting		9:	
chain for do		3:	6[61]

While on the basis of most probate inventory references it is difficult to distinguish a cane couch frame (see catalogue entries 59 and 60) from a frame of a couch covered with leather or with fabric, the references from the Fitch and Grant accounts make clear one thing: the frames of couches intended to receive either a cane seat or a cloth bottom—what Fitch calls a "duck bottom"—to support a more expensive textile-covered squab, were fundamentally the same. The two couches illustrated in catalogue entries 83 and 84 are of this type. They differ from the two cane examples illustrated in entries 59 and 60 only in their use of a canvas bottom and, in the case of no. 83, in that its seat rails are tenoned into the front posts, in the joiner's manner, rather than the legs tenoned into the underside of the rails, in the turner's manner. In both couches, the wide seat rails gave the maker sufficient wood to cut a rabbet into the inside upper edge of the seat rails to accept the tacked edge of the cloth bottom.

Grant's bill to Davenport clearly refers to a couch that was to receive cloth or leather upholstery. Here, amid a listing of the textiles and foundation materials, Grant specifies "brass nails," which suggests that his couch was upholstered over the rails in much the same way that chairs were. With this in mind, the frame for this couch and others of its type that Grant made on a regular basis during the period must have differed from surviving couch frames in two important ways. First, its seat rails would have been oriented vertically and would have been about 2½″ (6.4 cm) high. They would have been joined into the rear stiles and the front foot posts. This in turn caused a second difference: the feet must have had a projecting shoulder that was placed inside the seat rails and screwed in place. That this was probably the case is suggested by the thickness of vertically oriented seat rails on surviving earlier examples. With an average width of ¾″ (1.9 cm), there was simply not enough wood to afford the cutting of a mortise without endangering the strength of the completed joint.

CONCLUSIONS

Although chairs made during the first century of settlement in America have been avidly collected for several generations, they have been unduly neglected by scholars. Part of this neglect can be traced to the fact that chairs are often difficult to identify by place of origin and hence are difficult to interpret. When we can bring together enough examples to reveal the outlines of the story of their development, they become an important means of getting at the social, cultural, and economic life of the period in which they were made. Indeed, one aspect of these chairs makes them the *most* valuable tool for such a study; they were relatively inexpensive to buy when they were new—much less costly, for example, than case furniture—which implies that they could be acquired or replaced with relative frequency by moderately upwardly mobile families who responded to the dictates of fashion. Moreover, chairs are public rather than private furniture and can be used in the public rooms of a home as a subtle signal of changes in the status of their owners. From the craftsman's viewpoint, the chair is a supple medium for reflecting changes of fashion. It is a simple task for him to modify a few details of his product and create the impression of a newer style, without basically altering his model. This process can be traced in the cane chairs made in Boston between 1700 and 1730 and is likewise apparent in the leather chairs made in urban centers of colonial America prior to 1750 (see, for example, catalogue entry 77). Thanks to the perseverance of Brock W. Jobe in retrieving the Thomas Fitch and Samuel Grant ledgers and letterbooks from obscurity, some of the vagaries that have inhibited the study of upholstered chairs have been dispelled; leather chairs of the types that were popular between 1695 and 1730 can now be approached with confidence—a possibility that was but a dream of researchers prior to 1971. The variations that occur among these chairs impel us to consider their broader implications.

The Fitch and Grant documents confirm the idea only hinted at in the case of Cromwellian-style leather chairs: Boston, with its almost 200 furniture craftsmen in the first century of settlement, was the center for the production and distribution of chairs in quantities that stagger the imagination. The Fitch and Grant records represent only the tip of the iceberg. These records reveal that the upholsterer played an important role in the production of chairs in Boston, and they give us, for the first time, firm points of reference by which to date the leather chairs of New England that have survived. Fitch's letters to his customers confirm the long-held notion, extrapolated from the observation of English cane chairs, that leather chairs with turned rear stiles and carved crest rails were made in New England earlier than those with molded rear stiles. In letters to two New York customers during the winter of 1705, Fitch reveals that he has sold the carved-top version of these turned-stile chairs "for many year" and a "plain" version of them without a carved crest rail and carved front stretcher. "Many year" is an unfortunately inexact span of time. Since we know that Fitch was born in 1669, he could not have set up as an upholsterer on his own account before 1690, even if he were precocious. Furthermore, it is improbable that he began upholstering high-back leather chairs from his first day in business. Entries in the inventories of Essex County, Massachusetts, show that Cromwellian chairs remained in vogue in the early 1690s and provide further evidence for the axiom that styles overlap each other. The household inventory of Capt. John Price of Salem, for example, lists "12 New Turkey Wrought Chaires" at £4.16 or 8s. each on November 24, 1691.[62] The low valuation assigned to these *new* chairs, combined with the fact that no American-made high-back chairs in the William and Mary style with turkey-work upholstery have survived, suggests that Captain Price's chairs were the older fashioned low-back chairs rather than the high-back turned-stile chairs under discussion here.

One caveat must be added. Even though American high-back chairs in the William and Mary style upholstered with turkey work have not survived, a reference in the 1697 inventory of Capt. Thomas Berry of Boston suggests that at least one set of them existed. Berry possessed considerable worldly goods at the time of his death: his estate amounted to £1,172.3.10. Among the furniture in his "Hall—the main and, therefore, most public room in his house—were 12 turkey-work chairs valued at 30s. each. This valuation might be interpreted as an aberration, except that the inventory takers assessed the "6 old-fashioned Turkey workt chairs" "in the Dining room chamber," a somewhat more private room, at 9s. each. But Berry's references are atypical. Even in New England, the fashion for turkey work was on the wane by the 1690s. Most of the turkey-work chairs listed in the inventories of Boston in this decade are characterized by the adjective *old*, and are appraised at a fraction of their former values. By June 1, 1711, when the inventory of the wealthy and respected merchant Charles Chauncey was taken, among the things found "in the several rooms in the upper stories," were "6 old Turkey chairs" valued at only 3s. each.[63] The belief that it was possible for chairs upholstered in turkey work to exist in urban America on some chair form other than the Cromwellian is not confirmed by a single surviving example. That chairs upholstered in turkey work were chosen for the "State and Official apartments in the 'House of Peers'" in London between 1734 and 1740 may have been a political move to support English manufactures rather than one of fashion.[64]

On the basis of Fitch's letters and accounts, we can conclude that a new kind of high-back chair appeared in urban Massachusetts sometime around 1696 (a date that neatly coincides with the production of the earliest known case furniture in the William and Mary style in Boston). The first phase of William and Mary chairs persisted for nearly thirty years and beginning in 1722 gradually gave way to a second phase in which the chairs had molded stiles and crook backs, again illustrating the overlap of styles in preindustrial "bespoke" work to suit particular customers' tastes. The change was not abrupt, and the second-phase chairs were more expensive. Even when we calculate the 100 percent inflation rate between 1717 and 1723, the new molded-stile chairs still commanded a price that was 3s. higher than was asked for the turned-stile carved-top variety, and this tends to demonstrate anew that joiner's work was more expensive than turner's work; planing and shaping the rear stiles of the embowed-back chairs required more time to execute than did turning the stiles on the earlier type.

The end of the molded-stile crook-back version as the most fashionable in Boston can be traced in the accounts of Samuel Grant. The style itself persisted into the 1740s, although some evidence, albeit sparse, suggests that most of the later chairs in this manner were consciously made for the export trade.

The overlapping conflux of fashions and the economic interests represented by the chairs being made and exported to Philadelphia and New York during the first third of the eighteenth century enables us to reconstruct an unexpectedly complex picture whose details belie the facile generalizations that so often plague the study of furniture history. On one hand, craftsmen of Philadelphia—such as upholsterer Plunkett Fleeson—commissioned and marketed their own versions of Boston leather chairs as late as 1744. On the other hand, merchants of Philadelphia imported and sold true Boston chairs. It is obvious that both were simultaneously catering to a class of customer that either did not desire the high-style Philadelphia Georgian chairs of walnut or could not afford them.

In the case of New York, Boston chairs were imported for social as well as economic reasons. In many instances, New York merchants had ordered them. But in many others, even at the beginning of the century, the chairs were shipped to New York on speculation. That Boston chairs or copies of them could be sold there speaks of the cultural diversity of New Yorkers. One group of Anglo-colonists looked to Boston as its intermediate contact with England. Another group, New Yorkers of Dutch extraction, was accommodating to the English presence in what had been New Netherland. A third group, Dutchmen who resisted acculturation, in many ways offers the most fascinating subject for study; for the distinctively New York chairs that were made for them by New York's chairmakers and upholsterers define their character as surely as if they had left us their autobiographies. Once we begin to look at the chairs dispassionately, we quickly perceive that the New York versions with stiff back legs and thickly turned rings differ substantially from the analogous parts on their Boston equivalents.

The profusion of surviving American leather chairs gives us, for the first time in this study, enough examples to compare in a general way. Up to this point, we have had to struggle to achieve regional identifications. With the high-back leather chairs, however, the variety of models that emerged from a relatively few urban shops and the variations among them reveal that change is as powerful a force as stasis in determining the way an object looks. While it is always more convenient for teachers and writers to freeze time and deal with related objects as if their popularity suddenly began and suddenly ended, chairmaking in early eighteenth-century America was part of a continually changing process. Yet we must also acknowledge that some chairs continued to be made over a protracted period of time without change. Such continuity might be represented by furniture made in rural areas where the rhythm of life does not encourage rapid change and the occasional demands for certain forms did not encourage craftsmen to update a form; or in urban shops that specialized in inexpensive or utilitarian furniture made for a clientele that, bluntly stated, could afford only the merest wisp of a suggestion of fashion; or for a customer who eschewed fashion for ethnic or religious reasons, or who intended the object to be used in a nonfashionable context. In addition to the shops emphasizing continuity, the urban centers of colonial America were full of highly competitive craftsmen whose fashionable furniture, judging from the surviving examples, was almost identical to that being made in the shop next door yet was simultaneously in the process of changing and thus was subject to new influences arriving on every ship that brought furniture, ideas, or craftsmen into port.

Even in the products of shops that made furniture in large quantities and standardized the forms by using patterns (the workmanship of certainty) to achieve the economies of efficient production, the changes of time can be seen in the character of the hand work not governed by patterns (the workmanship of risk). This kind of change may be seen by comparing the rear stiles of the two Boston chairs in figure 169. The base under the finial on the left (probably earlier) chair is full and broad, that on the right (probably later) chair is attenuated and abrupt. The ball above is full on the chair to the left, flattened on the chair to the right. The bottom of the column on the left chair has a ring turned on it, the one on the right chair has incised grooves. The collarino of the left boldly flares outward, that of the right is merely a thin ring. These kinds of changes are subtle, their implications elusive, and their reality not easy to interpret.

The process of change is highly visible at those moments when the pressure to be fashionable dictates the introduction of a new style. Such a moment comes for the crook-back leather chair with the introduction of the crook-leg style. We have long referred to furniture that intermingled features of two styles as "transitional" and dated it accordingly. In the case of the leather-upholstered chairs itemized in the accounts of Samuel Grant between 1729 and 1733, we can, for the first time, study documents that show how the process of transition worked in a specific case. As we read Grant's notes in chronological order, it becomes obvious that we are witnessing the emergence of one Boston chairmaker's version of a new style. New feature after new feature is added to the well-known Boston leather-chair form. In our mind's eye we are able to see and recognize the permutations that transform an existing model into something

Fig. 169. LEFT. Detail of the rear stiles of two Boston chairs dating from 1695–1710 and 1710–ca. 1723. The chair on the left is catalogue entry 64, the chair on the right is catalogue entry 66. (Winterthur 58.553, 54.540.)

Fig. 170. RIGHT. Leather chair with molded stiles and crest rail, a straight back with a banister, and carved horsebone legs; Boston, 1730–32. Front seat rail, white pine (*Pinus strobus*); H 45⅞" (116.5 cm), W 19" (48.3 cm), D 15½" (39.4 cm), SH 17" (43.2 cm). (Winterthur 66.1311.)

quite new. It is as if reading the Grant ledger had placed us in a sort of time machine, and model after model, each varying slightly from the previous one—all of them incidentally, transitional chairs—appears before our eyes. It is clear from these documents that the concept of transition is valid and, moreover, that we have no reason, given the documentation available, not to assign a specific date range to the transition in Boston.

Yet the concept of transition reveals a chink in the armor of our ideas about how styles change. The rare and unusually fine chair illustrated in figure 170 reveals that transitional chairs, such as the kinds described in the Grant accounts, were not designed to represent a new idea. They represent instead an older form that has been updated to give the appearance of something new by incorporating into it more current stylistic elements. The chair in figure 170 is basically a stiff-back cane chair of the Boston school—molded stiles, great heels, Spanish front feet, stretchers, double-ogee front apron (now integrated into the seat rail)—with overtones of the crest rail and rectilinear seat of the leather chair, onto which have been grafted elements of the "newest fashion," carved horsebone legs (in what may properly be called the "Kent manner"), banister splat, and cushion seat. But the observable and demonstrably

new features of this chair do not answer the most important question: Where do these features come from, and how does the craftsman know to incorporate them into his product?

The answer to this question cannot be found in the documents available to us, but is implied by the chair itself. First we must relinquish the cherished notion that furniture made in the colonies was unique; colonists had a derivative culture. It seems clear that the attributes of the new style were brought to the colonial culture either in the form of new-style chairs imported from the parent culture(s) or in the mind of an immigrant craftsman. The design of the chair illustrated in figure 170, for example, cannot have been crystallized much earlier than that of the chair in figure 156. The latter is a reasonable facsimile of a well-known English type and is evidence of the presence of English models in Boston, although our museums and private collectors have not collected them. It further reveals that the chair in figure 170 is not the *only* solution to the problem of making a fashionable chair in Boston. Since the details of the turning indicate that these two chairs did not come from the same shop, no reason exists to believe that the chair in figure 156 was necessarily made later in time than that in figure 170. Thus it follows that the idea of new style is already present in the derivative culture before the craftsman who makes the transitional object begins to grope toward it, else he would not know what style he is groping toward! If any time lag exists in the taste of a derivative culture, as we have often been led to believe, then this point is all the more forcefully emphasized. If there is a transition to a new style, it is the transition of the individual craftsman in finding his own means of accommodating to the new style. Since the chair in figure 170 has none of the features of the chair in figure 156, which became the standardized Boston chair of its time, it cannot be said that the chair in figure 170 is transitional to anything but oblivion! In short, use of the word *transitional* can create more problems than it solves.

The chair in figure 156 well illustrates the second way of inaugurating a new style—copying. It need scarcely be pointed out that the derivative culture has not evolved the style at all: here is substitution rather than transition. Indeed, we could easily argue that major styles do not evolve, but are created, although they may be created out of elements already present in a culture. Often they are created out of totally exotic elements; the early phase of the Queen Anne style, with all its oriental allusions, is a classic example of this. But a style can also represent, and often does, a total reaction *against* what had previously been fashionable, and the Queen Anne style does this too: its sensuous and boldly curvilinear forms represent a positive rejection of the small, tight, overly ornamented curves and formal rectilinearity that preceded it.

If the Boston chair in figure 170 were made (as the Grant records could be construed to suggest) between November 1730, when the horsebone foot was first mentioned, and January 13, 1731/32, when the first horsebone *round* foot is noted, we can date it with unusual precision and understand it as a product of its time and place of origin. In the case of upholstered chairs of the Boston school, we have a large body of furniture made in an urban community that has every reason to be the aesthetic and formal arbiter of its region. Further, Boston has a flexible and multifaceted professional chair industry. Its products represent a cohesiveness typical of the cooperation/competition that characterizes the work of an urban center. Here the idea of transition makes sense because we feel that—as had happened twice before in Boston with upholstered chairs and once before with cane chairs—the product will eventually become standardized and settle down into a long run of production.

Problems arise when we branch out from the known facts of this urban context and apply the concept of transition to the village products inspired by these urban examples. It is difficult to equate the transitional features with a period of time for which we have only a few surviving objects upon which to base a judgment. They do not allow us to take into account the different production circumstances, the mental attitudes and experiences of the potential customers, and the very rhythm of life and notions of fashion. What was fashionable to a Boston chairmaker and how he could express his concept of fashion with the resources at his command must have been quite different from what was possible for a village chairmaker, whether he lived close to or far from that urban center. No discoverable principle of historical method will tell us when Ipswich, Portsmouth, Albany, or Charlestown made its transition; each of these places is subject to cultural influences that cannot be documented.

These observations are not intended to denigrate the accomplishments of the craftsmen who made the chair in figure 170 or those of the other American craftsmen who made their transition to the newest fashion in other places. Indeed, the appearance of such chairs are an occasion for admiration and pride in our cultural past. Far from being slavish copies of a style produced in our parent cultures, chairs such as these ought to be viewed as monuments in the history of our arts: they are the result of a single craftsman's efforts to arrive at a new expression, all the more valuable to us because we know that he is making a piece of furniture in a style that he was never academically trained to make. Often these objects are unique expressions because they externalize the ingenious craftsman's struggle to create his own version of something new. It is, thus, repeating a similar process that had already taken place in England, for the Queen Anne style was not invented in England nor even the Lowlands from whence English craftsmen received their inspiration.

The documentable appearance of the cabriole leg (horsebone foot) in Boston furniture in 1730 is one of the pivotal moments in American decorative arts. It prompts us to ask why it took so long for the style to reach this continent. A set of dining-room chairs at Blenheim Palace reveals that the form was made in England more than a decade earlier. One explanation may be that Boston's seventeenth-century woodworking dynasties continued to exert control over shop production in the early eighteenth century.[65] Another equally possible explanation is that the so-called lag did not exist at all, and perhaps our European colleagues have tended to date their examples somewhat too early. The introduction of the cabriole leg also forcibly brings to our attention the role of the turner in the production of furniture: the turner's lathe is the tool of rapid production, and rapid production leads to a savings in time, which in turn means that the product will be relatively less expensive and hence can become "popular" in all the meanings of that word.

1 See Edwards and Jourdain, *Georgian Cabinetmakers*, p. 19.

2 Symonds, DMMC, microfilm M-285, unpaged (Symonds' notes state that this is in the British Museum's Department of Printed Books, ref. HARY. 5947).

3 "Account-books of Treasures of Harvard College, 1669–1752," p. 353 (I am indebted to Richard H. Saunders for this reference), and Thomas Brattle's Journal, 1693–1713, p. 50. Although one of these chairs was in existence in 1863, recent searches of the Harvard premises by Margo Scott did not find it.

4 Fitch to Pease, May 8, 1705, Fitch to Carr, November 19, 1705, Fitch to Benjamin Faneuil, July 11, 1709, Fitch letterbook, AAS. I am deeply indebted to Brock W. Jobe for calling the Fitch manuscripts and those of Fitch's former apprentice, Samuel Grant, to my attention.

5 The high-back leather chair illustrated in Edwards, *English Chairs*, pl. 25, is a rare English example with a carved stretcher in the London cane-chair manner of 1680–85. The turned feet are not original to the chair and are, in any case, inappropriate on the rear legs. The medial stretcher between the lower side stretchers is not original to the chair either. Considering these replacements, we must also suggest the possibility that the front stretcher may not be what it appears to be; otherwise, its presence on this chair suggests that the Cromwellian style enjoyed an extremely long life in England's metropolis, just as its American analog did in Boston.

6 Randall, "Boston Chairs," pp. 12–20; Swan, "Coastwise Cargoes," pp. 278–80.

7 November 27, 1722, Fitch account book, MHS.

8 Bruce T. Sherwood to Forman, June 22, 1980; the front stretcher on the Henry Ford Museum armchair is a restoration. I am indebted to Carol Gordon for calling the Munson-Williams-Proctor chair to my attention.

9 *Account of Her Majesty's Revenue in the Province of New York*, p. 35, item 28; I am indebted to Lois Olcott Price for this reference.

10 Fitch to Faneuil, April 22, 1707, March 8, 1707/8, April 16, June 21, July 19, 1708, and Fitch to Abram Wendell, March 28, May 16, 1709, Fitch letterbook, AAS.

11 Fitch to Ti[e]nhoven, October 30, 1710, Fitch letterbook, AAS.

12 Fitch to Atkinson, April 14, 1717; Fitch to Crouch, November 23, 1715, Fitch to Arnold, [ca. November 25, 1715], Fitch letterbook, NEHGS.

13 "Massachusetts Shipping Returns 1686–1719," folios 40, 56, CO 5.848; "New York Treasurer's Accounts," CO 5.1222.

14 Knight to Livingston, July 10, 1721, Livingston Papers; I am indebted to Ruth Piwonka for sharing these materials and for her transcription of them with me.

15 February 27, 1722/23, Fitch account book, MHS.

16 Fitch to Powell, March 20, 1723[/24], April 4, 1724, Fitch letterbook, MHS.

17 Blackburn, *Cherry Hill*, pp. 66, 172, fig. 33. An additional chair of this type is displayed at Fort Crailo, Rensselaer, New York.

18 See, for example, a London-made chair of this type in the great hall of the Treasurer's House, York, England.

19 Hempstead, *Diary*, p. 70.

20 Contract between Edward Skate, carpenter, and John Hill, April 6, 1698, SPNEA (I am indebted to Joseph W. Hammond for calling this contract to my attention). See also Goodman, "Woodworking Apprentices and Their Tools in Bristol, Norwich, Great Yarmouth, and Southampton," p. 389.

21 Suffolk Probate 27:341. Crook-back chairs with flag or bass bottoms are relatively rare. An excellent Boston chair with turned front legs and a rush "slip" seat is in the collection of the Old Gaol Museum, York, Maine. A related example was illustrated in an advertisement by Henry V. Weil, *Antiques* 9, no. 3 (March 1926): 134.

22 Samuel Grant's journal, more properly termed a "daybook," contains detailed entries that are a painstaking record of his daily business transactions. These would have been transferred to an alphabetized account book, which does not survive. All entries are in chronological order and can be located by date. Grant's billhead, with an engraved picture of his shop sign is illustrated in Means, "Early American Trade Cards," pp. 13–14; and in Jobe, "Boston Furniture Industry" (conference report), p. 33.

23 Perkins and Leach are frequently mentioned. Johnson and Baxter are less so (e.g., January 12 and 29, 1732/33, Grant daybook). Johnson (w. 1732) is not further identified. Nathaniel Holmes, a Boston joiner who made some of the case furniture sold by Grant, apparently did not make leather chairs, since he bought 6 from Grant on February 18, 1729/30.

24 January 14, February 4, 1728/29, May 19, 1733, March 8, 1732/33, September 24, 1733, Grant daybook. Surviving chairs in this style with turned feet are rare.

25 Fitch to Pease, May 8, 1705, Fitch letterbook, AAS.

26 One such instance is the "Elbow" leather chair sold to Capt. John Morke, May 27, 1730, Grant daybook.

27 October 14, 1729, November 21, 1730, Grant daybook. In shop parlance of this period, "feet" means "legs."

28 October 8, 1731, January 22, and February 4, 1731/32, Grant daybook. The August 29, 1732, inventory of Col. William Tailer of Boston values "6 new fashion chairs" a total of £6. If these are Queen Anne–style chairs of Boston manufacture, the appraised worth of each is exactly half of the cost of a new chair, which reveals an important correlation between inventory values and new costs (Suffolk Probate 31:56).

29 September 8, 1732, Grant daybook.

30 March 30, 1737, Grant daybook.

31 Rutherford, "Furnishings of Hampton Court Palace," p. 17 (I am indebted to Colin Streeter for calling this reference to my attention); Edwards and Jourdain, *Georgian Cabinetmakers*, p. 19.

32 I am indebted to Bruce T. Sherwood for first calling this chair to my attention and for insisting that it was of New York origin.

33 Sack, *Opportunities in American Antiques* 4, no. 177.

34 Although the legs and top are of mahogany, the frame of the Johnson table is made of American red gum (*Liquidambar styraciflua*), a wood common in New York furniture, but rarely used elsewhere. I am indebted to Roderic Blackburn for providing samples of this table for microanalysis.

35 Lockwood, *Colonial Furniture* (1st ed.), p. 143. It is also illustrated in Butler, *Family Collections at van Cortlandt Manor*, p. 42 (acc. no. 58:432). I am indebted to Anne T. Larin for providing a wood sample for analysis.

36 Singleton, *Furniture of Our Forefathers*, p. 241; Nutting, *Furniture Treasury*, no. 1930, *Furniture of Historic Deerfield*, p. 29, no. 36.

37 Forman interview with Jonathan Fairbanks, February 24, 1975; Vogelsang, *Le meuble Hollandais*, fig. 133.

38 Vogelsang, *Le meuble Hollandais*, figs. 137, 138, 144; Failey, *Long Island Is My Nation*, p. 25, no. 21.

39 Kane, *Three Hundred Years of American Seating Furniture*, p. 61, pl. 39; Lyon, *Colonial Furniture*, fig. 69.

40 Joseph Downs, *Loan Exhibition of New York State Furniture*, no. 5.

41 This chair was owned by Fred J. Johnston of Kingston, N. Y., when it was illustrated in *Antiques* 104, no. 5 (November 1973): 824. It is said to be identical to a chair once owned by the Van Der Lyn family of Kingston (Johnston to Forman, November 13, 1973).

42 Nutting, *Pilgrim Century* (1st ed.), p. 221; (2d ed.) p. 325.

43 Fitch to Faneuil, April 22, 1707, Fitch letterbook, AAS.

44 See Failey, *Long Island Is My Nation*, no. 23.

45 This chair is owned by the Nordiska Museet, Stockholm. I am indebted to Dr. Elisabet Hidemark for making it available to me for examination.

46 Fitch to Faneuil, April 22, 1707, Fitch letterbook, AAS; Fitch to Faneuil, February 8, 1715/16, Fitch letterbook, NEHGS.

47 Matzkin, "Inventories of Estates in Philadelphia County," pp. 104–5.

48 Philadelphia Wills, 1708-83, 1708-101, 1709-141, 1722-251. The relatively low valuation of these chairs may partially be explained by the higher value of Pennsylvania currency which was not subject to the inflationary pressures on New England paper money at this period.

49 Philadelphia Wills, 1708-113.

50 Savage, *Genealogical Dictionary*, 4:87; Cowan, *Members of the Ancient and Honorable Artillery Company*, p. 43; *Suffolk Deeds*, 10:241, 11:297 (this is the earliest datable use of "upholsterer" yet found in an American document). Fitch to Clement Plumsted and Charles Read, February 14, 1714/15, Fitch letterbook, NEHGS.

51 *Suffolk Deeds*, 14:270.

52 See Barnsley, *Newtown Library under Two Kings*, p. 15. I am indebted to Nancy D. Kolb for calling this chair and reference to my attention.

53 These two chairs are illustrated in Kindig, *Philadelphia Chair*, figs. 15, 64.

54 Randall, *American Furniture*, no. 128; Hornor, *Blue Book*, pl. 16.

55 Leibundguth, "Furniture-Making Crafts in Philadelphia," p. 37, quotes an advertisement of Peter Baynton in *Pennsylvania Gazette* of February 1, 1738/39, offering "New England red Leather chairs." Two men of that name lived in Philadelphia during the 1720s and 1730s. One was a joiner (Hornor, *Blue Book*, pp. 2, 26), the other, probably the man whose advertisement is quoted above, was at one time a supercargo working in the coastal trade to the southern colonies and later a merchant in Philadelphia. He was not an upholsterer. His letterbook is in the manuscript collection of the Historical Society of Pennsylvania.

56 Prime, *Arts and Crafts in Philadelphia, Maryland and South Carolina*, pp. 201–2. Fleeson's remark about the possibility of damage in shipment is confirmed by a letter from Fitch to Richard Wibird of Portsmouth, N.H., dated February 22, 1706/7 (Fitch letterbook, AAS): "yor chairs are done but neither Webber or Giddins can stow them so but they'l be exposed to the weathr, wherefore I chuse to take the next better opportu[nity] to send yo the Chairs."

57 Hornor, *Blue Book*, p. 34; Fussell account book, p. 3: "9/11/1742 2 Crookt feet Chairs . . . £1."

58 Suffolk Probate, 13:408, 16, 259.

59 Fitch to Faneuil, April 22, 1707, Fitch letterbook, AAS; June 11, 1723, August 17, 1724, Fitch account book, MHS.

60 October 4, 1729, Grant daybook.

61 May 27, 1730, August 6, 1730, Grant daybook.

62 Docket 22733, Essex Probate Files; see Trent, "History for the Essex Institute Turkey Work Couch," pp. 29–37, for evidence that this style was being made in Boston after 1697.

63 Suffolk Probate, 8:139; 17:440–41.

64 Symonds, "Turkey Work, Beech and Japanned Chairs," p. 224.

65 See Henretta, "Economic Development and Social Structure in Colonial Boston," pp. 75–92.

61.
CARVED-TOP LEATHER CHAIR WITH BANISTER BACK
Boston, Massachusetts
1690–1710
WOOD: A maple of the soft group, probably red maple (*Acer rubrum*), definitely not European field maple (*Acer campestre*)
OH 52⅜″ (133.0 cm)
SH 17⅝″ (44.8 cm), SW 18″ (45.7 cm), SD 15½″ (39.4 cm)
PROVENANCE: History of ownership in the Cobb family; Rockwell Gardiner; purchased by the museum
59.28.1

62.
CARVED-TOP LEATHER CHAIR WITH BANISTER BACK
Boston, Massachusetts
1690–1710
WOOD: A maple of the soft group, probably red maple (*Acer rubrum*), definitely not European field maple (*Acer campestre*)
OH 52⅛″ (132.4 cm)
SH 18″ (45.7 cm), SW 18⅛″ (46.1 cm), SD 15⅝″ (39.7 cm)
PROVENANCE: History of ownership in the Cobb family; Rockwell Gardiner; purchased by the museum
59.28.2

In the early eighteenth century, chairs with banister backs and upholstered seats were among the rarest forms made in colonial America and were equally rare in Europe. The pair illustrated in this entry are clearly of urban origin and may be like those listed in the inventory of Boston taverner Thomas Selby, whose parlor contained "23 Leather Chairs, Banister Backs" valued at £8.1 or 7s. each on October 21, 1727. In the same inventory were "12 high back Leather chairs" appraised at £5.8 or 9s. each, which indicates that all else being equal banister-back leather-bottom chairs were less expensive than chairs with both seat and back upholstered.[1]

A few examples of this form are to be found in the museums of western Europe. An outstanding Dutch example, in the collection of the Rijksmuseum, Amsterdam, is illustrated in Willem Vogelsang's *Le meuble Hollandais* as fig. 145. It has boldly carved Flemish-scroll front legs that rest upon tiny ball feet (restored) and two-axis-turned rear stiles; the seat appears to have been framed to receive upholstery of textile or leather. An English banister-back chair that may have once had a similar bottom was illustrated by Nutting as no. 1922 in *Furniture Treasury*. An exquisite example, which looks to be of northern European origin, was once owned by Mabel Brady Garvan and is also illustrated in *Furniture Treasury* as no. 2011. It differs from the other examples in that it had a cane seat, as did a chair now upholstered in green velvet in the collection of the Victoria and Albert Museum. The most striking thing about all these chairs is that they are of high quality urban design and workmanship, and, like the Winterthur examples, go far to refute the popular notion that banister-back chairs are inelegant.

Winterthur's chairs have all the stylistic attributes of Boston manufacture, yet they have spent most of their lifetime in Parsippany, Morris County, New Jersey. They were acquired in 1959 from direct descendants of Edward Cobb, who apparently brought them with him from Taunton, Massachusetts, when he settled in New Jersey.[2] On the basis of the style alone, we are now certain that these chairs were not originally made for Edward Cobb because he was not born until 1731. More likely the original owner was either Edward's father, Ebenezer (b. 1688), or grandfather, Jonathan (b. 1660, m. 1683), of Barnstable (assuming that these chairs descended to Edward Cobb in the direct paternal line).[3] A 1690–1710 date has been assigned to the two chairs because they so closely resemble the earliest style of cane chair definitely known to have been made in New England (see fig. 126). The details of the chairs are closely modeled on urban English examples of moderate quality, so closely that we might be tempted to see the hand of an English chairmaker at work here, if only the records had clearly revealed that one worked in New England in the 1690s. The finials are a classic London type—the beautifully articulated and fully rounded compressed ball is common on English cane chairs of that period. The columnar shapes on the rear stiles are carefully turned; that they narrow slightly just above the base gives the appearance of entasis in the academic-classical manner employed by contemporary London chair-making shops. Vertical slats, carefully rounded on their front edges, further heighten the English cane-chair impression, as does the dip of the lower back rail, which also echoes the crest rail and emphasizes the symmetrical design of the back. The design and arrangement of the stretchers are also modeled on those of English cane chairs and reinforce a probable early date of manufacture (furthermore this type of stretcher owes no debt to American leather-upholstered chairs of the previous generation). The front legs are based on a type that commonly appears on English cane chairs as well. The outward cant further emphasizes the rarity of these American examples.[4] The columnar shape between the scrolls of the leg and the seat rail is often seen in English examples, as opposed to the more usual baluster shape found on American chairs of a slightly later date. Indeed, if the wood were not an American maple, it would be difficult to state with conviction that those two chairs are American made.

A cane chair made of American beech (*Fagus grandifolia*), in the collection of the Wadsworth Atheneum (Nutting, *Furniture Treasury*, no. 1985) is closely related to the Winterthur chairs and suggests that all three were executed by the same turner or at least in the same shop; the differences may be explained by the varying construction techniques necessary to make a frame for cane upholstery as opposed to leather upholstery. The Wadsworth chair retains a remnant of the ball feet under the scroll legs, which the Winterthur chair also once possessed. Inasmuch as this is one of the few instances in which a cane chair and an upholstered example from the same shop may be identified, it is perhaps appropriate to speculate for a moment on the wood, the one feature that differentiates them. The wood selected for all of the New England cane chairs (except those of the relatively late I group) is beech; the wood used for the upholstered chairs is maple.[5] As we have seen in the discussion at catalogue entry 54, maple is perfectly satisfactory for cane chairs, and, conversely, beech could have served for upholstered chairs in America, just as it did in Europe. At first blush it might appear that beech with its more prominent ray structure might be stronger than maple and therefore would stand up better to the drilling of holes necessary for caning. This, however, does not invariably appear to be the case. Some American maples, including those used in chair frames during the eighteenth century, are harder woods than

cat. 61

cat. 62

beech.[6] Maples were plentiful in colonial New England, less subject to insect damage than beech, and when cut into lumber could supply a greater proportion of sound wood than could beech. Furthermore, chairmakers in New England had been using maple in their frames since the middle of the seventeenth century. Nonetheless, the earliest American cane chairs were beech, not maple. The best possible explanation is that the first craftsman to make cane chairs in New England was a recent immigrant who preferred beech because he had used it to make similar chairs in England. (Compare these chairs, for example, with the American cane chair in fig. 126.) Similarly the earliest of the I-group cane chairs was made of beech in the English manner, probably the product of a recently immigrated craftsman. The rest of the I group, made at least a full generation after the cane-chair style was introduced into New England, and the leather-upholstered chairs have maple frames.

A close examination of the two leather chairs further reinforces the idea that they were made at an early date. The columnar shapes on the legs and stretchers are well articulated and have bold rings. Similar shapes appeared on the earliest cane chairs of New England and were replaced by baluster forms fairly early in the eighteenth century. The care with which the collarino on each of the rear stiles is articulated is much like the way this same element is executed in architectural work. It is clearly more academic than that on the chair in catalogue entry 64, for example, in which the collarino is combined with the capital and becomes little more than a spool. A detail that chairs in catalogue entries 61, 62, 64, and 66 share is a scribed line at each end of the barrel-shape element on the lower stile between the lower back rail and the rear seat rail. Scribes also appear on the turned portions of the lower back legs. Probably the earliest features on the chairs in this entry are the outward canted legs. Both the Winterthur and Wadsworth chairs give lie to the fondly held notion that the carved crest rail and front stretcher of chairs of this type should be of the same pattern: that phenomenon did not occur until the standardized chair was produced (catalogue entry 66).

The finish—a walnut-grained effect composed of two layers, a transparent reddish-brown glaze over a white lead and yellow ochre undercoat—is not original to these chairs. There is a layer of black paint next to the wood. It is not possible with present techniques to determine whether the graining was applied in the eighteenth or the nineteenth century. The top crest of the chair in entry 61 is a replacement, while the balls originally under the feet of both examples are missing.

NOTES
[1] Suffolk Probate, 25:530–35.
[2] Rockwell Gardiner to Charles Montgomery, quoting *History of Morris County, New Jersey*, in object files 59.28.1 and 59.28.2, Registrar's Office, Winterthur.
[3] Savage, *Genealogical Dictionary*, 1:413.
[4] Symonds, "Cane Chairs of the Late 17th and Early 18th Centuries," p. 179, fig. 11, is, in many ways, the prototype for the Cobb family chairs.
[5] The exception is the crest rail of certain late leather chairs; see catalogue entry 77.
[6] The load required to impress a ball .444 inches (1.128 cm) to half of its diameter into the side of a piece of unseasoned American beech (*Fagus grandifolia*) was 850 pounds (384.5 kilos). For sugar maple (*Acer saccharum*) the load required was 970 pounds (436.5 kilos). Figures were not available for red maple (*Acer rubrum*) (*Wood Handbook*, pp. 50–52).

63.
CARVED-TOP LEATHER CHAIR or LOW-BACK LEATHER CHAIR
Boston, Massachusetts
1695–1705
WOODS: All American red maple (*Acer rubrum*), except the three rectangular rails of the back panel and the rear and side seat rails of red oak (*Quercus rubra*)
OH 38⅜″ (97.5 cm)
SH 18½″ (47.0 cm), SW 17¾″ (45.1 cm), SD 14⅜″ (36.5 cm)
PROVENANCE: Bequest of Henry Francis du Pont
59.2115

The fine quality of workmanship and the diminutive size of this leather chair place it in the category of rare and desirable collectors' items. The style in which it is made suggests that it is an anomaly: a low-back chair made in an age of chairs with high backs. The bold design and deeply incised carving of the crest rail also set it apart; the average American leather chair usually had carving of feathery designs executed in a competent but somewhat careless manner.

The most striking aspect of the crest rail, a carefully molded scoop (or hollow, as it would have been described in the early eighteenth century), is the predominant design feature. This feature is common on American chairs in the Queen Anne style and would superficially seem to suggest that this chair was made late in its period. But, the same motif is on English cane chairs that date from around 1700, such as a low-back chair formerly at the Art Institute of Chicago (fig. 171), which suggests that the present chair is a predecessor of the related high-back chairs. This idea is enhanced by the presence of turned rear stiles rather than molded ones.

The quality of workmanship lavished on the turning of this chair is generally superior to that of the Boston chairs dating from the 1705–22 period and further suggests an early date of manufacture. A comparison of this chair with the slightly later versions of the style (see catalogue entries 65, 66, and 85) reveals familial resemblances as well as differences. All have seat and back rails of red oak, all were originally stained brown to simulate walnut, and all possess backward-canting heels on the rear legs, single side stretchers, and a higher rear stretcher (as in the standard Boston type). The front legs on this chair are identical in design to those of the chair in entry 65, and the bilobe front stretcher is similar to that in entry 66, although on this early chair it is more complex, bolder, and has numerous refinements in its turning, such as a fillet below the collar on the neck of the baluster and more elaborate and larger profiles at the

cat. 63

Fig. 171. Cane chair with low back, England, ca. 1700. (Present location unknown, formerly owned by the Art Institute of Chicago.)

stretcher on this early chair bears further comparison with the one on the textile upholstered chair illustrated in entry 85, to which it is nearly identical. The front stretcher on that chair, however, is slightly more attenuated and less refined in execution, which suggests it was made at a later date. (This notion is supported by the fact that the upholstered chair has grooves on the cylinder of the rear stiles between the seat and lower back rail, in the manner of the standardized Boston chairs, as opposed to the half-round rings turned at the top and bottom of the analogous elements on the present example.)

The stiles likewise exhibit affinities to and differences from the standardized Boston leather chair. A sharply tapered column is the primary decorative feature here. The plump ring turned at its base is reminiscent of those on the chairs illustrated in entries 61, 62, 64, and on the side stretchers of entry 84. The column has the incised groove near the base that appears on the chairs in entries 65 and 66, the shaft of the column lacks entasis, and the distinct collarino has a fillet beneath it instead of being compressed with the capital. The lower edge of the crest rail arches upward in all three examples. The feature that sets this chair apart from its fellows is the construction of the crest rail itself. Here it sits atop the round tenons turned at the tops of the stiles, simulating the appearance of numerous English cane chairs. This feature suggests that this chair was a design worked out early in the period during which leather chairs vied for popularity with cane chairs. It further indicates turnerly thinking on the part of its designer, a notion reinforced by the observably high quality of the turning itself. The crest rail, however, also betrays the American copyist origins of this maker. On English chairs each stile usually has a rectangular tenon cut upon its topmost turning, and that tenon is fitted into a rectangular mortise hole in the crest rail, where it is firmly glued or pinned. On this chair the crest rail, sitting as it does on round tenons, is constructed in a dangerously weak fashion indicating an imperfectly worked-out design.

The modern upholstery and tacks on this chair replaced original upholstery that was single nailed. The side stretchers are reinforced with narrow strips of sheet copper held in place with nineteenth-century machine-made wrought tacks.

extremities. This stretcher further differs from that of the later chair in that the round tenons (about ¾″ [1.9 cm] in diameter), which fit in the auger holes on the front legs, are pinned in place; the ones on the later chair are much smaller—as if the style had been simplified and "streamlined" for rapid, hence inexpensive, production—and are glued in place. The

64.
CARVED-TOP ELBOW CHAIR WITH DOUBLE-NAILED RUSSIA LEATHER
Boston, Massachusetts
1695–1710
WOODS: Stiles, legs, arms, crest rail, front stretcher, right and bottom rails of back panel, and front seat rail, American sugar maple (*Acer saccharum*); left back rail and remaining seat rails, red oak (*Quercus rubra*)
OH 53¼″ (135.3 cm)
SH 17¾″ (45.1 cm), SW 22⅞″ (58.1 cm), SD 17″ (43.2 cm)
PROVENANCE: Helen T. Cooke, Wellesley, Mass.; Henry Francis du Pont
58.553

In many ways this chair represents the adoption of the Anglo-Dutch cane-chair style as the model for the earliest American-made high-back leather chairs. The bold turning of the stretchers as well as their placement heightens the resemblance of this chair to English cane examples and suggests that this chair is of an earlier date of manufacture than the standardized Boston side chair (see catalogue entry 65). An identical chair, presently displayed at the Smithtown Historical Society on Long Island, is believed to have been owned originally by Richard Smith II. A third chair in the Munson-Williams-

cat. 64

Proctor Institute differs only in the pattern of the crest rail and stretchers (see fig. 180). And that chair is identical to a chair in the Henry Ford Museum with a history of ownership in the Schuyler family of Albany.[1]

The evidence points to a New York origin for Winterthur's chair, but the only features that it shares with the identified New York chairs are the form of the finial—the compressed ball of the top is separated from its base by a hollow—and the turned ring at the base of the column on the stiles, details that may have made their way to Boston from New York. In contrast, numerous attributes of the New England school are present on the chair: the distinctive arm support consisting of compressed baluster, elongated baluster, ball, and grooved cone; lines scribed on the part of the stile between the lower back rail and the rear seat rail; collarino combined with a capital on the columns; backward raking rear feet; and the tapered columnar forms on the stretchers; all of which bear comparison with the Boston cane chair illustrated in catalogue entry 55. Moreover, the turning on this chair and on all of the Boston examples is executed with a crispness and delicacy not usual in the New York versions.

Some evidence of a New England origin for this chair can be assumed on the basis of a plain-top chair with a history of ownership by the Reverend Benjamin Prescott (1687–1777) of Peabody, Massachusetts, in the collection of the Historical Society of Peabody.[2] In style, the Prescott chair is somewhere between the chair in the previous entry and the one in this entry. It is a plain chair with medial and rear stretchers, stiles, and finials like the present example. It has, however, turned elements on the stiles between the lower back and seat rails like the previous example and turned columns on the front legs, like the chairs in entries 61 and 62. As is true with most of the plain-top leather chairs of colonial America, the front stretcher of the Prescott chair is composed of baluster forms.

Winterthur's chair was once in the collection of Helen T. Cooke of Wellesley, Massachusetts. When illustrated in Nutting's *Furniture Treasury* (no. 1979), it was described as "a handsome shape, ram's horn arm, stretcher repeated in crest, rare." It was not included in *Pilgrim Century*, consequently we have no further comment by Nutting. Nutting was quite right about the chair's rarity: no side chair versions are known.

Perhaps the rarest aspect of the chair is that it retains its original russia-leather covers. But, as pointed out in the introduction to Cromwellian chairs, russia leather has qualities of pliability and durability: most of the leather chairs which have survived from the seventeenth or early eighteenth centuries with their upholstery intact are of this type. The thickness of the leather on this chair suggests that it was made from cowhide.

No evidence has survived from the early eighteenth century to suggest that russia leather was made in America or even in England. The russia that was used in Boston was imported from England, as several letters from Boston upholsterer Thomas Fitch confirm, but English merchants in turn had imported it from the Continent. The Fitch letterbooks also reveal that the supply was often uncertain and costly. In spring of 1725, he informed customer Arnold Collins in New York that he "expected to have had . . . some Rushias Leather to have suited You with the Chairs you wrote for, but this day I recd my Letters . . . advising me that Rushia Leather is Extream Scarce and dear in London so that I can't have any untill the Fall"; in 1726 he wrote to Anna Hooglant in New York that he had "no Rushia Leather [it] being very scarce and dear in London, but being desirous to Sute your occasions I have sent you a dozen of very good New fashion'd chairs of Neats Leather." A year later, he wrote to a Colonel Coddington, "Rushia Leather is so high at home that It won't answer. . . . I think Mr. Downs has NewEngland red Leather, but there's no Rushia in Town." William Downs, a Boston upholsterer, occasionally worked for Fitch and in 1723 had once provided him with "3 hides of Russhia leather [weighing] 10 lb. 27 oz. [each?] at 4[s.] £5:8:0." In contrast, the value per pound in 1653 had been 20d.[3]

In 1707 Fitch began selling New York bound side chairs with New England leather at 14s. each; those with russia leather sold at 16s., and "Russhia Leath[er] Elbow chairs" he priced at 28s. each.[4]

Of course, Fitch's entries tell us very little about details of style and ornament; they merely inform us that parts of these chairs were decorated. It seems fairly certain that the crests of the vast majority of carved-top, double-nailed russia-leather chairs sent to New York by Fitch were not exactly like those on the present example, but were similar to that on the chair illustrated in the next entry. Nonetheless, the presence of a chair like this one in the vicinity of Smithtown indicates that the trade to the New York area existed before the Boston chair became standardized and that this example is one of them.

The upholstery on Winterthur's chair has been removed, new girt web installed, and the upholstery replaced as it originally was. The tenons on the arms have been restored. Approximately ¾" (1.9 cm) is missing from the bottoms of the feet.

NOTES
[1] See Failey, *Long Island Is My Nation*, p. 27, no. 23; Davidson, *American Heritage History of Colonial Antiques*, p. 73. The front stretcher is restored.
[2] This chair is illustrated in Sherman, *Sherman Genealogy*, p. 105; Perley, *History of Salem*, 3:390–91. I am indebted to Nancy Goyne Evans for calling this chair to my attention.
[3] Fitch to John Crouch, November 23, 1715, Fitch letterbook, NEHGS; Fitch to Collins, April 18, 1725, Fitch to Hooglant, March 9, 1725/26, and Fitch to Col. Coddington, June 26, 1727, Fitch letterbook, MHS; January 6, 1723, Fitch account book, MHS; Suffolk Probate, 2:74.
[4] Fitch to Faneuil, April 22, 1707, Fitch letterbook, AAS.

65.
CARVED-TOP LEATHER CHAIR
Boston, Massachusetts
1700–ca.1723
WOODS: Stiles, crest rail, and stretchers, striped maple (*Acer pennsylvanicum*); seat frame, back bottom, and side rails, red oak (*Quercus rubra*)
OH 48¾″ (123.8 cm)
SH 19½″ (49.5 cm), SW 17⅞″ (45.4 cm), SD 14¾″ (37.4 cm)
PROVENANCE: 1750 House, Inc., Sheffield, Mass.; Henry Francis du Pont
54.541

In his inimitable prose style, Wallace Nutting wrote, "A class of chairs which we may call leather-backs is very satisfactory because while their general outlines are in good style, there is a simplicity and homelikeness about them which appeals."[1] In describing the charm of such plain-top chairs, Nutting, as he often did, hit upon their salient characteristic: they are "in good style" because they represent the mature fruit of Boston commercial chairmaking of the time.

Winterthur's chair is remarkable in that it is the sole example of its group that still retains the pad under its baluster-shape feet; on most of the surviving examples this pad has worn or rotted away. Since the chair cannot have lost more than a fraction of an inch of this pad, we may conclude that the present seat height, 19½″ (49.5 cm), is very nearly the original seat height of these chairs. Moreover, the lack of wear on the feet gives us a good opportunity to see the heels of the rear legs to their best advantage. These heels are less exaggerated than those on numerous English chairs of this period, or even on a few American cane chairs, but they do reveal that heels of this type on Boston chairs raked backward on both their front and rear surfaces, in contrast to the New York type which were chamfered on the front surfaces only (compare catalogue entries 69 and 70 and fig. 161).

On the negative side, this example had lost its carved front stretcher prior to being acquired for the Winterthur collection. In its place was a stretcher that was rectangular in section, similar to the side stretchers, and probably of nineteenth-century origin. (The crazing pattern of the varnish on this stretcher was not the same as that on other parts of the chair.) Since this stretcher was fitted into the original rectangular mortise holes in the front legs, it was evident that the chair had originally had a stretcher with rectangular tenons. Inasmuch as the only chairs of this type that have front stretchers with rectangular tenons are those with carved ornament, it was decided to restore the chair to its original appearance on the basis of similar examples in numerous private collections and museums. The present stretcher was patterned on that of one of the four chairs in Hasbrouck House at Washington's Headquarters, Newburgh, New York—a set of chairs that had been shipped to New York within weeks of their manufacture in Boston.

Chairs of this type were produced in great quantities, usually in sets of a dozen supplemented by one or two armchairs. If this is an example of the carved top, double-nailed russia-leather chair that Thomas Fitch wrote about in his letter and account books, as it ought to be, it sold for 16s. in 1707, 21s. in 1714/15, 22s. in 1717, 23s. in 1719/20, and 27s. in 1722, the year in which "new fashion" leather chairs with crook backs, molded stiles, and double-hollow-corner crest rails were first made in Boston.[2] These prices reflect the steady depreciation of Massachusetts currency during this interval rather than any basic modifications of the details of the chairs themselves, and because the general form of this chair was produced over a long period of time, it has been referrred to in the introduction and previous entries as the "standardized Boston leather chair."

Much as we would like to believe that the high prices such chairs bring today are an acknowledgment of the affectionate and careful workmanship lavished on them by the craftsmen who made them, the comparison of the relatively large number of surviving chairs of this type reveals little generic difference among them, although they vary in details. The materials used in them are uniformly the same: maple for the crest rail, stiles, legs, and stretchers; maple or oak in the back and seat rails; russia or neat leather, depending upon price and availability, for the upholstery. Carving on the crest rails and stretchers is of excellent quality, but rarely superb; the back sides are uniformly rough. With the exception of the chair in entry 64, the balusters are seldom painstakingly well-proportioned and the turning is seldom executed with refinement. In short, the standardized Boston chairs are strictly the output of professional chair-frame shops, usually working at the behest of the upholsterer who commissioned frames and sold finished chairs, and represent a high level of competence but rarely more than the standards of professional production demanded. Gone is the entasis that makes the columns on the stiles of the chairs in entries 61 and 62 remarkable; in its place is a tapered cone. Gone is the slender ring at the base of the columns of the chair in entry 64; in its place are two lightly incised grooves. Gone is the elaborately turned base of the finial that appears on the previous chair with its rounded shoulders and slender fillet; in its place is a flat-edge ring. Gone are the turned side, medial, and rear stretchers of the previous chair; in their place are the rectangular stretchers of the Cromwellian style leather chairs, which give these chairs a less busy but somewhat behind-the-times look.

It requires little imagination to visualize an apprentice or journeyman sawing boards into framing pieces, planing them smooth, cutting them into proper lengths—for 24 side stretchers, 24 side seat rails, 12 rear stretchers, 12 rear seat rails, 12 front seat rails, 12 bottom back rails, and 24 back side rails, then cutting 240 tenons for each dozen chairs (and an additional 48 for the carved crest rails and stretchers). Add to this 288 rectangular mortise holes and the 264 pin holes that must be drilled (the rear seat rail is not pinned), and we have a picture of the colossal amount of labor—none of it very highly skilled—needed to make a single set of chairs. This is not a labor of love, it is an industry. It is thus a tribute to the artistry of the turners and carvers involved in producing this style over a documentable period of fifteen years or more that these chairs achieve the effect that was intended.

Our connoisseurship is not sufficiently refined to permit us to tabulate the subtle differences among the surviving chairs, nor are we ever likely to gather together in one place all of the surviving examples that would permit us the luxury of such a study. Considering the quantities in which they were made and the long period of time that they were popular, it would be

cat. 65

foolhardy to believe that all of these chairs were made in the same shops or that the same men made the same parts of all of them.

As in London during the last quarter of the seventeenth century when cane chairs became popular, the growing demand for new fashionable upholstered chairs among colonial America's elites stimulated both master joiners and master turners to make them. Henry Allen (w. 1644, d. 1696), a long-time resident of Boston, is always referred to in the records as a "joiner," and yet, at the time of his death, the chamber over the hall in his house contained "7 frames for chairs 18 frames for stools" and 3 chests all valued at only £2.8, an indication that these were not easy-chair frames (discussed in the next section). The references are significant because the room also contained girt "web" and 46 yards of "new cloth," which suggest Allen was in the upholstered-chair business.[3]

Of the same generation as Allen was Samuel Mattocks, Sr. (b. 1659), who was sometimes called a "turner" and other times called a "chairmaker." His son, Samuel, Jr., was invariably called a "chairmaker." There is reasonable evidence to support the notion that in urban eighteenth-century New England "chairmaker" meant a maker of *framed* chairs. In October 1723, Samuel, Jr., sued John Lincoln, a Boston carver, for "work" owed to him in the amount of £4, clear evidence that Lincoln did carving on Mattocks's chairs. At the same court session, Mattocks sued John Davis, a Charlestown joiner, for a debt of £4.19.1, suggesting that Mattocks did turned work for Davis. On June 17 of the following year, Mattocks sued Edmond Perkins, the best documented of Boston's joiner/chairmakers, for a debt on his account, suggesting that Mattocks had done work for him as well.[4] Mattocks may also have handled the chairmaking department of James Mattocks's cabinetmaking business. James, a leading cabinetmaker, was Samuel's uncle.

Edmond Perkins (1683–1761) enjoyed a career that spanned the William and Mary, the Queen Anne, and the early years of the Chippendale styles. Although his activities as a cane-chair maker for Thomas Fitch are best documented, he also supplied frames for leather chairs to Samuel Grant once the fashion for cane chairs began to wane. Working with Perkins were sons William and Henry. Other chairmakers working in Boston prior to 1728 were Jabez Hunt (1698–post-1734), Fitch's nephew; John Humphrey (w. 1698–1704); Henry Maddox (w. 1697–1709); Benjamin Davis (w. 1714–18); Thomas Odell (w. 1724–28; the only Boston furniture-maker also known to have been a counterfeiter or "coiner"); and Anthony Underwood (1680–1749) and John Leach (m. 1713, d. 1748), perhaps the most successful of the group, since both left estates valued at more than £2,000.[5]

Having listed the most obvious men who could have made these chair frames, we have still covered only one of three groups of craftsmen involved in the production of leather chairs; the other two are the carvers and upholsterers. The dean of Boston's carvers was Edward Budd, Sr., who lived in Boston several years before he purchased a piece of land in the North End in 1668. Budd had a son, also named Edward, and it is not clear whether the "Edward Budd, carver" mentioned in a lawsuit on June 14, 1709, was father or son.[6] In any event,

this family maintained a continuity of craft well into the period in which carved-top leather chairs were made. In 1681, George Robinson, described as a carver, purchased land in the North End. Robinson, then 23 years old, had a son, also named George (b. 1680), who also became a carver. Both men were working in the period in which Winterthur's chair was made. The younger Robinson appears to have been particularly successful at his trade since his inventory included £139.19.8 worth of "shop goods" and £58.10.1 worth of silver "plate" at the time of his death.[7] "Richard Knight, caruer" appears on the Boston tax list of 1685, and a "Richard Knight, carver" is mentioned in the records of the Court of Common Pleas in Boston on January 22, 1701/2, but whether these two references are to the same man or a father and his son is unknown.[8] In 1713 the names of two more carvers appear in public records—William Shute and Jacob Crouch. Crouch is never mentioned again in the records. Shute became a successful craftsman and apparently continued working at his trade. At his death (1746) he owned "20 carving tools" worth 2s.6d., 73 worth 1s., and other tools worth £21.18.3.[9] In 1721, Gabriel Habbot, a stranger, arrived. On November 24, 1730, he was still working in Boston, for Samuel Grant paid him £12 for carving "a Sion [sign] 8 feet long" for the ship *Success*.[10] And John Lincoln worked in Boston in 1723 and was sufficiently well established to have another carver, Thomas Mellens, working for him.[11] The records of no other town in colonial America reveal so many carvers at work.

The final process for a leather chair was upholstering. While the books of Thomas Fitch suggest that he dominated the trade in Boston between 1695 and 1730, he was by no means the only upholsterer there. Jonathan Everard (d. 1705), identified as an "upholsterer" in 1699 and an "upholder" in 1704, first appears on a Boston tax list in 1688. In December 1696, Everard "sold and delivered . . . to John March of Newbury . . . twelve chairs alias leather chairs" worth £7.16. These chairs, valued at 13s. apiece, were undoubtedly of the high-back type. When Everard's estate was inventoried in 1705, his shop wares included "Six chair frames at 3[s. each,] Six chair frames at 2[s. each,] . . . 3 Leather Chairs at 7 [s. each,] a pc red leather at 6[s.,]" and sundry upholstery wares.[12] The listing of the chair frames in the inventory suggests that they were Everard's property; items on consignment or belonging to someone else would not have been inventoried as his. The three leather chairs appraised at 7s. each may indicate the wholesale value of a leather chair at this time. Other Boston upholsterers in this period were Francis Righton (w. 1710 or earlier, d. 1748), William Whetcomb (b. 1681, w. 1714), and William Downes (1675–1747), who amassed considerable wealth perhaps equal to Fitch's. Downes's inventory itemizes an estate worth £6,761.0.2 at the time of his death.[13]

Perhaps more significant than these native-born upholsterers are the two who came to Boston in 1700—John Cutter (or Cutler) and George Baker, "late of London."[14] By 1714 or 1715 Rupert Lord was in Boston and two years later "Samuel Gifford from London, Upholsterer" arrived. Lord may have had little impact, since his stay was short, but

Gifford was still there in 1723, despite having been "warned to depart the town" six years earlier.[15]

The listing of eleven chair-frame makers, eight carvers, and nine upholsterers working in Boston makes several points. Most obviously it shows, by the sheer numbers, that Boston must have dominated the furniture trade of New England in the first quarter of the eighteenth century. Second, it illustrates how a quality object can be produced in an urban setting: it is the result of combined special skills. Third, it shows how impossible it is to attribute a surviving object to one craftsman or one shop and how meaningless such an attribution would be. Last, it points out that new craftsmen coming into a community may interject, at crucial moments, new ideas about styles.

The original walnut stain on Winterthur's chair is covered by a modern varnish. Its front stretcher was made by Mervin Martin in 1977. The top ¼″ (0.6 cm) of all the seat rails is replaced, indicating that the seat was originally double nailed with a strip of leather between the rows of nails, as on the chair in the preceding entry. The back was probably double nailed

as well. The feet have lost a fraction of an inch, and the leather currently on the chair is modern.

NOTES
[1] Nutting, *Pilgrim Century* (2d ed.), pp. 330, 322.
[2] Fitch to Faneuil, April 22, 1707, Fitch letterbook, AAS; Fitch to Faneuil, February 8, 1714/15, Fitch to Atkinson, April 17, 1714, Fitch letterbook, NEHGS; January 21, 1719/20, June 9, 1722, Fitch account book, MHS.
[3] Suffolk Probate, 11:163–64.
[4] Suffolk Superior Court Files, 111: leaf 33, 127: leaf 40; Suffolk Common Pleas, 9:199, 10:346–47, 9:353, 11:65.
[5] Sewall, *Diary*, 1:607–8; Suffolk Probate, 42:123–24; January 21, 1720/21, February 19, 1721/22, March 4, 1722/23, Fitch account book, MHS; Kaye, "Eighteenth-Century Boston Furniture Craftsmen," p. 287; Jobe, "Boston Furniture Industry" (conference report), p. 45.
[6] Savage, *Genealogical Dictionary*, 1:287; *Suffolk Deeds*, 5:553; Suffolk Common Pleas, 4:181.
[7] *Suffolk Deeds*, 12:231; Savage, *Genealogical Dictionary*, 3:550; Suffolk Probate, 33:271, 338; Cowan, *Members of the Ancient and Honorable Artillery Company*, p. 41.
[8] *Boston Records*, 1:79; Suffolk Common Pleas, 3:13.
[9] Suffolk Common Pleas, 5:320; Suffolk Probate, 39:38–40.
[10] November 24, 1730, Grant daybook.
[11] Suffolk Common Pleas, 10:232, 319.
[12] Suffolk Common Pleas, 2: leaf 5 verso; 3:143; *Boston Records*, 1:142. Suffolk Probate, 16:44.
[13] Suffolk Probate, 40:441.
[14] Suffolk County Court of Common Pleas, 2: leaves 104, 108 verso; 5:134.
[15] Dow, *Arts and Crafts of New England*, p. 106; Suffolk County Common Pleas, 6:326; 10:346; *Boston Records*, 13:29.

66.
CARVED-TOP LEATHER CHAIR
Boston, Massachusetts
1700–ca.1723
WOODS: All a maple of the soft group, except seat rails and right and bottom rails of back panel, red oak (*Quercus rubra*)
OH 47⅛″ (119.7 cm)
SH 18¼″ (46.4 cm), SW 18″ (45.7 cm), SD 15″ (38.1 cm)
PROVENANCE: Gift of Henry Francis du Pont
54.540

In the previous entry, it was asserted that the standardized Boston leather chairs were virtually identical in genre but differed in detail. This chair, which at first glance seems identical to the previous example—given the differences in the front stretchers—is in fact quite different in the articulation and disposition of its elements. The differences are easy to tabulate; they are more difficult to explain. On the front legs of the previous chair the lower balusters are compressed, on this chair they are less so; the distance from the beginning of the rake of the back on the former chair to the top of the finial is 28½″ (68.5 cm), on this chair it is 28″ (71.1 cm); the column on the previous chair measures 10¾″ (27.3 cm), on this chair it is 9½″ (24.1 cm); the blocks into which the back rails fit are also of different size on the two chairs. Although it is easy to see that these chairs are more or less the same type and style, when looked at singly it is clear that they are not made from the same patterns; the vergiers, or sweeps, that were used to lay out turnings on the legs of the two chairs were not the same nor really closely related (fig. 172). The same may be said for the patterns that were used to lay out the crest rails prior to carving. The crest rail of the former chair is 6¾″ (17.15 cm) high, and the pattern is more vertical in appearance than that of the

Fig. 172. Detail of the turning on the stiles of two Boston leather chairs dating from 1700 to 1723. The chair on the left is catalogue entry 65, the chair on the right is catalogue entry 66. (Winterthur 54.541, 54.540.)

cat. 66

present chair, which is 6⁵⁄₁₆″ (16 cm) high. Any thought that these are the inevitable changes that occur in a man's work over time may be dismissed; time affects only the workmanship of risk (details of the execution) and not the workmanship of certainty (the pattern used). Thus the chairs prove that at least two sets of patterns existed. It is unlikely that these two sets of patterns were used in the same shop in order to permit more than one craftsman to produce parts at the same time, because within a shop the patterns would have to be the same to insure uniformity of chairs within the sets. The inescapable conclusion is that more than one shop was producing these chairs.

In the introduction to this section, it was stated that chairmakers offered numerous optional variations for the chairs. It is clear that a banister-back version with flag or rush bottoms (see fig. 153) was available. A chair of this description was itemized in the Fitch accounts for November 27, 1722, when he billed "18 carved flag chairs" to Timothy Woodbridge of Newbury at 10s.[1] The additional option—plain as opposed to carved-top chairs—is also well documented. These plain-top chairs, with a simple, chamfered crest rail, have survived in some numbers and may be identified by the rear stiles, which are identical to those on Winterthur's chair. The front stretcher design on the majority of those chairs, however, is usually different from this one. It consists of balusters and rings, as is illustrated in figure 152. It is similar in the style but not the execution to the stretchers of the New York chairs (see catalogue entries 69, 70, and 71). Boston chairs of this type usually have one stretcher on each side, New York chairs have two.[2]

A curious chair of this group is illustrated as no. 389 in Nutting's *Pilgrim Century*. Since it was well known that crest rails which project above the stiles of these chairs are easily broken, the dealer or collector who had acquired that chair probably assumed that the top rail had been broken and then chamfered to clean it up and retain the chair's usefulness; thus he had a restorer carefully piece a "proper" carved top onto the obviously old piece of wood that was there (the joint clearly shows in the photograph). This little exercise in connoisseurship would merely be academic except that Nutting chose this chair to make a comment that is true but does not apply in that instance. Nutting advised, "It is a curious fact that carving on chairs of this type . . . is done much better, in most cases, than the carving on cabinet furniture."[3] While the carving on this group of eighteenth-century chairs is good, Nutting was admiring a piece of twentieth-century restoration. His comment teaches another lesson as well; we must exercise caution in making generalizations and comparisons on the basis of estimated dates. Nutting dated these chairs in the period 1680 to 1700, a full generation earlier than they were

actually made, because of his knowledge about case furniture. The analogy was false. We now know that this carving on chairs was most fashionable during the first quarter of the eighteenth century, a time when urban carving on American case furniture was rare, indeed, even unfashionable.

Winterthur's chair illustrates one further option of the customer for leather chairs in the first quarter of the eighteenth century: the pairing of a carved top with a turned front stretcher. This option may have reduced the price of a chair by 1s. or so and saved 14s. on a set of 12 side chairs and 2 armchairs, and this may explain the shilling or so variation in the cost of chairs billed in the Fitch accounts. For example, on June 2, 1722, Fitch billed Estis Hatch for "12 rushia leather chairs" 23s. apiece" and 7 days later billed William Dyre for "6 carved Russhia Chairs" at 24s. each.[4] In short, it cannot be assumed that the turned stretcher represents a later version of these chairs: doubtless the options were available from the time the chairs were first introduced.

The symmetrical turned stretcher is of larger significance. On either side of the central spool is a baluster and a ring that is slightly concave on its outside face. This turning may be associated with a number of upholstered Boston chairs and appears to define the turning style of one of the major shops of Boston in this period (see figs. 153 and 160, and catalogue entry 75). For the sake of convenience, this type of turning has been called "bipartite" in this book, to differentiate it from the "tripartite" type that appears on the I group of cane chairs, the Boston leather armchairs with crook backs, and one upholstered chair (catalogue entries 54, 76, 79, 85). The turning also may have been the source for those on the front stretcher of Philadelphia leather chairs made in the Boston manner (catalogue entry 80).

Although we know that the second version of the Boston leather chair—the type with molded stiles and Spanish feet—began to appear in 1722, it is quite likely that the carved-top version continued to be made throughout the 1720s. Presumptive evidence of this is furnished by a chair in a private collection in Connecticut. That chair is identical to Winterthur's in every respect except one—it has a banister, or "splat," in place of the leather back.[5] All evidence indicates that the banister is original on that chair and thus dates the chair from no earlier than 1729 or 1730, when this stylistic device began to appear in Boston.

NOTES
[1] November 27, 1722, Fitch account book, MHS. An armchair of this type is illustrated in Lockwood, *Colonial Furniture* (2d ed.), fig. 463.
[2] Lyon, *Colonial Furniture*, fig. 69 appears to be a New York chair, but contrast with it fig. 159.
[3] Nutting, *Pilgrim Century* (2d ed.), pp. 325, 335.
[4] June 2 and 9, 1722, Fitch account book, MHS.
[5] I am indebted to Robert F. Trent for calling my attention to this chair.

cat. 67

67.
CARVED-TOP BANISTER-BACK CHAIR
Boston or Charlestown, Massachusetts
1710–1740
WOODS: Left rear leg, poplar (genus *Populus*); bottom back frame, an American ash
OH 48¾″ (123. 8 cm)
SH 18″ (45.7 cm), SW 19″ (48.3 cm), SD 14″ (35.6 cm)
PROVENANCE: Gift of Henry Francis du Pont
57.530

Winterthur's fine example of the inexpensive, banister-back version of the leather-upholstered chairs made in Boston is similar to that illustrated as figure 153 and displays a number of features that were later widely copied by country turners. One important design shift was the adoption by Boston shops of the flatwise-framed seat with prominent exposed front corner blocks. While it provided a neater-looking, more comfortable seat than earlier versions where the front posts projected above the rush seat, this solution left a gap between the upper stretcher blocks on the front posts and the seat, a space that chairmakers frequently filled with a combination of turned vases and reels. Later versions of the same chair, updated with crook-back rails, rounded crest, and vasiform banister of the Queen Anne style, improved this formula by elongating the last vase turning on the front posts until it reached the corner block. Another detail seen here that influenced many rural turners is the profile of the lower back rail, which takes the form of two console brackets set back-to-back. Most rural versions did not have carved crests and instead had flat crests scalloped in any one of a variety of "crown" profiles. This may indicate that rural turners generally did not have access to professional carvers or that their clients could not afford the added cost of carved rails.

68.

CARVED-TOP LEATHER CHAIR
England or America
1710–1720
WOODS: All black walnut (*Juglans nigra*)
OH 44⅞″ (114.0 cm)
SH 18⅜″ (46.7 cm), SW 17⅜″ (44.1 cm), SD 14⅞″ (37.8 cm)
PROVENANCE: Bequest of Henry Francis du Pont
59.2116

Fig. 173. Leather chair with turned stiles and molded and carved crest rail, England, 1690–1720. European beech (*Fagus sylvatica*) with walnut stain, H 47⅛″ (119.7 cm), W 17¼″ (43.8 cm), D 14⅝″ (37.1 cm), SH 18⅛″ (46.1 cm). (Winterthur 58.586.)

Despite the knowledge that this chair is made totally of American black walnut (*Juglans nigra*) and, therefore, stands a very good chance of having been made in America, none of the stylistic devices or quirks of articulation on it relate to any of the identified American examples in the collections surveyed for this catalogue. The columnar shapes on the stiles do generally relate to those on the Bybee chair (fig. 157), although here they are rather more coarsely executed. Both have a prominent collarino on the rear stiles, and the rings above the bases of the columns are similar, but these are common features on European chairs, too, and offer poor grounds for attribution. The columns lack entasis, and the blocks are much squarer than those usually found on American urban chairs of this period. The finials are rather fatter than those on either New England or New York examples, and the topmost element has an unusual extra fillet turned on it. The balusters on the front legs also differ from the more common American types in that they are large, pearlike forms set upon well-articulated compressed spools, or reels. The carving is much deeper than that found on the typical American chair of this period and represents the highest level of workmanship of any of the crafts employed in making this chair.

Documentary evidence that some American black walnut was shipped to Europe at the turn of the eighteenth century has prompted a search for furniture of that wood in the then current styles in England today. The search has not been rewarding. Those few pieces of English furniture made of black walnut are usually of a much higher quality than is this chair. The expenses involved with cutting and transporting that wood to England made it a costly investment for furniture. Price may explain why the English used black walnut primarily for wainscotting rooms. In aesthetic terms, however, chairs were a more logical use of black walnut in England because the absence of the dark striations in the wood would not have been considered detrimental to a turned and carved chair. Black walnut rarely appears as a veneer; the beautifully striated European walnut (sometimes called "Circassian" today and "French" in the eighteenth century, although both are botanically the same wood, *Juglans regia*) was most often used for that purpose.

References to walnut chairs occasionally appear in early eighteenth-century American inventories, particularly those of New York and further south. Where these walnut chairs originated is never clear from these documents, and we cannot automatically assume that they were made in America. In at least two widely separated instances, black walnut chairs were ordered from England by distinguished and wealthy Americans, James Logan in 1712/13 and Samuel Sewall in 1719/20.[1]

One aspect of the Winterthur chair that would be unusual

in an English chair is that the seat rails, normally covered with upholstery, are made of black walnut—a profligate use if the wood were imported. Such use was unusual in New England or New York; oak was often more common for the rails of upholstered chairs at that period. A close examination of the rails under the upholstery of Winterthur's chair revealed that the seat was never half-upholstered over the rail, unlike the middle-colonies chairs illustrated in entries 73 and 82.

Walnut chairs occasionally appear in the inventories of Massachusetts during the last quarter of the seventeenth century, but were by no means common until the advent of the cabriole-leg style, and even then they were still valued at advanced levels.[2] The taste for walnut chairs was undoubtedly present early in the eighteenth century since most of the urban New England examples from that time were stained or "colored" walnut; the scarcity of walnut chairs reflected the scarcity of native walnut itself, which grew in New England only in isolated clumps. Further evidence of the scarcity of walnut in Massachusetts may be inferred from shipping records. On November 20, 1718, the brig *Elizabeth*, with Joseph Prince as master, set sail from Virginia for Boston with a load of "walnut plank," which surely would have been the American equivalent of carrying coals to Newcastle had the wood been readily available in New England.[3] Walnut is most common in Pennsylvania furniture, but no Philadelphia-made leather chairs with turned stiles have been positively identified.

The possibility of a New York origin for Winterthur's chair is suggested by the double side stretchers. This trait, however, carries little weight in this instance inasmuch as Winterthur owns a closely related chair made of European beech (*Fagus sylvatica*) with the same characteristic (fig. 173). The two

cat. 68

chairs are similar in size, design, and articulation, and are related to a chair owned by SPNEA and displayed in the Rundlett-May House, Portsmouth, New Hampshire. The SPNEA chair is also made of beech and varies from the Winterthur example slightly in the internal carving of the crest rail. It is possible that both it and the Winterthur beech chair may have been imported into this country during the period in which the William and Mary style was fashionable.[4] Winterthur's beech chair retains its original simulated-walnut stain.

On balance, the unfamiliar characteristics of Winterthur's walnut chair outweigh the familiar ones. In spite of this, the chair may someday be proved to have been made in an urban center such as Charlestown, Cambridge, Salem, Newport, or Philadelphia, for which we have been unable to identify any pre-cabriole-leg–style leather chairs, or in New York where only one such school of chairmaking has been identified.

If Winterthur's black walnut chair can someday be proved to have been made in America, it is possible that its design was developed from the imported examples: a clever craftsman would need to see such a chair only once to be able to duplicate its attributes. And if it is American, then the existence of almost identical European examples has frightening implications for the dealer, collector, or scholar who would assert the American origin of chairs in this early period solely on the basis of stylistic attributes.

Approximately 1″ (2.5 cm) is missing from the bottoms of all four feet of this chair.

NOTES
[1] Logan to Askew, February 20, 1712/13, August 1, 1713, correspondence book, Logan papers, HSP (I am indebted to Bradford L. Rauschenberg for these references); Sewall, memoranda [to Samuel Storke], February 20, 1719/20, Sewall, *Letter-Book*, 2:106; Sewall, *Diary*, 2:954–55.
[2] See Jobe, "The Boston Furniture Industry 1720–1740" (conference report), and Saltar, "New England Timbers."
[3] Massachusetts Shipping Returns, 1686–1719, folio 116, CO 5.848.
[4] I am indebted to Richard Nylander for providing samples of the SPNEA chairs for microanalysis. A chair that combines features of the Winterthur chair and the SPNEA chair is illustrated in Nutting, *Pilgrim Century* (2d ed.), fig. 385.

69.
PLAIN-TOP CHAIR WITH DOUBLE-NAILED LEATHER
New York, New York
1707–1725
WOODS: All turned elements, a maple of the soft group; stretchers, back rails, and seat rails, red oak (*Quercus rubra*)
OH 43⅜″ (110.2 cm)
SH 19¾″ (50.2 cm), SW 17⅝″ (44.8 cm), SD 14⅜″ (36.5 cm)
PROVENANCE: Gift of Henry Francis du Pont
54.547

70.
PLAIN-TOP CHAIR WITH DOUBLE-NAILED LEATHER
New York, New York
1707–1725
WOODS: All turned elements, a maple of the soft group; stretchers, back rails, and seat rails, red oak (*Quercus rubra*)
OH 43⅛″ (109.5 cm)
SH 19¾″ (50.2 cm), SW 17¾″ (45.1 cm), SD 14½″ (36.8 cm)
PROVENANCE: Gift of Henry Francis du Pont
54.548

Although the Winterthur collection does not include a Boston-made example of the plain-top leather chair, it does have three New York examples, of which the present two chairs form a pair, while the third chair is the focus of catalogue entry 71. Only one other plain-top side chair (see fig. 174) has a New York history of ownership. That chair possesses rear stiles of the same general design as the present chairs, but does not appear to have been made in the same shop.

Winterthur's chairs display several distinctive quirks of workmanship not found in the Boston examples, even though all the American-made leather-upholstered chairs in this style are framed in the same basic manner. Here the crest and lower back rails bow backward slightly, and every turned ring is fat and full; a flat-bottom cap tops the lower baluster on each stile—a characteristic also visible on a Dutch chair illustrated by Willem Vogelsang in *Le meuble Hollandais* as figure 151. This flat-bottom turning, which joins the baluster beneath it rather abruptly, is also visible on the Bybee chair and on another plain-top New York armchair (see figs. 157 and 159). The rear feet are chamfered on the front face but are straight on the rear surface and thus do not rake backward to suggest the heels so common on Boston chairs. The double side stretchers of the Cromwellian style are retained, as opposed to the single ones on the chairs of the Boston school in this period and, further, they are made of oak, rather than the maple so common on Boston chairs. The rear stretcher enters the legs on the same level as the side stretcher, which is also different from the Boston type. That the legs and stiles are of maple and the stretchers, back rails, and seat are of oak is a clear indication that the maker intended to stain or paint the chairs. Microscopic analysis of a small section of no. 70 reveals that at some time in its history this chair was covered with a coat of black paint. Under the paint is a layer of brown stain, which may be original.

Old tack holes near the top of the seat rails reveal that the double-nailed upholstery now on the chairs is a proper restoration. Double-nailed seats are always accompanied by a band of leather between the rows of tacks. This band functions visually in the same way that fringe does on a cloth-upholstered chair of this period: the ornamental border and decorative brass nails conceal the unsightly row of upholstery tacks, which actually hold the leather bottom in place. The presence of rings on the barrel turnings between the seat and the bottom back rail, as opposed to the scored lines in the analogous position of

Fig. 174. Plain-top leather chair, New York, ca. 1718. (Private collection.)
The chair has a history of ownership in Kingston, N.Y.

under the influence of these Dutch ideas, and it is equally possible that the style made its way to New York directly from England, since the colonial records of New York reveal that chairs were shipped there from England as well as from Boston. For example, on March 11, 1701, John Potter of New York imported six chairs from London on the *Antiqua Merchant*, so there is no question that the English fashion in chairs was known there at the beginning of the eighteenth century.[2] But the resemblance to Dutch chairs with similar elaborately turned stiles suggests that either furniture from the Netherlands continued to come into New York as it had in the previous century, or a chairmaker from the North Netherlands had emigrated to New York and brought this style of turning with him. In the absence of documents that would confirm either conjecture, perhaps all we can safely argue is that the stiles of these chairs are unlike those on the Boston examples.

A provocative series of letters from Thomas Fitch in Boston to Benjamin Faneuil in New York gives us a number of insights into the story of plain-top chairs in New York. On June 23, 1707, in the first of what would ultimately be a lengthy correspondence on this topic, Fitch enclosed "a receipt for . . . six Neats leather chairs double nail'd in my acco[un]t for tryale at 14s/6d apcs." On March 8, 1707/8, he sent six more and with instructions "please to make the most ye can of them and Invest the produce in good Spring beavers when at 4[s.]6d. or not exceeding 4[s.]9d." On April 12 he sent a half-dozen more "chairs double nail'd," and on April 16 he mentioned that they are "consigned yo for sale. The lowest price of them here is 16s. a pcs." On June 21 he sent 6 more and on July 19 he wrote, reassuringly, "they sell very readily here and doubt not of yor ease to sell them there." On July 11, 1709 —almost a year later—Fitch queried "I wonder the chairs did not sell; I have sold a pretty many of that sort to Yorkers . . . and tho some are carv'd yet I make Six plain to one carv'd; and can't make the plain so fast as they are bespoke, so you may assure thm that are customers that they are not out of fashion here. . . . I submit the price of them to yor prudence. Its bettr to sell than let them lie; It might be best to have them rub'd over that they may look fresher." In 1711, "Sir, by yours of the 21 of May I perceive yo had finished the sale of my chairs"—three years and two months after they had been sent to New York.[3]

There are three possible explanations for the sequence of events: perhaps plain-top chairs were not considered fashionable in New York, or perhaps the demand for plain-top chairs in New York was being satisfied by New York chairmakers, or perhaps plain-top chairs did not become popular in New York until a later date.

Lacking as we do any clues other than a few histories of ownership and the chairs themselves, it is difficult to extract the names of the men who could have made these chairs from the lists of New York craftsmen at work during the first quarter of the eighteenth century. The records have revealed the name of only one carver there at this time, John Price who lived at Turtle Bay. It is not known how long he worked, but his will was proved on June 1, 1715.[4]

The unusual articulation of the arm of the van Cortlandt family chair (see fig. 158) suggests the frame maker was of northern European or perhaps French extraction. Among the

the Boston chairs, is a distinctive feature. The design of the column on the stiles of these particular examples differs slightly from the usual type in that the collarino, which has a fillet turned beneath it (as on the Bybee chair), is very near the top of the column while the capital itself has additional elaborations that detract from its academic character. Indeed, all of these turnings exhibit an elaboration and complexity of elements that would never be confused with those of the Boston version.

It is not certain how the idea for the design of the turned stiles on these chairs found its way into New York. The identical idea of a column upon a small baluster upon an elongated baluster appears on a highchair of European beech (*Fagus sylvatica*) in the collection of the Rijksmuseum, Amsterdam (see fig. 163). That chair is of North Netherlands origin and was made in the last quarter of the seventeenth century.[1] It has fat rings on the stiles, a dropped collarino on the column, and a flat-bottom cap turned on the arm support. In addition it has a finial that is very much like those on the Bybee chair and related examples, and may even have been the inspiration for the finials that appear on the Boston-made chairs illustrated in entries 64 and 66, so many of which were made to be shipped to New York.

Countless English chairs of this period were also made

cat. 69

cat. 70

New York joiners there are several candidates: John le Chevalier, admitted as a freeman on October 1, 1695; Frans Cowenhover, admitted as a freeman on August 30, 1698 (d. 1748); Jean (later John) Suire, naturalized in 1701 and who possessed "8 leather chairs and 1 old Elbow chair" valued at £4 at the time of his death on March 12, 1715; James Gautier, who took James Davy as apprentice for seven years on December 7, 1718; John Pelletreau, admitted as a freeman on April 2, 1719, and Francis Clerembault, who was likewise admitted on October 13, 1724.[5]

The tragic loss of New York probate records in a fire in 1911 has prevented us from gathering the information we need to be more precise about the makers of New York's chairs; however, at least John Suire's estate inventory has survived. Suire, who came from "St. Seurin de Montagne, Saintonge, France"— perhaps the modern town called *Saintes* on the Bay of Biscay —had unfinished case furniture in his shop, but more importantly possessed "7 matted chair[s]" valued together at 9s. 6d. He also had "a parcel of rushes for chairs," which suggests that he made the matted chairs. His "3 Indian drest [dressed] Deerskins" valued at £1.3 and "2 skins of Neat [ox] Leather" valued at a little less than £1 could have been used for upholstering.[6] Since the rush-bottom chair illustrated in Nutting's *Furniture Treasury* as no. 1930, the Pruyn family chair illustrated in Singleton's *Furniture of Our Forefathers* (p. 241), and the van Cortlandt leather chair are the only group of chairs from New York that exhibit an identifiable familial resemblance, it does not seem illogical to suggest that they may have been made by a craftsman like Suire.

A number of turners with northern European names were also working in New York between 1699 and 1726 and they too may have had a hand in these chairs. Among them are Johannes Tiebout, made a freeman of New York on February 2, 1698/99; Jacob Blom, freeman on July 26, 1699, and still working in 1723; William Bogaert, who took Jacob Coursen as an apprentice for six years beginning October 20, 1701; Aaron Boagard, who apparently had an active shop inasmuch as he took apprentices in 1718, 1719, and 1720; Aaron or Arent Bloom, made a freeman on September 6, 1698 (d. 1709); Johannes van Gelder, called a "carpenter" when he was made a freeman on August 30, 1698, but called a "turner" when he and Johanes Brestead, also a turner, executed the estate of Hans Kierstede on March 3, 1712; Adrian Bogard, who took Louis Boumie apprentice on April 13, 1724; and Joh[anes?] Breedsteed, who took Gabriel van Laer as an apprentice for seven years beginning February 1, 1719.[7]

Of course, the idea that the chairs betray a northern European stylistic influence may be mere wool gathering, since England's chairmakers were influenced by this same source. In this respect, consideration of the Dutch/English/German arts of New York always poses a problem. If these stylistic ideas were coming from England, however, then we must ask ourselves why we do not see their attributes more often in New England furniture and why there are no documented examples of this type of chair with histories of ownership in Massachusetts.

To some extent the argument that these chairs are not recognizably English confirms the idea advanced in the introduction to this section that they were not made for an English taste. English taste was undoubtedly satisfied in New York by the chairs imported from Boston or by direct copies, such as the Van Alen House chair (see fig. 160). But the role of customer preference in the style of an object cannot be ignored and may be especially relevant here inasmuch as three of the four upholsterers who can be identified from the New York records appear to be Englishmen. The earliest upholsterer's name to appear in the New York documents surveyed for this catalogue is that of Anthony Chishull who was made a freeman on January 28, 1701/2. Five and a half years later comes the first mention of a second upholsterer, Richard Lott, who was made a freeman on September 30, 1707. On October 12, 1714, an upholsterer with the unusual name of Germanicus Andrews—perhaps a second generation New Yorker—was also made a freeman. His career was brief, for his death is recorded in 1718. Thomas Wenman, the last upholsterer on the list, was made a freeman on November 10, 1719.[8] The short list of upholsterers suggests that there was relatively little upholstering to be done there. That the first man to practice that trade does not appear in the town until the year 1702 additionally suggests that the competition from the merchants of the town for the textile aspect of the upholstery trade was significant and that perhaps the activities of the four upholsterers we have identified in the little community were confined to the more menial and less lucrative aspects of journeyman upholstering.

The upholstery on both of Winterthur's chairs has been replaced, and the original walnut stain on their frames has been removed.

NOTES

[1] Lunsingh Scheurleer, *Catalogus van meubelen*, p. 216, no. 228. I am indebted to Mr. R. J. van Wandelen, furniture conservator at the Rijksmuseum, for the wood analysis of the chair.

[2] *Account of Her Majesty's Revenue in the Province of New York*, p. 4.

[3] Fitch to Faneuil, June 23, 1707, March 8, 1707/8, April 12, 16, June 21, and July 19, 1708, July 11, 1709, and September 10, 1711, Fitch letterbook, A.A.S.

[4] *Abstracts of Unrecorded Wills*, pp. 13–14. Price died childless, and we do not know if he ever trained apprentices.

[5] Le Chevalier, Cowenhoven, Pelletreau, and Clerembault are included among *Burghers . . . and Freemen*, pp. 58, 66, 98, 105. Gautier is specified in *Indentures of Apprentices*, p. 117. New York Probate mentions Cowenhoven in Liber 4:208, and Suire in Liber 2:256. Suire is also listed in Secords, *Biographical Sketches . . . of New Rochelle*, p. 50 (I am indebted to Mrs. William Heidgerd for this reference).

[6] Secords, *Biographical Sketches . . . of New Rochelle*, p. 50. New York Wills, Liber B: pt. 2, pp. 256–57 (I am indebted to Neil Duff Kamil for calling this portion of the inventory to my attention).

[7] See *Burghers . . . and Freemen*, p. 72 (Tiebout), p. 63 (Blom), p. 600 (Bogaert & Courson), p. 70 (Bloom), p. 68 (van Gelder); Lois Olcott Price notes, in Forman files (Blom); *Indentures of Apprentices*: (Boagard) p. 114, (Bogard) p. 164, (van Laer) p. 156; *Abstracts of Unrecorded Wills*: (van Gelder) p. 173; and New York Probate: Liber 3:30 (Bloom). The Bogaert, Boagard, and Bogard families were all probably one and the same.

[8] *Burghers . . . and Freemen*, pp. 76, 87, 92, 99.

71.
PLAIN-TOP LEATHER CHAIR
New York, New York
1710–1725
WOODS: All turned members are American silver maple (*Acer saccharinum*); seat rails, back and side stretchers, and back panel rails, red oak (*Quercus rubra*)
OH 43⅝″ (110.8 cm)
SH 19½″ (49.5 cm), SW 17⅝″ (44.8 cm), SD 14¾″ (37.4 cm)
PROVENANCE: Gift of Henry Francis du Pont
58.570

Since this chair is closely related to the previous two examples, it raises the issue of chronology. The evidence is mixed. On this chair the finials, lacking the characteristic compressed ball at the top, suggest a carelessness in workmanship that might well indicate the kind of change that usually occurs with the passage of time. Balanced against that is the much more academic rendering of the columns, which suggests that they are closer to the prototype and hence earlier than those of the previous example. That the balusters on the rear stiles between the seat and bottom back rail have replaced the ringed barrel shapes of the previous chairs would seem to indicate a later date of manufacture. The absence of any quarter-round turnings with a flat bottom suggests that this chair and the previous examples were not made in the same shop.

A clue to the approximate date of manufacture for this chair is contained in the history of ownership of a closely related chair (fig. 174), now in a private collection in Massachusetts. It has features that relate to the previous two chairs and the present one, although it is somewhat more loosely turned. It retains the knot at the top of each finial which reveals that the finials of no. 71 have not been greatly altered, as we might suspect when comparing them with the Bybee chair (see fig. 157), although they have been abused. The chair pictured in figure 174 was purchased from Fred J. Johnston of Kingston, New York, on October 23, 1974, at which time the following information was made available to the present owner: "This chair," wrote Johnston, "belonged to Pieter Vanderlyn, descended to his son, Nicholas, and to his son, John on his death. All the Vanderlyn heirlooms went to an Aunt Kate Vanderlyn, on her death to Judge Schoonmaker, and to his daughter, Mrs. Lawton. From her estate it was purchased."[1] If Pieter Vanderlyn (1687–1778) was the original owner of the chair and bought it new, it is possible that he acquired it at about the time he emigrated from Holland to New York, circa 1718. The Winterthur example ought to date from about that same time.

One additional chair of this type, formerly owned by Joseph Downs, but with no history of family ownership, is now in the Hendrickson House, Wilmington, Delaware. This chair enlarges our knowledge of the upholstery trade in New York by one more mite: it has its original upholstery, and that upholstery is russia leather.[2]

It is obvious that high-back plain-top leather chairs must have replaced chairs in the Cromwellian style in New York just as they did in Boston. The inventories of early eighteenth-century New York are so scarce that it is virtually useless to try to interpret the references to leather chairs in them statistically. The 1686 inventory of Cornelis Stenwick, a wealthy merchant, reveals that "5 rush leather Chayers" in his kitchen chamber were valued at 6s. each. They were the most expensive chairs in his estate, of which the movables amounted to £2,664.18.9. It is likely that these chairs were low-back chairs in the earlier style, and their value reflects the appraisals of such chairs in Boston at this period. This notion is further strengthened by the mention, two years later, of a dozen turkey-work chairs in the estate of Francis Richardson, a New York merchant, appraised at £7 or 11s. 8d. each—about the proper ratio between turkey-work and leather chairs. On May 18, 1704, 13 leather chairs were valued at £3.5 or 5s. each in the inventory of Col. William Smith, a well-to-do mariner whose estate amounted to £2,589.4. In 1715, when the goods of joiner John Suire were inventoried, his leather chairs were appraised at 8s. 6d. each.[3] Since Suire did not arrive in New York until after 1701, it is possible that his leather chairs, valued at almost a third more than the seventeenth-century examples in much grander estates, are of the new style. Even after we calculate level of inflation during the first two decades of the eighteenth century, these chairs probably cost about as much as the plain-top chairs that Fitch was sending to Faneuil priced at 14s. 6d. and 16s. between 1706 and 1715.

No inventory references reveal how long the taste for plain-top leather chairs persisted in New York, but it is probable that it did not long survive the introduction of the "Rushia Leather Chairs newest fashion" with molded stiles and embowed backs that Fitch shipped to Adam Powell in New York in April 1724. A chair of this type branded with the initials of Robert Sanders and his grandson Philip van Rensselaer (Albany Institute of History and Art) shows that the style made its way to Albany, perhaps with some speed. In spite of this, it is possible that the old style, "being so sutable for Country people and really cheap," continued to find a ready market.[4]

The paint on Winterthur's chair probably dates from the middle of the nineteenth century. It consists of a black wash over an ocher ground.

NOTES

[1] Johnston to owner, October 23, 1974; owner to Forman, June 11, 1977.
[2] I am indebted to Deborah Dependahl Waters for calling this chair to my attention (DAPC 76.472, Winterthur Library).
[3] New York Probate, Liber 19B: pt. 2, p. 220; Liber 14A: 46; Liber 6: 123; and Liber 19B: pt. 2, p. 256.
[4] Fitch to Powell, April 4, 1724, Fitch letterbook, MHS. The Fitch account book, [ca. March 19,] 1723/24, MHS, reveals that these side chairs had "crook'd backs" and were priced at 27s. each. Rice, New York Furniture, p. 20; Fitch to Wendell, May 16, 1709, Fitch letterbook, AAS.

72.
CARVED TOP, BANISTER-BACK ELBOW CHAIR WITH
WOODEN BOTTOM
Probably Philadelphia, Pennsylvania
1710–1730
WOOD: Black walnut (*Juglans nigra*)
OH 52½″ (133.4 cm)
SH 18″ (45.7 cm), SW 26½″ (67.3 cm), SD 17¾″ (45.1 cm)
PROVENANCE: Mary Thornton collection, Milan, Ohio; Timothy and Pamela
Hill, American Antiques, South Lyon, Mich.; purchased by the museum
76.173

This great chair, like cane chairs attributed to Philadelphia
elsewhere in this catalogue, is somewhat controversial. Its only
wood is American black walnut, the wood of choice for the
finest furniture made in Philadelphia before 1725, and although that wood was exported, there are reasons that strongly
suggest that this is a Philadelphia product.

At first glance, the chair seems peculiar. Its arms, framed
board seat, and flat carving on the front stretcher and crest are
reminiscent of joiner's work, while its basic structure is the

work of an able turner. The back, composed of two uprights run with moldings flanking four narrower plain struts, calls to mind certain English upholstered chairs. Some of the turned ornament, particularly the stretchers, hints at Scandinavian or North German influence. And the chair's great size makes most American collectors judge it on instinct to be English.

The key feature that points to a Philadelphia origin for the chair, aside from the confluence of stylistic traits, is the carving. Without question, the maker of the chair trained in northern England, probably Lancashire, where the same style of carving is found on joined back stools (fig. 175). There, low-relief carving articulated with incised veins is often contained within arched crests and flanked by a simple molded surround. The same joiners and turners who were responsible for some of the so-called Chester County wainscot chairs may have experimented with the cane-chair style before migrating to Pennsylvania. Once in the colony, they may have been further influenced by Scandinavian turning.

Most of the chair is intact, but 3½″ (8.9 cm) of the four feet have been pierced out, and the form of the feet, while plausible, is conjectural.

73.
LEATHER CHAIR WITH TURNED CREST RAIL
Possibly Delaware, or perhaps New Jersey or Pennsylvania
1690–1720
WOOD: American beech (*Fagus grandifolia*)
OH 46⅛″ (117.2 cm)
SH 19″ (48.3 cm), SW 17⅞″ (45.4 cm), SD 15″ (38.1 cm)
PROVENANCE: Bequest of Henry Francis du Pont
54.519

Students of American decorative arts whose knowledge of leather-upholstered chairs is based upon familiarity with those of New England and New York greet this chair and its relatives with uncertainty. The form of these chairs is so startlingly different from that of their better-known contemporaries that it is difficult to believe that they were all being made in colonial America at the same time. At first, the chair seems to be a country chairmaker's rather bizarre interpretation of the Anglo-American leather chair of its period. The overall attenuation of its members, including the remakably thin seat rails, gives the chair a spare look. This effect is heightened by the wide gap between the seat and the lower back rail. That the rear legs are decoratively turned below the seat rail, however,

vividly demonstrates that this is no ordinary chair made by a country chairmaker, for two-axis turning, of which this is a classic example, requires a fairly sophisticated lathe and the ambition to do such work. The technique was not used by the village chairmakers of New England. Although it appears on New England chairs made in the first decade of the eighteenth century, it was not used on leather chairs prior to about 1730. Moreover, the turning on the rear legs of this chair is ornamental in design and not the plain sort so common on English-inspired cane chairs.

Closer examination reveals that the chair has other novel features. The half-round crest rail with moldings "laid on it," as Joseph Moxon would say, is obviously half of a board that was turned on its face in a lathe.[1] In addition, the absence of tack holes in the seat rails other than those needed for the present upholstery, which is original to the chair, reveals that the chair was never upholstered in any other way, and thus we may conclude that the seat was always intended to appear as it does today. Finally, the chair is made totally of American beech (*Fagus grandifolia*), an uncommon wood in middle-colonies furniture and indeed a wood not extensively used in any other

cat. 73

group of leather-upholstered American chairs, no matter where they were made.

The uprights of the back that support the upholstery and the lower margin of the lower back rail were molded with the same plane. That the moldings cut into the crest rail are not of the same profile as those of the back supports—as opposed to those on the chair illustrated in catalogue entry 82—has provoked many connoisseurs to suggest that either the crest rail or the back rails of this chair are replaced. The chair offers no evidence that this is so. The rails are made of the same wood as the rest of the chair; they have the same tool marks on them that appear on other parts of the chair and the same vestiges of the original walnut stain; and the upholstery is original. The only explanation that fits these facts is that the man who made this chair primarily thought as a turner and literally was carried away with the exhilaration of turning the crest rail and gave no thought to matching up the moldings to the rather conventional ogee plane that he possessed. The chair displays one other note of professional refinement. When stiles are turned on a man-powered lathe, the points where the wood is fitted between the puppets for turning are invariably left on the bottom of the foot and on the top of the finial. On this chair, the depressions left by the lathe points have been drilled out and filled in with tiny plugs, a unique instance of a maker's care and attention to detail on the leather-upholstered chairs of its time. The tenons that hold the crest rail in place are glued and wedged rather than pinned—a technique not found on American chairs made in the English tradition.

The immediate impulse upon approaching a piece of middle-colonies furniture about which little is known and which is not related to urban high-style prototypes is to seek northern European influences in its makeup. Confirmation of this suspicion would appear to be found in the design of the rear legs—essentially an attenuated version of the inverted baluster that is an almost ubiquitous turned form on the legs of American William and Mary-style case furniture, especially a northern European version with an elongated cap. In this case, however, the overall slimness of the turning could equally be a result of a cultural habit brought to this country by the maker of the chair. The rounded crest rail is also a motif that is fairly common in northern Europe, but it is also often seen in English West Country and North Country chairs from Derbyshire, Lancashire, and Yorkshire (see fig. 175). This last item complicates the attempt to explore the cultural origins of the craftsman who made this chair because West and North Country craftsmen as well as German and Scandinavian ones were living in Pennsylvania by the close of the seventeenth century.

The rounded crest rail and the great heels are the only aspects of the chair that can be related to the English chairmaking tradition, and even so, they are not conclusive evidence. Great heels appeared on continental chairs before they found their way onto English chairs, and on English chairs the rounded crest rail was usually sawed out, not turned.

The vast majority of the remaining details are continental. Prominent among them are the ornamentally turned rear legs, a treatment that appears to have originated in France, was quickly adopted in Scandinavia, and was abundantly used on both joined and upholstered chairs made in Sweden in

Fig. 176. Leather chair with turned stiles and carved crest rail, Sweden, 1680–1710. Beech; H 49¼″ (125 cm), W 18⅝″ (48 cm). (Göteborgs Historiska Museum, Göteborg, Sweden.) The chair is painted green and the sculptured parts are highlighted with red and gold. The black oilcloth covering the stuffed seat and back is not original.

mid century styles as well as in the later high-back chairs represented by the present example. Sigurd Erixon illustrated a number of them in *Möbler och heminredning i Svenska bygder*.[2] These chairs, although admittedly influenced by French, Dutch, and English styles, have all the characteristics of design that are visible in the American example. The inverted baluster with an elongated cap is illustrated in Erixon as fig. 678; the arched crest rail—in these instances not turned on a lathe—is to be seen on the chairs illustrated as his figs. 685 and 686, which share with the American example the great heels, a high front stretcher, low side stretchers joined by a medial stretcher, and thin seat rails. The seats of a number of these chairs (Erixon's figs. 670, 678, 679, 681, 682, and 685) are half upholstered over the rail in the same fashion as the Winterthur example. In numerous instances the upholstery is held in place by a single row of widely spaced, decorative tacks with a narrow strip of leather under them, as on Winterthur's. An unusually elaborate example in the collection of Göteborgs Historiska Museum (fig. 176), whose seat no longer has its original upholstery, reveals most of the attributes of the Swedish group and additional motifs that can be seen on the American chair. Particularly noticeable are the conically topped balusters on the front legs, the rounded top of the upholstered back, the widely spaced nails, and the great heels on the rear legs. The conical element that tops the rear stiles is almost identical to the analogous motif on the rush-bottom chair illustrated in catalogue entry 74. The resemblance between the Swedish chairs and the American example is too close to be mere coincidence; it must represent a tradition that was brought to America in the mind of a craftsman.

The American chair demonstrates the transplanted tradition in several ways. First, it, like the Göteborg example, is made of beech, rather than readily available walnut or maple, which indicates the strong hold of tradition on the maker.[3] Beech, birch, and ash are the most common woods used to make turned chairs in northern Europe. Birch was a rare wood in the temperate parts of the middle colonies, and ash was rarely used there except as seat lists and stretchers. Second, that only the seat rails are pinned and the rest of the joints are wedged demonstrates the persistence of learned techniques. And, third, that the crest rail is turned rather than sawed and carved suggests that the maker, faced with a problem, solved it in a turnerly way rather than spoil the chair with a poorly carved crest rail, there being no professional carver in the neighborhood. This in turn implies the maker of this chair had trained in an urban setting where the division of crafts was sufficiently strict that a specialist carver would have executed crest rails, and thus the turner/joiner who made the frames was taught carving. And, because there is a European prototype for every other detail of the chair, undoubtedly there is one for the crest rail.[4]

Winterthur's chair was made by a craftsman who knew the urban European prototypes. The high quality of the workmanship on this chair suggests that its maker had undergone a traditional apprenticeship with a skillful craftsman in an urban center, although at the time he was making it the craftsman may have been living in a rural setting. In short, this is not a country chair.

The upholstery on the seat of the present example has been removed, the girt webbing replaced, the leather repaired, and the seat restuffed and reinstalled. Most of the leather strip under the tacks is modern and was probably restored by Ernest LoNano prior to 1954.

NOTES
[1] *Moxon's Mechanick Exercises*, p. 217.
[2] Erixon, *Möbler*.
[3] I am indebted to Ingmar Hasselgreen of Göteborgs Historiska Museum for information about the Swedish chair. Hasselgreen to Forman, August 30, 1977.
[4] The crest rail of a chair said to be of New England origin (Nutting, *Furniture Treasury*, no. 1942), if in fact of American origin and if not a replacement, shows that another turner reached a similar solution to this problem.

74.
BANISTER-BACK LEATHER CHAIR
New Castle County, Delaware
1720–1750
WOODS: Striped maple (*Acer pennsylvanicum*) and ash
OH 48⅜″ (122.9 cm)
SH 17⅞″ (45.4 cm), SW 19¼″ (48.9 cm), SD 14⅞″ (37.8 cm)
PROVENANCE: Bequest of Henry Francis du Pont
54.520

While this chair, with distinctive reeded banisters and turned crest, has no known history, a nearly identical chair has a strong history of having been owned by William Shipley, who was born in Leicestershire, England, in 1693, immigrated to Philadelphia about 1725, and settled in Wilmington, Delaware, in 1735, where he lived until his death in 1768.[1] A similar but more complex chair with carved ornament on the crest and with vase-and-column turnings on two front stretchers has a tradition of ownership in the Gill family of Haddonfield, New Jersey.[2] There is good reason to think that these three chairs were the work of Scandinavian craftsmen working in the former Swedish colony of New Amstel (now New Castle, Delaware). Although some of the turned ornament is similar to English motifs, notably the tripartite front stretcher, the overall form of the chair recalls Scandinavian chairs, and abundant documentary evidence of Scandinavian craftsmen working in that town survives.[3] One such craftsman is "John Hendrixon the Torner." On February 21, 1682/83, Henrickson, whose first name had been Jan and whose last name was anglicized to Henricks, applied to become a naturalized citizen of the English colony. He may well have been in New Castle since 1657 during the time of Swedish settlement; he died in 1689.[4] Numerous craftsmen with Swedish names listed in the records throughout the eighteenth century may have trained in Henrickson's shop tradition.

NOTES
[1] See DAPC 65.3742, Winterthur Library.
[2] *Early Furniture*, pp. 6–7.
[3] Sharp, "Janvier Family of Cabinetmakers," appendix.
[4] *Records of the Court of New Castle*, 2: 7, 37, 71, 198.

cat. 74

75

CROOK-BACK CHAIR WITH DOUBLE-NAILED LEATHER AND
SPANISH FEET

Boston, Massachusetts

1722–1732, except examples made for export into the 1740s

WOODS: All soft maple (genus *Acer*), except seat rails and lower back panel rail,
American red oak (*Quercus rubra*)

OH 45⅝″ (115.9 cm)

SH 18⅛″ (46.0 cm), SW 17⅞″ (45.4 cm), SD 14½″ (36.8 cm)

PROVENANCE: Israel Sack, Inc.; purchased by the museum

58.57.4

Considering the relatively large number of chairs of this type that have been found along the eastern seaboard in every place except Boston in the twentieth century, the attribution of crook-back-style chairs to Boston smacks of temerity. Early in the twentieth century, six of these crook-back chairs were illustrated, but only one had a vague association with Boston. Irving W. Lyon in 1891 illustrated a chair owned by Walter Hosmer, collector, dealer, upholsterer, and restorer, of Wethersfield, Connecticut. When Luke Vincent Lockwood published the second edition of *Colonial Furniture* (1913), the chair was then in the Metropolitan Museum of Art, having first passed to Horace Eugene Bolles, who with his cousin George A. Palmer had purchased the Hosmer collection in the early 1890s. In 1895, E. E. Soderholtz published photographs of two chairs: one was in the home of George Curwen, an early collector who lived in Salem, Massachusetts; the other was merely captioned "Furniture in Boston, Mass." Nutting illustrated a fourth chair with unusual double side stretchers in *Furniture Treasury* (no. 2681); it was in a collection in Wickford, Rhode Island. Two associated with the van Rensselaer family of Albany were illustrated in *New York Furniture*.[1] Only one of the chairs, that published by. Soderholtz, points to Boston as the place of origin.

In 1965, Richard Randall published a catalogue of furniture in the Museum of Fine Arts, Boston, and finally a chair of this type with a firm Boston history of ownership appeared in print.[2] That chair was an heirloom of the Lamb family and had been given to the museum in 1956. Although it may be mere coincidence, Brock W. Jobe has shown that a chairmaker named Edward Lamb was working in Boston in 1741. The Lamb-family chair is somewhat related to Winterthur's chair; however, another chair in the Museum of Fine Arts collection, a bequest of Bostonian Charles Hitchcock Tyler who formed his collection from objects found in his immediate environs, is strikingly similar to the Winterthur chair which is, in turn, similar to the Curwen chair illustrated by Soderholtz.

The Winterthur chair has an old label written in brown ink attached to one of the modern corner blocks under the reupholstered seat. The writing is in a nineteenth-century hand and, frustratingly, is not completely legible. It reads "George B. _____ [Dunlap?], Boston, Mass." The Winterthur chair and possibly the Curwen chair have rosewood graining. Although graining was used to decorate woodwork in seventeenth-century America, rosewood furniture enjoyed a short-lived popularity during the nineteenth century—from about 1820 to about 1860.[3] Tack holes that pierce the surface of the graining and go into the inner margin of the rear stiles as well as the bottom surface of the seat rail confirm that Winterthur's chair was grained prior to being completely upholstered, perhaps in the late nineteenth or early twentieth century, since the areas that were overupholstered are also grained.

The structure of these crook-back chairs does not materially differ from that of the carved-top variety popular during the first two decades of the eighteenth century. Following practices that the Boston chairmaking industry established in the seventeenth century, oak continued to be used for the seat rails and lower back rail, while everything else was of maple. Many decorative features are retained. The rear feet rake backward. The rear stretcher is slightly offset above the single lower side stretchers. Double-nailed leather upholstery is attached in the same fashion. Balusters still decorate the front legs, but the blocks between them are smaller since only turned stretchers were ever destined to be fitted into them. The characteristic terminus used by the craftsman who had made turned front stretchers earlier (see catalogue entry 66) is still used, although the stretcher itself is tripartite rather than bipartite.

A host of new features also appears. The upper rear stiles are molded on their front surface and are crook'd or embowed in profile. The lower rear legs sweep dramatically down and back from the seat to the bottoms of the feet. (This bold shape is also apparent on the cane chair illustrated at catalogue entry 54, although that chair retains the straight upper stiles of the earlier style, perhaps as much for the convenience of the caner as for stylistic considerations.) The most important iconographic feature to appear on the crook-back leather chairs is the Spanish foot, which without exception replaces the ball and pad foot of the earlier style.

The crest rail, too, has been redesigned and has to be executed by a carver because planes do not negotiate compass shapes easily. This crest, slightly reminiscent of the crest rail on some of the cane chairs, is easier to carve than the floriated type and may not have required the services of a highly skilled carver in a separate shop. It is flat on the top with rounded corners sculpted in the hollow-round-hollow shape, and flows into the molding planed on the rear stiles. A flat crest, generally with rounded corners, appears on English cane chairs of the early eighteenth century, but here it has been given additional refinement by being carefully rolled backward on its front surface. There is an analogous element on easy chairs, the earliest surviving New England examples of which date from this period. Chairs with this feature would be handsome en suite with easy chairs and suggest that those who could afford it were giving increased attention to furnishing their rooms harmoniously during this period. This flat-top motif is also found on English looking glasses and other forms of furniture, but it is doubtful that it appears in furniture available to people of a socioeconomic level comparable to that of the Americans before the death of Queen Anne. Thus, it is equally doubtful that the sudden appearance of crook-back chairs in Boston in 1722 represents quite such a time lag as would appear at first glance.

Winterthur's chair has been reupholstered and repainted. Its well-executed feet are original.

cat. 75

NOTES
[1] Lyon, *Colonial Furniture*, fig. 70; Lockwood, *Colonial Furniture*, fig. 481; Saunders, "American Decorative Arts Collecting in New England," p. 79; Soderholtz, *Colonial Architecture and Furniture*, pl. 26 (also illustrated in Saunders, "American Decorative Arts Collecting in New England," p. 96, fig. 30, and pl. 58); Rice, *New York Furniture*, p. 20.
[2] Randall, *American Furniture*, no. 129; Randall, "Boston Chairs," pp. 12–20. Suffolk County Inferior Court, September 18, 1741, as cited in Jobe, "Boston Furniture Industry" (thesis), craftsmen list no. 19.
[3] An advertisement by Richard Martin in the Charleston, S.C., *Gazette*, no. 132 (July 31–August 7, 1736), offers "House, Sign and Ship—painting and glazing Work done after the best manner, imitation of Marble, Walnut, Oak, Cedar & c. at five shillings a yard"; I am indebted to Susan B. Swan for this reference.

76.

CROOK-BACK CHAIR WITH DOUBLE-NAILED LEATHER AND SPANISH FEET

Boston, Massachusetts

1722–1735

WOODS: All American sugar maple (*Acer saccharum*), except seat rails and lower back rail of red oak (*Quercus rubra*)

OH 44½″ (113.0 cm)

SH 19¼″ (48.9 cm), SW 17⅞″ (45.4 cm), SD 14½″ (36.8 cm)

PROVENANCE: Bequest of Henry Francis du Pont

54.533

Between January 1719/20 and June 1722 Thomas Fitch sold numerous carved-top leather chairs, with russia-leather upholstery, at a uniform price of 23*s*. (46*s*. for an armchair). But the entry of February 27, 1722/23, contains a notation that reveals he was selling a new type of leather chair: "1 doz. crook'd back chairs . . . £16:4:0," or 27*s*. each. Eleven days later he billed Edward Bromfield, Jr., for "10 russhia Chairs" also at 27*s*. each, and three months later he billed Jacob Wendell for "1 dozen russhia leather crook Chairs" again at 27*s*. each. The following November he charged Samuel Thaxter and Samuel Holmes, both of whom bought six, the same 27*s*. price. And when Fitch exported the first chairs in the new style to New Yorker Adam Powell in the following March, he billed him 27*s*. per chair. The combined billings also allow us to identify both the components of the new style and the established price. "John Otis, Esq." of Boston purchased "1 doz Carv'd Tops rushia Chairs" at 24*s*. each on January 4, 1723/24. Thus the former style was still available, and its price was firmly 3*s*. less than that of crook-back chairs.[1]

The additional 3*s*. cost can be easily explained. The new-style chairs differ from the earlier, carved-top version in two important ways: first, the rear stiles are sawed out of a board and are molded by hand with a plane; second, the front feet are of the Spanish type and are carved. On the earlier chairs, both of these elements were executed on a lathe by a turner; the planing and carving for the new style therefore represented a considerable expenditure of time and money.

Unlike the numerous entries in the Samuel Grant accounts that reveal the cumulative addition of Queen Anne–style elements to a previous style and ultimately resulted in the emergence of a completely new chair, the crook-back chair suddenly appears full blown in the Fitch manuscripts. Neither the Fitch nor the Grant accounts reveal the terminology for any parts of these chairs except the crook back: no hint gives us the New England name for what we now call Spanish feet, no allusion is made to the form of the crest rail, and no reference is made to the molded stiles. And the sole pertinent comment that emerges from Fitch's letterbook is on March 23, 1724, "I intend next week to send you Dozn of Rushia newest fashiond chairs," and notes them again in this book as he did in the account book, "12 Rushia new fashion'd chairs @ 27[*s*.] £16:4:9."[2]

We cannot help but wonder if Fitch's use of the phrase "newest fashiond" was confined to the idea of what constituted the newest fashion in Boston or if it included London, with which he was in monthly contact. In 1704, Fitch recognized differences between the two cities and informed his English counterpart that certain types and colors of textiles "do not at all take [well] with our people." Five years later he wrote Messrs. Phillip Blow and Co., his London factors: "The old fashion Tables & stands woud do well" in Boston. In the very next sentence he added, "Looking glasses from 18 Inches long to 30 inches that are fashonable, not too broad would sell well."[3] The Boston taste was current with that of London in some respects but not all. We also know that "London taste" was not monolithic; fashions there were spread over a wide spectrum of social and economic gradients, and the most expensive furniture was doubtless somewhat more advanced in styling than the least expensive.

While it is difficult to deal with the abstractions that appear in the Fitch correspondence, his accounts reveal that he was purchasing chair frames from at least two craftsmen—Edmond Perkins and John Leach—during the periods in which he was selling the "carved top" variety and the "newest fashiond" type.[4]

A close comparison of the chairs in catalogue entries 75, 76, and 77 confirms the notion that three separate shops produced these chairs and that each shop had a different set of patterns. The rear stiles of all three, although superficially similar, embow differently. And different marking sticks or sweeps were used to determine the positions and sizes of the balusters and blocks on the front legs (fig. 177).

The Lamb-family chair in the Museum of Fine Arts, Boston (Randall, *American Furniture*, no. 129), came from yet another pattern, which suggests that a fourth shop in the Boston area made the chairs. On that chair the inner bead of the stiles is carried upward to the upper bead that outlines the crest rail. (It is indubitably original to the chair since the carved miter that is normally seen at the corners of the crest rail is not in evidence.) The balusters of the front legs are set off by fillets at their extremities, an extra touch of flamboyance. The tripartite

cat. 76

Fig. 177. LEFT. Detail of the legs of three Boston-made leather chairs in catalogue entries (left to right) 75, 76, 77. (Winterthur 54.533, 58.57.4, 76.31.)

Fig. 178. ABOVE. Detail of the front stretchers on three Boston-made leather chairs in catalogue entries (top to bottom) 75, 76, 77. (Winterthur 54.533, 58.57.4, 76.31.)

front stretcher is also different: the balls are quite round, and the transition to the rest of the stretcher is abrupt. The termini are likewise distinctive in that their extremities do not taper. Last, the carved feet are incised with three broad channels instead of the usual two.[5]

That at least four shops in Boston were making chairs of this model comes as a surprise since only two shops—those of Perkins and Leach—are consistently mentioned in Fitch's accounts. Undoubtedly one of these shops belonged to Samuel Mattocks, Sr., and his son Samuel, Jr., who, along with other possible makers are discussed in the introduction to this section.

If different marking sticks were used to lay out the front legs of the three Winterthur side chairs and different patterns were used to lay out the rear stiles, then that the front stretchers are also different in design, proportion, and details of workmanship suggests these stylistic details have meaning. Figure 178 illustrates the stretchers of Winterthur's three chairs. (They are in the same order as the legs illustrated in figure 177.) Stretcher A, from catalogue entry 75, is tripartite. It has the concave termini like those on the stretcher of the carved-top leather chair illustrated in entry 66, although that stretcher is of the bipartite design. Stretcher C, from entry 77, is bipartite, has a fillet turned at the base of each terminus, and has less pearlike balusters. Stretcher B, from the chair in this entry, is the most common type among the surviving crook-back Boston leather chairs and is nearly identical to the stretcher that appears on the cane chair illustrated in entry 54. In scale it is somewhat more robust than that one, as if its maker intended the fullness of the turning here to be appropriate to the mass of an upholstered chair, as opposed to the lightness of design appropriate to a cane chair whose minimal woodwork is echoed by the open weave of cane upholstery.

If the quirks of workmanship on the three stretchers represent in effect the signature or trademark of the shop in which each of these chairs was made, then the identicality of stretcher pattern of this chair and the one on the cane chair in entry 54 suggests that both examples were made in the same shop. It is perhaps foolhardy to attempt to put a name to this shop, but, considering that this is by far the most common type of stretcher on both the surviving Boston cane and leather chairs and the documentary evidence shows that the largest number of chair frames furnished to Thomas Fitch came from the shop of Edmond Perkins, the Perkins shop is the logical place for this particular chair to have been manufactured, admittedly assuming that Fitch and his suppliers operated the most important shops in Boston in their day.

Of course, the chairs themselves do not offer proof of authorship, and until some proof may be found, we are left with speculation. But the existence of four chairs of the same model made from different patterns is provable and is in itself sufficiently important to reinforce our explanation of interdependent Boston chairmaking shops. It is also further evidence that the masters of these shops were willing to supress stylistic individuality to obtain the commercial advantages of making a popular chair. This in itself raises a question: if chairs of the same model are being made in different shops, which of the shops was responsible for the introduction of the design? While we cannot answer this question on the basis of any firm date, it seems likely that the masters of *none* of the shops conceived this design, but that the upholsterer who commissioned them was responsible for their ultimate form.

The seat of the present chair has been reupholstered, and its original walnut stain has been removed. Chiseled on the underside of the right side stretcher is XIII.

NOTES

[1] January 21, 1719/20 to June 9, 1722, passim, February 27, March 10, 1722/23, June 11, November 23, 1723, January 4, 1723/24, April 4, 1724, Fitch account book, MHS; Fitch to Adam Powell, March 23, April 4, 1724, Fitch letterbook MHS. Bromfield was probably furnishing a new home; he had married Abigail Coney on February 21, 1722/23 (Savage, *Genealogical Dictionary*, 1:258).

[2] Fitch to Adam Powell, March 23, April 4, 1724, Fitch letterbook, MHS.

[3] Fitch to Jno Crouch & Co., April 22, 1704, Fitch to Phillip Blow & Co., August 13, 1709, Fitch letterbook, AAS.

[4] Fitch account book, MHS: "Mar. 7, 1719/20 . . . Shop [debtor to] Edmund Perkins for bedsteads, chair frames, benches &c as pr his accot settled in his book . . . £63:7:00"; "February 19, 1721/22 . . . Sundry Accounts Debtor to John Leech . . . for chair frames &c. as p[er] his Ascot. to this day £25:1:4." After the change in styles: "February 1722/23 . . . Shop [debtor to] Edmund Perkins for Chair Fraims &c. as p[ser] his accot £77:12:6"; "Mar. 4, 1722/23 . . . Sundry Accounts debtor to John Leech . . . for Chair fraims &c. as,pr accot settled this day £15:12:6."

[5] I am indebted to Jonathan L. Fairbanks and Robert F. Trent for information on the Lamb family and for the loan of a photograph of the chair to compare with the Winterthur examples.

77.

CROOK-BACK LEATHER CHAIR

Boston, Massachusetts

1722–1730, perhaps as late as the early 1740s

WOODS: All exposed members of silver maple (*Acer saccharinum*), except crest rail, a beech (genus *Fagus*), and seat rails and lower back rail, white oak (*Quercus alba*)

OH 44⅞" (114.0 cm)

SH 18¼" (46.4 cm), SW 18" (45.7 cm), SD 14½" (36.8 cm)

PROVENANCE: Tradition of ownership in the Shirley family of Virginia; gift of Mrs. Henry H. Tweed

76.31

Fig. 179. Detail of shape of stiles on two Boston crook-back leather chairs dating from ca. 1732 and 1722–30. The chair on the left is figure 156, the chair on the right is catalogue entry 77. (Winterthur 54.523, 76.31.)

The third of the Winterthur crook-back leather chairs differs from the previous examples in two significant ways: its crest rail is of beech, making it the only leather-upholstered Boston chair in the Winterthur collection that contains this wood, and its front stretcher is of the bipartite type with hollow-turned (concave) termini. This stretcher also differs from a similar one on the carved-top chair illustrated in entry 66 in that the central balls are somewhat rounder and each terminus is preceded by a small fillet.

The conventional concepts of furniture dating would suggest that chairs in this style enjoyed a rather short popular life, from 1722 when they were first introduced until around 1732 when the cabriole-leg style can be shown to have completely emerged in Boston. The daybook of Samuel Grant shows that such chairs as these continued to be made and sold in Boston and in the export trade well after the cabriole-leg style was introduced. In December 1731 Grant was selling the chairs at 26s. 6d., only 6d more than he had sold them for during the preceding two years. On March 8, 1732/33, he shipped Peter Faneuil in New York "4 doz: Leathr chairs claw feet" at 27s. each, and in September he sold Caleb Richardson six at 26s. apiece. Three years later, the price of old-style chairs had risen to 30s.; in June 1737, the price of chairs with "compass," or rounded, seats had risen to 55s.[1]

That the leather chairs gradually inched up in price may be explained by the inflationary trend of this period. But this does not explain why Grant was selling leather chairs for 26s. early in his career instead of the 27s. that his former master, Fitch, charged. It is possible that Grant's chairs were upholstered with domestic leather, which was less expensive than the russia leather Fitch used (Grant never specifies the imported material

in his accounts). An alternate explanation may be that Grant was selling a version of these chairs that differed slightly from Fitch's model, a prospect that is more fully discussed at entry 81. A final reason might be that he lacked the clientele.

Although Grant did buy individual chair frames from James Johnson, whom Grant identifies as a "chairmaker" in January 1732/33, most of the time he, like Fitch, bought large numbers of chair frames from Edmond Perkins, one of the investors in Grant's business, and John Leach.[2]

The frame of Winterthur's chair cannot be attached documentarily to any of the chairmakers. The fillet at the base of the hollow-turned terminus of the stretcher is a motif that cannot be associated with either the largest group of Boston cane chairs or the carved-top leather chairs. The rear stiles, however, are virtually identical in outline to those of the cabriole-leg chair, attributed to the shop of John Leach, illustrated in the introduction to this section (see fig. 156). As shown in figure 179, both embow at the same angle, are of the same thickness and breadth, rake backward below the seat from the same point, and generally coincide with each other to such an extent that it is difficult to resist the temptation of

cat. 77

attributing this chair to the Leach shop. While no written evidence survives to support (or deny) the attribution, at the very least the resemblance between the two stiles illustrates how a patternmaker in an urban shop approached the problem of updating a style. Probably in the early 1720s a designer took the carved-top-chair design, retained the essential outline of the seat and front legs, and added a crook in the back and a new style of crest rail. About a decade later as styles again changed, he retained the outline of the crook back—perhaps even continued to use the same patterns for the stiles—but changed most other features.

While we cannot state with certainty that any one of Winterthur's chairs was more likely to have been first, that the relatively rare bilobe front stretcher on this particular chair was the model for the front stretcher of the chair in catalogue entry 80 indicates the version was still being produced in the 1740s.

The original upholstery and the glued-on sections for the feet are missing. The legs have lost approximately ½″ (1.3 cm) of their original height.

NOTES
[1] December 20, 1731, March 8, 1732/33, September 24, 1733, March 28, 1736, June 3, 1737, Grant daybook.
[2] January 29, 1732/33, November 28, 1728, Grant daybook.

78.
CROOK-BACK ELBOW CHAIR WITH DOUBLE-NAILED LEATHER AND SPANISH FEET
Boston, Massachusetts
1722–1745
WOODS: All soft maple, except bottom back rail and right seat rail of oak and vertical back rails of white elm (*Ulmus americana*)
OH 47⅞″ (121.6 cm)
SH 17¾″ (45.2 cm), SW 22¾″ (57.8 cm), SD 16⅞″ (42.9 cm)
PROVENANCE: Gift of Henry Francis du Pont
58.556

79.
CROOK-BACK ELBOW CHAIR WITH DOUBLE-NAILED LEATHER
Boston, Massachusetts
1722–1745
WOODS: All soft maple, except rear seat rail of white oak (*Quercus alba*)
OH 47″ (119.4 cm)
SH 16¼″ (41.2 cm), SW 23″ (58.4 cm), SD 17″ (43.2 cm)
PROVENANCE: Howard Reifsnyder; Henry Francis du Pont
54.539

One of the questions that armchairs raise for the furniture historian is whether to characterize them as "great," "elbow," or "armed" since all three descriptive adjectives are used in early colonial records.[1] In the eighteenth century the last two are used repeatedly and often interchangeably in inventory and shop records. Carved top, "Russia Leathr, Elbow chairs" were mentioned in Thomas Fitch's letterbook twice in 1707 and were sold for 28s. each, but in 1709 he referred to the same type as "arm d[itt]o." In May 1720, he sold "1 Russia leather elbow chair" for 46s. When Samuel Grant noted the first crook-back leather chairs in his journal on April 22, 1729, he identified some as "armed," but over the next three years he consistently used the phrase "elbow leather chairs" whether describing the examples with overupholstered seats, of the "Boston" type, or those with cushion seats in the Queen Anne style.[2] Normally one and sometimes two armchairs accompanied the sets of a dozen or half dozen. On occasion, Grant sold armchairs singly, a happenstance that almost never occurred with side chairs. Thus the relative rarity of Boston-type armchairs today is a direct reflection of their relative rarity in their time.

As far as we can determine from inventory references, the crook-back chairs differ from the Cromwellian type in two ways: their owners do not appear to have used cushions with them (although cushions were being used on cane chairs at that time) and footstools are rarely paired with them, perhaps because the armchairs were primarily intended to be used in dining rooms.[3] Armchairs differ from side chairs in size: they are roughly 5″ (12.7 cm) wider and 2½″ (6.4 cm) taller. Their seats are generally about 2″ (5.1 cm) deeper, and the extra depth is compensated for by making the seats ½″ (1.3 cm) or so closer to the floor. These dimensions graphically reveal that the craftsmen made a different set of patterns for armchairs. Structurally armchairs that stylistically predate the mid 1740s differ from side chairs only in that the front legs are extended upward to form arm supports and in that the arms themselves are added. The leather seat had to accommodate the front corners, an extension of the technique used at the rear corners of side-chair seats. Double-nailed decorative upholstery is the invariable rule on the New England examples of these chairs and the piece of leather trim was used in the same way that gimp or decorative fringe was used on textile-upholstered chairs, it extended around the juncture of seat rails with front legs and rear stiles.

A comparison of a prestandardized leather armchair (catalogue entry 64), a standardized armchair (fig. 180), and the two crook-back armchairs in this entry reveal subtle changes. The first elements to disappear between the time of the prestandardized chair and the period of the standardized chair are the turned medial, side, and rear stretchers arranged in the cane-chair manner; they are replaced by rectilinear stretchers reminiscent of the Cromwellian style. The small baluster at the base of the arm support also disappears with the introduction of the standardized model, and the remaining large baluster is elongated. On the arm support of standardized and crook-back chairs, the longer baluster is topped by a ring, a com-

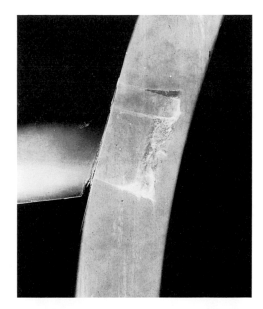

Fig. 181. X-ray photograph of the arms and stile of the chair in catalogue entry 78 showing the tenon half dovetailed on its lower edge and the wedge inserted along the upper edge. (Winterthur 58.556.)

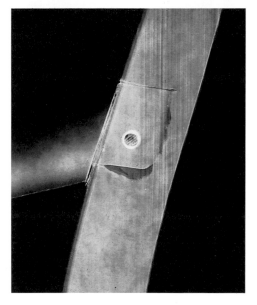

Fig. 182. X-ray photograph of the arm of the chair in catalogue entry 80 showing the pinned mortise-and-tenon joint. (Winterthur 58.555.)

Fig. 180. Carved-top leather armchair, Boston, 1700–ca. 1723. Maple; H 50¾″ (128.9 cm), W 23″ (58.4 cm), D 17″ (43.2 cm), SH 17½″ (44.5 cm). (Courtesy Munson Williams Proctor Institute, Utica, N.Y.)

pressed ball, and a small tapered baluster. The tapered cone at the top of the arm support on the prestandardized chair is much more like the analogous element on the armchair in catalogue entry 81, and both are found on Boston-made chairs.

One significant difference between the chairs in catalogue entries 78 and 79 and those in catalogue entry 64 and figure 180 is the way in which the arms are attached to the rear stiles. On the earlier chairs, the back end of the arm is tenoned into a flat-face block on the rear stile and is held in place with a wooden pin—a technique almost invariably used on contemporary cane armchairs. On the later chairs the molded rear stile is planed smooth at the point where the arm meets it. The tenon on the arm is notched on its lower surface to form a half dovetail and the mortise hole in the stile is cut downward on its bottom surface to form a notch on which the half dovetail literally is hung. Since the mortise hole is taller than the tenon, a wedge has been inserted on the upper surface, which also holds the arm in place (fig. 181). Lest we become overly enthusiastic about this extraordinary manner of affixing the arm to the stile, we must also note that the crest rail and the vertical and lower back supports have been repaired, all of

which suggest that this joint is also a repair; indeed the outline of the mortise hole is irregular and has been covered with a filler that had been varnished to match the rest of the chair. The reliance on the wedge mildly suggests that this repair may have been done fairly early and done in the middle colonies, quite possibly in Pennsylvania, where the northern European technique of wedging tenons in mortises on chairs became common after 1735. (It was used in the leather chair of a much earlier style illustrated in catalogue entry 73.) In any event, the method of cutting a mortise hole that is half-dovetailed on its bottom edge into the rear stile and hanging the arm on it is a fascinating device that is cosmetically superior to an exposed pin on the outer edge of the stile but may not be structurally better than the pinned joint (fig. 182) on the Philadelphia chair illustrated in catalogue entry 80, which survived the years without mishap.

The lower rail of the back of the chair in entry 78 has been pieced out about ½″ (1.3 cm) across its bottom edge, and circular-saw marks are visible on its surface; these repairs may have been made to strengthen the rail after repeated upholstery tackings had weathered the wood. The crest rail has been

cat. 78

cat. 79

broken, indicating the chair at sometime fell over backwards and was repaired. The vertical supports of the back panel are of white elm (*Ulmus americana*) and lack the same walnut stain that covers the rest of the chair, suggesting that these, too, are a repair. (The upper tenons of the original supports may have been damaged when the crest rail was broken.) That these supports are covered with a modern varnish, which does not quite match the original stain, heightens this impression. Furthermore, the presence of elm in a piece of New England urban furniture of this period is unusual, even though white elm grows abundantly there. In contrast, the use of oak (right seat rail and lower back rail) is common on the rest of the Boston chairs of this type. The toes of no. 78 are restored, the leather is modern (although old tacks were used again). The strip of leather between the rows of tacks around the seat frame was not restored.

Although it does not appear to be so now, each element of no. 79 is sufficiently like the corresponding part of no. 78 to suggest that both were made from the same patterns and that both were made in the same shop. Well-executed repairs, probably made in the twentieth century, replaced the missing Spanish feet with the present baluster-shape ones (a feature unknown on Boston chairs of this type). The rear legs are likewise pieced out from the bottom of the rear stretcher to the bottom of the feet, a repair that has diminished the original bold backward sweep of the rear feet. Most dimensions of these two chairs are nearly identical.

Recent attempts to find Boston-made leather chairs with histories of ownership in Philadelphia have been unsuccessful. Nevertheless, the idea that the present chair may have been in the middle colonies during the period in which it was fashionable is suggested by its presence in Howard Reifsnyder's collection, which was composed almost exclusively of items he had found in the immediate Philadelphia area.[4]

Presumptive evidence of the shipment of chairs from Boston to Philadelphia in the first third of the eighteenth century may be found in the characteristic Boston tripartite stretcher, which became naturalized in middle-colonies slat-back chairs prior to that date. Such a stretcher also occurs on a Pennsylvania leather chair (see fig. 168), which is contemporary with or predates the present example. It is therefore somewhat surprising that the documents of Philadelphia and vicinity do not allude to New England chairs in Philadelphia prior to the advertisement of February 1, 1738/39, in the *Pennsylvania Gazette* in which Peter Baynton, a Philadelphia joiner turned merchant, offered "New England red Leather chairs" for sale.[5]

In the years between 1754, when Charles Willing owned "1 doz. Boston Chairs at Farm," and 1773, when Thomas Turner had "6 Boston chairs," there were "new England leather," "leather bottom," and numerous "Boston made Leather Bottom Maple" chairs present in great and modest Philadelphia homes. The appraised values assigned to several such chairs in 1760 and 1764 suggest that by that time they were no longer considered very stylish nor very highly valued. "Boston chairs" in 1760 were worth only 5s. each, but the following year six others were appraised at twice that sum. Others ranged between 6s. 8d. and 7s. 6d. Even if appraisal values were 50 percent of sale prices this amount is still quite a comedown from the 26s. and 48s. Samuel Grant had charged for similar chairs in Boston in 1729 (and Grant's price did not include the markup of the Philadelphia retailer).[6]

NOTES
1 Suffolk Probate, 2:138; 9:148; 10:52, 412; 13:408; 14:146.
2 Fitch to Faneuil, April 22, June 23, 1707, and Fitch to Wendell, March 28, 1709, Fitch letterbook, AAS. April 22, 1729, May 27, 1730, December 20, 1731, September 15, 1732, and March 8, 1732/33, Grant daybook.
3 Customs may have differed in Philadelphia. An advertisement in Philadelphia's *American Weekly Mercury* dated October 30, 1729, for a vendue, reveals that among the goods of Samuel Gifford was "one elbow leather chair with a board to write on . . . one feather cushion for an elbow chair"; I am indebted to Arlene Palmer Schwind for this reference.
4 *Reifsnyder Sale*, no. 373. No history of ownership accompanied the illustration.
5 Leibundguth, "Furniture-Making Crafts in Philadelphia," p. 18. A decade earlier, Baynton had apparently been importing "Very good Red Leather Chairs, the newest fashion" from England and "sundry other *European* Goods" (advertisement, *Pennsylvania Gazette* [January 20, 1728/29] cited in Prime, *Colonial Craftsmen of Pennsylvania*, p. 1, no. 2).
6 Philadelphia Wills, 1760-03, 1761-37, 1762-220, and 1764-53; I am indebted to Arlene Palmer Schwind for these references.

80.
NEW ENGLAND–FASHION CROOK-BACK ELBOW CHAIR WITH DOUBLE-NAILED LEATHER AND SPANISH FEET
Probably Philadelphia, Pennsylvania
1735–1745
WOOD: All red maple (*Acer rubrum*)
OH 49″ (124.5 cm)
SH 18½″ (47.0 cm), SW 23″ (58.4 cm), SD 17¼″ (43.8 cm)
PROVENANCE: Gift of Henry Francis du Pont
58.555

The two advertisements of 1742 and 1744 by the Philadelphia upholsterer, Plunkett Fleeson, have been a source of fascinating speculation to students of American furniture ever since they became widely known in 1929 with their publication in Alfred Coxe Prime's *Arts and Crafts in Philadelphia, Maryland,* *and South Carolina*. In these ads, Fleeson states that he sells locally made chairs that are of quality comparable to and cheaper than those imported from Boston. Were the advertisements idle boasts? If not, what could these Philadelphia chairs, designed to compete with the Boston type, have looked like? Obviously Fleeson's chairs could not have varied from the prototypes to a great extent or they could not have competed with them effectively. But if they were closely similar to the Boston examples, how can we possibly hope to identify them today? These chairs, which have eluded identification for so long, would have to capture the essence of the Boston style but ought to differ in details of execution that should betray their Philadelphia origin.

Although the present chair has no provenance that ties it to

cat. 80

Philadelphia, it varies from the usual Boston chair of this type in seven small but significant details, and more to the point, one of these is a prominent Philadelphia characteristic. When compared with a typical Boston chair, the following differences may be observed:

Philadelphia chair	*Boston chair*
1. Made totally of maple	1. Made primarily of maple but usually having oak in seat rails and back supports
2. Very slight chamfer on front of rear stiles at the junctures with arms and side seat rails	2. Prominent chamfer on front of rear stiles at the junctures with arms and side seat rails
3. Pin through tenon of each arm visible on outer edge of rear stile	3. Tenon of each arm held in place in rear stile by half dovetail and glue
4. Scroll feet not glued up, i.e., front leg is one piece of wood	4. Scroll feet glued up before being carved
5. Scroll feet incised with narrow gouge	5. Scroll feet carved with wide gouge, usually 2 grooves on each foot.
6. Front leg has a baluster and a compressed ball between seat and front stretcher	6. Front leg has 2 balusters between seat and foot
7. Baluster of arm support has only 1 ring above it, is scored around its middle, and rests upon a spool	7. Baluster of arm support has turned elements above it and is not scored about its center

Students of Philadelphia furniture of the eighteenth century will immediately recognize in item 7 a feature that is familiar. Figure 183 illustrates the arm support of a Philadelphia chair that probably was made in the shop of William Savery circa 1750.[1] This arm support, with the rounded knob that is characteristic of the early production of his shop, is a version of the arm support of the earlier turned chair illustrated in figure 184, although a somewhat evolved form of it. While it can only be argued that the present chair emerged from the shop of Savery, the similarity of its baluster to the cited examples emphasizes that the form remained remarkably unchanged and was used over a long period of time in Philadelphia by a number of eighteenth-century craftsmen who continued to score a groove around the widest part of the baluster, as their masters' masters had in the seventeenth century, and thus produced a recognizable regional attribute. This grooving of the baluster does not appear to be an element of the New England style introduced into the middle colonies and may have come either from the Germanic, perhaps Lower Saxony, vocabulary of ornament introduced into Germantown, Pennsylvania, toward the end of the seventeenth century or, less likely, from the west of England. It would be futile to search for this stylistic touch in Boston work of the eighteenth century since no German or West Country English craftsmen were working there at that time.[2] While points 1 through 6 may merely represent observable differences between two chairs, point 7 is a distinctive characteristic of early eighteenth-century Pennsylvania chairs in general and Philadelphia chairs in

Fig. 184. Dr. Christopher Witt, *Johannes Kelpius.* Germantown, Penn., ca. 1705. Watercolor on paper. (Historical Society of Pennsylvania, Philadelphia.) Note the chair upon which Kelpius sits.

particular; it seems to be as good a piece of evidence that we shall find to identify the leather chairs of Philadelphia.

The second Plunkett Fleeson advertisement appeared in the *Pennsylvania Gazette* on June 14, 1744:

Plunket Fleeson, Upholsterer, at the Easy-Chair, in Chestnut-Street, Philadelphia, Knowing that People have been often disappointed and impos'd upon by Master Chair Makers in this City, to the Prejudice of his Part of that Business, by Encouraging the Importation of Boston Chairs, Has ingaged, and for many Months, employed several [of] the best Chair-makers in the Province, to the End he might have a Sortment of Choice Walnut Chair Frames; Gives Notice that he now has a great Variety of the newest and best Fashions, ready made, whereby all Persons who want, may be supply'd without Danger of Disappointment or Imposition, at the most reasonable Rates; and Maple Chairs as cheap as from Boston. Also Feathers; Feather Beds, Bed Bottoms, Sea Beds, &c.—Ready Money for Horse Hair and Cow Tails.[3]

Proof that Winterthur's chair is one of the "Maple Chairs as cheap as from Boston" mentioned in the ad cannot be produced. It is entirely possible that Fleeson was offering a crook-leg, cushion-seat, and round-top Queen Anne chair—for we have only the presumption that the labels "Boston chair" and "New England chair" refer to stylistic attributes rather than merely their place of origin. But other traditionally styled furniture owned by the clientele in the vast hinterland surrounding Philadelphia to whom Fleeson could have been selling chairs suggest that the taste in furniture there was influenced by a number of factors other than pursuit of the chimera of fashion.

Although Philadelphia's upholsterers such as Edward Shippen and, later, his son Joseph maintained Boston connections, and although chairmaker Thomas Stapleford came from Boston, evidence of Boston or New England leather chairs in Philadelphia prior to 1710 was not turned up by Ruth Matzkin. Nor does Hornor mention any of them in the *Blue Book*. The February 1738/39 advertisement by Peter Baynton, mentioned in catalogue entry 79, may be the earliest reference. The negative results of this research suggest that Fleeson's advertisements of 1742 and 1744 were published in reaction to a situation that was becoming intolerable. This is important to know, since it suggests that the present Philadelphia-made Boston chair may very well date from about the time of the Fleeson ads. This, too, suggests that the "5 Leather Bottom chairs New England fashion" valued at 10s. each and listed among "what the widow took" in the 1762 inventory of Solomon Fussell, a chairmaker turned merchant who was working in Philadelphia between 1724 and 1750, may well have been like the present chair.[4] That they were valued at only 10s. each does not suggest that they were conspicuously new.

The phrase "leather bottom," and especially the word *bottom*, are potentially troublesome. Susan Prendergast Schoelwer has argued that the phrasing is important; "leather bottom chair" suggests a chair with a cushion or slip seat, "leather chair" indicates a chair of the Boston type in which the leather is tacked to the chair frame. The idea is highly attractive and would be most helpful if it can be proved to be a generally reliable assumption. Contradictory evidence abounds, even in Fussell's inventory. Fussell had "6 maple Rush Bottom chairs & a Leather Bottom Arm d[itt]o . . . £3," and "4 Rush Bottom chairs and 2 small d[itt]o . . . 10[s]." None of these could be slip-seat chairs, especially those with rush bottoms,

since rush-bottom slip seats are unknown among middle-colonies chairs, and the values are also too low for slip seats. Alexander Moore, a Philadelphia peruker whose estate amounted to £2,262, died the year before Fussell. His inventory contained "6 Boston chairs" valued at 10s. each, 6 additional ones valued at 6s. 8d. each, and "6 compass seat chairs" with "red damask bottoms," clearly the Queen Anne style, valued at 26s. 8d. each. His second set undoubtedly had slip seats.[5]

From the standpoint of economics, it should be pointed out that Fleeson's chairs could not have been a great deal cheaper than their Boston counterparts because the labor and materials involved are about equivalent. Savings could only be on shipping costs and middleman profits, for Fleeson was not competing against Boston chairmakers but against the import-export activities of merchants, some of whom were, according to his 1744 advertisement, "Master chairmakers," for whom chairs were merely another commodity in commerce.

We have no way of knowing to what extent Fleeson's advertisements reflected the trade in chairs flowing from Boston to Philadelphia, but a manuscript entitled "Clearances of the British Colonies in America," in the collection of the Boston Athenaeum, reveals that large quantities of chairs were shipped from Boston in the 1740s, which suggests that the Philadelphia production of them affected the trade very little. On April 21, 1744, the snow *Friendship* cleared the port of Boston for Philadelphia with "8 doz. & 2 Leather Chairs" aboard. On April 26, the schooner *Boston* headed for Philadelphia with "3 doz. Leather Chairs here made." Others were shipped as follows:

1744

September 1	sloop *Wallis*—"3 chairs"	
September 20	sloop *Mary*—"1 doz. chairs here made"	
December 17	schooner *Betty*—"4 doz. Chairs" (shipped by Samuel Grant)	

1745

May 9	sloop *Ranger*—"6 chairs"	
May 28	sloop *Dolphin*—"4 doz. chairs"	
June 12	schooner *Betty*—"18 Leather Chairs"	
June 18	sloop *Industry*—"1 doz. Chairs"	
July 11	sloop *Lidia*—"2½ doz. Leather Chairs"	
August 30	sloop *Ranger*—"20 Chairs"	
October 3	sloop *Willing Mind*—"1 doz. Chairs"	
October 12	sloop *Greyhound*—"5 doz. of Chairs"	
October 18	schooner *Betty*—"1 dozn. Chairs" (shipped by Samuel Grant)	

Of the 817 chairs, 72 are specified as "leather chairs." These records begin April 3, 1744, and end September 19, 1748. Philadelphia was the third best customer for Boston-made chairs. The best customer—which should also have been Philadelphia's best customer—was Maryland, where 1,013 were shipped, followed by New York, to which 979 were sent. It is surprising that two of the cities where Boston chairs were sold were cities that had sizable furniture-making industries. Excluding those sent to Newfoundland, the total number of chairs shipped from Boston during this period was 4,193. Other recipients were the West Indies—578; Virginia—354; South Carolina—193; North Carolina—181; Rhode Island (principally Providence)—66; and New Jersey—12.[6] The continued popularity of Boston-made chairs, combined with the aggressiveness of Boston merchants, may account for the rarity of Philadelphia examples: only two others—both armchairs—have been located in American museums, one at New York's Metropolitan Museum of Art and the other in the Detroit Institute of Arts. None has been found in Philadelphia.[7]

Winterthur's Philadelphia-made leather chair offers us a rare opportunity to stop time for a moment, as decorative arts objects often do, and see if we can distill from its reality as an object something of the mind of the craftsman who made it. Of the upholsterer-entrepreneur who commissioned the frame, little individuality emerges or can be expected to emerge. The frame itself reveals that the original upholstery was double nailed, but the ribbon of leather that was once present between the rows of tacks was not restored when the chair was reupholstered. Double nailing, according to the Fitch and Grant accounts, was the most popular method of upholstering a leather chair and, of course, more expensive than single nailing because it required more time and materials. The mentality of the upholsterer is revealed by his commission of a virtual replica of the competing Boston chair, a "copy," as it might be called in art historical circles, a "knock-off," as it would be called in modern furniture-making circles.

At almost every step, the framemaker complied with his commission. Virtually every detail is rendered exactly as it is in the Boston prototype: the crest rail is nearly identical to that on Boston-made examples, including such details as a gouged chamfer that feathers out at the extremities on the rear top edge; the stiles are virtually identical to those of the previous example in this catalogue; so, too, are the arms. Indeed, these parts are so much alike in the two chairs that they could be interchanged. For reasons known only to the framemaker and the man who commissioned it, the decision was made to change the way in which the front feet were executed and to substitute a Pennsylvania form of baluster on the arm support. The difference in making the foot of one piece of wood might say to us that maple cost less in Philadelphia than in Boston and was therefore worth less than the time the maker would use in gluing it up, except that the Philadelphia-made example in the Metropolitan Museum of Art (acc. no. 23.80.6), nearly identical to the Winterthur chair in every other respect, has glued-up feet.

The substitution of the characteristic Philadelphia arm support for the Boston one is another matter. While some might argue that the articulation of the Philadelphia baluster is less baroque than its Boston counterpart, others would respond that Philadelphia's baluster is visually more pleasing, more graceful, and less bottom heavy than Boston's. Indeed, Philadelphia turning has refinement and sharpness. The delicate neck of the baluster, with the long slender taper below and above the tiny ring set off by groove and fillet above, is a masterfully calculated curve. The baluster between seat and front stretcher is also artfully articulated. Why then does the Philadelphia maker insert the compressed ball between front stretcher and foot? Certainly it was no lack of design capability or absence of skill, as the balusters above so well demonstrate. Perhaps the designer of this chair believed it was more important to equalize the size of the blocks on the front legs, a consideration which left insufficient room for another baluster. Or perhaps the craftsman decided to mark his work for the future, to impress his own identity on it, to identify himself as an individual rather than a slavish copyist.

Although the aesthetic merits of the Philadelphia version versus the Boston type may be argued according to personal taste, the chair stands as the physical embodiment of a complex of cultural and economic forces that, at least in this one instance, can be shown to have affected furniture design. Moreover, the chair is living evidence that the chairmakers of Boston had continued to make an older style of chair for the export trade more than a decade after the crook-leg, compass-shape chair seat had been introduced in Boston, for the Philadelphia version was clearly made to compete with imported Boston chairs. Equally to the point is that there was a market among a certain clientele for this type of chair in Philadelphia and vicinity as late as the 1740s.

The upholstery on this chair is modern.

NOTES
[1] For an explanation of this attribution, see Forman, "Delaware Valley 'Crookt Foot' and Slat-Back Chairs," pp. 41–64.
[2] Grooved balusters are found on the chairs of Thomas Gaines, ca. 1735, but this individualistic touch is not derived from the high-style William and Mary chairs made by his father; for a summary of their production, see Hendrick, "John Gaines III and Thomas Gaines I," pp. 56–150.
[3] Prime, *Arts and Crafts in Philadelphia, Maryland, and South Carolina*, p. 202.
[4] Philadelphia Wills, 1762-148.
[5] Philadelphia Wills, 1762-148, 1761-37.
[6] I am indebted to Brock W. Jobe for his generosity in supplying me with a copy of his notes from the original manuscript. For additional references, see Swan, "Coastwise Cargoes," pp. 278–80.
[7] I am indebted to Frances Gruber Safford, Nancy M. Rivard, and Beatrice Garvan for this information.

Fig. 185. Dining room of the Pickering house in Salem, Mass., showing the 1 armchair and 7 of the 10 side chairs, all with crook backs, molded stiles, and leather seats. The chairs were probably made in Boston between 1722 and 1745. (From a ca. 1910 photograph in the Mary B. Northend Collection, DAPC, Winterthur Library.)

81.
CROOK-BACK ELBOW CHAIR WITH DOUBLE-NAILED LEATHER
Probably Boston, Massachusetts
1722–1745
WOOD: A soft maple
OH 46″ (116.8 cm)
SH 17¼″ (43.8 cm), SW 23″ (58.4 cm), SD 16½″ (41.9 cm)
PROVENANCE: Gift of Henry Francis du Pont
58.554

To all outward appearances, this chair varies only slightly from the preceding examples and by all rights ought to have been made in Boston. It most obviously differs from the others in that the front feet are turned baluster shapes rather than claw feet, and the crest rail consists of what might have been termed a double-round rather than the more familiar hollow-round-hollow molding of the previous chairs.[1] Two less obvious features prevent an unhesitating attribution to Boston: oak was not used as a secondary wood in it, and the volute of the handholds consists of a single spiral rather than the double spiral that is common among the identified Boston group (see, for example, catalogue entries 56 and 78). That no oak was used in the seat rails and lower back rails here may merely represent a shop preference, a regional variation, or it may be of no significance whatsoever, perhaps indicating that the shop in which it was made was out of oak on the day it was put together. A closely related chair formerly owned by Luke Vincent Lockwood and now in the Mabel Brady Garvan Collection at Yale has a lower back rail and rear seat rail of maple, while the other three seat rails are oak.[2] The variation of the handhold presents a problem. Minor deviations from the

standard type such as this have normally been rationalized as differences among shops in the same town, but the recent identification of Philadelphia-made chairs, which almost exactly duplicate the appearance of the Boston examples (see catalogue entry 80), implies that the explanations of the past are inadequate data on which to make a firm attribution.

A similar set of chairs in Massachusetts has a history of ownership by the Pickering family of Salem. The Pickering set consists of 1 armchair and 10 side chairs, most of which are illustrated in figure 185. According to family tradition, those chairs were made by the Reverend Theophilus Pickering (1700–1747), who was born in Salem, was graduated from Harvard College in 1719, and was minister in Chebacco Parish of Ipswich from 1725 until his death. Family tradition has long held that Pickering was an amateur woodworker. The Pickering armchair varies from Winterthur's in two important respects: first, its arm and arm support are of the conventional type, usually found on Boston armchairs, such as the one illustrated on the chair in entry 78; and second, the front stretcher is highly attenuated and differs markedly from the stretchers of the side chairs of the set, all of which are the conventional Boston tripartite type and are identical to the stretcher on the Winterthur example. These side chairs are so close to numerous examples that have no association with the Pickering family that we must question the family tradition. Unfortunately Pickering's craftsmanship cannot be confirmed by an independent document. No inventory of his estate was ever filed, and his will mentions only bequests of money to his sisters and their children. The residue of his unitemized estate was left to his brother Timothy in Salem.[3] It is certainly

cat. 81

possible that Pickering copied an armchair being made in urban Massachusetts at the time, since the variation of the stretcher would not have occurred in a professional shop that made such a chair en suite with the existing side chairs. Indeed, the stretcher cannot be explained away and may very well have been replaced, perhaps by an amateur woodworker. Two additional chairs of this type are owned by the Essex Institute, but no history of ownership is known for them. [4]

Since all 13 chairs are present in Essex County and none with Boston associations is known, it is possible that the style was being made there. The search for the makers, however, is impeded by the absence of identifiable upholsterers in the county records, even in those of Salem—the most important town in the area—during the first third of the eighteenth century. If upholstered chairs were being made there, it is likely that they were made by craftsmen called "chairmakers," but this search is likewise disappointing. Benjamin Gray of Salem is a typical candidate. Gray, the son of Benjamin Gray, a turner, called himself "turner alias chairmaker" in his will. He was born October 3, 1700, and should have been at the height of his career during the years in which chairs of this type were popular, but the February 20, 1761, inventory of his home and shop noted only 8s. worth of "chairmaker's tools" and numerous "maple chairs" valued between 8s. for 1 armchair and 16d. for a group of "old" chairs. None of them is said to be upholstered with leather nor was any leather or other upholstery material listed in his shop. [5]

While it is possible that such chairs were being made in Salem and that their makers have merely eluded our researches, that the surviving examples are obviously of commercial origin and that others have been found throughout the northern colonies implies dissemination possibly through migration or through the export trade at the time that they were made. Two examples, which appear to have New York histories of ownership, were illustrated in books by Esther Singleton. The first, which appeared in *Furniture of Our Forefathers* (1900) was owned by Mrs. Cuyler Ten Eyck of Albany and was in the Gansevoort family home, Whitehall. The second was in the collection of the Colonial Dames of New York and was at the van Cortlandt mansion in 1902 when it was illustrated in *Social New York under the Georges*. [6] Another example found in Hartford, Connecticut, was owned by George Dudley Seymour when it was pictured in Nutting's *Furniture Treasury* as no. 2090. It is now in the collection of the Connecticut Historical Society. [7] An additional example that may have been found in the Hartford area was illustrated by Lockwood in *Colonial Furniture* (2d ed.) as fig. 484. This chair—the only one with Spanish front feet—was then owned by William Meggatt, an early dealer in antiques who lived in Wethersfield, Connecticut. An armchair, then in a collection in Wickford, Rhode Island, was illustrated in Nutting's *Furniture Treasury* as no. 2681. Another armchair descended in the Hartshorn family of northern New Jersey and is now in the collection of the Monmouth County Historical Association. [8] A pair of chairs which take the story back to eastern New England were found in Kittery, Maine, some years ago by distinguished collector Joseph Parsons. They had a tradition of local ownership in the family of Capt. Nathaniel Sparhawk and are

unusual because both retain the original leather back and one retains its original leather seat. That leather is not russia leather, but the domestic product referred to in Thomas Fitch's accounts as "New England leather." [9] Since none of these chairs betrays the local characteristics of the places in which they were found, it seems logical to assume that they all originated in an urban chairmaking center, such as Boston. [10]

Although there is a dearth of leather chairs of this type known to have been made there, there are two cane chairs with double-round crest rails that could have originated nowhere except in Boston. One of these cane chairs appeared in *Harvard Tercentenary*. At that time it had been covered with leather, but the manner in which the seat overhangs the legs clearly indicates that the seat at least was originally upholstered with cane. The chair is said to have been made by the Reverend Edward Holyoke (1689–1769), president of Harvard College from 1737 until his death. [11] The medial stretcher of the chair appears to be a replacement, but the rear stretcher exhibits the deep central groove and swelled outline found on the stretchers of a chair that, although also said to be by Holyoke, is among the professionally made Boston cane chairs (see catalogue entry 54). Thus it appears likely that neither chair attributed to Holyoke was made by him. A second cane chair, also unmistakably the product of a professional chairmaking shop, is illustrated by Downs in *American Furniture* (no. 12). That chair, made of American beech and soft maple, is of superior quality and appears to retain much of its original black lacquer. Although the handgrip of the arm has two spirals at the volute rather than the single one, that chair is more closely related to catalogue entry 81 than to the previous catalogue entries. Its front legs are similar to those of the Boston side chair illustrated in figure 161. The presence of the double-round-corner crest rail on the second cane chair, which could not have been made much earlier than 1730 when the cabriole leg first appears in the accounts of Samuel Grant, suggests that chairs with double-round-corner crests were being made at that time, when the crook-back type with the hollow-round-hollow crest rail should have been on the wane. There is, however, no reason to believe that this type of crest rail was not a variation available as early as the hollow-round-hollow type, although neither stylistic treatment is specifically mentioned either in Grant's records or those of his former master, Thomas Fitch.

When Grant began working on his own account around 1728, crook-back leather chairs became a staple item of his shop almost immediately. On January 14, 1728/29, he billed "6 Leather chairs" at 26s. each to Rufus Green, "Goldsmth at the soth End." On February 4, 1728/29, he billed William Clear, a merchant in New York, for 2 dozen leather chairs at 26s. each, which he notes were shipped "on my acco[un]t," meaning that they were sent on speculation and not in response to an order. On April 27, 1729, Grant billed Daniel and Andrew Oliver, of Boston, for "3 arm'd Leather Chairs at 48s.," the same price that Fitch charged for this form. [12] As hinted at in the discussion of the chair in entry 77, the price that Grant charged for his leather chairs is provocative. At 26s. for a side chair, the cost to Grant's customers was 1 s. less than the price Thomas Fitch had been charging in 1723, but, in terms of actual money, Grant's price was even lower since the value of Massachusetts currency had depreciated in the 6 intervening years.

At first glance, it would appear that Grant was in a competitive situation with his former master, but his accounts reveal that this is not so. First, Grant was dependent upon Fitch for business, and second, Fitch was the second largest investor in Grant's enterprise and thus was more a partner than a competitor.[13] It is possible that the differential in price between the chairs of Grant and Fitch was caused by the use of New England leather, but it is equally possible that Grant's chairs varied in style from those of Fitch and were of the present type, which almost invariably has a turned baluster foot and is therefore less expensive to make than the carved Spanish foot usually found on the model with the hollow-round-hollow crest rail.

On September 24, 1733, Grant was still selling leather chairs at 26s. each.[14] How much longer he contined to sell them is not known, but 12 years later leather chairs were still being shipped from Boston to Philadelphia.

The upholstery on the chair is modern.

NOTES
[1] London Cabinet Maker's Union Book of Prices (1811, 1824, 1836), pl. 1, as quoted in Montgomery, American Furniture, pp. 358–60.
[2] Kane, Three Hundred Years of American Seating Furniture, pp. 61–62, fig. 40; Lockwood, Colonial Furniture, no. 485.
[3] Fales, Essex County Furniture, no. 32; John J. Costello, registrar of the Essex County Probate Court, to Forman, January 29, 1978; will and bond docket no. 21820, Essex Probate Files.
[4] Soderholtz, Colonial Architecture and Furniture, pl. 22; also illustrated in Chamberlain, Salem Interiors, p. 21.
[5] Docket 11585, Essex Probate Files; Perley, History of Salem, 3:9; Forman, "Salem Tradesmen and Craftsmen," pp. 62–81.
[6] Singleton, Furniture of Our Forefathers, p. 249; Singleton, Social New York under the Georges, p. 54.
[7] It is also published in Comstock, American Furniture, fig. 28.
[8] Joseph W. Hammond to Forman, June 27, 1979.
[9] DAPC 75.992, Winterthur Library. The chairs were illustrated in the catalogue of Sotheby Parke Bernet, Sale no. 3866, Fine Americana, lot 483.
[10] A set of chairs of this type is presently displayed in the Old State House, Boston. The records of the Colonial Society of Massachusetts do not reveal that the chairs have a history of ownership in that city. The termini of their front stretchers consist of a ring and a bulbous baluster, not unlike the baluster at the top of the arm of the chair in entry 78 and not unrelated to the termini of the front stretchers of labeled William Savery chairs. See Hornor, Blue Book, pl. 462.
[11] Harvard Tercentenary, no. 210, pl. 34.
[12] January 14, February 4, 1728/29, April 27, 1729, Grant daybook.
[13] November 28, 1728, Grant daybook, shows that Fitch had advanced him £156.15.3 in merchandise and credits with which to set up trade.
[14] September 24, 1733, Grant daybook.

82.

ELBOW LEATHER CHAIR
Probably Philadelphia, Pennsylvania, possibly Delaware or New Jersey
1725–1745
WOOD: Black walnut (*Juglans nigra*)
OH 49⅞" (126.7 cm)
SH 15½" (39.4 cm), SW 23⅜" (59.3 cm), SD 17⅞" (45.4 cm)
PROVENANCE: Joe Kindig, Jr.; Henry Francis du Pont
54.518

While furniture historians may be able to identify some objects so thoroughly that the written exposition of their identification becomes tedious, other objects that are very nearly but not quite the same elude identification completely. Such is the case with the present chair, one of four in the Winterthur collection whose crest rails show different uses of the same idea—a semicircular arch (see catalogue entries 73 and 74). Like the others, this chair is made of an American wood, in this case black walnut (*Juglans nigra*), including the seat rails and the turned stretchers. Unlike the other two, it has provenance but no history. Joe Kindig, Jr., the distinguished antiques dealer of York, Pennsylvania, from whom the chair was acquired, recalled a year prior to his death that it was one of two of identical appearance that he had handled during his long career. This one, which Kindig referred to as "the Moravian chair," was acquired in Bethlehem, Pennsylvania. The identical mate was purchased in Michigan and is now in a private collection in Florida.

Like the Scandinavian-inspired example of an earlier date (catalogue entry 73), this chair is very different from the more familiar Boston leather chairs in the Anglo-American

tradition. Unlike the chair in entry 73, the legs and stretchers of this example do not have the easily recognized attributes of northern European turning. Like that chair, this example has none of the softness of transition from one turned element to another that would suggest it either was made late in its period or is a rural product. Moreover, it is an upholstered chair, a form that is rarely essayed outside an urban area. The high back here has lingered on from the earlier style, but the molded stiles and handsomely sculpted arms place this chair squarely within the second quarter of the eighteenth century and reveal that its maker was well aware of the stylistic attributes of contemporary Boston or English chairs since he had absorbed these elements into his design. The distinctive form of the balusters that support the arms suggests that the maker of this chair was aware of the traits of Germanic turning that had appeared in the middle colonies slightly earlier but is probably not German himself since the arms differ greatly from the type made by immigrant craftsmen of German extraction.

The most unusual feature of this chair is the distinctive crest rail. Rounded crest rails are often illustrated in Sigurd Erixon's *Möbler*, and one of these (fig. 709) from the collection of the Nordiska Museet, Stockholm, closely resembles a simplified village version of the present one, complete with notched corners.[1] Although the moldings on the crest rail form a perfect semicircle and superficially appear to have been turned on the face plate of a lathe, in the manner of the crest rail of the related chair illustrated in catalogue entry 73, they could not have been turned because the angled blocks extending to the sides here, unlike those of the former chair, are not recessed and

cat. 82

indeed have the outer molding carried around their rectangular perimeters. The moldings could have been carved with gouges, but their surfaces, although less mechanical than those turned on a lathe, are somewhat more regular than surfaces that are hand carved. A possible way of accomplishing this—a technique that would explain the close match of the profiles of the moldings on the crest rail with the moldings on the uprights of the upholstered back—is often used by modern craftsmen and was published by Joseph Moxon. With customary pithiness, Moxon described the process of "laying moldings either upon Mettal, or Wood, without fitting the work in a Lathe":

I Had, soon after the Fire of *London*, occasion to lay Moldings upon the Verges of several round and weighty flat pieces of *Brass*: And being at that time, by reason of the said Fire, unaccommodated of a *Lathe* of my own, I intended to put them out to be *Turned*: But then *Turners* were all full of Employment, which made them so unreasonable in their Prizes, that I was forc'd to contrive this following way to lay Moldings on their Verges.

I provided a strong Iron *Bar* for the *Beam* of a *Sweep*: (For the whole *Tool* marked in *Plate 16* [see fig. 21, above], is by Mathematical *Instrument-makers* called a *Sweep*.) To this *Tool* is filed a *Tooth* of Steel with such *Roundings* and *Hollows* in the bottom of it, as I intended to have *Hollows* and *Roundings* upon my Work: For an Hollow on the *Tooth*, makes a *Round* upon the Work; and a *Round* upon the *Tooth*, makes an *Hollow* on the Work; even as they do in the *Molding-plains Joyners* use. Then I placed the *Center-point* of the *Sweep* in a Center-hole made in a square *Stud* of *Mettal*, and fixed in the *Center* of the Plain of the Work; and removed the *Socket* that rides on the *Beam* of the *Sweep*, till the *Tooth* stood just upon its intended place on the Verge of the Work, and there screw'd the *Socket* fast to the *Beam*.

To work it out, I employ'd a Labourer, directing him in his Left Hand to hold the Head of the *Center-pin*, and with his Right Hand to draw about the *Beam* and *Tooth*, which (according to the strength) he us'd, cut and tore away great Flakes of the *Mettal*, till it receiv'd the whole and perfect Form the *Tooth* would make; which was as compleat a Molding as any Skillful *Turner* could have laid upon it.

Having such good Success upon *Brass*, I improv'd the invention so, as to make it serve for Wood also. And make a *Plain-Stock* with my intended Molding on the *Sole* of it, and fitted an *Iron* to that *Stock* with the same Molding the *Sole* had.

Through the sides of this *Stock* I fitted an Iron *Beam*, to do the Office of the *Beam* I used for the *Sweep*, viz. to keep the Plain always at what position I listed from the Center (from thus the Iron in the Plain wrought about the Center, even as the Tooth in the *Sweep* (before rehearsed) and to that purpose I made a round Hole of about an Inch Diameter near the end of the Iron: Then in the Center of the Work I fixed a round Iron *Pin*, exactly to fit the said round Hole, putting the round Hole over the *Pin*, and fitting the *Iron* into the *Stock* commodious to work with. I used this Plain with both Hands, even as *Joyners* do other *Plains*: For the *Iron Pin* in the Hole of the *Beam* kept it to its due distance from the Center; so that neither hand was ingaged to guide it.

But note, The *Stock* of this *Plain* was not straight (as the Stocks of other Plains are) but by Hand cut Circular pretty near the size of the Diameter of the intended Molding: And yet was made to slide upon the *Beam*, farther from or nearer to the Center, as different Diameters of Verges might require.[2]

The implications of the use of this technique by the maker of Winterthur's chair are of great interest to historians of furniture, for here is the work of a craftsman committed to a stylistic idea —the arched crest—that he may have been trained to use when he was taught to make chairs in an earlier era, during which arched crest rails were tenoned *between* the turned stiles of a chair. By the time this chair was made, fashion dictated that crest rails be tenoned *onto the ends* of stiles that are rectangular in section and molded on their front surfaces. The technique that Moxon describes, or one very like it, would solve his problem and gives us a rare insight into what happens when a craftsman is caught between new fashions and the comfortable solution of traditional ideas.

The question of the Scandinavian as opposed to the German ancestry of the maker of this chair could be endlessly debated, since we know painfully little about the furniture-making activities of either group in early eighteenth-century America. The chair, however, did originally display one trait that is known to have been used in Sweden: its seat was half upholstered over the front rail. The rails are made of walnut, as is the rest of the chair, instead of some inferior wood.

Despite the lingering touch of Scandinavian practices that can still be seen in this chair, it is clear from the related banister-back chair in catalogue entry 74 that the Swedish school of chairmaking in the middle colonies absorbed so many influences from the dominant Anglo-German majority during the first half of the eighteenth century that the Swedish characteristics of the later chair can scarcely be recognized. The famous Swedish traveler in America, Peter Kalm, commented on the assimilation of the Swedish minority, but he noticed only the assimilation into the English strain. "Before the English settled here," he wrote, "the colonnists of New Sweden followed the customs of Old Sweden; but after the English had been in the country for some time, the Swedes began gradually to follow theirs. When [the Swede whom Kalm was quoting] was but a boy, there were two Swedish smiths here who made hatchets, knives and scythes, exactly like Swedish ones. . . . The hatchets now in use are often of the English style."[3]

The upholstery on the chair is modern but approximates the appearance of the original.

NOTES
[1] Nordiska Museet, acc. no. 88.087.
[2] *Moxon's Mechanick Exercises*, pp. 217–19.
[3] Kalm, *Travels in North America*, p. 273; I am indebted to Ellen M. Rosenthal for this reference.

83.
COUCH
Boston, Massachusetts
1722–1740
WOODS: Left side rail and left rear leg, soft maple; crest rail, a maple; rear stretcher
peg, an ash
OH 38¼″ (97.2 cm)
SH 15½″ (39.4 cm), SW 61¼″ (155.6 cm), SD 21½″ (54.6 cm)
PROVENANCE: Philip Flayderman; Henry Francis du Pont
58.550

See p. 356 for text

84.
COUCH
Boston, Massachusetts
1722–1740
WOODS: Frame, soft maple; pins, soft and hard maples
OH 38″ (96.5 cm)
SH 15″ (38.1 cm), SW 62″ (157.5 cm), SD 21⅞″ (55.8 cm)
PROVENANCE: Bequest of Henry Francis du Pont
69.818

These two Boston couches in the molded-stiles manner of the 1720s and 1730s provide examples of variations available within the tradition: no. 83 has tripartite turned stretchers, front legs that project above the seat rails, and an ogee-shape crest; no. 84 has bipartite stretchers and a stepped, rounded crest. Bipartite stretchers are, generally speaking, an earlier feature. Both couches have adjustable backs. Rabbets in the seat rails indicate that the frames originally had laced sacking bottoms that supported a quilted pad. The backs were upholstered with linen linings, a small amount of hair stuffing, a linen undercover, and a cover textile matching the cover of the pad. The Mabel Brady Garvan Collection, Yale University Art Gallery, has a couch identical to no. 84 that retains its original sackcloth layer and a fragment of green moreen or harrateen under an original tack. Since the cover was tacked in place, the edges of the cover were probably trimmed with binding or galloon.

EASY CHAIRS AND
LOW CHAIRS

The easy chair, characterized by a fully upholstered back, wings, and arms that end in one or two great scrolls, plus a cushion seat, evolved not from a seventeenth-century Cromwellian armchair or couch, but from an older tradition of invalid chairs. One such chair was made for the ailing Philip II of Spain in the 1590s. It had a padded seat, hinged but open arms that had padding on top, a padded footrest and back which could be adjusted at various angles with ratchets, and lignum vitae casters. (The similarity of that sixteenth-century form to the twentieth-century recliner is obvious and pertinent.) By the 1670s, chairs with square cheeks attached to the hinged back were made for the royalty and the nobility and were called "sleeping chairs"; however, the association of heavily padded chairs with the aged and the infirm also persisted. The sumptuously upholstered chairs and *canapés*, or sofas, made for the Dauphin (son of Louis XIV) in the 1690s, had closed arms, dust ruffles, and silk covers with gold and silver trim. These shocked some observers who thought it effete for healthy young people to use such soft, comfortable seating furniture. The stylistic connection between such luxurious seating forms and the upholstered alcoves of Turkish harems, a theme revived in the nineteenth century, also played a part in the philistine disapproval of the Dauphin's rooms.[1]

On the Continent the *fauteuil de commodité* (literally, an armchair of ease or comfort) may have been the full-blown easy chair of the 1690s. In England the duke of Ormonde, a member of Charles II's court, had what was termed an "easy chair" in 1684; however, surviving examples of upholstered furniture from this period, at Ham House in Surrey and at Knole in Kent, suggest that the only difference between a sleeping chair and an easy chair in the 1680s was that the back

of a sleeping chair was hinged to recline, while that of an easy chair was fixed. Other features of both could vary: an easy chair could have either a tight (stuffed) or a cushion seat and either open or closed arms. The first unambiguous reference to a furniture form identical to the modern easy chair dates from 1697. A kind of double easy chair, then called a sofa (but by the 1720s called a settee), had been introduced from France. The sofa made for William III of England by a French upholsterer working in London was described as "of a new fashion, filled up with down [in the seat cushion], the frieze [crest] and cheeks [wings] all molded [padded, with curled horsehair?] and fringed."[2] Certainly many sofas and easy chairs with these characteristics that are thought to date from the 1690s survive, and it seems reasonable to date the plainer examples no earlier than 1700. Thus the obvious relationship between the emergence of easy chairs and of sofas and settees underscores their quite obviously minimal relationship to armchairs and couches in the Cromwellian style; they represented innovations and were consciously assigned new names.

The heavy padding attached to the wings and scrolled arms of easy chairs required new upholstery techniques. The padded areas had to conform to the complex curves of the frames, and marsh grass was too stiff and hard a stuffing material for that purpose. Curled horsehair had been used to stuff chair and couch backs since the 1660s, but now it came into its own as the stuffing that could be caught under twines, picked to a desired contour, and further molded under linen undercovers with the upholsterer's regulator or utility needle.[3] (Linen undercovers also protected the show covers and the sitters from the prickly horsehair.) After 1700 easy chairs were always

Fig. 186. Easy chair, Boston, 1695–1705. Maple and pine, original underupholstery; H 42½″ (108 cm). (Private collection. Photo: Benno M. Forman.) The chair was formerly in the collection of Roger Bacon.

provided with deep, down-filled, boxy cushions that, although loose, fitted the contours of the seat, arms, and back. The great down pillows laid on the seats of chairs of state and couches between 1575 and 1680 provided a precedent for the new contours of boxy cushions with welted, or piped, edges. Unlike the knife-edged pillows used on chairs, the edges of these cases were boxed 4″ to 6″ (10.2–15.2 cm.) On easy chairs, cushion casings were made of soft leather, fustian, or linen ticking, all sturdy textiles that could resist the tendency of down-and-quill mixtures to work through seams. A range of options existed for the ends of the arms, including single vertical scrolls, single horizontal scrolls, and combinations of vertical and horizontal scrolls connected by C-shape panels. Undercarriages of the earliest examples were often elaborately carved in the cane-chair manner or in the gilded-architectural manner of the influential Daniel Marot.

Exactly when easy chairs were first made in Boston and New York City is not known. Among the very earliest to survive is a small easy chair made in Boston (fig. 186). This chair, which retained most of its original upholstery foundation until 1969, has a number of peculiarities that set it apart from its more standardized counterparts dating from the second decade of the eighteenth century. Among these are the flat crest embellished with a grass roll, straight arms with backswept stumps or supports, a tight seat, and stretchers running between the four legs. This somewhat cramped frame

is 6″ (15.2 cm) shorter than easy chairs with curved crests that evolved in the 1710–20 period, but it is strikingly close to a London easy chair from the 1700–1710 period (fig. 187). The design of the London chair, however, is a little more advanced: its crest is rounded, the seat is provided with a heavy cushion, and the undercarriage of the frame has a medial stretcher (the carved front stretcher was probably an optional feature). A side view of the London example (fig. 188) reveals the slight heels at the bottom of the rear legs and the astonishing backward cant of the frame, which extends far to the rear of the legs in a dramatic and precarious sweep. All these features were incorporated in American easy-chair frames of the 1710–30 period in the Winterthur collection.[4]

The earliest American reference to an easy chair is to one "lined with red" valued at £2.10 in a 1708 New York inventory. Four years later an easy chair was cited in a Boston inventory. After that time, easy chairs are cited with increasing frequency in the inventories of prosperous individuals. Inventories and the daybook of upholsterer Samuel Grant demonstrate that the preferred covers were sturdy wools with calendered patterns like harrateen, moreen, and cheny, rather than silk textiles like bourette.[5]

The frames and the materials used to fashion the upholstery foundations warrant attention insofar as they represented new ideas in American chairmaking. A Boston easy chair with its upholstery removed (fig. 189) shows the wooden components common to all frames of this period. The wood of preference for both the exposed undercarriage and the parts to be covered was maple. Because the rear legs were continuous with the rear posts, they had to be stained when the show wood of the undercarriage was walnut. Each arm-and-wing assembly consisted of an upright and rail outlining the wing, a horizontal arm cone with a vertical upright, a spacer block, and an extension of the front leg with an applied roll. Many of these components were simply nailed together.

An invoice dated December 8, 1729, in the Grant accounts lists the textile and other fixtures attached to the frame of an easy chair. The invoice, made out to Nathaniel Green of Boston, specifies:

	[£ s. d.]
1. Easie chair fraim	2: :
6½ Yd. chainy @6[s.]8[d.]	2:13: 4
1 Yd ⅛ print 4[s.]	: 4: 6
18 Yd. silk bindg 12[d.]	:16: 6
Tax 5[s.] girtweb Thred & line 3[s.]	: 8:
4 lb. curld hair 10[s.] 4 lb. feathrs. 14[s.]	1: 8:
1½ Yd Ticken 9[s.]4[d.] crocus & Ozna: 12[s.]	1: 1: 4
makg: an Easie chair	1:15:
Total:	10: 6: 8[6]

Setting aside the faulty arithmetic, Grant's invoice demonstrates that easy chairs were, without question, the most costly seating furniture available. The frame itself and the upholsterer's labor accounted for a third of the cost (£3.15), while the cheny and the silk binding used for the cover represented roughly another third (£3.14). The remaining part (£2.16.4) was spent on girt web, crocus (coarse linen sackcloth), curled horsehair, feathers (usually a mixture of fine down and larger quills), and oznaburg (durable linen

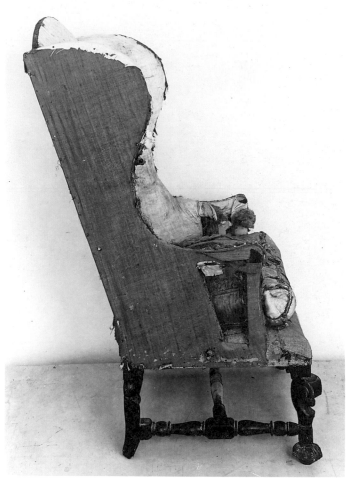

Fig. 187. ABOVE LEFT. Easy chair, London, England, 1700–1710. Beech and a conifer; original upholstery; H 52½″ (133.4 cm), W. 28″ (71.1 cm), D 23½″ (59.7 cm). Victoria and Albert Museum, London.) The chair has a history of ownership in Chastleton House near Oxford.

Fig. 188. ABOVE RIGHT. Side view of the easy chair in figure 187. (Victoria and Albert Museum, London.)

Fig. 189. LEFT. Easy chair, Boston, 1710–20. (Present location unknown. Photo: Archives of American Art on deposit at Winterthur Museum.)

undercover), and ticking. The girt web was used only in the seat and back panels, while the crocus was used to line the seat, back, and inside face of the arms and wings. Upon this foundation was laid horsehair stuffing in the arms, wings, and back. In most easy chairs whose stuffing has been preserved, the horsehair does not appear to have been affixed with systematic twining. Although the invoice does not mention marsh grass or reeds, such stiff stuffings were employed in the rolls tacked to the front seat rail and the edges of the arms and wings; these rolls are visible in figures 186 and 189. A skimmer layer of grass was also used to line the surface of the seat. All stuffings were contained by undercovers made of linens like oznaburg, duck, and canvas. The ticking was made up into the case for the cushion and filled with feathers.[7]

A number of inexplicable quirks of period practice complicate our understanding of this seemingly straightforward procedure. The "print" listed in Grant's invoice, perhaps a printed cotton cloth, appears in every invoice for an easy chair in both Fitch's and Grant's papers, yet no printed fabric

Fig. 190. Profiles of chairs in catalogue entries (left) 88 and (right) 92. (Winterthur 58.558, 58.537.)

survives on an easy chair; perhaps the print was used to line the seat or to cover the outside back. No undercover was used on the outside arms, wings, and back, which made them extremely vulnerable to punctures. Above all, the eighteenth-century easy-chair frame differed from its modern counterparts in its lack of medium struts. These mediums, as they are called today, are auxiliary rails set just in front of the rear posts and just above the side seat rails. They provide stretching and tacking surfaces for the upholsterer at those points in the frame where materials have to be drawn through and attached, known as tuck-aways. In modern work, tuck-aways modeled over mediums produce a harsh, rigid line and promote heavier stuffing to hide the mediums from view. A Newport easy chair of the 1750s or early 1760s, upholstered using exactly the same types and amounts of materials enumerated in the Grant invoice, exemplifies the lean, wavering lines expected of an easy chair when the undercovers and covers of the arms, wings, and back are drawn through tuck-aways without mediums (fig. 190).[8]

Among the rarest survivals of the eighteenth-century upholsterer's work are high-back low-seat chairs occasionally made en suite with easy chairs. The only reference to such a chair in the Grant account book is in an invoice dated January 25, 1731/32, for "1 Crimson Chainy Easy Chair" and "1 Low chair horse bone foot cush[io]n seat." Two such low chairs in the Winterthur collection parallel a well-known low chair with matching easy chair made in Newport about 1750.[9] What the purpose of low chairs was is not clear, but the persistent use of easy chairs in chambers throughout the eighteenth century suggests that their accompanying low chairs may have served as the functional ancestor of the Victorian slipper chair.

[1] Thornton, *Seventeenth-Century Interior Decoration*, pp. 197–201, 210–16.

[2] Thornton, *Seventeenth-Century Interior Decoration*, pp. 195–96, 220, 213.

[3] For more detailed information on upholsterer's tools and materials, see Passeri and Trent, "Two New England Queen Anne Easy Chairs," pp. 26A–28A.

[4] For more background on the easy chair illustrated in fig. 186, see Trent, "Franklin Chair," pp. 26B–29B.

[5] Unspecified New York inventory as cited by Lockwood, *Colonial Furniture* (2d ed.), 2:64.

I am indebted to Wendy Kaplan, whose paper "Catalogue Entry for the Flock Room Easy Chair" written for Art History 803–804 in the Winterthur Program in Early American Culture in 1978, has provided many useful references.

[6] December 8, 1729, Grant daybook.

[7] Passeri and Trent, "Two New England Queen Anne Easy Chairs," p. 28A.

[8] Passeri and Trent, "Two New England Queen Anne Easy Chairs," p. 28A.

[9] January 25, 1731/32, Grant daybook; Sack, *Fine Points of Furniture*, p. 65.

85.
LOW CHAIR
Boston, Massachusetts
1710–1720
WOOD: Medial stretcher, right rear leg, and right seat rail, a soft maple
OH 48¼″ (122.6 cm)
SH 15″ (38.1 cm), SW 19½″ (49.5 cm), SD 15⅛″ (38.4 cm)
PROVENANCE: Luke Vincent Lockwood; Henry Francis du Pont
58.569

cat. 85

This extraordinary low chair is the earliest known American example and the earliest object in the sequence of easy chairs and low chairs in the Winterthur collection.[1] The bipartite front stretcher and cane-chair-style columnar-shape turnings on the stretchers indicate its early date. The frame has sufficient height between the seat rails and the lower back rail to have accommodated a cushion, although not one with the usual 4″ to 6″ (10.2 to 15.2 cm) height.

Although the back is practically as tall as that of an easy chair, it does not have a strong backward rake, while the great heels of the rear legs are more than adequate to prevent the chair from tipping over backwards. The trapezoidal nature of the seat is more pronounced than are those of comparable leather-chair frames, increasing in width from 14½″ (36.8 cm) at the rear to 19½″ (49.5 cm) at the front. (This may also have been intended to give the frame stability.)

Lest it be thought that the chair is an innovative Boston design, it must be pointed out that sets of high-back upholstered chairs with matching armchairs occasionally were provided for aristocratic homes in England en suite with a state bed. This Boston-made frame has distinctive scalloping that establishes its relationship to easy chairs; the English sets that accompany state beds generally have straight stay rails, and their seat rails are intended to be trimmed with fringe.

That the frame has survived intact is rendered all the more remarkable by the crest rail that sits atop the rear posts and is mortised between them. In order to provide enough wood from which to fashion the deep scalloping, the crest rail is 6″ (15.2 cm) high. Underneath the present varnish are traces of an old if not original walnut-color stain.

NOTE
[1] The chair was owned by Luke Vincent Lockwood in 1913, but it does not appear in the sale catalogue of his collection (Lockwood, *Colonial Furniture* [2d ed.], p. 50; *Lockwood Sale*).

cat. 86

86.
LOW CHAIR
Boston, Massachusetts
1730–1740
WOODS: All maple, except the front seat rail of birch
OH 43⅜″ (100.2 cm)
SH 15¾″ (40.0 cm), SW 19¾″ (50.2 cm), SD 16½″ (41.9 cm)
PROVENANCE: Bequest of Henry Francis du Pont
66.778

In 1952 Joseph Downs identified this chair as a Connecticut product perhaps because the reddish varnish on the maple frame made it resemble cherry. Subsequent research has shown that some Queen Anne–style chairs from the Norwich area of Connecticut have square cabriole legs and baluster stretchers much like those seen here, precisely because the Norwich craftsmen were copying Boston chairs like this.[1] In addition, the baluster side stretchers demonstrate that the chair was probably made to accompany an easy chair, for the side stretchers of most Boston Queen Anne side chairs shifted to the columnar style of stretcher turnings by the mid 1730s. Unlike that in entry 85, this frame has a high seat that was not intended to receive a cushion. The retention of a backswept scroll crest is a surprisingly late feature for a chair made in the 1730s.

NOTE
[1] Downs, *American Furniture*, no. 96; Lyman Allyn Museum, *New London County Furniture*, p. 30. Also, see the so-called Southmayd-type Norwich chair illustrated and discussed as no. 102 in Downs, *American Furniture*.

cat. 87

87.
EASY CHAIR
Boston, Massachusetts
1715–1730
WOODS: Front seat rail, a hard maple; right seat rail, red oak (*Quercus rubra*); left
rear stile, a soft maple
OH 50¾" (128.9 cm)
SH 12½" (31.8 cm), SW 27" (68.6 cm), SD 21" (53.3 cm)
PROVENANCE: Gift of Henry Francis du Pont
58.538

See p. 365 for text

cat. 88

88.
EASY CHAIR
Boston, Massachusetts
1715–1730
WOOD: Front skirt, front right leg, a soft maple
OH 51¼" (130.2 cm)
SH 13" (33.0 cm), SW 25⅞" (65.7 cm), SD 21" (53.3 cm)
PROVENANCE: Gift of Henry Francis du Pont
58.558

See p. 365 for text

89.
EASY CHAIR
Boston, Massachusetts
1715–1730
WOODS: Front stretcher, chestnut; both side stretchers, oak; left front leg, medial stretcher, soft maple; front seat rail, a maple
OH 49¼″ (125.1 cm)
SH 13⅝″ (34.6 cm), SW 26¾″ (68.0 cm), SD 21″ (53.3 cm)
PROVENANCE: Bequest of Henry Francis du Pont
66.1309

The earliest fully developed easy-chair frames, dating perhaps a decade after the frame shown in figure 186, all display undercarriages with medial stretchers, scalloped skirts, double-scroll arms with C-shape panels, and rounded or scalloped

crests. The variations to be seen among these three examples represent both the conflicting influences of cane and leather-upholstered styles and the quirks of individual chairmaking shops. While the difficulties in assigning a chronological order to some of these variations are apparent, the broad development of the easy-chair frame in Boston between the emergence of the fully developed frame about 1710 to 1715 and the introduction of the crook foot in 1730 can be isolated with some exactitude.

Easy chairs nos. 87 and 89 have side stretchers turned with abstract, strongly tapering columns (frequently used on the undercarriages of English and some Boston cane chairs) and baluster ornament on the front stretchers, medial stretchers, and rear stretchers (similar to that on leather-chair frames being produced in a number of Boston shops). This admixture of turning vocabularies suggests that the same chairmakers were producing both cane chairs and leather chairs. Variants of the dominant short-baluster–long-baluster formula include the elided medial stretcher on no. 88, where the two central small balusters are united, base to base, into a single ball-like form. This formula undoubtedly was prompted by this particular frame, which is 1″ (2.5 cm) narrower than most other easy chair frames of this period, and the turner was forced to adapt his formula to fit the measurement. A virtually identical easy chair by the same maker displays a different solution to this problem—the two central short balusters of the medial stretcher are squashed together.[1]

The symmetrical ogee scalloping of the skirt of the chair in entry 87 is the classic formula for this detail; it was also used on the Franklin-family easy chair at the Museum of Fine Arts, Boston (acc. no. 1976.727).[2] The elaborate scalloping seen on no. 88 is exceptional, while the shallow, simple, skirt profile of no. 89 can tentatively be identified as a progressive streamlining of easy-chair frames that took place in the late 1720s and early 1730s. Similar permutations of the rounded crests seen on all three examples have the identical significance. A number of frames have the backswept scroll crest seen on no. 87, and such crest scrolls may have been more common than is now apparent. The extraordinary cant of many frames made it easy to overturn the chairs, and numerous frames that originally had crest scrolls probably lost them in just that way. Of course not all frames have a backward rake as extreme as that of no. 88, as a view comparing its profile with the chair in catalogue entry 92 indicates (see fig. 190).

Almost all Boston easy-chair frames dating from 1715 to 1730 have double-scroll arms whose lower level is set flush with the front rail. The offset scrolls of no. 89 are extremely rare, and like other features they seem to relate to the frame—simplified skirt profile, suppressed crest profile, and T-shape cushion—that they may reflect an "advanced" taste for overall compactness and leanness; similar qualities are found in Queen Anne easy chairs made between 1740 and 1800 in both Boston and Newport (fig. 191).

While the foundations and covers on these three chairs are not original to the frames, it is important to note that their cushions are all far too thin by early eighteenth-century standards. The invoices for easy chairs in the Fitch and Grant papers all specify between 3 and 4 pounds (1.4 and 1.8 k) of feathers for the cushions, an amount which probably brought the cushions level with the tops of the forward arm scrolls. As the cushions were routinely boxed, this also implies a more

Fig. 191. Easy chair, Newport, R.I., 1750–65. Walnut, maple, chestnut; H 47″ (119.4 cm), W 33¼″ (84.5 cm), D 21½″ (54.6 cm), SH 13″ (33 cm). (Colonel Daniel Putnam Association on loan to Connecticut Historical Society, Hartford, Conn.) Godfrey Malbone owned the chair when he retired in 1766 and moved from Newport, R.I., to his farm in Brooklyn, Conn.

widely boxed cushion than is now on the chairs.

The examples in nos. 87 and 88 have both suffered some loss in their original height and have thus been restored at the feet. The chair in entry 89 has been pieced out a full 1½″ (3.8 cm) at the bottom, its front feet are complete restorations, and its front stretcher is a modern addition which was not present originally.

NOTES
[1] The identical example is illustrated in an advertisement of John Walton, Inc., *Antiques* 120, no. 2 (August 1981): 206.
[2] Trent, "Franklin Chair," p. 26B.

90.
EASY CHAIR
Boston, Massachusetts
1730–1740
WOOD: Left rear seat rail, front seat rail, left front leg, and left side stretcher, a soft
maple
OH 48⅜″ (122.9 cm)
SH 13″ (33.0 cm), SW 27⅜″ (69.6 cm), SD 21″ (53.3 cm)
PROVENANCE: Bequest of Henry Francis du Pont
58.576

See p. 369 for text

cat. 91

91.
EASY CHAIR
Boston, Massachusetts
1730–1740
WOOD: Maple
OH 48″ (121.9 cm)
SH 13″ (33.0 cm), SW 28″ (71.1 cm), SD 21″ (53.3 cm)
PROVENANCE: Bequest of Henry Francis du Pont
58.1504

See p. 369 for text

92.
EASY CHAIR
Boston, Massachusetts
1730–1740
WOODS: Front rail, right rear leg, soft maple; left side stretcher a walnut; right seat rail, hard maple
OH 48″ (121.9 cm)
SH 11½″ (29.2 cm), SW 27¾″ (70.5 cm), SD 21″ (53.3 cm)
PROVENANCE: Gift of Henry Francis du Pont
58.537

The easy-chair format changed in about 1730 with the introduction of crook feet and the tripartite medial stretcher. The heavy scalloped skirts of the earlier style were displaced by a simpler skirt profile consisting of quarter-round or bracket-like cutouts and a straight front, while the high crests of the earlier style gave way to gentle ogee curves occasionally embellished by breaks near the sides. The double-scroll arm continued to be fashionable until the late 1730s, when the single vertical scroll set back from the seat rail was introduced. A subtle adjustment of the placement of the medial stretcher brought it about 2″ (5.1 cm) or more forward of its prior placement near the center of the side stretcher, and eventually the resultant longer vases at the rear of the side stretchers were replaced by columns, while the shorter vases at the front became mere ogee stops.

These three nearly identical frames clearly point toward a higher degree of standardization in chair-frame production. While it was not possible to uncover the vertical arm scrolls of no. 90, it seems likely that the unusual extension of the scrolls all the way to the rear posts is a later alteration, perhaps one made to brace the wings. The ambiguous turnings of the medial stretcher on this example, so unlike the vigorous ball-reel-ball turnings on the medial stretchers of nos. 91 and 92, suggest that the chair was made at a time when the transition from vasiform turnings to tripartite turnings was taking place.

The rear posts on no. 90 have been pieced out 1½″ (3.8 cm), and the front feet are restored. Four brackets are missing from the side rails of no. 91, and its rear turned stretcher is missing. About 1½″ (3.8 cm) is missing from the bottom of the frame of no. 92.

APPENDIX 1

THE 1708 INVENTORY OF CHARLES PLUMLEY, PHILADELPHIA JOINER

[IN HIS HOME]

	[£ s. d.]
Cash	5: 7: —
Thomas Biddle bill for	6: —: —
John Moses bill for	6: —: —
3 Silver Spoones	£2: 6: 0
6 Knives and 6 forks with Silver ferrills &c	1: 4: —
1 Pockett knife and forke and 2 Eggs Spoones	—: 8: —
2 flannell Vests	—:10: —
1 Speckled Linnen Vest and briches	1: 4: —
1 Leather Jackett and 1 pr. briches Cullird	2: 5: —
1 Ticken Jackett 10[s.] 1 old Stuft one 5[s.]	—:15: —
1 broad Cloth Coat Lined	2:15: —
1 Kersy Coat Close boddyed Lyned with Red	2: 5: —
1 Loose Kersey Coat Lyned wth Redd	2: 5: —
1 New hatt 20[s.] 1 old Ditto 12[s.]	1:12: —
3 pair of Shoes	—:12: —
2 pair shoes & 1 pr Steel Buckles	—:10: —
1 feather bedd wt 60 [lb. feathers] at 14[d.]	4: —: —
1 feather bedd and bolster wt. 55[lb.] at 18[d.]	4: 2: 6
1 Sea feather bed and 2 old Pillows wt 35 [lb.] at 12 d.	1:15: —
1 New Tick and bolster Case & 2 [lb.] feathers	2:10: —
1 old Bedd Quilt	—: 6: —
1 White old Rugg	—:12: —
3 old Blanketts	—:10: —
1 Flock bedd & 1 Bagg feathers	—: 15: —
1 Bedd stend Bottom Iron Rodds and Cornishes &c	2:10: —
1 pr Green Curtains and Vallins	1:15: —
1 pr blew Printed Curtains fringed	1:15: —
1 small Sacking bedd stend	—:15: —
1 pr Ozenb sheets and Two Pillow Cases	—:18: —
1 pr. fine holland sheets & 1 pr Pillow Cases	1:10: —
1 odd old Sheet	—: 5: —
1 new Cotton sheet 15[s.] 2 old Ditto 10[s.]	1: 5: —
1 Dyaper Table Cloth and Six napkins	1: 4: —

	[£ s. d.]
2 small Table Cloths and Six napkins	—:13: —
4 Window Curtaines	—: 5: —
1 black Cherry tree Chest Drawers	2:10: —
1 black screettore	3: 5: —
6 black Caine Chairs	3: —: —
6 leather Chairs	2:10: —
1 looking glass 30[s.] 2 smaller Ditto 3[s.]	1:13: —
1 Close Stool 12[s.] 2 sconces 5[s.]	—:17: —
1 fender with brass knobbs & 2 pr Iron Tongs	—:18: —
3 pictures in frames	—: 4: —
1 folio bible 50[s.] 2 small Ditto 6[s.] 6[d.]	2:16: 6
7 small books	—: 3: —
1 Walking Cane 4[s.] 1 Darke Lanthorne 2[s.]	—: 6: —
36 [lb.] Pewter at 18[d.]	2:14: —
3 brass Candlesticks 1 brass Ladle	—: 9: —
1 best metle old pott and hooks	—:10: —
1 Iron pott and hooks	—:10: —
1 pr Pott Racks	—:10: —
2 pr andirons 11[s.] 1 frying pann 5[s.]	—:16: —
1 box Iron & 2 heaters 5[s.] 2 Iron Candlesticks 2[s.]	—: 7: —
1 Pine Dough Trough 10[s.] 1 Salt box 1[s.]	—:11: —
a pekill of beef and Porke in ye Cellar	2:10: —
1 hhd [hogshead] of 76 Gallons of mollasses at 20[d.] p. gallo	6: 6: 8

[IN HIS SHOP]

	[£ s. d.]
5 handsaws	1: 8: —
4 Tennant Saws	—:16: 6
3 beam Saws	—: 7: 6
3 small saws	—: 3: —
33 formers and broad Chisells	1: —: —
14 gowges	—: 6: —
5 mortice chissells	—: 4: 2
2 Wyreable bitts	—: 4: 6

4 Center bitts and 1 Dott bitt	—: 5: —
2 Wimble stocks 1 iron 1 wood	—: 4: 6
1 drawing knife 15d. 2 hatchetts 5[*s*.]	—: 6: 3
2 Long plaines 1 Jack Plaine 2 Swich blocks 3 Smoothing plaines new	—:12: —
1 Jointer Yellow Jaunders 7[*s*.] 6[*d*.] 2 Ditto beach 7[*s*.] 6[*d*.]	—:15: —
3 Long plaines 7[*s*.] 6[*d*.]: 3 Jack plaines 4[*s*.] 6[*d*.] 3 strike blocks 4[*s*.] & 3 Smoothing plaines 3[*s*.]	—:19: —
5 Hammers 7[*s*.] 3 Raysors 3[*s*.]	—:10: —
1 Morris [mortise?] fraime	—: 6: —
1 chalk Role 10[*d*.] 1 hand Vice 2[*s*.] 6[*d*.]	—: 3: 4
3 gimbletts 1[*s*.] 2 punches 4[*d*.] : 2 saw setts 10[*d*.]: 3 compasses 18[*d*.]	—: 4: 5
4 wooden squares 2[*s*.] 8[*d*.] 2 bevells 1 setting square 2[*s*.] 6[*d*.]	—: 5: 2
The best bench 13[*s*.] 1 Ditto 10[*s*.] 1 ditto 7[*s*.]	1:10: 0
One Wheel and Layth &c	1:10: 0
22 hollows and rownds at 15d. Each	1: 7: 6
9 OGs at 15[*d*., each]. 6 belexions 14[*d*.] pr asticle 15[*d*.] 1 sash plain 15[*d*.] & 1 groove plaine	1: 2: —
3 Rabbitt Plaines 2[*s*.] 6[*d*.] 2 Philissers 2[*s*.] 6[*d*.], 1 pr Inch, 1 pr ½ Inch 3[*s*.] 4[*d*.]	0: 8: 4
2 Plougs 6[*s*.] 8[*d*.] 1 Revele Plaine 2[*s*.] 1 small cornish 3[*s*.]	—:11: 8
2 Rownd Smoothing Plaines & 1 hollow Ditto	—: 2: —
1 Upright Smoothing plaine 3 half upright Ditto	—: 2: 8
4 old chizzells 20[*d*.] 10 augers 15[*s*.] 3 screws & nutts 9[*s*.]	1: 5: 8
8 Turnings gowges 8[*s*.] 8 Turning Chissels 8[*s*.]	—:16: —
10 Ivory Turning tooles 8 Turning hooks 8 [*s*.]	0:16: —
5 Iron Turning Mandrells at 5[*d*.]	—: 2: 1
1 Looking Glass	—:16: —
2 Iron holdfasts 4[*s*.] 6[*d*.]. 6 glew potts wt 41 [lb.]	—:17: 1
1 Small Vice 5[*s*.] 29 pr. snipe bills 7[*s*.]3[*d*.]	—:12: 3
12 pr. chest hinges 2[*s*.] 1 Double Spring Chest Locks 6[*s*.]	—: 8: —
18 Outside box Locks 15[*s*.] 30 pr. Coffin handles 37[*s*.] 6[*d*.] 33 Square Ditto 2[*s*.]9[*d*.]	2:15: 3
30 pr. Duftailes 25[*s*.] 2 small Chest Locks 3[*s*.] 1 Desk Lock 18[*d*.].	1: 9: 6
2 pr. H hinges 3[*s*.] 35 Old fashioned scutcheons 18[*d*.]	—: 4: 6
30 old ffashioned Damnified Dropps 15[*d*.]: 15 La[rge] brass Rings 15[*d*.]	—: 2: 6
112 Dropps 28[*s*.] 53 Scutcheons 13[*s*.] 3[*d*.] 4 Sett Chest Draw Locks 16[*s*.]	2:17: 3
2 Rules 5[*s*.] 6[*d*.] 17708 Spriggs & Tacks at 4[*s*.]2[*d*.] p[r.] m [1000]	3:19: 3
3 pair box hinges Smooth filed 3[*s*.] 4 pr. Clock Ditto 6[*s*.]	—: 9: —
6 Clock Cace Locks 6[*s*.] 4 Dressing box Locks 4[*s*.]	—:10: —
1 Sett Screetore Locks 8[*s*.] 1 pr. Xnett [cross garnet] Dore hinges brass 2[*s*.]	—:10: —
8 Turning Strings 16[*s*.] 4 pr fish Skins 10[*s*.] 2 Screetore Joints 3[*s*.]	1: 9: —
22 new Wimble bitts 11[*s*.] 7 large ½ Round files 7[*s*.]	—:18: —
9 Small half Round files 10[*d*.]: 8 hand saw files 5[*s*.] 4[*d*.]	—:12:10

4 Small handsaw files 2[*s*.]: 12 molding plaine Irons 5[*s*.]	—: 7: —
3 Plow Irons—1[*s*.] 4 Dozn. Table Rivetts 4[*s*.] 4 Dozn Small brass Rings	—: 7: —
2 Oyle Stones 5[*s*.] 1 [lb.] bees wax 18[*d*.]: 2 pr Chest hinges 3[*s*.]	—: 9: 6
2 Screetore hinges 3[*s*.] 10 Long bedd screws 10[*s*.] 12 short ditto 6[*s*.]	—:19: —
7 New Plaine Irons 5[*s*.] 10[*d*.] 3 Tooth plaine Ditto 2[*s*.] 6[*d*.] 1 saw plate 10[*d*.]	—: 9: 2
3 Old Paring chissells 15[*d*.]: 2 New Varn[ish]ing brushes 2[*s*.]	—: 3: 3
3 Dore box Locks 15[*s*.] 7 plaine Irons 3[*s*.] 2 Tooth Plane Do. 1[*s*.] 8[*d*.]	—:19: 8
A parcell of wheel worke not finished	1:10: —
76 lb. of Glew [at] 14[*d*. per lb.] 8[*s*.] & 8[*d*.] 1 pr. Callipers 20[*d*.] 1 pr. pinchers 10[*d*.]	4:11: 2
3 Rasps 3[*s*.] 2 wood files 2[*s*.] 2 Quarts Varnish 25[*s*.]	1:10: —
2 pine Chests	1: 4: —
2859 feet Pine and oak boards at 8[*s*.] p [board foot]	11: 8: 8
311 Large Walnutt scantling at 12[*s*.] 6[*d*.]	1:19: 3
457 foot Small Walnutt Scantling at 8[*s*.] 4[*d*.]	1:17: 1
2738 foot Walnutt boards at 15[*s*.] p cen [hundred foot]	20:10: 8
734 foot Walnut Plank at 17[*s*.] p 100	6: 4: 9
2 Mohogany Planks 36 ½ feet at 16[*d*.]	2: 8: 8
3 inch board Ditto 48 feet at 6[*d*.]	1: 4: —
1 Walnut Table frame	1: 0: 0
1 pine Table	—: 5: —
7 sett Gum bedstead pillows at 2[*s*.] 4[*d*.]	—:16: 4
15 Sett [bedstead] Sydes and Ends at 2[*s*.] 4[*d*.]	1:15: —
160 foot pine scantling	—:11: —
8 parcels of Wallnutt & Pine Ends	1: 5: —
2 black Carved Chair frames	—:18: —
1 Walnut cace drawers, not finished	1:16: 0
6 Carved Maple Chairs ntt finished	3: —: —
1 Large frame saw	—: 9: —
a parcell of olive wood and other Veinarys	1:16: —
1 Grindstone	—: 7: —
6 ffeneaireing Screws at	—: 6: —
2 Ordinary benches in old house	—: 4: —
Brick House	100: —: —
Old House	10: —: —
Wooden House	50: —: —
Isaac his time to Serve	18: —: —
David his time to serve	12: —: —
	£389:16: 6

The above Inventorie was appraised too Three hundred Eighty nine pounds. Sixteen shills. Six pence. This 15th of 1obr 1708 by us

Joseph Shippen

John Jones

SOURCE: Philadelphia Wills, 1708-113.

NOTE: England adhered to the Julian Calendar until 1752. The tenth month was December.

APPENDIX 2

THE ART OF CANING

(Editor's note: The following text is Benno M. Forman's translation of the section on caning in André Jacob Roubo's essay on joinery [*menuisier*], which appears in volume 2 of *Description des arts et métiers* [1745–1761]. Roubo's is the earliest detailed description of that art.)

Cane-chair making in France is not very old and was introduced by the Dutch, who long monopolized the trade with the Indies, whence come the canes or reeds called *rotings* (rattan), which are of several kinds: those called *bamboo*, which are very large; those called *canes* or Indian bulrushes [*jonc des Indes*], which are used as walking sticks; finally, those known simply by their Dutch name *rattan*, which is a slender, ground-creeping kind of reed that grows to diverse lengths, sometimes extends 12, 18, or even 24 feet, splits like willow, and is used in the Orient to make baskets, beds, entire chairs, tables, and blinds. They are used in France only to upholster chairs, for which purpose they are both stronger and better looking than straw or rush. They are also used on coaches and sedan chairs, as I have indicated in their places, which are worked in the same way as chair upholstery, the description of which is the purpose of this section, which will be divided into three paragraphs. In the first I shall discuss the way to prepare the seats for caning; in the second, caning tools and the way to split the cane; and in the third, the way to upholster chairs, following all the operations necessary to this subject, which constitutes what is called the *Art of the Caner*.

I. HOW TO PREPARE CHAIRS FOR CANING

It is necessary to know two things in preparing chairs for caning: the way in which to lay out the holes designed to hold the cane and the way to drill these holes.

The first of these has the beauty and neatness of the caner's work as its object and is often most neglected, because it depends entirely upon the framemaker who, in drilling his holes, is very little concerned with what the caner's work will be like, for he regards the caner as a minor adjunct to his goal.

The second, which has the soundness of the furniture as its object, is a little better attended to, but often without neatness, as I shall explain below.

When chairmakers mark off the places where the holes will be drilled on the frames that are to be caned, they begin by finding the midpoint, from which they mark them off (making sure that the midpoint is in a void between the two centermost hole marks) without considering where their marks will come out [at the corners] and ignoring whether the frame is rectangular or curved. This can cause much difficulty; because, in the first instance, when the frame is rectangular, as in [fig. 192, upper left], it is necessary to manage the work for the last holes on each side to come out in a half space, so that they will receive all the perpendicular, horizontal, and diagonal strips of cane that they are supposed to without forcing any of them out of line. I have shown a properly laid out frame where the lines *ab*, *bd*, *cd*, and *ac* represent the proper spacing of holes, which receive all the slips of cane at the junctions, without disarraying them in any way. This could not be if the spaces at the extremities were equal to the others, as for example lines *ef*, *fh*, *gh*, and *eg*, where the diagonal slips of cane would have to be twisted underneath the frame in order to go into holes that would be on these lines. This would disarray the cane a great deal and would oblige the framemaker to drill additional holes to take the strips, which would weaken the structure too much and, in consequence, would render that expedient impossible. This alone ought to recommend the adoption of the method I now propose which, although different from the ordinary, requires but a little care, to wit: lay out the holes at intervals relative to the size of the work. This would require only a little reconsideration of the ordinary method and would require that the holes be marked off in such a way that there is ¾″ to ⅞″ [1.9 to 2.2 cm] between the midpoints of any two holes, or sometimes ¹⁵⁄₁₆″ [2.4 cm], which makes ⅜″ [1.0 cm] from the middle of one hole to the next, as I have shown full size in Fig. 3.

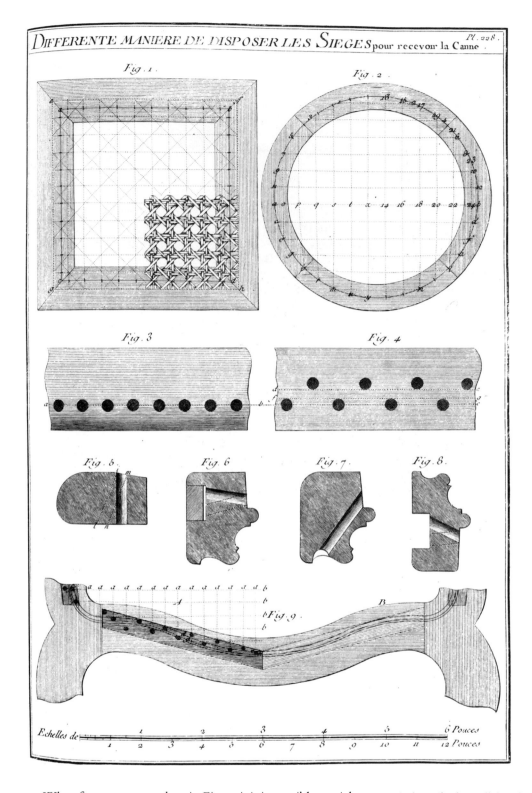

Pl. 228.

DIFFERENTE MANIERE DE DISPOSER LES SIEGES pour recevoir la **Canne** .

Fig. 1.

Fig. 2.

Fig. 3.

Fig. 4.

Fig. 5.

Fig. 6.

Fig. 7.

Fig. 8.

Fig. 9.

Echelles de

Fig. 192. Caning. From Roubo, *Description des arts et métiers*, 2: pl. 288.

When frames are curved, as in Fig. 2, it is impossible to stick to the same rules for spacing the holes as in rectangular figures; this is why furniture makers, after having marked the middle of each side, make the spaces between them equal; but the lines of cane that would intersect there would not be equidistant from each other, those at the extremities of the curves being squeezed together more than those toward the middle, which is quite natural; or even if they were equidistant at the middle, they would form crooked lines as those at *ab*, *cd*, *ef*, *gh*, *il*, and *mn*; and those *oe*, *pi*, *qr*, *sm*, *tu*, and *xy*, which not only are unsightly but are weaker, because, little by little, the cane tends to stretch, in view of the weight of people sitting down, which partially causes all cane seats in compass shapes to loosen.

Thus, I believe that, although it is not customary, one would do very well to overlay a square grid of equidistant lines onto the rounded frame and to drill holes at the junction of this grid with a

circle scribed parallel to the front of the frame and set back from it in proportion to its depth, as I have shown in the upper part, where lines 1–12 and 13–24 indicate the location of the holes without regard to the marking out of equal spaces.

When the frame is curved only slightly, the holes may be laid out in the customary manner, which is, however, inferior to the method I have proposed. I have laid out the holes in Fig. 9, side A, according to my rules. These holes are drilled at the juncture of the perpendicular lines *a, a, a,* and the horizontal ones *b, b, b,* with the curved line *cde*, which is in front of the holes, and *fgh*, on the back, from which lines the holes do not diverge except for reasons of strength, about which I am going to talk shortly.

Proper holes to receive the cane strips ought to be about ³⁄₃₂″ [0.2 cm] in diameter and ought to be drilled in pairs at least ⁷⁄₃₂″ [0.6 cm] from the edge of the frame, at the points indicated by the laying out method I have given above. These holes are not all drilled straight downward, but on the contrary, every other one is angled backward so that the holes, being thus varied, cut away less of the grain of the wood, leaving plenty of wood between the two rows of holes, as you can see in Fig. 4 (which represents the reverse of Fig. 3), where the full measure of wood remaining between the two rows of holes is indicated by the lines *de* and *fg*.

It is necessary to make certain that a portion of the holes in this frame are pierced perpendicularly, as indicated by line *abc*, which passes through the middle of the holes in both Figs. 3 and 4. You may do this on any chair frame, and you ought to each time, especially when you need not worry about the width (or size) of the piece. Fig. 5 represents the cutaway view of Figs. 3 and 4, in which the perpendicular hole is visible, and the slanted hole is indicated by the dotted lines *il* and *mn*.

When the rear of the back of a piece of cane furniture is going to be seen, as is true of all chair backs, it is the custom to plane a groove or rabbets that are later filled in by strips of wood glued over the cane so that it is not visible in any way. The depth of these rabbets is at least ⅜″ [1.0 cm], and the wooden filler strips put over them are about ⁵⁄₁₆″ [0.8 cm] thick, the cane taking up about ¹⁄₁₆″ [0.2 cm]. As to the width of the rabbets and their wooden fillers, they are ordinarily ²⁴⁄₃₂″ to ²⁷⁄₃₂″ [1.9 cm to 2.1 cm], at least those not constricted by curves, which will oblige them occasionally to be made narrower and ought to be avoided to preserve the soundness of the workmanship. These wooden filler strips are fitted into curved work, in two pieces. In Fig 9, side A, you may see the uncovered rabbet and the holes, drilled on the bias, for the reasons stated above. See this same figure, side B, where the filler is in place. I have drawn lines that indicate the location of the holes on the front of the work under the filler. On fairly straight parts the filler strips are made in one piece; on those that are rather more curved, one ought to lay the filler in two or even three pieces, according to what will be necessary, unless one prefers to run rabbets there, and consequently curved fillers which would thus remove all kinds of difficulties. In any case, the wooden rabbets and their fillers must not be sunk deeply at the intersection of framing members, lest they cut the joinery, as I have noted on the two straight pieces of Fig. 9, sides A and B. Fig. 6 represents the cut of a piece of frame with its rabbet, its wooden filler strip, and the two holes drilled on the bias, each toward the two sides of the rabbet.

There are some furniture makers who, to save work, never fit filler pieces either across the back or from top to bottom, but they drill their holes that emerge on the outside edge of the back, on which they run a little rabbet to hide the cane, which they later cover over with putty, which is both less neat and weaker; that is why one would do very well not to use this method, which I have only illustrated in Fig. 7 as an example to avoid. The same applies to work that is compass shape in a flat plane, where chairmakers never use rabbets on the pretext that they weaken the work, which is not true; the better reason, which they ought to give, is that doing so takes more time and makes the work harder. Fig. 8 represents the crest rail of a back with a rabbet run in it in the usual manner.

Generally, when one prepares seating furniture and all other works for caning, one must take care to plane down the upper surface of the inner perimeter of the frame by about ³⁄₃₂″ [0.2 cm] so that the thickness of the cane does not project above the molded surface. It is also necessary to slope carefully this part of the frame slightly inward so that the stress of weight on the cane will not score the cane at the sharp edge of the frame and break it, which will happen without this precaution. I have shown this slope in Figs. 5, 6, 7, and 8.

II. HOW TO CHOOSE CANE; HOW TO SPLIT IT; AND THE TOOLS OF THE CANER

When buying rattans, one ought to choose the longest and most uniform pieces possible, because the longer it is, the less waste there will be in using it; the same applies to its uniformity, which assures that the strips will be of similar width from one end to the other, and, thereby, you will suffer no loss from its thickness.

It is also important to be careful lest the cane be too dry, for then it is difficult to split and works up poorly. Caners attempt to remedy cane that is too dry by moistening it when they wish to use it; but this moisturizing has only a temporary effect, which will be found totally wanting, since this can never replace the sap, which has been expulsed. Thus drying weakens it and exposes it to vermin and consequently causes it to break easily. To understand whether a rattan is too dry or not, one must bend it in several ways; note the character of the natural varnish that is on its surface; does it tend to ravel at the ends, and does it fail to peel easily? These are the marks of overdryness.†

It is also necessary when buying canes or rattans to choose those that are the largest, that is to say, at least ⅜″ [1.0 cm] or so in diameter, so that when split, they yield more strips. Even though they contain more pith inside, and thus a part of the original weight is lost, the loss is a small matter when compared with the advantage of having good-size cane strips to work with. Moreover, they are stronger than the smaller rattans, having acquired their full growth, and are easier to split, which is a strong consideration.

When one has chosen his canes, it is necessary to remove the shoots which form knots or irregularities, [fig. 193, top] before splitting it, caners call this process "deknotting" or "picking the knots," i.e., removing the nodules. They do this by scraping the cane with a knife against the grain at the knot, as represented in Fig. 3, being careful to hold the knife slightly aslant, with its back edge facing outward, so as to avoid cutting the strand, but only to scrape it.

When the strand of rattan is deknotted, it is split, which is done in the following way:

One begins by considering the size of the rattan and consequently how many strips of cane may be contained in its circumference; then, with a knife, one splits it lengthwise into three or four parts, which parts are then split again with the knife, up to the point that these strips are wide enough to yield two strips of cane with one final splitting, after which one removes the pith from the inside by splitting the rattan down its whole length with the splitter, illustrated in Fig. 5. This device is nothing more than a piece of boxwood or other hardwood 1″ [2.5 cm] in diameter by 2″ or 2½″ [5.1 or 6.3 cm] long, which is rounded off on the bottom and sharpened at an angle on the top, so that it forms an X-shape wedge, which is used to split the rattan, pushed into slips with the knife; thus, one takes the splitter in the left hand, feeds the rattan started with a knife onto the splitter, and then pulls the rattan across it and downward with the right hand, being careful to maintain the pressure of the left thumb against it at the place where it is splitting, to prevent its coming loose from the splitter. See Fig. 6.

It is also necessary, when splitting rattan, to wear a leather finger staff on the thumb, lest the friction and unevenness of the cane hurt it, which could happen because of the force of friction.

Fig. 4 shows the section of a rattan slightly larger than ⅜″ [1.0

---

†Rattan is sold by the pound, at prices ranging from 7 or 8 cents, which is the usual price, up to 30 cents, which it is worth in wartime, or when the vendors do not have enough (which causes the caners to raise or lower their prices) or even to take a smaller size in order to get a greater quantity at the same weight, which weight is considerably diminished, because of the pith it contains. This is not a total loss for them, however, as they can then sell it for brooms to be used in courtyards, kitchens, and other inconsequential places.

cm] in diameter, split into three parts, which yields a triangle including the pith, *abc*; each of the three parts is then split into two each at points *def*, from which one removes the pith indicated by the line *ghi*, which one likewise does to the other parts; after which one makes the last split as indicated by these hints, which yields twelve strips of cane about 3⁄32″ [0.2 cm] wide that are split easily, without breaking, from a rattan with a circumference of about 1 1⁄16″ [2.7 cm]. This is the usual size for the caning that runs from front to back and side to side in seats; the strips that run diagonally ought to be narrower and either are split from smaller rattans or are made with strips that did not split well.

When the cane is split to the required width, one brings it to uniform thickness by running it through a drawknife/planing mill, a special kind of iron box *ab*, Fig. 10, uncovered at the top, in which

has been placed a thick plate of steel, Fig. 12 *cd* (which represents this plate or "bed" seen in this side view), that is attached to both sides of the box by a pin that functions as an axial pivot in such a way that one is free to raise or lower the bed at point *c* by means of a screw *e*, placed under the box. In so doing, one can adjust the bed so that the approach to the drawknife blade, Fig. 9, is as one needs it. This drawknife blade is a piece of steel, as wide as the bed, with a beveled cutting edge firmly attached to one side of the box in a notch that holds it rigid, and is held in place by means of a thumbscrew *h*. The bottom side of the cutting edge of this knife ought not to be parallel to the bed, but ought to be a little higher at the front, so that when the cane is passed over the bed and under the knife, one begins to cut away large irregularities, and ends by bringing the cane to a uniform thickness as it is drawn toward the back.

Fig. 14 represents a view of the planing mill, with the drawknife blade seen head on.

Inasmuch as the bed can be worn away by the continual friction of the cane that is fed over it, one can not only turn it over—the hole being placed midway between its faces—but can also turn it end to end, which is easy since it is drilled at both ends. The mill is attached to a horse or bench, with bolt *i*, which is fastened underneath the bench with wing nut *l*. See Figs. 10–15 which show the mill in front, rear, side, under, and transverse views as well as views of the unmounted cutting blade.

The caner's bench or horse, Fig. 7, is about 2′ long by 2′ high, and 8 to 9″ [61 × 61 × 21 cm] wide. A hole is drilled, *m*, at one of the ends, in order to insert and fasten the bolt of the planing mill, a little to the rear and at a convenient place, so that the screw, which is used to adjust the mill, overhangs the rear of the horse that has the corner rounded off; the mill, *q*, can turn at the pleasure of the workman, who is seated in front of the horse and holds it steady by putting his foot on the medial stretcher (see Fig. 9, which shows the layout of the horse). Then, to bring the cane to the desired thickness, having adjusted the mill to make a cut, which takes around 1/32″ [0.08 cm] from the bottom side, one takes the slip of cane in the right hand and feeds it (shiny side down) between the bed and the cutter with the fingers of the left hand as near as possible to the edge of cutter, so that in passing through the mill the cutter does not cut the cane in two. One repeats this same operation many times until the cane is of perfectly uniform thickness. Be careful, when sizing cane, to wear leather finger stalls on the first two fingers of the left hand, or at least on one, to prevent friction burns as well as cuts. See Fig. 10, wherein the cane, *no*, is shown passing under the cutter, which, at point *g*, forms a sliver, *p*, that, curling back, could cut the fingers of the workman's left hand were they not covered with finger stalls, as I have just recommended.

Having brought the cane to a uniform thickness, one now brings it to a uniform width by passing it between the blades of cutters, which are installed vertically in a piece of wood, *r*, Fig. 7, at the opposite end of the horse, and which are fastened there by a key wedge. These cutter blades are located exactly as far apart as is indicated by the desired width of the cane strips and flare outward a bit toward the top so that the cane enters between them easily. Fig. 2 shows the plan of this tool; Fig. 8 shows its elevation.

The tools I have just described are used only to prepare cane; those are used in caning itself are few in number, and are:

An awl, Fig. 16, that used to open up and enlarge holes when they already have two or three slips of cane in them. A peg, Fig. 18, holds the first slips of cane in their holes until the others are inserted and held by a permanent peg. A "darning awl," Fig. 17, used to pull the [diagonal] slips of cane through the mesh at the final stage of the work. Finally, strips of cane known as easers, about 9/32″ [0.7 cm] thick, Figs. 19 and 20, used to raise and lower the strips of cane in order to facilitate the passage of a needle of the same stuff, which serves to introduce the cane, about which I shall tell in its place.

III.   HOW TO CANE CHAIRS, AND THE VARIOUS TASKS OF A CANER

When the frames are ready, as I have described above, they are given to the caner, who, having prepared his cane, begins his first operation, warping, which is done in the following manner:

He begins by finding the middle of the front piece of the frame, [fig. 194, upper left]; he then passes a slip of cane up through the nearest hole, *a*, and affixes it with a knot on the underside, as I shall describe below; then he passes the cane over and down through the

hole directly opposite on the back piece of the frame *b*. The slip of cane, passing under the frame, reappears at *c*, and goes into the front part of the frame at hole *d*, which constitutes the basic weaving pattern for a single strand. He then doubles it by threading the cane from *d* cut B* under the frame, and threading it by way of hole *a* (also called hole *e*); whence he leads the thread from *e* to *f* (also called *b*), which doubles the first woven thread of cane. To double the second, he threads the cane downward, and makes it emerge again at point *g* (previously called *c*); he then threads it underneath as before, from *g* to *h* (also called *d*); thus doubling these as he did before. Then he threads the cane singly from *h* to *i*, leads it from *i* to *l*, then makes it go (always underneath the frame) from there to point *m*, whence it goes to point *n*, which completes the second basic pattern, which he doubles by threading the cane again from *n* to *o* and carrying it from *o* to *p*; then threading it from *p* to *g*, and leading it from *g* to *r*, he completes the second doubling. He does the same until he finishes, then he begins again on the other half, and the frame is then "warped"; with this exception: when it is perfectly square, as in Fig. 1, and the last hole becomes the first of a new step, he cannot double the last thread on itself, which he then has to run from *t* to *u*, where he fastens it with a temporary peg. When the hole *u* is needed in the weaving process, he takes another slip of cane, which he knows is under the seat frame and threads it upward through point *x*, whence he carries it over to point *y*, then under the frame to point *z*, where he fastens it with a pin. Note that in this operation, the canes not only pass through each hole two times, but they pass differently under each side because at the outset, the strands of cane passed singly over all the spaces; whereas, they pass twice over some of the spaces on the bottom, except where they do not pass at all in between operations. I have marked those places with an x in Fig. 1 to make it easier to understand what I have just said on the subject. It is easy to comprehend if you have paid the least attention to the way in which the caning has progressed—easier to do than to explain.

Before passing on to the second operation of the caner, I think it is necessary to show how to knot the cane, for one can not warp a frame without several slips of cane, and consequently, not without knotting them, which is done as follows:

If there is not enough cane left to go completely across the frame again, the caner inserts it into a hole, as in Fig. 4*b*, in the usual way, and passes it under the next hole; then he takes a new slip of cane *c*, which is passed through hole *a*; then in the space between the two holes and the first slip of cane, he inserts end *d* of the second, which he folds upward over the first and under itself, in such a way that in pulling through the end *c* of the latter, he ties the knot. See Fig. 3, where the underside of two pieces of knotted cane is shown, and Fig. 5, wherein the same knot is shown from the upper side, i.e., the side in contact with the frame. These are shown with the same letters as in Fig. 4, to make the discussion easier to understand.

When he ties slips of cane, he ought to make certain that the short end of the strand that has already been woven is no longer than is needed to knot it, because a short piece is of no use unless it is at least 8″ (18.7 cm) long; if there is less, he would do well to make his knot at the previous hole, and use the remainder to bind in short pieces of cane long enough to make two passes across the frame. This will save materials; a caner wastes enough as it is.

The second operation of the caner, mounting, is done as follows:

He takes a little rod of rattan, *CD*, Fig. 2, known as a staying easer because it stays in place until the work is finished, then threads

---

* You will observe that I have shown the basic step in weaving pieces of cane in Fig. 1, cut A; and that I then showed it completed by doubling in cut B, where I have engraved the same letters, so you can more readily observe the sequence of this basic operation, which would have been too involved had I not shown it in two stages.

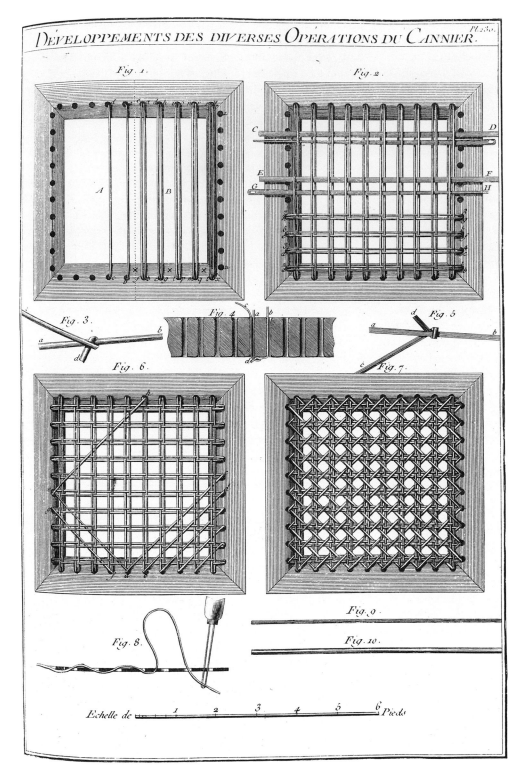

Fig. 194. Caning. From Roubo, *Description des arts et métiers*, 2: pl. 230.

it carefully between the strips of cane already warped, so that every other strip goes over it and the alternate strips go under; then he passes an easer *EF* through the warped strips so that the strips that go over the first easer go under the second, and those that went under the first go over the second; then from two corners of the frame ready to be mounted he threads two slips of cane; the first, *ab*, which he introduces with a needle, *GH*, passes between all the strips separated by the easer *EF*; then he moves this latter back, and passes the other slip of cane, *1 2*, with another needle, of the same, which is equal in size, according to the path opened up by the second staying easer; then he moves the second easer back, and threads the slips down through the holes in the frame; that is, the first designated by letters *b* and *c*; and the second designated by numbers *2* and *3*. Next, he repeats the operation by threading, with the needle, the first strip of cane from *c* to *d*, and the second from *3* to *4*, being careful to fasten

the slips of cane with a temporary peg each time it has been passed downward through a hole so that the work is kept tight. The remainder of the mounting is done in the same way, as one can see in the figure, where the letters and numbers indicate the pattern of the caning, which is easy to follow, according to the instructions I have just given.

The third and last operation of the caner, garnishing, consists of running slips of cane diagonally to the preceding slips. These slips are ⅓ wider than those used in the previous steps, but this difference should not be great, although it is in the work of several caners who for warping and mounting use overly narrow strips. They do this to save material, and not, as they claim, to make the work more perfect. One should mistrust perfection, especially when achieved at the expense of strength and when it has its foundation only in desire for profit and in saving of materials; a failing that is very common, not only in the works of which I speak, but also in all sorts of furniture which has, for the most part, only the appearance of strength, and to which, under pretext of fashion, makers give only half as much care and materials as is needed: resulting in so many people cheated, if indeed it is possible to be cheated when one pays or is willing to pay only about half or three-quarters of what things would be worth if they were good and well made.

The caner takes the ends of a slip of cane and threads them upward through two adjacent holes in the middle of the frame, Fig. 6, *ab*; then he runs them diagonally, so that they are either parallel to each other, like those illustrated at *ac* and *bd*, or form a right angle, as those at *ae* and *bd*, or *ac*, *fg*, and *eh*. These strips are passed downward with the left hand, and are pulled back up by a darning awl that is held in the right hand, see Fig. 8. The operation is then repeated to double the diagonal strips and thus completes the work, as shown in Fig. 7.

In general, as one goes through the various steps necessary to cane a chair, one must take care to pull each strip of cane tight each time one threads it through a hole, especially toward the end, and one ought to fasten the last ones tightly with small pegs which should be glued so that they will not come loose, and as a result allow the cane to sag, as often happens when caners do not take this very necessary precaution. This is neglected on almost all chair backs, which they generally peg only at those extremities they cannot knot, and it makes for shoddy work that easily sags and breaks.

And that is just about all one can say about the art of the caner. What I have said about it is applicable in every instance, for square frames, which were used herein for purposes of demonstration, as well as for hollowed or round ones, to which the same principles may be applied, provided one is willing to follow directions.

In general, cane chairs became fashionable in France only about 25 or 30 years ago [ca. 1740]. They are very serviceable, and much neater than straw- or rush-bottom chairs, whether the frames of these latter are made by joiners—very rare at present—or by turners—almost the only ones who make such chairs for the common folk or for inconsequential rooms. Cane chairs have the advantage of being much less expensive than upholstered chairs, and less easily soiled; that is why they are preferred for dining rooms and generally in all places where the air is damp.

BIBLIOGRAPHY

"Abstracts of the Earliest Wills upon Record in the County of Suffolk, Ms." *New England Historical and Genealogical Register* 2, no. 2 (April 1848): 181–86.

Abstracts of Unrecorded Wills prior to 1790 in the Surrogate's Office, City of New York. In *Collections of the New-York Historical Society . . . for 1902.* New York: By the society, 1903.

"Abstracts of Wills of the Mather Family." *New England Historical and Genealogical Register* 47, no. 3 (July 1893): 330–41.

"Account-books of Treasurers of Harvard College, 1669–1752," *Proceedings of the Massachusetts Historical Society*, 1st ser., 6: 337–57. Boston: By the society, 1862–63.

An Account of Her Majesty's Revenue in the Province of New York, 1701–09: The Records of Early Colonial New York. Facsimile reprint, edited by Julius M. Bloch et al. Ridgewood, N.J.: Gregg Press, 1966.

Agius, Pauline. "Late Sixteenth and Seventeenth Century Furniture in Oxford." *Furniture History* 7 (1971): 72–86.

Agricola, Georgius. *De re metallica.* 1556. Translated by Herbert Clarke Hoover and Lou Henry Hoover. 1912. Reprint. New York: Dover Publications, 1950.

Alberici, Celia. *Il mobile Lombardo.* Milan: Gölich Editore, 1969.

Albion, Robert Greenhalgh. *Forests and Sea Power: The Timber Problem of the Royal Navy, 1652–1862.* Cambridge, Mass.: Harvard University Press, 1926.

Alexander, John D., Jr. *Make a Chair from a Tree: An Introduction to Working Green Wood.* Newtown, Conn.: Taunton Press, 1978.

[Arches Wills]. Wills and Inventories, Deanery of the Arches. Lambeth Palace, London, England.

[*Aspinwall Notarial Records*]. *A Volume Relating to the Early History of Boston Containing the Aspinwall Notarial Records from 1641 to 1651.* Boston: Municipal Printing Office, 1903.

[Atwood Inventory]. *Mayflower Descendant* 5, no. 3 (July 1903): 153.

Austin, John Osborne. *The Genealogical Dictionary of Rhode Island.* 1887. Reprint. Baltimore: Genealogical Publishing Co., 1978.

Axtell, James. *The School upon a Hill: Education and Society in Colonial New England.* New York: W. W. Norton, 1976.

Baird, Charles W. *History of the Huguenot Emigration to America.* Vol. 2. New York: Dodd, Mead, 1885.

Banks, Charles Edward. *Topographical Dictionary of 2,885 English Emigrants to New England.* 1937. Reprint. Baltimore: Genealogical Publishing Co., 1969.

Barnes, Jairus B., and Moselle Taylor Meals. *American Furniture in the Western Reserve, 1680–1830.* Cleveland: Western Reserve Historical Society, 1972.

Barnsley, Edward R. *Newtown Library under Two Kings.* Newtown, Penn., 1938.

Bartlett, Daniel. Account book. Essex Institute, Salem, Mass.

Belknap, Henry Wyckoff. *Artists and Craftsmen.* Salem, Mass.: Essex Institute, 1927.

Belknap, Henry Wyckoff. *Trades and Tradesmen of Essex County, Massachusetts: Chiefly of the Seventeenth Century.* Salem, Mass.: Essex Institute, 1929.

Beman, David. *The Mysteries of Trade.* Boston, 1825.

[Bentley, William]. *The Diary of William Bentley, D.D.* 4 vols. Salem, Mass.: Essex Institute, 1905–14.

Bishop, James Leander. *A History of American Manufactures from 1608 to 1860.* 3 vols. Philadelphia, 1861.

Blackburn, Roderic H. *Cherry Hill.* Albany: Historic Cherry Hill, 1975.

Blackie and Son. *The Victorian Cabinet Maker's Assistant.* New York: Dover Publications, 1970. Reprint of *Cabinet Maker's Assistant.* 1853.

Bland, A. E. *English Economic History: Select Documents.* New York, 1919.

Bloch, Julius M., et al. See *Account of Her Majesty's Revenue.*

Bodge, George M. "Soldiers in King Philip's War." *New-England Historical and Genealogical Register* 39, no. 2 (April 1885): 175–79.

A Booke of Secrets Shewing Diuers Waies to Make and Prepare All Sorts of Inke, and Colours . . . also to Write with Gold and Siluer . . . with Many Profitable Secrets. Translated by W. P[hilip]. London, 1596.

[*Boston Records*]. Boston, Registry Department. *Reports of the Record Commissioners of the City of Boston: Records Relating to the Early History of Boston.* 39 vols. Boston: Rockwell & Churchill, 1876–1909.

Bowman, George Ernest, ed. "Elder William Brewster's Inventory and the Settlement of His Estate." *Mayflower Descendant* 3, no. 1 (January 1901): 15–22.

————. "Governor William Bradford's Will and Inventory." *Mayflower Descendant* 2, no. 4 (October 1900): 228–34.

————. "Alice (Southworth) Bradford's Will and Inventory." *Mayflower Descendant* 3, (July 1901): 144–49.

Bradford, William. *Of Plymouth Plantation, 1620–1647.* Edited by Samuel Eliot Morison. New York: Alfred A. Knopf, 1952.

Brears, Peter C. D., ed. *Yorkshire Probate Inventories, 1542–1689.* Yorkshire Archaeological Society Record Series, no. 134. By the society, 1972.

Bronowski, Jacob. *The Ascent of Man.* Boston: Little, Brown, 1973.

The Burghers of New Amsterdam and the Freemen of New York 1675–1866. In *Collections of the New-York Historical Society for . . . 1885.* New York: By the society, 1886.

Burr, Horace. *The Records of Holy Trinity (Old Swedes) Church, Wilmington, Delaware, 1697–1773.* Wilmington: Historical Society of Delaware, 1890.

Butler, Joseph T. *The Family Collections at van Cortlandt Manor.* Tarrytown, N.Y.: Sleepy Hollow Restorations, 1967.

Buxton's Guide to New England Antique Shops. Greenwich, Conn., 1963–64.

The Cabinet-Makers Philadelphia and London Book of Prices. Philadelphia: Snowden & McCorkle, 1796.

Campbell, R[obert?]. *The London Tradesman.* 1747. Reprint. Newton Abbot, England: David & Charles, 1973.

Caputo, Ginny. "Concord, N.H.: Bourgeault 'Country Sale.'" *Maine Antique Digest* 7, no. 9 (October 1979): 22C–27C.

Carroll, Charles F. *The Timber Economy of Puritan New England.* Providence: Brown University Press, 1973.

———. "The Forest Society of New England." In *America's Wooden Age*, edited by Brooke Hindle, pp. 13–36. Tarrytown, N.Y.: Sleepy Hollow Restorations, 1975.

Cary, Thomas G. "Some Notices of the Family of Perkins in America." *New England Historical and Genealogical Register* 10, no. 3 (July 1856): 211–16.

Catalogue of the Albany Bicentennial Loan Exhibition, 1686–1886. Albany: Albany Academy, 1886.

Cescinsky, Herbert, and Ernest R. Gribble. *Early English Furniture and Woodwork.* London: George Routledge & Sons, 1922.

Chamberlain, Samuel. *Salem Interiors.* New York: Hastings House, 1950.

Cheyney, Edward P. *An Introduction to the Industrial and Social History of England.* New York: Macmillan, 1925.

Chippendale, Thomas. *The Gentleman and Cabinet-Maker's Director.* 3d ed. London, 1762. Reprint. New York: Dover Publications, 1966.

[Company of Joyners]. Minutes of the Court of the Worshipful Company of Joyners of the City of London. Ms. 8046/2. Guildhall, London.

Contract between Edward Skate, carpenter, and John Hill, April 6, 1698. Society for the Preservation of New England Antiquities, Boston.

Comstock, Helen. *American Furniture: Seventeenth, Eighteenth, and Nineteenth Century Styles.* New York: Viking Press, 1962.

———. "Pilgrim Chairs." *Antiques* 68, no. 5 (November 1955): 450–51.

———. "Spanish-foot Furniture." *Antiques* 71, no. 1 (January 1957): 58–61.

Connecticut Chairs in the Collection of the Connecticut Historical Society. Hartford: By the society, 1956.

[Connecticut Records]. Trumbull, J. Hammond, ed. *The Public Records of the Colony of Connecticut.* Hartford: Brown & Parsons, 1850.

Cope, Gilbert, ed. *Genealogy of the Darlington Family.* West Chester, Penn., 1900.

———. *Historic Homes and Institutions and Genealogical and Personal Memoirs of Chester and Delaware Counties, Pa.* 2 vols. New York: Lewis Publishing Co., 1904.

Core, H. A., W. A. Côté, and A. C. Day. *Wood Structure and Identification.* 2d ed. Syracuse: State University of New York, School of Forestry, 1979.

Corwin, Jonathan. Ledger. Essex Institute, Salem, Mass.

Cowan, Maude Roberts. *Members of the Ancient and Honorable Artillery Company in the Colonial Period.* Boston, 1958.

Croker, Temple Henry, Thomas Williams, and Samuel Clark. *The Complete Dictionary of Arts and Sciences in which the Whole Circle of Human Learning is explained. . . .* Vol. 3. London, 1766.

Crouch, Nathaniel. *The English Empire in America; or, A Prospect of Their Majesties Domains in the West Indies. Namely New Foundland, New England, New York, Pennsylvania, New-Jersey, Maryland, Virginia, Carolina, Bermuda's, Berbuda, Anguilla, Montsevrat, Dominica, St. Vincit. . . .* 2d ed. London: Nathaniel Crouch, 1692.

Cummings, Abbott Lowell. *The Framed Houses of Massachusetts Bay, 1625–1725.* Cambridge, Mass.: Harvard University Press/Belknap Press, 1979.

———. ed. *Architecture in Colonial Massachusetts.* Publications of the Colonial Society of Massachusetts, vol. 51. Boston: By the society, 1979.

Cummings, Hubertis M. "An Account of Goods at Pennsbury Manor." *Pennsylvania Magazine of History and Biography* 86, no. 4 (October 1962): 397–416.

Currier, John J. *History of Newbury, Mass., 1635–1902.* Boston: Damrell & Upham, 1902.

[Cushing Sale]. Sale Catalogue no. 3821 (Nathan Cushing Collection, Providence R. I.) New York: American Art Association-Anderson Galleries, February 27, 1930.

Cust, Lionel. "Notes on the Collections Formed by Thomas Howard, Earl of Arundel and Surrey, K.G.," pts. 2, 3, 4. *Burlington Magazine* 20, nos. 94, 96, 97 (November 1911, January 1912, February 1912): 97–100, 233–36, 341–43.

DAPC. Decorative Arts Photographic Collection, Winterthur Library, Winterthur, Del.

Darlington, Amos. Account book. Chester County Historical Society, West Chester, Penn.

Davidson, Marshall. *The American Heritage History of Colonial Antiques.* New York: Simon & Schuster, 1967.

———. *Life in America.* 2 vols. Boston: Houghton Mifflin Co., 1951.

Davies, Margaret Gay. *The Enforcement of English Apprenticeship, 1563–1642.* Cambridge, Mass.: Harvard University Press, 1956.

d'Aviler, Charles Augustin. *Cours d'architecture qui comprend les ordres de vignole.* 2 vols. Paris, 1710.

Davis, Charles Thomas. *The Manufacture of Leather.* Philadelphia: Henry Cary Byrd, 1885.

Davis, Richard Beale, ed. *William Fitzhugh and His Chesapeake World, 1676–1701: The Fitzhugh Letters and Other Documents.* Chapel Hill: University of North Carolina Press, 1963.

de Félice, Roger. *French Furniture in the Middle Ages and under Louis XIII.* Translated by F. M. Atkinson. New York: Frederick A. Stokes Co., ca. 1924.

Defoe, Daniel. *The Complete English Tradesman.* 2 vols. 1726. Reprint. Oxford: Thomas Tegg, 1841.

Deneke, Bernward. *Bauernmöbel.* Munich: Keysersche Verlagsbuchhandlung, 1969.

Description of the Villa of Mr. Horace Walpole. 1784. Reprint. London: Gregg Press, 1964.

Diderot, Denis. *Recueil de planches, sur les sciences, les arts, libèraux, et les arts méchaniques, avec leur explication.* Vol. 2. Paris, 1762.

Diderot, Denis, and Jean d'Alembert. *Encyclopédie, ou dictionnaire raisonné des sciences, des arts, et des métiers, par un Société de Gens de Lettres.* 17 vols. Paris: Briasson et al., 1751–65.

Dilliard, Maud Esther. *An Album of New Netherlands.* New York: Twayne Publishers, 1963.

Ditchfield, Peter H. *Country Folk: A Pleasant Company.* London: Methuen, 1923.

DMMC. Joseph Downs Manuscript and Microfilm Collection, Winterthur Library, Winterthur, Del.

Doménech (Galissa), Rafeal, and Luis Pérez Bueno. *Antique Spanish Furniture.* Translated by Grace Hardendorff Burr. New York: Bonanza Books, 1965.

Donisthorpe, Wordsworth. *A System of Measures.* London: Spottiswoode, 1895.

Douglass, William. *A Summary Historical and Political of the First Planting, Progressive Improvements and Present State of the British Settlements in North America.* 2 vols. 1749–52. 3d ed. London, 1760.

Dow, George Francis. *The Arts and Crafts in New England, 1704–1775: Gleanings from Boston Newspapers.* Topsfield, Mass.: Wayside Press, 1927.

———. See also *Essex Quarterly Courts* and *Essex Probate.*

Downing, Antoinette F. *Early Homes of Rhode Island.* Richmond: Garrett & Massie, 1937.

Downs, Joseph. *American Furniture: Queen Anne and Chippendale Periods.* New York: Macmillan, 1952.

Downs, Joseph, and Ruth Ralston. *A Loan Exhibition of New York State Furniture.* New York: Metropolitan Museum of Art, 1934.

Drake, Samuel Gardner. "The Founders of New England." *New England Historical and Genealogical Register* 14, no. 4 (October 1860): 297–346.

Dreppard, Carl. *Handbook of Antique Chairs.* New York: Doubleday, 1948.

du Pont, Henry Francis. Accession books. Registrar's Office, Winterthur Museum, Winterthur, Del.

Eames, Penelope S. "Furniture in England, France, and the Netherlands from the Twelfth to the Fifteenth Century." *Furniture History* 13 (1977): xxiv–303.

Early Furniture Made in New Jersey, 1690–1870. Newark: Newark Museum, 1958.

Earwaker, John Parsons. *The Four Randle Holmes of Chester: Antiquaries, Heralds, and Genealogists, c. 1571–1707.* Manchester, 1892. Reprinted from *Journal of the Chester Archaeological and Historic Society.*

Eaton, Allen H. *Handicrafts of the Southern Highlands.* 1937. Reprint. New York: Dover Publications, 1973.

Edwards, Ralph. *English Chairs.* London: Victoria and Albert Museum, 1965.

———. *The Shorter Dictionary of English Furniture.* London: Country Life, 1964.

Edwards, Ralph, and Margaret Jourdain. *Georgian Cabinetmakers.* London: Country Life, 1946.

Emerson, George B. *A Report on the Trees and Shrubs Growing Naturally in the Forests of Massachusetts.* Boston: Dutton & Wentworth, 1846.

Encyclopédie méthodique, ou par ordre de matières par une société de gens de lettres, de savans et d'artistes. Vol. 4. Paris: Chez Pankoucke; Liège: Plomtoux, 1785.

The English Experience. New York: DaCapo Press; Amsterdam: Theatrum Orbis Terrarum, 1969.

Erixon, Sigurd. *Möbler och heminredning i Svenska bydger.* Stockholm: Nordiska Museets Förlag, 1926.

[Essex County Deeds]. Registry of Deeds. Essex County Courthouse, Salem, Mass.

Essex County Probate Files. Registry of Probate, Essex County Courthouse, Salem, Mass.

[Essex Probate]. Dow, George Francis, ed. *The Probate Records of Essex County, Massachusetts, 1635–1681.* 3 vols. Salem, Mass: Essex Institute, 1916–20.

[Essex Quarterly Courts]. Dow, George Francis, ed. *Records and Files of the Quarterly Courts of Essex County, Massachusetts, 1636–1692.* 8 vols. Salem, Mass: Essex Institute, 1911–21.

Evelyn, John. *Silva: or, A Discourse of Forest-Trees....* 5th ed. London, 1729.

An Exhibition of Furniture and Furnishings from the Collection of the New Jersey State Museum. Trenton: By the museum, 1970.

"Extracts from the Deed Books of the Plymouth Colony." *Mayflower Descendant* 10, no. 3 (July 1908): 140–44.

"Extracts from the Letter-Booke of James Claypoole." *Pennsylvania Magazine of History and Biography* 10, nos. 2, 3, 4 (1886): 188–202, 267–82, 401–13.

Failey, Dean F. *Long Island Is My Nation: The Decorative Arts and Craftsmen, 1640–1830.* Setauket, N.Y.: Society for the Preservation of Long Island Antiquities, 1976.

Fairbanks, Jonathan L. "Four Pilgrim Chairs." *Winterthur Newsletter* 9, no. 7 (September 1963): 1–2.

Fairbanks, Jonathan, and Robert F. Trent. *New England Begins: The Seventeenth Century.* 3 vols. Boston: Museum of Fine Arts, 1982.

Fairfield Probate District Records, Connecticut State Library, Hartford.

Fales, Dean A., Jr. *American Painted Furniture, 1660–1880.* New York: E. P. Dutton, 1972.

———. *Essex County Furniture: Documented Treasures from Local Collections, 1660–1860.* Salem, Mass.: Essex Institute, 1965.

———. *The Furniture of Historic Deerfield.* New York: E. P. Dutton, 1976.

Ferguson, John, ed. *Bibliographical Notes on Histories of Inventions and Books of Secrets.* 2 vols. London: Holland Press, 1959.

Fisher, George. *The Instructor or Young Man's Best Companion.* Glasgow, 1786.

Fitch, Thomas. Account book, 1719–1732. Massachusetts Historical Society, Boston.

———. Letterbook, 1702–1711. American Antiquarian Society, Worcester, Mass. (Microfilm, DMMC M-1423, Winterthur.)

———. Letterbook, 1714–1717. New England Historical and Genealogical Society, Boston.

———. Letterbook, 1723–1733. Massachusetts Historical Society, Boston. (Microfilm, DMMC M-1422, Winterthur.)

[*Flayderman Sale*]. *Colonial Furniture, Silver, and Decorations: The Collections of the Late Philip Flayderman.* New York: American Art Association-Anderson Galleries, January 2–4, 1930.

Forman, Benno M. "The Account Book of John Gould, Weaver of Topsfield, Massachusetts, 1697–1724." *Essex Institute Historical Collections* 105, no. 1 (January 1969): 36–49.

———. "Continental Furniture Craftsmen in London: 1511–1625." *Furniture History* 7 (1971): 94–120.

———. "Delaware Valley 'Crookt Foot' and Slat-Back Chairs: The Fussell-Savery Connection." *Winterthur Portfolio* 15, no. 1 (Spring 1980): 41–64.

———. "Mill Sawing in Seventeenth Century Massachusetts." *Old-Time New England* 60, no. 220 (Spring 1970): 110–30.

———. "Note." *Country Life* 152, no. 3924 (August 31, 1972): 519.

———. "Salem Tradesmen and Craftsmen Circa 1762." *Essex Institute Historical Collections* 107, no. 1 (January 1971): 62–81.

———. "The Seventeenth-Century Case Furniture of Essex County, Massachusetts, and Its Makers." Master's thesis, University of Delaware, 1968.

———. "Urban Aspects of Massachusetts Furniture in the Late Seventeenth Century." In *Country Cabinetwork and Simple City Furniture*, edited by John D. Morse, pp. 1–28. Charlottesville: University Press of Virginia, 1970.

Fowells, H. A., comp. *Silvics of Forest Trees of the United States.* Agriculture Handbook no. 271. Washington, D.C.: U.S. Department of Agriculture, 1965.

Fowler, H. W. *A Dictionary of Modern English Usage.* Oxford: University Press, 1944.

F[rothingham], R[ichard], Jr., trans. "A Declaration of the Affairs of the English People That First Inhabited New England by Phinehas Pratt." *Collections of the Massachusetts Historical Society.* 4th ser., 4: 474–91. Boston: Little, Brown, 1858.

Fussell, Solomon. Account Book, 1738–1750. Stephen Collins Papers, Manuscript Division, Library of Congress, Washington, D.C. (Microfilm, DMMC M-659, Winterthur.)

Garrett, Wendell D. "Furniture Owned by the American Antiquarian Society." *Antiques* 97, no. 3 (March 1970): 402–7.

[*Garvan Sale.*] *Important Americana Property from the Estate of Mabel Brady Garvan.* New York: Sotheby Parke Bernet, June 7, 1980.

A General Description of All Trades.... London: T. Waller, 1748.

The Georgian Period, Part II. New York: American Architect and Building News, 1898.

Gibbins, H. deB. *Industry in England.* London: Methuen, 1910.

Gilbert, Christopher G. "Furniture by Giles Grendy for the Spanish Trade." *Antiques* 99, no. 4 (April 1971): 544–50.

———. *The Life and Work of Thomas Chippendale.* 2 vols. New York: Macmillan Publishing Co., 1978.

———. "Regional Traditions in English Vernacular Furniture." In *Arts of the Anglo-American Community in the Seventeenth Century*, edited by Ian M. G. Quimby, pp. 43–77. Charlottesville: University Press of Virginia, 1975.

Gillingham, Harrold E. "The Estate of Jonathan Dickinson." *Pennsylvania Magazine of History and Biography* 59, no. 4 (October 1935): 420–29.

———. "Benjamin Lehman, a Germantown Cabinetmaker." *Pennsylvania Magazine of History and Biography* 54, no. 4 (1930): 289–306.

Gloag, John, and C. Thompson Walker. *Home Life in History.* New York: Coward-McCann, 1928.

Goodman, W. L. "Tools and Equipment of the Early Settlers in the New World." *Chronicle of the Early American Industries Association* 29, no. 3 (September 1976): 40–51.

———. "Woodworking Apprentices and their Tools in Bristol, Norwich, Great Yarmouth, and Southampton, 1535–1650." *Industrial Archaeology* 9, no. 4 (November 1972): 376–411.

Gould, John. Account book. Essex Institute, Salem, Mass.

Gowans, Alan. *Images of American Living.* Philadelphia: J. B. Lippincott, 1964.

Grant, Samuel. Daybook, 1728–1737. Massachusetts Historical Society, Boston. (Microfilm, DMMC M-1526, Winterthur.)

Greenwood, F. W. P. *A History of King's Chapel in Boston....* Boston: Carter, Hendee, 1833.

Gregory, Edward. *The Furniture Collector: An Introduction to the Study of English Styles of the Seventeenth and Eighteenth Centuries.* Philadelphia: David McKay, 1915.

Greguss, Pal. *Holzanatomie der europäischen Laubhölzer und Sträucher.* 2 vols. Budapest: Akademai Kiado, 1959.

Grieve, Hilda M. *A Modern Herbal.* London: Jonathan Cape, 1931.

Halliwell, James Orchard, ed. *Ancient Inventories of Furniture, Pictures, Tapestry, Plate &c. Illustrative of the Domestic Manners of the English in the Sixteenth and Seventeenth Centuries.* London: J. E. Adlars, 1854.

Hamlin, A. D. F. *A History of Ornament, Ancient and Medieval.* New York: Century Co., 1916.

Hartford County Probate Records. Connecticut State Library, Hartford.

Harvard College Book, No. 5, containing Harvard treasurer Thomas Brattle's Journal, 1693–1713. Harvard University Archives, Cambridge, Mass.

Harvard Tercentenary Exhibition Catalogue. Cambridge, Mass.: Harvard University Press, 1936.

Hatton, Edward. *The Merchant's Magazine or Trades Man's Treasury.* London: Chr. Coningsby & Dan. Midwinter, 1719.

Havard, Henry. *Dictionnaire de l'ameublement et de la décoration.* 4 vols. Paris: Maison Quantin, [1887–90].

Havinden, M. A., ed. *Household and Farm Inventories in Oxfordshire, 1550–1590.* London: Her Majesty's Stationery Office, 1965.

Hayden, Arthur. *Chats on Cottage and Farmhouse Furniture.* London: T. Fisher Unwin, 1912.

Heal, Ambrose. "A Great Country House in 1623." *Burlington Magazine* 82, no. 32 (May 1943): 108–16.

———. *London Tradesmen's Cards of the XVII Century.* London: B. T. Batsford, 1925.

Heckscher, Morrison H. "Lock and Copland: A Catalogue of the Engraved Ornament." *Furniture History* 15 (1979): 7–23.

[Hempstead, Joshua]. *The Diary of Joshua Hempstead.* New London, Conn.: New London County Historical Society, 1901.

Hendrick, Robert E. P. "John Gaines III and Thomas Gaines I, Turners of Ipswich, Massachusetts." Master's thesis, University of Delaware, 1964.

Henretta, James A. "Economic Development and Social Structure in Colonial Boston." *William and Mary Quarterly*, 3d ser., 22, no. 1 (January 1965): 75–92.

Hepplewhite, George. *The Cabinet-Maker and Upholsterer's Guide.* London, 1788.

Hill, Derek, and Oleg Grabar. *Islamic Architecture and Its Decoration,* A.D. 800–1500. London: Faber & Faber, 1967.

Hill, Donald Gleason. See *Town & Selectmen.*

Hinckley, F. Lewis. *Directory of Historic Cabinet Woods.* New York: Bonanza Books, 1959.

Historical Statistics of the United States, Colonial Times to 1970. 2 vols. Washington, D.C.: U.S. Bureau of the Census, 1975.

Hoadley, R. Bruce. *Understanding Wood: A Craftsman's Guide to Wood Technology.* Newtown, Conn.: Taunton Press, 1980.

Holme, Randle. *Academy of Armory; or, A Storehouse of Armory and Blazon.* Vol. 1, London, 1688. Vol. 2, London: Roxburghe Club, 1905.

Printing of the first volume of the *Academy* was begun in 1682 and was completed in 1688. It consisted of two complete "books" and 13 chapters of the third. The balance of the third book, chapters 14–22, and parts of a fourth book, chapters 4–13, were published from Holme's manuscript in 1905, and is generally referred to as volume 2. An inscription in Holme's handwriting at the beginning of Harleian MS. no. 2026 at the British Museum notes that "This is my first collection and draughts for the *Academy of Armory*, anno 1649." It is generally believed that the earliest materials were collected by Holme's father, also named Randle. I am indebted to Charles F. Montgomery for calling these books and Harleian MSS. 2026-2045 to my attention. For a biographical and analytical study of Holme, see Earwaker, *The Four Randle Holmes*; see also the introduction by I. H. Jeanes to the second volume of the *Academy of Armory*, esp. p. vi.

Holtzapffel, Charles, and John Jacob Holtzapffel. *Turning and Mechanical Manipulation*. 5 vols. London, 1843–84.

Hornor, William Macpherson, Jr. *Blue Book: Philadelphia Furniture, William Penn to George Washington*. Philadelphia, 1935.

Household Conveniences; Being the Experience of Many Practical Writers. New York: Orange, Judd, 1884.

Hulot. *L'art du tourneur mécanicien*. Paris: M. Roubo, 1775.

Indentures of Apprentices, 1718–1727. In *Collections of the New-York Historical Society for . . . 1909*. New York: By the society, 1910.

Israel Sack, Inc. *Opportunities in American Antiques*. No. 4. New York, May 1959.

―――――. *Opportunities in American Antiques*. No. 15. New York, February 1967.

―――――. *Opportunities in American Antiques*. No. 16. New York, December 1968.

Iverson, Marion Day. *The American Chair*. New York: Hastings House, 1957.

Jacquemart, Albert. *A History of Furniture*. Edited by Mrs. Bury Palliser (Fanny Marryat Palliser). London: Chapman & Hall, 1878.

[Jenny, John. Inventory]. *Mayflower Descendant* 6, no. 3 (July 1904): 171.

Jobe, Brock W. "Boston Cabinet Woods of the Eighteenth Century." *Boston Furniture of the Eighteenth Century*, pp. 251–53. Charlottesville: University Press of Virginia, 1974.

―――――. "The Boston Furniture Industry, 1725–1760." Master's thesis, University of Delaware, 1975.

―――――. "The Boston Furniture Industry, 1720–1740." *Boston Furniture of the Eighteenth Century*, pp. 3–48. Charlottesville: University Press of Virginia, 1974.

Johns, C. A. *The Forest Trees of Britain*. London: Society for Promoting Christian Knowledge, 1892.

Johnson, Philip A. "The Leffingwell Inn." *Antiques* 79, no. 6 (June 1961): 567–69.

Joiner's Company. See Company of Joyners.

Jorgenson, Neil. *A Guide to New England's Landscape*. Barre, Mass.: Barre Publishers, 1971.

Joseph Moxon's Mechanick Exercises; or, The Doctrine of Handy-works Applied to the Arts of Smithing, Joinery, Carpentry, Turning, Bricklaying. Introduction and captions by Benno M. Forman. Edited by Charles F. Montgomery. New York and London: Praeger Publishers, 1970.

Joseph Moxon. See also Moxon, Joseph.

Josselyn, John. *An Account of Two Voyages to New England*. London, 1674.

―――――. *New-England Rarities Discovered*. London, 1672. Reprinted in *Archaeologica Americana: Transactions and Collections of the American Antiquarian Society*. Vol. 4. Edited by Edward Tuckerman. Worcester: By the society, 1860.

Jourdain, Margaret. *English Decoration and Furniture of the Early Renaissance, 1500–1650*. London: B. T. Batsford, 1924.

This book is the most reliable survey of English furniture of this period.

Judd, Sylvester. *History of Hadley, Including the Early History of Hatfield, South Hadley, Amherst, and Granby, Massachussetts*. 1863. New ed. Springfield, Mass.: H. R. Huntting, 1905.

Kalm, Peter. *Travels in North America (1753–1761)*. Translated by Adolph B. Benson. New York: Dover Publications, 1966.

Kane, Patricia E. *Furniture of the New Haven Colony: The Seventeenth-Century Style*. New Haven: New Haven Colony Historical Society, 1973.

―――――. "Furniture Owned by the Massachusetts Historical Society." *Antiques* 109, no. 5 (May 1976): 960–69.

―――――. "The Joiners of Seventeenth Century Hartford County." *Connecticut Historical Society Bulletin* 35, no. 3 (July 1970): 65–85.

―――――. "The Seventeenth-Century Furniture of the Connecticut Valley: The Hadley Chest Reappraised." In *Arts of the Anglo-American Community in the Seventeenth Century*, edited by Ian M. G. Quimby, pp. 79–122. Charlottesville: University Press of Virginia, 1975.

―――――. *Three Hundred Years of American Seating Furniture: Chairs and Beds from the Mabel Brady Garvan and Other Collections at Yale University*. Boston: New York Graphic Society, 1976.

Kaye, Myrna. "Eighteenth-Century Boston Furniture Craftsmen." *Boston Furniture of the Eighteenth Century*, pp. 267–302. Charlottesville: University Press of Virginia, 1974.

Keyes, Homer Eaton. "Another Tea Chair." *Antiques* 8, no. 6 (December 1925): 355.

―――――. "Dennis or a Lesser Light?" *Antiques* 34, no. 6 (December 1938): 296–300.

―――――. "The Editor's Attic." *Antiques* 11, no. 4 (April 1927): 275.

―――――. "Some Pennsylvania Furniture." *Antiques* 5, no. 5 (May 1924): 222–25.

Kreisel, Heinrich. *Die Kunst des deutschen Möbels. . . .* Vol. 1. Munich: C. H. Beck, 1968.

Kindig, Joseph, III. *The Philadelphia Chair*. York, Penn.: Historical Society of York County, 1978.

Kircher, Athanasius. *An Embassage . . . to . . . the Emperor of China. . . .* Translated by John Ogilby. London, 1669.

Kirk, John T. *American Furniture and the British Tradition to 1830*. New York: Alfred A. Knopf, 1982.

―――――. "Sources of American Regional Furniutre, Part I." *Antiques* 88, no. 6 (December 1965): 790–98.

Konig, David Thomas. "A New Look at the Essex 'French': Ethnic Friction and Community Tension in Seventeenth Century Essex County, Massachusetts." *Essex Institute Historical Collections* 110, no. 3 (July 1974): 167–80.

LaCroix, Paul. *The Arts in the Middle Ages and at the Period of the Renaissance. . . .* Translated by W. Armstrong. 1870. Rev. ed. London: Virtue, 1876.

Lancaster County Deeds. Lancaster County Courthouse, Lancaster, Va.

Lancaster County Wills. Lancaster County Courthouse, Lancaster, Va.

Langley, Batty. *The City and Country Builder's and Workman's Treasury of Designs*. London: Thomas Langley, 1740.

Lauder, Sir Thomas Dick. *Sir U. Price on the Picturesque: With an Essay on the Origin of Taste*. London: William S. Orr, 1842.

Learmont, David. "The Trinity Hall Chairs, Aberdeen." *Furniture History* 14 (1978): 1–8.

Leibundguth, Arthur W. "Clues and Footnotes." *Antiques* 107, no. 6 (June 1975): 1158.

―――――. "The Furniture-Making Crafts in Philadelphia, ca. 1730–1760." Master's thesis, University of Delaware, 1964.

"Letters of William Penn." *Pennsylvania Magazine of History and Biography* 33, no. 4 (1909): 423–31.

Lewis, W. S., ed. *Horace Walpole's Correspondence*. Vol. 1. New Haven: Yale University Press, 1937.

Lidget/Waldron Legal Papers. Jeffries Family Papers. Vol. 6. Massachusetts Historical Society, Boston.

Little, Elbert L. *The Audubon Society Field Guide to North American Trees, Eastern Region*. New York: Alfred A. Knopf, 1980.

Littlehales, Henry, ed. *The Medieval Records of a London City Church (St. Mary at Hill)*, A.D. 1420–1559. London: Kegan Paul, Trench, Trübner, 1904.

Livingston Papers, Franklin D. Roosevelt Library, Hyde Park, N.Y.

Lockwood, Luke Vincent. *Colonial Furniture in America*. 1st ed. New York: Charles Scribner's Sons, 1901.

―――――. *Colonial Furniture in America*. 2 vols. Rev. ed. New York: Charles Scribner's Sons, 1913.

[Lockwood Sale]. *XVII & XVIII Century American Furniture and Paintings: The Celebrated Collection Formed by the Late Mr. & Mrs. Luke Vincent Lockwood*. New York: Parke-Bernet Galleries, 1954.

Lodge, G. Henry, trans. *The History of Ancient Art Translated from the German of John Winckelmann*. Boston: Little, Brown, 1856.

Logan Papers. Cash book. American Philosophical Society, Philadelphia.

Logan, James, Papers. Correspondence book. Historical Society of Pennsylvania, Philadelphia.

Lossing, Benson J. *The Pictorial Field-Book of the Revolution*. 2 vols. New York: Harper & Brothers, 1859.

Loudon, John Claudius. *Arboretum et Fruticetum Britannicum; or, The Trees and Shrubs of Britain*. 8 vols. 2d ed. London: Longman, Brown, Green, & Longmans, 1844.

―――――. *Encyclopedia of Cottage, Farmhouse and Villa Architecture and Furniture*. 1839. Reprint. Edited by Christopher G. Gilbert. London: Connoisseur, 1970.

Lowenthal, Helen. "History in Houses (Dyrham Park)." *Antiques* 101, no. 5 (May 1972): 864–69.

Lower Norfolk County Deed Books. Courthouse, Portsmouth, Va.

Lunsingh Scheurleer, T. H. *Catalogus van meubelen*. Amsterdam: Rijksmuseum, 1952.

―――――. "The Dutch and Their Homes in the Seventeenth Century." In *Arts of the Anglo-American Community in the Seventeenth Century*, edited by Ian M. G. Quimby, pp. 13–42. Charlottesville: University Press of Virginia, 1975.

Lyle, Charles T., and Philip Zimmerman. "Furniture of the Monmouth County Historical Association." *Antiques* 117, no. 1 (January 1980): 186–205.

Lyman Allyn Museum. *New London County Furniture, 1640–1840*. Catalogue entries by Edgar deN. Mayhew and Minor Myers, Jr. New London, Conn.: By the museum, 1974.

Lynes, Wilson. "Slat-Back Chairs of New England and the Middle Atlantic States." *Antiques* 25, no. 3 (March 1934): 104–7.

Lyon, Irving P. "The Oak Furniture of Ipswich, Massachusetts. Part I." *Antiques* 32, no. 5 (November 1937): 230–33.

. "Square-Post Slat Back Chairs." *Antiques* 20, no. 4 (October 1931): 210–16.

Lyon, Irving W. *The Colonial Furniture of New England.* Boston and New York: Houghton Mifflin Co., 1891.

McElroy, Cathryn J. "Furniture of the Philadelphia Area: Forms and Craftsmen before 1730." Master's thesis, University of Delaware, 1970.

McGrath, Patrick, ed. *Merchants and Merchandize in Seventeenth-Century Bristol.* Bristol Record Society publications, vol. 19. Bristol: By the society, 1955.

MacDonald, William H. *Central New Jersey Chairmaking of the Nineteenth Century.* Trenton, N. J., 1960.

Markham, Gervase. *The English Husbandman. . . .* Vol. 2. Rev. ed. London, 1635.

Marot, Jean. *Recueil de plusieurs portes des principaux et maisons de la ville de Paris. . . .* Vol. 2. Paris, [ca. 1680].

Maryland Probate Records. Maryland Hall of Records, Annapolis, Md.

[*Massachusetts Records*]. Shurtleff, Nathaniel B., ed. *Records of the Governor and Company of the Massachusetts Bay in New England (1628–86).* 5 vols. Boston, 1853–54.

Massachusetts Shipping Returns, 1686–1719. Ms. 5.848. Colonial Office, London.

Matzkin, Ruth. "Inventories of Estates in Philadelphia County, 1682–1710." Master's thesis, University of Delaware, 1959.

Maxwell, Sir Herbert. *Trees, A Woodland Notebook.* Glasgow: James Maclehose & Sons, 1915.

Mayhew, Edgar deN. See Lyman Allyn Museum.

Means, Mary Elizabeth. "Early American Trade Cards." Master's thesis, University of Delaware, 1958.

"Metcalf Family Treasures." *Dedham Historical Society Newsletter* (June 1966).

Michaux, François André. *The North American Sylva.* 6 vols. Philadelphia: J. Dobson, 1842.

Middlesex County Probate Records. Courthouse, East Cambridge, Mass.

Miller, Regis B. "Reticulate Thickenings in Some Species of *Juglans*." *American Journal of Botany* 63, no. 6 (July 1976): 898–901.

Miller, V. Isabelle. *Furniture by New York Cabinetmakers, 1652 to 1860.* New York: Museum of the City of New York, 1957.

Moens, William John Charles. *The Walloons and their Church at Norwich: Their History and Registers, 1565–1832.* Publications of the Huguenot Society, vol. 1. London: By the society, 1887–88.

Monmouth County Historical Association. *New Jersey Arts and Crafts: The Colonial Expression.* Catalogue entries by Charles T. Lyle and Milton J. Bloch. Freehold, N.J.: By the association, 1975.

Montgomery, Charles F. *American Furniture: The Federal Period.* New York: Viking Press, 1966.

Moxon, Joseph. *Mechanick Exercises; or, The Doctrine of Handy-works Applied to the Arts of Smithing, Joinery, Carpentry, Turning, Bricklaying.* 3d ed. London: Dan. Midwinter and Tho. Leigh, 1703.

. See also *Joseph Moxon's Mechanick Exercises.*

Myers, Minor, Jr. See Lyman Allyn Museum.

Naeve, Milo M. "English Furniture in Colonial America." *Antiques* 99, no. 4 (April 1971): 551–55.

New Hampshire Historical Society. *The Decorative Arts of New Hampshire: A Sesquicentennial Exhibition.* Concord: By the society, 1973.

New Jersey Probate Records. Superior Court of New Jersey, Trenton, N.J.

New York Probate Records. Wills. Queens College Historical Manuscripts Collection. City University of New York, New York.

New York Treasurers Accounts. Ms. 5.1222. Colonial Office, London.

Nichols, John Gough, ed. *The Unton Inventories.* London: Berkshire Ashmolean Society, 1841.

North Kingston Probate Records. Town Hall, North Kingston, R.I.

Norton, Malcolm A. "Joint Stool and Candlestick." *Antiques* 5, no. 5 (May 1924): 226–27.

Nutting, Wallace. *Furniture of the Pilgrim Century.* 1921. Reprint. New York: Bonanza Books, 1977.

. *Furniture of the Pilgrim Century.* 2d ed. Framingham, Mass.: Old America Co., 1924. Reprint. New York: Dover Publications, 1965.

. *Furniture Treasury.* 2 vols. Framingham, Mass.: Old America Co., 1928.

Object file. Registrar's Office, Winterthur Museum, Winterthur, Del.

[*OED*], *The Oxford English Dictionary. . . .* 22 vols. Oxford: Clarendon Press, 1888–1933.

Olive, Gabriel. "Furniture in a West Country Parish, 1576–1769." *Furniture History* 12 (1976): 17–23.

. "West Country Settles." *Furniture History* 17 (1981): 20–22.

Palardy, Jean. *The Early Furniture of French Canada.* Translated by Eric McLean. 2d rev. ed. Toronto: Macmillan of Canada; New York: St. Martin's Press, 1965.

Panofsky, Erwin. *Renaissance and Renascences in Western Art.* Stockholm: Almqvist & Wiskell, 1960.

Panshin, Alexis John, and Carl de Zeeuw. *Textbook of Wood Technology.* 4th ed. New York: McGraw-Hill, 1980.

Park, Helen. "Thomas Dennis, Ipswich Joiner: A Re-examination." *Antiques* 78, no. 1 (July 1960): 40–44.

Parley, Peter. *Recollections of a Lifetime, or, Men and Things I Have Seen. . . .* New York: Auburn, Miller, Orton, and Mulligan, 1857.

Passengers and Ships prior to 1684. Reprint. Baltimore: Genealogical Publishing Co., 1970.

Passeri, Andrew, and Robert F. Trent. "Two New England Queen Anne Easy Chairs with Original Upholstery." *Maine Antique Digest* 2, no. 4 (April 1983): 26B–28B.

Perley, Sidney. The History of Salem, Massachusetts. 3 vols. Salem, Mass., 1924–28.

. "Marblehead in the Year 1700, No. 5." *Essex Institute Historical Collections* 47, no. 1 (January 1911): 67–95.

Petition to the General Court, May 23, 1677. Facsimile. *Bulletin of the Public Library of the City of Boston* 4 (January 1894): 305–6.

Philadelphia Wills and Inventories. City Hall Annex, Philadelphia, Penn. (Microfilm, DMMC M-962–M1006, Winterthur.)

Phillips, Charles J. *History of the Sackville Family.* 2 vols. London: Cassell, n.d.

Phillips, Henry Laverock. *Annals of the Worshipful Company of Joiners of the City of London.* London, 1915.

Pickman, Benjamin. "Some Account of Houses and Other Buildings in Salem, from a Manuscript of the Late Col. Benjamin Pickman." *Essex Institute Historical Collections* 6, no. 3 (June 1864): 93–105.

Plymouth County Wills and Inventories. Plymouth County Courthouse, Plymouth, Mass.

Prerogative Court of Canterbury Probate Inventory Files. Public Record Office, London.

Prime, Alfred Coxe. *The Arts and Crafts in Philadelphia, Maryland, and South Carolina, 1721–1785.* Topsfield, Mass.: Walpole Society, 1929.

. *Colonial Craftsmen of Pennsylvania: Reproductions of Early Newspaper Advertisements.* Philadelphia: Pennsylvania Museum and School of Industrial Art, 1925.

Probate Files. Connecticut State Library, Hartford.

Proceedings of the Provincial Court, 1650–1657. Maryland Archives. Vol. 10. Baltimore: Maryland Historical Society, 1891.

Pye, David. *The Nature and Art of Workmanship.* London and New York: Studio Vista and Van Nostrand Reinhold Co., 1971.

. *The Nature of Design.* London and New York: Studio Vista and Van Nostrand Reinhold Co., 1972.

Quynn, William R., ed. *The Diary of Jacob Engelbrecht.* Frederick, Md.: Frederick Historical Society, 1976.

Randall, Richard H., Jr. *American Furniture in the Museum of Fine Arts, Boston.* Boston: By the museum, 1965.

. "Boston Chairs." *Old-Time New England* 54, no. 1 (July 1963): 12–20.

Records of the Court of New Castle on Delaware, 1681–1699. Vol. 2. Colonial Society of Delaware, 1935.

Records of the Town of Boston. See Boston Records.

[*Reifsnyder Sale*]. *Collections of the Late Howard Reifsnyder.* New York: American Art Association, April 24–27, 1929.

A Report of the Record Commissioners of the City of Boston. See Boston Records.

Reynolds, Ronna L. "The Towns of Glastonbury, Rocky Hill, and Newington." *Antiques* 109, no. 3 (March 1976): 518–27.

Rice, Norman S. *New York Furniture before 1840.* Albany: Albany Institute, 1962.

Ripley, S. Dillon. "An American Triangular Turned Chair?" *Antiques* 85, no. 1 (January 1964): 104–6.

Robbins, Thomas. Diary. Connecticut Historical Society, Hartford.

Robinson, John. *The Flora of Essex County, Massachusetts.* Salem, Mass.: Essex Institute, 1880.

Roe, Fred. *Ancient Church Chests and Chairs in the Home Counties Round Greater London.* London: B. T. Batsford, 1929.

Rose, Walter. *The Village Carpenter.* Wakefield, Yorkshire: EP Publishing, 1973.

Roubo, André Jacob, et al. *Descriptions des arts et métiers.* 45 vols. Paris, 1761–88.

Routh, C. R. N., and James Lees-Milne. *Charlecote Park.* London: National Trust, 1971.

Ruskin, John. *The Nature of Gothic.* London: George Allen & Unwin, 1905.

Rutherford, F. J. "The Furnishings of Hampton Court Palace 1715–1737." *Old Furniture*, 2 nos. 6, 7 (November, December 1927): 77–85, 180–88.

Rutman, Darrett B. *Winthrop's Boston: Portrait of a Puritan Town, 1630–1649.* Chapel Hill: University of North Carolina Press, 1965.

Ryder, Richard D. "Four-Legged Turned Chairs." *Connoisseur* 191, no. 767 (January 1976): 44–49.

Sack, Albert. *Fine Points of Furniture—Early American.* New York: Crown Publishers, 1950.

Sack, Israel. See Israel Sack, Inc.

St. George, Robert Blair. "The Staniford Family Chest." *Maine Antique Digest* 11, no. 2 (February 1983): 16B–18B.

———. "Style and Structure in the Joinery of Dedham and Medfield, Massachusetts." In *American Furniture and Its Makers: Winterthur Portfolio 13*, edited by Ian M. G. Quimby, pp. 1–46. Chicago: University of Chicago Press, 1979.

———. *The Wrought Covenant: Source Materials for the Study of Craftsmen and Community in Southeastern New England, 1620–1700*. Brockton, Mass.: Brockton Art Center/Fuller Memorial, 1979.

Salaman, R. *Dictionary of Tools Used in the Woodworking and Allied Trades, c. 1700–1970*. London: George Allen & Unwin, 1975.

[*Salem Records.*] *The Town Records of Salem, Massachusetts*. 2 vols. Salem, Mass.: Essex Institute, 1934.

Salmon, William. *Polygraphice; or The Art of Drawing, Engraving, Etching, Limning, Painting, Washing, Varnishing, Colouring, and Dying*. London, 1701.

Saltar, Gordon. "New England Timbers, with an Annotated Bibliography." *Boston Furniture of the Eighteenth Century*, Charlottesville: University Press of Virginia, 1974. pp. 251–64.

Sargent, Charles Sprague. *Manual of the Trees of North America*. 2 vols. 1922. 2d ed. New York: Dover Publications, 1965.

Saunders, Richard H. "American Decorative Arts Collecting in New England, 1840–1920." Master's thesis, University of Delaware, 1973.

Savage, James. *A Genealogical Dictionary of the First Settlers of New England*. 4 vols. 1860–62. Reprint. Baltimore: Genealogical Publishing Co., 1965.

———. "Gleanings for New England History." *Collections of the Massachusetts Historical Society*. 3d ser., vol. 8. Boston: Charles C. Little & James Brown, 1843.

Schiffer, Margaret B. *Chester County, Pennsylvania, Inventories, 1684–1850*. Exton, Penn.: Schiffer Publishing, 1974.

———. *Furniture and Its Makers of Chester County, Pennsylvania*. Philadelphia: University of Pennsylvania Press, 1966.

Seacord, Morgan H. *Biographical Sketches and Index of the Huguenot Settlers of New Rochelle, 1687–1776*. New Rochelle, N.Y.: Huguenot and Historical Association, 1941.

[Sewall, Samuel]. *Diary of Samuel Sewall, 1674–1729*. Edited by M. Halsey Thomas. 2 vols. New York: Farrar, Straus, & Giroux, 1973.

[———]. *The Letter-book of Samuel Sewall*. 2 vols. In *Collections of the Massachusetts Historical Society*. 6th ser., vols. 1, 2. Boston, 1886–88.

Sharp, L. Corwin. "The Janvier Family of Cabinetmakers of Odessa, Delaware." Master's thesis, University of Delaware, 1980.

Shepherd, Raymond V., Jr. "James Logan's Stenton: Grand Simplicity in Quaker Philadelphia." Master's thesis, University of Delaware, 1968.

Sherman, Thomas Townsend. *The Sherman Genealogy*. New York: Tobias A. Wright, 1920.

Shettleworth, Earle. "Clues and Footnotes." *Antiques* 103, no. 3 (March 1973): 470.

Shirley, Evelyn Phillip, ed. "An Inventory of the Effects of Henry Howard, K. G., Earl of Northampton." *Archaeologia* 42 (1869): 348–74.

Shipton, Clifford K. See *Sibley's*.

Shoemaker, Thomas A. "A List of the Inhabitants of Germantown and Chestnut Hill in 1809." *Pennsylvania Magazine of History and Biography* 15, no. 4 (1891): 449–80.

The Shoemaker Family. Privately printed, n.d.

Shurtleff, Nathaniel B. See *Massachusetts Records*.

[*Sibley's*]. Shipton, Clifford K. *Sibley's Harvard Graduates. . . .* Vol. 5: *1701–1712*; vol. 6: *1713–1721*; vol. 7: *1722–1725*. Boston: Massachusetts Historical Society, 1937, 1942, 1945.

Singleton, Esther. *The Furniture of Our Forefathers*. 1901. Reprint. Garden City, N.Y.: Doubleday, Page, 1913.

———. *Social New York under the Georges, 1714–1776: Houses, Streets, and Country Homes, with Chapters on Fashions, Furniture, China, Plates, and Manners*. New York: D. Appleton, 1902.

Skate, Edward. See Contract between Edward Skate and John Hill.

Smith, Helen Evertson. *Colonial Days and Ways as Gathered from Family Papers*. New York: Century Co., 1900.

Smith, Robert C. *The Art of Portugal, 1500–1800*. New York: Meredith Press, 1968.

Soderholtz, E. E. *Colonial Architecture and Furniture*. Boston: George H. Polley, 1895.

"Some Letters and an Abstract of Letters from Pennsylvania." *Pennsylvania Magazine of History and Biography* 4, no. 2 (1880): 187–201.

Sordelli, Angela Comolli. *Il mobile antico dal XIV al XVII secolo*. Milan: Görlich Editore, 1967.

Sotheby, Parke, Bernet, *Sale no. 3866: Fine Americana* (Public auction April 30–May 1, 1976). New York, 1976.

Sprat, Thomas. *History of the Royal Society*. 1667. Reprint, edited by Jackson I. Cope and Harold Whitmore Jones. St. Louis: Washington University, 1958.

Stanley-Stone, A. C. *History of the Worshipful Company of Turners of London*. London: Lindley-Jones & Brother, 1925.

The Statutes of the Realm. Vol. 3. 1817. Reprint. London: Dawson's of Pall Mall, 1963.

Steer, Francis W., ed. *Farm and Cottage Inventories of Mid-Essex, 1635–1749*. Essex Record Office Publications, no. 8. Chelmsford: Essex County Council, 1950.

———. "The Inventory of Anne, Viscountess of Dorchester." *Notes and Queries* 198 (March, April, September, October, November, December 1953): 94–96, 155–58, 379–81, 415–17, 469–73, 515–19.

[*Stokes Sale*]. *Early Pennsylvania and Other Colonial Furniture: From the Collection of the Late J. Stodgell Stokes, Philadelphia*. New York: Parke-Bernet Galleries, 1948.

[Suffolk Common Pleas]. Records of the Inferior Court of Common Pleas for Suffolk County. Suffolk County Courthouse, Boston.

Suffolk Deeds, 1629–1697. 14 vols. Boston: Rockwell & Churchill, 1880–1905.

[Suffolk Probate]. Probate Records of Suffolk County. Suffolk County Courthouse, Boston. (Microfilm, DMMC Mm-109–M-121, Winterthur.)

[Suffolk Superior Court]. Suffolk County Superior Court Files. Suffolk County Courthouse, Boston.

Swain, Margaret. "The Furnishing of Holyroodhouse in 1668." *Connoisseur* 194, no. 780 (February 1977): 122–30.

Swan, Mabel Munson. "Coastwise Cargoes of Venture Furniture." *Antiques* 55, no. 4 (April 1949): 278–80.

———. "Newburyport Furnituremakers." *Antiques* 47, no. 4 (April 1945): 222–25.

Symonds, George W. D. *The Tree Identification Book*. New York: William Morrow, 1958.

Symonds, R. W. "Cane Chairs of the Late 17th and Early 18th Centuries." *Connoisseur* 93, no. 391 (March 1934): 173–81.

———. "Charles II. Couches, Chairs, and Stools," pt. 1, "1660–1670," pt. 2, "1670–1680." *Connoisseur* 93, nos. 289, 390 (January, February 1934): 15–23, 86–95.

———. "English Cane Chairs," pts. 1 and 2. *Connoisseur* 127, nos. 520, 521 (March, May 1951): 8–15, 83–91.

———. "The Export Trade of Furniture to Colonial America." *Burlington Magazine* 77, no. 452 (November 1940): 152–63.

———. "Turkey Work, Beech and Jappanned Chairs." *Connoisseur* 93, no. 392 (April 1934): 221–27.

Symonds Collection. Photographs from the Robert Wemyss Symonds Collection filed in DAPC, Winterthur Museum Library, Winterthur, Del.

Symonds Papers. The papers of Robert Wemyss Symonds. DMMC, 75 × 65.33, 75 × 69.28, 75 × 69.25, and microfilm M-285. Winterthur Library, Winterthur Del.

Talbot, Charles W., ed. *Dürer in America: His Graphic Work*. Washington, D.C.: National Gallery of Art, 1971.

Tattersall, C. E. C. *A History of British Carpets*. Essex: F. Lewis, 1966.

Temple Newsam House. *Oak Furniture from Yorkshire Churches*. Catalogue by Christopher G. Gilbert, Anthony Wells-Cole, and Richard Fawcett. Leeds: Temple Newsam House, 1971.

Theus, Mrs. Charlton. *Savannah Furniture, 1735–1825*. Savannah, 1967.

Thornton, Peter K. "Back Stools and Chaises à Demoiselles." *Connoisseur* 185, no. 744 (February 1974): 98–105.

———. *Seventeenth-Century Interior Decoration in England, France, and Holland*. New Haven: Yale University Press, 1978.

———. "A Short Commentary on the Hardwick Hall Inventory of 1601." *Furniture History* 7 (1971): 15–40.

[*Town & Selectmen.*] Hill, Don Gleason, ed. *Early Records of the Town of Dedham*. Vol. 3, *Town and Selectmen, 1636–59*. Dedham, Mass.: Transcript Press, 1892.

The Town Records of Salem, Massachusetts. See *Salem Records*.

Trent, Robert F. "The Endicott Chair." *Essex Institute Historical Collections* 114, no. 2 (April 1978): 103–19.

———. "The Franklin Chair." *Maine Antique Digest* 7, no. 11 (December 1979): 26B–29B.

———. "A History for the Essex Institute Turkey Work Couch." *Essex Institute Historical Collections* 113, no. 1 (January 1977): 29–37.

———. "The Joiners and Joinery of Middlesex County, Massachusetts, 1630–1730." Master's thesis, University of Delaware, 1975.

———. "The Joiners and Joinery of Middlesex County, Massachusetts, 1630–1730." In *Arts of the Anglo-American Community in the Seventeenth Century*, edited by Ian M. G. Quimby, pp. 123–48. Charlottesville: University Press of Virginia, 1975.

————. "Two Seventeenth-Century Salem Upholstered Chairs." *Essex Institute Historical Collections* 116, no. 1 (January 1980): 34–40.

Trumbull, J. Hammond, ed. See *Connecticut Records*.

[Turners Company Minutes]. Minutes of the Court of the Worshipful Company of Turners. Vol. 1, 1605–1633, vol. 2, 1633–1688. Mss. 3295/1, 3295/2. Guildhall, London.

Twiston-Davies, L., and H. J. Lloyd-Johnes. *Welsh Furniture: An Introduction*. Cardiff: University of Wales Press, 1950.

Tyack, Norman L. "Immigration from East Anglia to New England, 1630–1650." Ph.D. diss., University of London, 1952.

U.S. Department of Agriculture. *Wood Handbook*. Washington, D.C.: Forest Products Laboratory, Government Printing Office, 1940.

"Unpublished Letters of Judge Sewall, John Adams, &c." *New-England Historical and Genealogical Register* 24, no. 3 (July 1870): 291–97.

van Laer, A. J. F., trans. and ed. *Correspondence of Jeremias van Rensselaer*. Albany: University of the State of New York, 1932.

Vasari, Georgio. *Lives of the Artists*. 1568. Reprint, edited by Betty Burroughs. New York: Simon & Schuster, 1959.

Vaughn, Rowland, Esq. *Most Approved and Long Experienced Water Works*. London, 1610.

Virkus, Frederick Adams, ed. *The Compendium of American Genealogy: The Standard Genealogical Encyclopedia of First Families of America*. 7 vols. Chicago: Institute of American Genealogy, 1924–32.

Vogelsang, Willem. *Le meuble Hollandais au Musée National d'Amsterdam*. Amsterdam: Van Rijkom Fréres, 1910.

Vose, Peter E. "The Great Boston Fire of 1760." *New-England Historical and Genealogical Register* 34, no. 3 (July 1880): 288–93.

Wadsworth Atheneum. *Connecticut Furniture: Seventeenth and Eighteenth Centuries*. Catalogue by John T. Kirk and Henry Maynard. Hartford: by the Atheneum, 1967.

Wallin, Sigurd. *Nordiska museets möbler fran svenska herremanshem*. Vol. 1. Stockholm: Nordiska Museets Förlag, 1931–35.

Walpole, Horace. *Anecdotes of Painting in England*. . . . 4 vols. 3d ed. London: J. Dodsley, 1782.

Warren, David B. *Bayou Bend: American Furniture, Paintings and Silver from the Bayou Bend Collection*. Houston: Museum of Fine Arts, 1975.

Waters, Henry F., ed. "Maverick's Account of New England." *Proceedings of the Massachusetts Historical Society*, 2d ser., vol. 1: 221–49. Boston: By the society, 1884.

Waters, Thomas Franklin. *Ipswich in the Massachusetts Bay Colony*. 2 vols. Ipswich: Ipswich Historical Society, 1905–17.

Weil, Martin E. "A Cabinetmaker's Price Book." In *American Furniture and Its Makers: Winterthur Portfolio 13*, edited by Ian M. G. Quimby, pp. 175–92. Chicago: University of Chicago Press, 1979.

Whipple, Stephen. Account book. Ipswich Historical Society, Ipswich, Mass.

Whitmore, William H., et al. See *Boston Records*.

Wigginton, Eliot, ed. *The Foxfire Book*. New York: Doubleday, 1972.

Williams, Edward. *Virginia's Discovery of Silke Wormes with Their Benefit And the Implanting of Mulberry Trees*. London: T. H. for John Stephenson, 1650.

Williams, Charles A. *Outlines of Chinese Symbolism and Art Motives: An Alphabetical Compendium of Antique Legends and Beliefs*. . . . 3d rev. ed. Shanghai: Kelly & Walsh, 1941.

Willison, George F. *Saints and Strangers*. New York: Reynal & Hitchcock, 1945.

Winsor, Justin, ed. *The Memorial History of Boston, Including Suffolk County, Massachusetts, 1630–1880*. 4 vols. Boston: James R. Osgood, 1881–83.

Winthrop's Journal: "History of New England, 1630–1649." Edited by James Kendall Hosmer. 2 vols. New York: Charles Scribner's Sons, 1908.

Wolsey, S. W., and R. W. P. Luff. *Furniture in England: The Age of the Joiner*. New York: Praeger Publishers, 1969.

Wood, William. *New England's Prospect*. 1634. Reprint. Edited by E. M. Boynton. Boston, 1897, pp. 16–18.

Wood Handbook. See U.S. Dept. of Agriculture.

Woodall, Mary. "The Furniture at Aston Hall: Some Pre-Restoration Treasures, with a Comment on Turkey Work." *Antique Collector* 31, no. 2 (April 1960): 59–64.

Wyman, Thomas Bellows. *The Genealogies and Estates of Charlestown in the County of Middlesex and Commonwealth of Massachusetts, 1629–1818*. 2 vols. Boston: David Clapp & Son, 1879.

York County Wills. Courthouse, Yorktown, Va.

York County Probate Records. Courthouse, Yorktown, Va.

Young, Alexander. *Chronicles of the First Planters of the Colony of Massachusetts Bay from 1623 to 1636*. . . . Boston: Charles C. Little & James Brown, 1846.

————. *Chronicles of the Pilgrim Fathers of the Colony of Plymouth from 1602 to 1625*. Boston: Charles C. Little & James Brown, 1841.

CONCORDANCE

GUIDE TO THE WINTERTHUR
OBJECTS ILLUSTRATED

ACC. NO.	ILLUS.	ACC. NO.	ILLUS.	ACC. NO.	ILLUS.
52.236	fig. 88	58.540	fig. 129	60.743	cat. entry 44
53.104	cat. entry 20	58.547	cat. entry 50	61.1143	cat. entry 21
54.73	cat. entry 18	58.550	cat. entry 83	61.1150	cat. entry 24
54.518	cat. entry 82	58.551	cat. entry 43	61.1151	cat. entry 26
54.519	cat. entry 73	58.553	cat. entry 64, fig. 169	61.1152	cat. entry 33
54.520	cat. entry 74	58.554	cat. entry 81	61.1153	cat. entry 28
54.523	figs. 156, 179	58.555	cat. entry 80, fig. 182	61.1154	cat. entry 22
54.524	cat. entry 46	58.556	cat. entry 78, fig. 181	64.152	cat. entry 51
54.525	cat. entry 11, figs. 54, 179	58.558	cat. entry 88, fig. 190	64.1780	cat. entry 25
54.526	cat. entry 12, fig. 54	58.569	cat. entry 85	64.1781	cat. entry 42
54.527	cat. entry 55	58.570	cat. entry 71, fig. 161	65.2004	cat. entry 37
54.528	cat. entry 56	58.576	cat. entry 90	65.2249	cat. entry 27
54.533	cat. entry 76, figs. 177, 178, 179	58.578	cat. entry 59	65.2833	cat. entry 41
54.539	cat. entry 79	58.586	fig. 173	66.698	cat. entry 31
54.540	cat. entry 66, figs. 169, 172	58.680	cat. entry 9, fig. 50	66.778	cat. entry 86
54.541	cat. entry 65, fig. 172	58.681	cat. entry 1, fig. 38(?)	66.1309	cat. entry 89
54.547	cat. entry 69	58.682	cat. entry 2, fig. 42	66.1311	fig. 170
54.548	cat. entry 70	58.683	cat. entry 13	66.1312	cat. entry 60
55.130	cat. entry 57, fig. 147	58.684	cat. entry 4, fig. 47	67.803	fig. 183
56.10.2	cat. entry 8	58.690	cat. entry 17	67.1166	cat. entry 32
56.94.6	cat. entry 40	58.691	cat. entry 15	67.1170	cat. entry 23
57.530	cat. entry 67	58.692	cat. entry 19	67.1172	cat. entry 29, fig. 83
57.537	cat. entry 35	58.693	cat. entry 3	67.1176	cat. entry 30, figs. 84, 85
57.538	cat. entry 36	58.694	cat. entry 45, figs. 104, 108, 161	69.818	cat. entry 84
57.539	fig. 10	58.695	cat. entry 47	70.428	fig. 138
57.541	fig. 2	58.698	cat. entry 49, figs. 113, 114	70.1349	cat. entry 38
57.542	fig. 3	58.964	cat. entry 53, fig. 137	71.135	fig. 53
57.598	cat. entry 10	58.1504	cat. entry 91	73.382	cat. entry 52, figs. 134, 135, 136
57.1367	fig. 20	59.28.1	cat. entry 61	74.40	cat. entry 16
57.1389	cat. entry 48, fig. 110	59.28.2	cat. entry 62	74.120	cat. entry 54, figs. 130, 131, 140,
58.57.4	cat. entry 75, figs. 177, 178	59.2115	cat. entry 63		141, 145, 146
58.521	cat. entry 5	59.2116	cat. entry 68	76.31	cat. entry 77, figs. 177, 178, 179
58.522	cat. entry 7, figs. 48, 49	59.2324	fig. 9	76.173	cat. entry 72
58.523	cat. entry 6	59.2499	fig. 20	77.60	cat. entry 58
58.537	cat. entry 92, fig. 190	59.2639	fig. 132	78.110	cat. entry 14, fig. 55
58.538	cat. entry 87	59.2640	fig. 132	81.290	cat. entry 34
58.539	fig. 128	60.189	cat. entry 39	82.276	fig. 63

INDEX